644
Ada

Adams, Jeannette T.

How to buy, re-
pair, and maintain
home systems & ap-
pliances

DATE DUE

JA 16 '87			
MR 8 '89			
NO 4 '89			
MR 7 '90			
JAN 0 6 '95			
MAY 1 6 '95			
JL 23 '97			
SE 11 '00			
SE 19 '00			

HOW TO BUY, REPAIR, AND MAINTAIN

HOME SYSTEMS & APPLIANCES

HOW TO BUY, REPAIR, AND MAINTAIN

HOME SYSTEMS & APPLIANCES

J. T. ADAMS

ARCO PUBLISHING, INC.
NEW YORK

Published by Arco Publishing, Inc.
219 Park Avenue South, New York, N.Y. 10003

Library of Congress Cataloging in Publication Data

Adams, Jeannette T
  How to buy, repair and maintain
    home systems and appliances.

  Includes index.
  1. Household appliances. I. Title.
TX298.A32   644   79–25773
ISBN 0–668–04530–2

Printed in the United States of America

Acknowledgments

The author desires to acknowledge with thanks the assistance of the following national organizations, colleges, and branches of the government that have cooperated in the production of this book.

Air Pollution Control Association; Amana Refrigeration, Inc., a subsidiary of Raytheon Co.; American Gas Association; American Petroleum Institute; American Society of Heating, Refrigeration, and Air Conditioning Engineers; American Standards Association; Association of Home Appliance Manufacturers; Bradford—White Corp.; Brown Stove Works; Chambers Corporation, a subsidiary of Rangaire Corp.; Con Edison; Corning Glass Works; Council of Better Business Bureau; Dunham-Bush, Inc.; Electric Energy Association; Electric Furnace Man, Inc.; Electrical Committee of the National Fire Protection Association; Energy Research and Development Administration; Federal Energy Administration; Federal Trade Commission; Friedrich Air Conditioning & Refrigeration Co., a division of Wylan, Inc.; Gaffers & Sattler, a subsidiary of Magic Chef; Gibson Products Corp.; Heat Controller, Inc.; Hobart Corp.—Kitchen Aid Division and Disposer Division; Litton Systems; McGraw-Edison; Minneapolis-Honeywell Co.; National Board of Fire Underwriters; National Oil Fuel Institute; National Association of Oil Heat Service Managers; National Bureau of Standards; National Electrical Code; National Technical Information Service; North American Systems; Northern Electric Co.; Oak Ridge National Laboratory; Procter-Silex—SCM Corp.; Ray Oil Burner Co.; Roper Sales; South Dakota State College; Sunray Stove Co.—Division of Glenwood Range Co.; Thermador—Norris Industries; University of New Hampshire; University of North Carolina; U.S. Department of Agriculture; U.S. Department of Commerce; U.S. Department of Health, Education, and Welfare; U.S. Environmental Protection Agency; U.S. General Service Administration; Weil McLain Co.; Westbend Co., a division of Dart Industries; Whirlaway—Tappan Division; White Consolidated Industries; White-Rodgers Co.; White-Westinghouse Co.

Preface

This book completely describes new home appliances, the latest methods of their use and upkeep, and provides generously-illustrated instruction for the homeowner. It is also designed to serve as a basic introductory text for training in high schools and vocational schools, technical institutes, and industrial training programs.

How to Buy, Repair and Maintain Home Systems and Appliances is a valuable introductory guide, with step-by-step procedures. Written in simple, straightforward language to aid any man or woman in the correct use and maintenance of home appliances, it provides detailed descriptions, general uses, correct uses, correct operation, and approved maintenance, whenever necessary, of the various electrical, gas, oil, or coal appliances in the home.

The outstanding features of the book are more than 800 illustrations (line drawings and photographs); plentiful tables and charts; appendices with useful data and illustrations; a glossary of terms; and an extensive index.

The author hopes that the information and suggestions in this book will help you attain delightful living and trouble-free comfort for your home.

J.T.A.

Energy Guide Labels on Major Household Appliances

Be sure to look for the yellow-and-black energy guide label when shopping for your major household appliances. These federal energy labels will tell you the estimated cost of operating the appliances, and help you decide which one to buy.

The labels are on new models of refrigerator-freezers, freezers, dishwashers, clothes washers, room air conditioners, furnaces, and water heaters.

The energy guide labels are required by the Federal Trade Commission on appliances manufactured since May 19, 1980.

ESTIMATED ENERGY COSTS

The energy guide labels will tell you the estimated yearly energy costs of operating the appliances; and they identify the lowest and highest energy costs for appliances of similar size. The costs are given both for electrical and gas appliances.

The seven appliances for which these labels are required account for more than 70 percent of most homeowners energy bills.

The room air conditioner labels have energy efficiency ratings (EER) based on the amount of cooling the appliance gives for the electricity it uses. The EER is shown as a number, usually between 7 and 12; the higher the EER number, the more efficient the unit. Furnace labels provide some energy conservation information, and they direct customers to fact sheets available at sales rooms and from building contractors.

Consumers who use the information on the energy guide labels can tell whether an appliance with a higher purchase price will prove to be a better buy in the long run because of lower operating costs.

Television sets, home heating equipment (excluding furnaces), kitchen ranges and ovens, clothes dryers, humidifiers, and dehumidifiers are not labeled because the Federal Trade Commission has determined that there is little difference in energy consumption between different makes and models.

Contents

SECTION III: ELECTRIC MOTORS, PHASE CONVERTERS, TRANSFORMERS, AND SOLDERING

SECTION IV: COMFORT CONDITIONING

SECTION V: FOOD PREPARATION

SECTION VI: FOOD PRESERVATION

SECTION VIII: HOUSEWARES

SECTION IX: HOW TO SAVE ENERGY IN AND AROUND YOUR HOME

HOW TO BUY, REPAIR, AND MAINTAIN

HOME SYSTEMS & APPLIANCES

Section 1

APPLIANCES FOR HOMEMAKERS

EQUIPMENT IN THE HOME falls into two groups: first, the commonly considered major appliances, and second, the items coming under the heading of portable appliances.

Chapter 1

Major Appliances for Homemakers

Responsibility for satisfactory performance of major home appliances falls upon three groups: the manufacturer, the retailer, and the family.

The manufacturer must search for better, safer, and more economical appliances to better serve the family. Through the Association of Home Appliance Manufacturers (AHAM), industry is working cooperatively on performance standards and certification programs for home appliances.

Manufacturers make appliance innovations known to the public through advertising and educational programs. Adequate instructions for operating the appliance should be provided with each sale.

Appropriate warranties or guarantees should be provided to protect the consumer who purchases the appliance against faulty merchandise. Replacement parts and training for servicemen must also be made available so that the appliances can serve a long and useful life.

The retailer must provide a suitable selection of each appliance to be sold so that each buyer can find the best appliance to meet his family situation. Salesmen should be trained to understand appliances and appliance features in order to explain them fully to prospective buyers. Such services as delivery, installation, and maintenance of appliances sold should also be provided at costs that are reasonable for the community served.

Additionally, the retailer is charged to serve as a liaison between the family and the manufacturer, seeing that the conditions of the warranty are met by the manufacturer to the general satisfaction of the family.

A reliable dealer is likely to retail reliable appliances and stand behind them.

The role of the family in appliance satisfaction is sometimes overlooked. Because appliances are purchased at infrequent intervals, new appliances may be different from what you now have. More choices may be available. As a result, you should take time to become fully informed before shopping.

Many people rely on information provided by consumer testing groups. This information can be helpful if you recognize that not all models and makes are studied, and then read carefully to make certain that appliances are compared on a basis important to you.

Knowing what appliance variations are available is only half the job. You must also evaluate your family's needs, at present and projected through the lifetime of the appliance.

1. Is your family large or small? What space is available? These may determine appliance size.

2. What can you afford and how will it be paid for? Spreading payments over a long period of time may ease the budget temporarily, but eventually it will cost you more money because of the effects of the credit service's finance charge.

3. What are the demands on your family time? Time and energy-saving features may help.

4. What is your family's life style? It is wasteful to purchase an appliance or feature you are unlikely to use.

When shopping for appliances you should ask about the availability and costs of appliance service. Carefully read warranties and check instruction books, too. Make sure the instructions are clear.

The American Gas Association (AGA) seal certifies that gas appliances have been tested for safety, performance, and durability. The Underwriters Laboratories, Inc. (UL) certifies that electrical appliances have been submitted by the manufacturer for testing and have met standards regarding life, fire, and casualty.

Read credit contracts before signing to be sure all spaces are filled in. It will help you understand what you are paying for.

When the appliance has been selected and installed the instruction book should be carefully studied and followed. Write the appliance model and serial number on the instruction book so it will be easy to find if you need service.

Instruction book, warranties, and sales receipts should be filed in a safe but handy place. If an appliance problem occurs, check the instruction manual. It will tell you what to do and may even save a service call. When service is required, call the dealer or service agency it recommends.

For service problems that cannot be resolved locally, feel free to write or call the manufacturer, giving all the details. His concern for consumer satisfaction will usually help.

SELECTION OF MAJOR APPLIANCES

Ranges. The appliance the homemaker uses most extensively is her *range*. She and her range form the team that cooks and serves food for the family. Along with cooking, many spills, spatters, and splashes occur, and the homemaker must spend much time and effort keeping her range clean.

When things go well with the homemaker and her range, she is a better cook. So it is important that she select a range that meets her needs and then make the best use of it and its features.

About five electric ranges are bought for every four gas ranges, but the choice is highly individual. Your satisfaction will depend on the availability and cost of each and your past experiences.

Many of the same features are to be found on either *gas or electric ranges.*

About 10 percent of the ranges bought are the high oven type, usually with two ovens.

A second oven may be useful for a large family, special occasions, or entertaining. This feature is available in both gas and electric models. It requires special space.

The upper oven may be smaller. Check size, if it is important to use large roasters or cookie sheets in it.

Look for take-apart units and burners and surface tops that can be lifted for easy cleaning underneath, and removable oven doors and oven liners that can be washed at the sink.

Two oven-cleaning arrangements are available in gas and electric ranges.

Self-cleaning ovens use high temperatures to remove oven soils.

Insulation should keep surface temperatures at a safe level during cleaning.

Continuous-cleaning ovens are lined with a material that encourages the breakdown of oven soils at baking temperatures. Thus, more time is needed for cleaning. If spatters occur with great frequency, keeping the oven clean may be difficult.

Programmed cooking is another feature. Delay-cook ovens have been available for some time on electric ranges. Gas range ovens with programmed cooking will usually be the cook-and-keep-warm type. Cooking begins when food is put into the oven. As the end of cooking time approaches, the oven temperature drops to about 170° F. and is held at that temperature until the food is removed.

Smooth-top ranges provide a new look for the kitchen. Glass ceramic materials have been developed to withstand normal banging and bumping and high cooking temperatures. Pans with smooth, flat bottoms should be used. A special product is available to clean cooked-on spots if they occur. The heat-up and cool-down times are longer than with normal gas or electric ranges.

The *microwave oven* is a new method of heating food. Microwave energy, much like radio and TV radiant energy, is produced and directed into the oven.

The oven has special locks and seals designed to keep microwave energy in and protect the user. Materials such as glass, glass ceramic, china, pottery, paper, and some plastics allow the energy to flow through and are used for cooking utensils.

Microwave energy enters food directly. Molecular agitation inside the food produces heat. Cooking times are much shorter than usual and browning will not take place, except for something as large as a roast that requires a long time to cook.

New utensils have been developed that absorb the energy, and if preheated will brown foods in the oven while cooking quickly with microwave energy.

The family that buys a microwave oven will probably enjoy quick heating and reheating of foods when many busy schedules must be observed. But they will need to spend time and effort to learn to make the best use of it. (Some heart pacemakers are affected by microwave energy, so a pacemaker wearer should consult his physician before purchasing a microwave oven.)

Some concern has been voiced about leaks of microwave energy creating hazards. It is important to point out, however, that microwave rays are longer than visible light and their effect is only to heat. This should not be confused with cosmic rays, gamma rays, X-rays, and ultraviolet rays which are all shorter than visible light and when strong enough can alter living cells.

Refrigerators. The primary function of the *refrigerator* is to provide storage that will keep foods fresh and safe for a long time. The size will depend on both the size of your family and how frequently you shop.

Since storage space is so important, special attention has been given to shelf and compartment design. Crispers should have tight covers to keep fresh vegetables and fruits from drying out. Adjustable shelves, pullout shelves, and door storage should all stretch space.

It is important for the family to consider what they like to put into the refrigerator when they shop—watermelons, turkeys, tall bottles, and other large items can influence their selection.

About a fifth of the refrigerators sold are *side-by-side refrigerator-freezers* and come in sizes that range from 30 to 60 inches wide. They offer storage at a convenient height for both refrigerator and freezer. Doors do not require as much space to open because they are narrow. Some have a third door for ice cubes.

Flush-mount refrigerators are built with the condenser coils (usually on the refrigerator back) under the refrigerator cold-food compartment. This allows the refrigerator to be pushed back against the wall, saving room space. A fan cools the condenser coils when the refrigerator is running.

In *frost-free refrigerators* the cooling coils are concealed behind the refrigerator and freezer compartments so as to completely eliminate the defrosting job. Refrigerated air is blown into the compartments.

Temperatures in frost-free refrigerators are even throughout the unit, and foods cool to safe storage temperatures faster. But unless foods are carefully wrapped and sealed they will dehydrate. The cost of a frost-free refrigerator may be almost double that of automatic defrost refrigerators with manual defrost freezers.

Icemakers eliminate the tray filling job. Add-on icemakers will be slower than some built-in types.

Compact refrigerators may be useful for the family room or a vacation home. They are usually manual defrost.

Freezers.   *Home freezers* are enjoying a spurt in popularity. The types and amounts of frozen foods have more than doubled in the last 10 years. We can expect them to double again in the next 10 years.

A freezer allows you to shop less frequently. This is important if the supermarket is distant, and it fits with the trend toward busy family lives and more working women.

Many families enjoy freezing fresh foods and preparing foods to freeze for later use as well.

An *upright freezer* has easy-to-see-and-use shelf space. Most are frost-free, but may cost more to operate.

A *chest-type freezer* costs less than an upright type, but takes up more floor space and makes reaching foods at the bottom more difficult. It needs defrosting one to three times a year. Some types have push button flash-defrost and a bottom drain to help in defrosting more quickly.

A *compact freezer* saves space.

Dishwashers.   Dishwashers were a luxury appliance 15 years ago. Today, one family in four has one and would hesitate to give it up. Estimates are that 40 percent of homes will have a dishwasher in only a few more years. It may be the next new appliance you buy.

Dishwashers are popular for several reasons: (1) They save an important block of time each day, (2) they reserve kitchen space because used dishes and utensils go right into the dishwasher instead of cluttering the counter, (3) and they get dishes cleaner and more sanitary than if hand washed and dried.

The family's role in getting clean dishes is important. Water must be soft and hot (140° F.–160° F.) and the proper amount of the right detergent must be used.

The dishwasher instruction book will say what can and what cannot be washed and provide charts for proper loading of racks.

In the water distribution system, spray arms direct water onto dishes. Water must reach every dish. A spray arm beneath each rack may be the best method for doing this.

Soft food disposers reduce the need for scraping and prerinsing while flexible rack designs allow random loading and easily accommodate mixed loads.

You have a number of cycle choices. Regular and rinse-and-hold are used the most. Also offered are soak, utensil, short, gentle, and fine china cycles.

Food-Waste Disposers.   *Food-waste disposers* eliminate the garbage chores and odors once associated with trash cans. To make the best use of a disposer, all wastes should be ground immediately. Foods decay rapidly and the acid that develops can corrode metal disposer parts and cause odors.

Cold water is a must in order to solidify fats so they will not congeal in drain pipes and clog them. Most disposers will grind small bones, fruit rinds, and seeds but metals, glass, and china should not be placed in disposers.

In a *continuous-feed disposer*, wastes can be fed into the machine continuously during the disposing process. A batch feed type will operate only with the cover on. It may be safer when the children are around, but may prove to be slower.

Antijamming and reset devices are features that protect the motor from overheating and allow you to get the disposer back into operation when stalled.

Waste Compactors.   *Waste compactors* are a new favorite in many households. They reduce the volume of trash leaving the home and simplify waste disposal. Bottles, cans, cartons, and waste paper can all be compacted. The compactor should be operated after each addition. It takes about a minute for each use.

Large bottles or cans should be laid on their sides near the center of the compactor. Keep hands and feet out when adding trash because of broken glass and sharp can edges.

Compacting food wastes may cause problems. Odors develop with the decaying process and disinfectant sprays delay but do not stop food decomposition.

Key locks are available on all models. In some they prevent operation of the compactors; on others they prevent opening the door as well.

Special trash bags may be required and can be relatively expensive. Sometimes, though, any standard-sized heavy-duty plastic bag can be used.

Washers and Dryers.   We expect more of laundry appliances than just clean, dry clothes. A family's clothes are made up of many fibers—from cotton and wool to polyesters and acrylics. Easy care finishes on clothes are plentiful, too. Laundry appliances must keep them all clean and protect the carefree qualities that are prized so highly.

Many *washers* and *dryers* are larger today than they used to be. They can handle more clothes at a time, but they also use more water and need more detergent and other laundry aids to wash big loads.

New washers and dryers offer more flexibility for better laundry results. However, making the best use of them may mean revising laundry practices. Most manufacturers include a laundry handbook with their washers and dryers to help. Now, 120-volt dryers are also available when a 220-volt circuit is not available. The 120-volt dryers will usually be slower, but are more economical to operate.

Water temperature selector switches allow a choice of wash and rinse water temperatures for many clothes load types.

Water level controls allow small loads to be washed with water and detergent savings.

Agitation and spin speed selectors give vigorous or gentle action for both normal and special loads.

With fully-programmed controls you select the button for the type of wash load, and the proper temperatures and speeds will automatically be used in the cycle.

In *dryers*, look for the following: lint filters, which make it easy to locate and empty lint; temperature choice, from air fluff to hot to suit all clothes load types; fan speed, from gentle to normal for delicate to normal loads; drying sensors, which stop drying when clothes are just right; a drying rack, to dry such things as canvas shoes without tumbling.

Compact washers and *dryers* are good for small families with small loads to wash or where space is limited. Compacts do not usually offer as many features as standard-sized washers and dryers.

Washer-dryer combinations are still around and may solve space problems. Both front-loading washers and washer-dryer combinations use much less water and detergent than the top-loading washers do.

Chapter 2

Buying Small Portable Appliances

Your pleasant plight as a consumer might well be expressed like this. You make yourself beautiful, your house clean and comfortable, and your family or friends happy with good food cooked and served anywhere in the house. And it is all done with appliances, most of them portable and quite inexpensive, but sometimes difficult to select because of the great variety of choices offered.

This chapter gives information that hopefully will help you make the *best buy*. For organizational purposes the appliances are classified as personal care, comfort, cooking, and kitchenware, and are discussed in that order.

As people have become "hair conscious," manufacturers have been busy producing appliances to care for it. There is quite an array of combs, brushes, stylers, dryers, hairsetters, and even "portable beauty salons."

PERSONAL CARE

Electric Combs and Brushes.   *Electric combs* and *brushes* are especially suitable for hair with "direction" or for the natural look. They may be sold as attachments for styling dryers or as hot combs, which are more lightweight and streamlined than dryers. In any case, they perform the same grooming jobs.

Brushes for shaping and combs for styling produce even drying by lifting and separating the hair. They help control cowlicks, unruly ends, and curly hair, and at the same time dry hair quickly and easily.

Most models have two temperatures or speed settings; hot for drying and a cooler one for styling. They may be marked "dry" and

11

"style" or "high" and "low." Many models have a mist feature for dampening hair as it is styled, resulting in a better set.

Detanglers are similar in appearance to hot combs but are made especially for combing out snarls and tangles with a gentle vibrating motion. There is a cordless one for use at the beach, pool, or even in the shower.

While hot combs and styling dryers may be used by all members of the family they are often designated for use by a color key—pastel for women, dark for men, bright or neutral for the family.

Hair Dryers.   *Regular hair dryers* are available in bonnet and more expensive salon types. Features of bonnet models are comb and brush, spot curl attachment for quick touchups, a cool setting for summertime drying, carrying strap, and loose-fitting bonnet with detachable featherweight motor floating on top.

Salon-type dryers have such features as spot mist for touchups, adjustable height, extra-large hood that tilts to allow you to read or sew, remote control, plastic shield for facial saunas, and folds into a compact case.

Hairsetters.   *Hairsetters* allow you to roll your hair on heated rollers for a quick set. Some models set hair dry and with mist or conditioner. A set contains about 20 to 27 or more rollers in three sizes.

Electric Manicure Set.   An *electric manicure set* consists of a power handle and attachments for shaping, buffing, handling cuticles, and smoothing calluses. The greatest advantage to you, other than saving time and money, is that nail edges are beveled to prevent splitting.

Toothbrushes.   If your children hate to brush their teeth or are in the brace stage, an *automatic brush* and *oral irrigator* may be just what they need. Happily, these appliances are geared to family use, so everyone benefits.

Toothbrushes are cordless when in use, but come with a charging unit that must be connected to a live outlet. Do not count on using one that is part of a light fixture unless it operates independently of the light switch. Choose a set that has the number of brushes that best suits your family size, and check on local availability of extra brushes.

Some models brush up and down or back and forth at the flick of a switch. Others brush up, down, and around at the same time.

An *oral irrigator* is designed to supplement brushing. With a pressure control, you send pulsating jets of water into your mouth which clean and stimulate around and between teeth. It is especially good for orthodontic or fixed bridge use.

Rather than two separate appliances, you might prefer having an oral hygiene center that combines the operations of brushing and irrigating.

PERSONAL COMFORT

Air Conditioners.   The best time to buy an *air conditioner* is when you least need it—in the middle of the winter. You have plenty of time then to make a careful selection, and the chances are that you will get a good buy.

Although cost is important, it is not the only factor. An air conditioner must be properly sized for the area it is to cool. When you shop, go armed with information that includes size and shape of the area to be cooled, number of people who normally use the area, exposure, type of windows, amount of glass, and insulation. A dealer then knows what to show you.

You must consider the cost of installation. You may be able to use an existing circuit, but be prepared to pay for additional wiring of perhaps 230 volts.

Operating cost may offset a low purchase price. A simple calculation that takes only a few seconds gives a means of comparing one unit with another. Look for the seal of the Association of Home Appliance Manufacturers (AHAM) which certifies that the British thermal unit (Btu) rating is correct. Divide this rating by the wattage of the unit to get its efficiency. The most efficient model will cost less to operate.

Look closely at the controls. They should be easy to reach and allow you to tailor the air conditioning to your needs. If you are noise conscious, you will enjoy having several speeds. Direction control louvers for air distribution are important, especially in the larger sizes.

Consider serviceability. Look at it from your ability or the repairman's ability to get to and remove the unit if necessary. Also consider filter accessibility because cleaning and changing filters is something you will be doing yourself.

Dehumidifiers.   As a rule, you will not need a *dehumidifier* if you have air conditioning. But you may want to consider one if you notice symptoms of excess moisture such as musty, moldy odors, mildew, peeling interior paint, sweating of cold pipes and basement walls, rusty metal objects, or warped or swelling wood.

A *dehumidifier* works by drawing room air over a cooling coil where it is relieved of some of its moisture. It is then heated slightly and returned to the room at just above its original temperature.

Size depends on a number of factors such as climate, house construction, and where used. But this rough rule of thumb will help you decide: The unit should have the capacity to remove at least a pint of water for every thousand cubic feet of space to be dehumidified.

Look for the Association of Home Appliance Manufacturers' certification of water removal capacity rating.

The unit's cost depends on its capacity, appearance, and features. Among the features are disposal of water by a drain hose or an easy-to-handle container, automatic shutoff to prevent overflowing, and a signal light telling when the container is full. Other features are easily moving wheels, long cord, and adjustable controls for operation.

The operating cost is fairly high but a bargain when balanced against moisture damage to your house and furnishings.

Humidifiers.   A *humidifier* performs exactly the opposite from a dehumidifier. Signs that you may need one are uncomfortably dry body conditions, static electricity, cracks in your house and furniture, and drooping plants.

There is a central type which is installed with a forced hot-air furnace and a self-contained console or tabletop appliance. Sizing is determined by size of the house, tightness of construction, amount of moisture from other sources such as laundering, and desired relative humidity.

Your best bet is to follow the manufacturer's recommendations for space that a unit can handle. If in doubt, buy an oversized rather than an undersized unit.

Humidifiers operate by evaporation or atomization. The latter may create housecleaning problems because the droplets evaporate, leaving mineral deposits on furniture. An evaporation humidifier emits pure vapor by moving air through or around wet pads or sleeves which must be removed by cleaning about once a month, and for replacement about once a year.

The operating cost is moderate but can be increased considerably if the unit has a heater for offsetting the air cooling effect of operation.

Check these features as you shop—furniture styling, automatic shutoff, signal light for filling, ease in filling and cleaning, plastic or stainless parts for hard water areas, air-flow louvers, good casters, and flexible controls for humidity and speed.

Vacuum Cleaners. Your choice of a *vacuum cleaner* should depend to a great extent on what you want it to do for you. As a rule, canister cleaners are easy to handle and do an adequate job of general house-cleaning. Some models feature power attachments that give them increased carpet cleaning efficiency. Uprights are made for carpets, but with a set of attachments they can also houseclean.

Hand vacuums are good for spot cleaning, auto interiors, or other light jobs. They should be used only to supplement full-size cleaners.

Many homes are fully or partially carpeted, some with as many as three or four pile heights. *Upright vacuum cleaners* that adapt to low (such as indoor-outdoor or kitchen carpet), medium, and shag are desirable for these situations. Some models adapt automatically, others must be set manually.

Standard models can be adjusted by changing the amount of suction to the point that the cleaner moves over the carpet without extra effort or without seeming to skim the surface.

Higher priced models may move around at the touch of a finger, a good point to keep in mind if you are troubled with arthritis or other handicaps.

Edge cleaning is a new feature, eliminating the need for using a tool next to walls and pieces of furniture.

You pretty well get what you pay for in a vacuum cleaner, although it is not necessary to buy a very high-priced model that seems out of line with the prices of similar models. Nor should you buy strictly on the basis of low cost. Power, design, and brand reputation are all important, and a good mixture of the three is desirable. Local service is also a plus.

Floor Polishers and Shampooers. Clean, attractive floors are no accident. Whether wood, carpet, or resilient or ceramic tile, any floor can be cleaned with an appliance that is simple and easy to use.

You can buy one that does nothing but shampoo carpets. Another scrubs resilient or ceramic floors, and polishes and buffs resilient, ceramic, and wood. It may also apply liquid polishing wax. Still another does all these jobs with a change of brushes and solution.

Prices vary accordingly, and there is no need to pay for one that does more than your needs require. Whatever your choice of floor polishers and shampooers, it should be easy to move around, have controls that are accessible while the appliance is in use, be easy to assemble and to fill during operation, and have a long cord.

It is important that you follow operating instructions in order to achieve good results. Therefore, be sure that the model you select has a good operations manual. For shampooing carpets, it is especially necessary that you follow instructions. The process is basically as follows:

1. Vacuuming to remove loose soil is the first step. Suds dispensed by the shampooer bring additional soil to the pile surface. The carpet should not be wet excessively and it does not need rinsing. You will notice that the suds disappear rapidly.

2. After the carpet is thoroughly dry, vacuum to remove soil that the shampooer brought to the surface. It is advisable to vacuum every day for about a week for a thorough cleaning.

COOKING

Fondue Pots.   A *fondue pot* is a fun appliance for a specialized type of cooking and a great gift for yourself or someone else. The basic unit consists of a pot, a stand on which it rests, and a burner for cooking or keeping the fondue mixture hot. As you shop you will find many colors, sizes, shapes, and deluxe models, but all fall into three groups, depending on the type of cooking for which they are suitable. They are metal, ceramic, and dessert.

Meats are cooked in oil and therefore require a *metal pot* that can withstand high heat. Frequently used metals are stainless steel, plain, enameled, or porcelainized aluminum, and copper. By regulating the heat, this type of pot can be used for cheese and dessert mixtures and is the best choice for all-purpose fondue cooking. A heavy-gage metal pot that is larger at the bottom than at the top holds heat well and helps prevent spattering. The interior may have a non-stick coating.

A *ceramic pot* shaped like a shallow casserole may be used for cheese fondues; it is not suited for hot oil cooking.

Most metal pots have two-quart capacity but a *dessert utensil* is smaller and may use a candle warmer since sauces require less space and heat than other mixtures. Heat for metal pots is supplied by alcohol, canned heat, or electricity. *Candle warmers* are for dessert fondues only.

Although alcohol burners have some means of regulating the amount of heat, the electric unit features a thermostat to eliminate guesswork.

Forks, plates, trays, and lazy-Susans are accessories that may accompany a fondue set. They can also be bought separately.

When making your selection, remember that it will be used on a table by a group of people. Choose a fairly heavy pot with a comfortable, heat-resistant handle that fits securely on its stand. Use it on its own tray or another that protects the tabletop as well as providing a firm foundation.

Toaster-Ovens. Although it is more than a toaster but less than a range-oven, a *toaster-oven* is a delightful tabletop appliance that does a variety of cooking jobs. Depending upon the manufacturer, it may broil, bake, roast, or toast. How these jobs are accomplished varies with the manufacturer.

All the methods are based on one principle: Heat for baking and roasting comes from the bottom. For broiling and top browning, heat comes from the top.

Some toaster-ovens have one heating unit but since the entire appliance can be flipped over, the unit for broiling and toasting is in the top, for baking and roasting in the bottom. Another type has both top and bottom units controlled by switches. Select the type of cooking you prefer and the appliance automatically does the rest.

These models generally toast one or both sides, automatically turn off, and may have a bell to signal that the food is ready.

Still another type opens from the front for baking and has slots in the top for popup toasting.

To be certain you know exactly what a particular model is capable of doing, take time to look at the operations manual. If it contains no instruction for broiling, the appliance will not broil. If there are no instructions for baking, it will not bake, and so on.

Although the temperature range is from 200° F. to 500° F., baking is necessarily limited by space, even in the larger models. Roasting, where possible, is also limited to small amounts.

As you shop and compare, ask yourself the following questions:

1. Does the toaster-oven perform the jobs you expect of it?

2. Is the size right for the space you have and the amount you want to cook?

3. Does it have features such as removable glass door, removable rack, or continuous clean liner to make cleaning reasonably easy?

4. Does it automatically turn itself off, and is there a signal to tell you that it has turned off?

5. Does it have adequate instructions for use, care, and service?

Rotisseries.   A *rotisserie* cooks meat to a beautiful brown by turning it on a spit in controlled heat. There are two types—open-air and covered. *Open-air models* do not have covers, are low in silhouette, store easily, and can be used for broiling. *Covered models* are larger and more difficult to store but can generally be used for other types of cooking.

The following are factors to consider when shopping for a rotisserie:

1. What you expect it to do—some models have adjustable heating elements and accessories that allow them to be used as a rotisserie, griddle, grille, broiler, and fryer.

2. Space to use and store it, in relation to the size of the appliance.

3. Distance between spit and drip pan below, in relation to what you plan to cook.

4. Features such as removable, immersible parts and continuous-clean liner to make cleaning reasonably easy.

MORE KITCHENWARE

Electric Can Openers.   An *electric can opener* works on cans of all sizes by piercing the lid, cutting it smoothly, and holding it with a magnet until the operation stops automatically. It may also sharpen smoothedge knives and scissors, juice fruit, or crush ice. Prices vary considerably, depending on the number of uses. Important features include good balance and stability, cutting assembly easy to take apart for cleaning, and space for excess cord storage.

Ice Crushers. You may prefer having a *separate ice crusher.* Features to check for are the amount of crushed ice the container can hold, choice of more than one texture of ice, and a powerful but quiet motor.

Mixers and Blenders. *Mixers* and *blenders* complement each other but one does not replace the other.

Three basic types of mixers are available: standard, heavy duty, and portable. For most families a *standard model* is the best choice. However, some homemakers prefer the *heavy duty* one because of its strength. Its main limitation is that the motor head may not be detachable for use at the range.

A *portable mixer* is easy to store and to use at the range but lacks the power to do heavy jobs well. Its very portability can be a tiring liability when you must hold it while mixing a cake or something requiring similar steps.

You may notice a substantial price difference between models made by the same manufacturer. This is sometimes due to the material of which they are made. For example, chrome is more expensive than enamel and glass. There may, however, be a difference in weight, power, number of speeds, or other features.

Some mixers have *attachments* that usually must be purchased separately. You should ask about this if you think that you might be interested at some later date.

Your one reason for buying a mixer is to be able to mix and beat with ease and efficiency. For this reason, you should check the number and sizes of bowls, number of speeds, power of motor at any speed, coverage of bowl by the beaters, beater insertion and ejection methods, ease of handling, the adequacy of the instruction book, and availability of service and parts.

A *blender* operates at very high speed, even on the lowest settings, and is especially good for chopping, blending, pureeing, shredding, whipping, grating, and liquefying. It mixes but cannot handle heavy batters. Neither can it beat egg whites or mash potatoes, both jobs that a mixer does easily.

There are blenders on the market at many prices. Differences are due to the materials of which they are made, number of speeds, type of controls, and power of the motor. Also affecting price are size of the container, whether or not there is a timer, attachments, and the amount of research that was done in development of the blender. The latter point shows up as a well made, sturdy appliance with a good instruction book, and service available in the region.

All blenders operate in a similar manner but subtle differences are important. You may, for example, prefer one that has removable blades or that can be used with regular screwtop jars. Design and color of the base, arrangement of pushbuttons, handle and lid style, and shape of the container are other "small differences" which may be of interest to you.

Both the mixer and blender should be kept where they are handy to use. There is a built-in type, with the motor installed in the countertop, that has attachments for mixing, blending, juicing, and a number of other operations. The one drawback is not being able to use the appliances elsewhere.

Coffeemakers.   As aromas go, freshly brewed coffee is hard to beat. It is possible to produce the aroma without having good coffee but there is no excuse for it. Delicious coffee depends on a number of factors but first and foremost is a good, scrupulously clean pot.

We cannot say that one type of coffeemaker makes better coffee than another because each one has its adherents who swear by it. There are three types—percolator, vacuum, and drip. Differences between the vacuum and drip may not be clear to you.

The *vacuum-type coffeemaker* has two bowls that fit tightly together. Cold water in the bottom bowl is heated and rises into the top bowl where it brews for a few minutes until the heat automatically cuts to a keep-warm position. The coffee then runs back into the lower bowl where it is kept hot for serving.

The lower part of a *drip coffeemaker* is empty until hot water runs through the coffee and a filter and drips into it, ready to serve. Recently this type of coffeemaker has become popular in a model similar to what is used is restaurants. At the moment, it is somewhat more expensive than other types.

Because spotlessness is so important, you should buy a model that is easy to clean. Regular washing with hot water is a must but special periodic cleaning is determined by the material of the coffee-maker's interior.

Oil from the coffee tends to cling to the interior parts and, if left, affects the taste of the coffee. It can be removed by going through the brewing process using a cleanser instead of coffee. For stainless steel or glass, use laundry or dishwasher detergent after removing aluminum parts. For aluminum, use cream of tartar or scrub with a soap-filled steel-wool pad.

Buy a coffeemaker that fits the amount you want to make. It is just as important to know how little it will make satisfactorily as how much. Generally the smallest amount is three or four cups. There is, however, a small basket that fits inside the larger one for making small amounts in some makes.

The spout of a percolator should pour without dripping and should be accessible for cleaning with a percolator brush. There should be a control that allows for flexibility in strength of the coffee and also allows you to reheat coffee without reperking.

IN SUMMARY

These buying hints about small appliances are necessarily limited and general in nature.

There are many good appliances on the market and the final choice may be difficult.

All else being equal, let the following factors weigh heavily:

1. Buy a recognized brand with service, if possible, available locally or not too far away. Some manufacturers maintain service centers in the larger cities where appliances can be carried in or sent to for repair.

2. Look for the Underwriters' Laboratories, Inc., seal of approval for safety, and the Association of Home Appliance Manufacturers' certification of rating for room air conditioners and dehumidifiers.

3. Take the time to look through the instructions, making a quick check for adequacy. This one factor is often a good indication of a quality appliance.

4. Once you have made your decision, return the warranty card, follow the instructions, and enjoy your new convenience.

Section 2

HOME ELECTRICAL WIRING SYSTEMS, ELECTRICIAN'S TOOLS AND TEST EQUIPMENT, AND MATERIALS

IN THE DESIGN OF an electrical system, there are two basic factors to be taken into consideration. One factor is *safety*—compliance with the local governing rules and with the regulations of the National Electrical Code. The other factor is *function*—the designing of a system that will permit the residents full and convenient use of the electrical equipment they now have and may procure in the future.

The National Electrical Code is prepared by the Electrical Committee of the National Fire Protection Association, which committee is representative of all the principal interests concerned with the safety of wiring. This code is a standard adopted by the National Board of Fire Underwriters and has the approval of the American Standards Association. Together with local ordinance, frequently based upon the Code, and rules and regulations of local utility companies, the National Electrical Code provides a standard governing the installation, and, to a certain extent, the use of electrical equipment.

An effective and efficient electrical system depends upon the following:

1. Sufficient circuits of sufficiently large wire to carry the various loads without uneconomical voltage drop.

2. Sufficient outlets to allow for convenient use of electrical equipment.

3. Well-placed control-centers equipped with modern circuit protection.

4. High-quality materials and workmanship.

A large variety of tools and equipment together with special equipment are used for repairs of electrical equipment and appliances. Therefore, it would be wise to become familiar with these tools and equipment, their proper names, and the purpose for which they are used.

Chapter 3

Home Electrical Wiring Systems

The home that is wired not only in accordance with the standards of safety, but also with the "ability to serve," will be capable of accommodating the lighting equipment and appliances that might be installed during its entire life. Thus, the owner need not suffer from the inconvenience and inefficiencies of overload circuits and insufficent outlets—nor will he or she suffer from the annoyance and expense of alterations necessary to accommodate the "electrical way of living."

ROUGH-IN WORK

There are two separate phases to the work performed by electricians on new residential construction—rough-in and finish. The electrician becomes involved in the construction process after the exterior walls and roof have been framed and the building dried in.

This is the time for the *rough-in phase*. Using the wiring blueprints, the electrician and his helpers locate the spot where the utility pole conductors will be tied to the building. The electrician assembles and installs the conduit, weather-head and meter loop, main disconnect and the interior circuit-breaker panels. This interior circuit-breaker panel will become the heart of all wiring inside and outside the building. Complying strictly to electrical codes and specifications, the electrician locates and sets utility and receptacle outlet boxes. Holes are bored and wires pulled through and stapled. Usually, romex wire is specified in residential construction.

Romex is a name given to a type of wire, and it is normally referred to by the size of the wire and the numbers of wires that are wrapped together in a plastic cover. A 12-2 with ground means there are two insulated wires or conductors, each with a sizing of 12. There would also be a ground wire. This wire with ground is the most common wire used in residential circuits.

All circuits originate at the circuit-breaker box and spread throughout the house. During the rough-in phase, all wiring must be completed before the walls and ceilings are insulated and covered with gypsum wallboard. Therefore, the electrician and his helpers must work rapidly, but exactly. Correcting wiring mistakes can be costly to the electrical contractor or homeowner if they have to be made after the walls and ceilings are covered.

After the rough-in phase is completed and before the walls are closed in, an electrical inspector must inspect and approve the wiring system. Strict code requirements must apply. Any improper wiring practices must be corrected and inspected again. Delay to the overall construction project, for whatever reason, will cost the contractor money.

To do rough-in wiring, electricians and the electrician's helpers read and accurately interpret blueprints and building specifications. They measure, cut, and bend rigid and thin wall conduit tubing. They measure, locate, and place various boxes and run wires to these boxes. All wiring connections must be made securely, correctly, and safely.

CIRCUITS

In residential construction, there are two basic circuits—230 volt and 115 volt. Electric ranges, water heaters, heating and cooling systems, and pumps and dryers are almost always wired for 230 volts. Lighting and outlet boxes are generally wired for 115 volts. They are wired with 12-2 wire and grounded circuits. They may be several lighting fixtures or outlets on one circuit. It is important that all of these items are wired using the two-color wiring code—black for hot wires and white for common wires. Ground wires are usually bare, but in some cases may be green in color. On outlet receptacles, the hot or black wire is tied to the gold terminal, and the common or white wire is tied to the silver terminal. The colored plastic insulation on each wire is stripped just enough to make the connecting loop if screwed terminals are used. On push-in quick connectors, a scale for stripping is usually printed on the receptacle.

Today, the most common type of connectors for wires are the solderless screw-on type. The wires are stripped and pig-tailed together, trimmed, and the connector is screwed on tightly. A wire coil inside of these connectors will draw and lock in the wires together. No bare conductor should show from under the shield of the connector. A firm tug should be applied to the connector to check for a secure connection. All connections, whether screw, push-in, taped, soldered, and the like, should be checked in the same manner.

WIRING OF SWITCHES

The wiring of single pole switches will not conform to the regular use of the two-color code. These wires should be thought of as both black, as switches should only open and close the hot side of the circuit. When wiring a single-pole single-throw (spst) switch, it will be necessary to connect a white wire to the black wire going to the light. Nearly all switches used in residential construction are placed in series with the circuit. Figure 1 shows how a switch is diagramed in series with a circuit.

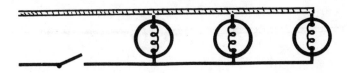

Fig. 1. Spot switch.

This circuit is now opened and the lights are not on. When the switch is closed the lights will burn if all of the bulbs are good (Fig. 2).

Fig. 2.

The lights of the circuit shown in Fig. 3 are parallel, and you can see the basic differences between series and parallel circuits.

A simple circuit only has one light or appliance and is diagramed as shown in Fig. 4.

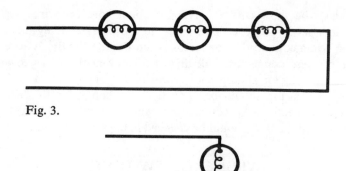

Fig. 3.

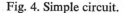

Fig. 4. Simple circuit.

You can see that this circuit can be described as either series or parallel, but, to avoid this problem, it is called a simple circuit.

Nearly all of the operational circuits in homes today are parallel, but there are other switches used in residential construction. The single-pole single-throw switch has been described previously and shown in Fig. 4. The three-way switch and its function is shown in Fig. 5.

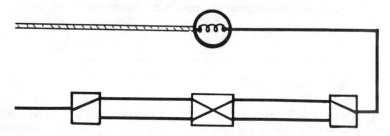

Fig. 5. Three-way switch.

The circuit can be opened and closed from either switch. As shown in Fig. 5, the light would be on. Use of these switches include control of lights in a large room, with switches placed at two entrances/ exits to the room. Also, garage lights can be wired this way to permit lights to be turned on and off from inside the house or garage.

Another type of switch that is sometimes used in residential construction is the four-way switch as shown in Fig. 6.

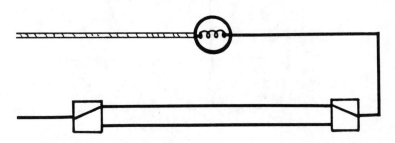

Fig. 6. Four-way switch.

You can see that it utilizes the basic three-way diagram, but now includes a four-way switch connected to the traveler wires between the 2 three-way switches. The light in the diagram would not be on. This light can now be controlled from three different positions in a room. This type of switch might be used in residential construction to control lights in hallways and stairways, in addition to lights in large rooms.

There are other kinds of switches that are used in homes today— push button, pull chain, timer, temperature controlled, photoelectric cell, pressure, and many others. Their functions are identical—to open and close the circuits that they control.

WIRING OF RECEPTACLES

In residential wiring there are many types of receptacles. The most common are shown in Fig. 7. A: Parallel slot—115-volt receptacle, usually one receptacle includes a pair of outlets; B, tandem slot— 230-volt receptacle, in pairs or single outlets; and C, crow foot—230 volt, usually mounted as a single outlet.

These three receptacles are by far the most common. There may be special outlets, however, for plugs on some appliances. An example of this would be receptacles required by different manufacturers of clothes dryers.

All of these receptacles should be wired properly, including the wiring of grounds.

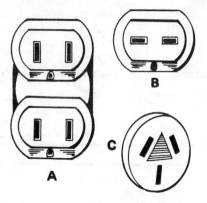

Fig. 7. Types of receptacles.

WIRING OF DIMMERS

Another device that is frequently installed to residential wiring is a light dimmer. There are two types of dimmers: One for fluorescent lights and one for incandescent lights. Dimmers for controlling fluorescent lamps are variable reactors or choke coils that control the amount of *current* flowing through the lamps. Dimmers for controlling incandescent lamps are variable resistors that control the *voltage* to the lamps. Let us first look at how incandescent dimmers are installed.

Incandescent dimmers are relatively simple. There are two types: Three-way dimmers and rotary dimmers. The three-way dimmer has three positions—high, low, and off. They are wired into circuit, as is any single pole switch, with two wires to connect. Rotary dimmers can be set to any degree of lighting, from zero lighting (off) to full lighting. As the switch knob is turned clockwise the light becomes brighter; when turned counterclockwise, the light dims. Rotary dimmers also have only two wires to connect and are wired in a single pole switch.

Fluorescent dimmers are similar to incandescent dimmers, but are somewhat more complicated. In addition to the dimming switch, a special transformer is installed. The transformer feeds current to the lamp. In turn, the transformer is fed current from a dimmer switch similar to those used with incandescent lights.

When the electrician installs dimmers, the first thing he does is to check the plans for the electrical system being installed to find the exact spots where the dimmer switches and connected wiring should be installed. Next, the proper distances from floor to ceiling are measured off, and boxes and wiring are "roughed in." Lighting fixtures are attached and wired in. The dimmer is then wired to the ground box and into the circuit. The circuit is connected to the power and tested.

FLUORESCENT LIGHTING

Fluorescent lighting was previously mentioned in the section on Wiring of Dimmers. One task that electricians frequently do is to install a fluorescent lamp controlled by a single-pole, single-throw switch. Let's look at some of the special requirements of fluorescent systems.

Incandescent lighting produces light by running electrical current through a tungsten thread, called a filament, inside the light bulb. As current flows through the filament, it becomes white hot. The light from incandescent lamps comes from this glowing white-hot filament. On the other hand, a fluorescent bulb produces light by heating mercury until it vaporizes. An electrical current is passed through the mercury vapor. Electrons from the mercury vapor strike a powder, called phosphor, and cause it to glow. It is the glow from the phosphor that creates the light from fluorescent lamps. High voltage is run through the tube when the light is started; then, when the mercury vapor has filled the tube, a low voltage is maintained. The voltage is raised and lowered by special transformers, called "ballasts," built into fluorescent lighting systems. The ballast also controls the exact amount of current flowing through the lamp at any given moment.

A second device used in fluorescent lamps is the lamp starter. In order to understand what a lamp starter does, let us look again at what happens in a fluorescent lamp. When the current is turned on, mercury is vaporized—that is, heated until it turns into a gas. Then current is set flowing through the gas. There are two steps in the process, and, in between the two steps, current in the bulb is turned off. It is the starter that shuts off the heating current and starts up the arc that actually lights the bulb.

CIRCUIT BREAKERS

When electricians wire a residence they install devices called circuit breakers. Circuit breakers shut off the flow of current when a circuit is overloaded. There are two types of devices that trip circuits. One is constructed with a bimetallic switch somewhat like a thermostat. When an overload occurs, the switch heats up and shuts off the circuit just as a thermostat does. The second tripping device is operated by an electromagnet that becomes strong enough to pull open the circuit when an overload occurs.

The National Electrical Code is now requiring the use of ground-fault circuit breakers on outlets located in *hazardous* locations. The intent of the ground-fault breaker is to protect the users of electrical appliances from electrocution. Its theory is that if more current is flowing in the "hot" wire than is returning through the neutral wire, then the extra current may be going to ground through the operator of some appliance. It interrupts the circuit before the "last" current reaches injurious proportions.

Circuit-breaker panels are installed in much the same way that other panel boards are installed. There are several different types of circuit breakers. Most of those installed in residences fit into panel boards. Circuit breakers are rated according to their capacity to carry amperage, that is, their ampacity. Circuit breakers on 120-volt lines use single pole switches; those on 240-volt lines use double pole switches. Each circuit is wired into its switch just as any other switch is wired. Panel covers have *twistouts* which are spots where metal plates may be knocked out with a screwdriver (Fig. 8) so that there will be a place for the breaker switches.

Circuit breakers and fuses provide a vital service. They are a safety valve to appliances fed by that circuit. Should something go wrong, the breaker or fuse will open at the source of power to that circuit. This action prevents abnormal heat build-ups in the wires. If not checked by a circuit breaker or fusing device, the wires of the circuit will heat up, and, at the very least, damage the entire circuit or cause a fire within the walls or ceiling of the residence. Therefore,

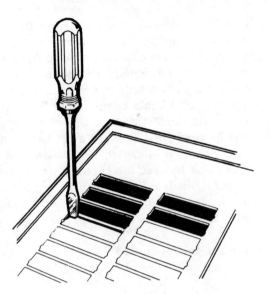

Fig. 8. Twistouts.

every circuit should include these very important safety devices. They should never be bypassed or tampered with in any way.

When an electrician installs a circuit breaker, the circuits are laid out in the house. Next, the panel board is attached to the wall either with clips or screws. All 120-volt circuits are identified and marked. Those circuits that are unidentified should be wired to single pole switches. Then all 240-volt circuits are located and connected to double pole switches. Grounding conductors are then fastened to the grounding conductor. The breaker board cover is attached. At last, a diagram of the circuits is attached to a card in the panel cover.

WIRING OF APPLIANCES

Electricians also connect wiring to electrical kitchen equipment such as ranges, cooking burners, ovens, garbage disposals, and electric clothes washers. One of the simplest operations is to install a *cook-top unit and a built-in oven.* When an electrician starts to install these units, calculations must be made on the circuit requirements for each appliance. Usually a circuit is run from the service entrance to a panel board in the kitchen. (*See* Fig. 9.) From there circuits are run to the different appliances. A cooking top will use about five or six kilowatts and should be wired to allow 30 amps to pass. A wall oven will use about four or five kilowatts and use about 26 amps. Usually No. 10-3 cable connected to 30 amp circuits is used. When an electrician is wiring in a cooking-top and oven, voltage drop must be considered. *Voltage drop*, or line drop, is the voltage lost in the circuit. It is caused by resistance in the wiring and A is turned into heat between the electrical source and the place where it will be used. Usually no more than a one percent line drop is allowable in circuits to cooking-tops and ovens. About 35 feet of No. 10 cable or 55 feet of No. 8 cable will give a one percent line drop.

After the electrician has calculated voltage drop and the circuits needed, the boxes that will be needed are roughed-in. Behind each

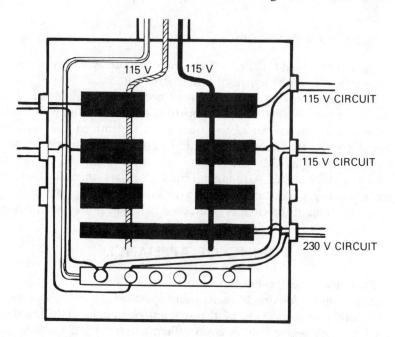

Fig. 9. Circuits.

unit—the cooking top and the oven—a four-inch box is installed. Cable is then attached to the wiring of the appliance.

The oven and the cooking-top are grounded to the neutral wire of the supply cable. This cable is at least No. 10. Finally, the covers of the boxes are attached and the appliances slid into place.

Another kitchen appliance frequently installed is a *garbage disposal unit*. Garbage disposals have certain circuit requirements. The electrician needs to check the directions supplied by the manufacturer of the equipment in order to determine exactly how the wiring should be connected to the unit itself. Plans are then checked to locate the garbage disposal. The boxes and wiring are roughed-in and the motor control switch is wired in. Then, leads from the box are connected to the disposal unit itself. Finally, the grounding conductor is connected to the disposal.

Another appliance often installed is the *dishwasher*. The appliance should be checked to determine the circuit load. Whatever boxes and wiring are needed should then be roughed-in. The dryer receptacle should be mounted on a four-inch box and the cover plate on the back of the dryer removed. The cord from the receptacle should be attached to dry terminals, flexible grounding braid should be attached to the grounding conductor, and the other end of the grounding braid should be attached to the grounding terminal on the dryer. Finally, the dryer should be leveled and pushed into place.

WIRING OF OTHER SYSTEMS

Electricians also install a variety of automatic (or servo-controlled) electrical systems, from heating and cooling systems to door chimes and remote-controlled lighting.

For instance, one job an electrician might be asked to do is install a 15-kilowatt *electric furnace* and its controls. An electrician should first have some knowledge of electric furnaces and other heating devices before beginning to install one. In an electric furnace, heating elements become red hot. After the elements heat up, fans blow air across the elements. This heats the air. It then flows down metallic ducts and out into the different rooms of the house. Smaller heaters are mounted in walls or ceilings and are used to heat individual rooms of a house. These types of electric heaters operate on the principle that when electric current flows through a high-resistance conductor, the conductor produces heat and light, as in an incandescent light bulb. (*See* Fig. 10.)

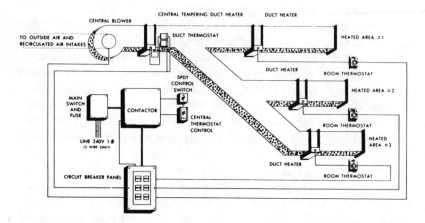

Fig. 10.

When an electrician installs an electric furnace, the first thing he does is check the designs to locate exactly where the furnace and its controls should be placed. The furnace manufacturer will have supplied exact wiring requirements for the furnace, either in a booklet, or engraved on a plate on the furnace itself. The size of wire and the number of circuits needed should be calculated. The wiring for the furnace circuits should be roughed-in from the main panel.

An electric furnace may be wired into a 115-volt, two-wire circuit, using No. 12 wire. Usually 15 or 20 amps will be a sufficient current limit. Then wiring should be roughed-in between the thermostat and the furnace. The wiring diagrams provided with the thermostat and the furnace should be followed exactly. The thermostat should be placed on an interior wall, away from drafts. Power should be turned on, and the operation of the thermostat and furnace should be checked.

Electricians also install *automatic controls* on natural gas furnaces. As with electric furnaces, the first step the electrician takes is to locate the exact spot where controls and their wiring should be placed. Then the operating manual, or nameplate rating of the furnace, should be checked to determine circuit requirements. With this information, circuits can be laid out.

To understand what circuits are needed, let us review what electric controls are available. First of all, thermostats of different types are used to turn a furnace on and off. The type used in any given place depends on the type of furnace used. One type, used with water heating systems, has the thermostat submerged in a pool of water. It is set to shut off when the water temperature reaches a certain level. Another device, called a pressurestat, is used with steam heating devices. Instead of turning the furnace off when a given temperature has been reached, the pressurestat turns it off when a set pressure is reached. Another device, called the furnacestat, is mounted in the bonnet of the furnace and keeps it going until the temperature rises to a preset air temperature.

The actual process of installing a thermostat begins with the electrician checking plans and determining exactly what type of thermostat should be installed and where it should be located. Then, the wiring is roughed-in. Relatively low voltage wiring is used to connect current from the thermostat to the furnace. A fused switch is placed near the external wall. A junction box is placed on the outside wall. The control cable is fed in. Conduit and wire are connected between the junction box, the switch box and the alternating current unit. Finally, the thermostat itself is mounted and wired in. Figure 11 shows a thermostat circuit diagram.

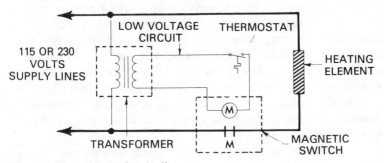

Fig. 11. Thermostat circuit diagram.

Besides installing electric heaters and thermostats, electricians also often install *door chimes*. Here is how a door chime with front and back door buttons would be installed. Circuits for door chimes are relatively simple—they consist of a power source, a low voltage transformer, a pushbutton, and a bell. Basically, the bell and the pushbutton are in a series circuit. Other pushbuttons may be wired in together, parallel to each other. The wiring used should be low voltage wiring, loosely stapled down with insulated staples. Frequently, chimes are installed that sound different tones, depending on whether the button at the front or back door is pressed. In this case, two chime units are connected in parallel. Each unit has three wires. If the front door button is pushed, the front chimes alone will sound. If the back door button is pushed, both chimes will sound. (*See* Fig. 12.)

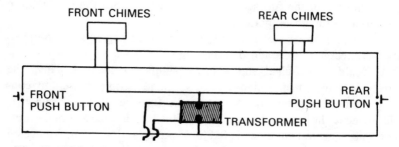

Fig. 12. Wiring for two-tone chimes with low voltage power supply.

When installing door chimes, the electrician first checks the blueprints to determine exactly where the chimes, the transformer, and the pushbuttons should be located. Next, the power circuit to the transformer box is roughed-in along with low voltage wiring. Care is taken in stapling it so that the insulation is not cut. The circuit is connected to the pushbuttons with the buttons mounted next to the doors with small nails or screws. The control and circuit wires of the chime are then connected. The grounding conductor is fastened to the transformer box. Finally, the circuit and low voltage wires are connected to the low voltage transformer.

Besides installing door chimes, electricians install low voltage *remote-control lighting systems*. These systems differ from ordinary switches in that they require 24 volts rather than 115 volts. Remote-control switches use a relay to switch the current on and off. An electromagnet pulls the switch off and on. The electrician checks the plans and locates where the fixtures and switches should be placed. The boxes and wiring for a 120-volt system are roughed-in. A four-inch square box is mounted to hold the transformer. Next, the necessary low voltage wiring is roughed-in. A low voltage relay is set in one of the ½-inch knockouts at each light or receptacle box. The low voltage leads and switch legs are spliced to the transformer leads. The 120-volt power leads are spliced inside the box. The light fixture or receptacle is wired into the box. Switch leg conductors are attached to each switch. Each switch should be mounted on a raised plaster ring. Each ring is then connected to the master selector switch. This switch is fastened to the wall, as are the others. Power is connected to secondary terminals.

Other voltage systems installed are home radio, intercom, and TV antenna distribution systems. When an electrician installs an *intercom system*, the first step is to check the blueprints to determine the type of system. The electrician locates where the control and slave stations should be placed. The boxes and wiring are roughed-in. The wiring for the intercom system should not be adjacent to the house wiring. A step-down transformer is mounted in the panel board. The line side of the circuit is wired into the transformer. Next, the low voltage cable from the transformer to the master station is wired in. Power leads are wired into the master station. Remote speakers are connected and mounted. The step-down transformer is mounted in the panel board and the line side of the transformer is wired in. Finally, the master unit is connected to an antenna mounted in the attic.

Electricians also install *TV antennas and lead-in cables*. There are many different types of antennas on the market. In order to install any given antenna properly, you should study the directions supplied by the manufacturer. Also check the blueprints and specifications to determine exactly where the antenna and television outlets should be placed. The next step is to install the antenna mast and the antenna. All lead-in cable should be roughed-in. This cable should be placed at some distance from all AC wiring. The coupler should be

Fig. 13. TV antenna.

mounted; the lead-in cables should be connected according to a diagram supplied with the coupler. (*See* Fig. 13.) The antenna mast should be grounded to an electrode driven into the ground. The lead-in cable should be connected to the antenna. Finally, the cable should be attached to a specially designed TV outlet.

Chapter 4

The Electrician's Tools and Test Equipment

The following lists includes common tools and equipment that are frequently needed for repairs and adjustments; and special tools and equipment for motor, generator, and other types of repair.

COMMON TOOLS AND EQUIPMENT

Machinist's hammers
Rawhide mallets
Rubber mallets
Hacksaw frame and blades
Handsaws (woodworker's crosscut and backsaw)
Chisels (machinist's and woodworker's)
Clamps (C clamps)
Files (bastard cut)
Rasps (woodworker's)
Knives (electrician's)
Scissors (straight blade)
Nippers (blacksmith's)
Pliers:
    Adjustable combination
    Long-nose (half-round)
    Diagonal cutting
    Flat-nose, parallel jaw
Punches:
    Prick punch
    Center punch

Pin punch
Taper punch
Hollow punch
Reamers:
    Straight reamers
    Adjustable aligning reamers
Screwdrivers:
    Standard
    Offset
    Phillips
Shears:
    Straight-blade tinners
    Aviation snip
    Bolt cutter
Rules (steel scales)
Micrometer calipers:
    Inside
    Outside
Calipers:
    Inside spring
    Outside spring
    Firm-joint hermaphrodites
Dividers
Soldering irons:
    Electric
    Gas
Taps:
    Taper
    Plug
    Bottoming
    Pipe
Dies:
    Round-split
    Pipe
Vises:
    Utility
    Pipe

Wrenches:
  Adjustable, open-end
  Socket
  Setscrew
  Pipe
  Box
Twist drills
Drill press
$\frac{1}{4}$-inch electric drill
$\frac{1}{2}$-inch electric drill
Small-engine lathe
Source of compressed air
Plumber's gasoline furnace
Solder pot
Braces and bits
Test lamp
Solder ladles:
  Common
  Long-spout
Blowtorch

SPECIAL TOOLS AND EQUIPMENT FOR MOTOR, GENERATOR, AND OTHER TYPES OF REPAIR

Spring balance
Plug gages (shop made)
Sleeve bearing arbors (shop made) (Fig. 1)
Extractor and inserter set (Fig. 2)
Arbor press
Arbor press plates
Wire hook (shop made)
Acetylene torch set
Coil-winder drive-and-head (Fig. 3)
Commutator dresser
Insulation former (Fig. 4)
Wire gage
Wire stripper

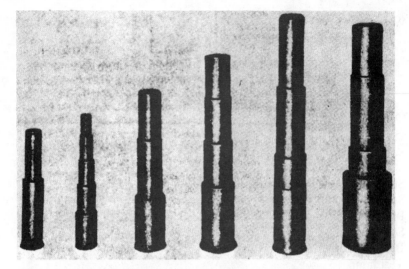

Fig. 1. Sleeve bearing arbors (shop made).

Fig. 2. Extractor and inserter set.

Fig. 3. Coil-winder drive-and-head.

Fig. 4. Insulation former.

Commutator stone dressing tool (Fig. 5)
Mica undercutting tool (Fig. 6)
Jackscrew- and plate-type bearing pullers
Hook-type bearing puller
Bar-type bearing puller
Air-gap feeler gage (Fig. 7)

TEST EQUIPMENT

Electric meters and other test equipment when necessary are as follows.

Circuit tester (Fig. 8).

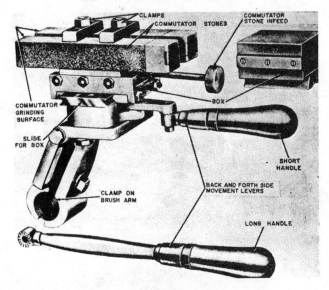

Fig. 5. Commutator stone dressing tool.

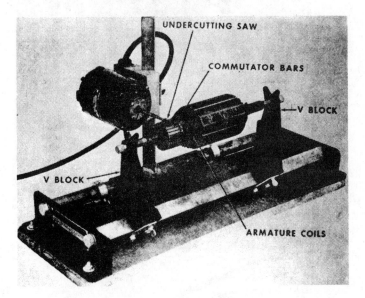

Fig. 6. Mica undercutting tool.

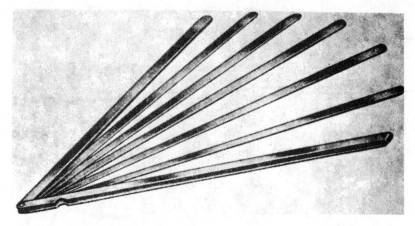

Fig. 7. Air-gap feeler gage.

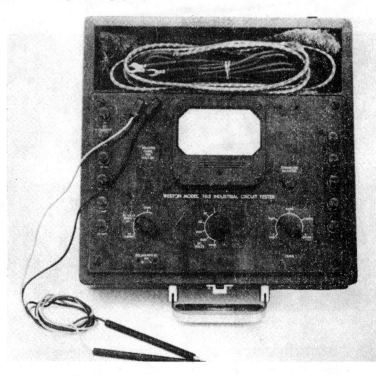

Fig. 8. Circuit tester.

Multimeter (Fig. 9). The multimeter is a versatile piece of equipment that can be used for many purposes, such as checking voltages, both alternating current (AC) and direct current (DC), amperes, resistances, and continuity. It will not check AC amperes.

Wattmeter, AC and DC.

Clamp-on ammeter (Fig. 10). The split core multimeter, commonly called a clamp-on ammeter, is a portable piece of equipment that can be used to check AC voltages or AC amperes in AC circuits only.

Coil and condenser tester (Fig. 11).

Power factor meter.

Frequency meter (Fig. 12). The frequency meter is used to check the 60 and 400 hertz (Hz) frequencies.

Electrical analyzer (Fig. 13). This analyzer is designed for AC circuits and should not be used on DC circuits. It consists of a voltmeter, ammeter, wattmeter, and power factor meter, together with two current transformers and the necessary switches suitably con-

Fig. 9. Multimeter.

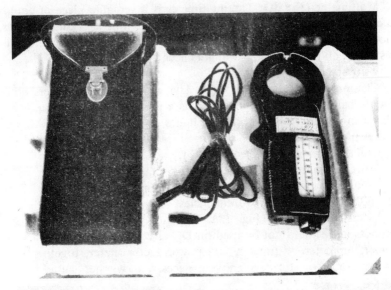

Fig. 10. Clamp-on ammeter.

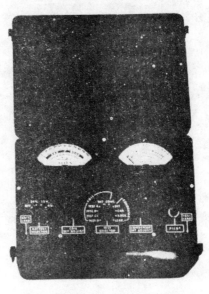

Fig. 11. Coil and condenser tester.

Fig. 12. Frequency meter.

Fig. 13. Electrical analyzer.

nected to facilitate the testing of three-phase three-wire loads. The analyzer can also be used for measurements on single-phase and other polyphase circuits.

Megohmmeter (Fig. 14). The megohmmeter, commonly called the megger, is used to check the quality of insulation around a wire. It can also be used to locate a ground coil. It may be used to check for shorts between coils only if a high-scale model is used.

Fig. 14. Megohmmeter.

Tachometer (Fig. 15). The magnetic tachometer is primarily a small electric generator coupled to a meter. The tachometer includes the generator, revolutions per minute (rpm) indicator, five-foot connecting cord, surface speed wheel attachment, and pointed and mushroom tips. To use the tachometer as a hand type, plug the generator into receptacle on indication, and twist to lock in position.

Fig. 15. Tachometer.

External growler (Fig. 16). The external growler is a versatile piece of equipment that can be used to test 2½-inch to 6-inch

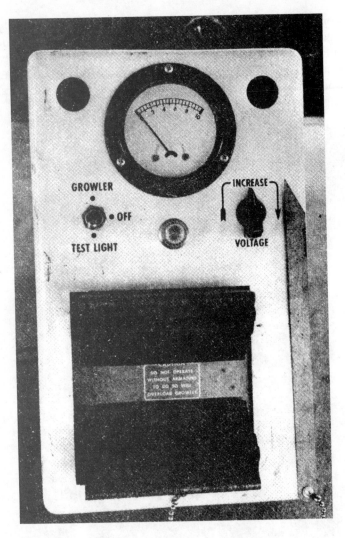

Fig. 16. External growler.

diameter armatures for opens, shorts, grounds, incorrect number of windings on the armature, and reversed coils.

Internal growler (Fig. 17). The internal growler is used to test 6-inch to 12-inch diameter AC stators for shorts between coil groups.

Fig. 17. Internal growler.

Oscilloscope (Fig. 18). The oscilloscope is a solid-state portable instrument that combines small size and light weight with the ability to make precision wave form measurements. It is mechanically constructed to withstand the shock, vibration, and other extremes of environment associated with portability. A DC to four megahertz vertical system provides calibrated deflection factors from 0.01 to 20 volts/division (0.001 volt/division minimum with reduced frequency response). The trigger circuits provide stable triggering over the full vertical band width. The horizontal deflection system provides calibrated sweep rates from 1 second to 5 microseconds/division. An X10 horizontal magnifier allows each sweep rate to be increased 10 times to provide a maximum sweep rate of 0.5 microsecond/division in the 5 μs position. X-Y measurements can be made by applying the vertical (Y) signal to the VERT INPUT connector and the horizontal (X) signal to the EXT TRIG or HORIZ INPUT connector (time/division switch set to EXT HORIZ).

Pen recorder or oscillograph (Fig. 19). Pen recorders are basically graphic DC milliammeters designed for laboratory and field use where analog signals in the DC to five-Hz range are to be recorded. An unusual feature is their straight line motion, especially important where a low-frequency, undistorted trace is required. The D'Arsonval galvanometers, coupled with unique pen systems, produce true sinusoidal input. In many applications, this will eliminate time-consuming data reduction and interpretation.

AC and DC digital voltmeter (Fig. 20). The digital voltmeter is a compact, economical, general purpose instrument with a high degree of accuracy and reliability. It features a servo-driven three-digit

Fig. 18. Oscilloscope.

Fig. 19. Pen recorder or oscillograph.

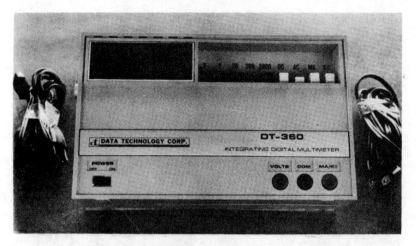

Fig. 20. AC and DC digital voltmeter.

counter with overranging and combines in one instrument many virtues of both digital and analog voltmeters.

Transistor tester (Fig. 21). The transistor tester is a solid-state portable instrument used to check transistors and diodes present in solid-state control devices of motors and generators.

AC power source (oscillator) (Fig. 22). The power oscillator is intended for use where requirements exist for AC signals over the frequency range of 0.1 to 100,000 hertz with a high degree of amplitude stability and purity wave form. It is used as a source in AC voltage and current calibration work, galvanometer calibration, precise distortion measurements, vibration calibration and testing, filter and transformer testing, and other applications in the subsonic through ultrasonic regions. The power amplifier section has extremely stable gain, very low distortion, and a high degree of regulation.

Electro-hydraulic actuator test stand (Fig. 23). The test stand was designed basically for a governing system on generator sets using the LEH control unit. The test stand may also be used to test and align other actuators provided the correct mechanical and electrical biases are available to the user. The stand has its own hydraulic system with three gages and connections to provide hydraulic fluid to the actuator. It has an electrical system that requires 120 volts to provide the correct power to the actuator being tested.

Fig. 21. Transistor tester.

Fig. 22. AC power source (oscillator).

Fig. 23. Electro-hydraulic actuator test stand.

Chapter 5

Materials

After determining the electrical equipment to plan for in the home, the next step is to determine outlets needed to properly serve this equipment.

OUTLETS

Care in determining the number and location of outlets—such as *lighting, switch-controlled convenience,* and *special-purpose* outlets— is of utmost importance. By having adequacy in the number of outlets, unsightly, inconvenient, and long extension cords will be unnecessary. Extension cords present a double hazard—one from tripping and the other from the electrical hazard of short circuits caused by frayed cords.

Location of Outlets.   The location of outlets must satisfy the original scheme of interior decoration and furniture arrangement and be flexible, so that future rearrangement of furniture can be equally well served electrically. Do not make the mistake of locating convenience outlets based on a given furniture layout. Interiors are often changed by the same family and certainly, when the house has a new occupant, the arrangement of furniture is bound to be different. Therefore, *place convenience outlets so they may serve any practical interior furniture arrangement.*

Outlets must be located conveniently to serve the desired lighting and portable appliances. Recommended heights of switches and convenience outlets are as follows:

Wall switches—on lock side of door, within six inches of door frame; and from 48 to 54 inches above finished floor.

Convenience outlets—locate 12 to 18 inches above finished floor, except in kitchen, dinette, laundry, bathroom, utility space, and garage where outlets should be approximately 48 inches above finished floor.

Master Switch Control. In determining the outlets required, a feature worthy of consideration is a master control of certain outlets from the owner's bedroom. This master switch makes it possible to turn on lights located at various points inside or outside the house, independently of local switch controls.

More specifically—when the master switch is in the off position, the outlets under its control may be controlled by local switches. When the master switch is in the on position, the outlets under its control will all be on regardless of whether the local switches are on or off.

Figure 1 shows wiring connections for one and two branch circuits. Where more than two branch circuits are to be controlled, single-pole magnetic switches are recommended in each circuit, actuated by a single-pole master switch.

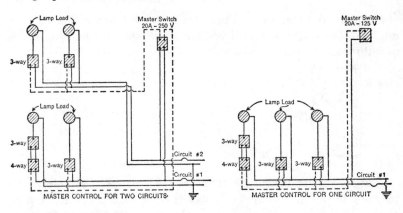

Fig. 1. Master switch control wiring.

Wiring Devices. Single-pole switch outlets and duplex receptacle outlets are quite common in use and therefore need no introduction. But there are many more wiring devices available—wiring devices designed for specific uses; that is, to render added convenience. These devices do not need special outlet boxes. They fit into standard outlet boxes.

A brief description of what some of these devices are and where they can best serve may not be amiss here. Although these small items are of modest cost, they are one of the many factors that can contribute to the difference between an *ordinary* or *common* installation and an *outstanding* installation. The following wiring devices are of particular interest.

Silent switches (Fig. 2). Mercury switches are very desirable in a home, as they lend added refinement. There being no "click" when the handle is moved makes for quietness in operation, and this is particularly desirable in bedrooms and bathrooms.

Fig. 2. Silent switch.

Night lights (Fig. 3). No one device in the wiring line adds so much to the house as night lights. They are ideal for halls, at stairs, in bathrooms, and in the children's bedroom.

Fig. 3. Night light.

Receptacles for cleaning equipment (Fig. 4). A ready means for plugging in portable cleaning devices such as vacuum cleaners, floor waxers, and the like, is very desirable. An ideal location is at the switch height immediately upon entrance to the room. This device is also frequently used in bathrooms where it is practical to combine the switch with the convenience outlet.

Fig. 4. Receptacles for cleaning equipment.

Indicators (Fig. 5). The basement and attic areas are often left lighted because these areas are unfrequented and the switch controlling the lights is out of sight. A pilot light in connection with the switch, properly located so it can be readily seen from some active area in the house, will overcome this.

Fig. 5. Indicators.

Controlling closet lights (Fig. 6). The convenience of opening the closet door and automatically having light is so outstanding that it is surprising that this type of installation has not been used more extensively. Particularly satisfying is this method of control in the coat closet at the entrance hall and also in the master and guest bedrooms.

Fig. 6. Controlling closet lights.

Controlling outside lights (Fig. 7). Control of lights from outside the house has merit and is often convenient in the control of patio or terrace lights, garden lights, lighting of walks and driveways. This device is available for this service in single-pole, double-pole, and 3- and 4-way switches. The weatherproof mat under the plate provides a weather-tight seal.

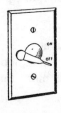

Fig. 7. Controlling outside lights.

Outside receptacles (Fig. 8). Weatherproof convenience receptacles around the outside of the house or throughout the yard area will be helpful in many ways. Weatherproof mat under the plate provides a weathertight seal. Some of the uses they may be put to are: garden lighting, electric cooking appliances on the terrace or in the garden, hedge cutter, lawn mower, and the like. It is desirable that the outlets be located so the equipment with their standard length cords can be used without extension cords.

Fig. 8. Outside receptacles.

OUTLET AND SWITCH CONTROL REQUIREMENTS

Living Room, Den, Library.   *Lighting.* Ceiling outlets—rooms twice as long as wide may require more than one outlet. Where desired, ceiling outlet may be substituted by (1) wall, cove, or valance lighting outlets or (2) switching two or more *two-circuit* duplex convenience outlets.

Outlets at bookcases, window valances, and the like.

Convenience outlets. Place outlets so that no point along floor line on any usable wall space, unbroken by a doorway, is more than six feet from an outlet. Wall spaces less than three feet in width are not considered usable.

Outlet flush in top of mantle shelf, construction permitting.

Television or radio outlet, combined with duplex power outlet.

Switch controls. Switch control all lighting outlets. Where commonly used doorways to a room are more than 10 feet apart, provide 3- and 4-way switch controls as needed.

Control two or more convenience outlets by a wall switch.

Dinette or Breakfast Nook.   *Lighting.* Ceiling outlet.

Convenience outlets. Place outlets so that no point along floor line on any usable wall space, unbroken by a doorway, is more than 10 feet from an outlet. Wall spaces less than three feet in width are not considered usable.

Switch controls. Switch control all lighting outlets. Where commonly used doorways to a room are more than 10 feet apart, provide 3- and 4-way switch controls as needed.

Kitchen. *Lighting.* Ceiling outlet, outlet over sink, and outlets under wall cabinets.

Convenience outlets. Outlet for every four-linear-foot frontage of kitchen work surface. Where surface is divided, provide one outlet at each work unit.

Switch controls. Switch control ceiling outlet at entrance door. Where commonly used doorways are more then 10 feet apart, provide 3- and 4-way switch controls as needed.

Wall switch control for light over sink.

Control each undercabinet light unit separately—by switch on fixture.

Special purpose outlets. Outlet for refrigerator, dishwasher, food waste disposer, range, ventilating fan, clock, and audible signals for responding to front and rear door push buttons. (Audible signals may be located in entrance hall instead of kitchen.)

Laundry Room. *Lighting.* Ceiling outlet at sorting, washing, and ironing center.

Switch controls. Switch control ceiling outlet at entrance door. Where commonly used doorways are more than 10 feet apart, provide 3- and 4-way switch controls as needed.

Special purpose outlets. Outlet for clothes washer, for clothes dryer, for ironer, for hand iron, and for hot plate.

Bedrooms. *Lighting.* Ceiling outlet—rooms twice as long as wide may require more than one outlet. Where desired, cove lighting or wall outlets (at least two) may be used instead of ceiling outlet.

Outlets at vanity table, bed recesses, valances, and the like.

Convenience outlets. Place outlets so that no point along floor line on any usable wall space, unbroken by a doorway, is more than six feet from an outlet. Wall spaces less than three feet in width are not considered usable.

Switch controls. Switch control all lighting outlets. Where commonly used doorways to a room are more than 10 feet apart, provide 3- and 4-way switch controls as needed.

Master switch (at master bed location) for controlling a predetermined number of outlets throughout the house.

Special purpose outlets. Night light outlets.

Bathrooms. *Lighting.* Light outlets on each side of mirror. Ceiling outlet for rooms greater than 60 square feet. Locating outlet over tub, particularly if tub is set in recess, is very desirable. Vaporproof ceiling outlet in shower compartment.

Convenience outlets. At lavatory, away from tub.

Switch controls. Switch control outlets at mirror and at ceiling from separate switches at entrance door. Control outlets for tub and shower from switch outside shower compartment and tub.

Special purpose outlets. Outlet for built-in heater, for sun lamp, and for night light.

Recreation Room. *Lighting.* Ceiling outlet for each 150 square feet, or major portion, of floor area. Rooms twice as long as wide may require more than one outlet. Cove lighting or wall outlets (at least two) may be used in place of ceiling outlet.

Convenience outlets. Place outlets so that no point along floor line on any usable wall space, unbroken by a doorway, is more than 10 feet from an outlet. Wall spaces less than three feet in width are not considered usable.

Outlet flush in top of mantle shelf, construction permitting.

Television or radio outlet, combined with duplex power outlet.

Switch controls. Switch control all lighting outlets. Where commonly used doorways to a room are more than 10 feet apart, provide 3- and 4-way switch controls as needed.

Special purpose outlets. Outlet for wall clock.

Utility Room. *Lighting.* Outlet for each enclosed space, for workbench lighting, and at furnace location. Sufficient additional outlets to provide one outlet for each 150 square feet of open space.

Convenience outlet. Near furnace.

Switch controls. At least one lighting outlet should be wall-switch controlled from entrance door; the remainder may be pull-chain controlled. Where a wall switch is at head of stairs, a pilot light is recommended.

Emergency switch control for heating furnace or boiler.

Special purpose outlets. Outlet at workbench, at air cleaner, at heating furnace or boiler, at water heater, at home freezer, at air conditioning unit, and at bell ringing transformer.

Closets. *Lighting.* Outlet at ceiling or on wall above door—at lock side of door.

Switch controls. Door-type switch control, or pull-chain lampholder.

Entrance (Front and Trade). *Lighting.* Exterior outlets—the number and location of outlets depend on architectural treatment of doorway.

Illuminated house number at front entrance may be combined with fixed lighting fixtures.

Convenience outlets. Weatherproof receptacle outlet at front entrance, 18 inches above grade. Additional outlets around perimeter of house desirable—spacing approximately 40 feet.

Switch controls. Control front entrance light outlets from switch inside front entrance door.

Control trade entrance light outlet from switch inside trade entrance door.

Control house number light from switch inside front door.

Control weatherproof receptacle at front entrance from switch inside front entrance door.

Special purpose outlets. Push button to ring buzzer, bell, or chimes. Locate outside of front and trade entrance doors.

Entrance Hall and Halls. *Lighting.* Outlet for each 15 linear feet, or major portion, of hall.

Convenience outlets. Outlet for each 15 linear feet, or major portion, of hall.

Switch controls. Switch control lighting of entrance door; where commonly used doorways are more than 10 feet apart, 3- and 4-way switches are recommended.

Stairways. *Lighting.* One outlet at head of and one at foot of each stairway (connecting finished floors).

Switch controls. Individual three-way switches at head and foot of stairs, for controlling each of the two outlets. (Locate switches away from top steps, to avoid falling resulting from misstep.)

Covered Porch. *Lighting.* Outlet for each 150 square feet, or major portion, of porch floor area.

Convenient outlets. Provide outlet along every 15 feet, or major portion, of wall.

Switch controls. Switch control, separately, the lighting and convenience outlets, from inside entrance door to porch.

Accessible Attic. *Lighting.* Outlet at head of stairs; also an outlet in each enclosed space.

Switch controls. Switch and pilot combination at foot of attic stairs, to control at least one attic light. On all other outlets in the attic use a pull-chain lampholder.

Garage. *Lighting.* Ceiling outlet over hood end, for 1- or 2-car garage. Exterior outlet over car entrance door.

Convenience outlets. One duplex outlet for 1- or 2-car garage.

Switch controls. Control interior light from switch at entrance door. Where commonly used doorways are more than 10 feet apart, provide 3- and 4-way controls.

Control exterior outlet from switch at car entrance door. If garage is detached from house, three-way control, at house and garage, is recommended.

Section 3

ELECTRIC MOTORS, PHASE CONVERTERS, TRANSFORMERS, AND SOLDERING

ELECTRIC MOTORS ARE EFFICIENT, compact, and a dependable source of power. Effective use, however, requires the selection of the best type for a particular job, proper installation, and the use of suitable controls for the operation and protection of the motor.

Single-phase motors are in general use because farm electric power service is usually single-phase. For some jobs, however, *three-phase motors* can be a better choice than single-phase motors. Also, they may be the only type readily available in the size needed.

Phase converters make it possible to operate three-phase motors from single-phase power lines when three-phase power is not available. They convert the single-phase line voltage into three-phase voltage.

Transformers. In alternating current circuits it is possible to change the value of the voltage by means of transformers.

Soldering is a very important part of electrical repairs, and much depends on the way it is performed.

Chapter 6

Single-Phase Motors

The seven general types of single-phase, alternating current (AC) motors are as follows:

1. Split-Phase (SP)
2. Capacitor:
     Capacitor Start (CS-IR) (Capacitor Start-Induction Run)
     Two-Value Capacitor (CS-CR) (Capacitor Start-Capacitor Run)
     Permanent Split Capacitor (PSC)
3. Wound-Rotor:
     Repulsion-Start (RS)
     Repulsion-Induction (RI)
     Repulsion (R)
4. Shaded-Pole
5. Universal or Series (UNIV)
6. Synchronous
7. Soft Start (SS)

Three-phase motors that are operated on single-phase power through phase converters may also be used for single-phase applications.

Motor types differ primarily in the amount of starting torque developed and in their starting-current requirements. The type to use depends on the starting requirements of the equipment to be driven and the maximum current that may be drawn from the single-phase power service. (Table 1 lists the important characteristics of each type of single-phase motor.)

TABLE 1

TYPES OF SINGLE-PHASE MOTORS AND THEIR CHARACTERISTICS

Type	Horsepower ranges	Load-starting ability	Starting current	Characteristics	Electrically reversible	Typical uses
Split-phase	1/20 to ½	Easy starting loads. Develops 150 percent of full-load torque.	High; five to seven times full-load current.	Inexpensive, simple construction. Small for a given motor power. Nearly constant speed with a varying load.	Yes.	Fans, centrifugal pumps; loads that increase as speed increases.
Capacitor-start	1/8 to 10	Hard starting loads. Develops 350 to 400 percent of full-load torque.	Medium, three to six times full-load current.	Simple construction, long service. Good general-purpose motor suitable for most jobs. Nearly constant speed with a varying load.	Yes.	Compressors, grain augers, conveyors, pumps. Specifically designed capacitor motors are suitable for silo unloaders and barn cleaners.
Two-value capacitor	2 to 20	Hard starting loads. Develops 350 to 450 percent of full-load torque.	Medium, three to five times full-load current.	Simple construction, long service, with minimum maintenance. Requires more space to accommodate larger capacitor. Low line current. Nearly constant speed with a varying load.	Yes.	Conveyors, barn cleaners, elevators, silo unloaders.
Synchronous	Very small, fractional	N/A[1]	N/A	Constant speed.	N/A	Clocks, timers.

[1] N/A = not applicable.

TABLE 1 (continued)

Type	Horsepower ranges	Load-starting ability	Starting current	Characteristics	Electrically reversible	Typical uses
Soft-start	10 to 75	Easy starting loads.	Low, 1.5 to 2 times full-load current.	Excellent for large loads requiring low starting torque.	Yes.	Crop driers, forage blowers, irrigation pumps, manure agitators.
Permanent-split capacitor	1/20 to 1	Easy starting loads. Develops 150 percent of full-load torque.	Low, two to four times full-load current.	Inexpensive, simple construction. Has no start winding switch. Speed can be reduced by lowering the voltage for fans and similar units.	Yes.	Fans and blowers.
Shaded pole	1/250 to ½	Easy starting loads.	Medium.	Inexpensive, moderate efficiency, for light duty.	No.	Small blowers, fans, small appliances.
Wound-rotor (Repulsion)	1/6 to 10	Very hard starting loads. Develops 350 to 400 percent of full-load torque.	Low, two to four times full-load current.	Larger than equivalent size split-phase or capacitor motor. Running current varies only slightly with load.	No. Reversed by brush ring re-adjustment	Conveyors, drag burr mills, deep-well pumps, hoists, silo unloaders, bucket elevators.
Universal or series	1/150 to 2	Hard starting loads. Develops 350 to 450 percent of full-load torque.	High.	High speed, small size for a given horsepower. Usually directly connected to load. Speed changes with load variations.	Yes, some types.	Portable tools, kitchen appliances.

SPLIT-PHASE MOTORS (SP)

Split-phase motors are inexpensive and widely used fractional horsepower motors (Fig. 1). They are only suitable for handling easy

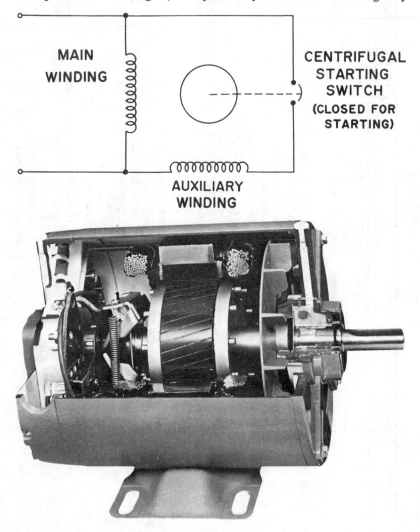

Fig. 1. Split-phase motor.

starting loads such as ventilating fans because of their low starting torque. They are rarely used in sizes larger than ½ horsepower because of their relatively high starting currents. Generally their use is limited to applications where their low cost is more important than their low torque and high starting currents.

Power is applied to a starting, or auxiliary, winding through a starting switch during the starting period. The direction of rotation can be changed by reversing the line connections to the starting, or auxiliary, winding.

CAPACITOR MOTORS

Capacitor-Start Motors (CS-IR).   This motor is a popular type for general use. *Capacitor-start* (capacitor-start-induction run) *motors* are similar in design to split-phase motors, with one important difference—a capacitor is placed in series with the auxiliary winding (Fig. 2). The capacitor gives the motor up to twice the starting torque of a split-phase motor with about one-third less current requirement. The capacitor-start motor is electrically reversible in the same manner as a split-phase motor. Line connections to the starting winding are interchanged to reverse the direction of rotation.

Starting torque of capacitor motors may be reduced when they operate at very low temperatures because the capacitance of the electrolytic starting capacitor is less at low temperatures. This factor should be considered when selecting the size of a capacitor-start motor to be used for hard starting loads in cold weather.

Two-Value Capacitor Motors (CS-CR).   *Two-value capacitor* (capacitor start-capacitor run) *motors* are similar to capacitor-start motors (Fig. 3). CS-CR motors use the same type of starting circuit as CS-IR motors, but a small capacitor remains in series with the auxiliary winding during running. This capacitor gives greater efficiency of operation by lowering the amount of line current required to run the motor.

These motors have slightly higher starting torque than capacitor-start motors and, therefore, can handle more difficult starting loads. The starting current requirement is about the same for both CS-IR and CS-CR types. Direction of rotation can be reversed electrically.

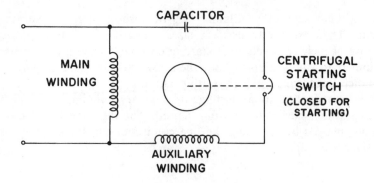

Fig. 2. Capacitor-start motor. Arrow points to capacitor.

Permanent-Split Capacitor Motors (PSC). *Permanent-split capacitor motors* are similar to capacitor-start motors except that the same value of capacitance is used for both starting and running conditions (Fig. 4). Starting torque is much lower than that for capacitor-start motors and the breakdown torque is suitable for loads that require load peaks no greater than normal load torque, such as fans and blowers.

Fig. 3. Two-value, capacitor-run motor.

No starting mechanism is used on PSC motors; therefore, they are adaptable to variable speed control and can be operated at reduced speeds (below design speed) by lowering the effective supply voltage. A PSC motor should not be operated at a speed less than that at which torque breakdown occurs. With a standard low-slip

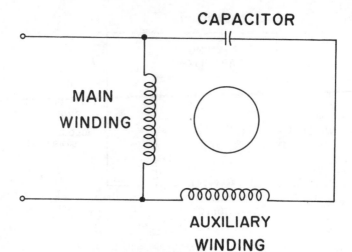

MAIN WINDING

CAPACITOR

AUXILIARY WINDING

Fig. 4. Permanent-split capacitor motor.

motor, torque breakdown occurs at about 75 percent of the motor's synchronous speed. With a high-slip design, torque breakdown occurs at less than 75 percent of the synchronous speed.

Motor current much higher than normal will be drawn if the PSC motor is operated at a speed lower than that at which torque breakdown occurs.

WOUND-ROTOR MOTORS

Wound-rotor, or *repulsion motors* are single-phase motors that have a stator winding arranged for connection to a source of power and a rotor winding connected to a commutator. The running current for wound-rotor motors varies little with variations in load, and heavy starting loads can be handled with low starting current. These motors are more expensive than split-phase or capacitor motors and require more maintenance because of brush and commutator wear. The three general subtypes of wound-rotor motors are discussed next.

Repulsion-Start Induction Motors (RS).   This kind of motor starts as a repulsion motor but operates as an induction motor with speed characteristics similar to a capacitor-start motor. *Repulsion-start induction motors* are the most common type among the wound-rotor motors. They have a rotor similar to the kind found in all wound-rotor motors (Fig. 5). At a predetermined speed, the rotor winding is short-circuited or otherwise connected to give the equivalent of a squirrel-cage winding.

Repulsion-Induction Motors (RI).   A *repulsion-induction motor* is a form of wound-rotor motor that has a squirrel-cage winding in the rotor in addition to the repulsion, or wound-rotor, winding. This motor may be either constant-speed or varying-speed, depending on design, and it is capable of starting very difficult loads with less voltage than other general-purpose motors.

Repulsion Motors (R).   This type of motor carries the name often applied to all single-phase, wound-rotor motors. Brushes on the commutator are short-circuited and placed so that the magnetic axis of the rotor winding is inclined to the magnetic axis of the stator. This type motor has varying speeds and is sometimes referred to as a variable-speed motor. This motor's speed is controlled by load.

The *repulsion motor* starts and runs as a repulsion motor. Brushes do not lift and the commutator is not shorted. Output torque and motor speed for a given load are controlled by the brush setting. The no-load speed of this type of motor is above synchronous speed.

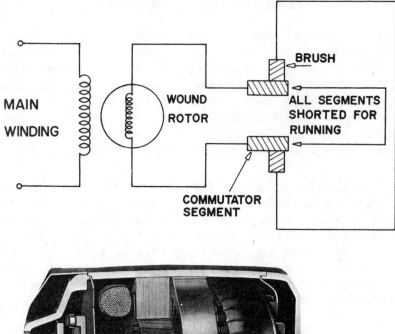

Fig. 5. Repulsion-start induction motor.

SHADED-POLE MOTORS

Shaded-pole motors are low-cost, low-starting-torque motors that are simply constructed. A short-circuiting ring of copper, or other conductor, in a slot in each pole face provides the electrical characteristics that enable the motor to start (Fig. 6). The low efficiencies of these motors in addition to their low starting torques limit their use to small-size loads.

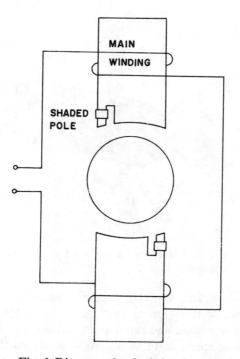

Fig. 6. Diagram of a shaded-pole motor.

UNIVERSAL OR SERIES MOTORS (UNIV)

The *universal* or *series motor* is a high-speed motor that will operate on either alternating or direct current (Fig. 7). It is usually a special-purpose motor, often built into portable equipment such as

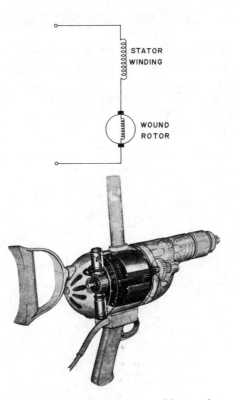

Fig. 7. A universal motor used in an electric drill.

drills, grinders, sanders, sprayers, vacuum cleaners, and food mixers. The advantages of this type of motor include high starting torque, high power-to-size ratio, and rapid acceleration of the load to speed.

The operating speed of these motors depends on the load. They do not operate at a constant speed, but run as fast as the load permits. If not loaded, they will overspeed, which may damage the motor.

SYNCHRONOUS MOTORS

Synchronous motors are constant-speed motors that are often used in clocks and timers. A most important characteristic is that their output speed is very exact. Synchronous motor speed is determined by the design and the alternate current (AC) line voltage frequency.

SOFT-START MOTORS (SS)

In large integral horsepower motors, starting currents may be high enough to restrict the use of large motor sizes on available single-phase power lines. *Special single-phase, soft-start motors* are available that have a reduced starting current as low as one and one-half to two times normal running current.

The lower starting currents in soft-start motors are usually obtained by suitable switching of the motor windings, such as using two windings placed in series for starting and in parallel for running. By reducing the high starting current, large motors may be operated on single-phase power lines. The reduced starting current results in lower starting torque (50 to 90 percent of full-load torque) than conventional single-phase motors. Therefore, this type of motor is best suited to easy starting loads such as crop drier fans, forage blowers, manure agitators, or saws.

Chapter 7

Three-Phase Motors

The rotating magnetic field provided by three-phase alternate current (AC) power permits a simple and low-cost means of constructing an electric motor. In general-purpose use, three-phase motors require no auxiliary winding switch and no starting or running capacitors. Therefore, these major sources of failure in split-phase and capacitor-start, single-phase motors are eliminated.

Three-phase motors may be made for either a y (Y) or delta (Δ) connection (Fig. 1). For balanced phase voltages, both types have similar performance. An important consideration in the application of either type is that the proper connections be made to the motor windings.

The horsepower of three-phase motors ranges from ½ to 400 and the starting current required is low to medium, about three to four times full-load current. Some typical uses of three-phase motors are for crop driers, elevators, conveyors, irrigation pumps, and hoists.

Three-phase motors can be easily reversed electrically, making them useful for applications involving control of direction or remote positioning. Several different speed-torque characteristics are also available so that the motor performance can be matched to a particular use.

Normally, the speed-torque characteristics and the rotor impedance are fixed. Motors are available, however, that have variable speed-torque characteristics in designs using a wound rotor and an external variable rheostat connected to the rotor by slip rings. The wound-rotor type is considerably more expensive than fixed-rotor types and requires more maintenance.

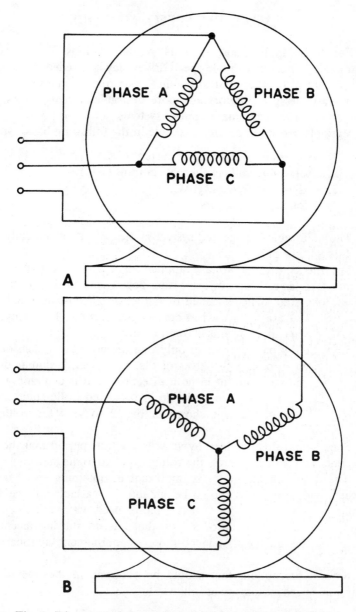

Fig. 1. Diagrams of three-phase motor electrical connections.
A, delta (Δ); B, y (Y).

VARIABLE-SPEED MOTORS

For some applications, such as ventilating fans, feed handling equipment, or tools, variable-speed drives may be needed. Mechanical speed control is often used to obtain the desired output speed. However, variable-speed motors are more desirable in many cases, particularly for use in automatic control systems.

Variable-speed motors are available in the following basic type:

    1. Adjustable-voltage direct current (DC).
    2. Adjustable-voltage alternate current (AC).
    3. Adjustable-frequency AC.
    4. Wound-rotor motors.

The adjustable-voltage AC system is the only type generally used on farms at the present time.

For the control of voltage applied to a motor, variable transformers, series resistors, or solid-state power control devices may be used. Solid-state switches called thyristors or silicon-controlled rectifiers (SCR's) are often used to control the portion of each cycle of the AC voltage that power is allowed to pass.

Since SCR's pass current in only one direction, two such devices are required to pass both halves of the AC cycle. A similar device, the triac, will pass current in both directions and is commonly used. Either SCR's or triacs are available in packaged, solid-state, motor-speed controls of the type shown in Fig. 2 to vary the voltage to the motor.

Speed control is obtained by varying the time period that the SCR or triac is on, which controls the voltage applied to the motor.

The design of the motor is important in obtaining speed control over a wide range and should be suitable for variable-voltage applications. It is also important that a motor used with variable-voltage motor speed controls be of a type that has no starting mechanism such as the universal, shaded-pole, or permanent split-capacitor motor.

Several precautions that should be observed in the operation of variable-speed motors are as follows:

    1. The lowest speed setting should be limited to provide proper bearing lubrication.

Fig. 2. Variable-voltage motor speed control used for ventilating fans.

2. The speed control used should provide sufficient voltage to start the motor under load at low speed settings.

3. The lowest speed setting should be high enough to provide sufficient ventilation to prevent overheating of the motor.

Because of the varied possibilities of variable-speed motors, selection and application of such motors should be done in consultation with the equipment manufacturer and the local power supplier.

PHASE CONVERTERS

Whenever it is desirable to operate three-phase motors but three-phase power is not available, phase converters make it possible to operate from single-phase power lines. It is essential, however, that the combination of converter and three-phase motor is properly selected and applied. Combinations of phase converters and three-phase motors are being used to successfully operate many types of loads, such as crop driers, grain handling systems, irrigation pumps, and animal feeding systems.

The two general types of *phase converters* that are available are *static* and *rotary*. Each type offers advantages for specific kinds of motor loads. Proper choice of a phase-converter type is determined by the motor loads that must be run.

Static converters with no moving parts other than relays are available in two general types: capacitor and autotransformer capacitor. Both types are generally used with a single motor. The full-load capacity of the three-phase motor may need to be reduced, depending on the exact type of static converter used. Care must be taken to see that the motor loading is such that the currents in each phase do not exceed motor nameplate rating and damage the motor. Also, motors may run rough if they are operated at loads substantially less than those at which the phase converter was balanced.

Rotary converters have a rotating unit and a capacitor bank. Rotary converters are more suitable for multimotor use than static converters and generally will operate any combination of motors up to approximately twice their rating for the maximum motor size that they will start.

For both types of converters, the starting torque of three-phase motors may be reduced to 50 to 80 percent of normal. The exact amount of reduction depends on the phase converter design, and this factor must be taken into account when selecting motor sizes.

If the phase voltages and currents from the converter to the motor are approximately balanced, motor starting currents are reduced at the same time that motor starting torque is reduced. This permits the use of a converter-operated three-phase motor that has more horsepower than a standard single-phase motor on a single-phase line. Therefore, converter-motor combinations are sometimes used as the equivalent of soft-start motors.

Proper phase converter selection, installation, and wiring are essential for satisfactory operation. Overcurrent protection for the motor should be used in all three motor leads. For more information on phase converters, *see* Chapter 11, Phase Converters for Operation of Three-Phase Motors from Single-Phase Power.

Chapter 8

Motor Selection

The choice of the proper electric motor depends primarily on the electrical service available, the size and type of load, and the environmental conditions under which the motor will operate.

ELECTRIC SERVICE

Single-Phase.   Electrical service is usually 120 or 240 volts, 60 hertz, and single-phase for operation of motors and equipment rated at 115 or 230 volts. Single-phase motors up to and including one horsepower can be operated on 115 volts. Generally, however, because of the large currents drawn by motors over ½ horsepower, particularly at starting, motor sizes larger than ½ horsepower should be operated on 230 volts.

Three-Phase.   Three-phase power is available for some locations. General-purpose, three-phase motors in sizes above two horsepower may be readily available and are generally less expensive than single-phase motors. Both y and delta three-phase systems are common. Figure 1 illustrates these two electrical systems and the phase-to-phase voltages as well as the phase-to-neutral voltages. It is important that a three-phase motor be chosen to match the phase-to-phase voltage of the electrical system available.

Three-phase motors can also be operated on single-phase power. This is discussed in Chap. 6, in the section on Phase Converters; *see also* Chap. 11, Phase Converters for Operation of Three-Phase Motors from Single-Phase Power.

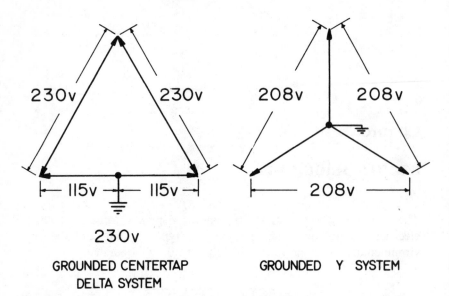

Fig. 1. Electrical systems of the delta and y types showing phase-to-phase and phase-to-neutral voltages.

EFFECTS OF VOLTAGE AND FREQUENCY ON MOTOR PERFORMANCE

For proper performance of an electric motor, the supply voltage and frequency at the motor terminals must match the values specified by the manufacturer as closely as possible. Motor performance is usually determined at rated voltage and frequency. Satisfactory performance is generally obtained over a range of plus or minus 10 percent from rated voltage and plus or minus five percent from rated frequency.

If you allow the applied voltage or frequency to vary from the nominal values specified on the motor nameplate, there will be changes in the motor torque from the values that are given at rated voltage and frequency. These changes in performance occur because torque developed by the motor is approximately proportional to the square of the voltage and inversely proportional to the square of the frequency.

The successful operation of a motor under running conditions, with the voltage and frequency variations within the allowable range, does not necessarily mean that the motor will start and accelerate the load under these conditions. Limiting values of voltage and frequency at which a motor will start and accelerate a load to running speed depend on the margin between the speed-torque curve of the motor at rated voltage and frequency and the speed-torque curve of the load under starting conditions.

Frequency variation is generally no problem, except for possible operation by standby power units. Low voltage from inadequate wiring or other causes, however, can cause severe problems because motor starting torque may be too low to start and accelerate the load. The section on wiring gives recommended minimum sizes of conductors.

Proper *motor voltage* is, therefore, particularly important for hard starting loads; at 80 percent of its rated voltage, a motor develops only 64 percent of the torque that is developed at nameplate voltage rating.

MOTOR TORQUE CHARACTERISTICS

An electric motor is simply a device for converting electrical power into mechanical power. Therefore, after the type of power source has been determined, the next step is to determine the motor size required for the load.

To start the load, a certain amount of *turning force*, or *torque*, the turning force available from the motor shaft, is required. A load such as a fan starts easily, and the shaft can be turned by hand (low starting torque). A load such as a filled grain auger is much harder to start (high starting torque), and a wrench is needed to rotate the shaft. An electric motor must be selected that will provide the starting torque required by the load as well as the torque necessary to bring the load to operating speed.

When the load is running, a given amount of turning force is required for rotating the load at the desired speed. This power that the motor must put out (*horsepower*) is proportional to the shaft speed and torque required. Thus, the horsepower required to turn the load determines the size of motor that must be selected. If too small a motor is selected, it will be overloaded and have a short life.

Certain equipment varies widely in the amount of power required for starting. For example, fans, bench saws, and grindstones are easy to start. Split-phase motors, which have low starting torque, will satisfactorily operate this equipment. Reciprocating compressors, auger conveyors, and vacuum pumps are harder to start and require motors with higher starting torque, such as the capacitor-start type. Bucket elevators, barn cleaners, silo unloaders, or similar equipment are very hard to start and require motors with high starting torque, such as two-value capacitor or repulsion types.

The torque characteristics of a load that a motor is required to start and run are therefore important in the choice of a motor. Typical torque characteristics of a load and a motor are shown in Fig. 2. Motor torque must exceed load torque requirements over the

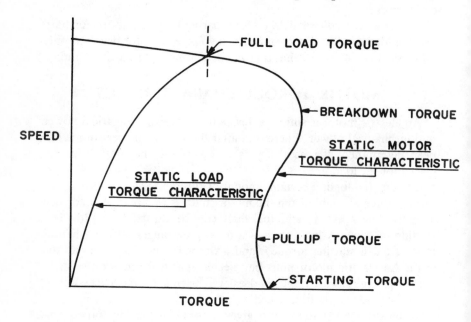

Fig. 2. Typical motor and load torque characteristics.

entire range of speed if the motor is to properly start and bring the load to operating speed. The motor torque characteristics that are important in matching a motor to a load are defined as follows:

Full-load torque. A full-load torque is the turning force that the motor will deliver continuously at rated voltage and speed without exceeding its temperature rating. Full-load torque usually determines the basic rating and, therefore, the size of the motor that must be used.

Starting torque (locked rotor). A starting torque is the amount of torque that the motor has available at zero speed. Starting torque is important and may dictate the type of motor that must be used.

Breakdown torque. A breakdown torque is the maximum torque that a motor develops at rated voltage without an abrupt drop in speed. Breakdown torque must be considered in relation to peak intermittent loads that may be encountered.

Pull-up torque. A pull-up torque is the minimum torque that is developed by the motor during the period of acceleration from zero speed to the speed at which breakdown torque occurs. Pull-up torque is generally of minor importance but must be adequate to accelerate a load up to its operating speed.

MOTOR LOADING

The life of an electric motor is reduced if the motor is overloaded for extended periods. Overload is indicated when the current is above the nameplate rating. One method of checking for motor overload is to measure the current drawn by the motor. A clamp-on ammeter may be used for this purpose as shown in Fig. 3.

Each of the conductors carrying power to the motor is passed through the clamp-on ammeter loop individually to determine the current of the motor under load conditions. Currents should be approximately equal and within the motor nameplate rating for both leads of a single-phase motor and for all three leads of a three-phase motor.

If motor current exceeds the motor nameplate current rating, the motor is most likely overloaded and motor temperature will rise above the rated value. Unless the load is of short duration or the cooling air temperature is below 104° F., motor life will be shortened. The load on the motor should be adjusted so that the current drawn by the motor is within the nameplate rating to obtain normal motor life.

Fig. 3. Clamp-on ammeter.

TEMPERATURE

Once the required motor torque characteristics are determined, motor temperature ratings should be considered. Both motor insulation and bearings have definite temperature limitations for long successful operation. Generally, however, bearing temperature limits will be met if insulation temperature is kept within the permitted range.

Four insulation systems are available for small induction motors. They are as follows.

| | *Maximum hot spot continuous* |
System	*temperature*
Class A	221° F.
Class B	266° F.
Class F	311° F.
Class H	356° F.

Temperature limits are established by Underwriters Laboratories, Inc., to protect against fire hazards and by the National Electrical Manufacturers Association (NEMA) to assure adequate motor life. Nameplate data generally give the permissible temperature rise above the ambient air or the maximum ambient temperature for motor operation that will keep the hot spot temperature of the motor within the specified value for the insulation system used. Normal maximum ambient temperature is 104° F. for most motor ratings.

Equipment manufacturers usually recommend the type and size of electric motor needed to operate their equipment. Their recommendations are generally based on the starting, pull-up, breakdown, and running torques required under normal operating conditions and serve as a basis for motor selection. For unusual conditions, consult the equipment manufacturer or power supplier, or both.

OPERATING CONDITIONS

Electric motors are often operated under adverse conditions where there is dust, dirt, or moisture or where there are explosive mixtures of gas or dust such as in feed or flour mills. Motors are available with different types of enclosures, or housings, for use under specific operating conditions. Selecting the proper type of enclosure is important for the protection of the motor and for safe operation.

Enclosures.   Two general types of enclosures are available: *open* and *totally enclosed.*

An *open motor* is one that has ventilating openings that permit the passage of external cooling air over and around the windings of the machine. Open enclosures may be drip-proof (Fig. 4) or splash-proof (Fig. 5).

Fig. 4. Drip-proof motor.

Fig. 5. Splash-proof motor.

A drip-proof enclosure protects a motor from liquids or solids falling zero to 15 degrees downward from vertical. It is designed for indoor use where the air is fairly clean and where there is little danger of splashing liquid.

A splash-proof enclosure protects the motor from liquids or particles that strike the enclosure at angles not greater than 100 degrees downward from vertical. Such motors may be used outdoors but must be protected from the weather (Fig. 6).

Totally *enclosed motors* are those where the enclosure prevents the free exchange of air between the inside and outside of the case but does not make the case completely airtight. They may be cooled

Fig. 6. Slash-proof motors installed outside should be protected from the weather by a suitable covering. The motor drive is covered as a safety precaution.

by a fan (totally enclosed fan-cooled, TEFC), or by direct radiation and convection of heat through the case (totally enclosed, non-ventilated). (*See* Fig. 7.)

Totally enclosed motors are also available in explosion-proof, dust-ignition-proof, and water-proof designs for operation under dirty or wet conditions or where explosive gas or dust mixtures are present.

Bearings. Electric motors are available with either *sleeve bearings* (Fig. 8) or *ball bearings* (Fig. 9). Operating conditions determine whether sleeve or ball bearings should be used. Sleeve-bearing motors are usually quieter and cost less than ball-bearing motors but generally require more maintenance.

Sleeve-bearing motors are usually designed to operate only in the horizontal position, although sleeve bearings are sometimes used in a vertical position in small motors. When sleeve bearings are lubri-

Fig. 7. Fan-cooled motor. Totally enclosed motors may be either nonventilated, disposing of heat by radiation, or fan cooled.

cated with oil, the reservoir must always be toward the bottom of the motor.

Ball-bearing motors may be operated in either a horizontal or vertical position and are better suited for end thrust and control of end play than sleeve-bearing motors. Ball bearings that are normally used in electric motors are designed to absorb some thrust, but if the thrust load is high, special thrust bearings must be used. Also, enclosed motors that are used in wet and dirty conditions usually have ball bearings.

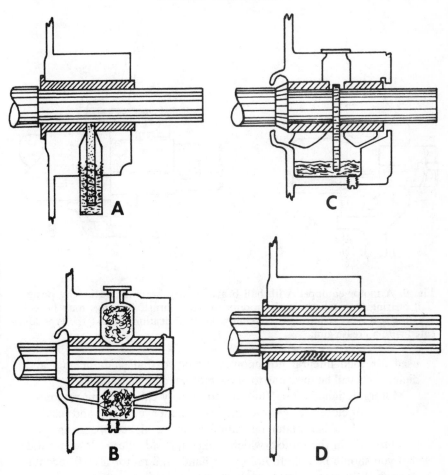

Fig. 8. Low-cost sleeve bearings are suitable for many motor applications. The motor shaft must be mounted horizontally with the oil reservoir underneath. Sleeve bearings will not absorb axial thrust. They may be lubricated by (A) oil wick, (B) yarn, (C) oil ring, or (D) impregnated permanent lubrication.

MOTOR RATINGS

Motors of a given horsepower rating are built in a certain size frame or housing. For standardization, the National Electrical Manufacturers Association (NEMA) has assigned the frame size to be

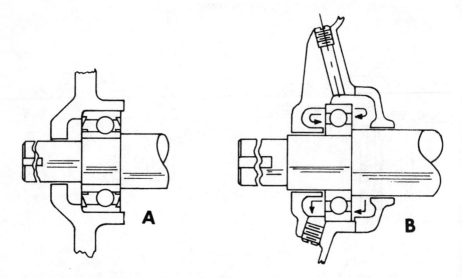

Fig. 9. A motor equipped with ball bearings may be mounted in any position. Ball bearings can take a small amount of axial thrust. Bearings may be either (A) the seal type, requiring disassembly for relubrication, or (B) the type lubricated with a grease gun.

used for each integral horsepower motor so that shaft heights and dimensions will be the same to allow motors to be interchanged.

Motors designed after 1964 are commonly called T-rate motors—the result of closer design tolerances and better magnetic and insulating materials. Also, better insulation allows a higher operating temperature within the motor, which makes the old rule no longer valid that you should be able to hold your hand on a motor for 10 seconds or more if the motor is not overheating.

Table 2 shows the motor frame sizes used for various sizes of integral horsepower motors. Shaft diameters for motors with a single straight shaft are shown in Table 3. The shaft height of integral horsepower motors may be obtained by dividing the first two numbers of the frame size by 4. Example: The shaft height for the 200-frame-size series is 20 divided by 4, or 5 inches.

The shaft height of fractional horsepower motors may be obtained by dividing the frame size by 16.

Because of tighter design tolerances, the temperature rise of T-

TABLE 2

MOTOR FRAMES FOR VARIOUS SIZES OF 1,800-R.P.M. MOTORS[1]

Kind and size of motor	Motor-frame sizes (NEMA frame series)							
	140	180	200	210	220	250	280	320
	Horsepower							
Single-Phase T-Rate (after 1964)	1 1½	2 3		5 7½				
Single-Phase, U-Rate (1952 to 1964)		1 1½		2 3		5 7½		
Three-Phase, T-Rate (after 1964)	1 1½ 2	3 5		7½ 10		15 20	25 30	40 50
Three-Phase, U-Rate (1952 to 1964)		1 1½ 2		3 5		7½ 10	15 20	25 30
Three-Phase (pre-1952)			1 1½		2 3	5	7½	10 15

[1] The information for this table was taken from NEMA tables MG 1-13.01, 1-13.02, 1-13.01a, and 1-13.02a (1968).

TABLE 3

SHAFT DIAMETER FOR FOOT-MOUNTED ELECTRIC MOTORS WITH A SINGLE STRAIGHT SHAFT EXTENSION[1]

Motor frame size	Shaft diameter inches
143, 145	¾
143T, 145T, 182, 184	⅞
182T, 184T, 213, 215	1⅛
213T, 215T, 254U, 256U	1⅜
254T, 256T, 284TS, 286TS, 284U, 286U, 324S, 326S	1⅝
284T, 286T, 324TS, 326TS, 324U, 326U, 364US, 364TS, 365US, 365TS	1⅞
324T, 326T, 364U, 365U	2⅛
364T, 365T	2⅜

[1] The information for this table was taken from NEMA tables MG1-11.31 and MG1-11.31a.

rate motors will stay within specifications only if the motor terminal voltage is kept within plus or minus 10 percent of the nameplate rating. The motor winding temperature will exceed specifications and motor life will be shortened unless the specified range of motor terminal voltage and load are maintained.

Motors are designed for continuous or limited duty. Those designed for continuous duty will deliver the rated horsepower for an indefinite period of time without overheating. General-purpose motors should always be the continuous-duty type.

Limited-duty motors will deliver rated horsepower for a specified period of time but cannot be operated continuously at the rated load. A typical use of a limited-duty motor is as a silo unloader. A limited-duty motor will operate the unloader satisfactorily for a short time and it costs less than a continuous-duty motor. However, if the operating period is extended, the limited-duty motor will overheat and may burn out prematurely.

Motor nameplates carry the essential information regarding a motor's characteristics. A typical nameplate is shown in Fig. 10. The information generally given on the nameplate includes the following:

Frame and type. The NEMA designation for frame designation and type.

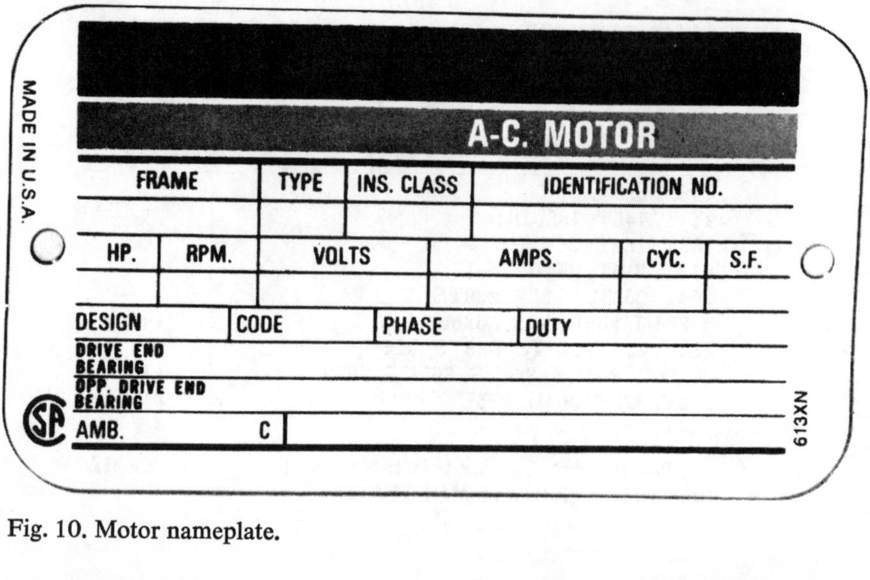

Fig. 10. Motor nameplate.

Horsepower. The horsepower rating of the motor.

Motor code. Designated by a letter indicating the starting current required. The higher the locked-rotor kilovolt-ampere (kva), the higher the starting current surge. Table 4 shows the most common letter designations and the locked-rotor kva they represent.

TABLE 4

MOTOR CODE LETTERS USUALLY APPLIED TO RATINGS OF MOTORS
NORMALLY STARTED ON FULL VOLTAGE[1]

Code letter	Locked rotor[2] kva per horsepower	Horsepower sizes	
		Single-phase	Three-phase
F	5.0 to 5.6		15 up
G	5.6 to 6.3	5	7½ to 10
H	6.3 to 7.1	3	5
J	7.1 to 8.0	1½ to 2	3
K	8.0 to 9.0	¾ to 1	1½ to 2
L	9.0 to 10.0	½	1

[1] The information for this table was taken from NEMA table MG 1-10.37.

[2] Locked rotor kva is equal to the product of line voltage times motor current divided by 1,000 when the rotor is not allowed to rotate; this corresponds to the first power surge required to start the motor. Locked-rotor kva per horsepower range includes the lower figure up to but not including the higher figure.

Cycles, or hertz. The frequency at which the motor is designed to be operated.

Phase. The number of phases on which the motor operates.

Revolutions per minute (rpm). The speed of the motor at full load.

Voltage. The voltage or voltages of operation.

Thermal protection. An indication of thermal protection provided for the motor, if it is provided.

Amps. The rated current (amperes) at full load.

Time. Time rating of the motor showing the duty rating as continuous or as a specific period of time the motor can be operated.

Ambient temperature, or temperature rise. The maximum ambient temperature at which the motor should be operated, or the temperature rise of the motor above the ambient air at rated load.

Service factor. The amount of overload that the motor can tolerate on a continuous basis at rated voltage and frequency.

Insulation class. A designation of the insulation system used, primarily for convenience in rewinding.

NEMA design. A letter designation for integral horsepower motors specifying the motor characteristics.

In addition, the bearing designations are often given on the nameplate for both ends of the shaft for convenience in replacement.

Generally, a motor with a continuous-duty rating and a 72° F. temperature rise is a good motor capable of operating satisfactorily for an indefinite period of time if properly serviced and operated under normal conditions. However, with the development of improved insulating materials, it is possible to have general-purpose motors that will operate at a rise of 158° F. or more above ambient temperature.

Chapter 9

Installation and Wiring of Electric Motors

Proper installation of an electric motor is essential for satisfactory operation, maximum service, and personal safety. The *installation* and *wiring* should conform to the recommendations of the National Electrical Code (NEC) and to any local code that has more restrictive requirements.

CAUSES OF MOTOR FAILURE

Motors properly selected and used will give many years of satisfactory service. Failures are most often due to overheating, moisture, bearing failure, or starting mechanism failure. Preventive maintenance and proper motor loading are the best insurance against motor failure. Motor life is prolonged by keeping the motor cool, dry, clean, and lubricated.

Overheating.   Heat is one of the most destructive agents causing premature motor failure. *Overheating* occurs because of motor overloading, low voltage at the motor terminals, excessive ambient temperatures, or poor cooling caused by dirt or lack of ventilation. If heat is not dissipated, insulation failure and possibly bearing failure can ruin a motor.

Moisture.   Moisture should be kept from entering a motor. The proper motor should be chosen for use in a damp environment and it should be covered to protect it from the weather, particularly during periods when it is not used.

Bearing Failure.   Bearings should be kept properly lubricated. Bearings in seldom-used motors such as crop driers may fail after going unrotated for extended periods of time. Special care in lubrication may be required for these motors.

Starting Mechanism Failure.   Choice of a well-built motor will help to solve this problem. Also, the starting mechanism must be kept free of dirt and moisture, the same as bearings and motor windings.

MOUNTING

Secure mounting and correct alignment with the load are essential for proper motor performance. The motor should be positioned where it is readily accessible, but not in the way. If possible, the motor should be located so that it will not be exposed to excessive moisture, dust, or abrasive material.

Mount the motor on a smooth, solid foundation and fasten the mounting bolts tightly. If mounted on an uneven base or fastened insecurely, the motor may become misaligned with the load during operation. This will throw unnecessary strain on the frame and bearings, causing rapid wear and overheating. Loose mounting also causes vibration and noise during operation.

CONNECTING TO THE LOAD

Motors may be connected to the load by direct drive, belt and pulley, or chain and sprocket.

Direct drive can be used only when the motor and the driven equipment operate at the same speed. A flexible coupling should be used, and the motor shaft and driven shaft should be in near perfect alignment. This prevents excessive wear of the shaft bearings.

Using a V-belt is the most common and the easiest way of connecting a motor to the load.

High-speed chain drives are used when a positive drive is necessary or when the torque required is more than a V-belt drive can transmit.

Proper belt tension must be maintained. If a belt is too loose, it will slip on the drive pulley, overheat, and wear out quickly. If it is too tight, it will cause the belt and bearings to wear excessively.

To properly tension a V-belt drive, measure the span between shafts as shown in Fig. 1. Measure the force required to deflect the belt $\frac{1}{64}$ inch for each inch of span. The force required should be within the values shown in Table 5 for the type of belt used.

Most motors available for farm use operate at about 1,800 rpm. Equipment generally operates at much slower speeds. Provision for the required load speed can be made by using the proper size pulley

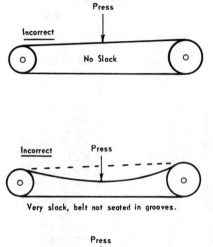

Some give in belt and seated in pulley grooves.

Fig. 1. Adjusting V-belt tension correctly.

on the driven equipment in relation to the motor pulley. To determine the load-pulley size, multiply the speed of the motor by the diameter of the motor pulley, then divide by the speed of the driven equipment.

Example:
A load needs to run at 600 rpm. The driving motor operates at 1,725 rpm and has a six-inch diameter pulley.
Equipment pulley diameter—

$$\frac{\text{motor speed} \times \text{motor pulley diameter}}{\text{equipment speed}}$$

Equipment policy diameter =

$$\frac{1,725 \times 6}{600} = 17.25 \text{ inches}$$

TABLE 5
RECOMMENDED DEFLECTION FORCE FOR V-BELT TENSIONING[1]

V-belt cross section	Small sheave diameter range	Small sheave r.p.m. range	Speed ratio range	Deflection force	
				Minimum	Maximum
type	inches			pounds	pounds
A	3.0 to 3.2		2.0 to 4.0	2.3	3.2
	3.4 to 3.6		2.0 to 4.0	2.5	3.6
	3.8 to 4.2		2.0 to 4.0	2.9	4.2
	4.6 to 7.0		2.0 to 4.0	3.5	5.1
B	4.6		2.0 to 4.0	4.0	5.9
	5.0 to 5.4		2.0 to 4.0	4.5	6.7
	5.6 to 6.4		2.0 to 4.0	5.0	7.4
	6.8 to 9.4		2.0 to 4.0	5.8	8.6
C	7.0		2.0 to 4.0	7.1	10.0
	7.5 to 8.0		2.0 to 4.0	7.9	11.0
	8.5 to 10.0		2.0 to 4.0	9.3	13.0
	10.5 to 16.0		2.0 to 4.0	11.0	16.0
D	12.0 to 13.0		2.0 to 4.0	16.0	24.0
	13.5 to 15.5		2.0 to 4.0	18.0	27.0
	16.0 to 22.0		2.0 to 4.0	21.0	31.0
E	21.6 to 24.0		2.0 to 4.0	33.0	47.0
3V	2.5 to 3.5	1,200 to 3,600	2.0 to 4.0	3.0	4.3
	3.51 to 4.50	900 to 1,800	2.0 to 4.0	3.5	5.3
	4.51 to 6.0	900 to 1,800	2.0 to 4.0	4.3	6.0
5V	7.0 to 9.0	600 to 1,500	2.0 to 4.0	8.8	13.0
	9.1 to 12.0	600 to 1,200	2.0 to 4.0	9.5	14.0
	12.1 to 16.0	400 to 900	2.0 to 4.0	11.0	15.0
8V	12.5 to 17.0	400 to 900	2.0 to 4.0	22.0	31.0
	17.1 to 24.0	200 to 700	2.0 to 4.0	23.0	34.0

[1] Pressure must be applied at midspan perpendicular to the belt. Example: For a span of 32 inches, the measured deflection should be $1/64 \times 32$, which is ½ inch. For a Type A belt with a small sheave diameter of 3 inches, the pressure to produce the ½-inch deflection should be 2.3 to 3.2 pounds.

The motor pulley and equipment policy must be correctly aligned to avoid excessive wear of the belt and bearings (Fig. 2). Pulley alignment can be checked by laying a straight ruler along the outside edge of the pulleys (Fig. 3).

Fig. 2. Slotted motor base for aligning the motor with the load and for adjusting the belt tension.

Fig. 3. Align motor and load pulleys so that the belt is perpendicular to each shaft.

WIRING

For safety, a good ground should be provided to the frame of all electric motors. If an electrical fault develops in the motor or wiring, the ground will prevent hazardous voltages from appearing on the motor frame.

Motors perform best at rated voltage and when adequate wiring is provided to the motor. Operating motors with a terminal supply voltage within the range of rated voltage makes motors less subject to damage during reductions in power system voltage. Adequate voltage also provides better motor performance than that obtained at voltages below the nameplate rating.

Table 6 gives full-load currents of single-phase motors and Table 7 gives full-load currents of three-phase motors. Current values shown in these tables should be used for wire size selection unless the motor nameplate current is larger; in that case, use the nameplate current value. Branch-circuit conductors to an individual motor should be selected to carry 125 percent of the full-load current of the motor.

TABLE 6
FULL-LOAD CURRENTS FOR SINGLE-PHASE A.C. MOTORS[1]

Motor horse-power	115 volts		230 volts	
	Full load	125% full load	Full load	125% full load
	amps	amps	amps	amps
1/6	4.4	5.5	2.2	2.8
1/4	5.8	7.2	2.9	3.6
1/3	7.2	9.0	3.6	4.5
1/2	9.8	12.2	4.9	6.1
3/4	13.8	17.2	6.9	8.6
1	16.0	20.0	8.0	10.0
1½	20.0	25.0	10.0	12.5
2	24.0	30.0	12.0	15.0
3	34.0	42.0	17.0	21.0
5	56.0	70.0	28.0	35.0
7½			40.0	50.0
10			50.0	62.0

[1] To obtain full-load currents for 208-volt motors, increase corresponding 230-volt motor full-load current by 10 percent.

TABLE 7
FULL-LOAD CURRENTS FOR THREE-PHASE A.C. MOTORS[1]

Motor horse-power	Full load	125% full load
	amps	amps
1/2	2.0	2.5
3/4	2.8	3.5
1	3.6	4.5
1½	5.2	6.5
2	6.8	8.5
3	9.6	12.0
5	15.2	19.0
7½	22.0	28.0
10	28.0	35.0
15	42.0	52.0
20	54.0	68.0
25	68.0	85.0
30	80.0	100.0
40	104.0	130.0
50	130.0	162.0
60	154.0	192.0
75	192.0	240.0
100	248.0	310.0
125	312.0	390.0

[1] To obtain full-load currents for 208-volt motors, increase corresponding 230-volt full-load current by 10 percent.

When conductors supply more than one motor on a single circuit, the wire size is determined by taking a current value of 125 percent of the full-load current of the largest motor plus 100 percent of the current for each additional smaller motor.

The following measures must be taken when wiring to motors:

1. Branch-circuit overcurrent protection to protect the conductors of the motor circuit.

2. A means to disconnect the motor from the electrical supply.

3. Motor overcurrent protection to prevent overloading the motor under running conditions.

4. A controller to stop and start the motor.

Wire Sizes.   Tables 8 to 11 show the required wire size for cop-

TABLE 8

SIZES OF COPPER WIRE FOR SINGLE-PHASE, 115-120 VOLT MOTORS AND A 2-PER CENT VOLTAGE DROP[1]

Note: Compare the size shown below with the size shown in the column to the left of the double line and use the larger size.

Wire size (AWG or MCM)[3]

Load in amps	Minimum allowable wire size			Length of wire to motor in feet													
	Wire in cable, conduit, or earth		Bare or covered wire overhead in the air[2]	20	30	40	50	60	80	100	120	160	200	250	300	400	500
	Types R,T,TW	Types RH, RHW, THW															
5	12	12	10	12	12	12	12	12	12	12	12	10	10	8	8	6	6
6	12	12	10	12	12	12	12	12	12	12	12	10	8	8	8	6	4
7	12	12	10	12	12	12	12	12	12	12	10	10	8	8	6	6	4
9	12	12	10	12	12	12	12	12	12	10	10	8	8	6	6	4	4
10	12	12	10	12	12	12	12	12	10	10	8	8	6	6	4	4	3
12	12	12	10	12	12	12	12	12	10	8	8	6	6	4	4	3	2
14	12	12	10	12	12	12	12	12	10	8	8	6	6	4	4	3	2
16	12	12	10	12	12	12	10	10	8	8	6	6	6	4	3	2	1
18	12	12	10	12	12	12	10	10	8	8	6	6	6	4	3	2	1
20	12	12	10	12	12	10	10	8	8	6	6	4	4	3	2	1	0
25	10	10	10	12	10	10	8	8	6	6	4	4	3	2	1	0	00
30	10	10	10	12	10	8	8	8	6	4	4	3	2	1	1	00	000
35	8	8	10	10	10	8	8	6	6	4	4	3	2	1	0	00	000
40	8	8	10	10	8	8	6	6	4	4	3	2	1	0	00	000	0000
50	6	6	10	8	8	6	6	4	4	3	2	1	0	00	000	0000	250
60	4	6	8	8	8	6	4	4	3	2	2	0	00	000	000	250	300
70	4	4	8	8	6	6	4	4	3	2	1	0	00	000	0000	300	350

[1] Use 125 percent of motor nameplate current for single motors.

[2] The wire size in overhead spans must be at least number 10 for spans up to 50 feet and number 8 for longer spans.

[3] AWG is American wire gauge and MCM is thousand circular mil.

TABLE 9

SIZES OF ALUMINUM WIRE FOR SINGLE-PHASE, 115-120 VOLT MOTORS AND A 2-PER CENT VOLTAGE DROP[1]

Load in amps	Minimum allowable wire size			Length of wire to motor in feet													
	Wire in cable, conduit, or earth		Bare or covered wire overhead in the air[2]	Wire size (AWG or MCM)[3] (Note: Compare the size shown below with the size shown in the column to the left of the double line and use the larger size.)													
	Types R,T,TW	Types RH, RHW, THW		20	30	40	50	60	80	100	120	160	200	250	300	400	500
5	12	12	10	12	12	12	12	12	12	10	10	8	8	6	6	4	
6	12	12	10	12	12	12	12	12	10	10	10	8	6	6	6	4	4
7	12	12	10	12	12	12	12	12	10	10	8	8	6	6	4	4	3
9	12	12	10	12	12	12	12	10	10	8	8	6	6	4	4	3	3
10	12	12	10	12	12	12	10	10	8	8	6	6	4	4	3	2	2
12	12	12	10	12	12	10	10	10	8	6	6	4	4	3	3	1	1
14	12	12	10	12	12	10	10	8	8	6	6	4	4	3	2	1	0
16	10	10	10	12	10	10	8	8	6	6	4	4	3	2	1	0	0
18	10	10	10	12	10	8	8	8	6	6	4	4	3	2	1	0	00
20	10	10	10	10	10	8	8	6	6	4	4	3	2	1	0	00	00
25	8	8	10	10	8	8	6	6	4	4	3	2	1	0	00	000	000
30	6	8	10	10	8	6	6	6	4	3	3	1	0	00	00	0000	250
35	6	8	10	10	8	6	6	4	4	3	2	1	0	00	000	0000	300
40	4	6	10	8	6	6	4	4	3	2	1	0	00	000	0000	250	300
50	3	4	8	8	6	4	4	3	2	1	0	00	000	0000	250	300	400
60	2	2	6	6	6	4	3	3	1	0	0	000	0000	250	300	350	500
70	2	2	6	6	4	4	3	2	1	0	00	000	0000	300	350	500	600

[1] Use 125 percent of motor nameplate current for single motors.

[2] The wire size in overhead spans must be at least number 10 for spans up to 50 feet and number 8 for longer spans.

[3] AWG is American wire gauge and MCM is thousand circular mil.

TABLE 10

SIZES OF COPPER WIRE FOR SINGLE-PHASE, 230-240 VOLT MOTORS AND A 2-PER CENT VOLTAGE DROP[1]

(Note: Compare the size shown below with the size shown in the column to the left of the double line and use the larger size.)

Wire size (AWG or MCM)[3]

Load in amps	Minimum allowable wire size — Wire in cable, conduit, or earth. Types R,T,TW	Types RH, RHW, THW	Bare or covered wire overhead in the air[2]	Length of wire to motor in feet — 20	30	40	50	60	80	100	120	160	200	250	300	400	500
2	12	12	10	12	12	12	12	12	12	12	12	12	12	12	12	12	12
3	12	12	10	12	12	12	12	12	12	12	12	12	12	12	12	12	10
4	12	12	10	12	12	12	12	12	12	12	12	12	12	12	12	10	8
5	12	12	10	12	12	12	12	12	12	12	12	12	12	10	10	10	8
6	12	12	10	12	12	12	12	12	12	12	12	12	12	10	8	8	8
8	12	12	10	12	12	12	12	12	12	12	12	10	10	8	8	6	6
10	12	12	10	12	12	12	12	12	12	12	12	10	8	8	8	6	6
12	12	12	10	12	12	12	12	12	12	12	12	10	8	8	8	6	4
14	12	12	10	12	12	12	12	12	12	12	10	10	8	6	6	6	4
17	12	12	10	12	12	12	12	12	12	12	10	10	8	6	6	4	4
20	10	12	10	12	12	12	12	12	10	10	10	8	6	6	4	4	3
25	10	10	10	12	12	12	10	10	8	8	8	6	6	4	4	3	2
30	10	10	10	12	12	10	10	10	8	8	8	6	4	4	4	2	1
35	8	8	10	12	12	10	10	8	8	8	6	6	4	4	3	2	1
40	8	8	10	12	12	10	8	8	6	6	6	4	4	3	2	2	1
45	6	6	8	12	10	10	8	8	6	6	4	4	4	2	2	1	0
50	6	6	8	12	10	8	8	8	6	4	4	3	3	2	1	1	0
60	4	6	8	12	8	8	6	6	4	4	4	3	2	1	1	0	0
70	4	4	6	10	8	8	6	6	4	4	4	2	2	1	1	00	00
80	2	4	6	10	8	6	6	4	4	4	3	1	1	0	00	000	000
100	1	3	6	10	8	8	6	6	4	3	2	1	0	00	000	0000	250

[1] Use 125 percent of motor nameplate current for single motors.

[2] The wire size in overhead spans must be at least number 10 for spans up to 50 feet and number 8 for longer spans.

[3] AWG is American wire gauge and MCM is thousand circular mil.

TABLE 11

SIZES OF ALUMINUM WIRE FOR SINGLE-PHASE, 230-240 VOLT MOTORS AND A 2-PER CENT VOLTAGE DROP[1]

(Note: Compare the size shown below with the size shown in the column to the left of the double line and use the larger size.)

Load in amps	Minimum allowable wire size			Length of wire to motor in feet — Wire size (AWG or MCM)[3]													
	Wire in cable, conduit, or earth		Bare or covered wire overhead in the air[2]	20	30	40	50	60	80	100	120	160	200	250	300	400	500
	Types R,T,TW	Types RH, RHW, THW															
2	12	12	10	12	12	12	12	12	12	12	12	12	12	12	12	12	10
3	12	12	10	12	12	12	12	12	12	12	12	12	12	12	12	10	8
4	12	12	10	12	12	12	12	12	12	12	12	12	12	10	10	8	8
5	12	12	10	12	12	12	12	12	12	12	12	12	10	10	8	8	6
6	12	12	10	12	12	12	12	12	12	12	12	10	10	8	8	6	6
8	12	12	10	12	12	12	12	12	12	12	12	10	8	8	6	6	4
10	12	12	10	12	12	12	12	12	12	12	10	10	8	6	6	4	4
12	12	12	10	12	12	12	12	12	10	10	10	8	6	6	6	4	3
14	12	12	10	12	12	12	12	12	10	10	10	8	6	6	4	3	3
17	10	10	10	12	12	12	12	10	10	10	8	8	6	4	4	2	2
20	10	10	10	12	12	12	12	10	8	8	8	6	4	4	3	1	1
25	10	10	10	12	12	12	10	8	8	8	6	6	4	3	2	0	0
30	8	8	10	12	12	10	10	8	6	6	6	4	3	2	1	0	00
35	6	8	10	12	12	10	8	8	6	6	6	4	3	2	0	00	00
40	6	8	10	12	10	10	8	6	6	4	4	3	2	1	0	000	000
45	4	6	8	12	10	8	8	6	6	4	4	3	2	1	00	000	000
50	4	6	8	10	10	8	8	6	6	4	3	2	1	0	00	0000	0000
60	2	4	6	10	8	6	6	4	4	3	3	1	0	00	000	0000	250
70	2	2	6	10	8	6	6	4	4	3	2	1	0	00	0000	250	300
80	1	2	6	8	6	6	4	4	3	2	1	0	00	000	0000	300	300
100	0	1	4	8	6	4	4	3	2	1	0	00	000	0000	250	300	400

[1] Use 125 percent of motor nameplate current for single motors.

[2] The wire size in overhead spans must be at least number 10 for spans up to 50 feet and number 8 for longer spans.

[3] AWG is American wire gauge and MCM is thousand circular mil.

per and aluminum conductors for single-phase motors and a two-percent voltage drop. Tables 12 and 13 show equivalent information for three-phase motors. To prevent low voltage from causing improper operation, wiring should be selected to limit the voltage drop under full-load conditions to two percent for branch circuits and to a total voltage drop of five percent for the branch circuit and service wiring combined.

Connections.   *Single-phase, single-speed motors* usually have from 2 to 6 leads. The number of leads depends on the type of motor and on whether it is a single- or dual-voltage unit.

Split-phase and capacitor motors that are single-voltage and are not reversible (the direction of rotation cannot be changed) have only two leads. Split-phase and capacitor motors that are single-voltage and are reversible have four leads—two for the main winding and two for the auxiliary, or starting, winding.

Dual-voltage capacitor motors have a minimum of six leads—four leads for the main winding and two for the auxiliary winding. For low-voltage operation, all windings are connected in parallel to the line. For high-voltage operation, the main windings are wired in series and the auxiliary winding is connected to the center leads of the main winding and to one of the supply lines.

The direction of rotation can be changed in split-phase or capacitor motors by reversing the electrical connections of either the main winding or the auxiliary winding to the line (Fig. 4). The terminals may be located on a terminal board or brought out of the motor frame into a terminal box as numbered leads. The wiring diagrams for the specific motor that is being wired must be followed when making connections.

Repulsion-start induction motors and repulsion-induction motors are usually dual-voltage units with four winding leads. For low-voltage operation, the main windings are wired in parallel. For high-voltage operation, the windings are wired in series. No changes in the rotor-brush connections are necessary for operation at either voltage.

Motors of the repulsion type can be reversed by rotating the brush ring to the alternate position (Fig. 5). The brush ring of a repulsion motor is held in position by a locking screw or a spring clip. When released, the brushes may be rotated. The two brush positions are marked on the ring with an index on the frame. When the brush position is changed, the direction of rotation is reversed.

TABLE 12
SIZES OF COPPER WIRE FOR THREE-PHASE, 230-240 VOLT MOTORS AND A 2-PER CENT VOLTAGE DROP[1]

(Note: Compare the size shown below with the size shown in the column to the left of the double line and use the larger size.)

Load in amps	Minimum allowable wire size			Length of wire to motor in feet													
	Wire in cable, conduit, or earth — Types R,T,TW	RHW, THW Types RH	Bare or covered wire overhead in the air[2]	20	30	40	50	60	80	100	120	160	200	250	300	400	500
				Wire size (AWG or MCM)[a]													
2	12	12	10	12	12	12	12	12	12	12	12	12	12	12	12	12	12
3	12	12	10	12	12	12	12	12	12	12	12	12	12	12	12	12	12
4	12	12	10	12	12	12	12	12	12	12	12	12	12	12	12	12	10
5	12	12	10	12	12	12	12	12	12	12	12	12	12	12	12	10	10
6	12	12	10	12	12	12	12	12	12	12	12	12	12	10	10	10	8
8	12	12	10	12	12	12	12	12	12	12	12	12	12	10	10	8	8
10	12	12	10	12	12	12	12	12	12	12	12	12	10	10	8	8	6
12	12	12	10	12	12	12	12	12	12	12	12	12	10	8	8	6	6
15	12	12	10	12	12	12	12	12	12	12	12	10	10	8	8	6	4
20	12	12	10	12	12	12	12	12	12	12	12	10	10	8	6	6	4
25	10	12	10	12	12	12	12	12	10	10	10	8	8	6	6	4	3
30	10	10	10	12	12	12	12	10	10	8	8	8	6	6	4	4	2
35	8	8	10	12	12	12	10	10	8	8	8	6	6	4	4	3	1
40	8	8	10	12	12	12	10	10	8	8	6	6	6	4	4	2	1

TABLE 12 (continued)

Load in amps	Minimum allowable wire size			Length of wire to motor in feet — Wire size (AWG or MCM)[3]													
	Wire in cable, conduit, or earth — Types R, T, TW	Types RH, RHW, THW	Bare or covered wire overhead in the air[2]	20	30	40	50	60	80	100	120	160	200	250	300	400	500
45	6	8	10	12	12	10	10	8	8	6	6	4	4	3	2	1	0
50	6	6	10	12	12	10	10	8	8	6	6	4	4	3	2	1	0
60	4	6	8	12	10	10	8	8	6	6	4	4	3	2	1	0	00
70	4	4	8	12	10	8	8	8	6	4	4	3	2	1	1	00	000
80	3	4	6	12	10	8	8	6	6	4	4	3	2	1	0	00	000
100	1	3	6	10	8	8	6	6	4	4	3	2	1	0	00	000	0000
120	0	1	4	10	8	6	6	4	4	3	2	1	0	00	000	0000	250
150	000	0	3	8	6	4	4	4	3	2	1	0	00	000	0000	250	300
180	0000	000	1	8	6	4	4	3	2	1	0	00	000	0000	250	300	400
210	250	0000	0	8	6	4	4	3	2	1	0	00	000	0000	250	350	500
240	300	250	00	6	4	4	3	2	1	0	00	000	0000	250	300	400	500

(Note: Compare the size shown below with the size shown in the column to the left of the double line and use the larger size.)

[1] Use 125 percent of motor nameplate current for single motors.

[2] The wire size in overhead spans must be at least number 10 for spans up to 50 feet and number 8 for longer spans.

[3] AWG is American wire gauge and MCM is thousand circular mil.

TABLE 13

SIZES OF ALUMINUM WIRE FOR THREE-PHASE, 230-240 VOLT MOTORS AND A 2-PER CENT VOLTAGE DROP[1]

Load in amps	Minimum allowable wire size			Length of wire to motor in feet													
	Wire in cable, conduit, or earth		Bare or covered wire overhead in the air[2]	20	30	40	50	60	80	100	120	160	200	250	300	400	500
	Types R,T,TW	Types RH, RHW, THW		Wire size (AWG or MCM)[3] (Note: Compare the size shown below with the size shown in the column to the left of the double line and use the larger size.)													
2	12	12	10	12	12	12	12	12	12	12	12	12	12	12	12	12	12
3	12	12	10	12	12	12	12	12	12	12	12	12	12	12	12	10	10
4	12	12	10	12	12	12	12	12	12	12	12	12	12	12	10	10	8
5	12	12	10	12	12	12	12	12	12	12	12	12	12	10	10	8	8
6	12	12	10	12	12	12	12	12	12	12	12	12	10	10	8	8	6
8	12	12	10	12	12	12	12	12	12	12	12	10	10	8	8	6	6
10	12	12	10	12	12	12	12	12	12	12	12	10	8	8	6	6	6
12	12	12	10	12	12	12	12	12	12	12	10	8	8	6	6	4	4
15	12	12	10	12	12	12	12	12	10	10	10	8	6	6	4	4	4
20	10	10	10	12	12	12	12	10	10	10	8	6	6	4	4	3	3
25	10	10	10	12	12	12	10	10	8	8	8	6	4	4	3	2	2
30	8	8	10	12	12	10	10	8	8	8	6	4	4	3	2	1	1
35	6	8	10	12	12	10	8	8	6	6	6	4	3	2	2	0	0
40	6	8	10	12	10	10	8	8	6	6	6	4	3	2	1	0	00
45	4	6	10	12	10	8	8	6	6	4	4	3	2	1	0	00	000

TABLE 13 (continued)

Load in amps	Minimum allowable wire size			Length of wire to motor in feet													
	Wire in cable, conduit, or earth		Bare or covered wire overhead in the air[1]	20	30	40	50	60	80	100	120	160	200	250	300	400	500
	Types R,T,TW	Types RH, RHW, THW		Wire size (AWG or MCM)[3] (Note: Compare the size shown below with the size shown in the column to the left of the double line and use the larger size.)													
50	4	6	8	12	10	8	8	6	6	4	4	3	2	1	0	00	000
60	3	4	6	10	8	8	6	6	4	4	3	2	1	0	00	000	0000
70	2	3	6	10	8	6	6	6	4	3	3	1	0	00	00	0000	250
80	1	2	6	10	8	6	6	4	4	3	2	1	0	00	00	0000	300
100	0	1	4	8	6	6	4	4	3	2	1	0	00	000	0000	300	350
120	00	00	2	8	6	4	4	3	2	1	0	00	000	0000	250	350	400
150	0000	000	1	6	4	4	3	2	1	0	00	000	0000	250	300	400	500
180	300	0000	0	6	4	3	2	1	0	00	000	0000	250	300	350	500	600
210	350	300	00	6	4	3	2	1	0	000	000	0000	300	350	400	600	700
240	500	350	000	4	3	2	1	0	00	000	0000	250	350	400	500	700	800

[1] Use 125 percent of motor nameplate current for single motors.

[2] The wire size in overhead spans must be at least number 10 for spans up to 50 feet and number 8 for longer spans.

[3] AWG is American wire gauge and MCM is thousand circular mil.

THERMALLY PROTECTED

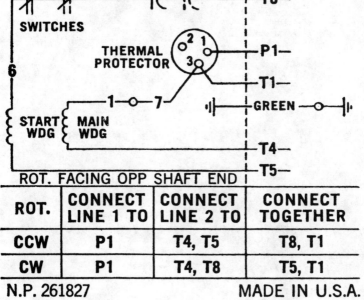

ROT. FACING OPP SHAFT END			
ROT.	CONNECT LINE 1 TO	CONNECT LINE 2 TO	CONNECT TOGETHER
CCW	P1	T4, T5	T8, T1
CW	P1	T4, T8	T5, T1

N.P. 261827   MADE IN U.S.A.

Fig. 4. Wiring diagram of a split-phase or capacitor motor shows which leads to interchange to reverse the direction of rotation.

Special-purpose or special-duty motors may differ in their wiring and method of reversing direction. Consult the manufacturer's instructions.

Fig. 5. Repulsive-induction motors. The double arrow indicates rotation.

Chapter 10

Motor Protection and Control, and Motor Servicing and Repairs

MOTOR PROTECTION

Motors must be protected against both excessive current and excessive winding temperature caused by faults, overloads, or low supply voltage.

An overloaded motor draws excessive current from the line. This causes overheating that destroys the winding insulation and causes bearings to fail. Maximum temperature at which a motor can operate depends on its construction and the type of insulation used for the windings.

Motor current required for starting will usually be 2 to 8 times that for running at full load. Short-circuit protection devices must be able to carry this high current for a short time.

Branch circuit fuses or circuit breakers do not adequately protect the motor; they primarily protect the circuit wires and give limited protection to the motor for short-circuit conditions only. Additional overcurrent protection for the motor is therefore needed.

Fuses. Time-delay fuses afford both short-circuit and overload protection (Fig. 1). Short circuits melt the fusible link in the fuse almost instantly, which breaks the circuit. For small continuous overloads, heat developed in the second element of the fuse weakens the eutectic solder connections, and permits a spring to break the connection (Fig. 2). Time-delay fuses must be properly sized to protect the motor.

Other Overload Protective Devices. *Motor-starter switches,* both manual and electromagnetic, are available with built-in overload protection. Thermal overload relays with either a bimetallic or eutectic element are commonly used protective devices (Figs. 3 and 4).

123

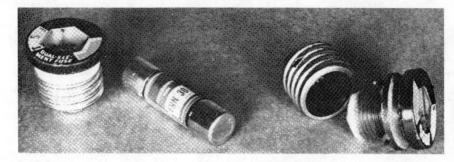

Fig. 1. Time-delay fuses (left fuse) can replace a common plug fuse on old installation. The middle fuse is a cartridge fuse that should be used in 230-volt circuits. The right fuse, when placed in a fuse socket, cannot be replaced with any fuse except one with equal rating.

If the overload relay elements are not thermally compensated, allowance must be made for ambient temperature. Your power supplier or electrician should be consulted for recommendations. The combination overload switch-relay unit should preferably be installed so it will be under the same operating conditions as the motor.

A *thermal-overload switch* built into the motor affords the best protection against overload (Fig. 5). The switch generally opens the line directly on fractional horsepower motors. With larger motors, a relay may be needed. Built-in thermal protective units may be automatic-reset or manual-reset types. The manual-reset unit is usually recommended for general-purpose use because the cause of the overload can be corrected before the motor is restarted and unexpected startup of equipment is avoided.

Overcurrent protection in the ungrounded conductor is adequate for single-phase motors. Overcurrent protection, however, should be provided in all three conductors supplying a three-phase motor to insure protection for all fault conditions.

The overcurrent device should be rated or selected to trip at no more than the following percent of motor full-load current rating:

     1. Motors with a service factor of 1.15 or greater—125 percent.
     2. Motors with a marked temperature rise of not over 104° F.—125 percent.
     3. All other motors—115 percent.

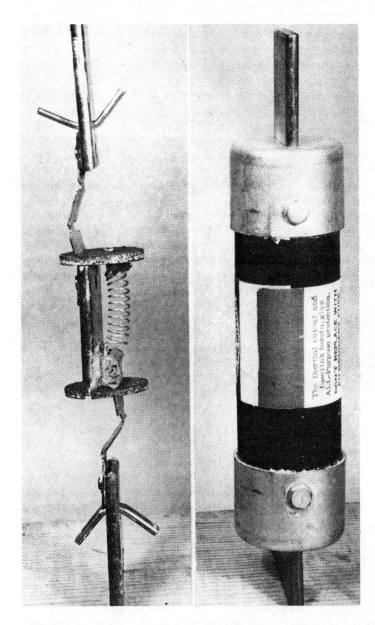

Fig. 2. Time-delay, two-element fuses (left), shows the two elements, one for short-circuit protection (fusible links) and one for brief overload (the spring-loaded eutectic solder link in the center of the fuse).

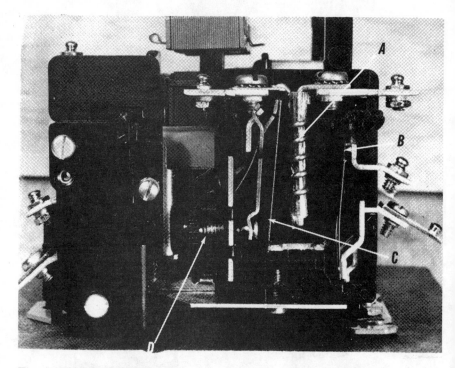

Fig. 3. Thermal overload relay (bimetallic-type shown). Most often used for manual and electromagnetic starter switches. (A) heater; (B) interlock contacts; (C) bimetallic strip; (D) compensation adjustment.

Where these values cannot be matched exactly with standard sizes or settings, higher ratings or settings may be used, but they must not exceed the following percentages of motor full-load current rating:

    1. Motors with a service factor of 1.15 or greater—140 percent.
    2. Motors with a marked temperature rise not over 104° F.—140 percent.
    3. All other motors—130 percent.

The values listed are maximum. Better protection will be afforded the motor if values are chosen at nameplate current rating or less. Most overcurrent devices will pass currents exceeding their rating for extended periods without tripping.

Fig. 4. Thermal overcurrent relay elements are resistance units that generate heat in proportion to the current flowing through them: (left) heater for a bimetallic overcurrent relay; (middle) eutectic solder unit; (right) heater. These are used in small manual starter switches.

CONTROLS

Controls for electric motors vary from a simple on-off toggle switch to complex automatic systems. Motor controls have two purposes: (1) to start and stop the motor and (2) to protect the motor from damage caused by excessive current. Only simple controls are discussed in this chapter. Advice on more complex systems should be obtained from your local electrician or power supplier.

Manually Operated Switches.   Manual switches are used most often to control small motors of ½ horsepower or less. These switches are low-cost devices. They are available with a built-in over-current cut-out that can be sized to the current demand of a particular motor. If the switch does not provide over-current protection, these motors must be provided with a suitable overload device such as a dual element fuse, sized specifically to protect the motor, or by a thermal overload built into the motor. Typical manual switch motor-control circuits are shown in Fig. 6.

Control switches for electric motors must be able to withstand

Fig. 5. Thermal overload switch. Arrow points to reset button.

the high starting current and the arcing that occurs when the circuit is opened (Fig. 7). Quick-make, quick-break switches equipped with arc quenchers are used. These are rated by horsepower and voltage.

T-rated, tumbler-type light switches should not be used to control electric motors. They can withstand the high starting current but are not equipped with arc quenchers and usually burn out quickly.

Magnetic Motor Starters.   A magnetic motor starter is the best kind to use for controlling a motor. This type of starter should be used for all motors larger than one horsepower and is essential in automatic control systems. A magnetic coil allows operation from either local or remote locations and will remove the motor from the

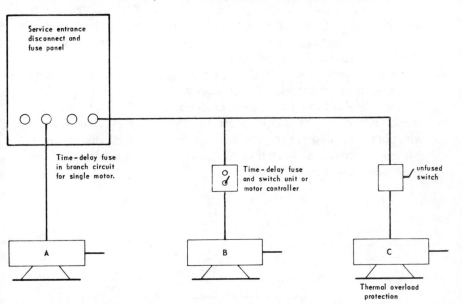

Fig. 6. Typical manual-switch, motor-control circuits.

Fig. 7. Control switches for electric motors. From left: magnetic motor starter with self-contained push-button switches; a push-button start-and-stop station for remote installation with a magnetic starter, a manual starter switch for integral-horsepower motors; and a manual switch for fractional-horsepower motors.

line if there is a loss of power. Built-in thermal or other types of overload elements provide overcurrent protection for the motor and should be sized for the specific motor that is to be controlled.

There are many ways to connect the control circuits of magnetic motor starters. A commonly used circuit for a 230-volt single-phase motor is shown in Fig. 8. A more complex circuit is shown in Fig. 9, which provides a sequenced start for three motors. Simultaneous stopping of all motors is provided and overload contacts are interlocked to provide shutdown of all motors if any one of the motors is shut down because of overload.

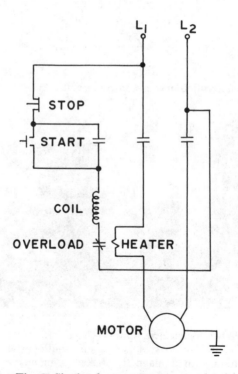

Fig. 8. Single-phase motor starter circuit with 230-volt holding cell.

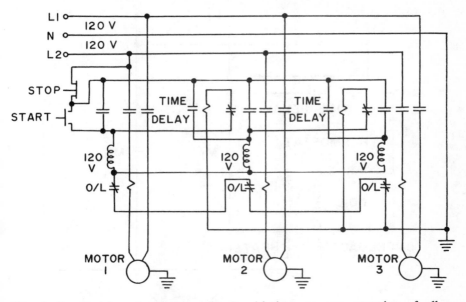

Fig. 9. Sequenced motor starting circuit with instantaneous stopping of all motors and interlocked overload relays.

Generally, motors should not be allowed to restart automatically after a loss of power. If automatic operation is necessary, provision should be made for random restarting to prevent the excessive voltage drop in the wiring that would occur if all motors came at one time. This can be accomplished by including a low-cost time-delay relay in the magnetic motor starter-control starter as shown in Fig. 10. This random restart feature is especially desirable for large-horsepower motors, such as those often found in crop-drying fans.

MOTOR SERVICING AND REPAIRS

A well-made and properly installed electric motor requires less maintenance than many other types of equipment. However, for the best and most economical performance, *periodic servicing* is required.

The service operations listed should be performed at least once a year or more often if the motor operates under severe heat, cold, or dust conditions.

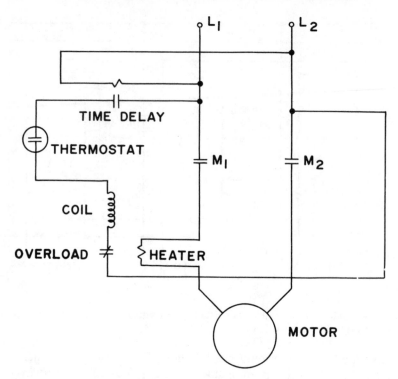

Fig. 10. Circuit for random restarting of motors under automatic control after a loss of power.

1. Remove dust and dirt from the air passages and cooling surfaces of the motor to insure proper cooling. Plugged air passages of an open motor, or a coating of dust on a totally enclosed motor, will cause the motor to overheat under normal operation.

2. Check bearings for wear. Excessive side or end play may cause the motor to draw higher than normal starting current, develop less starting torque, and may damage the motor.

3. Make sure the motor shaft turns freely. Tight or misaligned bearings will cause the motor to overheat.

4. Lubricate the motor according to the manufacturer's specifications. Do not overlubricate. Too much lubricant is as bad as too little.

5. Check all wiring for frayed or bare spots. Repair or replace as needed.

6. Clean the starting-switch contacts of split-phase and capacitor motors and the commutator and brushes in wound-rotor (repulsion-type) motors. Use very fine sand paper; *do not use emery cloth.*

7. Replace worn brushes and make sure the brush-lifting and shorting-ring action works smoothly in wound-rotor motors.

8. Check belt pulleys to be sure they are secure on their shafts. Align the belts and pulleys carefully. Improper alignment causes excessive wear on belts and pulleys. Check and adjust belt tension. Replace belts that are badly worn.

Properly installed and maintained electric motors should give trouble-free service for many years. Occasionally, however, a motor may give trouble or fail to operate. Some repairs require the services of an experienced electrician or motor serviceman; others can be made by the operator.

Caution: Do not attempt to service or repair an electric motor until it has been disconnected from the circuit.

Chapter 11

Phase Converters for Operation of Three-Phase Motors from Single-Phase Power

Proper selection, installation, and protection of both the phase converter and the three-phase motors are essential for satisfactory performance from a converter-motor combination.

Converter-motor combinations are being used to successfully operate many kinds of loads. Some examples are crop driers, grain handling systems, irrigation pumps, and animal feeding systems (Fig. 1).

Fig. 1. Converter-motor combination operating crop drier.

ADVANTAGES OF THREE-PHASE MOTORS

Three-phase motors are used instead of single-phase motors for a number of reasons when three-phase power service is available.

In the larger sizes (above two-horsepower), the motors are generally more readily available and less expensive than single-phase motors of the same horsepower rating. Also, they are usually smaller, lighter, and offer you a greater choice in the type of enclosure and horsepower rating that you can buy.

Three-phase motors are very simple in construction. No starting windings or starting devices (such as internal centrifugal switches) are required. Fewer parts generally mean less maintenance and service problems.

The direction of motor rotation is easily reversed with three-phase motors: you interchange the connections to any two of the motor leads.

WHEN TO USE PHASE CONVERTERS

There are three ways to power motor loads.

1. Single-phase motors operating on single-phase power.

2. Phase-converter, three-phase motor combination operating on single-phase power.

3. Three-phase motors operating on three-phase power where the service is available.

Before investing in a phase converter, you need to determine if a converter-motor combination will be the best source of power for your loads.

Draw up a list of your jobs that require electric motors. Include the sizes of motors required, the expected hours of use, and possible future loads. These will be important factors in your decision.

For example, power suppliers often limit the size of motors that may be used on single-phase power lines because of the high currents that large single-phase motors draw in starting. These high currents reduce the line voltage and may affect service to other customers and equipment.

Converter-motor combinations, however, generally draw less starting current than comparable size single-phase motors (but there is a corresponding decrease in the starting torque). Consequently, power suppliers may permit the use of higher horsepower converter-motor combinations than single-phase motors on their power lines.

Because the choice of the best method of operation depends on so many factors, you will need to consult with your electric-power supplier, the equipment dealer, and, if possible, phase converter manufacturers. Points to check with them are as follows:

1. The cost and availability of single-phase motors and three-phase motors of the required sizes and starting characteristics.

2. Motor size limitations on the single-phase power lines.

3. The availability and cost of three-phase power service.

4. The cost of operation for a converter-motor combination compared with the cost of operation for the other choices. All costs, including the cost of equipment, installation costs, and power rates, should be considered.

Use of a converter-motor combination is often the best choice:

1. When the cost of the line extension to bring three-phase power to your home or farm is high because of the wire and construction costs for the length of three-phase line required.

2. When the cost per kilowatt-hour for three-phase service is substantially higher than for single-phase service because of the additional investment your power supplier must make to give three-phase service. Over a period of time, the difference in the rates may add up to more than the cost of a converter.

3. When you need to use a larger motor, but the starting current of a standard single-phase motor of the required size is too high to use on single-phase lines.

4. When you need temporary three-phase service until regular three-phase service is available.

5. When you buy equipment with a three-phase motor as an integral part of the unit, and replacement of the motor is either too difficult or costs more than a converter.

6. When you need a number of motors and the most of three-

phase motors plus converter is less than the cost of single-phase motors.

TYPES OF PHASE CONVERTERS

Two general types of converters are available—*static* and *rotary*. Each type offers advantages for specific kinds of motor loads.

You can choose the type of converter to use on the basis of the motor loads to be run, but a specific unit should be chosen in consultation with the manufacturer, if possible. Recommendations of the manufacturer are desirable because of the variations in design between the different manufacturers' units. These design differences can make a difference in motor performance, particularly in such important factors as motor starting torque and temperature rise.

STATIC CONVERTERS

Two general kinds of static converters are available—*capacitor* and *autotransformer capacitor*. These converters have no moving parts other than switching relays that operate during the starting cycle. Thus, the name static (or nonmoving).

The *capacitor converter* is the simplest kind of converter. A typical unit, as shown in Fig. 2, consists essentially of an enclosure, a bank of capacitors, and relays.

Figure 3 shows simplified diagrams for two different designs of capacitor converters. In connection (a), two of the three-phase motor terminals are connected directly to the single-phase power lines (through switching and overcurrent protection in the complete installation). The third motor terminal is connected to one of the single-phase lines through the bank of capacitors of the converter. The capacitors shift the phase (or electrical position) of the voltage to the third winding. The phase-shifted voltage, in combination with the physical position of the motor windings, produces the rotating magnetic field to start and run the motor.

In connection (b), the third motor winding—the one supplied through the capacitor bank—connects to the line, L1, instead of to the common motor winding point as in (a).

Fig. 2. Capacitor phase converter.

Close check must be kept on the loading of motors operated on converters; particularly with the capacitor converter. The currents in the motor windings may exceed the nameplate rating of the motor only for short periods and when air temperatures are favorable for cooling (below 104° F.); otherwise, the motor may become overheated and damaged.

Currents drawn by motors operated on capacitor converters may increase rapidly with increases in the motor load. Care must be taken to prevent higher than rated currents when loading the motor above approximately 75 percent of its full-load rating. For some capacitor converters, it may be necessary to limit the motor load to less than the full-load rating of the motor to insure maintaining the currents within the nameplate rating.

An autotransformer-capacitor converter is shown in Fig. 4. The major difference between this kind of converter and the capacitor

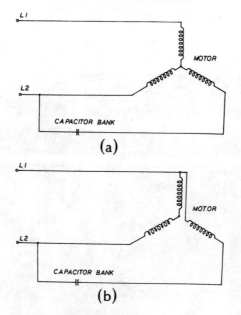

Fig. 3. Diagrams for two designs of capacitor converters.

converter is the autotransformer unit. The addition of this unit allows the currents in the motor windings to be balanced at full horsepower output.

Figure 5 shows a simplified diagram for an autotransformer-capacitor converter. Two of the three-phase motor terminals are connected directly to the single-phase lines. The third terminal is connected through the capacitor bank to the autotransformer. Taps on the autotransformer make it possible to adjust the voltage supplied to the capacitor bank. This allows the currents in the motor windings to be balanced at a specific load for a given motor.

Motors operated on this kind of converter—as on the capacitor converter—will have less starting torque than if they were operated on regular three-phase power. This must be taken into account when sizing the converter, particularly if the load is hard to start.

More than one motor can be operated at a time on this kind of converter, but the capacitance in the circuit must be changed as the number of motors operated is changed to prevent overheating and

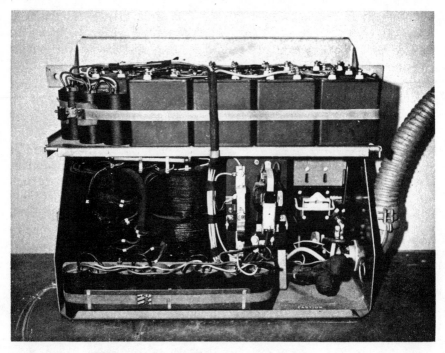

Fig. 4. Autotransformer-capacitor converter.

damage to the motors. Because this extra care is required, multiple-motor operation is not recommended for this kind of converter unless approved by the manufacturer.

To improve the starting torque of static converters, additional capacitors are connected into the circuit at starting. Electrolytic capacitors are generally used because, for a given capacitance, they are smaller and lower in cost than other types. However, these capacitors have a short duty cycle, or period of operation for which they may be used without overheating and failure. This must be considered where motors are started frequently or are slow to reach operating speed. The number of starts per hour or other period of time must be limited to the manufacturer's recommendation. A typical maximum service rating recommended by one manufacturer is 20 starts per hour of no more than three seconds duration for each start.

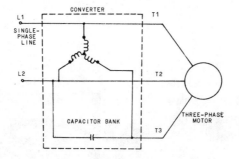

Fig. 5. Diagram for autotransformer-capacitor converter.

ROTARY CONVERTERS

A *rotary converter* is shown in Fig. 6. It consists of a rotating unit similar to a motor (on the left) and an enclosure containing capacitors.

Figure 7 shows a simplified diagram for the converter. Two of the three rotating converter terminals are connected directly to the single-phase power lines. The third rotating converter terminal is connected to one of the single-phase lines through the capacitor bank. The capacitors provide the rotating magnetic field to start and operate the converter. The generating action of the rotating converter, in combination with the phase shift of the capacitors, produces the three-phase voltage to operate the motor.

With a rotary converter, you can operate a number of motors under varying load conditions. The converter is started with no load connected. Then, while it is running, motors of sizes up to the rated starting horsepower of the converter may be started, one at a time. The horsepower rating of the largest motor to be started determines the minimum converter rating needed.

The total horsepower load that can be carried by a rotary converter is determined by its design and the method of switching capacitance when motor loads are connected. Generally this will be from 2 to 4 times the horsepower of the largest motor that may be started.

Fig. 6. Rotary converter.

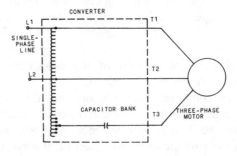

Fig. 7. Diagram for rotary converter.

The total horsepower rating indicated by the manufacturer should be with the motors fully loaded and operating at the rated temperature. This rating can be exceeded for short periods if air temperatures are favorable for motor cooling or some motors are not fully loaded.

There is also a minimum size of motor that should be operated alone on a rotary converter to prevent overheating of the motor. The size may vary with converters from $\frac{1}{10}$ to $\frac{1}{4}$ of the converter rating.

Follow the manufacturer's recommendations for both maximum and minimum loading of a converter. Improper loading can result in overheating and damage to motors or the converter.

As with the static converters, the starting and breakdown torques of motors are generally reduced when used with the rotary converter. On some converters, the starting torque for the largest motor may be as little as half that obtained if the motor were operated on regular three-phase power. You must allow for this possible reduction in motor torque when selecting a converter for loads requiring high starting torque.

Some rotary converters connect additional electrolytic capacitors into the circuit at starting to increase the starting torque. Up to 80 percent or more of normal motor torque is obtained in this way.

However, as indicated previously in the section on Static Converters, electrolytic capacitors have a short duty cycle. This must be kept in mind when selecting a converter for high inertia loads that start slowly or for loads that require frequent starts. Such loads require special consideration, and you should consult with the converter manufacturer, if possible.

In cold weather, capacitors lose capacitance, and the starting torque of the converter will be less. Also, the starting torque of equipment will be greater because of stiff bearings. The converter and motors must be large enough to provide cold-weather starts.

Additional starting torque may also be obtained by oversizing the converter—using one with a rating greater than that of the largest motor to be started. This will also allow you to increase your motor loads in the future. If you oversize the converter, remember that there is a minimum size for motors that are operated alone on a converter.

Motor performance may also be improved by adding capacitance to the circuit when larger motors are connected. These capacitors should be sized in accordance with the converter manufacturer's recommendations and connected as indicated in the section on Connection of Capacitors later in this chapter.

CHOICE OF PHASE CONVERTER

Considerations in determining the type of converter to use include the following: the number of motors to be operated, the kinds of loads and any load variations, the motor torque or turning power required to start and run the loads, and the cost of the converter unit.

The following guidelines will be helpful for selecting a converter:

1. For a single fixed load (minimum variation in the load) a capacitor static converter may offer a cost advantage. Allowance must be made for the possible reduction in horsepower available from the motor.

2. For a single load that varies over a wide range and for full horsepower output from the motor without exceeding the temperature-rise rating of the motor, consider the autotransformer-capacitor static converter specifically designed for single-motor operation.

3. For operation of several motors, the loads of which may vary over a wide range, the rotary converter is probably the best choice. An autotransformer-capacitor static converter could be used, but requires proper switching of capacitors as motors are connected and disconnected, and more care in the use and loading of the motors.

Note: If the loads are widely spaced or at a distance from the rotary converter, it may be desirable to provide means for turning the converter on from the motor location. Also, if the motors are subject to infrequent automatic starts, make provision for automatic starting of the converter before the motor loads are connected.

Select the size of the converter carefully. It should be chosen to match the characteristics and size of the motor load. The rating for motor starting must be at least as large as the rating of the largest motor to be started. The total-motor-load rating must equal the total motor load to be run at one time.

Oversizing a static converter will result in improper motor operation unless you adjust the converter to the actual load.

Oversizing a rotary converter will result in a slight loss of efficiency. This loss may be unimportant, however, and you may prefer.to over-size the converter for improved motor starting torque or to allow for future increases in the motor load.

Undersizing any converter will result in improper motor operation and, possibly, damage to the converter itself.

INSTALLATION

Phase converters, like any piece of electrical equipment, should be installed and serviced by an experienced person. Many of the problems reported with these units have been due to improper installation—incorrect connection of wires to the converter, loose connections, or undersized wiring.

Connection and sizing of the wiring and other installations should be in accordance with the requirements and recommendations of the converter manufacturer, your electric power supplier, and the national and local electrical codes.

The following information is intended as a guide.

SERVICE WIRING

Connection of Wiring from Converter to Motor. The wiring from the converter to the three-phase motor may be connected in two ways:

1. In the connection shown in Fig. 8, power is switched to the converter only. Other loads can be supplied with power from the motor location at all times. The disadvantage of this method is that single-phase power will be applied to the motor if you close the motor

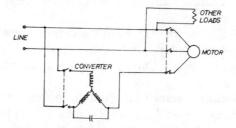

Fig. 8. Wiring of converter so that single-phase power can be supplied to other loads with the converter off.

switch without the converter being turned on. This could damage the motor.

2. In the connection shown in Fig. 9, power cannot be supplied to the other loads unless the converter has power. While this is a disadvantage, you cannot accidentally apply single-phase power to the three-phase motor.

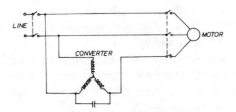

Fig. 9. Wiring of converter so that single-phase power cannot be supplied to other loads unless the converter has power.

Wire Size from Converter to Motor.   The *wiring* from the converter to the motor must be of the proper size. If it is too small, there will be excessive voltage drop. This will reduce the motor starting torque, and the motor may not start the load or bring it up to speed. The motor may also draw excessive current and overheat.

You can determine the minimum size of wire that should be used for 230-volt, three-phase motors as follows:

1. First, determine the total motor current that must be supplied on the circuit. For a:

(a) *Single-motor load:* Find the current value for the horsepower rating of the motor from Table 14, Column 3 (125 percent full-load amps). *Example:* Current value for a single five-horsepower motor is 19 amperes.

(b) *Multiple-motor load:* Find the current value for the largest motor to be used from Table 14, Column 3 (125 percent full-load amps). Then find the current value for each additional motor to be used on the circuit from Column 2 (full-load amps). Add the values to find the total current requirement. *Example:* One 10-horsepower motor and one 3-horsepower motor will be used on the circuit. The current value for the larger motor, from Table 14, Column 3 is 35

TABLE 14
MOTOR-CURRENT VALUES FOR 230-VOLT, THREE PHASE MOTORS

Col. 1	Col. 2	Col. 3	Col. 4	Col. 5
Motor Horsepower	Full-Load Current Amperes [1]	125% Full-Load Current Amperes	150% Full-Load Current Amperes	250% Full-Load Current Amperes
½	2.0	2.5	3.0	5.0
¾	2.8	3.5	4.2	7.0
1	3.6	4.5	5.4	9.0
1-½	5.2	6.5	7.8	13
2	6.8	8.5	10.2	17
3	9.6	12	14.4	24
5	15.2	19	23	38
7-½	22	28	33	56
10	28	35	42	70
15	42	52	63	105
20	54	68	81	136
25	68	85	102	170
30	80	100	120	200
40	104	130	156	260
50	130	162	195	325
60	154	192	231	385
75	192	240	288	480
100	248	310	372	620
125	312	390	468	780

[1] Current values taken from table 430-150 of the 1971 National Electrical Code. If motor nameplate current exceeds this value, use nameplate current.

amperes. Value for the smaller motor, from Column 2, is 9.6 amperes. Total current requirement is 35 + 9.6, or 44.6 amperes.

2. Next, determine the minimum size of wire required to carry the current determined in step 1(a) or step 1(b), according to the type of wire, type of wire insulation, and method of installation. Refer to Table 15 for copper wire or Table 16 for aluminum wire.

If your current value falls between those given in the table, use the next higher value. *Example:* Copper wire, Type TW and direct burial, will be used to carry the current of 44.6 amperes determined in the example in step 1(b). That current value is not listed in Table 15, so the next higher value, 55, must be used. The minimum size of copper wire required for 55 amperes is number 6.

3. Next, determine the minimum size of wire required to prevent excessive voltage drop for the length of service, or wire run, from the converter to the motor. Refer to Table 15 for copper wire or Table 16 for aluminum wire. If your current value falls between those listed in the table, use the next higher value. *Example:* Distance from the converter to the motor is 300 feet. The current value of 44.6 amperes is not listed in Table 15 for copper wire, so the next higher value, 45, must be used. Minimum size of wire required to prevent excessive voltage drop is number 2.

4. Choose the larger of the two sizes of wire determined in steps 2 and 3 for service from the converter to the motor. *Example:* Number 2 wire, the size required to maintain the voltage level (in the example in step 3) is the larger. That size should be used for service to the motor.

Wire Size from Power Source to Converter. The wires from the single-phase power source to the converter must also be large enough to prevent excessive voltage drop.

These wires will carry greater current than the wires from the converter to the motor. The single-phase current will be approximately $1\frac{1}{2}$ to 2 times the total current of the motors as determined in step 1(a) or step 1(b) of the preceding section.

You can determine the minimum size of wire required as follows:

1. First, determine the current value to use for selecting the wire size. For a:

(a) *Single-motor load:* Use twice the current value found for a single-motor in step 1(a) of the preceding section. (*See* Table 17, Column 5.) *Example:* Current value for the motor in the example in step 1(a) of the preceding section was 19 amperes. For sizing the wires from the power source to the converter, use a value of 2×19, or 38 amperes. (*See* Table 14, Column 5.)

(b) *Multiple-motor load:* Use twice the current value determined for the largest motor in step 1(b) of the preceding section plus

TABLE 15
ALLOWABLE CURRENT-CARRYING CAPACITY OF INSULATED
COPPER CONDUCTORS IN AMPERES

Wire size (AWG or MCM)	Not more than three conductors in raceway or cable, or direct burial		Single conductor in free air [1]	
	Rubber type R, RW, RU, and RUW, and thermoplastic type T and TW	Rubber type RH, RHW, and RUH, and thermoplastic type THW and THWN	Thermoplastic type TW	Weatherproof type WP
	Amperes	Amperes	Amperes	Amperes
12	20	20	—	—
10	30	30	40	55
8	40	45	55	70
6	55	65	80	100
4	70	85	105	130
3	80	100	120	150
2	95	115	140	175
1	110	130	165	205
0	125	150	195	235
00	145	175	225	275
000	165	200	260	320
0000	195	230	300	370
250	215	255	340	410
300	240	285	375	460
350	260	310	420	510
400	280	335	455	555
500	320	380	515	630
600	355	420	575	710
700	385	460	630	780
750	400	475	655	810
800	410	490	680	845
900	435	520	730	905
1000	455	545	780	965

[1] Overhead conductors shall not be smaller than number 10 for spans up to 50 feet in length and not smaller than number 8 for longer spans.

TABLE 16
ALLOWABLE CURRENT-CARRYING CAPACITY OF INSULATED ALUMINUM CONDUCTORS IN AMPERES

Wire size (AWG or MCM)	Not more than three conductors in raceway or cable, or direct burial		Single conductor in free air [1]	
	Rubber type R, RW, RU, and RUW, and thermoplastic type T and TW	Rubber type RH, RHW, and RUH, and thermoplastic type THW and THWN	Thermoplastic type TW	Weatherproof type WP
	Amperes	Amperes	Amperes	Amperes
12	15	15	—	—
10	25	25	30	45
8	30	40	45	55
6	40	50	60	80
4	55	65	80	100
3	65	75	95	115
2	75	90	110	135
1	85	100	130	160
0	100	120	150	185
00	115	135	175	215
000	130	155	200	250
0000	155	180	230	290
250	170	205	265	320
300	190	230	290	360
350	210	250	330	400
400	225	270	355	435
500	260	310	405	490
600	285	340	455	560
700	310	375	500	615
750	320	385	515	640
800	330	395	535	670
900	355	425	580	725
1000	375	445	625	770

[1] Overhead conductors shall not be smaller than number 10 for spans up to 50 feet in length and not smaller than number 8 for longer spans.

1½ times the current value determined for each additional motor. (*See* Table 14, Columns 4 and 5.) *Example:* Current value for the larger (10-horsepower) motor in the example in step 1(b) of the preceding section was 35 amperes. Value for the smaller (three-horsepower) motor was 9.6 amperes. For sizing the wires to the converter, use a value of 2 × 35, or 70, plus 1.5 × 9.6, or 14.4—a total of 84.4 amperes.

2. Next, determine the minimum size of wire required to carry the current determined in step 1(a) or step 1(b), according to the type of wire, type of wire insulation, and method of installation. Refer to Table 15 for copper wire or Table 16 for aluminum wire. If your current value falls between those listed in the table, use the next higher value. *Example:* Copper wire, Type TW and direct burial, will be used to carry the current 84.4 amperes determined in the example in 1(b). That current value is not listed in Table 15, so the next higher value, 95, must be used. Minimum size of copper wire required for 95 amperes is number 2.

3. Next, determine the minimum size of wire required to prevent excessive voltage drop for the length of service, or wire run, to the converter. Refer to Table 17 for copper wire or Table 18 for aluminum wire. If your current value falls between those listed in the table, use the next higher value. (Tables 17 and 18 are actually for sizing three-phase wiring, but for simplicity are being used to size the single-phase wiring. Use of the next higher current value partially compensates for possible differences in wire size requirements. For a more conservative estimate of the proper wire size, increase your current value by 16 percent and then use the closest value in the tables.) *Example:* The distance from the single-phase power source to the converter is 50 feet. The current value of 84.4 amperes determined in step 1(b) is not listed in the table, so the next higher value, 90, must be used. Minimum size of copper wire required to prevent excessive voltage drop for a current of 90 amperes and a length of service of 50 feet is number 6.

4. Choose the larger of the two sizes of wire determined in steps 2 and 3. Number 2 wire is the larger. That size should be used from the power source to the converter.

TABLE 17

COPPER WIRE SIZE REQUIRED AT 230-240 VOLTS, THREE-PHASE, BASED ON TWO PER CENT VOLTAGE DROP

Load in amperes	Length of wire run in feet																
	25	50	75	100	125	150	175	200	225	250	300	350	400	450	500	550	600
	Wire Size (AWG or MCM)[1]																
5.0	12	12	12	12	12	12	12	12	12	12	12	10	10	10	10	8	8
7.5	12	12	12	12	12	12	12	12	12	10	10	10	8	8	8	8	6
10.0	12	12	12	12	12	12	10	10	10	10	8	8	8	6	6	6	6
15.0	12	12	12	12	10	10	10	8	8	8	6	6	6	6	4	4	4
20.0	12	12	12	10	10	8	8	8	6	6	6	4	4	4	4	3	3
25.0	12	12	10	10	8	8	6	6	6	6	4	4	4	3	3	2	2
30.0	12	12	10	8	8	6	6	6	6	4	4	4	3	2	2	2	1
35.0	12	10	10	8	6	6	6	4	4	4	4	3	2	2	1	1	1
40.0	12	10	8	8	6	6	4	4	4	4	3	2	2	1	1	0	0
45.0	12	10	8	6	6	6	4	4	4	3	2	2	1	1	0	0	0
50.0	12	10	8	6	6	4	4	4	3	3	2	1	1	0	0	00	00
55.0	12	8	8	6	4	4	4	3	3	2	2	1	0	0	00	00	00
60.0	12	8	6	6	4	4	4	3	2	2	1	1	0	0	00	00	000
70.0	10	8	6	4	4	4	3	2	2	1	1	0	00	00	000	000	000
80.0	10	8	6	4	4	3	2	2	1	1	0	00	00	000	000	0000	0000
90.0	10	6	6	4	3	2	2	1	1	0	0	00	000	000	0000	0000	250
100.0	10	6	4	4	3	2	1	1	0	0	00	000	000	0000	0000	250	250
115.0	8	6	4	3	2	1	1	0	0	00	000	000	0000	0000	250	250	300

[1] AWG = American Wire Gage, and MCM = thousand circular mils. Table 2 must be referred to at the current value used to check the minimum wire size for proper current carrying capacity and the larger of the two sizes used.

Wire sizes are based on *voltage drop only*.

Wire in overhead spans must also have adequate mechanical strength and should not be smaller than number 10 for spans up to 50 feet or smaller than number 8 for spans greater than 50 feet.

TABLE 17 (continued)

Load in amperes	Length of wire run in feet																
	25	50	75	100	125	150	175	200	225	250	300	350	400	450	500	550	600
	Wire Size (AWG or MCM)¹																
130.0	8	6	4	3	2	1	0	0	00	00	000	0000	0000	250	300	300	350
145.0	8	4	3	2	1	0	0	0	00	000	0000	0000	250	300	300	350	350
160.0	8	4	3	2	1	0	00	0	000	000	0000	250	300	300	350	350	400
175.0	6	4	3	1	0	0	0	000	000	0000	0000	250	300	350	350	400	500
200.0	6	4	2	1	0	00	000	000	0000	0000	250	300	350	400	400	500	500
225.0	6	3	2	0	00	00	000	0000	0000	250	300	350	400	400	500	500	600
250.0	6	3	1	0	00	000	0000	0000	250	250	300	350	400	500	500	600	600
275.0	4	2	1	00	000	000	0000	250	250	300	350	400	500	500	600	600	700
300.0	4	2	0	00	000	0000	0000	250	300	300	400	500	500	600	600	700	750
350.0	4	1	0	000	0000	0000	250	300	350	350	500	500	600	700	700	800	900
400.0	4	1	00	000	0000	250	300	350	400	400	500	600	700	750	800	900	1000
450.0	3	0	00	0000	250	300	350	400	400	500	600	700	750	800	900	1000	
500.0	3	0	000	0000	250	300	350	400	500	500	600	700	800	900	1000		
550.0	2	00	000	250	300	350	400	500	500	600	700	800	900	1000			
600.0	2	00	0000	250	300	400	500	500	600	600	750	900	1000				

¹ AWG = American Wire Gage, and MCM = thousand circular mils.
Wire sizes are based on *voltage drop only.* Table 2 must be referred to at the current value used to check the minimum wire size for proper current carrying capacity and the larger of the two sizes used.
Wire in overhead spans must also have adequate mechanical strength and should not be smaller than number 10 for spans up to 50 feet or smaller than number 8 for spans greater than 50 feet.

TABLE 18

ALUMINUM WIRE SIZE REQUIRED AT 230-240 VOLTS, BASED ON TWO PER CENT VOLTAGE DROP

Load in amperes	Length of wire run in feet — Wire size (AWG or MCM)[1]																
	25	50	75	100	125	150	175	200	225	250	300	350	400	450	500	550	600
5.0	12	12	12	12	12	12	12	12	10	10	10	8	8	8	8	6	6
7.5	12	12	12	12	12	10	10	10	8	8	8	8	6	6	6	6	4
10.0	12	12	12	12	10	10	8	8	8	8	6	6	6	4	4	4	4
15.0	12	12	10	10	8	8	8	6	6	6	4	4	4	3	3	3	2
20.0	12	12	10	8	8	6	6	6	4	4	4	3	3	2	2	1	1
25.0	12	10	8	8	6	6	4	4	4	4	3	2	2	1	1	0	0
30.0	12	10	8	6	6	4	4	4	3	3	2	2	1	0	0	0	00
35.0	12	8	8	6	4	4	4	3	3	2	2	1	0	0	00	00	00
40.0	12	8	6	6	4	4	3	3	2	2	1	0	0	00	00	000	000
45.0	10	8	6	4	4	3	3	2	2	1	0	0	00	00	000	000	0000
50.0	10	8	6	4	4	3	2	2	1	1	0	00	00	000	000	0000	0000
55.0	10	6	6	4	3	3	2	1	1	0	0	00	000	000	0000	0000	0000
60.0	10	6	4	4	3	2	2	1	0	0	00	00	000	0000	0000	0000	250
70.0	8	6	4	3	2	2	1	0	0	00	00	000	0000	0000	250	250	300
80.0	8	6	4	3	2	1	0	0	00	00	000	000	0000	250	300	300	350
90.0	8	4	3	2	1	0	0	00	00	000	0000	0000	250	300	300	350	350
100.0	8	4	3	2	1	0	00	00	000	000	0000	250	300	300	350	350	400
115.0	6	4	2	1	0	00	00	000	000	0000	250	300	300	350	400	400	500

[1] AWG = American Wire Gage, and MCM = thousand circular mils.

Wire sizes are based on *voltage drop only.* Table 3 must be referred to at the current value used to check the minimum wire size for proper current carrying capacity and the larger of the two sizes used.

Wire in overhead spans must also have adequate mechanical strength and should not be smaller than number 10 for spans up to 50 feet or smaller than number 8 for spans greater than 50 feet.

TABLE 18 (continued)

Load in amperes	Length of wire run in feet																
	25	50	75	100	125	150	175	200	225	250	300	350	400	450	500	550	600
	Wire size (AWG or MCM)¹																
130.0	6	4	2	1	0	00	000	000	0000	0000	250	300	350	400	500	500	500
145.0	6	3	1	0	00	000	000	0000	0000	250	300	350	400	500	500	600	600
160.0	6	3	1	0	00	000	0000	0000	250	300	350	400	500	500	600	600	700
175.0	4	2	1	00	000	000	250	250	250	300	350	400	500	500	600	700	700
200.0	4	2	0	00	000	0000	250	300	300	350	400	500	600	600	700	700	800
225.0	4	1	0	000	0000	250	250	300	350	400	500	500	600	700	750	800	900
250.0	4	1	00	000	0000	250	300	350	400	400	500	600	700	750	800	900	1000
275.0	3	0	00	0000	250	300	350	350	400	500	600	700	700	800	900	1000	
300.0	3	0	000	0000	250	300	350	400	500	500	600	700	800	900	1000		
350.0	2	00	000	250	300	350	400	500	500	600	700	800	900	1000			
400.0	2	00	0000	300	350	400	500	600	600	700	800	900					
450.0	1	000	250	300	400	500	500	600	700	750	900	1000					
500.0	1	000	250	350	400	500	600	700	750	800	1000						
550.0	0	0000	300	350	500	600	700	700	800	900							
600.0	0	0000	300	400	500	600	700	800	900	1000							

¹ AWG = American Wire Gage, and MCM = thousand circular mils.
Wire sizes are based on *voltage drop only*. Table 3 must be referred to at the current value used to check the minimum wire size for proper current carrying capacity and the larger of the two sizes used.
Wire in overhead spans must also have adequate mechanical strength and should not be smaller than number 10 for spans up to 50 feet or smaller than number 8 for spans greater than 50 feet.

OVERLOAD PROTECTION

Your motors, service and branch circuit wiring, and phase converter should be protected against overload—the drawing of an excessive amount of current. Too much current causes overheating and damage to equipment.

The overload protection should be provided in accordance with the requirements and recommendations of your power supplier, motor and phase converter manufacturers, and the National Electrical Code and local regulations.

The overcurrent protection for motors should have a rating of not more than 125 percent of the current rating of the motor. If motor fuses are used, they should be the dual-element type and may be the next larger available size.

The overcurrent protection for the single-phase wiring to the converter should have a rating in accordance with the size of wiring chosen in the Service Wiring section under Installation, previously discussed. This may not provide adequate protection for the converter, particularly in multiple-motor installations. The converter manufacturer should be consulted for his recommendations for overcurrent protection of the converter.

With static converters, the recommended overload protection may not allow the use of full horsepower from the motor. But, as indicated in the section on this type of converter, the load should be limited to prevent excessive currents and damage to the motor.

MAGNETIC STARTERS

Magnetic starters are a combination of a magnetic controller, or relay, and overload protection for the motor. Use of one for each motor is highly recommended and may be required by many power suppliers.

It is essential to use a magnetic starter with a rotary converter to provide the means of disconnecting the motors in case of power interruption. Otherwise, when power is restored, the motors will try to start on single-phase power before the converter reaches operating speed and may be damaged.

For maximum protection of the motors, use magnetic starters that have thermal overload protection in each line.

CONNECTION OF CAPACITORS

As indicated previously in the section on Types of Phase Converters, capacitors may be added to the circuit as additional motors are connected to improve motor performance. These capacitors must be connected between the contacts and heaters as shown in Fig. 10, so that they will be disconnected. Unless some capacitance is removed from the circuit as larger motors are disconnected, small motors operating on the converter will have badly unbalanced voltages and most likely will overheat. In some cases, the converter may also overheat and be damaged.

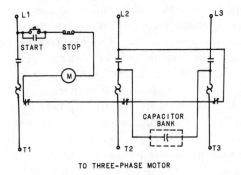

Fig. 10. Proper connection of extra capacitance into the circuit.

When capacitor banks are connected as shown in Fig. 10, their current will not flow through the heater coils of the starter. This will help prevent false tripouts of the starter.

Consult the phase converter manufacturer for the recommended value of capacitance and method of connection to be used for multiple motor loads.

Chapter 12

Transformers

The efficient use of electrical energy, like the efficient use of mechanical energy, often requires the introduction of some means of converting the form of the energy at the source to a form that can be used at the load. A gear train, for instance, introduced between a gasoline engine and certain power saws may be designed in such a way that the gear can be adjusted to turn the saw slowly with great force, or with great speed and less force, depending on the quality and hardness of the material being milled. In the same manner, it is often necessary to adjust electrical circuits so that the power available may appear at the load as one of various combinations of voltage and current—as high voltage with low current, as high current at low voltage, or as any convenient combination of the two. The electrical device that corresponds to a gear train in mechanics is the *transformer*, which converts the electrical power available from one voltage-current level to another voltage-current level. It should be noted, however, that neither the gear train nor the transformer changes the *amount of power* available. The amount of power used by the saw, at any instant, is the power delivered by the gasoline engine (less friction losses); and the amount of power dissipated by the load in an electrical circuit is the same as the power delivered by the source (less internal losses); but in either case, the power to be used can be adapted to the particular work to be done.

The operation of a transformer depends on the principle of electromagnetic induction. Basically, a transformer consists of any two inductors (in separate circuits) so placed physically that the changing electromagnetic field set up by an alternating current in one induces an alternating electromotive force (emf) in the other. Thus, mutual inductance exists between the coils, and the two circuits are said to be inductively coupled. Figure 1 shows such a basic transformer connected between an alternating-current generator and a resistance

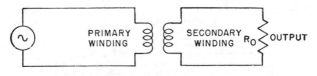

Fig. 1. Basic transformer.

load. The coil connected to the source of power is called the *primary* winding, and the coil connected to the load is called the *secondary* winding. The power delivered by the generator passes through the transformer and is delivered to the load, although no direct connection exists between the primary and the secondary winding or between generator and load. The connection that does exist is the flux linkage between the coils, and power is effectively transferred by induction. Thus, the power consumed by the primary winding is equal to the power delivered by the secondary winding, thus: $P_p = P_s$. If the coils of a transformer were completely shielded from each other, no power transfer could take place and the transformer would be useless.

For a maximum transfer of power from the primary winding to the secondary winding of the transformer, the flux linkage must be complete; that is, all of the lines of force set up by the primary winding must link the secondary winding. For this reason, the secondary is often wound directly on the primary with only protective insulation separating the two coils. Then, since the reluctance of air is very great and its permeability small, the introduction of a soft-steel core of high permeability in the transformer increases the flux linkage between the coils and makes possible a high percentage of power transfer. Even with the use of high permeability cores, a few of the flux lines fail to link the secondary winding and are effectively lost, constituting a flux leakage that prevents the transformer from being a perfect conductor of power from the generator to the load. However, a well-designed iron-core transformer may effect a 98 percent flux linkage, which means that K, the coefficient of coupling between the coils, is .98. Figure 2 shows a typical iron-core transformer with the flux lines set up by the primary linking the secondary by means of the low reluctance path of the core. The small flux leakages are also shown. Figure 3, A, shows the shell type of transformer core, which is the most efficient core type, and Fig. 3, B, is a cross section of the windings as they usually appear. Each layer of wire is

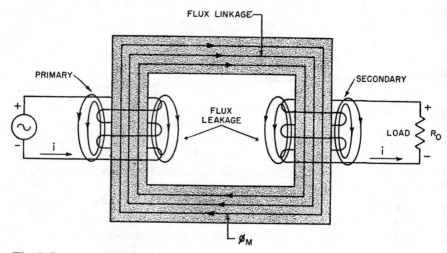

Fig. 2. Iron-core transformer.

separated from the other by sheets of waxed paper, and the primary winding is separated from the secondary winding by thick varnished paper or cardboard.

TRANSFORMER OPERATION

The ability of a transformer to transfer energy from its primary winding to its secondary winding through the agency of flux linkage is a function of inductive coupling or high mutual inductance. This means that the inductance of each winding should be as great as possible. If the transformer were ideal (the windings showing infinite inductance), the inductive reactance of the primary would also be infinite for any alternating-current (AC) frequency. At the usual 60-cycle power-line frequency, however, the inductance of the primary must be large in order to generate an appreciable reactance. Thus, if the iron core of a 60-cycle transformer were removed, the inductive reactance would fall and the primary circuit would show a high current even with no load on the secondary. This initial *magnetizing* current in the primary of a transformer under no load should be kept as low as possible since it represents a loss. The greater the inductance, the greater the reactance, and the less magnetizing current needed to set up the flux linkage.

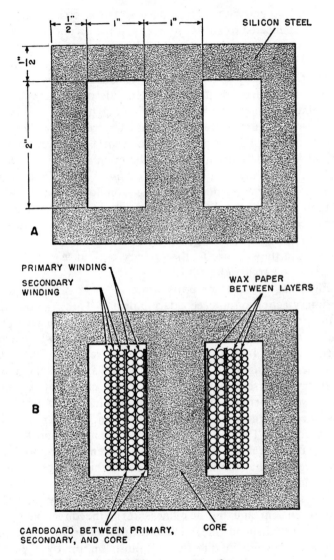

Fig. 3. Cross section of iron-core transformer.

The importance of the reactance of the primary, and the effect of the secondary winding on the primary, may be understood by a series of step-by-step analyses. In Fig. 4, A, a simple transformer with primary and secondary windings on a soft iron core is shown. The primary is connected to an AC source, and the secondary is left open so that it has no appreciable effect on the first analysis. The primary winding is then, in effect, nothing but a simple iron-core inductance. As such, the primary offers inductive reactance to the source, and current which is dependent on the magnitude of the reactance flows in the primary circuit, causing a changing magnetic field to be set up in the core. The current through the inductor and the voltage across it are 90 degrees out of phase, the current lagging. At any given instant of time, the current is in the direction shown. The direction of the flux line is determined by the *left-hand rule:* if the fingers of the left hand point in the direction of electron flow in the coil winding, the thumb points in the direction of the magnetic field. At this same instant, a counter emf, E_p', is set up in the primary 180 degrees out of phase with the applied voltage E_p, and 90 degrees out of phase with the current in the primary I_p, the primary current leading, as shown by the vector diagram in Fig. 4, B.

In Figure 5, A, the same transformer is shown with the effect of this primary action on the secondary indicated (for ease of explanation, the primary action is not shown). Thus, it will be seen that the secondary alone also constitutes a simple inductance in which a voltage has been induced by the changing flux lines set up by the primary. This induced voltage has the same direction as the counter emf of the primary. The secondary circuit is shown closed by a resistance so that a small current may flow in the circuit. The induced voltage is conceived as a generator in series with the secondary considered as an inductance. The current through the secondary and the voltage across it are 90 degrees out of phase, the current lagging as shown at Fig. 5, A. Note that the initial direction of the voltage is the same as that of the primary counter emf in Fig. 4, B.

At the same instant in time taken for the primary analysis, the secondary current and the flux lines are in the direction shown in Fig. 5, A (the left-hand rule). The flux lines set up by the secondary current are opposite in direction to those set up by the primary current. Therefore, the secondary current I_s effectively decreases the impedance of the primary circuit by opposing the flux lines set up by the primary current. The primary current must accordingly increase to maintain the flux linkage between the two coils. If the load

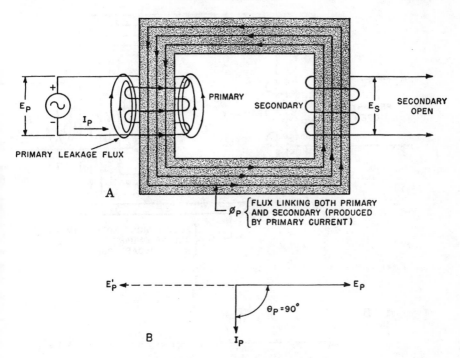

Fig. 4. Direction of flux lines produced by primary current.

on the secondary causes more current to flow in the secondary, more current flows in the primary from the source. This opposition in flux lines in a transformer is in accordance with the Lenz Law, which states that an induced voltage (and the current resulting from it) is always in such a direction as to oppose the force setting it up. If the action of the secondary aided the lines of flux set up by the primary, an increase in secondary current would effect an increase in flux lines, an increase in the inductance and inductive reactance of the primary, and a corresponding decrease in primary current—an impossible condition, since the secondary would then be delivering more power to the load than the primary receives from the source.

The effect of the secondary upon the primary of a transformer may be considered from another point of view. The secondary current sets up an emf of self-induction or counter emf E_s' in the secondary 180 degrees out of phase with the secondary voltage, and at the

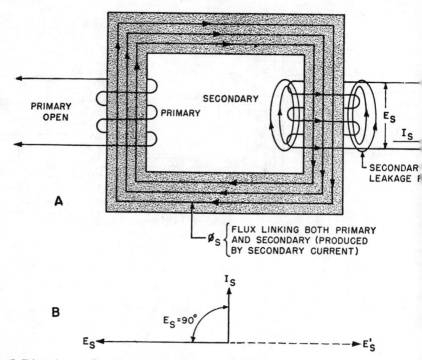

Fig. 5. Direction of flux lines produced by secondary current.

same time an induced voltage in the primary in phase with this counter emf. Since the voltage induced in the primary is 180 degrees out of phase with E_s, the voltage of the secondary, it is in phase with E_p, the voltage applied to the primary, and 180 degrees out of phase with E_p', the counter emf of the primary. Therefore, the effect of current in the secondary is to cancel to some extent the counter emf of the primary, or to increase the applied voltage, thereby allowing more current to flow in the primary. These induced voltages are shown as dotted line vectors in Figs. 4 and 5, B.

The total action of the transformer may now be understood in terms of the vector diagrams of Fig. 6. With a token current flowing in the secondary of the circuit shown in Fig. 6, A, the vector diagram of voltages and currents is as shown in Fig. 6, B. Voltages across the transformer are 180 degrees out of phase, and currents are

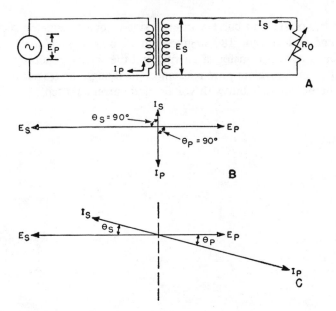

Fig. 6. Phase relationships of voltage and current in a transformer.

180 degrees out of phase. The phase angle between voltage and current in the secondary is also 90 degrees, with current lagging. As R_o—the load resistance—is decreased, the load is said to increase, and current in the secondary increases. Since R_o is shunted directly across the secondary, the resistive current increases and the circuit becomes more and more resistive; that is, voltage and current in the secondary circuit approach an in-phase condition and the phase angle θ_s approaches zero degrees. Since primary current increases with an increase in secondary current, as previously described, the inductive reactance of the primary has been, in effect, reduced and therefore the circuit appears more resistive. Hence, voltage and current in the whole primary circuit approach an in-phase condition and θ_p approaches zero degrees. The vector diagram of Fig. 6, C, shows these phase relationships for the transformer of A operating under the load for which it was designed. An ideal transformer would show the current and voltage vectors superimposed (θ_s and θ_p equal to zero degrees);

that is, voltage and current in each side-in phase, and the secondary voltage and current 180 degrees out of phase. Such a transformer effects a perfect transfer of energy, and the source generator sees the load as an equivalent pure resistance (as though the transformer were not in the circuit), but with voltage and current shifted 180° degrees.

Chapter 13

Soldering

Soldering is a metal-joining process in which a lower melting-point metal (called solder) is heated to the point where it melts and wets the joint surface and then is allowed to solidify in place. To enable the solder to wet the surfaces readily and be drawn into fine cracks, the surfaces and the solder must be clean and free of oxide film. When necessary, the cleaning is done with chemicals or abrasives. One cleaning substance frequently used is called *flux*. Copper, tin, lead, and brass are examples of metals that are easy to solder. Galvanized iron, stainless steel, and aluminum are difficult to solder and require the use of special techniques.

Soldering is a practical method of forming reliable electrical connections where bare wires are twisted together or are wound on terminals. Soldering is also used to make tight joints, such as lap seams of sheet metal, and to hold parts together physically. Soldered joints, however, do not support loads for long periods of time as well as welded joints do. Where load support is a governing factor, the usual practice calls for riveting, bolting, or using another means of fastening followed by sealing of the joints with solder.

In soldering the readily solderable metals, you only need the solder, a flux, and a heat source.

SOLDERS

By definition, *solders* are joining materials or alloys that melt below 800° F. They are available in various forms—wire, bar, ingot, paste, and powder. *Solders* used for *electrical connections* are alloys of tin and lead whose melting points range between 360° F. and 465° F. (both endpoints are approximate).

A *tin-lead solder alloy* is usually identified by two numbers indicating the percentages of tin and lead in the alloy. The first number is the percentage of tin. For example, a 30/70 alloy is made of 30 percent tin and 70 percent lead. Likewise, a 15/85 alloy is made of 15 percent tin and 85 percent lead. In general, the higher the percentage of tin in a solder alloy, the lower the melting point.

FLUXES

Soldering fluxes are agents that clean solderable metals by removing the oxide film normally present on the metals and also prevent further oxidation. Fluxes are classified as noncorrosive, mildly corrosive, or corrosive, ranging from mild substances such as rosin to chemically active salts such as zinc chloride. *Rosin* is an effective and nearly harmless flux used for electrical connections that must be reliable, tight, and corrosion-free. Rosin flux is available in paste or powder form for direct application to joints before soldering, or incorporated as the core of wire solders. Unless washed off thoroughly after soldering, salt-type fluxes leave residues that tend to corrode metals. Because of their corrosive effects, so-called acid core solders (which incorporate salt-type fluxes) must *not* be used in soldering electrical connections.

SOLDERING TOOLS

The source of heat for melting solder is a *soldering gun* (electric) or a *soldering iron* (electric or nonelectric), sometimes called a copper.

Soldering Gun.   The *soldering gun* (Fig. 1) operates from any standard 115-volt outlet and is rated in size by the number of watts it consumes. All good quality soldering guns operate in a temperature range of 500° F. to 600° F. The important difference in gun sizes is not the temperature, but the capacity of the gun to generate and maintain a satisfactory soldering temperature while giving up heat to the joint soldered. The tip heats only when the trigger is depressed, and then very rapidly. These guns afford easy access to cramped

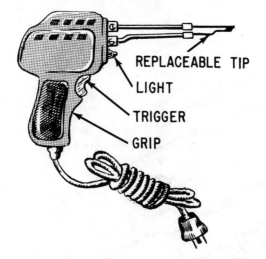

REPLACEABLE TIP

LIGHT

TRIGGER

GRIP

Fig. 1. Electric soldering gun.

quarters because of their small tip. Most soldering guns have a small light that is focused on the tip working area.

The *tip* of a soldering gun should be removed occasionally to permit cleaning away the oxide scale that forms between the tip and metal housing. Removal of this oxide increases the heating efficiency of the gun. If for any reason the tip does become damaged, replaceable tips are available.

Never use a soldering gun when working on solid-state equipment. Serious damage to diodes, transistors, and other solid-state components can result from the strong electromagnetic field surrounding the tip of the soldering gun.

Soldering Irons.   There are two general types of soldering irons. One is electrically heated and the other is nonelectrically heated. The essential parts of both types are the tip and the handle. The tip is made of copper.

A *nonelectric soldering iron* (Fig. 2) is sized according to its weight. The commonly used sizes are the ¼-, ½-, ¾-, 1-, 1½-, 2-, and 2½-pound irons. The 3-, 4-, and 5-pound sizes are not used in ordinary work. Nonelectric irons have permanent tips and must be heated over an ordinary flame, or with a blowtorch.

The *electric soldering iron* (Fig. 2) transmits heat to the copper tip after the heat is produced by electric current that flows through a

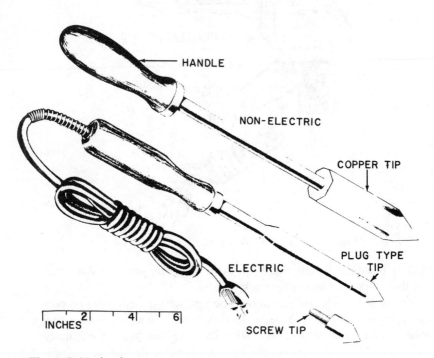

Fig. 2. Soldering irons.

self-contained coil of resistance wire, called the heating element. Electric soldering irons are rated according to the number of watts they consume when operated at the voltage stamped on the iron. There are two types of tips on electric irons: plug tips, which slip into the heater head and are held in place by a setscrew, and screw tips, which are threaded, and which screw into or on the heater head. Some tips are offset and have a 90-degree angle for soldering joints that are difficult to reach.

Electric iron tips must be securely fastened in the heater unit. The tips must be clean and free of copper oxide. Sometimes the shaft oxidizes and causes the tip to stick in place. Remove the tip occasionally and scrape off the scale. If the shaft is clean, the tip will not only receive more heat from the heater-element, but it will facilitate removal when the time comes to replace the tip.

Tinning a Soldering Iron.   If a soldering iron is new or has just been forced, it will need to be *tinned* (coated with solder). To do so, hold it in the vise and "dress" the point with a well-chalked file. By "dressing" is meant filling to remove hammer marks resulting from the forging process and to round off the sharp corners slightly. This is not always required when a tinned iron is to be retinned. Inspection will reveal if it is necessary. Then heat the copper tip so that it will readily melt solder. Try melting solder with the copper frequently as it is being heated, and as soon as it will melt solder, it is ready for tinning.

To tin the copper, quickly dip it into rosin or apply rosin-core solder to the tip of the iron. The coating of solder is bright and shiny and very thin. It aids in the rapid transfer of heat from the iron to the work.

SOLDERING PROCEDURE

Many equipment failures can be attributed to poorly soldered joints. The following suggestions are presented in an effort to assist in effecting a good job of soldering.

The parts to be soldered must be absolutely clean (free from oxide, corrosion, and grease). During the cleaning process, when removing insulation from wire, care must be taken to avoid producing cuts or nicks that greatly reduce the mechanical strength of the wire, especially under conditions of vibration.

The joint should be prepared just prior to soldering since the prepared surface will soon corrode or become dirty if it remains exposed to the air.

The parts to be joined must be securely joined mechanically before any soldering is done.

To *solder electrical connections* (Fig. 3), hold the soldering iron (copper) beneath the splice being soldered with as much mechanical contact as possible to permit maximum heat transfer. Apply the rosin-core solder to the splice. The tinning on the soldering iron aids the transfer of heat to the spliced wire that, when hot enough, will melt the solder. Before this temperature is reached, the rosin core will have melted and run out over the wire to flux the splice.

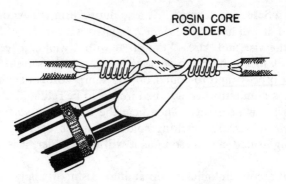

Fig. 3. Soldering an electrical connection.

When the solder has coated the splice completely, the job is finished. No extra solder is needed.

A good, well-bonded connection is clean, shiny, smooth, and round. It also approximately outlines the wire and terminal as shown in Fig. 4.

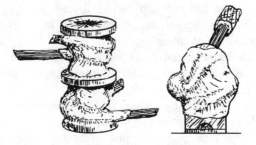

Fig. 4. Examples of properly made soldered joints.

PRECAUTIONS

One sizzling burn experience is usually enough to breed a healthy respect for hot objects. When using a soldering iron or gun always bear in mind the following:

1. Electric soldering irons must not remain connected longer than necessary and must be kept away from flammable material.

2. In order to avoid burns, always assume that a soldering iron is hot.

3. Never rest a heated iron anywhere but on a metal surface or rack provided for this purpose. Faulty action on your part could result in fire, extensive equipment damage, and serious injuries.

4. Never swing an iron to remove solder because the bits of solder that come off may cause serious skin or eye burns or ignite combustible materials in the work area.

5. When cleaning an iron, use a cleaning cloth or damp sponge, but *do not* hold the cleaning cloth or damp sponge in your hand. Always place the cloth or damp sponge on a suitable surface and wipe the iron across it to prevent burning your hand.

6. Hold small soldering jobs with your pliers or a suitable clamping device. Never hold the work in your hand.

7. After completing the task requiring the use of a soldering iron, disconnect the power cord from the receptacle and, when the iron has cooled off, stow it in its assigned storage area. Do not throw irons into a toolbox. When storing irons for long periods of time, coat the shaft and all metal parts with a rust-preventive compound and store in a dry place.

Section 4

COMFORT CONDITIONING

AIR CONDITIONING IS A field of engineering dealing with the design, construction, and operation of equipment used in establishing and maintaining desirable indoor air conditions. It is the science of maintaining the atmosphere of an enclosure at any required temperature, humidity, and purity. As such, air conditioning involves the cooling, heating, dehumidifying, ventilating, and purifying of air.

Room fans stir up the air. The temperature inside your house can be several degrees cooler than outside, but it can seem warmer if the air does not move. Also, air movement increases moisture evaporation, and moisture evaporation cools the body, or skin surfaces.

Attic and *window fans* exchange inside air for outside air.

Humidifiers, air cleaners, and *dehumidifiers* clean and filter the air in your home, removing air-borne pollen and dust particles.

Another method of air cooling you should consider is the *heat pump.* The heat pump is a single unit that replaces the conventional furnace air conditioner system. It removes heat from your home in the summer and supplies heat to your home in the winter. The heat removed in the summer is discharged to the outside air.

For years the best engineering minds have been working on *home heating systems* with the result that today there is a vast array of devices that solve many more heating, cooling, and air conditioning problems than we ever thought existed a few years ago.

Since our body creates its own heat, the purpose of a home heating system is simply to control the amount of heat our bodies give off.

In the past, the most important reason for the adjustment of *oil burners* has been to ensure reliable automatic operation. A second important reason has been to provide efficient fuel utilization. Common practice of adjusting a burner for minimum air setting, consistent with acceptable smoke levels, is an effective way of meeting both objectives.

Recently, a third objective has been added—that of minimizing air pollution. It is important to recognize that any burner adjustments for this purpose must also meet the former requirements. Fortunately, adjustments for low air-pollutant emissions can still meet the objectives of reliable and efficient operation.

Oil burners are small, highly efficient burners of rugged industrial design and construction. They are applicable to any heating application where oil or equivalent capacity is now being used or as an integral component of a new boiler-burner system.

Oil furnaces are much like the human body. The motor driven fan is the "lung" that provides the necessary oxygen. The oil supply from the fuel tank is the blood stream, and the fuel pump is the heart that keeps the oil supply circulating to the proper parts. The electric spark brings the whole system to life.

Gas furnaces are designed for the addition of central air conditioning from 1½ to 5 tons cooling in every furnace for year round living comfort.

Electric furnaces deliver dependable heat-up to 45 kilowatts (kw) and 153,585 British thermal units/hour (Btu's/hr). When used in conjunction with air conditioning they deliver up to 60,000 Btu's/hr cooling. No flue or chimney is required.

An *electric stoker* is a complete automatic unit designed to feed and fire coal.

Chapter 14

Selection of Air Conditioners

Air conditioning is the best way to keep your house at a constant, cool temperature. But it is also more expensive than other methods of cooling.

There are two types of air conditioners.

1. Room units.
2. Central-system units.

The cooling operation of both types of air conditioners is the same. Air passes through filters that remove large dust particles, and over a series of refrigeration coils, where it is cooled and dehumidified. A fan then blows the cooled air into your home.

Most air conditioners have either built-in thermostats or provisions for wiring the conditioners to remote temperature controls. Some of the small units are not thermostat equipped, but you may find a thermostat is available as optional equipment.

Room air conditioners cool one or more rooms. They range in output from about 5,000 to 32,000 British thermal units (Btu's) per hour. They operate on electricity only, and should have separate electrical circuits (this may require adding a circuit to your home).

You may choose from many available models—models for conventional windows, models for casement windows, models for in-front-of-window consoles, and models that mount in special wall openings.

But before you buy a room unit, think. You will probably need several small units to cool your whole house. A single, large room unit will be less expensive, but it will not cool your home evenly.

A central air conditioning system might be a better buy.

Central air conditioning systems are generally more efficient than room air conditioners. They also seem less noisy because they are located out of the living area.

But a central system may be unnecessarily expensive to install if you live in an older house, in an apartment, or in a climate where air conditioning is needed only occasionally for short times. One or more room conditioners may be the answer.

Central air conditioning systems can be separate systems with their own ducts, or they can be combined with forced air heating systems.

Cooling requires a greater amount of air flow than heating. If you choose an add-on system it will probably be necessary to increase the fan capacity of your furnace, and it may be necessary to enlarge and even relocate the distribution ducts. Larger ducts also decrease the velocity of the cooled air and reduce the noise of air conditioning.

For greatest uniformity in room comfort conditions, cold air supply grilles should be high in walls or in the ceiling and hot air supply grilles should be near or in the floor. If economy dictates use of only one grille for both heating and cooling, the near floor location is preferred.

The cost of purchasing and installing a central air conditioning system will depend, to a large extent, on whether you choose a separate central system, or a system to be added to your heating system.

Most room air conditioners have air-cooled condensers. This means that the condenser must be outside the cooled room, that it must have unrestricted air circulation over the condenser coils, and that it should be shaded from the sun.

Some air conditioners have water-cooled condensers. They require large quantities of water to disperse the heat—approximately 70 gallons to 150 gallons per hour for each 12,000 Btu's of cooling capacity. This water can be cooled in a cooling tower and reused. Locate the tower outdoors, away from your house; it is noisy.

Air-cooled units require more electric energy than water-cooled units. This increased cost is usually offset by water supply and disposal (or cooling tower) costs.

Air conditioners are rated by heat-removing capacity in British thermal units (Btu's). Where temperatures do not usually exceed 95° F., an air conditioner rated at 6,000 Btu's per hour will cool a room with 100 to 230 square feet of floor space. Where temperatures exceed 95° F. but do not exceed 100° F., an air conditioner rated at 6,900 Btu's is required to cool the same area.

Approximately one kilowatt-hour of electricity is required to remove each 6,500 Btu's with an electrical air conditioner. This is the same amount of electricity that is required to operate ten 100-watt light bulbs for one hour.

A water-cooled gas air conditioner requires about 13 cubic feet of gas (plus a small amount of electricity) to remove each 6,500 Btu's. An air-cooled gas air conditioner requires 21 cubic feet of gas (plus a small amount of electricity) to remove each 6,500 Btu's.

Central-system air conditioners are sometimes rated in "tons." One ton of refrigeration equals 288,000 Btu's per 24 hours, or 12,000 Btu's per hour.

Not all air conditioners dehumidify adequately during humid, muggy weather. The result is that the cooled air they put out feels clammy. This clamminess can be reduced, to a certain extent, by operating a dehumidifier when you operate your air conditioner.

When you set out to buy a room air conditioner, remember that it is essentially a heat pump. Its main job is to take heat from your room and discharge it into outside air. To be able to do this efficiently, a conditioner must fit its window and be compatible with your home wiring. With these requirements in mind, you can concentrate on four main questions in selecting a conditioner to fit your particular needs.

1. How much cooling should the conditioner provide?
2. What kind of window will it have to fit?
3. What is the electrical capacity of the wiring in your home?
4. What practical and convenience features should you look for?

The answers to these questions may save you a great deal of expense and trouble. (*See* the following sections in this chapter for help in making your decisions.)

HOW A ROOM AIR CONDITIONER WORKS

An air conditioner has four jobs to do in making you comfortable on a hot, humid day: it cools the air; it removes moisture from the air; it filters out dust; and it circulates the air inside the room.

Figure 1 illustrates a complete cooling cycle. The compressor (Fig. 1, A), a kind of pump, compresses the refrigerant gas, thereby raising its temperature to about 210° Fahrenheit.

The hot gas is forced through the pipe (Fig. 1, B) and carried outside the room to the hot pipe coil (Fig. 1, C).

A fan (Fig. 1, D) blows outside air across the coil, cooling the gas to about 115° F. and turning it into a liquid. Excess heat is discharged to the outdoor air.

The refrigerant liquid is now forced through the pipe (Fig. 1, E) and back into the room through an expansion device (Fig. 1, F), where it rapidly expands and drops sharply in temperature to a chill 45° F.

The chilled refrigerant liquid flows to the cooling coils (Fig. 1, G) while the fan (Fig. 1, H) blows room air across the coils (Fig. 1, G) through the filter (Fig. 1, I), and into the room. In the process, the room air is both cooled and circulated.

As the air is cooled, it loses moisture, which collects on the cooling coils and then drips into a pan (Fig. 1, J).

From this indoor pan, water flows downhill through the tubing (Fig. 1, K) to the outdoor pan (Fig. 1, L). Usually excess water is sprayed by the fan (Fig. 1, D) onto the hot pipe coils (Fig. 1, C), where it evaporates and joins outdoor air.

In the meantime, the refrigerant gas is warmed to 60° F. by room air and travels through the pipe (Fig. 1, M) back to the compressor and starts the cycle over again.

HOW TO ESTIMATE NEEDED COOLING CAPACITY

Before you can select a room air conditioner for your home, you must know the cooling capacity you need to keep you comfortable. You can arrive at a cooling capacity estimate in several ways.

Professional Estimate.　　A salesman at a reputable air conditioner dealer can make an estimate for you if you bring him accurate information. Usually, the answers to the following questions are all he or she needs.

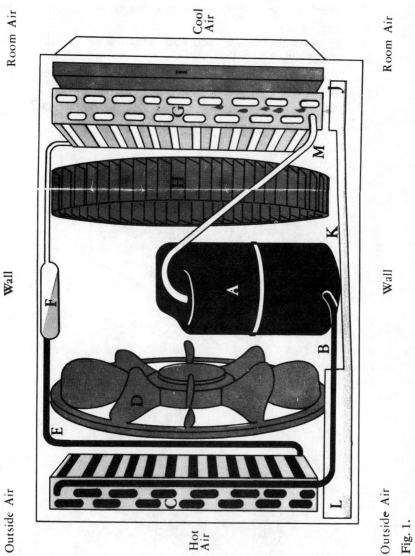

Fig. 1.

1. What are the height, width, and length of the area to be cooled? (*See* Fig. 2).

2. What are the number and sizes of windows and the directions they face? (*See* Fig. 3.)

3. Where is the space to be cooled located in the building? (*See* Fig. 4.)

4. Does the longest side face north, east, south, or west? (*See* Fig. 5.)

Fig. 2.

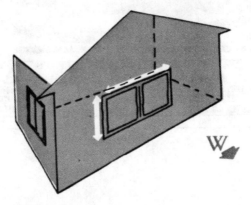

Fig. 3.

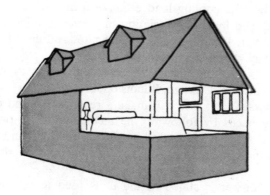

Fig. 4.

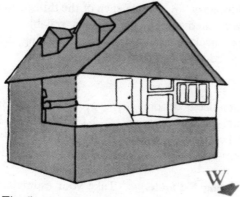

Fig. 5.

If you have already chosen your dealer, telephone and ask if he needs any other information to make a cooling estimate. Different dealers and salesmen use different estimating methods.

Some dealers offer free home surveys. If you plan to cool several connected rooms, professional advice will be specially valuable. One large room conditioner may be all you need if air flow between rooms is free enough; but in other homes two or more smaller units in separate rooms may be more efficient and economical.

Cooling Load Estimate Form. One way of finding your cooling needs is to use the cooling load estimate form for room air conditioners developed by the Association of Home Appliance Manufacturers (AHAM). If you are good with figures and used to filling out forms, you may wish to try this method.

The form is free and can be obtained by writing to AHAM, 20 North Wacker Drive, Chicago, Illinois 60606.

Do It Yourself.   You can make a reasonably good estimate of your cooling needs by following the method outlined on the work sheet shown in Fig. 6. Just follow the instructions and fill in the blanks as in the sample problem. Substitute the numbers that apply to your room.

The final answer is stated in the units used to measure cooling capacity in conditioners—Btu's/hr.

If you plan to cool several rooms, do a calculation for each room and then add the answers to find your total cooling needs.

Estimate Summary.   While each of the three estimation methods previously mentioned should give you a reliable answer, you can make a quick check by looking at the following list. It compares space to be cooled with the cooling capacity needed.

Space to be cooled	Cooling needed
Medium-size bedroom	5,000 to 6,000 Btu's/hr
Medium-size living room	8,000 to 12,000 Btu's/hr
Several connected rooms	15,000 to 20,000 Btu's/hr
Medium-size house	24,000 or more Btu's/hr

Using a Cooling Estimate.   Take your estimate with you when you go shopping for an air conditioner. If you are using your own figures, you can ask the dealer to check them to see if you have analyzed the situation correctly. In the store, compare your estimate to the cooling capacities listed in Btu's/hr units on the hang tags or labels on conditioners.

Select a machine that is close to your estimate—within 1,000 Btu's/hr for smaller conditioners or 2,000 or 3,000 Btu's/hr for larger ones. A conditioner with too little cooling will not do the job on hot days; one with too much will keep the space cool but will not take out enough moisture to prevent it from feeling damp and uncomfortable.

Cooling Need Work Sheet

1 Find the volume of the room by multiplying the width, length, and height, in feet.

Width _12_ X Length _15_ X Height _8_ = Volume _1,440_

2 Multiply the volume by 10 if the roof or attic is well insulated or if another room is above. If the room has many windows or an uninsulated ceiling or roof, multiply by 18. Cross out the multiplier you don't use.

Volume _1,440_ X $\frac{10}{\cancel{18}}$ = _14,400_

3 Multiply the answer above by 16 if the longest wall faces north; by 17 if it faces east; by 18 if it faces south; by 19 if it faces west. Cross out the multipliers you don't use.

$$\underline{14,400} \ \text{X} \ \begin{matrix} \cancel{16} \\ \cancel{17} \\ 18 \\ \cancel{19} \end{matrix} = \underline{259,200}$$

4 Divide the answer above by 60.

_259,200_ ÷ 60 = _4,320_ Btu/hr

Fig. 6.

HOW TO CHOOSE THE RIGHT LOCATION, DIMENSIONS, AND SHAPE

The shape and dimensions of the room air conditioner you need depend on the shape and dimensions of the window where it will be installed. If the conditioner does not approximately fit the window selected, an exact, airtight installation will be difficult to achieve. If you do not have an airtight installation, the conditioner will never cool up to its rated capacity.

Before you can choose the correct conditioner shape or dimensions for your window, you must decide on the window to place your conditioner in.

A window that faces north (Fig. 7) is best because it is shaded most of the day.

Fig. 7.

Do not install your conditioner in a window where outdoor airflow will be blocked by a nearby building (Fig. 8) or dense bushes.

Inside, avoid room corners or places where large pieces of furniture could hinder air circulation.

Be sure that the open space in the window you have selected for your conditioner is large enough. Take accurate measurements before you shop, and look for a conditioner that approximately fits your window space.

For a sash window, measure the width and height inside the frame

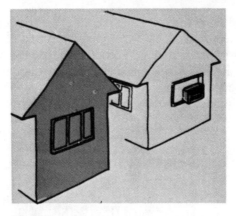

Fig. 8.

when the window is open (Fig. 9). Make sure the conditioner model you buy comes with side panels that will cover the full window width.

If your window is 40 inches or more wide, you may have to pay for an accessory mounting kit.

For open casement and sliding windows, measure the width and height inside the frame when the window is open. Be sure the conditioner's mounting materials will extend to the full height of the window opening.

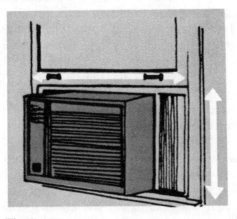

Fig. 9.

For a closed casement window, measure the width and height of the glass to be removed.

Sash windows, which slide up and down, accept conventional conditioners that are box shaped and wider than they are high. When such a conditioner is installed, the bottom window half rests on the top of the conditioner (Fig. 10); panels fill in side space.

Fig. 10.

Casement windows, which swing back and forth like a door, and windows that slide horizontally usually require tall, narrow conditioners (Fig. 11). Such conditioners are installed in windows left completely or partly open.

For closed casement windows, a specially shaped conditioner is available that has a small front and is deep from front to back. It is installed by removing one or two small panes of glass and inserting the unit in the opening (Fig. 12).

For both sash and horizontally sliding windows, U-shaped, split-unit conditioners are also available. This type allows installation with a minimum of open window space that must be sealed by panels or other devices (Fig. 13).

In some areas local laws or building regulations require that a conditioner must not project more than a certain distance from a building wall. Check to see if such rules apply to your home. If they do, ask your salesman to tell you about special room air conditioners designed to have a small overhang (Fig. 14).

Fig. 11.

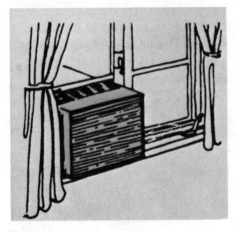

Fig. 12.

Another special type can be installed so that the front of the machine is almost flush with the window in which it is placed. You may consider this type more attractive; drapes can be pulled across the machine when it is not operating.

Note: When you are selecting a conditioner, see if the machine has a label that tells you how many inches it extends into and outside of the room from the mounting. Ask the salesman to give you these dimensions if they are not listed.

Fig. 13.

Fig. 14.

HOW TO FIND THE BEST AIR CONDITIONER FOR YOUR HOME WIRING

The electric motors in air conditioners are built with different volt and ampere ratings to fit different home wiring systems. Motors operate on 115 volts, 208 volts, or 230 volts, and they draw currents ranging from less than 7.5 amperes to over 25 amperes.

To find the conditioner best suited to your home, you need to know the electrical capacity of your wiring in volts and amperes, the codes in your area about connecting conditioners to home wiring, and the electrical load already on the wiring.

A conditioner that draws more current than the wiring can safely carry can cause fuses to blow or create a fire hazard. If your wiring is inadequate for the conditioner you want to buy, you have only two choices: buy a smaller conditioner or have higher capacity wiring built into your home.

Home Wiring Capacities.   Circuits in most houses and apartments supply electricity at about 115 volts and 15 amperes. Kitchens and laundry rooms may have circuits that supply 20 amperes.

Before you buy a conditioner, find out the amperage of the outlet where the conditioner will be located. One way to do this is to check your house or apartment fuse box and read the amperes from the correct fuse or circuit breaker.

If you have any doubt about the amperage or voltage of the outlet, consult a licensed electrician.

Local Electrical Codes.   In most of the United States, conditioners that draw 7.5 amperes or less at 115 volts may be connected to household circuits; in some areas and buildings, conditioners with ratings up to 12 amperes may be plugged into 115-volt, single-outlet circuits; but nowhere should machines drawing more than 12 amperes be connected to 15-ampere, 115-volt circuits.

Few houses or apartments are equipped with single-outlet, 115-volt circuits. Installing them requires a licensed electrician and the cost depends on the capacity of the existing building wiring and the location of the outlet.

To find out the electrical rating allowable for a conditioner connected to your home wiring, telephone the city or county engineer's office, a licensed electrician, or the local electric utility company.

You can also consult a local air conditioner dealer. Some offer a free home survey to determine what electrical circuit changes would need to be made in your home to install various air conditioners.

If you live in an apartment, check with the building manager before you purchase an air conditioner. Many buildings have strict rules about the maximum amperages allowed for air conditioners.

Loads and Wiring.   Even if you follow the rules of your local electrical code, it may be possible for you to overload a circuit's current-carrying capacity if you plug too many appliances into it in addition to your air conditioner. The combined load could result in blown fuses or an electrical fire if the circuit is improperly wired or fused. To avoid this situation, either determine the circuit's load yourself or consult your air conditioner dealer or an electrician.

You can check the total load yourself if you know all the appliances and lights that are already on the circuit to which you plan to connect the air conditioner. Add the wattages of the appliances and lights usually functioning and divide by 115 volts. The answer is the ampere load on the circuit without the conditioner. Then add the ampere rating of the conditioner.

If the total is more than 12 amperes on a 15-ampere circuit, or more than 16 amperes on a 20-ampere circuit, consider the following: put the conditioner on a circuit with fewer appliances; buy two small-amperage conditioners rather than one large one and put them on two different circuits; or have an electrician install another circuit. (*See* Table 19.)

TABLE 19

WATTAGES OF SOME COMMON ELECTRIC APPLIANCES

Small table lamp	75 watts
Floor lamp	400 watts
Overhead light	150 watts
Television set	300 watts
Radio-phonograph	300 watts
Vacuum cleaner	400 watts
Iron	1,100 watts
Coffeemaker	600 watts
Toaster	1,100 watts
Large fan	250 watts
Hair dryer	600 watts

Special High-Voltage Check.   Any person considering buying a 208- or 230-volt conditioner should consult a qualified electrician, your dealer, or the local power company about the actual voltage delivered to your home. It may be anywhere from less than 200 volts to more than 240 volts.

While some high-voltage conditioners are rated 208/230 volts and operate at either end of this range, many are not so flexible. If the voltage on your wiring is low, buy a conditioner rated 208 volts or one with a dual rating. If the voltage is high, buy a machine rated at 230 volts or with a dual rating.

FEATURES TO LOOK FOR

Keep certain practical and convenience features in mind when you go air conditioner shopping.

Practical Features.   *Electrical safety* should be indicated by a safety seal of approval, such as that of Underwriters Laboratories, Inc.

Ratings for amperes, watts, and Btu's/hr should have been tested on each room air conditioner model and a seal should be attached to the model saying "AHAM certified."

The *warranty* should clearly state how many years of free repair parts and labor you are buying with a conditioner and whether you have to pay for servicemen's travel time or for conditioner transport, if necessary. Be sure the warranty will be honored at a local authorized service shop.

The *filter* should be easy to remove and reinstall and either simple to clean or inexpensive to replace. Have the dealer demonstrate filter care.

The *initial price* depends mainly on a conditioner's cooling capacity and the number of control features; but you may be able to save money by doing some comparative shopping. However, if you find a bargain, be sure you are getting the features and services you want with the cheaper machine.

Operating costs can be kept down by buying a conditioner that is an efficient user of electricity. Check its efficiency by dividing the cooling in Btu's/hr listed on the machine by the watts, as in this example:

$$\frac{22{,}500 \text{ Btu's/hr}}{2{,}500 \text{ watts}} = 9 \text{ Btu's/watt-hour}$$

A conditioner that achieves 8 to 9 Btu's of cooling per watt-hour will ease your electric bills substantially during its lifetime.

Convenience Features.   Common features offered for improved convenience or flexibility of operation of conditioners are as follows:

Thermostat settings (Fig. 15) to regulate conditioner operation and room temperature for your comfort.

Heat controls (Fig. 16) for turning on heat (usually limited) on cool days.

Vents (Fig. 17) that open and close for bringing outside air into a room.

Fan settings (Fig. 18) for additional cooling, humidity, and sound control. Some conditioners also have a *fan-only* choice for circulating fresh air.

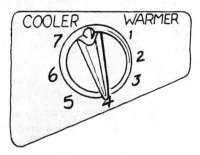

Fig. 15.

Fig. 16.

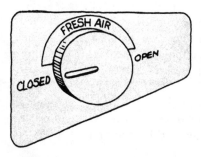

Fig. 17.

Fig. 18.

Chapter 15

Room Air Conditioners

Air conditioning is accomplished by applying the principles of mechanical refrigeration into an air recirculation system arranged to absorb heat from the air within a contained space (room or house) and transfering the heat to the outside of the structure.

A properly designed air conditioner should do the following:

1. Regulate and control temperature.
2. Regulate and control humidity.
3. Furnish proper ventilation.
4. Recirculate the contained air within the conditioned space.
5. Filter and clean the air.

For a better understanding of the application of the mechanical refrigeration machine for the air conditioner, you should be familiar with certain thermodynamic facts dealing with heat and its transfer from one form of energy to another and from one medium to another.

REFRIGERATION CYCLE

The refrigeration cycle is a series of changes of state of the refrigerant (Fig. 1). In this process the refrigerant is changed from a liquid to a vapor and then restored to a liquid. The energy (heat) changing the liquid refrigerant to a vapor is the heat extracted from the air in the conditioned space.

The complete cycle consists of the following four processes:

1. Heat gain in the evaporator.
2. Pressure rise in the compressor.
3. Heat loss in the condenser.
4. Pressure loss in the capillary.

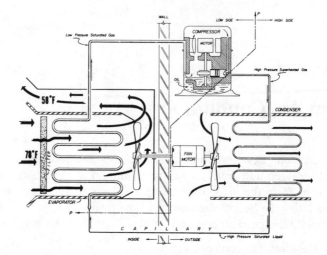

Fig. 1. Refrigeration cycle of air conditioner.

Basically, the refrigeration cycle consists of two heat transfer processes and two pressure change processes.

Heat Gain in the Evaporator.   The heat laden air inside the house is constantly recirculated through the coils of the evaporator. Heat from the air is transferred to the coils of the evaporator, which results in the heat gain in the evaporator (Fig. 2, A).

Pressure Rise in the Compressor.   When the compressor is started, the pressure in the evaporator is reduced, causing the liquid refrigerant in the evaporator to vaporize or boil.

Since the pumping capacity of the compressor is constant, the pressure in the low side is balanced between the inflowing liquid from the capillary and the compressor intake. This process results in the use of the heat in the air to bring about a change of state—liquid to vapor—of the refrigerant; and, in doing so, each pound of liquid refrigerant that is "boiled off" will absorb a considerable amount of heat, the heat being carried out of the evaporator with the vapor.

The vapor being pumped out of the evaporator is termed a *low pressure saturated gas*; that is, it is said to be saturated with the heat that came out of the air in the house. When heat is held in a vapor the heat energy is called *latent heat of evaporization.*

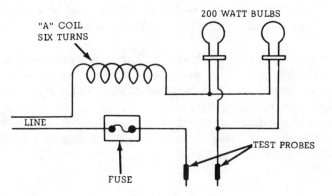

"A" COIL
SIX TURNS

200 WATT BULBS

LINE

FUSE

TEST PROBES

Fig. 2. Heat gain in evaporator.

When the low pressure saturated gas enters the compressor it is compressed and forced into the condenser coil under high pressure.

The process of compression requires power from the compressor motor; this power is expended to compress the gas. As the low pressure gas enters the compressor at 40° F. to 50° F., the temperature is increased by the compression action to 150° F. to 180° F., and the pressure evaluated to 225 pounds to 250 pounds per square inch gage (psig). After the gas leaves the compressor it is referred to as *high pressure superheated gas.*

Heat Loss in the Condenser. As the hot gas passes into the condenser, heat flows from the gas to the tubing and to the fins, where the heat is transferred to the cool air flowing through the coil. Under the high pressure condition, the heat saturated gas (refrigerant) undergoes another change of state—from vapor to liquid.

As the process of condensation takes place, the refrigerant gives up all the heat it absorbed in the evaporator and the compressor. When this heat is released to cause the vapor to change back to a liquid, the process is also referred to as *latent heat of evaporization.*

Heat flows from a warm to a cool body; therefore, in order to handle the heat being removed from the condenser coil, the coil is situated in the rear end of the unit and is isolated from the air inside the house by the weatherproof bulkhead. The fan circulates outside air through the coil and the heat is then transferred to the cooler air and is carried away from the building. (*See* Fig. 1.)

The liquid refrigerant flows to the lower area of the condenser coil, where it is accumulated and impounded ahead of the capillary tube.

Pressure Loss in the Capillary.   The capillary is a small tube that serves to change the high pressure liquid to a low pressure liquid. This is achieved by the flow resistance of the liquid refrigerant through the small bore of the capillary tube.

Another important function of the capillary is to regulate the liquid flow into the evaporator at a rate sufficient to replenish the liquid refrigerant just as fast as it boils off.

ROOM AIR CONDITIONER FUNCTIONS

Coils.   These systems are so arranged that the cooling coils—which absorb heat—are located on the room side of the window, and the condensing unit—which rejects heat—is on the outside of the window. It is important that no intermingling of the hot condenser air and cooled room air takes place. A partition (bulkhead) inside the air conditioner separates the room air from the condenser air. The rubber seals and panels at the window prevent exchange of inside and outside air. Good, tight insulation at the window is of the utmost importance.

Air Flow.   The *window-type air conditioner* is equipped with two separate air systems.

System one. The air system on the outside includes the condenser fan and dissipates the heat taken from the cooled area to the outside atmosphere. The condenser fan also picks up and dissipates into the outside atmosphere the condensate (water), which has been removed from the air in the cooled area. The slinger ring on the outer periphery of the fan performs this function.

System two. The air system within the cooled area circulates room air over the cooling unit. In so doing, the air loses sensible heat (*see* following sections) to the cooling unit. The cooling unit also condenses water vapor (latent heat) from the room air. A solid, insulated partition (bulkhead) inside the air conditioner separates these two air systems.

CERTIFIED COOLING CAPACITY TEST

The heat removal capacity of the room air conditioner is based upon tests made in accordance with *American Society of Heating, Refrigeration, and Air Conditioning Engineers* (ASHRAE) test conditions. The test conditions are as follows:

Outside Air Temperature
95° F. D. B. (Dry bulb) 75° F. W. B. (Wet bulb)

Inside Air Temperature
80° F. D. B. (Dry Bulb) 67° F. W. B. (Wet bulb)

The approximate rate of moisture extraction for a typical model under the above test conditions may be nine pints (approximately nine pounds) per hour.

Note: This quantity of water, removed from the air, represents approximately 9,000 British thermal units/hour (Btu's/hr) of cooling capacity.

Therefore, for a unit rated 30,000 Btu's/hr, the difference between 30,000 and 9,000 leaves approximately 21,000 Btu's/hr for sensible reduction of the air temperature. Each pound of water removed from the air represented a latent heat load of approximately 1,000 Btu's.

SOURCES OF HEAT GAIN

Sensible Heat. *Sensible heat* is that portion of the heat load that causes a sensible elevation or lowering of temperature that can be read on a common dry bulb thermometer. For instance, if we lower the temperature of a room from 85° F. to 80° F., we must remove sensible heat.

Latent Heat. *Latent heat* is that portion of the heat load represented by water vapor present in the air. It is possible to add water vapor to the air or, conversely, to take water vapor away from the air without changing the temperature of the air. A dehumidifier installed in a basement will remove moisture without reducing the base temperature. Roughly, 1,000 Btu's of heat per pound of water is required to make the physical change in water from liquid state to vapor state. Conversely, every pound of water that the air conditioner removes from the air represents approximately 1,000 Btu's of its capacity.

TROUBLE ANALYSIS—COMPRESSORS

Permanent Split Capacitor (PSC).   When a compressor is turned off in an air conditioner, the high pressure in the condenser drops rapidly because the liquid refrigerant in the lower portion of the condenser flows through the capillary tube into the evaporator. This results in an equalization of system pressures in both the low side and high side. Under equalized pressure conditions in both the compressor suction and discharge lines, the starting load on the compressor is very low; and, consequently, the extra starting torque that can be derived by adding a starting capacitor and relay is not necessary.

The term *permanent split capacitor*, or PSC for short, is the term most commonly applied to compressors that do not normally use a starting capacitor and relay.

The running capacitor is connected in series with the starting winding of the compressor, which helps to improve the power factor; and, with proper voltage and sufficient time for the refrigeration system to equalize pressure during the off-cycle, the PSC compressor will function just as well as a capacitor start relay (CSR) compressor.

PSC compressors may be converted to CSR compressors by adding the proper relay and starting capacitor; however, this procedure is rarely necessary.

Initial break in. Occasionally a new air conditioner may fail to start because of the "tightness" of the moving parts of the compressor. *Caution: Do not* declare the compressor defective. The compressor may cycle on the overload protector for 10 or 15 minutes before starting. Such compressors will usually require a brief run-in period after which they will start satisfactorily.

A temporary expediency to start a "stiff" compressor is outlined below and may be employed by the serviceman for the initial starting or breaking-in of the compressor.

1. Use a starting capacitor of approximately 150 microfarad (MFD)-250-volt capacity and connect a pair of lead wires 12 to 15 inches long to the terminals of the capacitor.

2. Expose the terminals of the running capacitor of the air conditioner.

3. Plug the service cord into the wall receptacle and set the switch to the cooling position.

4. Momentarily contact the starting capacitor wires to the compressor and hermetically on the running capacitor terminals. The compressor should start instantly. *Caution: Do not* leave the starting capacitor connected for more than one or two seconds.

5. Once the compressor is started, allow the air conditioner to run several hours for the break-in period. After this, the compressor should start satisfactorily without the aid of the starting capacitor.

Low voltage conditions. Under normal conditions the PSC compressor should start if the voltage applied to the service cord is within 10 percent of the voltage rating on the air conditioner nameplate. In cases where the customer reports that the air conditioner will not start, a voltage test should be made as follows.

1. First determine if the customer operates any other appliances such as an electric iron, grille, toaster, and so on, that might be connected to the same power circuit and turn all such appliances on.

2. Connect a reliable alternating current voltmeter across the circuit at the service cord and set the switch on the air conditioner to the Hi-Cool position.

3. Observe the voltage indicated on the voltmeter while the compressor is trying to start. If the voltage is less than 104 volts for a regular 115-volt circuit, or less than 188 volts for a regular 208-volt circuit, or less than 207 volts for a regular 230-volt circuit, or less than 197 volts for a dual voltage 208/230-volt air conditioner, the house wiring is inadequate to carry the load and the compressor motor may only hum and fail to start.

Low voltage conditions must be corrected if the air conditioner is to be used and operated successfully.

Starting capacitor and relay. When reliable voltage tests reveal that the power circuit has ample voltage (as outlined previously in the section on Low Voltage Conditions, paragraph 3), and the compressor will not start, a starting capacitor and relay may be added to the circuits to convert the PSC-type compressor to a CSR-type compressor. The CSR compressor will develop a considerable starting torque and overcome any abnormal loading conditions imposed on the compressor by high ambients or close tolerances.

For installation instructions of starting capacitors and relays, select the proper wiring diagram for your air conditioner.

GENERAL SYSTEM TEST—ELECTRICAL

Conditions for Test.   Remove service cord from power outlet. Set switch for Cooling and set thermostat on the Coldest position.

Test for Grounded Circuit.   Using either a test light or an ohm meter, apply the test leads to one of the flat blades and the ground prong of the service cord plug.

1. If the lamp lights, or if the ohm meter shows resistance, the circuit is grounded.

2. If the lamp does not light, or if the ohm meter shows no deflection, the circuit is not grounded.

A grounded circuit indicates trouble in the compressor motor, fan motor, or a capacitor. An open circuit indicates trouble in the switch, a broken wire in the service cord, or a loose connection on the terminal board.

Remove the air conditioner from the window and open the compartment that houses the electrical components. Examine the capacitors. If a capacitor has an internal short, the case may appear bloated or bulged, or it may have ruptured with the case and other nearby components covered with a whitish colored material from the capacitor.

If no obvious source of trouble is visible, proceed to test each electrical component separately.

Thermostat.   *Gas type.* The switch action in a thermostat is single-pole, single-throw. Pressure from the bellows will hold the switch contacts closed when the thermostat is set for deep cooling.

Bi-metal. The switch action in a thermostat is single-pole, single-throw. The switch mechanism is actuated with a bi-metal element. The bi-metal element senses the temperature from the sampling of room air. The evaporator fan draws a small continuous stream of room air through the air chute and over the bi-metal element.

Testing. Set the thermostat at its coldest position and the switch for cooling and connect the service cord to the power outlet. With the bare ends of a short piece of No. 12 insulated wire, shunt across the electrical terminals of the thermostat. If the compressor runs with the jumper wire attached, but will not run without it, the thermostat is defective and must be replaced.

Anti-Ice Control. *Function.* The switch action in the anti-ice control is single-pole, single-throw. Pressure from the bellows will hold the switch contact closed until the sensing element of the control gets a temperature of 28° F. The controls will then open the circuit to the compressor. The fan motor will continue to run as the coil de-ices and reaches a temperature of 58.5° F., then the control closes the circuit to the compressor and the air conditioner continues to cool.

Feeler bulb location. The anti-ice control feeler tube (capillary) is located at the centertop edge of the evaporator. Count down to the space between the first and second tube from the top and insert the anti-ice control feeler tube $2\frac{1}{2}$ inches between the vertical fins. (*See* Fig. 1.)

Test. To test the anti-ice control, prepare a solution of ice, water, and salt. Use a mercury-filled thermometer to determine the solution temperature. Place the feeler bulb into the solution. When the thermometer reads 28° F. $\pm$ 1°, the switch contacts should open. Warm the water to 58.5° F. $\pm$ 1°; the switch contacts should close. If the control is not defective, rinse off the solution with clear water and remount into the original position.

Switch. To test a switch, insert the service cord into the power outlet and set the thermostat on the Coldest position. Review the schematic wiring diagram (Fig. 1) and engage the switch into all of the various positions. If the fan motor or compressor fails to operate in any one of the particular switch positions, use an insulated jumper wire and shunt across the particular switch element by connecting the wire from the "hot" side of the switch to the terminal that feeds the high or low speed circuit of the fan motor in case the fan motor fails to run on either speed; or, to the circuit feeding the thermostat (or the overload) in case the compressor fails to run.

If the fan motor or compressor runs with the jumper wire connected, but will not with the wire removed, the switch is defective and must be replaced.

If the compressor does not run, check the continuity of the overload.

Overload.   In normal use, the overload contacts are closed. The overload protects the compressor by opening the circuit when excessive heat or current conditions prevail.

If there is no external overload mounted in the compressor terminal compartment, the overload is located in the compressor motor windings and must be tested as a part of the compressor motor.

Caution: Do not perform a continuity test on the motor windings or condemn the compressor motor until the compressor has been out of electrical circuit for at least 20 minutes. This will allow the compressor to cool down and give sufficient time for the internal overload to reset. The overload is not replaceable. To test external overload, remove it from the terminal box of the compressor, disconnect the wires, and test for continuity between all terminals. If the overload is defective it must be replaced. Current will flow between all terminals of a good overload.

Relay.   The relay may be tested by momentarily connecting an insulated jumper wire between the compressor terminals marked "S" and "R" with the switch set on the Coldest position. When the compressor starts, remove the jumper wire. If the compressor continues to run with the jumper wire removed, the relay is defective and must be replaced. If the compressor fails to start or runs for only a brief interval, the relay is probably satisfactory and the trouble is being caused by other defective electrical components.

Capacitor.   Test method No. 1: If a capacitor is suspected of being defective, the simplest and best means of testing is to replace the suspected capacitor with a new one of the same rating and test run the air conditioner.

If a new capacitor is not available, use a *volt ohm meter* to check suspected defective capacitor. *Do not* use ohm scale on an ampere probe meter. Use of an ampere probe meter will give a false reading.

A defective capacitor may have either an internal short or an open circuit.

If shorted, an ohm meter will show very little or no resistance when connected across the terminals of the capacitor.

If an open circuit, the ohm meter will show no deflection.

If the capacitor is good, the ohm meter will register a sharp deflection and, as the capacitor begins to load up, the needle on the ohm meter will begin to drift back to very low resistance.

Building a test device. You can build an inexpensive device that can be used to test capacitors. This tester can be used to test for a short between the plates and the can on the running capacitors or an open circuit inside the capacitor. You can establish the approximate microfared (MFD) of a capacitor. The following parts are required to build a test device.

1. Two flush mount receptacles that will accommodate a standard base light bulb.

2. Two 200-watt incandescent light bulbs.

3. A snap-on volt ohm meter.

4. One flush mount receptacle that will accommodate a standard base fuse.

5. One standard-base quick-acting fuse plug, not to exceed 10 amperes.

6. Two test probes.

7. Approximately 10 feet of No. 16 wire.

8. A service cord of No. 16 wire equipped with a 115-volt plug.

Mount the two light bulbs and fuse receptacles onto a base and install the light bulbs and the fuse. Form the coil of wire by wrapping the wire around a $1\frac{1}{2}$ inch cylinder six full turns. Remove the wire from the cylinder and tape the wires with electrical tape in a couple of places to keep the coil together. (*See* Fig. 2, A for coil of wire.) To wire and complete the tester, see the circuitry in Fig. 2.

Testing device check-out. Plug the tester into 115-volt power source and touch the test probes together. The bulbs will light to full brilliance if the tester is in proper working condition.

Test method No. 2—use of test device. Clamp a snap-on ammeter into coil "A" and momentarily touch the test leads to the capacitor terminals as outlined on the next page and note the ampere reading.

1. Two terminal capacitors.
   a. Take the ampere reading between the two terminals.
2. Three terminal running capacitors.
   a. Take the ampere reading between the terminals marked C and HERM for the high MFD factor.
   b. Take the ampere reading between terminals marked C and fan for the low MFD factor.
3. Four terminal running capacitors.
   a. Take the ampere reading between terminals marked HERM for the high MFD factor.
   b. Take the ampere reading between terminals marked fan for the low MFD factor.

Caution: Before handling the capacitor as outlined, discharge the capacitor through a 10,000 ohm, 1 watt resistor placed across the terminals for one minute.

Note: Do not discharge any capacitor by means of a direct short as this will cause di-electric breakdown; and in the case of an internal fused capacitor the fuse may blow—necessitating the replacement of the capacitor.

Note the ampere reading of the capacitor under test and determine MFD capacitance shown in Table 20. If the ammeter does not show an ampere reading, the capacitor being tested is open and the capacitor must be replaced.

If both test bulbs light to full brilliance when the test probes are touched to the capacitor terminals, the capacitor is internally shorted and must be replaced.

Compressor.   To test a compressor, remove the wiring from the three compressor terminals. Continuity between any one of the three terminals and the case indicates that the compressor is grounded, or if the continuity shows an open circuit between any two terminals, the compressor is defective and the complete chassis must be delivered or shipped to the nearest authorized factory service station for replacement.

Fan Blades.   Set the switch in the off position and examine clearance of both the evaporator fan and condenser fan blades. Rotate the blades slowly by hand and listen for a scraping or grating noise.

TABLE 20

CAPACITOR TEST

STARTING CAPACITOR	AMPERES FACTOR	MICROFARAD RATING
	4.9 - 5.2	21/25
	5.9 - 6.2	25/36
	10.6 - 11.0	38/46
	12.0 - 12.4	50/56
	14.8 - 15.2	72/87
	14.8 - 15.2	86/103
	15.0 - 15.4	88/108
	16.0 - 16.4	108/120
	16.8 - 17.2	121/146
	16.9 - 17.3	135/155
	18.4 - 18.8	161/193
RUNNING CAPACITOR	AMPERES FACTOR	MICROFARAD RATING
	1.1 - 1.5	5
	1.5 - 1.9	8
	3.3 - 3.7	15
	4.4 - 4.8	20
	5.9 - 6.2	25
	6.9 - 7.2	30
	7.9 - 8.2	35

If blades are hard to turn, or if any scraping or grating noise is felt or heard, the air conditioner chassis must be removed from the cabinet to permit a complete examination to determine the cause of the trouble and its proper correction.

Occasionally a fan-blade set-screw becomes loosened and develops a clicking sound between the fan blade hub and the motor shaft. Loosened set screws can be detected by rocking the blades of the evaporator fan. As the fan blades and motor shaft assembly change direction of rotation, the loosened set screw will bump on the shaft. To tighten a loosened set screw, the air conditioner chassis will have to be removed from the cabinet.

Fan Motor. Before checking a fan motor for electrical defects, first study the schematic wiring diagram (Fig. 1), then make sure that all electrical connections between the power source and the fan motor are good.

Some fan motors are equipped with a capacitor that may be tested in the same way as previously outlined for capacitor testing.

To test the fan motor windings, remove the motor leads from their terminal connections and check the continuity of the windings with a test light or an ohm meter. An open circuit indicates a defective winding, a broken connection, or a bad motor protector inside the motor. Continuity between the windings and the frame indicates an internal short or ground and the motor must be repaired or replaced.

Another testing procedure for a fan motor is to disconnect the motor wires and energize the motor independently with a test cord. With a test cord properly connected, the motor should operate if the motor is in good condition.

Fan motor lubrication. The fan motors are equipped with oiler tubes (Fig. 3). The recommended type of oil is SAE No. 20 weight of a non-detergent type. A detergent-type oil must not be used.

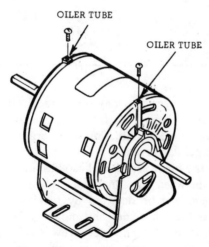

Fig. 3. Fan motor lubrication.

The fan motors have oilite bearings and a detergent oil can ruin the oil-absorbing quality of bearings.

If your motor does not have oiler tubes it has a lasting lubricant and therefore requires little attention.

Caution: Do not over-oil as the reservoir may overflow and damage the motor. Add five or six drops of oil to each bearing. Be sure to replace the oiler plugs to keep water and dirt from getting into the fan motor bearings.

FREEZE-UP

An evaporator freeze-up may result from a specific cause or a combination of causes. The following are the most common of these causes.

Reduced Air Volume Through Evaporator Coil.

1. Clogged or dirty filter.

Remedy: In cleaning extremely dirty filters, the bulk of dirt can be removed with a vacuum cleaner. If the filter is still dirty, it can be washed in a solution of warm water and liquid detergent. Flush the filter with clear water after each washing. Shake the excess water from the filter and allow to dry. *Caution:* Bleach solutions or dry detergents should never be used to clean filters.

2. Substitute filter, or wrong type of filter is being used.

Remedy: Replace with manufacturer-approved filter.

3. Clogged or dirty evaporator coil.

Remedy: Clean coil and fins with wire brush and vacuum cleaner. If coated with grease, the air conditioner should be removed and steam cleaned.

4. Loose evaporator fan.

Remedy: Tighten set screw.

5. Fan motor stalled or running too slow.

Remedy: Check and repair or replace fan motor if defective. Check for low-voltage conditions. Switch to Hi-Cool for a higher speed operation of the fan motor to gain more air volume on the evaporator.

Recirculation of Discharged Air.   Operation of the air conditioner with the cold discharged air deflected back into the return air stream entering the intake grille will result in the recirculation of chilled air. This condition may reduce the amount of heat normally delivered to the evaporator coil by the evaporator air, causing the internal coil temperature to fall to 32° F. or lower. With the coil temperature running below freezing temperature, the moisture in the air collects onto the surfaces of the metal and quickly freezes into ice, thus blocking or impeding the air flow.

Remedy: Adjust all discharge air louvers or relocate any furniture that might deflect the air back into the intake opening.

Prolonged Operation with Low Outside Temperature. In some cases, especially air conditioners installed in large apartment houses, freeze-ups occur when the air conditioner is operated during periods with outside temperature dropping below 70° F. to 75° F. at night.

Remedy: Suggest that the thermostat be set on a lower position to allow the air conditioner to cycle more frequently. Also, during such conditions the user should be instructed to operate the air conditioner on Hi-Cool position only.

Thermostat Sensing Tube Incorrectly Positioned. When the sensing tube from the termostat is in direct contact with the evaporator, as can easily happen on some models, only the coil temperature will be detected. This condition will cause the air conditioner to cycle frequently and the unit will never run long enough to produce any noticeable air conditioning.

In some cases the sensing tube may be mislocated, so that cooled air entering the coil is not drawn across the sensing tube. In this condition, the air conditioner will continue to run even though the average room temperature is reduced to a cut-out setting on the thermostat. Continued or prolonged running with this condition will cause an evaporator freeze-up.

Remedy: Check position of sensing tube and relocate to correct position. The correct location of the sensing tube is outlined below for different models.

In the air conditioner shown in Fig. 4, the sensing tube is mounted across the front edge of the base pan and is held in position with two mounting clips.

In the air conditioner shown in Fig. 5, the sensing tube extends through the bottom of the control panel. The sensing element is formed and mounted to the right hand side of the control panel in a vertical position.

In the air conditioner shown in Fig. 6, the sensing element tube is mounted to the evaporator header sheet (in a vertical position) directly below the control knobs.

Fig. 4. Position of sensing tube.

NOISY CHASSIS OPERATION AND VIBRATION

Excessive noise and vibration is usually traced to a faulty or careless installation.

Deteriorated Compressor Mounting Grommets. Compressor rubber mounting grommets may have deteriorated, causing the vibration noise from the compressor to travel into the air conditioner chassis. The chassis will transmit and amplify the noise, making it objectionable to the customer. The grommets will then have to be replaced.

Fig. 5. Position of sensing tube.

Failure to Loosen the Compressor Hold-Down Nuts. Failure to loosen the compressor hold-down nuts on compressors mounted on external springs will cause excessive noise and vibration. Hold-down nuts on external spring compressors must be backed off to the top of the stud bolt at time of installation.

This will allow the compressor to ride freely on the springs and absorb vibration from the compressor motor.

All compressors that are mounted directly to the base require no adjustment at the time of installation as the compressor motor is mounted on springs inside the hermetically sealed case.

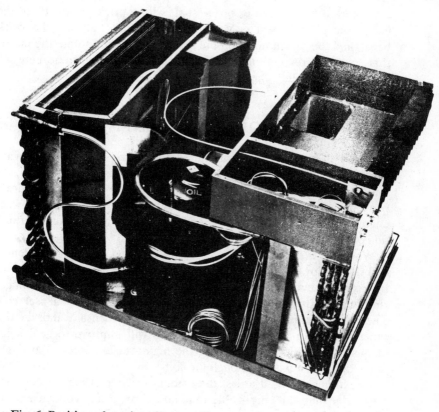

Fig. 6. Position of sensing element tube.

Imbalanced Fan Blades.   An out of balance condenser fan blade or evaporator blower wheel will also cause excessive vibration. Out of balance fan blades or blower wheels can be detected by removing the chassis from the window and observing the rotation of the blade with the fan motor operating.

Bent Motor Shaft.   A bent motor shaft will cause a fan to run out of track or wobble. A bent shaft can usually be detected by rotating the shaft and observing the extreme outer end of the shaft. If the shaft is bent, the outer end will not run true and the motor must be replaced. Another method of checking the fan motor shaft is to mark the exact center of the shaft with a prick punch. Place the motor on a work bench. Measure the distance between the work bench and the punch mark on the motor shaft. Then rotate the motor shaft one-half revolution. If the distance remains the same between the above two points, the motor shaft is straight.

MOISTURE PROBLEMS

Base Pan Water.   Warm humid air passing over the cold evaporator coil will result in the formation of condensate on the coil. As the condensate is formed it flows down the coil and into the drain pan through the drain hose. It then flows into the base pan. The accumulation of water in the base pan is a natural and important function of the air conditioner.

When the air conditioner is correctly installed, with the condenser end slightly lower than the evaporator end, the water will flow toward the rear of the air conditioner, where it will be picked up by a slinger ring on the condenser fan blade and blown into the condenser coil. The hot condenser coil will evaporate the condensate and, in this process, evaporization of the condensate will improve the efficiency of the air conditioner by cooling the high-pressure, superheated gas much faster as it passes through the coil.

In extremely humid areas, the amount of condensate formed may be greater than the unit is able to handle through the condenser coil; therefore, a slot hole is provided on the rear side of the base pan that will allow surplus water to overflow onto the ground. When the air conditioner is installed in a location where water from the overflow slot is objectionable, a special overflow connection may be added so that a drain tube can be attached. (This special connection may be obtained from the factory with instructions for installation.) With the special overflow attachment installed, a sufficient amount of water will be retained in the base pan to maintain proper operating efficiency.

Note: Never drill holes in the base pan bottom to prevent the base pan from accumulating water to a depth sufficient to submerge the slinger ring.

Water Dripping in Room. Water dripping from the front is usually the result of an improper installation. The air conditioner must be installed with a slight slope toward the outside. This slope will allow evaporator condensate to flow toward the rear of the air conditioner and be disposed of as previously described. Dripping water may also be the result of blocked water channels in the bulkhead. This condition can be easily corrected by taking the chassis from the window and removing any obstructions from the drain hose, which passes from the drain pan through the upright bulkhead located behind the evaporator coil. These obstructions may be in the form of foreign material or algae. A thick, yellowish, jelly-like substance in the base pan could be a form of algae.

To clean the base pan, move the chassis from the building. Flush the base pan with water by using a hose with a high pressure nozzle. If algae is suspected, a reoccurrence may be prevented by adding an algaecide. Several types of algaecides are on the market to prevent algae from forming. *Caution:* Never use copper sulphate as an algaecide.

Condensation on the Decorative Front. Condensation on the decorative front may occur if the insulation on the rear side of the front panel is broken, dislocated, or missing. In such cases, the insulation must be repaired or replaced.

Under extremely humid conditions, condensate may form on portions of the discharge louvers of the front panel. This condition may prevail even though the insulation described in the previous paragraph is in good condition. Such "sweating" will usually disappear after the air conditioner runs for a few hours or long enough to dehumidify the air in the room.

IMPROPER COOLING

Cooling Performance Test. *A cooling performance test* enables the serviceman to accurately determine if the air conditioning unit is operating satisfactorily. A simple and reliable test of an air conditioner can be performed by checking the temperature of the air stream that enters the evaporator through the front panel and the temperature of the outlet air that is discharged through the discharge louvers.

1. Suspend a thermometer in the stream of air entering the evaporator coil.

2. Suspend another thermometer in the cold stream of air that is discharged from the evaporator.

3. Operate the air conditioner for 15 minutes with controls set for maximum cooling. Close fresh air vents (if used) and put the thermostat on its coldest setting.

4. Obtain temperature differential (TD) by subtracting inlet air temperature from discharge air temperature.

5. Compare temperature differential (TD) of unit under test with the TD shown in the applicable performance chart for the model being tested.

An air conditioner that produces a temperature differential of 15 degrees to 20 degrees under average conditions is considered to be operating properly. In extreme humid weather, a temperature differential of 10 degrees would be considered adequate, due to the loss of cooling capacity in dehumidifying the air.

IMPROPER COMPRESSOR AMPERAGE

Current Check.   Analysis of any air conditioner system would not be complete without performing a check on the amount of current being drawn by the compressor. The amount of load or work being done by the compressor is in direct relation to the amount of amperes or current being consumed.

The performance chart shows the normal amount of current the compressor should draw, and allowing for local variations in temperatures and humidity, the serviceman can utilize the current data as an aid to diagnose certain troubles.

High Amperage.   Abnormally *high ampere draw* would indicate trouble in one or more of the following areas:

1. Recirculation of condenser air.
2. Obstruction of condenser air.
3. Leaking or partially shorted running capacitor.

4. Partially shorted or grounded compressor winding.
5. Overcharged system.

Low Amperage. Abnormally *low ampere draw* would indicate trouble in one or more of the following areas:

1. Clogged intake filter.
2. Dirty evaporator coil.
3. Recirculation of evaporator air.
4. System partially discharged—refrigerant leak.
5. Partially restricted capillary.
6. Partially restricted strainer.
7. Undercharged.
8. Inefficient compressor.

CASEMENT WINDOW ROOM AIR CONDITIONERS

In the application and sizing of room air conditioners for cooling, it is important to give full consideration to all factors that may contribute to the heat loss or gain of the space to be conditioned. It is therefore necessary to make a survey of the space to be conditioned and to calculate the load requirements before a selection of the size of the equipment needed can be made.

The load requirement may be determined very easily by simply using the standard AHAM Load Calculating Form shown in Fig. 7. This form is very easy to use and is self-explanatory throughout. It is only necessary to insert the proper measurements on the lines provided and multiply by the given factors, then add this result for the total load requirements.

Cooling load requirements are generally based on the cooling load for comfortable air conditioning that does not require specific conditions of inside temperature and humidity. The load calculation form is based on outside design temperature of 95° F. and 75° F. It can be used for areas in the continental United States having other outside design temperatures by applying a correction factor for the particular locality as determined from the map shown in Fig. 7.

When sizing a Twin-Temp unit (Fig. 9) for cooling and heating, we must remember that the heating capacity of any given unit varies directly with the outdoor ambient temperature. Also, we must keep in

HEAT GAIN FROM	QUANTITY	FACTORS DAY				BTU/Hr (Quantity x Factor)
		No Shades°	Inside Shades°	Outside Awnings°	(Area x Factor)	
1. WINDOWS: Heat gain from sun.						
Northeast	sq ft	60	25	20	Use	
East	sq ft	80	40	25	only	
Southeast	sq ft	75	30	20	the	
South	sq ft	75	35	20	largest	
Southwest	sq ft	110	45	30	load.	
West	sq ft	150	65	45	Use	
Northwest	sq ft	120	50	35	only	
North	sq ft	0	0	0	one.	

°These factors are for single glass only. For glass block, multiply the above factors by 0.5; for double-glass or storm windows, multiply the above factors by 0.8.

HEAT GAIN FROM	QUANTITY			
2. WINDOWS: Heat gain by conduction. (Total of all windows.)				
Single glass	sq ft		14	
Double glass or glass block	sq ft		7	
3. WALLS: (Based on linear feet of wall.)		Light Construction		Heavy Construction
a. Outside walls				
North exposure	ft	30		20
Other than North exposure	ft	60		30
b. Inside Walls (between conditioned and unconditioned spaces only)	ft		30	
4. ROOF OR CEILING: (Use one only.)				
a. Roof, uninsulated	sq ft		19	
b. Roof, 1 inch or more insulation	sq ft		8	
c. Ceiling, occupied space above.	sq ft		3	
d. Ceiling, insulated with attic space above	sq ft		5	
e. Ceiling, uninsulated, with attic space above	sq ft		12	
5. FLOOR: (Disregard if floor is directly on ground or over basement.)	sq ft		3	
6. NUMBER OF PEOPLE:			600	
7. LIGHTS AND ELECTRICAL EQUIPMENT IN USE	watts		3	
8. DOORS AND ARCHES CONTINUOUSLY OPENED TO UNCONDITIONED SPACE: (Linear feet of width.)	ft		300	
9. SUB-TOTAL	x x x x x		x x x x x	
10. TOTAL COOLING LOAD: (BTU per hour to be used for selection of room air conditioner(s).)	(Item 9) x		(Factor from Map) =	

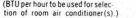

Fig. 7. Factors and map.

Fig. 7a. Casement unit.

mind the average low temperatures that might be experienced in the locality where the unit is to be installed. Therefore, when sizing a Twin-Temp unit, both cooling and heating requirements must be calculated. Do not oversize or undersize one phase of the unit's capacity at the expense of the other. In those cases where the unit will provide satisfactory cooling at all times but will be inadequate for those few times that the outdoor temperature is below the maximum low for the unit, additional auxiliary heating facilities must be provided to insure that adequate heat is available at all times.

HOW TO USE COOLING LOAD ESTIMATE FORM FOR ROOM AIR CONDITIONERS

A. This cooling load estimate form (Fig. 7) is suitable for estimating the cooling load for comfort air conditioning installations that do not require specific conditions of inside temperature and humidity.

B. The form is based on an outside design temperature of 95° F. dry bulb and 75° F. wet bulb. It can be used for areas in the continental United States having other outside design temperatures by applying a correction factor for the particular locality as determined from the map shown in Fig. 7.

C. The form includes "day" factors for calculating cooling loads in rooms where daytime comfort is desired (such as living rooms, and the like).

D. The numbers of the following paragraphs refer to the correspondingly numbered items on the form.

1. Multiply the square feet of window area for each exposure by the applicable factor. The window area is the area of the wall opening in which the window is installed. For windows shaded by inside shades of venetian blinds, use the factor for "inside shades." For windows shaded by outside awnings or by both outside awnings and inside shades (or venetian blinds), use the factor for "outside awnings." "Single glass" includes all types of single-thickness windows, and "double glass" includes sealed air-space types, storm windows, and glass block. Only one number should be entered in the right-hand column for item 1, and this number should represent *only the exposure with the largest load.*

2. Multiply the total square feet of all windows in the room by the applicable factor.

3a. Multiply the total length (linear feet) of all walls exposed to the outside by the applicable factor. Doors should be considered as being part of the wall. Outside walls facing due north should be calculated separately from outside walls facing other directions. Walls that are permanently shaded by adjacent structures should be considered as being "north exposure." Do not consider trees and shrubbery as providing permanent shading. An uninsulated frame wall or a masonry wall eight inches or less in thickness is considered "light construction." An insulated frame wall or a masonry wall over eight inches in thickness is considered "heavy construction."

3b. Multiply the total length (linear feet) of all inside walls between the space to be conditioned and any unconditioned spaces by the given factor. Do not include inside walls that separate other air-conditioned rooms.

4. Multiply the total square feet of the roof or ceiling area by

Specifications

BTU/HR	6000	7500
E.E.R. BTU/Watt	7.0	5.7
Volts	115	115
Amperes	7.5	12.0
Total Watts	860	1325
Hertz	60	60
Fuse/Breaker Size	15	15
Fan RPM	1550	1550
Evap. Air CFM	160	160
Dehumidification Pts/HR	1.6	2.3
Width	14-11/16	14-11/16
Height	10-13/16	10-13/16
Depth	27	27
Min. Ext. into Room	1-7/8	1-7/8
Min. Ext. to Outside	15-1/2	15-1/2
Net Weight	95	95
Shipping Weight	105	105

Performance Data

EVAPORATOR AIR TEMP. °F	DISCHARGE AIR	55.9	51.8
	TEMP. DROP °F	24.1	28.1
OPERATING PRESSURES	SUCTION	71	69
	DISCHARGE	285	330
ELECTRICAL RATINGS	AMPS	7.5	12.0
	LOCKED ROTOR AMPS	35.0	47.0
R-22 REFRIG.	CHARGE IN OUNCES	17.5	21
COMP. OIL	CHARGE IN FLUID OZ.	17	17

*Rating Conditions:

80°F Room Air Temperature and 50% Relative Humidity with 95°F Outside Air Temperature at 40% Relative Humidity.

Fig. 8. Specifications and performance data.

the factor given for the type of construction most nearly describing the particular application. (Use one line only.)

5. Multiply the total square feet of the floor area by the factor given. Disregard this item if the floor is directly on the ground or over a basement.

6. Multiply the number of people who normally occupy the space to be air-conditioned by the factor given. Use a minimum of two people.

7. Determine the total number of watts for lights and electrical equipment, except the air conditioner itself, that will be *in use* when the room's air conditioning is operating. Multiply the total wattage by the factor given.

8. Multiply the total width (linear feet) of any doors or arches

Fig. 9. Twin temp unit.

that are continually open to an unconditioned space by the applicable factor. *Note:* Where the width of the doors or arches is more than five feet, the actual load may exceed the calculated value. In such cases, both adjoining rooms should be considered as a single large room, and the room air-conditioner unit should be considered as a single large room. The room air-conditioner unit or units should be selected according to a calculation made on this new basis.

9. Total the loads estimated for the foregoing eight items.

10. Multiply the sub-total obtained in item 9 by the proper correction factor, selected from the map shown in Fig. 7, for the particular locality. The result is the total estimated design cooling load in Btu's per hour.

E. For best results, a room air-conditioner unit or units having a cooling capacity rating (determined in accordance with the NEMA Standards Publication for Room Air Conditioners, CN 1-1960) as close as possible to the estimated load should be selected. In general, a greatly oversized unit that would operate intermittently will be much less satisfactory than one that is slightly undersized and that would operate more nearly continuously.

F. Intermittent loads such as kitchen and laundry equipment are not included in this form. (*See* Fig. 8 for specifications and performance data for models described.)

INSTALLATION OF CASEMENT WINDOW AIR CONDITIONERS

The air conditioners shown in Figs. 10 and 11 will fit casement window openings as follows:

Height: $10^{13}/_{16}$ inches minimum to $11\frac{3}{4}$ inches maximum.
Width: $14\frac{3}{4}$ inches minimum to $18\frac{3}{8}$ inches maximum.

Note: An optional kit is available at extra cost for installations in conventional sash-type windows up to 42 inches wide.

Fig. 10.

1. Remove unit from shipping carton. Remove tape holding decorative front in place. Remove front and place out of the way.

2. Remove glass, putty, and window crank, if necessary. Measure horizontal width dimension "W" or window frame opening. If dimension "W" (Fig. 11) is 16 inches or less, no adjustments of side

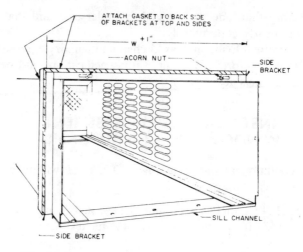

Fig. 11.

bracket is necessary. *If dimension is over 16 inches,* loosen two top acorn nuts and slide side brackets out. (Add one inch to measured "W" dimension for this adjustment.) Tighten acorn nuts (Fig. 11).

3. Remove paper backing from 36-inch strip of foam gasket ($\frac{3}{8}$ inch by $\frac{3}{4}$ inch) and attach to back side of top and side brackets (Fig. 11). Edge of gasket and brackets should be flush. Press gasket firmly in place.

4. Slide outer shell into window opening as far as the sill channel will permit. Back side of sill channel must be in contact with the front side of window frame (Fig. 12). Drill two $\frac{9}{64}$-inch diameter pilot holes in the lower part of window frame. *Note:* Use the first empty hole in the bottom side rails of the shell, just back of the steel sill channel, as a guide. Secure the shell to the window channel with two hex-head self-tapping screws $1\frac{1}{8}$ inches long in the pilot holes (Fig. 12).

5. Position support brackets as shown in Fig. 16. Attach the shell with four Phillips head 10-24 machine screws and four flat nuts. Secure bottom of support brackets to wall with the wood screws. Check shell to allow for $\frac{1}{4}$-inch downward slope toward the outside. If used on other than wood construction, screw support brackets to a piece of 2 by 4 material.

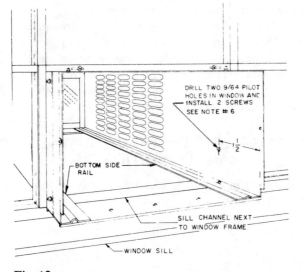

Fig. 12.

6. If installation is on the swing-out part of the window, be sure the window is closed and locked. Then slide the chassis into the shell, as far as it will go.

7. Place filter in pocket, in front of coil, install decorative front over edge of shell, and secure with two No. 10 $\times$ ½-inch slotted head screws (Fig. 13).

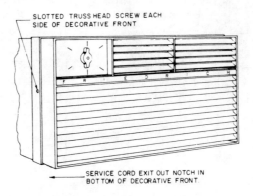

Fig. 13.

8. Plug service cord into electrical outlet.

Warning: This appliance is equipped with a three-prong grounding plug for your protection against shock hazards and should be plugged directly into a properly grounded three-prong receptacle. Where a two-prong receptacle is encountered, it must be replaced with a properly grounded three-prong receptacle in accordance with the National Electrical Code and local codes and ordinances.

INSTALLATION OF THRU-THE-WALL-TYPE AIR CONDITIONERS

The unit shown in Figs. 14, 15, and 16 may be installed in walls up to nine inches thick.

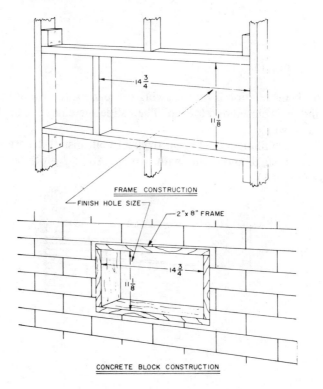

Fig. 14.

Procedure. Remove unit from shipping carton: remove tape holding decorative front in place; remove front and place out of the way; slide unit out of shell.

Layout. Cut and frame-in an opening in the desired wall area as shown in Fig. 14. Remove two screws and relocate sill plate back one inch to next set of holes in shell rail. Place shell in the wall opening with the front flange tight against the wall surface. Drill three $\frac{3}{32}$-inch diameter pilot holes. Secure with three Phillips screws $1\frac{1}{4}$-inches long in sill plate (Fig. 15).

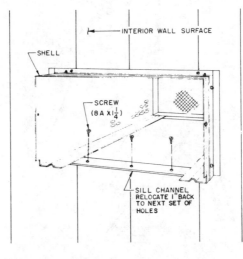

Fig. 15.

Attach brackets to shell with screws and nuts furnished (Fig. 16). Secure lower end of support brackets to wall (Fig. 16). If other than wood construction, use a piece of 2×4 lumber to attach support brackets (Fig. 16). Caulk all around shell on outside to insure a weathertight seal. Slide unit into shell. Place filter in position. Place decorative front in position on shell and secure with two slotted sheet-metal screws $\frac{1}{2}$ inch long. Plug service cord into electrical outlet.

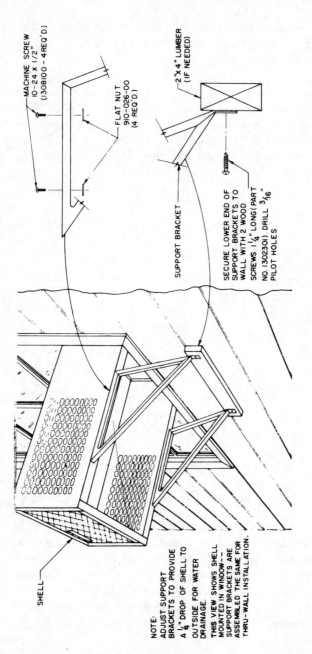

MACHINE SCREW
10-24 X 1/2"
(130BI00 - 4 REQ'D.)

FLAT NUT
910-026-00
(4 REQ'D.)

2"x 4" LUMBER
(IF NEEDED)

SUPPORT BRACKET

SECURE LOWER END OF
SUPPORT BRACKETS TO
WALL WITH 2 WOOD
SCREWS 1 1/4" LONG (PART
NO. 1302301). DRILL 3/16"
PILOT HOLES.

SHELL

NOTE:
ADJUST SUPPORT
BRACKETS TO PROVIDE
A 1/4" DROP OF SHELL TO
OUTSIDE FOR WATER
DRAINAGE.

THIS VIEW SHOWS SHELL
MOUNTED IN WINDOW --
SUPPORT BRACKETS ARE
ASSEMBLED THE SAME FOR
THRU-WALL INSTALLATION.

Fig. 16.

Hardware Required.

Quantity	DESCRIPTION
2	Support brackets
2	No. 12 × 1¼ RH. wood screws
4	10-24 × ½ machine screws
4	10-24 flat nuts
1	36-inch strip foam gasket
2	10 BP × ½ slotted truss head screws
3	8A × 1¼ Phillips head screws
2	8-32 × 1⅛ hex-head self-tapping screws

SERVICING AND TESTING PROCEDURES

Warning: Disconnect electrical power to unit before servicing or testing.

Compressor Test. Remove compressor terminal box cover and disconnect wires from terminals. Using an ohm meter, check across the following. (*See* Fig. 17.)

1. Terminals C and S—no continuity—open start winding—replace compressor.

2. Terminals C and R—no continuity—open run winding—replace compressor.

3. Terminal C and shell of compressor—continuity—grounded motor—replace compressor.

Note: If a new compressor is hard to start due to being stiff, the problem may be solved by wiring a capacitor in parallel with the run capacitor. If the compressor starts consistently after that, leave the capacitor on the unit or replace both capacitors with one that is larger than the original capacitor.

Thermal Overload Test (Compressor—external type).

1. Remove overload.

2. Allow time for overload to reset before attempting to test.

3. Apply ohm meter probes to terminals on overload wires. There should be continuity through the overload.

Fan Motor Test.

1. Determine that capacitor is serviceable.

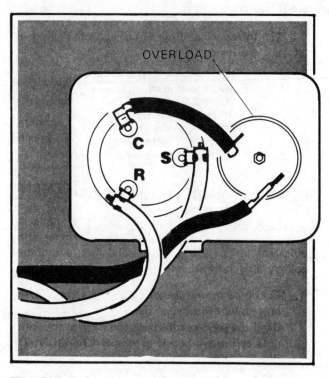

Fig. 17.

2. Disconnect fan motor wires from control switch.

3. Using a *live* test cord, apply test cord probes on black wire and (C) common terminal of capacitor. Motor should run at high speed.

4. Apply *live* test cord probes on red wire and (C) common terminal at capacitor. Motor should run at low speed.

Servicing and oiling. After the first year, add 30 drops of SAE No. 20 grade oil (non-detergent) and every year thereafter.

Capacitor Test.

1. Remove capacitor from unit.

2. Check for visual damages or defects such as bulges, cracks, or oil leaks.

3. Apply one ohm meter probe to (C) common terminal and the other probe to (HERM) compressor side terminal. The ohm meter needle should jump, then gradually move back to infinity.

4. Reverse probes. Ohm meter should react the same as in step 3.

5. Repeat steps 3 and 4, applying probe to fan motor terminal instead of compressor side terminal.

6. Apply one ohm meter probe to capacitor case and the other probe to each of the capacitor terminals. In each instance there should be an infinity reading on the ohm meter.

System Control Switch—Fan speed test.   *See* Fig. 18.

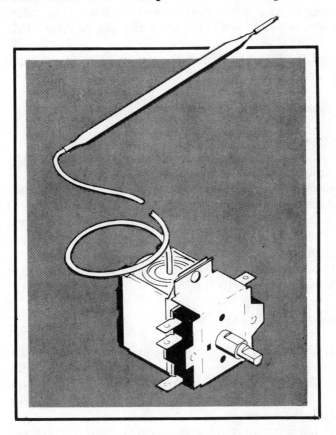

Fig. 18.

1. Disconnect wires from switch.
2. There must be continuity as follows:
    (a) Low fan position—between terminals 1 and B.
    (b) High fan position—between terminals 1 and A.
    (c) Low cool position—between terminals 1 and B, 1 and D.
    (d) High cool position—between terminals 1 and A, 1 and D.

This is a combination on-off switch, fan-speed switch, and thermostat. *To test thermostat*, check continuity between terminals 1 and 2 while turning knob through entire range and listening for a click indicating contacts have either opened or closed. The range of the thermostat is 65° F. to 85° F., with a four-degree differential.

Sealed Refrigeration System Repairs.   Equipment required for repairs are as follows:

Voltmeter
Ammeter
Ohm meter
Vacuum pump (capable of 200 microns or less vacuum)
Acetylene welder
Electronic Halogen leak detector (G.E. type H-6 or equivalent)
Accurate refrigerant charge measuring device such as: (1) Balance scales—½ ounce accuracy, (2) changing board—½ ounce accuracy.
High pressure gage (0–400 pounds)
Low pressure gage (30 inches–150 pounds)
Vacuum gage (0–1000 microns)

Equipment must be capable of:

1. Evacuation from both the highside and lowside of the system simultaneously.
2. Introducing refrigerant charge into highside of the system.
3. Accurately weighing the refrigerant charge actually introduced into the system.
4. Facilities for flowing nitrogen through refrigeration tubing during all brazing processes.

HERMETIC COMPONENT REPLACEMENT

The following procedure applies where replacing components in the sealed refrigeration circuit or repairing refrigerant leaks (compressor, condenser, evaporator, capillary tube, refrigerant leaks, and the like).

1. Discharge the refrigerant from the system at the process tube located on the highside of the system. Bend the process tube back and forth at the crimp until the refrigerant begins to escape. *Caution:* Do this operation slowly and cease the instant that the freon starts escaping. This will prevent rapid boiling of the refrigerant to reduce the amount of oil released. Place a cloth around the break point on the process tube to absorb any oil that might have mixed with refrigerant.

2. Break the process tube at the pinch-off on the suction side of the compressor.

3. Connect the line from the nitrogen tank to the suction process tube.

4. Drift dry nitrogen through the system. Unsolder the more distant connection first (filter drier, highside process tube, and so on).

5. Replace inoperative component, and always install the new filter-drier. Drift dry nitrogen through the system when making these connections.

6. Pressurize system to 30 pounds per square inch gage (psig) with proper refrigerant, and boost refrigerant pressure to 150 psig with dry nitrogen.

7. Leak-test complete system with electric halogen leak detector, correcting any leaks found.

8. Reduce the system to zero gage pressure.

9. Connect vacuum pump to highside and lowside of system with deep vacuum hoses, or copper tubing. (Do not use regular hoses.)

10. Evacuate system to maximum absolute holding pressure of 200 microns or less. *Note:* This process can be speeded up by the use of heat lamps, or by breaking the vacuum with refrigerant or dry nitrogen at 5,000 microns. Pressure the system to 5 psig and leave in the system for a minimum of 10 minutes. Release the refrigerant, and proceed with evacuation of a pressure of 200 microns or less.

11. Break vacuum by charging system from the highside with the correct amount of refrigerant specified. This will prevent boiling

the oil out of the crankcase. *Note:* If the entire charge will not enter the highside, allow the remainder to enter the lowside in small increments while operating the unit.

12. Check the system's operation.

13. Restart unit several times after allowing pressures to stabilize. Pinch off process tubes, cut and solder the ends. Remove pinch-off tool, and leak-check the process tube ends.

SPECIAL PROCEDURE IN CASE OF MOTOR COMPRESSOR BURN-OUT

1. Discharge all refrigerant and oil from the system.

2. Remove compressor, capillary tube, and filter-drier from the system.

3. Flush evaporator condenser and all connecting tubing with R12, or equivalent, to remove all contamination from system. Inspect suction and discharge line for carbon deposits. Remove and clean if necessary.

4. Reassemble the system, including new drier-strainer and capillary tube.

5. Proceed with processing as outlined under Hermetic Component Replacement section.

Chapter 16

Component Replacement and Maintenance of Room Air Conditioners

COMPONENT REPLACEMENT

Systematic servicing is a logical series of steps to follow in analyzing a problem in an air conditioning system with a minimum amount of lost time or call backs. Every possible source of trouble is checked to prevent the use of unnecessary material and to be assured that the system will operate satisfactorily.

To analyze a cooling system systematically, there are five basic areas that must be checked: (1) Evaporator, (2) condenser, (3) compressor, (4) metering devices, and (5) electrical components. (*See* Fig. 1.)

There is no set order in which you would check out a system, as the type of complaint would determine your starting point. For instance, if the unit ran all of the time and did not produce sufficient cooling, you would not start at the condenser blower motor. A complete system check would include all of the check points. The initial complaint would indicate what area you would start your check. All check points in that area would be made prior to starting in another area. If you suspect a low refrigerant charge and you notice a loose fan belt while checking the superheat, you would correct this before making any further checks.

Your job would not be complete if you found a defective expansion valve and did not check the compressor. The defective expansion valve may have allowed the refrigerant to flood back and damage the compressor. If the compressor was damaged, it would save time and material to replace it at the same time the expansion valve was being replaced. A costly service call would be prevented.

Fig. 1. Components of air conditioner.

Systematic servicing is habit forming. It is one habit you cannot afford to be without.

Basic Tools.   The following basic tools are required to properly service residential cooling units.

Good tools and equipment require a substantial investment. Failure to use the correct tool while troubleshooting or making a repair is time-consuming and in most cases does not get the job done. (*See* Fig. 2.)

Fig. 2. Basic tools required.

Volt-ohm meter	Charging manifold with gages
Capacitor tester	Vacuum pump
Scales	Thermometers
AMP meter (snap-on)	Potentiometer
Oil sample test kit	Leak detectors
Oil sampler	Halide torch
Refrigerant 22	Electronic
Flaring tools	Soap bubbles
Manometer	Assorted hand tools
Refrigerant valve wrenches	Tachometer

Fan Motor Replacement.

1. Remove the cabinet.

2. Remove the condenser mounting screws and bend up the clip that holds the capillary line in position.

3. Lift the condenser to clear the base pan and pull forward approximately three inches. *Caution:* Do not kink tubing.

4. Loosen the Allen set screw in the condenser fan hub and slide the fan from the shaft.

5. Remove the air deflector assembly.

6. Remove the electric control panel mounting screws and pull the assembly out of position so that the motor lead terminals can be disconnected and the fan motor wires can be pulled into the unit compartment.

7. Remove the evaporator mounting screws.

8. Lift the evaporator three inches and slide it out of the mounting position, then swing the evaporator away from the base. *Caution:* Do not kink tubing.

9. Loosen the Allen set screw in the evaporator fan hub.

10. Remove and discard the through bolt, which passes through the motor mount into a weld nut that is welded into the bulkhead.

11. Remove the motor-mounting hold-down bolt.

12. Remove the fan motor and reinstall the motor onto the new fan motor.

13. Reverse procedure for installing the new fan motor.

Switch and Thermostat Replacement.

1. Disconnect power cord; remove front panel and filter.

2. Remove control knobs and control plate.

3. Remove air discharge louvers and pull control-mounting bracket out to gain access to thermostat and switch.

4. Remove wires and mounting screws on the part to be replaced and remove part.

5. Reverse procedure to install new part.

Run Capacitor Replacement.

1. Disconnect power cord; remove front panel and filter.

2. Remove control knobs, control plate, and air discharge louvers.

3. Pull control-mounting bracket out to gain access to run capacitor.

4. Remove wires and capacitor clamp; then remove capacitor.

5. Reverse procedure to install new capacitor.

Overload Replacement.

1. Disconnect power cord; remove front panel and filter.

2. Remove complete air conditioner from the installation. *Caution:* Check the condensate level in the base pan; if the water level is high keep the base pan level to avoid spilling water on the floor.

3. Remove the cabinet from the air conditioner.

4. Remove the compressor terminal cover to gain access to the overload.

5. Remove the wires and overload lock spring and remove the overload.

6. Reverse procedure to install new overload.

Condenser Fan Replacement.

1. Remove the cabinet.

2. Remove the condenser mounting screws and bend the clip that holds the capillary line in position.

3. Lift the condenser to clear the base pan and pull forward approximately three inches. *Caution:* Do not kink tubing.

4. Loosen the Allen set screw in the condenser fan hub and slide the fan from the shaft.

5. Reverse procedure to install the condenser fan.

6. *See* Fig. 3 for correct positioning of the condenser fan.

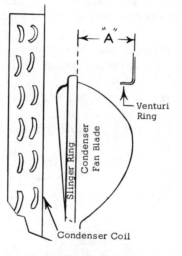

Fig. 3. Positioning condenser fan.

Evaporator Fan Replacement.

1. Remove the cabinet.

2. Remove the condenser mounting screws and bend up the clip that holds the capillary line in position.

3. Lift the condenser to clear the base pan and pull forward approximately three inches. *Caution:* Do not kink tubing.

4. Loosen the Allen set screw in the condenser fan hub and slide the fan from the shaft.

5. Remove the air deflector assembly.

6. Remove the evaporator mounting screws.

7. Lift the evaporator two inches and slide it out of the mounting position; swing the evaporator away from the base. *Caution:* Do not kink tubing.

8. Remove the through bolt, which passes through the motor mount into a weld nut that is welded into the bulkhead.

9. Remove the motor-mount hold-down bolt.

10. Loosen the Allen set screw in the evaporator fan hub.

11. Remove the scroll mounting screws and release the two tabs that are bent over the top flange of the bulkhead.

12. Pull the motor shaft from the evaporator fan.

13. Remove the fan motor and reinstall the motor mount onto the new fan motor.

14. Remove the scroll from the chassis and install the new one. Be sure the new scroll has permagum on the flanges to form a seal against the bulkhead.

15. Replace the evaporator fan and reverse the procedure to reassemble.

16. *See* Fig. 4 for correct positioning of the evaporator fan.

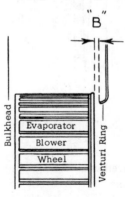

Fig. 4. Positioning
evaporator fan.

Evaporator Fan Scroll Replacement.
1. Remove the rear casing (cabinet).
2. Remove the air deflector assembly.
3. Remove the evaporator mounting screws.

4. Lift the evaporator three inches and slide out of mounting position. Swing the evaporator away from the chassis. *Caution:* Do not kink tubing.

5. Remove the scroll mounting screws and release the two tabs that are bent over the top flange of the bulkhead.

6. Remove the scroll from the chassis and install the new one. Be sure the new scroll has permagum on the flanges to form a seal against the bulkhead.

7. Reverse procedure to install the new scroll.

Drain Pan Replacement.

1. Remove the rear casing (cabinet).

2. Remove the air deflector assembly.

3. Remove the evaporator mounting screws.

4. Lift the evaporator three inches and slide out of mounting position. Swing the evaporator away from the chassis. *Caution:* Do not kink tubing.

5. Remove the scroll as outlined in evaporator fan scroll replacement.

6. Pull the drain pan from the base.

7. Put in the new drain pan. Be sure the hose has permagum packed around it to insure a watertight seal between the hose and drain pan.

8. Reverse procedure to install the new drain pan as outlined in steps 1 through 5.

MAINTENANCE

Fan Motor Lubrication.   The fan motors are equipped with oiler tubes (Fig. 5). The recommended type of oil is SAE No. 20 weight of a non-detergent type. A detergent-type oil must *not* be used.

The fan motors have oilite bearings and a detergent oil can ruin the oil absorbing quality of bearings.

The motors should be oiled at the beginning of each cooling season or every six months.

If your motor does not have oiler tubes it has a lasting lubricant and therefore requires little attention.

Caution: Do not over-oil as the reservoir may overflow and damage

OILER TUBE

OILER TUBE

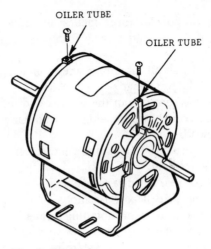

Fig. 5. Oiler tubes.

the motor. Add five or six drops of oil to each bearing. Be sure to replace the oiler plugs to keep water and dirt from getting into the fan motor bearings.

Cleaning of Filter.

1. Remove front panel.

2. For an extremely dirty filter, remove bulk of dirt with a vacuum cleaner.

3. Wash filter in a solution of warm water and mild liquid detergent.

4. Flush filter with clear water after each washing.

5. Shake the excess water from filter and allow to dry.

Caution: Do not use bleach solutions or dry detergents to clean filters. *Never operate air conditioner for extended periods of time without filter.*

Cleaning of Front Panel.   All plastic front panels should be cleaned with warm—not hot—soapy water; then rinsed and dried. *Do not* use cleanser or solvents.

Cleaning of Condenser Coil.   The condenser coil must be kept clean for the air conditioning system to operate at full efficiency. The location of this coil exposes it to dust, dirt, and air-borne foreign material that may clog the coil if it is not inspected and cleaned at regular intervals. The dust, dirt, and air-borne foreign material will collect on the back side of the condenser coil and may go unnoticed as the outside of the coil will be clean. The condenser coil may be cleaned with a stiff brush and a regular household vacuum cleaner.

How to gain access to the condenser coil for cleaning.

1. Disconnect power cord and remove the front panel.

2. Check the condensate level in the base pan. If the condensate is high, keep the air conditioner level when removing it from the installation.

3. Remove the air conditioner from the installation and remove the cabinet to gain access to the condenser coil for cleaning.

Chapter 17

Fans

There are two types of cooling fans available—room fans, and attic and window fans.

Room fans stir up the air. The temperature inside your house can be several degrees cooler than outside, but it can seem warmer if the air does not move. Also, air movement increases moisture evaporation, and moisture evaporation cools the body, or skin surfaces.

A good *room fan* has large blades, turns at about 1,000 revolutions per minute (rpm) (it may have a speed adjustment), operates quietly, and has an oscillating mechanism.

Attic and *window fans* exchange inside air for outside air. You can use them for night cooling, or whenever the temperature inside your home is greater than the temperature outside. A time switch can be installed in the electrical circuit to your fan to cut it off automatically at any time you desire. When you have cooled your house at night, keep the windows and doors closed during the next day as long as it is cooler inside than it is out.

You will find that *window fans* are easier to install than attic fans— no construction is required—but you will also find that they are usually noisier.

Fans are rated by the amount of air they move in cubic feet per minute (cfm). Fans rated by an association are more likely to deliver approximately the quantities of air stated.

For best results, you will need the help of an engineer in determining the size of *attic* or *window fan* needed for your house (some retail dealers provide the services of a trained technician). The air inlets and outlets, the horsepower of the fan motor, and the revolutions per minute of the fan blade all should be taken into consideration. However, you can determine the approximate size yourself and probably get satisfactory results.

To determine the size fan you will need, proceed as follows:

1. Find the volume of the area you want to cool. Multiply the length of the rooms by the width. Then multiply that by the height.

2. If you live in the dark area of the map (Fig. 1), divide the volume by 1.5. This will give you a minimum cfm requirement. If you live in the undotted area, your minimum cfm requirement will be the same as the volume you want cooled.

3. Pick a fan that has a cfm requirement—a larger rating will allow for slight differences in test procedure and efficiency.

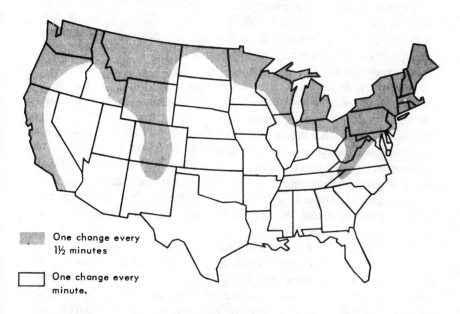

One change every
1½ minutes

One change every
minute.

Fig. 1. Minimum air changes recommended for fan cooling.

If you choose a fan that is driven with pulleys and a belt, rather than one that is driven directly by the motor, the size of the pulleys can be varied slightly to adjust the amount of air moved. Models with 2- and 3-speed motors are also available.

Normally, a ⅓-horsepower, 36-inch attic fan will provide 40 air changes per hour for the average three-bedroom house. This is sufficient ventilation in the dark area (Fig. 1).

A larger attic fan is required in the white area (Fig. 1)—a ⅓- or ½-horsepower, 42-inch fan that will normally provide 60 air changes per hour for the average three-bedroom house.

Window fans are usually smaller. They range in size from 20 to 30 inches. The 20-inch size is the most popular. It will generally provide about 15 to 20 air changes per hour for the average three-bedroom house.

When cooling with a fan, you should close off any portion of the house that you do not wish to cool; otherwise, the fan will not provide the proper number of air changes per unit time.

You can also remove accumulated attic heat during the day with an attic fan. Often an attic is 25 degrees or more hotter than outside; even if the ceiling of your house is insulated, this additional heat will warm your house.

When you remove attic heat with an attic fan during the day, close the attic off from the rest of your house. Otherwise the fan will draw hot, outside air into your house.

Suppose you decide to cool your home with an evaporative cooler (cooling with water) or air conditioning, but wish to ventilate the attic anyway. A fan—smaller than the usual size attic fan—will do that; it should be capable of changing the air in the attic at least once per minute, and should operate continuously when the temperature in the attic exceeds 110° F. It may be controlled by thermostat, time clock, or manual switch.

Cooling with fans has some disadvantages. Dust and pollen are likely to be drawn into your home. Fans are noisy. The cost of a good attic fan plus installation may be as much as a room air conditioner. While the attic fan may cool the entire house in some areas at night, it may not help much during the day because of high outside air temperatures. And remember, a fan will cool your house to only approximately the temperature of the outside air. On the other hand, the room conditioner will usually cool only one or two rooms, but it will cool during the day and night.

Chapter 18

Humidifiers, Air Cleaners, and Dehumidifiers

HUMIDIFIERS

A humidifier is a self-contained appliance that is used to increase the humidity within the space of operation.

Dry room air is drawn into the back of the humidifier by means of the circulating fan. This air passes through the water-saturated vaporizer-filter. The filter rotates through the water reservoir on a revolving drum. As the dry air passes through this material, needed moisture is absorbed. This results in increased relative humidity within the enclosed space.

OPERATION

Humidistat. The humidistat automatically opens and closes the electrical circuit according to the percent of relative humidity and the position of the humidistat setting.

When the humidifier is placed in operation, it may operate continuously or have short off-and-on cycles for several days. This is normal. The space that is to be humidified, plus the walls, furnishings, drapes, carpet, and the like, will absorb moisture from the humidified air. When all of these articles have absorbed moisture and no longer pull it from the air, the humidistat will cycle off-and-on in accordance with the control setting and maintain the desired level of humidity.

If you are not comfortable and want either more or less moisture in the air, turn the control setting to a higher or lower setting.

Air Flow Control and Selector Switch. Units equipped with variable speed controls allow you to select the correct fan speed suitable for maintaining the correct humidity output for existing conditions.

MAINTENANCE

Fan Motor.   It is recommended that approximately four drops of SAE No. 20 non-detergent motor oil be added to the front and back bearings at the beginning of each operating season.

Drum Drive Motor.   The drum drive motor has a sealed lubricant and doesn't require the user's attention. This motor is bi-directional and when starting will rotate either clockwise or counterclockwise.

Cleaning of Water Container.   *See* wiring diagrams shown in Figs. 1 and 2. *See also* Figs. 11 and 12, showing parts and parts lists.

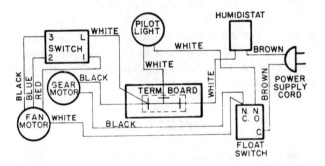

Fig. 1.

Clean container as follows:

1. Disconnect unit from power supply.

2. Remove evaporator drum from unit by lifting up slightly and moving it forward, against front of cabinet. This will disengage the drum from the drive and idler pulleys. Remove by carefully lifting straight up.

3. Reach down through top of unit, lift up float arm, and hook in slot.

4. Unlatch the lower back panel and swing it down. The container may now be pulled out.

5. When replacing water container, make certain the drum guide

(post in bottom of container) is toward back of unit.

Note: Be sure and unhook float arm before returning unit to operation.

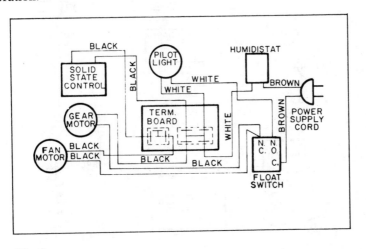

Fig. 2.

For cleaning containers see wiring diagrams shown in Figs. 1, 3, and 4. *See* also Figs. 8, 9, and 10, and proceed as follows:

1. Disconnect unit from power supply.

2. Lift straight up on complete unit, and water container will remain on floor.

3. Remove evaporator drum from unit by lifting up slightly and moving it forward against front of cabinet. This will disengage the drum from the drive and idler pulleys. Remove by carefully lifting straight up.

4. Raise float arm and hook in slot (Figs. 4, 5, 9, and 10).

5. Clean container and carefully replace unit and drum wheel.

Note: Be sure and unhook float (Figs. 4, 5, 9, and 10) before returning to operation.

Exterior Finish. The exterior finish requires only an occasional wiping with a soft, damp cloth. If desired, regular household furniture wax may be applied.

Vaporizer-Filter. The vaporizer-filter, which is stretched over the perimeter of the rotating drum, cleans and moistens the air passing

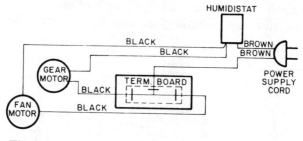

Fig. 3.

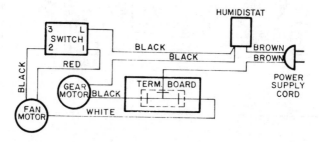

Fig. 4.

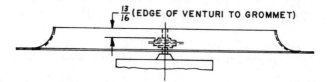

Fig. 5.

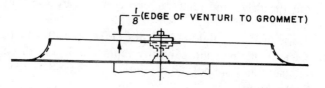

Fig. 6.

through it. The accumulation of foreign material from the air and mineral deposits from the water will require periodic replacement of this filter. Providing your humidifier runs constantly, a noticeable

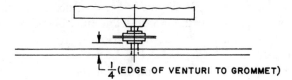

$\frac{1}{4}$(EDGE OF VENTURI TO GROMMET)

Fig. 7.

decrease in water consumption or the symptoms of low humidity in your home (such as static electric shock) are indications that the vaporizer-filter pad should be replaced.

The frequency with which this replacement is required will naturally vary, according to local water conditions. The accumulation of minerals on the exterior of the filter does not necessarily mean that replacement is required or that the efficiency of the unit is seriously impaired.

ELECTRICAL SYSTEM TESTS

Humidistat.   Turn the humidistat control knob to the highest position. If the unit is connected to the power source and the water container is full but the unit will not run, connect an insulated jumper wire between the two terminals on the humidistat. If the unit then runs, the humidistat is defective and must be replaced.

Refill and Signal Light Control Switch.   Models shown in Figs. 10, 11, and 12 are equipped with a refill switch.

The switch is mounted on the back of the control panel and is actuated by the float arm assembly. It is a double-action-type switch. The contacts that control the refill signal light are open until the water container is empty. When the water container is empty, the float arm actuates the switch causing the contacts to the refill light to close, and the contacts to the motor to open. Thus the light will be on and the unit will shut off. The humidifier will remain off, and the refill signal light on, until the water container is filled.

Fan Motor.   If the fan blade spins freely, test for electrical failure. If the fan blade does not turn freely, the motor bearing may be set up. Check the electrical connections to make sure that all connections between power source and the motor are good.

To test the fan motor windings, disconnect motor leads from the terminal board. Check the continuity of the windings with a test light or an ohm meter. An open circuit indicates a defective winding or a broken connection inside the motor. Continuity between the windings and the frame indicate an internal short or ground and the motor must be replaced.

Refill Signal Light.   The function of the refill signal light is to signal when the water container is empty. The signal light will remain on when the water container is empty and the humidistat is calling for humidification. If the refill signal light fails to light when the water container is empty and the humidistat contacts are closed, proceed to test as follows:

1. Disconnect the service cord from the power supply.

2. Remove the louvered back panel to gain access to the control panel.

3. Remove the signal light wires from the terminal board and float switch.

4. Test for continuity at the refill signal light blade.

5. If this test does not show continuity, the light assembly must be replaced.

6. If the above test shows continuity, check the humidistat and float switch.

Air Flow Speed Control.   The function of the speed control is to vary the fan speed. The float switch contacts must be closed to complete the circuit through the speed control to operate the fan motor.

After checking the fan motor as previously outlined in this section and the above conditions exist, remove the speed control leads from the terminal board.

1. Connect the speed control in series with a 75-watt light bulb. Turn the control to low and record the voltage with a Weston No. 433 voltmeter. Voltage should read approximately 94 volts.

2. If the speed control has a lower voltage drop, or an open circuit under load, it would indicate a defective control and it must be replaced.

Selector Switch.   When testing selector switch on model shown in Fig. 9, proceed as follows:

1. Remove the connecting wires from the switch.

2. Turn switch to low position. Continuity should be between terminals L and 1 only.

3. Turn the switch to high position. Continuity should be be-

tween terminals L and 2 only. Number 3 terminal on switch is not used.

When testing selector switch on models shown in Figs. 11 and 12, proceed as follows:

1. Remove the connecting wires from the switch.
2. Turn the switch to low position. Continuity should be between terminals L and 1 only. Turn switch to medium position. Continuity should be between terminals L and 2 only. Turn switch to high position. Continuity should be between terminals L and 3 only.

Drum Drive Motor.   Check the electrical connection to make sure that all electrical connections between power source and the motor are good.

To test the drum drive motor, check voltage between terminal connections. (Humidistat contact must be closed.) Check continuity of the windings with a test light or ohm meter. An open circuit indicates a defective winding. Continuity between windings and frame indicates an internal short or ground, and the motor must be replaced.

If continuity tests check out and the motor shaft fails to turn when proper voltage is applied, it would indicate defective gears and the motor must be replaced.

Note: Extreme care must be taken *not* to turn shaft by hand since this will damage gears.

COMPONENT REPLACEMENT

Electrical Components.   All electrical components are equipped with plug in quick connectors.
See Figs. 1, 2, 11, and 12.

1. Disconnect power supply cord.
2. Remove the back louvered panel to expose the electrical components for replacement.

See Figs. 1, 3, 4, 8, and 9.

1. Disconnect power supply cord.
2. Remove all knobs from controls. Remove screws from electrical cover. On models shown in Figs. 9 and 10, raise float lever arm and hook in slot before removing screws from electrical cover.

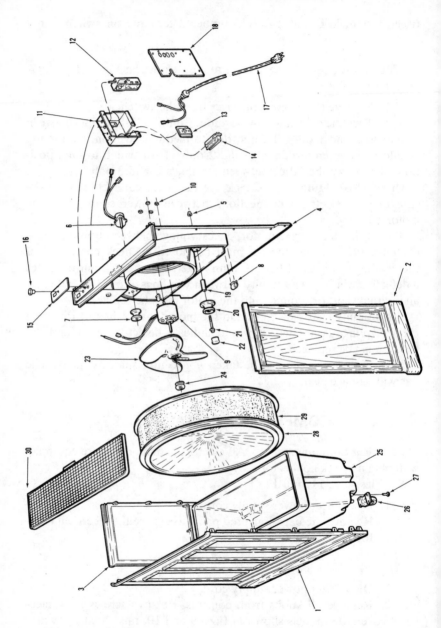

SPECIFICATION CHART

MODEL					
Volts – Hertz	120-60	120-60	120-60	120-60	120-60
Watts	68	88	88	75	85
Fan Motor	1 Speed	2 Speed	3 Speed	3 Speed	Variable
Fan Motor RPM – High Speed	1150	1400	1400	1400	1400
Fan Motor RPM – Med. Speed	–	–	1150	1150	–
Fan Motor RPM – Low Speed	–	900	900	900	700
Air Volume CFM – High	265	325	325	375	385
Air Volume CFM – Med.	–	–	250	300	–
Air Volume CFM – Low	–	200	200	225	175
Normal Tank Capacity – Gals.	7.5	7.5	7.5	10	10
Gear Motor RPM	4	4	4	4	4
Drum Speed RPM	1 Foot Per Minute	1 Foot Per Minute		1 Ft. Per Min.	1 Ft. Per Min.
Variable Air Flow Switch	No	No	No	No	Yes
Humidistat	Yes	Yes	Yes	Yes	Yes
Refill Signal Light	No	No	Yes	Yes	Yes
Top Fill	Yes	Yes	Yes	Yes	Yes
Water Level Indicator	No	Yes	Yes	Yes	Yes

Fig. 8. Humidifier. (1) Front panel (2) Side panel (right) (3) Side panel (left) (4) Back panel (5) Nut-stud (idler roller) (6) Gear motor (7) Drive roller (8) Clip "U" type (drum guide) (9) Fan motor (10) Whiz lock nut (fan motor) (11) Control housing (12) Humidistat (13) Terminal board (14) Strain relief (15) Control plate (16) Knob (humidistat) (17) Power supply cord (18) Control cover (19) Sleeve (idler roller) (20) Idler roller (21) Screw (idler roller) (22) Cap (idler roller) (23) Fan blade (24) Grommet (fan mounting) (25) Water container (26) Caster (27) Screw (caster) (28) Evaporating drum assembly (29) Filter (30) Grille

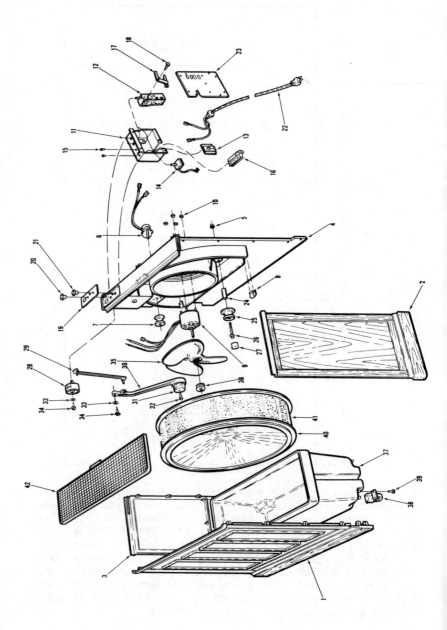

Fig. 9. Humidifier. (1) Front panel (2) Side panel (right) (3) Side panel (left) (4) Back panel (5) Stud nut (idler roller) (6) Gear motor (7) Drive roller (8) Clip "U" type drum guide (9) Fan motor (10) Whiz lock nut (fan motor) (11) Control housing (12) Humidistat (13) Terminal board (14) Switch (2-speed) (15) Screw (switch) (16) Strain relief (17) Arm-humidistat shut-off (18) Shoulder bolt (arm) (19) Control plate (20) Knob (humidistat) (21) Knob (switch) (22) Power supply cord (23) Control cover (24) Sleeve (idler roller) (25) Idler roller (26) Screw (idler roller) (27) Cap (idler roller) (28) Indicator (float) (29) Tie bar (float indicator and lever) (30) Float lever (31) Float (32) Screw (33) Washer (float indicator and lever) (34) Screw (float indicator and lever) (35) Fan blade (36) Grommet (fan mounting) (37) Water container (38) Caster (39) Screw (caster) (40) Evaporating drum assembly (41) Filter (42) Grille

3. Remove electrical cover. *Note:* When replacing humidistat (Fig. 9), remove plastic arm that actuates the humidistat when the water pan is empty.

Fan Motor.   *See* Figs. 1 and 5; *see also* Figs. 2 and 6.

1. Disconnect power supply cord.

2. Remove louvered panel and hinged top.

3. Remove the plastic fill spout from left side of unit by lifting straight up.

4. Remove drum by lifting up slightly before moving it forward against front of cabinet to disengage from pulleys. When drum is disengaged, lift straight up.

5. Remove fan blade. (*See* Figs. 5 and 6 for location of fan grommet when reassembled.)

6. Unplug motor leads from terminal board.

7. Remove motor mounting nuts.

8. Place new motor in position and reverse steps 1 through 7 to reassemble.

See Figs. 8, 9, and 10.

1. Disconnect power supply cord.

2. Remove drum by lifting up slightly before moving it forward against front of cabinet to disengage it from pulleys. When drum is disengaged, lift straight up.

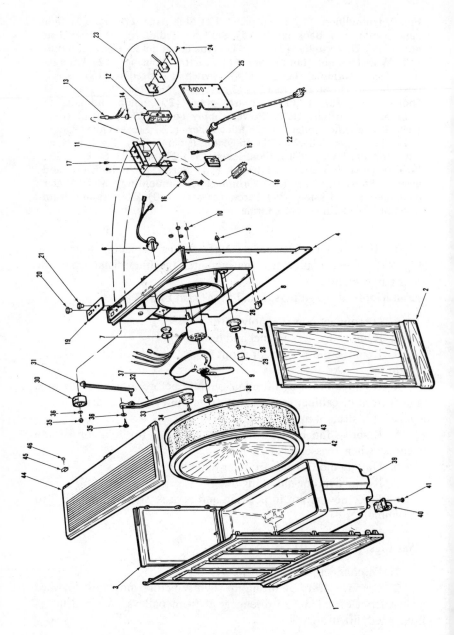

Fig. 10. Humidifier. (1) Front panel (2) Side panel (right) (3) Side panel (left) (4) Back panel (5) Stud nut (idler roller) (6) Gear motor (7) Drive roller (8) Clip "U" type (drum guide) (9) Fan motor (10) Whiz lock nut (fan motor) (11) Control housing (12) Humidistat (13) Refill light (14) Push nut (refill light) (15) Terminal board (16) Switch (17) Screw (switch) (18) Strain relief (19) Control plate (20) Knob (humidistat) (21) Knob (switch) (22) Power supply cord (23) Float switch assembly (24) Screw (switch to humidistat) (25) Control cover (26) Sleeve (idler roller) (27) Idler roller (28) Screw (idler roller) (29) Cap (idler roller) (30) Float indicator (31) Tie bar (float indicator and lever) (32) Float lever (33) Float (34) Screw (float) (35) Washer (float indicator and lever) (36) Screw (float indicator and lever) (37) Fan blade (38) Grommet (fan mounting) (39) Water container (40) Caster (41) Screw (42) Evaporating drum assembly (43) Filter (44) Top panel (45) Nut (46) Screw

3. Remove fan blade. (*See* Fig. 7 for location of fan grommet when reassembled.)

4. Remove electrical cover from back panel and disconnect motor.

5. Remove four nuts holding motor to grille.

6. Place new motor in position and reverse procedure to reassemble.

Fan Blade.

1. Disconnect power supply cord. Raise or remove top.

2. On models shown in Figs. 11 and 12, and in Figs. 1 and 2, wiring diagrams, remove plastic fill spout from left side of unit by lifting straight up.

3. Remove drum by lifting up slightly before moving it forward against front of cabinet to disengage it from pulleys. When drum is disengaged, lift straight up.

4. Slide fan blade and grommet off motor shaft. (*See* Fig. 7 for location of fan grommet when reassembled.

5. Place new fan blade and grommet in position and reverse procedure to reassemble.

Vaporizer Filter.

1. Disconnect power supply cord. Raise or remove top.

2. Remove plastic fill spout from left side of unit by lifting straight up (Figs. 11 and 12).

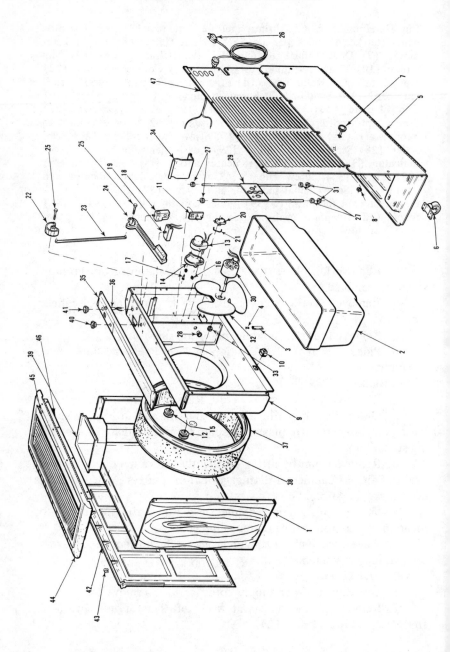

Fig. 11. Humidifier. (1) Cabinet wrap (2) Water container (3) Wear shield (4) Push rivet (5) Bottom panel assembly (6) Caster (7) Knob latch (8) Latch washer (9) Venturi housing assembly (10) Latch receptacle (11) Terminal board (12) Idler roller (13) Gear motor (14) Vibration dampener (motor) (15) Driver roller (16) Spacer (17) Screw—shoulder (18) Humidistat (19) Switch (20) Float switch (21) Retainer wire (switch) (22) Float indicator (23) Tie bar (float indicator) (24) Float lever assembly (25) Shoulder screw (float lever) (26) Power supply cord (27) Grommet (fan motor bracket) (28) Bushing (motor baffle) (29) Fan motor bracket (30) Fan motor (31) Pal nut (fan motor bracket) (32) Fan blade (33) Grommet (fan mounting) (34) Humidistat housing (35) Control panel (36) Refill light (37) Evaporator drum assembly (38) Filter (39) Fill spout assembly (40) Knob (switch) (41) Knob (Humidistat) (42) Front panel (43) Clip "U" (front panel) (44) Top panel (45) Lens (46) Hinge (top panel) (47) Back panel

3. Remove drum by lifting up slightly before moving it forward against front of cabinet to disengage from pulleys. When drum is disengaged, lift straight up.

4. Remove vaporizer-filter pad—which is stretched over perimeter of drum.

5. Stretch new vaporizer-filter pad over drum and reverse steps 1 through 3 to reassemble. *Be certain* that the inside rim of the drum is resting firmly on the two pulleys. (*See* Figs. 8, 9, 10, 11, and 12 showing parts and parts lists.)

PORTABLE DEHUMIDIFIER

To get maximum moisture removal from the air, a *dehumidifier* must move the correct amount of air over the evaporator coils efficiently. It must be able to continue to keep the humidity under control through a wide range of temperatures without icing up, and it must do it quietly.

The dehumidifier shown in Fig. 13 can be moved from room to room with ease. If your unit has rollers, just lift one end of the unit with the built-in handle and roll it anywhere you choose. Most of the weight is concentrated over the wheels.

Features.   The portable dehumidifier shown in Fig. 14 has the following features:

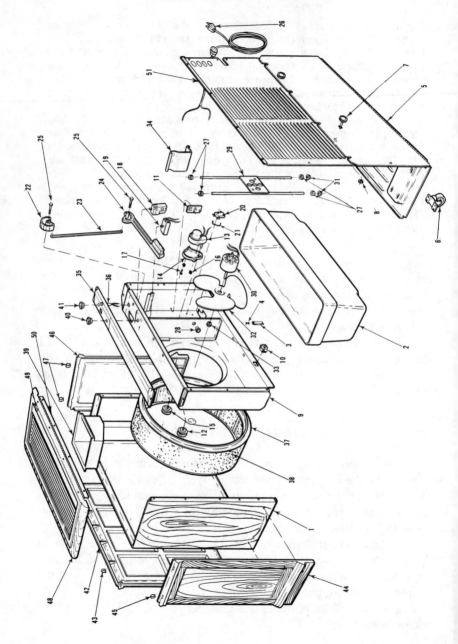

Fig. 12. Humidifier. (1) Cabinet wrap (2) Water container (3) Wear shield (4) Push rivet (5) Bottom panel assembly (6) Caster (7) Knob latch (8) Latch washer (9) Venturi housing assembly (10) Latch receptacle (11) Terminal board (12) Idler roller (13) Gear motor (14) Vibration dampener (motor) (15) Drive roller (16) Spacer (17) Screw—shoulder (18) Humidistat (19) Speed control (20) Float switch (21) Retainer wire (switch) (22) Float indicator (23) Tie bar (float indicator) (24) Float lever assembly (25) Shoulder screw (float lever) (26) Power supply cord (27) Grommet (fan motor bracket) (28) Bushing (motor baffle) (29) Fan motor bracket (30) Fan motor (31) Pal nut (fan motor bracket) (32) Fan blade (33) Grommet (fan mounting) (34) Humidistat housing (35) Control panel (36) Refill light (37) Evaporator drum assembly (38) Filter (39) Fill spout assembly (40) Knob (speed control) (41) Knob (humidistat) (42) Front panel (43) Clip "U" (side panel, right) (44) Side panel assembly (right) (45) Clip "U" (side panel, left) (46) Side panel assembly (left) (47) Clip "U" (side panel, left) (48) Top panel (49) Lens (50) Hinge (top panel) (51) Back panel

1. A powerful high speed compressor designed to give you top performance even under extreme conditions. It is internally spring-mounted to eliminate natural vibrations. Low current consumption makes it economical to operate.

2. A large, low speed fan that moves volumes of air over the evaporator coils slowly enough to allow the maximum amount of moisture to be removed from the air.

3. An air control shroud that directs all air over evaporator coils and puts more moisture-laden air in direct contact with moisture-removing coils.

4. All copper condenser coils with aluminum fins that provide longer life. Air-conditioner-type condenser is more efficient, gives greater capacity.

5. All copper evaporator coils. Puts more coiling (up to $34\frac{1}{2}$ feet) directly in the air stream.

INSTALLATION

Warning: Do not under any circumstances cut or remove the round grounding prong from the plug. (*See* Fig. 15.)

The appliance shown in Fig. 13 is equipped with a three-prong

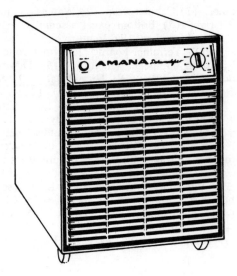

Fig. 13.

grounding plug for your protection against possible shock hazards. Where a two-prong wall receptacle is encountered, it is the personal responsibility and obligation of the customer to contact a qualified electrician and have it replaced with a properly grounded three-prong wall receptacle in accordance with the National Electrical Code.

Where a two-prong adaptor is required temporarily, it is your personal responsibility and obligation to contact a qualified electrician and have the adaptor properly grounded and polarized.

ELECTRICAL REQUIREMENTS

Most dehumidifiers are furnished with an eight-foot cord. The voltage of the electrical outlet must correspond with the requirements shown on the serial number and data plate. Voltage requirement is 115 volts, single-phase, 60 cycle.

LOCATION

The dehumidifier should be located in the area where you want to remove excess moisture from the air. In order to get the most efficient and effective use from your dehumidifier, follow these suggestions:

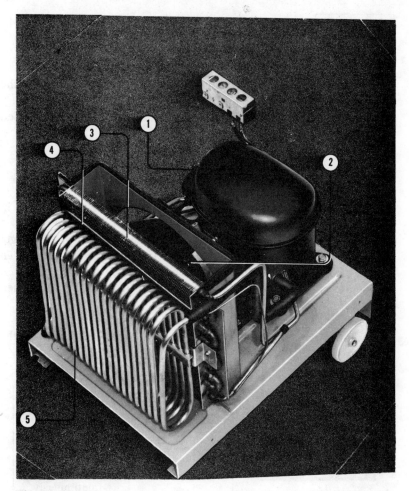

Fig. 14.

1. Locate it at least three feet from the nearest wall to permit free passage of air through the dehumidifier.

2. Close doors and windows to prevent moisture-laden air from entering from the outside.

3. Moisture removed from the air may be disposed of by using the condensate pan provided with the unit; by placing the unit directly

Fig. 15.

over a floor drain; or by attaching a garden or laundry hose to the fitting on the bottom of the unit.

4. When using the condensate pan, it must be emptied periodically.

HUMIDISTAT CONTROL

The humidistat (Fig. 16) employed on the dehumidifier shown in Fig. 13 is very sensitive and controls the relative humidity just as a thermostat controls the temperature. Simply set the control and forget about it. When the humidity in a room increases above the chosen setting, the humidistat will automatically start the unit, and allow it to operate until the humidistat setting is satisfied. The unit will then turn off automatically.

When setting the humidistat, use the chart shown in Fig. 16 as a guide for the amount of relative humidity corresponding to the number on the dial.

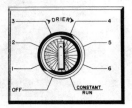

Humidistat Setting	% Relative Humidity
Position #1	70
Position #3	42
Position #5	23
Position #7	Unit Operated Continuously

Fig. 16.

THREE-WAY MOISTURE REMOVAL

Water pan. The dehumidifier comes equipped with a water pan that is set under the chassis inside the cabinet. As moisture is removed from the air it drains into the water pan. If your dehumidifier does not have an overflow control, you will have to empty the pan when it gets about one inch from the top of the pan. If you do not empty it, the water will flow over the top of the pan.

Drain connection. There is a standard drain hose connection on the bottom of the chassis. You can attach a standard hose and drain the water directly to a nearby drain or other area. You should remove the water pan when using the drain hose connection.

Set unit over drain. The entire unit can be set over a drain to allow condensate to flow directly into a drain. The water pan should be removed.

OVERFLOW CONTROL

If your dehumidifier has the overflow control and warning light, the unit will shut itself off when the water in the water pan is about one inch from the top. The warning light on the control on the front of the unit will turn on to tell you the water pan needs to be emptied.

The unit will not operate when the warning light is on. You must empty the water pan and replace it before the unit can continue to dehumidify the air.

OPERATION

The operation of the dehumidifier shown in Fig. 13 is easy to understand. Moisture-laden air enters the unit through the perforated metal section and is passed over the cold tubing. This causes the moisture to be condensed from the air. The dehumidified air then passes across the warm condenser coil, through the fan blades, over the compressor, and out the decorative front. The air that blows out the front of the unit is slightly warmer than the air entering the unit. However, considerable moisture has been removed.

A small amount of frost may build up on the dehumidifier coil during the first 10 to 15 minutes of operation. This frost will disappear, providing the air temperature is above 63° F. Continuous operation in a room temperature below 63° F. may result in a heavy layer of frost on the coil tubing. Under these conditions, little or no moisture is deposited into the condensate pan. This layer of frost will not damage the unit.

MAINTENANCE

Proper care and maintenance of your dehumidifier will ensure long life and trouble-free service. The compressor and refrigeration system is of the hermetically-sealed type and requires no oiling. The fan motor is oiled at the factory. It should be oiled once a year with 5 to 10 drops of SAE No. 20 oil. *Do not* use an excessive amount of oil. To oil the fan motor, the chassis must be removed from the outer shell by removing the necessary screws, control knob, and discharge air front, and disengaging the humidistat from its normal location.

To remove chassis from outer case use the following procedure.

1. Pull plug from electrical outlet.
2. Remove drain pan.
3. Remove control knob.
4. Remove six screws each on the side and front, and tilt front forward.
5. Remove humidistat mounting screws. Disconnect warning light wires on all units that have them.
6. Place the humidistat in a location where it cannot be damaged.
7. Pull chassis from outer case.

Use a vacuum cleaner periodically to remove accumulated dust and lint from the front and back of the dehumidifier. It is also advisable to remove the chassis once a year to clean all interior parts.

HUMIDIFIER/AIR CLEANER

The *humidifier/air cleaner* (Fig. 17) is designed to satisfy two home air comfort requirements.

1. Removal of air-borne particles by electrostatic precipitation.
2. Humidity requirements through the principle of evaporation.

Dust, dirt, and dry room air is drawn into the back of the unit by means of the circulating fan. This air first passes through the prefilter, where most of the large visible-to-the-eye matter, mostly lint, is removed. The air then passes through the electronic cell, where the remaining air-borne particles are given an intense electrical charge. As these charged particles continue through the cell, a series of metal

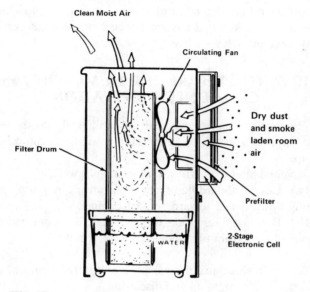

Clean Moist Air

Circulating Fan

Dry dust
and smoke
laden room
air

Filter Drum

Prefilter

2-Stage
Electronic Cell

Fig. 17.

plates, having an opposite electrical charge, attract and collect the particles similar to the way a magnet attracts iron filings. The metal plates hold the particles until they are washed off. (*See* Washing Instructions, in the Maintenance section, later in this chapter.) The air then passes through the drum filter that rotates in the water reservoir. As the dry, electronically filtered air passes through the drum filter, needed moisture is absorbed. This clean, highly humidified air passes out of the top grille area into the home.

Ozone. This is a fresh, pleasant odor similar to that experienced out-of-doors after an electrical storm. The strong electrical field in your air cleaner similarly creates a trace of ozone usually noticeable only when entering the space. Ozone odor may be more noticeable during the first few days of "break-in" operation. If your air cleaner is operated in a small confined space, the ozone odor may be objectionable. Opening the doors to adjoining rooms will reduce the ozone odor.

Arcing-normal operation. You may notice an occasional, infrequent, sharp snapping sound coming from the unit when operating in the humidifier-and-air-cleaner or air-cleaner-only position. This sound is known as *arcing*. Arcing is a normal occurrence that can result when unusually large particles are being collected.

HOW TO PREPARE THE HUMIDIFIER/AIR CLEANER FOR OPERATION

1. Remove the service cord, which is plugged into the water-fill spout for shipping and storing, then remove water-fill spout by lifting straight up.

2. Remove filter drum from cabinet as follows:

   (a) Lift cardboard flap from top of drum by grasping at side and pulling upward and toward rear of cabinet.

   (b) Remove filter drum from cabinet by lifting straight up. Hold against inside front of cabinet (be careful not to damage the fan blades).

   (c) Fold side flaps of inner packing toward center of cabinet. Lift inner packing straight up and discard.

Caution: Be careful not to misalign or bend the fan blade when removing the filter drum or interior packing.

Note: The float assembly may become hooked in the upper position during shipment. *To avoid overfilling*, check the float to be certain it is unhooked and free for operation.

3. Reinstall filter drum and fill spout in unit. *Note:* Inside rim of drum must rest in the two grooved pulleys.

Location.   You can place your humidifier/air cleaner almost anywhere in the living area as long as the air can circulate freely throughout the house. Avoid placing the unit near cold, outside walls or in the bathroom, kitchen, or laundry area.

It is recommended that the unit be placed where family activity is busiest for the best air cleaning operation possible. If the unit was purchased to obtain relief from a dust-borne allergy, locating the unit in the bedroom or bedroom wing of the home is recommended. Your unit should be positioned so the air intake grille on the back and the outlet grille on the top are unobstructed by walls or furniture. A minimum clearance of three inches is recommended for maximum air circulation. Free air circulation through the unit is required for maximum efficiency.

Caution: To avoid possible damage to plastic components, do not place it close to radiators, hot air registers, or other sources of heat.

Effective Cleaning Area. Your air cleaner will effectively clean the air that is circulated through the electronic cell in an area of up to 960 square feet (with an eight-foot-high ceiling). In an area of this size the unit will circulate and clean the air approximately three times per hour. Humidified air has a broader circulation and will be distributed quickly and evenly throughout your entire home.

CONTROL OPERATION

Selector Switch. The *selector switch* (Fig. 18) is the main operating control of your combination humidifier/air cleaner. The functions of this control are as follows:

Off. In this position all operating functions of the units are de-energized.

Humidifier only. In this position only the humidifying mechanism (drum and fan) is energized. Both drum and fan will cycle on and off as required to maintain selected humidity.

Humidifier and air cleaner. In this position both the air cleaning and humidifying mechanisms of your unit are energized. *Note:* When the humidifier drum turns off automatically because room humidity has been satisfied, the air cleaner and fan operation will continue.

Dry. In this position only, the circulating fan operates to dry the de-energized electronic cell after washing. (*See* Washing Instructions, in the Maintenance section, later in this chapter.)

Air cleaner only. In this position only, the electronic air cleaner and fan will operate.

Fig. 18.

Air Flow Control.   The solid-state air-flow control allows you to select the correct humidification/air cleaning output for existing home conditions. High speed should be used when maximum air cleaning and/or rapid humidification is desired. A lower speed should be used to maintain home comfort under normal operating conditions. The ideal setting is the minimum fan speed that will match the humidification/air cleaning output of the unit with the requirements of the area being conditioned. This setting will be influenced by the user's personal preference as to the percentage of relative humidity maintained, building construction (infiltration of outside air), household activities, outside temperature, operating sound level of unit, and size of area being cleaned or humidified.

Cell Indicator Light.   The *indicator light* signals that sufficient power is being delivered to the electronic cell for efficient air cleaning. If the indicator light flickers continuously or goes out completely when the unit is operating in the humidifier-and-air-cleaner or air-cleaner-only positions, the electronic cell should be washed according to instructions. (*See* Maintenance section later in this chapter.)

Refill Signal Light.   The *signal light* indicates that the water reservoir requires refilling, and humidistat is calling for humidification. *Note:* Both conditions (empty reservoir plus humidistat calling for humidification) must exist before signal light is activated.

Water Supply Indicator.   The *water supply indicator* shows at a glance when water supply is adequate or when reservoir requires refilling. To assure continuous humidity output, refill tank before gage reaches the empty mark.

Automatic Shut-Off Switch.   An internal switch that operates in conjunction with the water supply indicator, the automatic shut-off switch turns your humidifier off when the water supply reaches the empty mark.

Humidistat.   The unit is equipped with a built-in humidistat (humidity control) that controls its operation automatically. You may set the automatic humidistat as desired. Whenever the relative humidity falls below the setting that you select, the humidistat will turn your humidifier on. As soon as the relative humidity rises to the setting you have selected, the humidistat will turn the humidifier off. If you desire a higher humidity level, turn the humidistat knob counterclockwise to a lower number. Continuous run non-automatic operation may be obtained by turning the humidistat control to the extreme clockwise

Cont position. Turn humidistat knob to the extreme counterclockwise Off position at the end of the humidifying season. *Note:* When your unit is being operated in the humidifier-and-air-cleaner selector-switch position, the humidistat will control only the humidifier operation. Therefore, when the unit turns off automatically because room humidity requirements have been satisfied, the air cleaner mechanism will continue to operate as an air cleaning device.

To prevent overhumidification, make certain you properly adjust the humidistat, preferably when there is a major change in outdoor temperature. Condensed moisture or frost on inside windows is a good sign that your controls are set too high.

Note: When your unit is first placed into operation for humidification, it may operate continuously for several days. However, when furniture, drapes, carpets, and the like have absorbed adequate moisture and the humidity in your home rises, the humidifying mechanism of the unit will cycle on and off automatically to maintain the desired humidity level.

MAINTENANCE

Electronic Cell. To keep your electronic air cleaner operating at peak efficiency, it is recommended that the electronic cell be washed about every two months. Since there are naturally more particles, dust, smoke, and the like in some locations than others, it is advisable to make an inspection every few weeks until some idea of the normal cleaning interval is established.

If an excessive amount of particles are allowed to build up on the electronic cell, very rapid and frequent arcing may occur—which indicates that cleaning is required. If the *cell on* signal light flickers continuously or goes out, the cell should be washed. Visual inspection of the electronic cell plates may also be made to detect excessive buildup of accumulated particles. After the first few months of use, a regular washing schedule should be established to assist you in obtaining efficient operation from your unit.

Procedure for washing the cell is as follows:

1. Unplug power supply cord.
2. Open filter access door on back of unit by turning the two

black knobs counterclockwise. Tilt door back, then lift the electronic cell from the unit.

Note: When handling collector cell, extreme care should be taken so as not to damage the fine ionizer wires or bend the collector plates.

3. If you have an automatic dishwasher large enough to accommodate the electronic cell, it can be washed according to steps (a) through (e) below. If an automatic dishwasher is not available, proceed to step 4.

(a) Place electronic cell carefully into dishwasher racks. Select position in dishwasher that will permit best penetration of water into cell.

(b) Use an automatic dishwasher detergent that dissolves readily in hot water.

(c) Follow dishwasher manufacturer's recommendations for heavily soiled dishes or pots and pans.

(d) Remove cell from dishwasher, shake to remove any remaining water and replace in unit.

(e) Proceed to step 5.

4. To manually wash the electronic cell, obtain a plastic or metal container large enough to completely immerse the cell. *Note:* A plastic pan designed specifically for washing the electronic cell is available through your dealer. Wash the cell as follows:

(a) Select an automatic dishwasher detergent that dissolves readily in hot water. Depending on local water conditions, some brands may form a precipitate or scum. If a noticeable scum floats to the surface, try another brand.

Caution: Do not splash the detergent solution in eyes, and avoid prolonged contact with skin. Keep detergent and solution out of reach of children.

(b) Before placing cell in washing container, pour in one cup of detergent. Add enough very hot water (up to 160° F. is permissible) to cover the electronic cell.

(c) When detergent has completely dissolved, place electronic cell in the tub.

(d) Soak the electronic cell for 15 to 20 minutes, slosh several times and remove.

(e) Rinse cell with hose nozzle or running water.

(f) Fill tub with clean, hot water and soak cell for 5 to 15 minutes.

(g) Remove cell, standing it on end to let water drain. If water draining feels slippery, detergent still remains. Repeat rinsing until water no longer feels slippery.

(h) Inspect cell for cleanliness.

(i) Let cell drip for a few minutes and then replace in air cleaner cabinet.

5. Close tilt-out filter-panel and plug power cord into electric receptacle. Place selector switch on dry with variable speed control at high speed. Allow unit to operate on dry for a few minutes.

6. Set selector switch to humidifier-and-air-cleaner or air-cleaner-only. If electronic cell makes a repetitive arcing (snapping) sound, additional drying time is required.

Prefilter. As previously described, the function of the prefilter is to remove the large particles, such as lint, before they enter the electronic cell. This helps to reduce the frequency of cleaning the cell and minimizes arcing. Clean prefilter, when required, as follows:

1. Unplug power supply cord. Turn the two door latches located on rear tilt-out filter-access panel counterclockwise. Tilt the panel back.

2. Remove the foam-type filter.

3. Vacuum the filter thoroughly to remove the accumulated lint and dust.

4. Vacuum the air inlet holes in tilt-out back panel. For added convenience and operating efficiency, it is suggested that the prefilter be cleaned each time the electronic cell is washed.

5. Carefully replace filter in unit.

Vaporizer-Filter. The *vaporizer-filter*, which is stretched over the perimeter of the rotating drum, cleans and moistens the air passing through it. The accumulation of foreign material from the air and mineral deposits from the water will require periodic replacement of this filter. Providing your humidifier runs constantly, a noticeable decrease in water consumption or the symptoms of low humidity in your home (such as static electric shock) are indications that the vaporizer-filter pad should be replaced. The frequency with which this replacement is required will naturally vary, according to local water conditions. The accumulation of minerals on the exterior of the filter does not necessarily mean that replacement is required or that the efficiency of the unit is seriously impaired.

To *replace the vaporizer-filter*, proceed as follows:

1. Unplug power supply cord. Raise hinged top and remove plastic fill spout from left side of unit by lifting straight up.

2. Remove drum by lifting it up slightly, then move it forward against front of cabinet to disengage from the pulleys. Remove drum from unit by lifting drum straight up. Exercise care to avoid damaging fan blades.

3. Remove vaporizer-filter pad, which is stretched over perimeter of drum.

4. Stretch new vaporizer-filter pad over drum and replace in cabinet with inside rim of drum resting in the two pulleys.

5. Replace fill spout and reconnect power supply cord.

Drum Drive Motor.   The drum drive motor has a sealed lubricant and doesn't require the user's attention.

Exterior Finish.   The exterior finish requires only an occasional wiping with a soft, damp cloth. If desired, regular household furniture wax may be applied.

Water Additive.   To combat stale water odors, it is suggested that humidifier tablets be used. Refrain from using other substitutes or additives as they might have a damaging effect on the plastics and vaporizer-filter.

Fan Motor Lubrication.   It is recommended that the fan motor be lubricated once each year. Use a good grade of SAE No. 20 non-detergent motor oil. *Do not use light household oil.* Put three drops of oil in each of the two oil ports as shown in Fig. 19. *Do not over-lubricate.*

Water Reservoir.   The *water reservoir* should be emptied and cleaned periodically; the frequency depends upon conditions of use. Under average conditions the unit should be cleaned once every three months, or whenever excessive amount of minerals or foreign matter build up on the vaporizer-filter pad or in the water reservoir. The average cleaning time requires about 10 minutes.

Note: The first time the water reservoir is cleaned, four bright-colored screws in the lower hinged panel must be removed and discarded (required for shipping only).

1. Clean when water level is low. Approximately one gallon of water will remain in reservoir after unit turns off automatically.

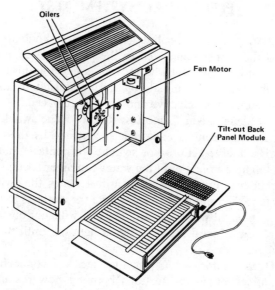

Fig. 19.

2. Unplug the power supply cord. Raise hinged top and remove plastic fill spout from left side of unit by lifting straight up.

3. Remove drum by lifting up slightly, then move it forward against front of cabinet to disengage from the pulleys. Remove drum from unit by lifting drum straight up. Exercise care to avoid damaging fan blades.

4. Reach through top of unit, lift float lever, hook in slot.

5. Turn the two black knobs on lower back panel counterclockwise to release panel and slide container out.

6. Dispose of loose sediment in water reservoir. A mild detergent and warm water may be used to remove mineral deposits from inside of reservoir.

7. Replace water container. (*Note:* Projections on inside bottom of container should be toward rear of unit.)

8. Unhook float lever.

9. Replace filter drum and fill spout.

10. Reconnect unit to power supply.

ELECTRICAL SYSTEM TESTS

Humidistat. Turn the humidistat control knob to the highest position. If the unit is connected to the power source and the water container is full but the unit will not run, connect an insulated jumper wire between the two terminals on the humidistat. If the unit then runs, the humidistat is defective and must be replaced.

Refill and Signal Light Control Switch. The switch is mounted on the back of the control panel and is actuated by the float arm assembly. It is a double-action-type switch. The contacts that control the refill signal light are open until the water container is empty. When the water container is empty, the float arm actuates the switch, causing the contacts to the refill light to close, and the contacts to the motor to open. Thus the light will be on and the unit will shut off. The humidifier will remain off, and the refill signal light on, until the water container is filled.

Drive Drum Motor. Check the electrical connection to make sure that all electrical connections between power source and the motor are good.

To test the drum drive motor, check the voltage between terminal connections (humidistat contact must be closed). Check continuity of the windings with a test light or ohmmeter. An open circuit indicates a defective winding. Continuity between windings and frame indicates an internal short or ground, and the motor must be replaced.

If continuity tests check out and the motor shaft fails to turn when proper voltage is applied, it would indicate defective gears and the motor must be replaced.

Note: Extreme care must be taken *not* to turn shaft by hand since this will damage gears.

Fan Motor. If the fan blade spins freely, test for electrical failure. If the fan blade does not turn freely, the motor bearing may be set up wrong. Check the electrical connections to make sure that all connections between power source and the motor are good.

To test the fan motor windings, disconnect the motor leads from the terminal board. Check the continuity of the windings with a test light or a ohmmeter. An open circuit indicates a defective winding or a broken connection inside the motor. Continuity between the windings and the frame indicate an internal short or ground and the motor must be replaced.

Refill Signal Light.   The function of the *refill signal light* is to signal when the water container is empty. The signal light will remain on when the water container is empty and the humidistat is calling for humidification. If the refill signal light fails to light when the water container is empty and the humidistat contacts are closed, proceed to test as follows.

1. Disconnect the service cord from the power supply.
2. Remove the louvered back panel to gain access to the control panel.
3. Remove the signal light wires from the terminal board and float switch.
4. Test for continuity at the refill signal light leads.
5. If this test does not show continuity, the light assembly must be replaced.
6. If the above test shows continuity, check the humidistat and float switch.

Cell Light.   The minimum operating voltage for the cell light is 72 volts. If the cell light does not operate when connected to the powerpack and if the voltage between the cell light connection and ground at the powerpack is in excess of 72 volts, replace the cell light.

Selector Switch.

1. Remove the connecting wires from the switch, leaving the white jumper wire between L1 and 3.
2. Turn the switch to the Off position; continuity should be between terminals L1 and 2, L1 and 4, L1 and 1.
3. Turn switch to Humidifier position; continuity should be between terminals L1 and 1, N and 2.
4. Turn switch to Humidifier/Air Cleaner position; continuity should be between terminals L1 and 1, L1 and 4, N and 3 .
5. Turn switch to Dry position; continuity should be between terminals N and 3.
6. Turn switch to Air Cleaner position; continuity should be between terminals L1 and 4, N and 3.
7. Should any of the above tests fail to show correct continuity, the switch is defective and should be replaced.

Air Flow Speed Control.

1. Disconnect power cord from wall outlet.

2. Disconnect the speed control lead wires from terminal board.

3. Connect the speed control in series with a 75-watt light bulb, using a 115-volt test cord.

4. Plug in test cord, turn speed control to low setting, and record the voltage. Voltage should read approximately 63.

5. If the speed control has a lower voltage drop, or an open circuit under load, it would indicate a defective control and it must be replaced.

Electronic Cell.   For excessive or continuous electrical arc at the cell, proceed to check as follows:

1. Disconnect the power cord from wall outlet.

2. Open cell-access door panel and remove cell.

3. Check the collector plates to be sure they are equally spaced.

4. Examine the cell for burrs or nicks on the ionizer wire retainer. Emery cloth or a burn-off period (operating the unit for two or three days) will correct this problem.

5. Check for broken ionizing wire and remove and replace. If necessary, the cell may be used temporarily with one wire short.

High Voltage Ground Strap.   Should it be necessary to remove or replace the high-voltage ground strap, care must be taken to reinstall properly. The terminal side *must* be facing toward the front of the humidifier/air cleaner.

Power Pack.   The *power pack* is a sealed unit; therefore, replacement of capacitors, rectifier, and the like is not possible.

With 120 volt, 60 hertz, AC, the open circuit voltage (without cell in place) should be approximately 6900 volts DC (VDC).

The output voltage at 1.0 MA load (with cell in place) is approximately 6200 VDC.

If output voltages are not in this range, replace the power pack.

High Voltage Contact Spring.   Arcing may take place between the contact spring and the cell frame if the contact spring is too close to the frame of the cell. Often arcing will also occur between adjacent plates of the cell.

Reshape the contact spring so that the projection into the cell area is reduced to $7/16$ inch. Bend the spring at the terminal so that there is a $3/32$ inch to $1/8$ inch gap between the spring and the mounting board. The loose end of the spring should clear the board by approximately $3/8$ inch. (*See* Fig. 20.)

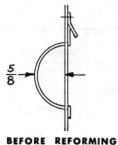

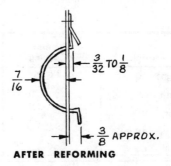

BEFORE REFORMING

AFTER REFORMING

Fig. 20.

POWER HUMIDIFIER

Discriminating homeowners, aware as never before of ecology needs outdoors, are also turning their attention indoors. Proper humidification of the home during the heating season has long been overlooked by many people. Studies indicate that many homes are actually drier than the earth's deserts. The *power humidifier* (Fig. 21) provides proper humidification automatically.

The power humidifier shown in Fig. 21 is designed to provide controlled humidification to complete the "total comfort" concept of heating and air conditioning. It is made of strong polyester fiberglass for strength and durability. No tools are required for servicing and maintenance is simplified by the detachable base and removable grid. Operation is controlled by a humidistat either in the duct or mounted on the wall.

The complete humidifier package includes a universal humidistat for duct or wall mounting, saddle valve assembly, supply tubing, flexible plenum duct, humidistat wire, and plenum fasteners. (*See* Specifications Chart 1; *see also* Comfort Chart 2.)

Features.

1. Made of strong polyester fiberglass.

2. Styled for attractive appearance, if it is necessary to install in living area.

3. Firm and durable structure.

4. Lightweight. Needs a minimum of structural support.

5. Universal humidistat for either duct or wall mounting.

CHART 1
SPECIFICATIONS

Dimensions		Plenum Opening	By-Pass Tube	Motor	Drain Connection
Height - 10''		7½'' x 6¼''	6''	Synchronous	Water Supply:
Width - 12½''				24v 3 watt	¼'' OD
Depth - 10½''					Compression
Weight - 10 lbs.					Overflow Conn.
					5/8'' ID

Temp.	Lbs. Hr.	Gal./Day		Temp.	Lbs. Hr.	Gal./Day
170	8.40	24		140*	6.45	18
160	7.70	22		130	5.65	16
150	7.00	20		120	5.30	15

*140°F. and 0.20S.P. Suggested ARI Standard Rating Conditions

Loose Construction (no insulation) . . . . .1670 Sq. Ft.
Average Construction (some insulation) . . . . .3340 Sq. Ft.
Tight Construction (heavy insulation) . . . . .4560 Sq. Ft.

CHART 2
COMFORT CHART

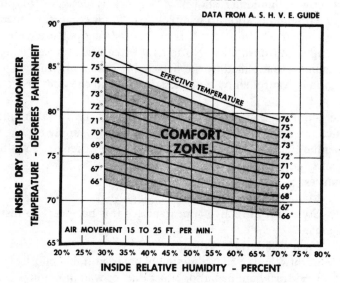

DATA FROM A. S. H. V. E. GUIDE

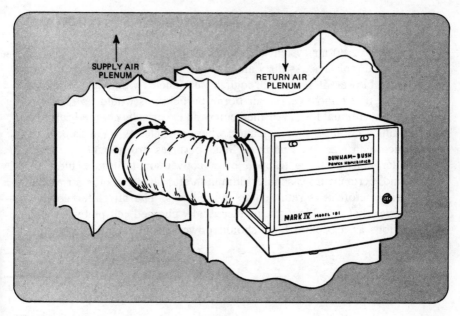

Fig. 21.

6. The complete package contains, in addition to the humidistat, a saddle valve assembly, supply tubing, flexible plenum duct as well as humidistat wire and plenum fasteners.

7. The humidistat can be located either in the duct or on the wall.

8. Base easily detachable without tools for any service that might be required. Front plate and grid removable.

9. An auxiliary transformer is optional where equipment wiring does not already provide 24-volt power.

10. This power humidifier, as adapted to the space-pak system, has a daily capacity of from 9 to 11 gallons.

ELECTRONIC AIR CLEANERS

In this section we will describe the forced air system, electronic air cleaners, and the return air grille electronic air cleaners.

FORCED AIR SYSTEMS FOR DUCT INSTALLATIONS

These forced air system electronic air cleaners (Figs. 22 and 23) filter air three ways. As dirty air is drawn to the air cleaner by the air moving blower, it passes through a permanent washable aluminum prefilter that removes large air-borne particles, as would be removed by a conventional filter. Air then enters an electrically charged cell, the working section of the air cleaner, where particles as small as 0.01 of a micron in size are removed. Such particles are about 500 times smaller than particles trapped by a conventional furnace filter. A second, permanent, washable, aluminum afterfilter gives the air a final filtering before it is returned to living areas. The afterfilter collects particles that may blow off the electrically charged cell plates. It also functions as a backup filter should power be interrupted to the air cleaner.

Fig. 22.

Fig. 23.

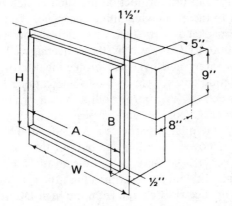

Fig. 24.

Specifications. The electronic air cleaner is available in three models to cover residential and commercial applications up to 2,000 cfm (five tons of cooling or 200,000 Btu's of input heating). Any of these models may be easily combined in a multitude of arrangements to cover large requirements. (*See* Fig. 24.) *Note:* All duct flanges are one inch.

Maintenance. Prefilters and afterfilters are easily removed for washing as required. You can remove cells easily for less frequent washing. No tools are required for filter or cell removal. All components are accessible for testing and replacement. (*See* Fig. 25.)

Equipment. The cleaners shown in Figs. 22, 23, and 25 are fully assembled units—enamel finished, rugged 22-gage steel cabinet with duct-flanged inlet and outlet; unique, patented aluminum collector cell(s) in durable non-corrosive casing; aluminum permanent-type pre- and afterfilters; complete powerpack assembly, including high voltage, heavy-duty transformer, and adjustable voltage-input control; six foot insulated electrical supply cord with three-prong plug attached.

Operating Principle. The electronic air cleaners are composed of three basic components—the ionizing section, the collecting section, and the powerpack.

The ionizing section and the collecting section combine to form the collecting cell. The collecting cell, along with the air cleaner housing, is installed in the return air duct on the suction side of the air moving unit, as close to the air moving unit as possible.

The powerpack converts 115 VAC house current to both 4,000 VDC and 8,000 VDC for use by the collecting cell. The powerpack also provides safety and overload protection for the unit as well as voltage regulation and system operation indication.

How It Works. Air-borne pollution is drawn through the return air ductwork (Fig. 26, A) and passes first through the lint screen (Fig. 26, B), where large particles are removed. This is about all the normal filter removes, returning the bulk of the contamination to the home. However, in the base of the electronic air cleaner, air next passes through the ionizing section (Fig. 26, C) where all particles receive a strong electrical charge from the high DC voltage applied to the ionizing wires. The highly charged particles then pass into the collecting cell where an additional electrical field then repels the

Fig. 25.

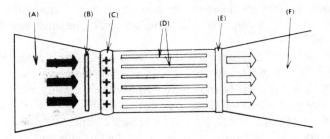

Fig. 26.

charged particles to alternately spaced ground collector plates (Fig. 26, D). The effect is similar to that of a magnet. The particles adhere to the plates. Should excessive build-up of particles occur and be blown off the plates, these accumulations are trapped by the afterfilter (Fig. 26, E). The clean air (Fig. 26, F) then moves on to be heated and cooled and returned to the conditioned space.

Electrical Circuit.   In the primary circuit, 115-Volt, 60 hertz, single-phase, AC enters the powerpack through an extension cord plugged into a grounded outlet. Current requirement is 0.9 amps maximum. The current flows first through a normally open safety interlock switch that must be depressed by a collecting cell handle before power can flow. Primary current then flows, in order, through a 1-amp fuse, on-off switch, milli-ammeter, rheostat, transformer, and then to ground.

The secondary circuit consists of the high-voltage side of the transformer, which supplies power to a standard voltage doubler circuit. This circuit consists of a dual selenium rectifier and two capacitors and provides 8,000 volts direct current for the ionizer wires and 4,000 VDC for the collector plates. For safety, a resistor is provided to discharge the capacitors when the unit is switched off. It takes several seconds for the resistor to completely discharge the unit. For this reason, wait one minute after turning the unit off before removing the power supply for servicing.

Installation.

1. The electronic air cleaner is pre-wired and pre-assembled. No changes or electrical connections need to be made during installation. The unit requires no clearance for service on three sides and only 16 inches on the powerpack side. The unit may be installed in any position.

2. Remove powerpack and sub-base (end panel) from the unit by releasing the white latches on both sides of the powerpack.

3. Remove cells from case, with lint screen and afterfilter intact to protect plates and ionizing wires during installation.

4. Determine where the electronic air cleaner is to be installed in the return air duct system; either in the duct or adjacent to the cabinet of the air handling unit. Provide transitions as necessary to attach the duct to flanges of the air cleaner case with sheet metal screws and tape all joints for airtight connections. Do not use screws in any portion of the case other than the flanges, as they will interfere with the cells. Refer to the following typical applications to determine that which best fits your type of furnace and duct system.

5. Be sure case is installed square. This can be checked by replacing the cells and powerpack in the cabinet before making up the duct connections.

6. If the unit is installed in suspended ductwork, be sure there is adequate support for the weight of the unit. Use duct hangers if necessary.

7. The cabinet of the units shown in Figs. 22, 23, and 25 has

been designed so that it is possible to install the cabinet inside the ductwork by inserting it through a hole cut in the duct. If this type of installation is made, it will be necessary to fasten an angle frame around the opening to support the unit and for an airtight connection. Use sheet metal screws and tape all connections carefully.

8. If the cabinet is inserted in the ductwork, be sure *no* air can by-pass the air cleaner. Use airtight baffles if required. Remember, once the case is installed, it will be difficult to tell if there is by-pass; and if there is, the whole purpose of the installation will have been defeated.

9. Be sure all ductwork—particularly any portion from the air cleaner to and including the blower unit—is airtight as possible.

10. After installing the case, replace the cells in the case, oriented so that the arrows on the ends of the cells are pointing in the direction the air is moving. No internal wiring changes are necessary. Be certain the unit is correctly aligned. Check this by installing the cells, filters, and control panel to see if these can be easily installed and removed.

11. Be sure contacts on the exposed ends of the cells and the mating contacts on the back of the powerpack sub-base are clean.

12. Mount powerpack on end of case and engage both latches.

13. Plug in power cord to a 115-volt grounded receptacle. (If permanent wiring is used in lieu of plug furnished, refer to wiring diagrams in Figs. 35, 36, and 37.)

14. Turn operating switch on.

15. Needle on performance level indicator (milli-ammeter) should move into the white area.

16. Set voltage control (rheostat) to highest position, unless arcing (crackling) results. Give unit time to pick up residual dust in the unit and ductwork. If constant arcing should continue, check section on Service, later in this section.

17. You, the homeowner, should learn all about the operation of the unit. (*See* Suggestions for Homeowner, later in this section.)

Typical Installations. Figure 27 shows a typical furnace installation side inlet.

Fig. 28 shows a typical duct installation, turning vanes. Where return duct drop connects to furnace as shown in Fig. 28, turning vanes installed in elbow help distribute air evenly over full surface of air cleaner.

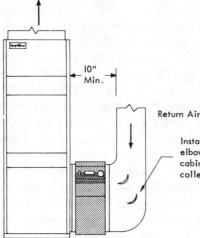

Fig. 27.

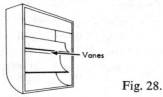

Fig. 28.

Figure 29 shows a lowboy installation, top return, with air cleaner installed horizontally.

Figure 30 shows a highboy furnace with return air entering bottom, with air cleaner horizontally installed at bottom.

Figure 31 shows a counterflow furnace with air cleaner installed at top in return air duct.

Figure 32 shows a typical return air duct.

Note: In all installations, allow 16-inch minimum service access clearance at powerpack side of unit.

Figure 33 shows a closet installation air cleaner on side, no return duct.

Figure 34 shows a horizontal furnace installation.

Note: It is recommended that the air moving blower operate continuously for maximum cleaning. If blower is to operate intermit-

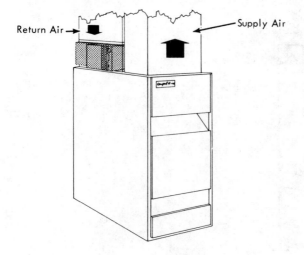

Fig. 29.

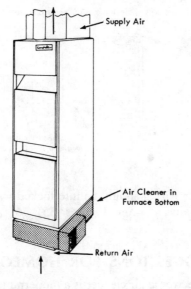

Fig. 30.

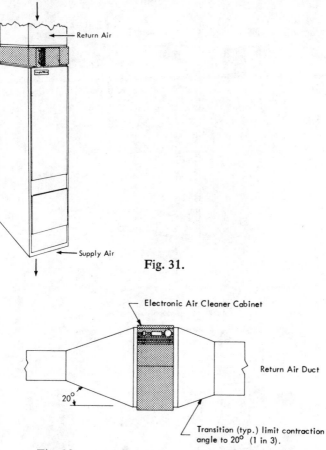

Return Air

Supply Air

Fig. 31.

Electronic Air Cleaner Cabinet

Return Air Duct

20°

Transition (typ.) limit contraction
angle to 20° (1 in 3).

Fig. 32.

tently, air cleaner wiring should be interlocked with the blower.

Wiring Diagrams.   *See* Figures 35, 36, and 37 for wiring diagrams.

SUGGESTIONS FOR HOMEOWNER

1. Your electronic air cleaner is a modern marvel, but remember that it can only clean air that passes through it. So good, unobstructed air circulation is necessary.

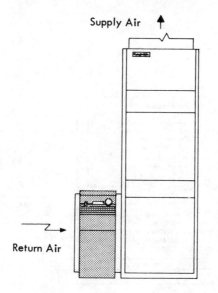

Supply Air

Return Air

Fig. 33.

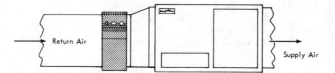

Return Air

Supply Air

Fig. 34.

2. The unit uses less electrical power than a 25-watt light bulb. It should never be turned off unless your air conditioner/furnace blower is off. For best results, operate your blower and electronic air cleaner continuously.

3. The purpose of the *voltage control* is to adjust your unit to minor neighborhood power variations. The control should be set at the highest position possible without causing excessive arcing (crackling) in the unit. Do not be concerned over occasional crackling as this simply indicates a large particle passing through the lint screen has been collected by the cell.

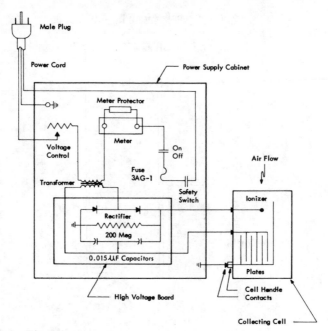

Fig. 35.

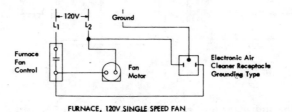

FURNACE, 120V SINGLE SPEED FAN

Fig. 36.

4. The *performance level indicator* gives you a constant visual check on the operation of the unit. If the needle moves out of the proper operating gage (white area), first be sure the unit is plugged in and power is on. After you are sure the unit has power, turn the unit off, and remove and wash all filters and cells. Replace them and leave the switch off for one hour with your air handling unit running. Then turn the switch on. If indicator is still out of the proper range, check the following section on Service or call servicer.

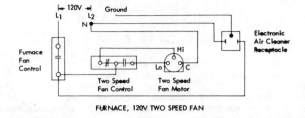

FURNACE, 120V TWO SPEED FAN

Fig. 37.

5. The aluminum lint screens and afterfilters should be removed and washed periodically on a *regular schedule*. The cleaning intervals should be determined by experience, but generally a monthly washing is sufficient. *Do not* neglect this simple chore, as it will assure constant high cleaning efficiency.

6. At less frequent intervals, generally no more often than every six months, the cells should be removed and washed with hot water. *Do not* use a brush or other cleaning instrument. The preferred method is in a sink with a spray nozzle or in the dishwasher, being careful not to damage the ionizing wires at the front of the cell.

Service.   Your electronic air cleaner is designed to give years of trouble-free operation. Eventually the unit will require some minor service. Although your dealer is familiar with the unit, you should be able to spot any trouble when it occurs, and in most cases correct it yourself, resulting in minimum loss of air cleaning time.

Any problems arising with your electronic air cleaner can be spotted from the indication of the performance level indicator (Fig. 38).

RETURN AIR GRILLE

Return air grille electronic air cleaners are designed for installation in the return air intake of forced air heating and/or cooling systems. (*See* Figs. 39, 40, and 41.) The return air grille units install flush in any position in wall or ceiling and are completely serviceable from the front. Two sizes of the filter grille model are available, for applications of 1,400 cubic feet per minute (cfm) and 2,100 cfm. All exposed parts are finished in aluminum and may be painted to match any room decor. Cabinets are constructed of 20-gage galvanized welded steel construction with two ½-inch electrical knock-outs.

Fig. 38.

Fig. 39.

The electronic air cleaner operates on 120 volts, 60 hz., ¼-amp operating, at .9 amps maximum. An on-off switch is located on the front panel behind the louvered grille. A safety switch is operated when the louvered door is opened. The switch interrupts current flow to the high-voltage transformer and high-voltage circuit components. Proper operation of the power supply is indicated by a neon lamp located on the front panel.

Fig. 40.

Fig. 41.

Electronically charged cleaning cells remove dirt particles from the air as small as 0.01 of a micron in size. Air-borne pollen, dust, smoke, aerosols, bacteria, and the like are drawn into the electronic cell after passing through a lint screen that mechanically traps large particles with similar efficiency to a disposable-type filter. Those particles too small to be trapped by the prefilter are carried into the ionizing section, where they receive an electrical charge. The charged particles pass over alternately charged aluminum plates where they are collected on the plate surface. Each electronic cell contains 6,164 square inches of collecting surface. Cells may be cleaned in a household dishwasher with hot water and detergent.

Specifications.   (*See* Fig. 42.)

Electrical. 120 volt, 60 Hz, ¼ ampere operating, at .9 amperes maximum.

Housing. 20 gage galvanized steel, welded construction.

Controls. On-off switch, safety switch, and operating lamp.

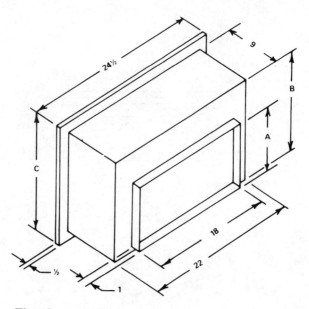

Fig. 42.

Installation.   The steel cabinet can be mounted in any position in a wall or ceiling. The galvanized steel cabinet is permanently mounted to the structure of the wall or ceiling, and the duct to air system is connected to the flanges provided.

Fig. 43. Electronic air cleaner. (1) Aluminum louvered return air grille door. (2) Chrome ¼-turn locking screws and interconnecting electrical safety switch. (3) Electronic cell hinged retaining bracket. (4) Aluminum electronic plates. Ionizing wires are positioned between the front of the plates. (Not visible in illustration.) (5) Modular electronic cell case. (6) Galvanized welded steel cabinet. (7) Aluminum mesh washable pre-filter. (8) On-off switch with operating light. (9) Electrical knock-outs. (10) Neon lamp indicates if unit is operating properly. (11) High voltage section access panel.

Carefully remove all parts from the carton and remove any packing material inside the unit. Remove the power access panel and the louvered door-plaster frame assembly. Remove the cell before proceeding to install the unit.

Cell removal and replacement.

1. Open the louvered door by turning chrome knob(s) one-quarter turn counterclockwise and pulling the door toward you.

2. Press the cell latch, grasp the cell handle, and pull it toward the front of the unit.

3. Holding the cell handle with one hand, push gently on the other end of the cell until it is free from the hinged retaining bracket.

4. Lift the cell out of the cabinet.

5. When replacing the cell, reverse the procedure. Be sure the latch engages the handle.

Site preparation and sheet-metal installation.

1. Prepare the duct entrance to fit the cabinet flange. See specification chart for the dimensions of the model being installed.

2. Frame the wall or ceiling opening to accept the cabinet. Add $\frac{1}{8}$ inch to the sizes shown for the rough opening dimensions.

3. Fit the cabinet into the rough opening and attach to the framing, using No. 10 × 1 inch screws or 8d nails through the holes provided in the flanges. (*See* Fig. 44.)

4. Attach the duct to the cabinet flange using sheet metal screws. The outside of the connection should be sealed with duct tape to prevent the leakage of dirty air into the system.

5. Install the plaster frame and the door assembly using the eight No. 8 pan-head screws provided. (Position the latch on the door at the same end of the cabinet as the rocker switch.)

Electrical installation. (*See* Fig. 45, wiring diagram.)

1. Wire a 120-volt circuit to the unit.

2. The circuit should be wired through a sail-switch (air-flow switch) so the electronic air cleaner will operate only when the blower is operating. As an alternative, the unit may be wired directly through

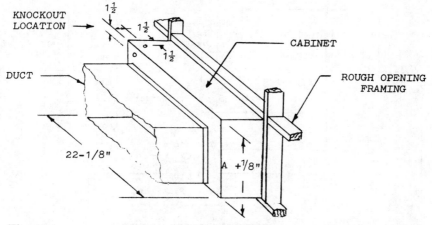

Fig. 44.

the system blower control. In either case, the unit will be most effective if the blower is operated continuously.

3. Bring the 120-volt circuit cable into the cabinet through either of the two ½-inch knock-outs provided. Use wire nuts to connect the two leads provided. A safety ground wire should be connected to the screw on the side of the switch bracket.

4. Replace the power supply access panel.

Operational check list.

1. Place the electronic cell(s) into the cabinet with the "air flow" label pointing inward. Position the end panel opposite the handle of the cell into the hinged bracket and swing the cell into the cabinet. *Place the lint screen in place. Be sure* the latch engages the cell handle.

2. Depress the on-off switch. The indicator lamp should now glow. (The unit is on when the side of the switch adjacent to the plaster frame is depressed.)

3. Close and latch the door.

4. The homeowner or maintenance personnel should be familiar with the operation and maintenance of the unit. Be sure to have the operating instructions and warranty card handy if needed.

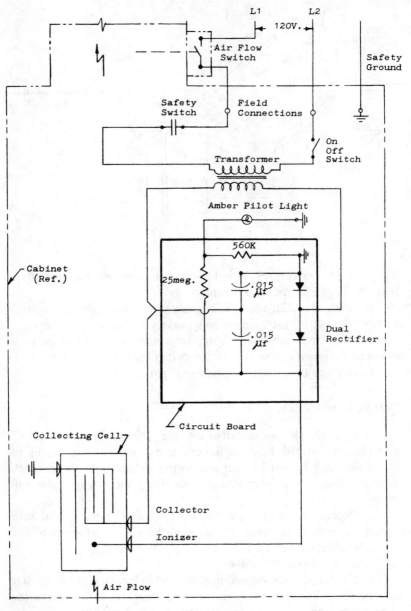

Fig. 45.

PRINCIPLES OF OPERATION

The electronic air cleaner operates on the principles of electrostatic precipitation (Fig. 46). Air-borne particulate matter (pollen, dust, smoke, aerosols, bacteria, and the like) is drawn into the electronic cell after passing through a lint screen (A) that mechanically traps large particles with similar efficiency as a disposal-type filter in most return air systems. Those particles too small to be trapped by this prefilter are carried by the air stream into the ionizing section (B), where they receive an electrical charge from high DC voltage applied to the ionizing wires. Passing through the ionizing section into the collecting cell (C), the charged particles pass over alternately charged aluminum plates. The positively charged plates repel the particles and the negatively charged plates attract the particles. The end result is that the particles are collected on the surfaces of the plates. (The effect is similar to the action of a magnet.) The cleaned air then moves through the duct to be heated or cooled and is returned to the conditioned space.

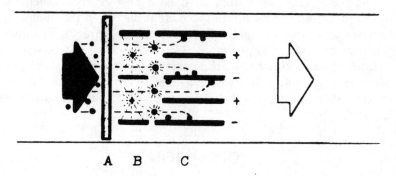

Fig. 46. Principle of operation.

Chapter 19

Heat Pumps for Heating and Cooling Homes

Heat pumps are being used increasingly for year round air conditioning in homes, especially in the southern part of the country. Whether such equipment will satisfactorily and economically meet a family's requirements is best determined by consultation with builders, engineers, electric power supply representatives, and heat pump equipment dealers.

The heat pump is a single unit that can both heat and cool the home or one or more rooms.

The pump takes heat from an outside *heat source* (water, air, earth) to warm the conditioned space in the winter. In the summer, it removes heat from the conditioned space and discharges it to an outside *heat sink* (water, air, earth).

Units of the air-to-air type are commonly used for heating and cooling homes. Air-to-air indicates that outside air is used as the heat source and heat sink, and that air is used as the heating and cooling medium.

OPERATION

A heat pump works on the same principle as a household refrigerator or other refrigeration system. In effect, it transfers heat from one place or source at a relatively low temperature to another at a higher temperature.

Figure 1 shows how an air-to-air unit heats. Outside air passes over the cold evaporator coil. Heat is transferred from the air to the refrigerant in the coil, raised to a higher temperature by compression, and discharged to the heating medium—air—at the condenser. A fan

304

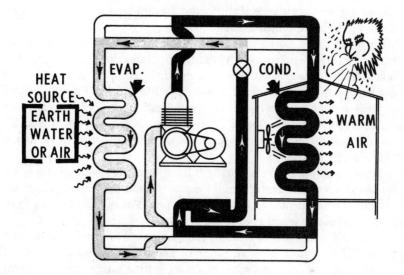

Fig. 1. Heating cycle of a heat pump.

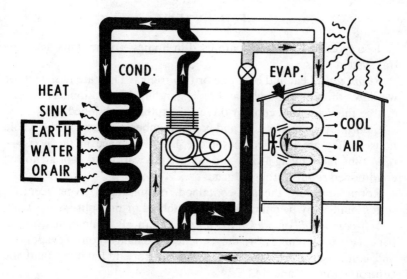

Fig. 2. Cooling cycle of a heat pump.

blows the warm air directly into the conditioned space or through ducts to the conditioned areas or rooms.

Figure 2 shows how an air-to-air unit cools. The heating and cooling cycles are identical except that the operation is reversed. Heat is taken from the warm air from the conditioned space or rooms and discharged to the outdoor air. Cool air is blown back into the house.

Heat pumps generally switch from heating to cooling, and vice versa, by *refrigerant reversal*. Valves (not shown in Figs. 1 and 2) reverse the directions of refrigerant flow, and the two heat-exchange coils, in effect, trade jobs.

Heat pump operation is usually fully automatic. A thermostat is set for the desired temperature, and then automatic controls regulate operation. On a spring or fall day, the pump may heat during cool periods of the day and cool at other times.

For fully automatic operation, the thermostat is usually set so that there will be a nonoperative range of about 2 to 4 degrees between the heating and cooling cycles. A closer setting might cause frequent cycling between the heating and cooling operations.

EQUIPMENT

Two types of heat pumps are used in homes—room units and central-system units.

Room units heat and cool one or two rooms. They are designed for window, through-the-wall, and free-standing installation. They discharge the warm and cool air directly into the conditioned area.

Central-system units heat and cool a number of rooms or the whole house. They are installed in some convenient place in the house—out of the main living area—and deliver the warm and cool air to the conditioned rooms through ducts.

Room units are the self-contained, or packaged, type. Central-system units may be either the self-contained or the split-system type.

Self-contained, or *packaged, units* contain all components in one package—the compressor, the two heat-exchange coils (evaporator and condenser), the two fans or blowers for air handling, and the controls (Figs. 3 and 4).

Split-system units consist of two sections. One section includes the indoor heat-exchange coil, a blower, and electrical controls; it is in-

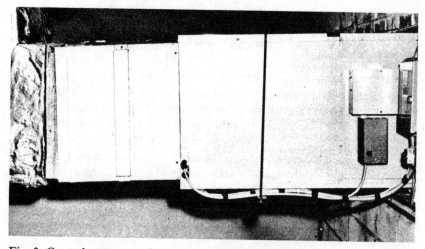

Fig. 3. Central-system, packaged-type heat pump installed.

Fig. 4. Components and controls of heat pump.

stalled *inside* the house. The other section includes the outdoor heat-exchange coil, a fan, and controls; it is installed *outside* the house. The two sections are interconnected by refrigerant lines and electric control wiring.

Heat pumps are rated according to their heating capacity and according to their cooling, or heat-removal, capacity. This is usually indicated in terms of British thermal units of heat per hour (Btuh). Central-system units may be rated in tons. A ton of cooling capacity equals 288,000 Btu's per 24 hours, or 12,000 Btu's per hour.

Room heat pump units are available in cooling capacities up to about 20,000 Btuh. Larger self-contained, or packaged, units are available in capacities of 2 to 6 tons. Split-system units are available in capacities of 2 to 15 tons.

HEATING AND COOLING REQUIREMENTS

Factors that determine heating and cooling requirements include area of the country, size and orientation of the house or room, construction, insulation, glass area, and shading.

Heat pumps are usually sized for the summer cooling load and supplemented with auxiliary heaters for the winter heating load.

Heating and cooling loads are calculated on the basis of the outside design temperatures recommended for the area and are indicated in terms of Btu's of heat to be supplied or removed per hour. (Outside design temperatures is a value used in design of heating and air conditioning systems. Heating values are related to minimum winter temperatures. Cooling values are related to maximum summer temperatures.)

Heating and cooling loads should be estimated by an experienced person. Heat pump dealers and electric power suppliers can assist and usually have special forms available for that purpose.

Proper sizing of the heat pump is important. Oversizing on cooling capacity, for example, can result in inadequate dehumidification; the pump may not operate long enough during the cooling cycle to properly dehumidify the house or room.

The additional heat in winter is supplied by electric-resistance-type heaters. These units provide approximately 3,413 Btu's of heat per hour per kilowatt of size. They are installed in the heat pump unit or in the duct work.

INSTALLATION

Installation of a central system heat pump is similar to that for central air conditioning or warm-air-heating equipment. The unit (the indoor heat-exchange coil) is connected to the conditioned rooms by supply and return air ducts. The same ducts carry the cool air in summer and the warm air in winter.

Proper design and installation of the airflow (duct) system are essential. An engineer or other qualified person should design the system. The following paragraphs contain general installation requirements or recommendations.

Basements (Fig. 3) and garages are favorite locations for central system heat pumps (packaged units or the indoor section of split-system units). Size of the pump can determine the best location; there must be adequate clearance for duct connections and for servicing.

Short outside-air supply and discharge ducts for packaged units (Fig. 4), and short air-distribution and return ducts for all units, save duct and insulation costs and improve air handling. A location near the center of the house, offset to an outside wall, will permit the shortest duct runs. (*See* Fig. 5.)

The pump should not be located where operating noise can bother occupants. A basement installation with the unit cushion mounted on a concrete block will reduce noise and vibration and place the air outlet up near the ceiling for easy connection to an air handling system. For quieter operation, asbestos cloth collars (or other suitable nonflammable material) should be used to connect pump unit and ducts, and the inside of ducts near the blower should be lined with sound-absorbing insulation.

The outdoor section of a split-system unit should be located where it cannot be damaged or blocked by snow (Fig. 6). There must be adequate clearance around the section for proper air intake and discharge and for servicing. A shaded or a north-side location will reduce solar heat load on the coil in summer and increase cooling efficiency.

The outdoor section should be mounted on a substantial, level

Fig. 5. View, from outside the house, of heat pump installation shown in Fig. 3.

base that cannot shift or settle. Movement of the base could cause strain on the refrigerant lines, which could cause leaks. For ground level installation, a concrete slab with footings extending below the frostline is recommended.

Refrigerant lines between the two sections of a split-system unit should be well insulated outside the house. If properly protected, the lines can be run underground. Electric control wiring must be properly protected and must be installed in accordance with the National Electrical Code and local codes.

Air distribution and return ducts should be as short and as straight

Fig. 6. Outside section of a split-system heat pump unit should be mounted on a substantial, level base. (Concrete is recommended.)

as possible—no unnecessary lengths or sharp changes in direction. Long, uninsulated distribution ducts—particularly those running through a cool basement or crawl space—reduce delivered air temperature during heating and may cause condensation trouble during cooling.

(A central system heat pump requires an airflow (duct) system designed especially for it; as an old warm-air-heating or air conditioning duct system cannot be used. Large heat pump units can also be installed for direct discharge of warm and cool air into a large room or area.)

Ducts should be insulated whenever heat loss or gain may be excessive. In general, insulate ducts in attics, crawl spaces, and other unconditioned areas, and ducts over 50 feet in length. One to two inches of insulation is recommended. For maximum heating comfort, an outlet should be located on the outside wall under the window to blanket the wall with a curtain of air and offset any downdraft of cold air.

HOUSE DESIGN

Insulation of walls, floors, and ceilings and reduction of the solar heat load in summer can reduce heating and cooling requirements and increase heat pump effectiveness and personal comfort.

A vapor barrier should be installed in walls to prevent moisture damage to insulation and construction during heating.

Insulation is specified in terms of inches of thickness and in terms of resistance (R) to heat flow when installed. The higher the R value, the greater the resistance to heat flow.

For comfort and economy in electric heating and cooling, minimum insulation values of R-19 for ceilings, R-11 for walls, and R-13 for floors are recommended. Because heat loss is greater through ceilings than through floors or walls, insulation values as high as R-30 may be desirable for ceilings. Floor and wall insulation of R-16 will improve personal comfort.

Table 21 lists the types of insulation commonly used in houses and an approximate R value for each. *Foamed* plastic, an efficient type of insulation, may be too expensive for general use.

Loose-fill insulation (mineral wool, macerated wood pulp, or treated, shredded-wood fiber) may be blown in the walls and ceilings to insulate houses already built.

Vermiculite (expanded mica) may be used to fill the cores of concrete block to reduce heat loss or gain. It insulates the core space only and does not reduce heat loss or gain through the web sections of the block. A new form of vermiculite does not absorb moisture as readily as the old type. Concrete block or other masonry walls should be further, or more effectively, insulated by fastening furring strips on the inside and applying another type of insulation to or between the strips.

Bat and *blanket types* of insulation are most commonly used in new construction and sometimes in remodeling.

Board-type insulation is often used in remodeling because it provides a finished interior as well as some insulation. (*See* Table 21.)

TABLE 21
INSULATION

Types of insulation	Approximate R value per inch of thickness [1]
Loose fill:	
Mineral wool (glass, slag, or rock)_____	3. 33
Macerated wood pulp_____	3. 57
Vermiculite (expanded mica)_____	2. 08
Bat and blanket:	
Fibrous mineral wool_____	3. 70
Wood fiber_____	4. 00
Cotton fiber_____	3. 85
Board and slab:	
Ceiling tile, ½-inch thick_____	2. 38
Sheathing (impregnated or coated), ½-inch thick_____	2. 63
Roof insulation (above deck), ½-inch to 3-inches thick_____	[2] 2. 78 to 8. 33

[1] For total R value, multiply by inches of thickness.
[2] Total R value.

Double- and triple-glazed windows (called insulating glass) reduce heat transfer from or to the outside. However, if exposed to direct sunlight, they transmit almost as much solar heat as single-glazed windows.

Walls below ground need not be insulated as well as those above ground because of the lower heat gain from the cooler ground.

Concrete block or masonry walls must be waterproofed to prevent moisture from reaching the insulation. Moisture reduces the effectiveness of insulation and may shorten its life. Exterior waterproofing is recommended; interior waterproofing may not be effective. Exterior waterproofing should be supplemented by good footing drainage.

SOLAR HEAT REDUCTION

Protection from direct rays of the sun or the reflection of solar heat can reduce temperatures inside the house in summer. Methods by which this may be done include the following:

1. Orientation of the house so that major glass areas receive maximum protection from the direct rays of the sun.

2. Shading of the house, particularly glass areas, with roof overhangs, awnings, trees, and other devices.

3. Utilization of light-colored roofs, exterior walls, and window hangings.

VAPOR BARRIER

Summer air cooling does not normally cause serious vapor problems in exterior walls and ceilings, but winter heating can create very serious problems. In most areas, a vapor barrier should be installed in walls and ceilings to prevent moisture damage to insulation and construction.

Polyethylene, duplex sheet with aluminum foil on one side, or asphalt-saturated and asphalt-coated sheathing paper may be used for a vapor barrier. Ordinary 15- or 30-pound asphalt-saturated building paper is not satisfactory. Polyethylene film should not be less than 0.002 inch thick. Some insulations and building boards are foil backed, and this backing provides a vapor barrier if properly applied.

Vapor barriers should be placed between the inside finish and the insulation in houses that require more heating than cooling. If the cooling load is nearly equal to, or is greater than, the heating load, there should be vapor barriers on both sides of the insulation. Joints in the barrier should be held to a minimum and made by lapping over framing members. Vapor barrier sealing tape should be used to seal joints around pipes and wiring outlet boxes and to repair holes caused by installation.

Paints on the inside surfaces of a house have some value as a vapor barrier, but not as much as separate barrier material. Alkyd gloss or semigloss, primer sealer plus enamel, or rubber-resin lacquer paints have low vapor permeance. Two or three coats are necessary.

Sheathing papers under the outside finish should not be a vapor barrier type. Use a material that will let moisture escape from the wall. The ordinary building papers and felts are satisfactory.

OPERATING COSTS

Operating costs for *cooling by heat pump* are comparable with those for conventional electric air conditioning units or systems.

In a well-insulated house, operation costs for heating can be comparable with, or can be twice as much as, the operation costs for other types of heating. How the cost compares with the cost of operating other systems depends on the cost of electricity, gas, or other fuel.

Detailed information about operating costs and other factors may be obtained from electric power suppliers, heat pump dealers, and building engineers.

The power supplier may offer special rates for year-round electric air conditioning, which would reduce operating costs. And he can advise about modification of service entrance equipment and wiring required for installation of a heat pump. All electrical work must be done in accordance with the National Electrical Code and local codes.

The heat pump dealer can advise on selection, installation, and operation of the heat pump unit. This includes estimating heating and cooling loads to determine the size (capacity) of unit needed.

Availability of a good service organization is important. Proper installation and servicing are essential for satisfactory operation and a minimum of maintenance. The pump compressor should carry a five-year warranty. Since the warranty would not cover other components, it may be advisable to carry a maintenance service contract.

Chapter 20

How to Choose a Heating System for Your Home

Heat is transferred in three different ways—by conduction, by convection, and by radiation.

Conduction is the flow of heat through a solid, such as heat from boiling water passing along the handle of a silver spoon. So, in a lesser degree, the heat generated inside or outside a room flows through walls, ceilings, and floors.

Convection is a transfer of heat by moving currents of air. As such currents move past a warm surface they pick up the heat and carry it with them. Although hollow spaces in walls may be partly sealed, a difference in temperatures between the top and bottom of the sealed areas creates currents of air, which carry heat from the warmer side to the colder.

Radiation is the process by which the sun's energy is carried to the earth. Any warmer surface transfers heat by radiation to any cooler neighboring surface. This radiant transfer even takes place within a room and between the walls of a room; thus the warmer walls of a house radiate heat to the colder ones. The human body also radiates heat. When this radiation is too rapid due to the low temperature of surrounding objects, personal discomfort and chills will result at ordinary room air temperatures. When walls and other surroundings are at a reasonable temperature, comfort will ordinarily ensue.

UNITS OF HEAT

To measure the extent of heat transfer the British thermal unit (Btu) is used. One Btu is required to raise one pound of water 1° F.

under specified conditions (from 39° F. to 40° F. at sea level). Heat losses are measured in British thermal units per square foot of material one inch thick per hour per degree Fahrenheit temperature difference. This quantity is sometimes called the k-factor; and, as it is, the measure of heat loss.

A HEATING PLANT

In selecting heating equipment for a new house or for the modernization of an old house, the homeowner should remember that there are two costs—original cost and operating cost—to be considered. The cheapest heating system from the standpoint of first cost is very likely to be the most expensive to operate.

Talk over your plans for a heating plant for your house with a good heating contractor or heating dealer. Give preference to heating equipment made by manufacturers of national standing in the heating field—manufacturers of stability and integrity; that is, manufacturers who are sure to be in business years from now when you may need repairs.

There is only one test for building materials, and that goes for heating equipment as well: the time test. Laboratory tests, no matter how well conducted, cannot begin to provide the proof of satisfactory operation that is provided by actual use of equipment in the field under varying conditions of use, and unfortunately, sometimes of abuse.

AUTOMATIC HEATING SYSTEMS

The best system is the most consistent system, because the body is most comfortable when it loses heat in a steady, controlled manner. Room temperatures must be consistent, not changing appreciably from center to corner, from top to bottom, or from time to time.

There are three heating systems today that are the most commonly installed in new homes or used in modernization—the hydronic hot water system, the warm air system, and the electric resistance system. Before selecting a system for your home, you should know how each, in varying degrees, controls the loss of heat by your body, and keeps you comfortable.

HYDRONIC HOT WATER SYSTEM

Hydronic heating maintains comfort in your home with hot water circulating to every room through baseboard panels (Fig. 1). The system basically consists of a boiler, pump, and baseboards, connected by water piping. The principle of heating with water dates back to ancient times, when Romans used it by distributing heated water through the walls and under floors. But hydronics today bears no resemblance to ancient times. The system is as modern as any you can install, with such refinements as zoning, which allows you to vary temperatures in different areas of the house.

Perimeter Heating—Radiant and Convected.   Baseboard panels around the outer perimeter of the home provide a curtain of warmth that surrounds you with comfort. Radiant heat rays warm the room surfaces and, at the same time, gently rising currents of convected warm air block out drafts and cold. Walls stay warm and cold spots are eliminated.

Hot Water Boiler.   A boiler heats water to temperatures between 120° F. and 210° F., and the water is then pumped through

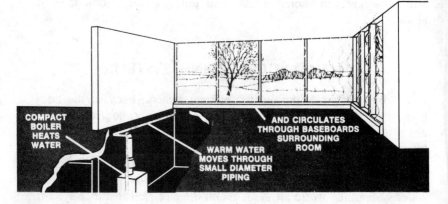

Fig. 1. Hydronic hot water heating system.

the piping in the baseboard. A modern cast-iron boiler used for home heating is very compact. Most units are the size of an automatic washing machine, and some are as small as a suitcase and can be hung on a wall.

WARM AIR SYSTEM

In a warm air system, air is used to conduct heat from the furnace to the rooms of the house. Air is warmed as it passes over a heat exchanger, then blown through the house by a motorized blower. Sheet-metal ducts channel the heated air to various areas of the house, and the heat enters each room through registers usually located in the floor. (*See* Fig. 2.)

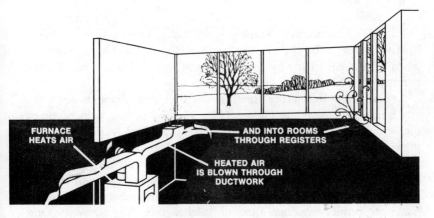

Fig. 2. Warm air heating system.

ELECTRIC RESISTANCE SYSTEM

To get an idea of resistance heating, think of the burner element on an electric range strung out in a straight line. Electricity heats the element, and this gives off heat to each room. Resistance heating cannot actually be called a central heating system, since it is basically a series of room units. Two types of resistance heating are discussed in this chapter.

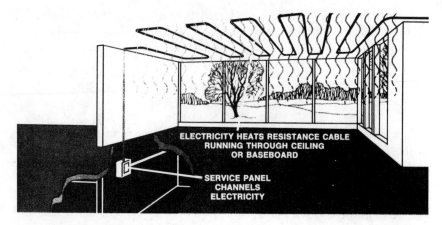

Fig. 3. Resistance heating system.

Baseboard Resistance Heating.   Electric elements in the baseboard are heated by the electric current (Fig. 3.) Elements turn on when heat is called for by the thermostat, turn off when room temperatures rise above the thermostatic setting.

Ceiling Cable Resistance Heating.   Electrical elements are actually buried in the ceiling plaster (Fig. 3). The ceiling then becomes the heating surface. In contrast to hydronics, electric resistance heating is an on-off system. Heat changes are sudden and noticeable. This is due to the fact that when room temperature drops slightly, the electric system is immediately activated to its highest temperature, which is often as high as 450° F. These sudden heat surges create *hot spots* in the immediate areas of baseboard heating elements. One major factor of comfort is lacking in this type of electric system—constant warmth.

Warm Air Heating.   An efficient home heating system must compensate for body heat losses by supplying the right amount of heat and the same type of heat. *Warm air systems* provide only convected heat through forced air movement and no radiation, even if the blower fan operates continuously. Like electric resistance systems, warm air operates on the on-off principle. It supplies heat in bursts rather than in a sustained flow, and the temperature continually varies up and down several degrees. Rooms are heated unevenly, the floors are often cold, and the ceilings are often hot. Warm air systems produce discomforting drafts and, in many cases, uncomfortable warm air turbulance.

CONSTRUCTION OF HOUSE

The way your house is built affects the amount of heat that escapes. That is why insulation, storm windows, and weather stripping are so important for economical heating. It would seem, then, that you should make your house as *light* as possible. However, extra-thick insulation and doors and windows that are too tightly sealed reduce the amount of fresh outside air that must enter your home to allow proper ventilation. If your house is too *tight*, air movement is restricted. It tends to stratify into separate layers of hot air at the ceiling and cold air at the floor. Room air becomes dead and stifling, and cooking odors linger.

There are established standards of house construction that allow your house to breathe. These standards apply, no matter what the heating system. But unless you can choose the most economical fuel in your community, you may be forced to tighten your house or be faced with high fuel bills.

There is no one temperature that is comfortable at *all* times. For example, if you are active, you need less heat to keep from feeling uncomfortably cool. If you are just sitting, you need more. The amount of heat your body requires to feel comfortable varies with your activities.

A *hot water heating system* can be installed with independent temperature controls for any area of your home, or even for each room, although this is not practical. Zone heating is the most practical and also the most economical. Bedrooms can be kept cool for a restful sleep, bathrooms warm for a comfortable morning shower. Kitchen and work areas can be maintained at one temperature, living and family rooms at another, while the garage is kept just above freezing. Or zoning can assure a constant temperature throughout the home, if desirable. And it is all done automatically. Zoning is also an important economic consideration because it eliminates wasteful heating in seldom used areas.

Electric resistance systems can be zoned, but usually by individual rooms only. This is actually a disadvantage. Room zoning means that the doors to each room must be kept closed at all times so that warm air will not dissipate into cooler areas. This, of course, cannot be done in many rooms, such as the living room, dining room, kitchen, and the like, which normally do not have doors. Individual zoning in these areas simply does not work.

A *warm air system* can be zoned, but this is more expensive and affects the balance, or comfort level, of the entire system.

CREATING DIRT

Contrary to many claims, heating systems, in themselves, *do not* create dirt. Dirt results from cooking, air infiltration, and tracking dirt in from the outside. However, both resistance and warm air heating systems spread dirt. A resistance system, which produces temperatures up to 450° F., moves the dust over the hot element and actually chars air-borne dust and lint, converting these substances into a fine soot that clings to walls and ceilings. Evidence of this can be seen in streaks above baseboards or along the paths of electric ceiling cables. Also, in resistance heating ceiling installations, plaster is apt to flake and crack because of the extreme expansion and contraction caused by wide temperature variations.

Warm air systems, as mentioned previously, create air turbulance because they operate with a blower. Rapid agitation of the air causes dirt particles to be deposited on walls, furnishings, and curtains and draperies. Even filters cannot affectively control this situation, inasmuch as they trap only larger particles of dirt, while the greatest portion of the dust and cooking vapor is left to circulate throughout the house.

With a hydronic system, warmed air is circulated uniformly and without sudden on-and-off cycles to create turbulance. This fact, plus the fact that a hydronic system operates at relatively low temperatures, allows you to keep a cleaner home.

HOT WATER FOR HOUSEHOLD USE

In a resistance or warm air system, a separate hot water heater is required. With a hydronic boiler, all the hot water your family will require can be supplied from the boiler all year round. A tank-less heater, which is no more than a coil through which tap water is circulated, can be installed in your boiler. During the summer months, when heat in your home is shut off, the boiler operates at a low fuel level, about the same as an ordinary hot water heater. The tankless hot water feature is a decided savings when figuring the initial cost of your heating system. It also saves space.

In addition, a hydronic system permits installation of a great modern labor-saver—a snow-melting system. Pipe coils may be installed under sidewalks and driveways. Hot water is circulated through them, and snow is melted as fast as it falls. A hydronic system is also easily adaptable to heating swimming pools, greenhouses, and separate garages.

Chapter 21

Oil Burners

The pressure-atomizing burner shown in Fig. 1 is a fully automatic type, consisting of a motor, fan, and pump directly coupled together. Oil is supplied by the pump to the atomizing nozzle under pressure, being regulated by an adjustable relief valve. Oil is ignited by means of a high-tension spark-ignition unit, voltage being furnished by a 10,000-volt transformer. The transformer is equipped with a built-in radio interference filter.

Housing. The main burner housing is an aluminum casting on which the motor, air inlet transformers, and so on are mounted.

Motor. The motor is a totally enclosed, flange-mounted type, usually split-phase induction with built-in, manually reset, thermal overload protection, and is equipped with waste-lubricated sleeve bearings.

Fan. The multivane fan is mounted directly on the motor shaft. It is balanced, and is quiet in operation.

Pump. The pump is connected to the fan hub by means of a flexible coupling. The coupling is fastened by set screws to the pump shaft, and by a spline to the fan hub. The pump is of the dual unit, gear type, and may be used with either a two- or single-pipe system. The two-pipe system is recommended for all installations, but a single-pipe may be used where the tank is above the level of the burner.

Blower tube. The blower tube is made of heavy gage steel tubing. It supports the front end of the fuel feed assembly. The component parts are designed to provide a minimum of resistance to the flow of air and at the same time develop the desired degree of turbulence for efficient combustion.

Fuel feed assembly. The fuel tube is fastened into a tailpiece at the back, and at the front is supported in the blower tube and carries a nozzle adapter into which the oil nozzle is screwed. A turbulator is also mounted on the fuel tube. This is provided to give a certain

Fig. 1. Oil burner.

degree of spin and turbulence to the air as it mixes with the oil spray to improve combustion.

On the burner shown in Fig. 1, the fuel tube is bent at 90 degrees and is screwed into the bottom of the cast plate on which the ignition transformer is mounted. An optional delay oil solenoid valve can be supplied on all burners. Included with the fuel feed assembly is the oil ignition system, consisting of the electrodes, porcelain insulators, bus bars, and high tension cables. On some burners a flame stabilizer is mounted on the nozzle adapter.

Ignition system. Ignition on all pressure atomizing burners is accomplished by direct spark from a 10,000-volt transformer. A single transformer is standard equipment.

Oil specification. The burner shown in Fig. 1 may burn No. 2 CS-

12-48, No. 3 CS-12-40, or lighter oils. Also Pacific Coast Specification 200, Diesel, or lighter oils may be burned. *Do not* use gasoline, crankcase oil, or oil containing gasoline.

Nozzles. Nozzles are available in sizes and angulation to meet requirements of load and firebox shapes. They should be selected to produce the heat required at the rated capacity, if possible. Some variation in firing rate may be effected by changing the pump pressure.

Primary control system. For detailed information on controls, refer to the literature supplied by the manufacturers of components or contact the dealer.

Temperature controller. A *plain thermostat* is furnished as standard equipment. The thermostat, to perform satisfactorily, should be located $4\frac{1}{2}$ to 5 feet above the floor. The location should be near the center of the space being heated, but it should not be located near a radiator, outside wall, a wall housing hot water pipes, cold water pipes, flues, chimney, or where it will be exposed to drafts from frequently opened doors or windows, but at a point of normal temperature and where there is a free circulation of air. With proper location, the thermostat should operate on a differential of approximately 2° F. (The selection of the thermostat will depend upon the type of control system employed.)

Clock thermostats may be substituted for plain thermostats, or a basement type of electric clock can be used in conjunction with a plain thermostat.

Air supply to burner room. It is important that provision be made for an adequate fresh air supply to the burner room. A permanent opening for fresh air having no less than twice the area of the stack should be installed.

TABLE 22

BURNER RATINGS

Hourly Capacity	Minimum	Maximum
Gallon oil/hour	1	3
Equivalent boiler horsepower (hp)	3	10
Equivalent pounds steam generated/hour	115	345
Thousands Btu input	140	420
Equivalent square foot of steam radiation	465	1400
Equivalent square foot hot water radiation	745	2240

The ratings shown in Table 22 are predicated upon specific conditions of draft and furnace design. It may be permissible, under favorable conditions, to operate at higher rates, or advisable, under restricted conditions, to operate at reduced rates.

Heating capacities are based on 140,000 Btu's per gallon of oil and upon an overall boiler efficiency of 80 percent.

INSTALLATION

In the application of heating units to specific buildings and other types of loads, it is recommended the Btu/hour requirements be estimated by methods set forth by a recognized authority, such as the American Society of Heating, Refrigeration, and Air-Conditioning Engineers' (ASHRAE) guide.

Be sure that a fresh air supply is available to the boiler room—twice the area of the stack as a rule. A check of the burner should be made for shipping damages. Check the combustion head dimensions against the manufacturer's recommendation. Mount the burner level or sloping slightly down toward the nozzle.

Wiring should conform to the National Electrical Code and any local codes. Check rotation of motor on three-phase installations and with all burners check nameplate data for conformity with local characteristics.

Placing the Burner in Service. After the burner has been properly installed in accordance with the foregoing instructions, the following method should be employed by placing it in service.

1. The firebox should be thoroughly dried out by means of slow, wood fire and that this fire be continuous during initial starting of the burner. The stack damper *must* be wide open.

2. Check all electrical connections. *Keep main switch open.* Place all reset buttons on motor, controls, and so on in running position.

3. Set the opening of the adjustable air shutter to a position proportional to the rate of firing to be employed.

4. Disconnect the burner from the oil feed line. If a stack-switch-type control is used, set it in Cold position. Also set the temperature control or operating control so that the circuit will be closed.

5. Close main switch, which will allow burner to operate. There may be a momentary flame from any residual oil in the pump.

6. Check lockout timing so that the timing period does not exceed the standards of the type of control being used. The end of the timing period is determined by the action of the lockout in the main control, which operates to cause the burner to shut down. It will be necessary to allow a period of about three minutes before the control lockout switch can be reset. During this initial operation, the presence of ignition spark can be checked with a flame mirror or through a furnace viewport.

7. Reconnect the oil feed line and open oil valves, if any, and reset the control. The burner will start and as soon as oil is delivered at the nozzle, ignition should occur.

8. The burner oil pressure is set at the factory from 90 to 100 pounds per square inch gage, and under normal conditions the best operation will be obtained within this range. Changes of operating pressure may be obtained by adjusting the regulating valve. The maximum operating pressure is 125 pounds and the minimum is 75 pounds. If proper size flame cannot be obtained when operating between these two limits, then a nozzle of proper capacity should be substituted.

ADJUSTMENT PROCEDURES

The following steps are emphasized from the viewpoint of minimizing air-pollutant emissions.

Preparation Steps.

1. *Clean and seal.* Make sure the burner blast tube, fan housing, and blower wheel are clean of dirt and lint. Seal any air leaks into the combustion chamber, especially joints between sections of cast-iron boilers (and around the fire door).

2. *Nozzle.* Annual replacement of nozzle is recommended. The nozzle size should match the design load. *Do not oversize.* Short cycles and low percent on time result in higher overall pollutant emissions and lower thermal efficiency. An in-line oil filter will reduce service problems due to nozzle clogging.

3. *Sampling hole.* Drill a ¼-inch hole in the stack or flue duct between the unit and the barometric draft regulator (if not already

drilled by the installer). This is for taking smoke and CO_2 samples. It can also be used to insert a stack thermometer.

If space permits, the hole (Fig. 2) should be located in a straight section of the stack, at least two stack diameters from the unit breeching and at least one diameter from the unit side of the draft regulator.

4. *Adjust electrodes.* Adjust ignition electrodes to assure prompt ignition.

5. *Operate burner.* Operate burner, adjust air setting for good flame by visual observation, and run for at least 10 minutes or until operation has stabilized.

6. *Check burner.* Bleed air from pump and nozzle piping. Check pump pressure and adjust to 100 pounds per square inch (psi), if necessary (or to manufacturer's recommendation).

Combustion Adjustment Steps.

1. *Set draft.* Check the draft reading over the fire with a draft gage through a $\frac{1}{4}$-inch hole drilled in the fire door or inspection door. (This hole should be in the inspection door for oil-fire-matched units, or in the fire door for conversion installations. If possible, the hole should be above the flame level.)

Adjust the barometric draft regulator on the stack to give the overfire draft recommended by the manufacturer. If no such recommendations are available, set overfire draft to assure a negative pressure within the combustion chamber (usually 0.02 inch water column).

With some equipment, it will not be possible to take draft readings over the fire. In this case, adjust the draft regulator to give a stack draft reading between 0.04 and 0.06 inch water column (taken at the stack sampling hole).

Seal draft or sampling hole in inspection or fire door after these tests have been made, using a plug, bolt, or high-temperature sealant. (It is not necessary to seal the stack sampling hole.)

2. *Check smoke.* After burner has been operating 5 or 10 minutes, make a smoke measurement in the stack, following the smoke tester instructions. Pump the tester slowly for 10 full strokes. On pull stroke, use a steady motion so that a full stroke is obtained in 3 or 4 seconds. Allow a two-second pause between pump strokes to insure a full sample.

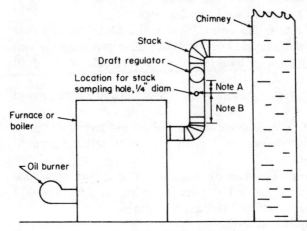

Horizonial Stack Connection

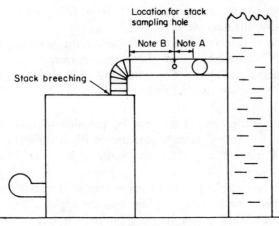

Vertical Stack Connection

Fig. 2. Typical stack connections.

Oily and yellow smoke spots on the filter paper are usually a sign of unburned fuel, indicating very poor combustion (and likely high emissions of carbon monoxide and unburned hydrocarbons). This condition can sometimes be caused by too much air, or by factors mentioned in the diagnosis section. If this condition cannot be corrected, a major renovation or even burner replacement may be necessary.

3. *Smoke-CO_2 curve.* Record measurements of smoke and CO_2 from the stack. (When making CO_2 readings, follow the instrument manufacturer's instructions.) Then establish the smoke-CO_2 curve by taking readings over a range of air settings, as shown in Fig. 3.

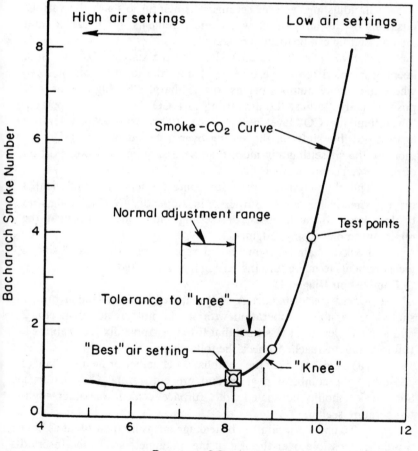

Fig. 3. Typical smoke-CO_2 characteristic for residential oil burner (with recommended air adjustment).

To do this, start with the air gate set at nearly full open and then take smoke and CO_2 readings at progressively lower air settings as necessary to visualize the general shape of the curve. (The CO_2 readings will increase as the air setting is decreased, unless combustion is incomplete.) Do not set air gate to give smoke reading above No. 4 or No. 5. Plot the points on graph paper, as shown in Fig. 4. Usually three or four readings are enough to establish the curve.

In adjusting each air setting, it is helpful to mark the various positions of the air gate at which measurements are made so that the final setting can be located quickly.

4. *Set air.* (*See* Table 23.) Examine the smoke-CO_2 plot and, keeping in mind the curve of Fig. 3, note the location of the *knee* where the smoke number begins to rise sharply. Noting the air gate position marks, adjust the air setting to a CO_2 level ½ to 1 percent lower than the CO_2 level at the knee. (This provides a tolerance against possible shifts in the setting over a period of time.) Do not increase the air setting any more than necessary on the lower portion of the curve below the knee.

The characteristic curve for some burners may not yield a distinct knee in the curve. Burner A in Appendix IX, Fig. 1, has no distinct knee. In such cases, the setting should be made near the minimum smoke (using judgment).

Lock the air adjustment and repeat draft, CO_2, and smoke measurements to make sure the setting has not shifted.

Combustion Diagnosis.

1. *Check performance.* A well-matched and well-tuned burner should be capable of operation with smoke not greater than No. 2 and at a CO_2 level not less than that listed in Appendix IX, Table 24. If this cannot be reached, check the following.

(a) Air leaks into the combustion chamber or heat exchanger can dilute the combustion gases and prevent normal CO_2 readings. Such leaks should be sealed with furnace cement or other high-temperature sealant.

To check for dilution by leakage, measure the CO_2 at as high a point as possible over the fire, using a stainless-steel tube inserted through the fire door sample hole (as described previously for overfire draft measurements), and compare this with the CO_2 measured in the

TABLE 23

TYPICAL AIR ADJUSTMENTS FOR DIFFERENT TYPES
OF RESIDENTIAL BURNERS

OIL-BURNER TYPE	Typical CO_2 in Flue Gas When Tuned*
HIGH-PRESSURE GUN-TYPE BURNERS	
• Old-Style Gun Burners	8 %
- No internal air-handling parts other than an end cone and stabilizer	
• Newer-Style Gun Burners	9 %
- special internal air-handling parts	
• Flame-Retention Gun Burners	10 %
- flame-retention heads	
OTHER TYPES OF BURNERS	
• Atomizing Rotary Burners	8 %
- ABC, Hayward, etc.	
• Rotary Wall-Flame Burners	12 %
- Timken, Fluid-Heat, Torridheet, etc.	
• Miscellaneous Low-Pressure Burners	**

* Based on acceptable Bacharach smoke -- generally No. 1 or trace, but not exceeding No. 2.

Caution should be used in leaving burners with CO_2 level higher than 13%.

** See manufacturer's instructions.

stack. A difference of more than one percent CO_2 between the stack and overfire readings usually indicates air entry through leaks that have not been properly sealed.

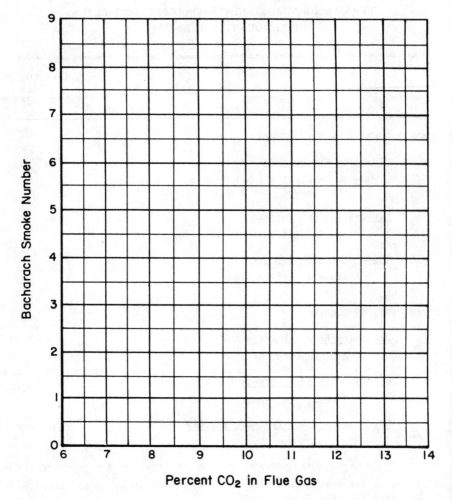

Fig. 4. Sample graph paper for plot of smoke-CO_2 characteristic.

Seal between the probe and fire door sample hole during testing (with asbestos rope, for example). The fire door hole should be sealed when not being used to avoid leakage of air through it. (*See* section on Combustion Adjustment, Step 1, Set draft.)

(b) If the CO_2 level in Appendix IX, Table 25, still cannot be reached without exceeding No. 2 smoke, poor mixing of air and fuel is likely.

This could be caused by a combustion head (blast tube nose piece) with too large a throat for good mixing, or an improper match between air pattern and nozzle spray pattern. Frequently, replacement of the nozzle with one having a different spray angle and pattern will improve performance.

It may be necessary to replace the combustion head or try different settings if the burner is equipped with an adjustable head or mixing devices. Modern flame-retention heads can be adapted to fit most blast tubes.

(c) The combustion chamber must be matched in size and shape to the nozzle spray and the burner air pattern. Oversized chambers do not insure adequate mixing. Undersized chambers may allow flame impingement on the chamber walls or heat exchanger.

Final Checks.

1. *Stack temperature.* Operating the unit at an excessive firing rate will generate more heat than the heat exchanger can use and result in unnecessary heat loss up the stack. Other causes of excessive heat loss are badly sooted heat-exchanger surfaces and excessive draft. The temperature of the flue gas provides an indication of these heat losses.

Measure stack temperature after at least five minutes of operation. Determine the net stack temperature by subtracting the room air temperature from the thermometer reading. Excessive stack loss is indicated if the net stack temperature during steady operation exceeds 400° F. to 600° F. for matched-package units, or 600° F. to 700° F. for conversion burners.

2. *Ignition.* Check operation over repeated cycles to insure prompt ignition on starting.

3. *Pump cutoff.* Slow pump cutoff at the end of a firing cycle can cause smoke and other pollutant emissions. Check for prompt pump cutoff by observing flame or by testing smoke at shutdown. If poor cutoff is observed, make sure air is purged from the pump and nozzle line. Air trapped in the pump or nozzle line will expand when heated, thus causing oil to drip into the combustion chamber after shutdown.

If poor cutoff persists, repair or replace pump. (A solenoid valve in the nozzle line should insure prompt cutoff. If it does not, replace or repair solenoid valve.)

4. *Controls.* Check settings of all operating and limit controls before leaving the installation.

5. *Annual cleanup.* An overall burner checkup and cleanup is recommended annually.

(*See* Appendix IX for Air-Pollutant Effects of Different Burner Adjustment Procedures.)

Chapter 22

Gas Burners

The gas burner shown in Fig. 1 is a fully automatic burner for natural gas. It provides 100 percent of the combustion air through the integral blower. It is used for operation at a fixed fuel input determined by orifice selection. The electric main gas valve, normally furnished, has a slow opening adjustment for *soft* light-off.

Two sizes are available as shown in Table 26. Both will operate with natural or induced draft. For forced draft operation against furnace back pressure the burner shown in Fig. 1 is recommended.

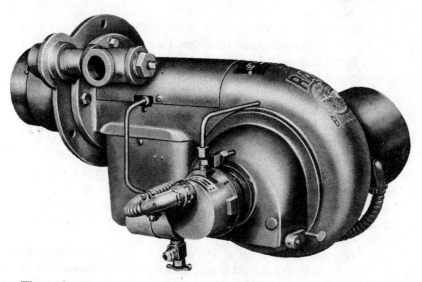

Fig. 1. Gas burner.

These burners are listed by Underwriters Laboratories, Inc., and have either a UV or flamerod combustion detector and control integrally mounted to provide safe ignition and combustion conditions.

TABLE 26

Type	Firing Rate BTU/hr	RPM	Motor HP	Main Valve Pipe Size
JGE-0	120,000-500,000	1725	⅛	¾"
JGE-1	120,000-1,000,000	3450	⅓	1"

They are available as a complete unit, and include the main and pilot electric valves, gas pressure regulators, and manual shut-off cocks. The gas manifold of the burner may be positioned for either a right-hand or left-hand approach of the main gas line.

Fuel. These burners are to be used with natural gas. Orifice selection and adjustment details are for natural gas. They can be used under most conditions with LP gas, LP/air-mixed gas, or manufactured gas with different orifice selections. The LP/air-mixed gas at 1,400 Btu's/cubic feet can be used with the natural gas pressure and orifice selections.

Main Gas Valve. The electric main gas valve, normally furnished, has an adjustment screw that allows a slow opening operation for a soft light-off under adverse firebox or back pressure conditions. If an alternate *snap acting* valve must be used, then the gas pressure regulator vent can be orificed to slow regulator response for the same results. Consult manufacturer's instructions.

Pilot Gas Valve. The electric pilot valve is burner mounted and has a needle valve for pilot adjustment installed in its inlet. (*See* Fig. 2 for gas supply piping to this valve.) For proper pilot gas input, this needle valve is opened one turn per 100,000 Btu's in main burner input.

Gas Pressure Regulators. Two regulators are furnished to be individually piped in the lines to the electric pilot and main gas valves. (*See* Fig. 2.)

The pilot regulator is pre-set at 3½ inches wc (water column) outlet pressure, but can be adjusted from 2 to 6 inches wc although this is not usually necessary. The needle valve piped into the electric pilot valve is used to adjust the pilot gas supply.

The main regulator can be adjusted from 3 inches to 7 inches wc, and must be finally set to produce three inches wc pressure at the orifice tee pressure tap to give proper Btu input for the orifice selected.

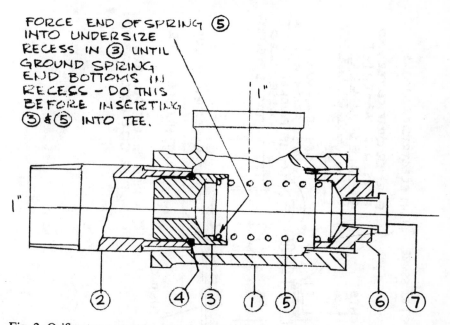

FORCE END OF SPRING ⑤
INTO UNDERSIZE
RECESS IN ③ UNTIL
GROUND SPRING
END BOTTOMS IN
RECESS — DO THIS
BEFORE INSERTING
③ & ⑤ INTO TEE.

Fig. 2. Orifice tee assembly. (1) Iron pipe tee (2) seat nipple (3) orifice (4) "O" ring (5) spring (6) cap (7) pipe plug

Maximum burner rating can be achieved with six inches wc incoming service gas pressure. The standard regulators are suitable for incoming gas pressure up to one psi. For higher gas pressures, special regulators must be substituted.

Orifice Tee. A special *tee* containing the removable gas input orifice is piped onto the burner with a special pipe nipple. *Do not change this nipple,* as it has a machined seat inside the tee to accept the changeable input orifice. (*See* Fig. 2.) The orifice is selected from the chart furnished by manufacturer for the input desired. Orifices can be changed or inspected by removing the large plug in the tee. The end of the spring that holds the orifice in position is then exposed. Pull the spring out gently and the orifice will come out with it. (*See* Fig. 3.) There is an *O* ring on the orifice. Place it on any other orifice being installed. Force the end of the spring into the recess of the orifice being installed. Then carefully insert into the tee, making sure the orifice slides into the internal machined seat

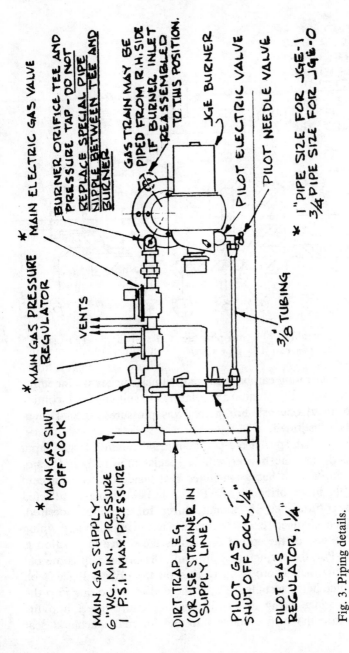

Fig. 3. Piping details.

provided in the nipple at the opposite end of the tee. Replace the large plug.

In the center of the large plug is a ⅛-inch pipe plug. This opening is used to read the orifice gas pressure during operation.

It is best to obtain properly sized orifices from the dealer or factory. Smaller orifices may be bored out, but be sure not to scar the stepped-down outside of the orifice that fits into the machined seat inside the tee.

A blank orifice (and *O* ring) can be installed to plug the line for testing the main gas valve for leakage. With the main electric valve closed, there should be no pressure built up at the ⅛-inch pipe tap for a period of one minute if the main valve is seating properly.

Air Shutter.   The burner *air shutter* has a lever and indicator that is locked into proper position for the firing rate used. The numbers on the indicator plate or multiples of 100,000 Btu's/hr input. For example, using 400,000 Btu's/hr input, set the lever at 4 for initial firing. Final adjustment, based on combustion analysis, may require a change from this position. For burners operating with high back pressure or high draft, the setting of the air shutter may have to be greater or less than indicated.

Air Supply Switch.   A *pressure switch* is mounted on the hub of the burner air inlet. This has both a suction and pressure pickup tube that runs into the housing to sense blower wheel operation and shut the burner and valves off should the blower stop or fail.

This switch can be adjusted by loosening the two set screws in the hub and pulling the switch out to expose its inner end, which has a central screw adjustment. (*See* manufacturer's instructions.)

Motor.   The *motor* (and blower) is mounted directly onto the burner housing. It is single-phase with integral manual reset overload protection. In case of overload or overheating, this switch will trip, shutting off the burner and requiring manual resetting. Motors with oil holes or cups over the bearings should be oiled annually with light engine oil (non-detergent).

Burner Gas Manifold.   The firing end of the burner consists of the gas manifold assembly, which also includes the mounting flange for the entire burner. The main gas stabilizing ring (of perforated metal), with stabilizing fingers, is mounted just inside the firing end of this assembly.

This assembly may be rotated 120 degrees to provide for a right-hand or left-hand entrance of the gas train. Merely remove the three bolts holding the burner housing to the manifold and remove the manifold. Then replace it in the desired orientation. Be careful to use the three bushings on the three bolts for proper centering of the parts when reassembling them. Also support or remove the central pilot assembly when making this change so that it does not droop and bend any parts when the manifold is removed. Be sure and check the location of the scanner or flamerod and entire pilot assembly.

You may turn the orifice tee to proper alignment with a pipe wrench but *do not replace* the special nipple between the tee and manifold casting.

Pilot Assembly.   The *pilot assembly* is located under the top access cover of the burner. It includes the pilot head and stabilizer, the ignition electrode, and scanner tube or flamerod. Its location can be shifted forward or backward by moving the slide through which the pilot gas supply tube enters the burner. *The location is important.* The front edge of the pilot head should be $\frac{3}{16}$ inch to $\frac{1}{4}$ inch back of the ends of the stablizing fingers of the main flame stabilizer. In this position, the top pin on this assembly should just touch the front edge of the top access opening of the burner so that replacement after service or inspection will reposition the assembly correctly. The assembly is removed by loosening the hex nut at the tubing connection on the rear of the assembly.

The rotational position of the pilot assembly is also important. The scanner tube or flamerod assembly must be just above the horizontal finger of the main stabilizer as shown in Fig. 4.

The location of the electrode and flamerod tips are also shown in Fig. 4.

Ignition Transformer.   The ignition transformer is a 6,000-volt, one end grounded type, mounted directly under the burner housing. The high tension terminal extends into the blower case and is connected to the ignition electrode by a short ignition cable.

Combustion Control.   The *combustion control* is mounted directly on the side of the ignition transformer if it is one of the standard controls normally furnished. Larger controls are shipped for separate mounting and wiring near the burner, and the burner wiring terminates in a junction box on the burner.

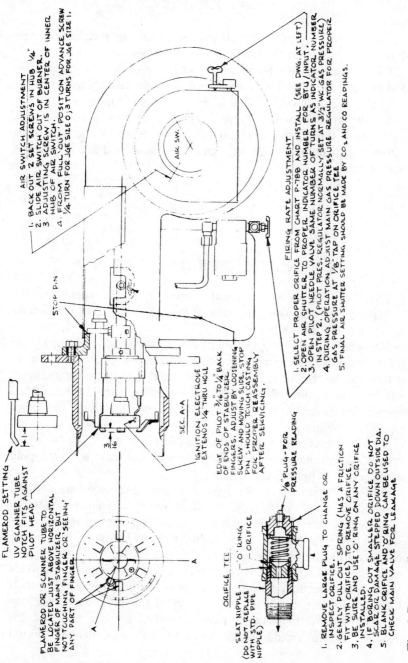

FLAMEROD SETTING

UV SCANNER TUBE
NOTCH FITS AGAINST
PILOT HEAD

|←—1—→|

FLAMEROD OR SCANNER TUBE TO
BE LOCATED JUST ABOVE HORIZONTAL
FINGER OF MAIN STABILIZER, BUT
NOT TOUCHING FINGER OR SEEING
ANY PART OF FINGER.

AIR SWITCH ADJUSTMENT

1. BACK OUT 2 SET SCREWS IN HUB.
2. SLIDE AIR SWITCH OUT OF BURNER.
3. ADJUSTING SCREW IS IN CENTER OF INNER
   HUB OF AIR SWITCH.
4. FROM FULL 'OUT' POSITION ADVANCE SCREW
   ¼ TURN FOR J&E SIZE 0, 3 TURNS FOR J&E SIZE 1.

AIR SW.

STOP PIN

SEC. A-A

IGNITION ELECTRODE
EXTENDS ¼ THRU HOLE

3/16

EDGE OF PILOT 3/16 TO ¼ BACK
OF ENDS OF STABILIZER
FINGERS. ADJUST BY LOOSENING
SCREW AND MOVING SLIDE, STOP
PIN SHOULD TOUCH CASTING
FOR PROPER REASSEMBLY
AFTER SERVICING.

FIRING RATE ADJUSTMENT

1. SELECT PROPER ORIFICE FROM CHART P-788 AND INSTALL (SEE DWG. AT LEFT)
2. OPEN AIR SHUTTER TO PROPER INDICATOR NUMBER FOR BTU/INPUT.
3. OPEN PILOT NEEDLE VALVE SAME NUMBER OF TURNS AS INDICATOR NUMBER
   IN STEP 2. (PILOT PRES. REGULATOR NORMALLY SET AT 3½" W.C. GAS PRESSURE)
4. DURING OPERATION ADJUST MAIN GAS PRESSURE REGULATOR FOR PROPER
   GAS PRESSURE AT 1/8" TAP ON ORIFICE TEE
5. FINAL AIR SHUTTER SETTING SHOULD BE MADE BY CO₂ AND CO READINGS.

A ———————— A

ORIFICE TEE

SEAT NIPPLE
(DO NOT REPLACE
WITH STD. PIPE
NIPPLE)

'O' RING
ORIFICE

1/8 PLUG — FOR
PRESSURE READING

1. REMOVE LARGE PLUG TO CHANGE OR
   INSPECT ORIFICE.
2. GENTLY PULL OUT SPRING (HAS A FRICTION
   FIT WITH ORIFICE) TO REMOVE ORIFICE.
3. BE SURE AND USE 'O' RING ON ANY ORIFICE
   INSTALLED.
4. IF BORING OUT SMALLER ORIFICE DO NOT
   SCAR OR DAMAGE STEPPED DOWN OUTSIDE DIA.
5. BLANK ORIFICE AND 'O' RING CAN BE USED TO
   CHECK MAIN VALVE FOR LEAKAGE

Fig. 4. Burner adjustment.

The control may utilize an ultraviolet scanner or rectification-type flamerod mounted on the internal pilot assembly.

The control provides for prepurge operation of the blower, ignition and proof of the pilot flame, ignition of the main flame, flame supervision, and rapid shut-off of fuel in event of flame failure.

See the manufacturer's wiring diagrams for two typical controls used. Read the control manufacturer's instruction sheets furnished with the control for details on control operation and flame response output readings.

PLACING THE BURNER IN SERVICE

There should be a permanently open, fresh air supply to the boiler room at least twice the area of the exhaust flue, or one square inch per 1,000 Btu's input.

Mounting.   See Fig. 5 for cut-out of the burner mounting plate on the combustion chamber. (*See* section on Gas Manifold to determine whether a right-hand or left-hand gas piping arrangement will be used, as this will influence the mounting plate cut-out. Check burner dimensions for proper clearance from the floor and other equipment (Fig. 5).

Check burner adjustment dimensions (Fig. 4) to be sure the critical dimensions shown are observed and that there is no shipping damage or misalignment.

Piping.   See Fig. 2 for typical piping. It is recommended the components shown be as close to the burner as convenient. Note the ⅜-inch tube for the pilot gas supply. Fittings are provided. (*See* section on Gas Manifold for right-hand or left-hand gas supply connection.)

A one- or ¾-inch line is recommended for maximum rating. Gas supply pressures may be any value between 6-inch wc and 1 psi. If higher or lower pressure is the case, special gas line components may have to be used in place of those furnished as standard. The gas pressure shown should be available to the main manual shut-off

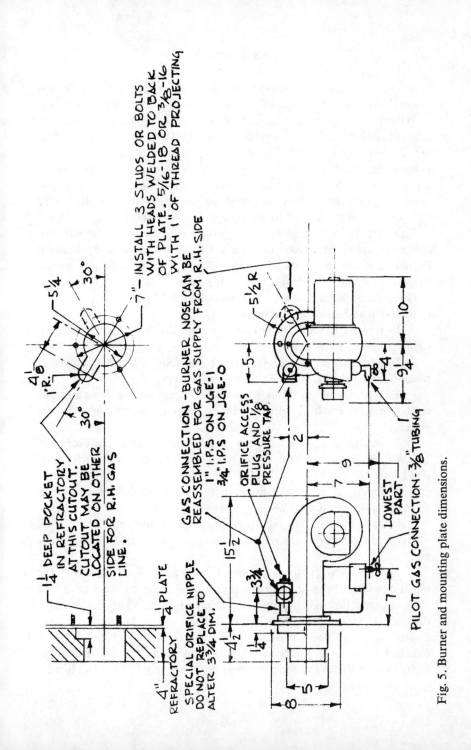

Fig. 5. Burner and mounting plate dimensions.

valve *during burner operation.* There is an extra pipe plug in the manual valve that can be used to check the gas pressure at this point.

Wiring. Make sure the motor and control electrical characteristic (110–120 volts, 60 cycles is standard) matches the electric service volts and cycles. The burner components and controls are completely wired with the exception of the main gas valve, which must be connected to the control after piping. Some larger controls, if used, cannot be burner mounted, so they must be installed near the burner and connected to the junction box on the burner.

The external limit and operating controls must be wired into the control system. See manufacturer's wiring diagrams for standard burner controls indicated on the diagrams, or obtain required diagrams for other controls from your dealer or factory.

Observe applicable codes when installing field wiring.

Start-Up and Adjustment Steps.

1. Be sure to read the foregoing sections of this chapter—it may save you time and difficulty.

2. Be sure the proper orifice for the required firing rate is in place in the orifice tee. (*See* section on Orifice Tee.)

3. With the main electric power off, press all the reset buttons on the motor, control, and any other manual reset devices in the system.

4. Set the burner air shutter to the proper number multiple of 100,000 Btu's/hr selected firing rate (for example, 4 for 400,000 Btu's/hr).

5. Open the pilot needle valve the same number of full turns as the number on the air shutter opening in step 4.

6. Loosen the small pipe plug in the main manual shut-off cock to bleed air out of the gas piping. Tighten the plug after bleeding the air.

7. With pilot and main shut-off cocks closed, turn on the electric power. If the limit circuit is completed, the burner motor will start and run through a prepurge period of from 30 to 90 seconds, depending on the particular control being used. At that time, the electric spark will be turned on for pilot ignition. (This can be checked through a rear view port on the boiler, or by lifting the burner cover slightly to look down at the spark gap in the pilot head.)

There should be no response of the control to the spark (flame relay pull-in, or *click* from operation of the main gas solenoid valve, or meter response if a meter is connected to the control-per-control instruction sheet.) The spark will continue for some seconds and then the control will lock out. Replace the cover.

8. Allow the control reset mechanism to cool for one minute and reset it. The burner will start again and prepurge. During this time, open only the pilot shut-off cock. Upon energizing the spark (and electric pilot valve), the pilot should ignite. The control should respond and energize the main fuel solenoid valve. Only the pilot will continue to operate since the gas cock to the main valve is closed. The pilot should continue without control drop-out or lock-out if the gas supply is correct. If not, try repeating the process with more or less gas as adjusted by the pilot needle valve until steady pilot operation and control hold-in is achieved. (Some larger, special controls will turn the pilot off after 20 seconds even when good pilot operation is present.)

9. With the pilot operating properly, and the main electric valve energized, open the main gas cock for main flame ignition. This should occur within 1 to 3 seconds depending on the slow opening adjustment of the main gas valve mechanism. If main flame ignition does not occur, shut off the main cock immediately and recheck the slow-opening screw on the standard main valve. (The standard main valve has a slow-opening adjustment screw that may prevent valve operation if it is completely screwed closed.)

It is helpful at this point to have a gas pressure gage or manometer attached at the $\frac{1}{8}$-inch pipe plug on the orifice tee. This will show positive pressure as soon as the main valve opens and indicates main gas delivery. Under firing conditions, this pressure should read about three inches wc. The pressure can be changed by adjusting the main gas pressure regulator to produce three inches wc at the orifice tee.

10. Shut the burner off electrically by the limit circuit or main power. Be sure the gas pressure at the orifice tee drops to zero, indicating closure of the main valve. Restart the burner with both pilot and main gas cocks open. Be sure gas pressure is zero at the orifice tee during prepurge operation. (This pressure may be slightly

negative due to the induction effect of the air stream in the burner.) The pilot should then turn on, the control responding to open the main valve and ignite the main flame.

11. After normal operation has been established, a final check of combustion quality should be made by CO_2 and CO readings and the air shutter readjusted if necessary for best efficiency. If the shutter is changed a great deal, the pilot may also have to be readjusted for the changed air supply.

12. The burner should be cycled several times to assure consistent operation. To check proper flame failure operation of the burner control, suddenly shut off both the main and pilot cocks during burner operation. The flame relay of the control should drop out immediately, de-energizing the pilot and main electric valves. Turn the cocks back on to see that there is no gas pressure at the orifice tee. This indicates closure of the main electric valve. The control may lock out or recycle the burner through another start, depending on the particular control being used.

Chapter 23

Oil Furnaces and Oil Heating

The oil furnace shown in Fig. 1 works as follows: on a call for heat, the thermostat switch closes and 24 volts AC power is supplied to the primary control, energizing the burner motor, ignition transformer, and safety timing circuit. Electrode spark is present for ignition. The fuel pump, driven by the burner motor, is operating. When fuel pump pressure reaches approximately 100 psi (pounds per square inch), the pump internal check valve opens. Combustion takes place. (The safety timing circuit monitors the burner flame by means of a light-sensitive cell, called a *cad cell*. Absence of burner flame causes the cell to send an electrical signal to the primary control sensitive relay, shutting down the burner assembly.) (*See* section on How the Primary Control Works.) With continued operation the cad cell remains in the flame monitoring mode. The fan-control helix assembly expands, closing the fan switch and starting the blower motor. If for some reason there is a loss of sufficient airflow, the limit switch opens, disconnecting 24 volts AC power from the primary control, shutting off the burner motor and ignition transformer. The fuel pump, driven by the burner motor, stops. As the fuel pump pressure drops to approximately 85 psi, the pump internal check valve closes, shutting off the fuel supply. The fan-control helix contracts, the fan switch opens, and 115 volts AC power is disconnected from the blower motor.

SERVICING OIL FURNACES

Fan Limit Controls. Fan limit controls serve two functions— they limit high temperature, and operate the on-off fan. The limit control is factory-set according to each unit's critical temperature.

Fan controls are adjustable. Recommended settings are 120° F.

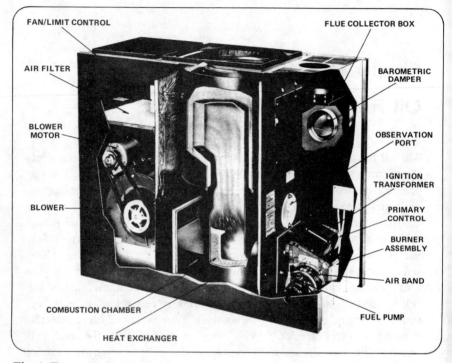

Fig. 1. Features of oil furnace.

for blower on, and 90° F. for blower off. Settings may vary, depending upon the system's design. Some models are equipped with a fixed differential between fan on and fan off. Only fan on requires setting. Figures 2 and 3 show the typical fan limit controls in use.

Primary Controls. The function of the primary control is to supervise and monitor the operation of the burner. It must provide system safety by sensing the presence or absence of flame and shutting down the system if the burner fails to function properly. The primary control must be subordinate to the limit control.

The flame monitoring safety control, which is used in conjunction with the primary control, is called the cad cell. The *cad cell* consists of a light-sensitive material called cadmium sulfide. In darkness, cadmium sulfide has a very high resistance to the passage of electrical current. In the presence of light in the visible range, its resistance

Fig. 2. Fan limit.

HELIX BIMETAL

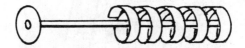

Expansion or contraction of bimetal element
causes shaft to rotate. Cam at end of shaft
activates switch.

Fig. 3. Fan cam and shaft.

becomes very low and electrical current is allowed to pass. The
current that is allowed to pass is used to actuate a sensitive relay in
the primary control, which in turn energizes or de-energizes the
control circuit in the presence or absence of flame. Figure 4 shows
a typical primary and cad cell control assembly with external reset.

How the Primary Cad Cell Control Works.   When the S-1 switch
is closed, supplying 115 VAC power, the T-1 transformer primary
is energized. Thermostat calls for heat, relay K-1 pulls in, energizing
burner motor and ignition transfer. Safety switch starts to heat. Cad
cell sees flame, relay K-2 pulls in, de-energizing safety switch heater.
Thermostat becomes satisfied, relay K-1 drops out, shutting off
burner motor and ignition transformer relay. K-2 drops out immediately when cad cell sees no flame. (*See* Fig. 5.) System will lock

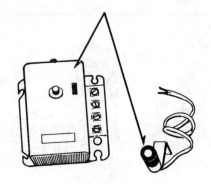

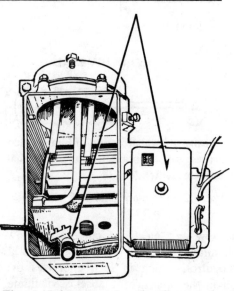

Fig. 4. Primary and cad cell control assembly.

out. Reset button must be depressed for a recycle. Safety switch timing will vary according to control design.

Oil Burner Assembly. The heat of the oil furnace is the burner itself. Several types of burners are available from those that have been manufactured. However, due to wide acceptance, the gun-type pressure burner is the most commonly used. The gun-type burner

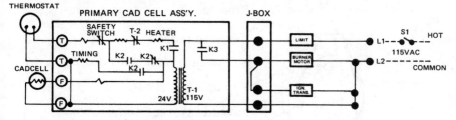

Fig. 5. Function of primary/cell control.

physically breaks the oil up into droplets, which are then mixed with air to form a combustible mixture. The oil is forced under ramp pressure through a calibrated nozzle, which then converts it to a fine spray. Figures 6, 7, and 8 show a typical gun-type burner.

How the Oil Burner Works.   The fuel oil is pumped from the tank through the pump gears, and oil pressure is regulated by an internal valve (check valve) that opens, developing approximately 100 psi at the burner nozzle. The oil is then atomized, ignited, and burned. The fine droplets of oil that are discharged from the nozzle are electrically ignited by a transformer, which raises the voltage from 115 volts to 14,000 volts. The electric spark is developed at the electrode gap located near the nozzle spray. The high velocity of air produced by a squirrel cage fan helps develop the ignition spark to the point where it will reach out and ignite the oil without the electrode tips actually being in the oil spray.

The nozzle is made up of two essential parts—the inner body, called the distributor, and the outer body, which contains the orifice that the oil sprays through. Under high pump pressure of approximately 100 psi, the oil is swirled through the distributor and discharged from the orifice as a spray. The spray is ignited by the spark and combustion takes place. (*See* Figs. 6, 7, and 8.)

ADJUSTING THE OIL FURNACE FOR MAXIMUM EFFICIENCY

For maximum efficiency of combustion it is important to be sure all checks are inclusive. To accomplish these goals it is recommended to use a complete combustion test kit, such as Bacharach Fyrite or its equivalent. (*See* Fig. 9.)

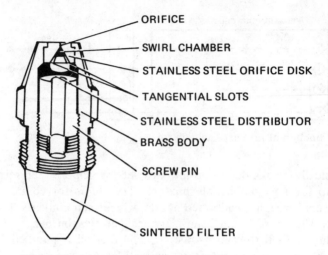

ORIFICE

SWIRL CHAMBER

STAINLESS STEEL ORIFICE DISK

TANGENTIAL SLOTS

STAINLESS STEEL DISTRIBUTOR

BRASS BODY

SCREW PIN

SINTERED FILTER

Fig. 6. Typical gun-type burner.

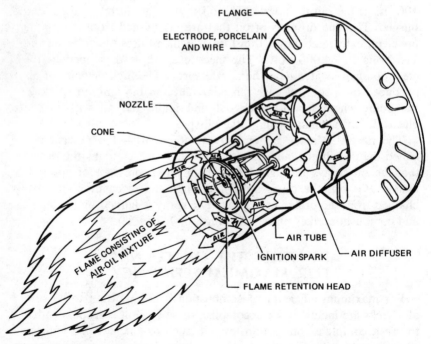

FLANGE

ELECTRODE, PORCELAIN AND WIRE

NOZZLE

CONE

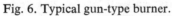
FLAME CONSISTING OF AIR-OIL MIXTURE

AIR TUBE

IGNITION SPARK

AIR DIFFUSER

FLAME RETENTION HEAD

Fig. 7. Typical gun-type burner.

Fig. 8. Typical gun-type burner.

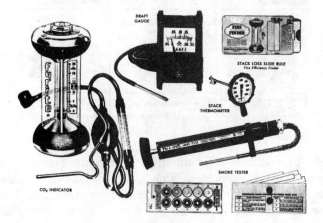

Fig. 9. Combustion test kit.

The following are recommended procedures for making the necessary checks and adjustments for maximum combustion efficiency.

Checking the Draft. The correct draft is essential for efficient operation. The intensity of draft determines the rate at which combustion gases pass through the furnace. The intensity of draft also governs the amount of air supplied for combustion. Excessive draft can increase the stack temperature and reduce the percent of CO_2 in flue gases. With the use of a draft gage, check the draft overfire.

This may be accomplished by inserting the sampling tube through the observation port. Normal reading should be —.01 to —.03 inch of water. (*See* Figs. 10 and 11.)

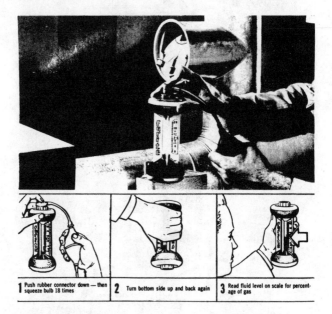

Fig. 10. Checking draft.

Always be sure to *zero in* the draft gage before taking a reading. Check the flue pipe draft by drilling a ¼-inch hole at the flue pipe, down stream of the barometric control damper. (*See* Fig. 12.) The flue pipe draft reading should be —.04 to —.06 inch water column. Should the reading not be within these tolerances, adjust the barometric control counterbalance, increasing or decreasing the draft.

Checking CO_2. CO_2 values may be obtained by using the CO_2 indicator. The CO_2, or carbon dioxide, indicator draws up a sample of the combustion gases that is read directly on the indicator. For taking the flue gas sample, use the hole previously drilled for the draft check. Turn the oil burner on and allow it to operate approximately five minutes before checking the CO_2. Insert the sampling tube of the CO_2 indicator's gas aspirating assembly into the hole in the flue pipe. The rubber cap end is placed on the top of

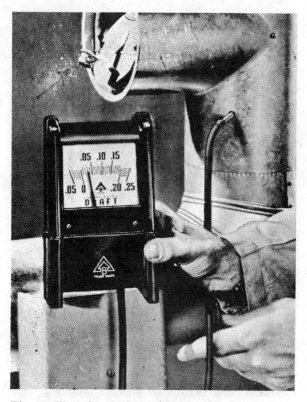

Fig. 11. Flue pipe draft reading.

the indicator plunger valve, and held in a depressed position. The aspirator rubber bulb is next squeezed 18 times. On the 18th squeeze, the depressed plunger valve is released before releasing the rubber bulb. The indicator is now turned over twice, permitting the test fluid to absorb the flue gas sample. The indicator is then held in an upright, level position. The percent of CO_2 is read directly on the indicator scale. (*See* Fig. 13.) The highest possible percent CO_2 reading should always be your goal. Readings will vary according to each unit. Readings from 9 to 10 percent are generally considered ideal. However, take into consideration other factors of your efficiency check, and instructions supplied with each oil furnace, since CO_2 values will vary.

Fig. 12. CO₂ indicator.

Checking the Stack Temperature. The stack thermometer is an instrument used in conjunction with your total test procedures, to diagnose and solve applications of the combustion process. The stack temperature may be checked using the same $\frac{1}{4}$-inch reference hole drilled in the flue pipe for draft and CO_2 readings. A high stack temperature may indicate any of the following conditions:

1. Excessive draft.
2. Sooted heat exchange.
3. Undersized furnace.
4. Defective combustion chamber.
5. Furnace over-fired.

Fig. 13. Thermometer reading.

As a rule of thumb, stack temperature readings in excess of the following figures may generally be considered abnormally high.

Packaged Units: 400° F.–500° F.

Such high temperature readings are cause for concern. Consult each unit's installation instructions for recommended stack temperatures. Determining the net stack temperature is accomplished by substracting the basement temperature from the actual stack temperature reading. For example, a thermometer reading 600° F. basement temperature, 70° F. net stack temperature: 600° F. minus 70° F. equals 530° F. (*See* Fig. 13.)

Checking the Combustion Smoke.   The objective of the smoke test is to measure the smoke content in the flue gases by means of a smoke tester and comparison scale. (*See* Fig. 14.) To check the smoke, operate the unit for approximately five minutes. Insert the free end of the tester's sampling tube into the ¼-inch hole used for previous tests. Place the filter paper in the *holding slot* of the tester. Pull the smoke tester handle 10 full strokes, hesitating a few seconds between each stroke. Remove the filter paper from the tester holding slot. Compare the smoke spot on the filter paper with the closest color on the smoke comparison scale. It should be emphasized that not all types of oil furnaces will be equally affected by the same smoke content in the flue gas, being regulated by the burner airband adjustment, fuel oil pump pressure, draft, and type of nozzle used. Recommended smoke scale comparison is a trace of number 1.

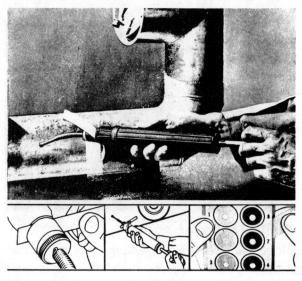

Fig. 14. Smoke tests and readings.

Table 27 shows the typical results for interpreting smoke readings. Smoke test values or a higher number may be caused by any of the following:

1. Improper fan delivery.
2. Poor draft.
3. Poor fuel supply.
4. Defective draft regulator.
5. Excessive air leaks.
6. Improper fuel-air mixture.
7. Defective combustion chamber.

Checking the Oil Pressure. Normal pump pressure is 90 to 100 psi. This is accomplished by installing a pressure gage at the pump gage port. The pump pressure is increased by turning the set screw in a clockwise direction. (*See* Fig. 15.) To determine the cause of improper cut-off at the nozzle, insert a pressure gage in the nozzle port of the pump. If the pump pressure drops approximately 15 psi from normal operating pressure, the pump is functioning properly, and air within the system is the cause of improper cut-off; if, however, the pressure drops to zero psi, the pump assembly should be replaced.

TABLE 27

SMOKE READINGS

BACHARACH SMOKE SCALE NO.	RATING	SOOTING PRODUCED
1	Excellent	Extremely light if at all
2	Good	Slight sooting which will not increase stack temp. appreciably
3	Fair	May be some sooting but will rarely require cleaning more than once a year
4	Poor	Borderline condition. Some units will require cleaning more than once a year.
5	Very Poor	Soot rapidly and heavily

TO INCREASE/DECREASE PRESSURE

Fig. 15. Pump pressure.

Checking the Temperature Rise.   After the unit has been adjusted for maximum efficiency, the final step is to check the temperature rise. This may be accomplished by drilling a ¼-inch hole in the supply air and return air ducts of the unit. Insert a thermometer in each duct hole (Fig. 16). Normal temperature rise is from 70° F. to 100° F.

> *Example:* Supply air temperature = 170° F.
>   Return air temperature = 75°
>   Temperature rise = 95°

Temperature rise may be increased or decreased by increasing or decreasing the blower speed.

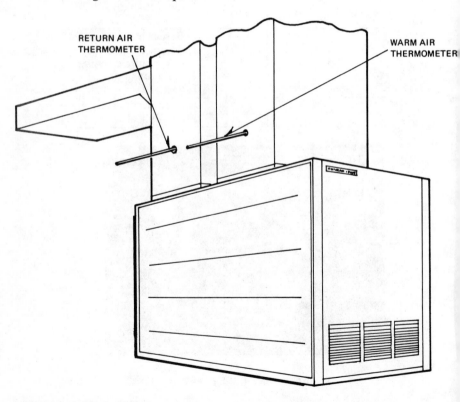

RETURN AIR
THERMOMETER

WARM AIR
THERMOMETER

Fig. 16. Adjusting blower speed for proper temperature.

Adjusting the Blower Speed for Proper Temperature. Adjust the blower speed on belt drive models by loosening the nut on the motor mount bracket and pushing the motor up to relieve belt tension. Remove belt, then loosen motor pulley with Allen wrench, and open adjustable pulley to decrease blower speed or close to increase speed. Be sure to adjust belt tension, so that the belt is as loose as possible without slippage. If belt tension is excessive, the blower motor will overload and cut off on thermal overload.

Adjust the blower speed on direct drive models with multi-speed motors by wiring the motor for higher or lower speed. Repeat these procedures until the desired temperature rise is obtained.

(*See* Fig. 17 for common chimney problems related to insufficient draft.)

PREVENTIVE MAINTENANCE FOR HEATING EQUIPMENT

At the beginning of each season, the unit should be checked as outlined below. (*See* Figs. 18 and 19.)

1. Check and clean blower assembly.
2. Lubricate blower motor, when possible.

(a) Motors without oiler plugs are pre-lubricated and permanently lubricated. No further lubrication is required.

(b) For motors with oiler plugs, add 8 to 10 drops of SAE No. 20 non-detergent oil. Some oilers may require a small piece of wire pushed into the oiler hole, to clear the oil wick for flow of lubrication.

3. Lubrication of blower bearings and pillow block bearing do not generally require lubrication and are permanently sealed.

If bearings are supplied with grease fittings, a good grade, wide temperature range lubricant is recommended, such as Lub-o-paste, an all temperature lubricant.

4. Always check unit's voltage underload and blower running amperes according to motor data plate.

5. Always check the air filters, especially since they can contribute to many problems, including excessive blower motor temperatures, resulting in excessive amperes. Clean or replace filters when

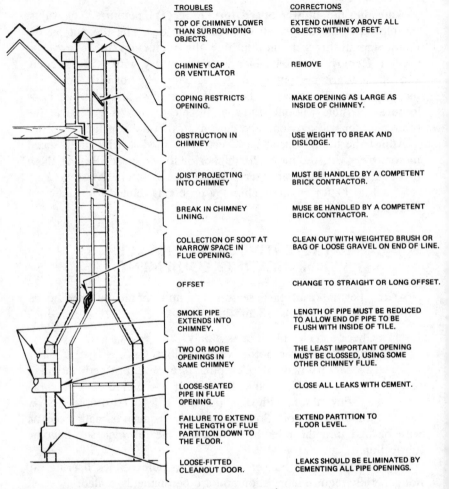

TROUBLES	CORRECTIONS
TOP OF CHIMNEY LOWER THAN SURROUNDING OBJECTS.	EXTEND CHIMNEY ABOVE ALL OBJECTS WITHIN 20 FEET.
CHIMNEY CAP OR VENTILATOR	REMOVE
COPING RESTRICTS OPENING.	MAKE OPENING AS LARGE AS INSIDE OF CHIMNEY.
OBSTRUCTION IN CHIMNEY	USE WEIGHT TO BREAK AND DISLODGE.
JOIST PROJECTING INTO CHIMNEY	MUST BE HANDLED BY A COMPETENT BRICK CONTRACTOR.
BREAK IN CHIMNEY LINING.	MUSE BE HANDLED BY A COMPETENT BRICK CONTRACTOR.
COLLECTION OF SOOT AT NARROW SPACE IN FLUE OPENING.	CLEAN OUT WITH WEIGHTED BRUSH OR BAG OF LOOSE GRAVEL ON END OF LINE.
OFFSET	CHANGE TO STRAIGHT OR LONG OFFSET.
SMOKE PIPE EXTENDS INTO CHIMNEY.	LENGTH OF PIPE MUST BE REDUCED TO ALLOW END OF PIPE TO BE FLUSH WITH INSIDE OF TILE.
TWO OR MORE OPENINGS IN SAME CHIMNEY	THE LEAST IMPORTANT OPENING MUST BE CLOSSED, USING SOME OTHER CHIMNEY FLUE.
LOOSE-SEATED PIPE IN FLUE OPENING.	CLOSE ALL LEAKS WITH CEMENT.
FAILURE TO EXTEND THE LENGTH OF FLUE PARTITION DOWN TO THE FLOOR.	EXTEND PARTITION TO FLOOR LEVEL.
LOOSE-FITTED CLEANOUT DOOR.	LEAKS SHOULD BE ELIMINATED BY CEMENTING ALL PIPE OPENINGS.

Fig. 17. Chimney problems—troubles and corrections.

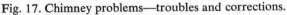

required. If the unit is equipped with permanent, washable filters, a viscous filter spray such as Filter Kote is recommended, and will add to their efficiency.

    6. Fan limit control. Check fan and limit control operation and settings.

    7. Burner assembly. The six main items to check are as follows:

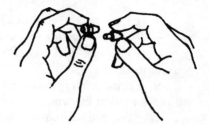

Fig. 18.

Fig. 19.

(a) Check the shut-off valve and fuel filter cartridge. Replace or clean cartridge if dirty.

(b) Check the nozzle assembly, disassembling and cleaning with lacquer thinner or kerosene.

(c) Check electrodes for deterioration, such as pitting of tips or cracked insulators, and readjust electrodes to unit's specifications.

(d) Check cad cell positioning (sighting). Clean the cell's lens surface.

(e) Check the combustion chamber for damage and soot accumulation. If soot remover is used, be sure to follow the manufacturer's directions.

(f) Check all electrical connections for tightness.

(g) Check all fuel piping connections for leaks and tighten as required.

8. Start the burner assembly. Check its efficiency.

(a) Draft over fire.

(b) Draft at flue and barometric damper operation.

(c) Stack temperature and smoke at the flue.

(d) CO_2 over fire and at the flue.

(e) Check fuel pump pressure, and internal pump check valve operation.

9. Check primary control safety lock-out operation by shutting off fuel supply at the tank.

10. The final recommended step is to check to see that extra fuses, a belt, and so on are available. You should always have an emergency number, in addition to the card at the unit.

TOOLS

Figure 20 shows the recommended tools for servicing oil furnaces; see also list of tools.

1. Screwdrivers and nutdriver set
2. Diagonal pliers
3. Six-inch long nose pliers
4. Five-inch short nose pliers
5. Stubby screwdriver
6. Pipe wrenches—10-inch and 12-inch
7. Open end wrench set
8. Wire strippers/crimper
9. Allen wrench set
10. Trouble light drop cord
11. Flashlight
12. Pocket thermometer
13. Draft gages
14. Incline manometer

Fig. 20. Tools for servicing oil furnaces:
1. Screwdriver and nutdriver set. 2. Diagonal pliers. 3. Six-inch long nose pliers. 4. Five-inch short nose pliers. 5. Stubby screwdriver. 6. Pipe wrenches: 10-inch and 12-inch. 7. Open end wrench set. 8. Wire strippers/crimper. 9. Allen wrench set. 10. Trouble light drop cord. 11. Flashlight. 12. Pocket thermometer. 13. Draft gages. 14. Incline manometer. 15. Amprobe. 16. Compound gage. 17. Volt, ohm, milliamp meters. 18. Stack thermometer. 19. Hand tachometer. 20. Feed oiler. 21. CO_2 indicator/checker. 22. Flame mirror.

15. Amprobe
16. Compound gage
17. Volt, ohm, milliamp meters
18. Stack thermometer
19. Hand tachometer
20. Feed oiler
21. CO_2 indicator/checker
22. Flame mirror

OIL HEATING

Fuel Oil.   In residential oil heating, No. 2 fuel oil is the primary fuel used. No. 2 fuel oil consists of 87 percent carbon, 10 percent hydrogen, and approximately 3 percent sulphur. The specific gravity is approximately 32–36. (*See* Table 28.) When completely burned, one gallon of No. 2 fuel oil will give up in heat content 138,000 to 140,000 Btu's. However, before the fuel oil can be used as a fuel in a residential oil furnace, the fuel must be changed from a liquid to a fine spray. This principle is called pressure atomization, or the process of preparing the fuel for combustion. This is accomplished by what we call the domestic-gun-type high-pressure atomizing oil burner, or the gun-type burner for short.

Details of its operation were explained previously in this chapter.

TABLE 28

FUEL OIL

CONTENT OF OIL	SPECIFIC GRAVITY	FUEL PUMP PRESSURE	HEAT CONT. PER/GALLON
CARBON HYDROGEN SULPHUR	32-36	90-100 P. S. I.	138-140,000 BTU per/gallon

TYPES OF OIL FURNACES

There are three types, or four styles, of residential oil furnace: upflow highboy, lowboy, counterflow, and horizontal.

The *upflow highboy* (Fig. 21) is by far the most popular. Its narrow width and depth allow for locations in closets and utility rooms. It can still be used in most basements. Blowers are usually direct drive multi-speed or may be belt drive. Air intake is optional from the sides or bottom.

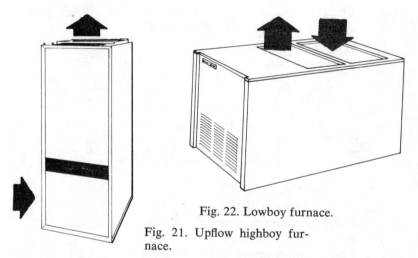

Fig. 22. Lowboy furnace.

Fig. 21. Upflow highboy furnace.

The *lowboy furnaces* (Fig. 22) are built low in height and are the necessary choice where head room is at a minimum. Supply and return ducts are on top for easy attachment. Blowers are usually belt drive. Many are sold for replacement equipment in older homes.

The *counterflow*, or *downflow*, is similar in design and style to the highboy, except the air intake and fan are at the top, with the discharge at the bottom (Fig. 23). They are widely used where the duct system is in concrete or beneath a crawl space. When mounted on a combustible floor, an accessory base is required, called a non-combustible base.

The fourth type is the *horizontal* furnace (Fig. 24) that is very adaptable for installation in crawl spaces, attics, or basements due to its low height. It requires no floor space. Inlet air is at one end and is discharged out the other. The furnace is designed to be field changeable from a left- or right-hand application.

Even though there are four different types of oil furnaces, the basic designs are similar. The components are grouped as follows:

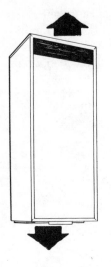

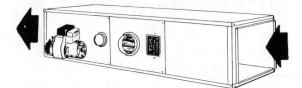

Fig. 24. Horizontal furnace.

Fig. 23. Counterflow or downflow.

1. Cabinet (Fig. 25).
2. Heat exchanger (Fig. 26).
3. Burner assembly and controls.
4. Barometric control.
5. Blower and motor.
6. Room thermostat.

The cabinet (Fig. 25) essentially serves to support the components and provides the necessary enclosure for air over the heat exchanger (Fig. 26), and also for safety purposes. Naturally, it should have good appearance and consumer approval. The heat exchanger, often called the radiator, is the drum type. The combustion chamber is sealed inside, which is made of a ceramic material.

Room air is forced over the outside surfaces, where it is warmed and returned to the conditioned space.

Clearances.   This leads to an important application discussion of clearances. When oil furnaces are approved and listed with UL (Underwriter Laboratories) test laboratories, they are done so with approved minimum clearances from combustible surfaces. (*See* Fig. 27.)

These necessary clearances are listed in the installation instructions for each model, and on a label attached inside the furnace cabinet by the manufacturer. The illustration shown in Fig. 22 is typical of

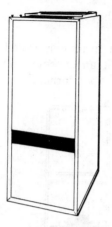

Fig. 25. Cabinet.

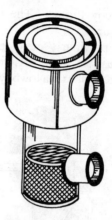

Fig. 26. Heat exchanger.

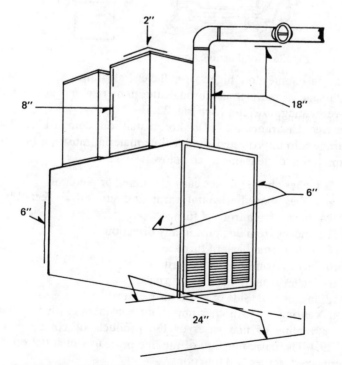

Fig. 27. Typical furnace clearances.

a lowboy furnace. The clearance label shown is from any surface enclosure.

As previously mentioned, when an oil furnace is installed on a combustible floor, UL requires the use of an approved floor base. Figure 28 shows a lowboy furnace and a highboy furnace.

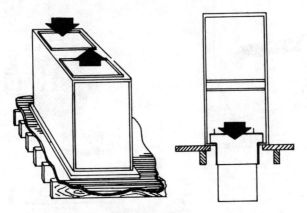

Fig. 28. Combustible floor base.

On the counterflow highboy, sufficient clearance space is allowed for passage of the plenum through the floor opening in the event of an overheating problem. (*See* Fig. 23.)

Service Clearances.   *Do not* install on combustible flooring. Clearances to unprotected combustible material must *not* be less than the minimum dimensions listed below.

  2 inches above furnace casing, bonnet, or plenum
  2 inches above horizontal warm air ducts with six feet of furnace
24 inches from front of furnace
18 inches from flue pipe in any direction
  6 inches from back of furnace
  6 inches from left side of furnace
  6 inches from right side of furnace
  8 inches from side of warm air plenum

Oil Venting.   Another important consideration is the matter of proper venting of flue gases or the products of combustion. (*See* Fig. 29.) The basic function of the flue pipe, to which the oil furnace is connected, serves two functions.

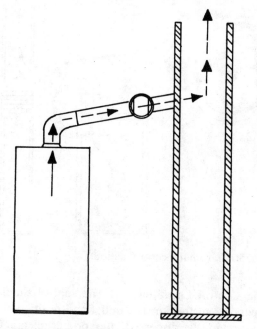

Fig. 29. Oil venting.

1. It provides a safe and effective means for moving the products of combustion from the flue outlet at the furnace to the outside atmosphere without contaminating the room air.

2. It provides the mechanics of producing and maintaining a draft and regulating a proper draft during any adverse changes in temperature, barometric pressure, or retarding *wind gusts*, all which affect draft action of a chimney.

Barometric Control Action. Under normal operation, the *barometric control* regulates the flue draft, removing or pulling the products of combustion from the furnace. The barometric control consists of a damper or gate, and a counterbalance (Fig. 30).

The counterbalance is adjustable, and is set according to the proper draft or negative pressure. This procedure is covered in the section on Servicing Oil Furnaces later in this chapter. The barometric control gate will regulate the draft, maintaining a constant draft, when the temperature or barometric pressure changes. Therefore, the control functions on pressure/temperature difference.

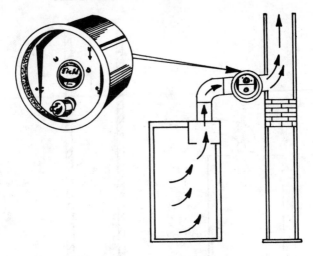

Fig. 30. Baromatic control action.

Barometric Control Locations.   The control should be located as close as possible to the furnace outlet and positioned as shown in Fig. 31. As previously discussed, the proper clearances must be followed when locating the barometric control in the flue pipe. Instructions for installation are supplied with each control. *Always* level the control with a spirit level.

Vertical Flue.   The types of vertical flues are *masonry chimneys*, which are field constructed and built in accordance with national and local codes. (*See* Figs. 33 and 34.)

The next item related to proper drafting is the flue pipe between the furnace outlet and the chimney connection. It is important to use a minimum length run and minimum elbows, using a flue pipe at least equal in size to the flue outlet size of the furnace. (*See* Fig. 32.)

Factory chimneys, which are factory built, are listed and approved by UL testing labratories.

Metal chimneys are made of metal of adequate thickness that is insulated, galvanized, and properly welded and riveted for maximum strength. This type is commonly called Class B Flues, or double-walled metalbestos. Double-wall design helps conserve heat in the flue gas, adds to more efficient draft, and allows lower surface temperatures of the outer wall surface. While the serviceman, in most

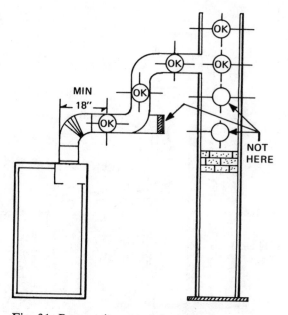

Fig. 31. Baromatic control locations.

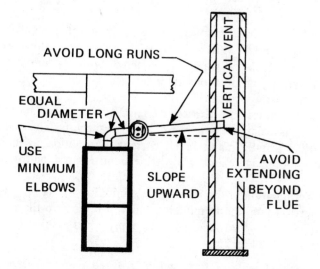

Fig. 32. Vertical flue.

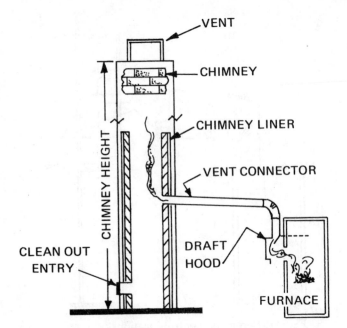

Fig. 33. Masonry chimney.

cases, will not be involved in the type or design of vertical flues, he may be confronted with a poor venting system, which requires replacing—particularly when encountered with a serious service problem. When you are replacing a furnace, always consider a close check of an existing system.

Most city codes are written using UL and the National Fire Protection Association as a basis. Local inspectors, city managers, and the like usually maintain all current information in their files. This information is generally available upon request or for a small charge.

Flue Termination at the Roof.   In addition to the flue type and size of vertical flue, the termination point in respect to the roof is of equal importance. Two separate rules apply when making the proper termination. (*See* Fig. 35.)

1. If the flue terminates within a listed cap and depends on natural draft, it must extend at least two feet above the point where

Fig. 34. Prefabricated chimney.

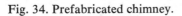

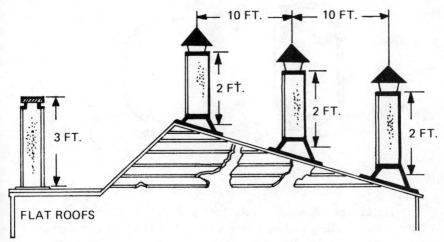

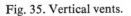

Fig. 35. Vertical vents.

it passes through the roof, and must be at least two feet higher than any building or obstruction within 10 feet of that point.

2. If the vent terminates with a listed or approved top, it must be arranged to terminate in accordance with the specified terms as listed. Additionally, type B flues must be equipped with an approved cap having a capacity at least as great as the vent stack, as far as critical temperatures are concerned.

Equal in importance to the flue is supplying sufficient air to the burner for combustion. Follow the recommended area for combustion air and ventilation as specified with each unit's installation instructions. With the tight construction of today's homes, together with storm doors and windows, infiltration alone is not sufficient air. This is particularly evident when the house is also equipped with exhaust fans, clothes dryer, and a fireplace, where each will contribute to the insufficient air problem.

Fuel Oil Storage Tanks.   The tanks for storage of fuel oil are commonly classified as inside or outside, depending on whether they are for use inside or outside the building or residence. (*See* Figs. 36 and 37.)

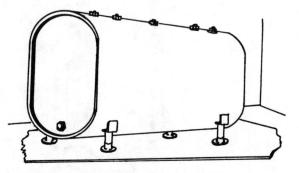

Fig. 36. Inside fuel tank.

Inside tanks or *basement tanks* are usually installed on the lowest floor of the installation. This is primarily a safety factor recommended by the National Fire Protection Association. In general, the following rules for installing fuel tanks should be followed.

1. The tanks must be located as close as possible to the inside

wall, either at the side adjacent to a driveway, or at the front of the building. This will allow easy access for filling.

2. The tank should be located to provide the shortest possible piping connection from the tank to the burner.

3. The tank must not be less than the minimum distance from the burner or any source of flame.

4. The tank should also be located in a manner that will permit the shortest fill connection as possible.

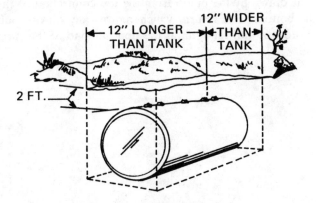

Fig. 37. Outside fuel tank underground.

The inside tank may be installed *underground*. However, underground tank installations should be carefully planned in advance so that all work can be completed in the same day. This is recommended to guard against cave-ins of the excavation, or possible flooding of the hole by a sudden rainstorm.

Proper Piping for the Burner and Tank. All *tank* and *burner* *piping* should be run as direct as possible. This, of course, follows the rules of yesteryear, that the fastest way home is a straight line, and also you avoid using too many fittings. (*See* Figs. 38 and 39.)

All piping connecting to the top of the tank should be sloped forward or toward the tank, thus preventing the formation of pockets of air. Swing joints should be used on all underground tanks, to prevent damage to tank or piping due to settling of the tank or frost action.

Fuel Lines to the Burner.   The first consideration is whether a *one-pipe* or a *two-pipe* system is to be used. A one-pipe system may be used (however, always be sure to check the instructions supplied with the pump). For satisfactory results, the bottom of the tank should not be below the level of the floor on which the burner rests, and the piping should be connected to the bottom opening of the tank to supply the burner. This is commonly called the *gravity flow system.*

The two-pipe system consists of a suction line and a return line, where fuel is drawn by the pump from the top connection of the fuel tank or the bottom. The return, which returns any oil not pumped, should be brought into the tank at the opposite end of the supply or suction line.

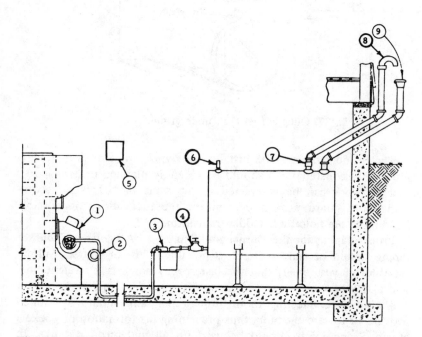

Fig. 38. Oil burner piping layout with basement storage tank. 1. Oil burner   2. Anti-pulsation loop   3. Oil filter   4. Globe valve   5. Instruction card   6. Oil gage   7. Vent alarm   8. Vent   9. Fill line cover

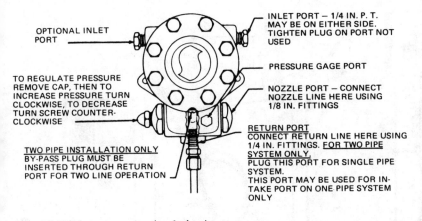

INLET PORT – 1/4 IN. P. T.
MAY BE ON EITHER SIDE.
TIGHTEN PLUG ON PORT NOT
USED

OPTIONAL INLET
PORT

PRESSURE GAGE PORT

TO REGULATE PRESSURE
REMOVE CAP, THEN TO
INCREASE PRESSURE TURN
CLOCKWISE, TO DECREASE
TURN SCREW COUNTER-
CLOCKWISE

NOZZLE PORT – CONNECT
NOZZLE LINE HERE USING
1/8 IN. FITTINGS

RETURN PORT
CONNECT RETURN LINE HERE USING
1/4 IN. FITTINGS. FOR TWO PIPE
SYSTEM ONLY.
PLUG THIS PORT FOR SINGLE PIPE
SYSTEM.
THIS PORT MAY BE USED FOR IN-
TAKE PORT ON ONE PIPE SYSTEM
ONLY

TWO PIPE INSTALLATION ONLY
BY-PASS PLUG MUST BE
INSERTED THROUGH RETURN
PORT FOR TWO LINE OPERATION

Fig. 39. Oil burner pump (end view).

When connecting fuel lines, never use compression fittings, as they nearly always admit air into the system. A shut-off and fuel filter should always be installed at the tank outlet or in the supply line.

The most popular type of lines used are soft, seamless, copper tubing with a minimum wall thickness of .035 inch.

Furnace Controls.   For a simple lowboy furnace, Fig. 40 illustrates the basic wiring of a furnace. Line voltage to the furnace should be fused and wired according to local codes. Always check the unit's specifications for the proper size wiring and fusing.

Basic Furnace Operation.   Line voltage passes through the normally closed limit switch before it goes to the primary control, where a step-down transformer provides a 24-volt secondary circuit.

The thermostat and primary control are in series in the 24-volt system. If the safety limit opens, all voltage to the primary control is killed and the burner shuts down.

The blower motor and fan control are also in series so that cycling of the fan can be set to cycle off-and-on as desired. Actually, the limit and fan control are physically in the same casing with temperature sensing elements projecting into the air stream. These sensing elements are also called a *helix*. When replacing the fan-limit control, always be sure the replacement has the same length helix.

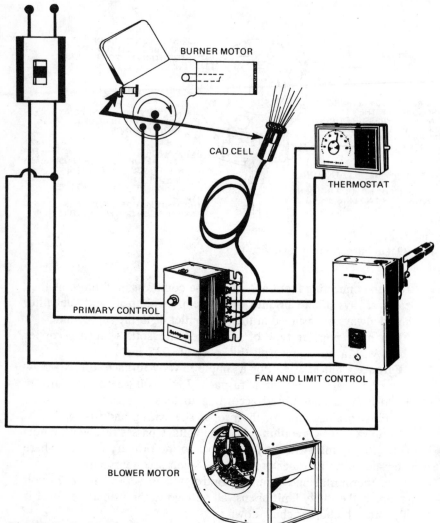

Fig. 40. Typical furnace wiring.

The primary control serves another safety function, which will stop burner operation. This is derived from the cad cell. The cad cell is sighted in view of the burner flame. In case of absence or loss of flame, the cad cell sends an electrical signal to the primary control, stopping the burner operation. To restart the burner, the manual reset button at the primary control must be pushed.

Room Thermostats.   Many complaints can be created from improper location and installation of the room thermostat (Fig. 41). The following suggestions are to help you do a better job of application.

1. Locate the thermostat five feet from the floor line, in the most lived-in room. Avoid rooms such as the kitchen and bathroom, or long hallways. The thermostat should be mounted on an inside wall, where it can respond to normal room conditions rather than a

Fig. 41. Room thermostat.

cold outside wall. Always seal off the hole in the plaster where the wires come through, since cold drafts may exist that will affect the thermostat operation.

2. The thermostat should be subject to natural air circulation, without obstruction from furniture. Never place the thermostat behind a door.

3. Avoid locating the thermostat where it is subject to sunlight, lamps, fireplace, warm air registers, electric appliances, and concealed hot-water pipes.

4. Before installing the thermostat, be sure to remove all devices used for protection during shipping. Follow the additional instructions packaged with each thermostat. Always make sure the thermostat is level.

Thermostat Heat Anticipator.   Most thermostats are equipped with a *heat anticipator*. The heat anticipator is actually an electrical resistance that produces a small amount of heat inside the thermostat cover (Fig. 42).

This heat will cause the mercury switch bi-metal to close a little sooner, and shut off the furnace burner shortly before the desired room temperature setting of the thermostat is reached.

The purpose of this is to prevent an overly warm or cold temperature. This is called *thermostat drift and override*. Wrong or incorrect heat anticipation can cause discomfort. So be sure it is matched to the amp rating on the primary control.

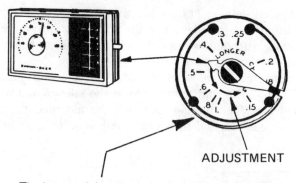

ADJUSTMENT

The heat anticipator setting inside the thermostat

Fig. 42. Heat anticipator.

The amp rating is stamped on all primary controls. An amp rating of .023 means the heat anticipator in the thermostat must be set at .023.

Furnace Blowers. The last major component is the *blower*, which provides the energy to distribute conditioned air to the living space. The two types of blowers used are the *belt-drive* (Fig. 43), or *direct-drive* centrifugal type (Fig. 44).

For detailed information on adjustments, see section on Servicing Oil Furnaces previously described.

INSTALLATION

The *upflow oil-powered furnace* (Fig. 21) is shipped as a packaged unit. The burners and controls are supplied as standard equipment, and may be shipped in a separate carton or completely wired and assembled in place.

The control compartment, which is an integral part of this furnace, is totally enclosed to provide a safe, compact, clean, and quiet control area.

The air handling capacity of this furnace is designed for cooling air flows.

(*Codes* and *local requirements* governing the installation of oil burning equipment, wiring, and flue connections must be followed.)

Location. This furnace is approved for reduced clearances to

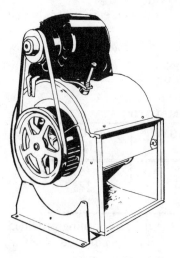

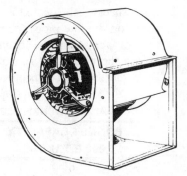

Fig. 44. Direct drive furnace blower.

Fig. 43. Belt drive furnace blower.

combustible construction; therefore, it may be installed in a closet or similar enclosure, and is generally located in the basement.

When this furnace is installed in a closet or enclosure, two ventilation openings, as shown in Table 29, are required for combustion air. These openings should be located about six inches from the top and bottom of the enclosure at the front of the furnace.

The minimum required clearances for this furnace are shown in Table 30.

When 85,000 and 100,000 Btu capacity furnaces are installed at the minimum clearances to combustible construction, two radiation shields must be used. These shields must be 9 inches by 12 inches,

TABLE 29

VENTILATION OPENINGS

Front	Sides & Rear	Top of Supply Plenum	Flue Pipe* Hori- zontal	Flue Pipe Vertical	Bottom
15	1	2	9	18	0

28 gage sheet steel, located at the top of the side casing panels and centered on the flue pipe. (*See* Fig. 45.)

The furnace should be located as close as possible to the chimney to reduce the horizontal run of flue pipe.

To *install* the furnace proceed as follows:

TABLE 30

MINIMUM CLEARANCES TO COMBUSTIBLE MATERIAL

BONNET CAPACITY 1,000 B.T.U./Hr.	LENGTH IN.	HEIGHT IN.
85	24	12
100	24	12
125	26	13

1. Attach the supply ductwork to the flanged opening provided at the top of the furnace. Dimensions for this opening are given in Fig. 48.

2. The return air duct should be attached to the external filter rack as shown in Fig. 49.

3. Knock-outs are provided on either side of the furnace so that the return duct work may be assembled on the right- or left-hand side of the furnace. (*See* Fig. 50.)

4. Provision is also made on this furnace for a bottom return air duct. The specifications for this opening are also illustrated in Fig. 46.

5. Flexible duct connectors are recommended to connect both the supply and return ducts to the furnace.

Before securing the flue pipe to the chimney, be sure that the chimney flue servicing the furnace is:

1. At least two feet higher than the ridge of the house. If it is only as high as the ridge it should be 10 feet from the nearest ridge.

2. Cleaned of any dirt or debris.

3. Not serving an open fireplace.

Connections from the furnace to the chimney should be:

1. Short and direct.

2. Pitched at $\frac{1}{4}$-inch per foot, downward toward the furnace.

3. Tightly joined and checked for leaks.

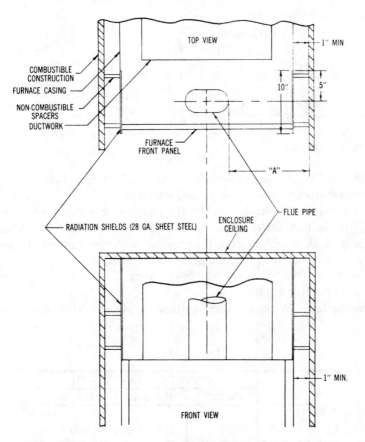

Fig. 45. Reduced clearance installation.

Burner.   The furnace is supplied with a high-pressure atomizing-type burner.

The air tube length, from the face of the mounting plate to the end cone extremity, must be as shown in Table 31.

Complete instructions for installation of the fuel oil piping will be found with the burner.

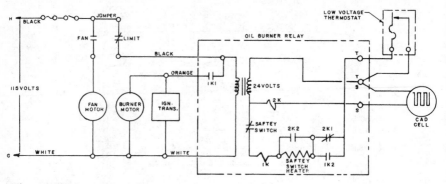

Fig. 46. Wiring schematic.

Lubricate the burner motor with SAE No. 10 oil. Once a year, pour two teaspoons of oil slowly into each oil cup.

Fan and Limit Control.   The fan and limit control must be installed in the hole provided on the front panel. (*See* Fig. 50.) When a ⅛-inch thick fiberglass gasket is provided with this control, it must be located between the furnace casing and the control.

Barometric Draft Control.   Instructions for installing pipe are packed with the control.

Electrical.   A separate line voltage supply should be used with

TABLE 31

	BONNET CAPACITY, BTU		
	85,000	**100,000**	**125,000**
AIR TUBE LENGTH, IN.	5	5	7

a fused disconnect switch between the main power panel and the unit. (*See* Figs. 47 and 48.)

All wiring must comply with local and National Electric Code requirements. The units operate on a 115–1–60 power supply. Be sure the jumper on the fan-limit switch is in place as shown in the connection diagrams.

Filters.   External filter racks are provided as standard equipment with this furnace. The assembly and installation of these filter racks are shown in Figs. 49 and 50.

Operational Checkout.   The installation of the furnace is now complete and the operational checkout may be performed.

Start-Up.

1. Check the wiring against the wiring diagram shown in Fig. 47.
2. Open the valve on the oil supply line.

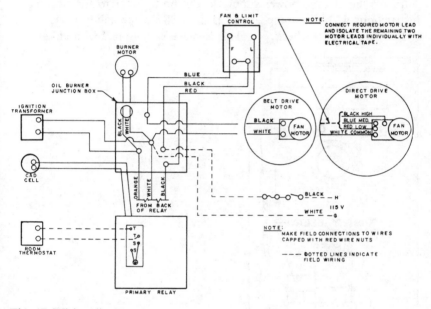

Fig. 47. Wiring diagram.

3. Reset the primary control.
4. Set the thermostat above room temperature.
5. Set the main electrical switch to On and the burner should start.

Combustion Check.

1. Adjust the primary air band to zero to smoke or until a hard clean flame is visible by eye. (Allow the furnace to run at least 10 minutes before final adjustments are made.)

2. Check the overfire draft. Adjust the overfire draft for a —0.01 to a —0.02 inch water gage. If necessary, adjust the barometric draft regulator.

Note: Whenever possible, use instructions to adjust the fire.

Oil Pump Check.   The oil pressure regulator is factory-set to give nozzle oil pressures of 100 psig. The firing rate, notes the nameplate, may be obtained with *standard* nozzles by adjusting the pump pressure as follows: (*See* Table 32.)

If the burner fails to pump oil and there are no leaks in the oil supply line to the furnace, it may be necessary to prime the pump. Turn off the electric power supply to the unit. Refer to the priming instructions with the pump. *Note:* Use an 80 degree solid nozzle.

Fan Adjustment Check.   This furnace is equipped with either a

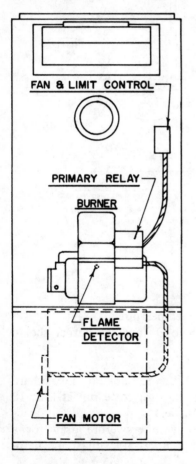

FAN & LIMIT CONTROL

PRIMARY RELAY

BURNER

FLAME DETECTOR

FAN MOTOR

Fig. 48. Wiring arrangement.

three-speed direct drive motor or a belt drive motor with a variable pitch motor pulley. The blower speed should be adjusted to deliver

TABLE 32

BONNET CAPACITY BTU/HR.	FIRING RATE GAL./HR.	STANDARD NOZZLE SIZE	PUMP PRESSURE PSIG
85,000	.76	.75	103
100,000	.90	.90	100
125,000	1.12	1.10	104

a differential air temperature of 85° F. between the return and supply plenums at the duct static pressure noted on the Underwriters Laboratories label.

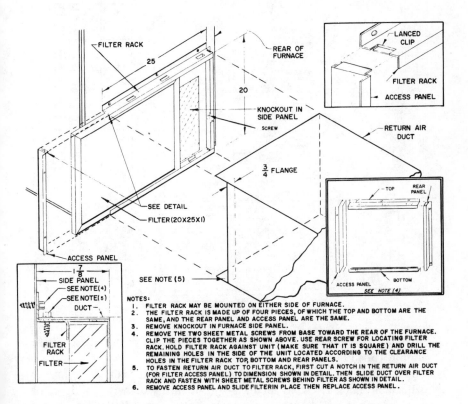

NOTES:

1. FILTER RACK MAY BE MOUNTED ON EITHER SIDE OF FURNACE.
2. THE FILTER RACK IS MADE UP OF FOUR PIECES, OF WHICH THE TOP AND BOTTOM ARE THE SAME, AND THE REAR PANEL AND ACCESS PANEL ARE THE SAME.
3. REMOVE KNOCKOUT IN FURNACE SIDE PANEL.
4. REMOVE THE TWO SHEET METAL SCREWS FROM BASE TOWARD THE REAR OF THE FURNACE. CLIP THE PIECES TOGETHER AS SHOWN ABOVE. USE REAR SCREW FOR LOCATING FILTER RACK. HOLD FILTER RACK AGAINST UNIT (MAKE SURE THAT IT IS SQUARE) AND DRILL THE REMAINING HOLES IN THE SIDE OF THE UNIT LOCATED ACCORDING TO THE CLEARANCE HOLES IN THE FILTER RACK TOP, BOTTOM AND REAR PANELS.
5. TO FASTEN RETURN AIR DUCT TO FILTER RACK, FIRST CUT A NOTCH IN THE RETURN AIR DUCT (FOR FILTER ACCESS PANEL) TO DIMENSION SHOWN IN DETAIL. THEN SLIDE DUCT OVER FILTER RACK AND FASTEN WITH SHEET METAL SCREWS BEHIND FILTER AS SHOWN IN DETAIL.
6. REMOVE ACCESS PANEL AND SLIDE FILTER IN PLACE THEN REPLACE ACCESS PANEL.

Fig. 49. Filter rack assembly.

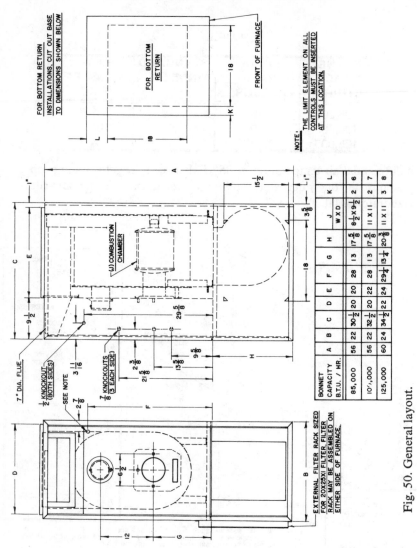

Fig. 50. General layout.

Refer to the wiring diagram for speed changes on the direct drive motor. (*See* Fig. 47.)

To adjust the belt drive motor policy, loosen the set screw on the adjustable hub. Then, to increase speed, turn clockwise to close, or to decrease speed, turn counterclockwise to open. Retighten the set screw on flat section of hub. The pulley belt tension should be

TABLE 33

FURNACE BONNET CAPACITY	FAN MOTOR HP.	BLOWER SIZE DXW	FAN PULLEY O.D. IN.	MOTOR PULLEY O.D. IN.	BELT LENGTH	MOTOR PULLEY TURNS-OPEN	BLOWER SPEED R.P.M.	AIR FLOW-EXTERNAL DUCT STATIC-IN. W.C. HEATING .20	COOLING .40	COOLING .45	COOLING .50
85,000	1/4	10 x 10	DIRECT DRIVE-MEDIUM SPEED BLUE LEAD				600	890			
			DIRECT DRIVE-HIGH SPEED BLACK LEAD				900		1115	1100	1085
85,000	1/3	10 x 10	DIRECT DRIVE-MEDIUM SPEED BLUE LEAD				800	1320			
			DIRECT DRIVE-HIGH SPEED BLACK LEAD				1030		1750	1720	1670
85,000	1/4	10 x 10	6	3¼	41	3½	720	890			
						0	900	*	1020	945	815
85,000	1/3	10 x 10	5	3¼	39	4½	790	1060			
						1	990	*	1330	1250	1230
100,000	1/4	10 x 10	DIRECT DRIVE-MEDIUM SPEED BLUE LEAD				600	920			
			DIRECT DRIVE-HIGH SPEED BLACK LEAD				900		1130	1100	1050
100,000	1/3	10 x 10	DIRECT DRIVE-MEDIUM SPEED BLUE LEAD				790	1300			
			DIRECT DRIVE-HIGH SPEED BLOCK LEAD				1050		1700	1660	1610
100,000	1/2	10 x 10	DIRECT DRIVE-LOW SPEED RED LEAD				720	1130			
			DIRECT DRIVE-HIGH SPEED BLACK LEAD				1100		1745	1705	1660
100,000	1/4	10 x 10	6	3¼	41	3	745	1065			
						0	900	*	1170	1090	890
100,000	1/3	10 x 10	5	3¼	39	4½	780	1170			
						2	940	*	1290	1220	1150
100,000	1/2	10 x 10	5	3¼	40	4½	790	1230			
						½	1050	*	1640	1575	1530
125,000	1/3	10 x 10	DIRECT DRIVE-MEDIUM SPEED BLUE LEAD				760	1330			
			DIRECT DRIVE-HIGH SPEED BLACK LEAD				1050		1700	1670	1630
125,000	1/2	10 x 10	DIRECT DRIVE-MEDIUM SPEED BLUE LEAD				930	1620			
			DIRECT DRIVE-HIGH SPEED BLACK LEAD				1100		1800	1750	1700
125,000	3/4	12 x 9	DIRECT DRIVE-LOW SPEED RED LEAD				620	1400			
			DIRECT DRIVE-HIGH SPEED BLACK LEAD				960		2120	2100	2060
125,000	1/3	12 x 9	7	3¼	46	2	690	1370			
						0	795	*	1440	1350	1265
125,000	1/2	12 x 9	6	3¼	44	4½	665	1350			
						1	855	*	1560	1540	1460
125,000	3/4	12 x 9	5	3¼	43	4½	800	1740			
						2	950	*	1930	1870	1820

*CAUTION: Operation of the blower motor under conditions established in these spaces on the chart will result in motor overloading and eventual motor failure.

adjusted to provide a one-inch deflection midway between the two pulleys.

Fans and Limit Check. After the furnace has been in operation for at least 15 minutes, restrict the return air supply by blocking the filters or closing the return registers and allow the furnace to shut down on high limit. The fan must continue to run. Remove the restriction and the burner should come on in a few minutes.

The optional checkout is now complete. *Be sure* to adjust the thermostat to the desired setting before leaving the installation.

Year Round Air Conditioning.   The furnace is designed for use in conjunction with cooling equipment to provide year round air conditioning. The blower has been sized for both heating and cooling; however, the fan motor may have to be changed to obtain the necessary cooling air flow.

Heating.   The blower speed is factory set to deliver the required air flow at normal duct static pressure.

Cooling.   The blower speed may be adjusted in the field to deliver the required air flow, for cooling applications, as shown in Table 33.

Chapter 24

Gas Furnaces

Gas furnaces are available in many styles, such as highboy, counter-flow, lowboy, and horizontal.

HIGHBOY

The *highboy* gas furnace (Fig. 1) is 55 inches high, and readily fits into any utility room, closet, or alcove. The extended flush jacket lets you install it next to an appliance or cabinet. Sizes range from 50,000 to 185,000 Btu's/hr.

Fig. 1. Highboy gas furnace.

They are available as direct drive gas fired, and belt drive gas fired. *See* Fig. 2 for dimensions.

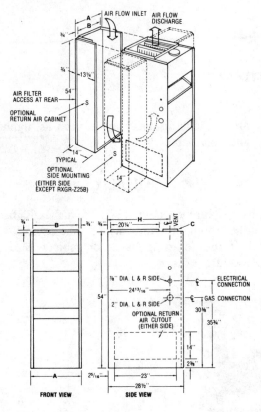

Fig. 2.

COUNTERFLOW

The *counterflow* gas furnace (Fig. 3) is designed for basementless homes. It is popular for perimeter heat systems, where ducts are installed in foundation slabs or crawl spaces. These systems surround the room with a blanket of hot air and warm the floor. Sizes range from 80,000 to 175,000 Btu's/hr.

See Fig. 4 for dimensions.

Fig. 3. Counterflow gas furnace.

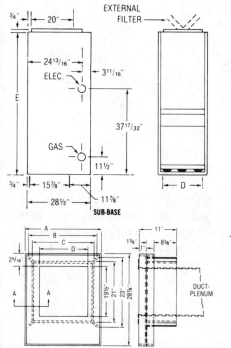

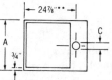

Fig. 4.

LOWBOY

The *lowboy* gas furnace (Fig. 5) is ideal for installations wherever overhead clearance is limited. It is only 43 inches high, and will fit into the lowest basements. This furnace is compact, powerful, and provides plenty of warm filtered air for complete winter comfort. Sizes ranges from 100,000 to 175,000 Btu's/hr.

See Fig. 6 for dimensions.

Fig. 5. Lowboy gas furnace.

HORIZONTAL

The *horizontal* gas furnace (Fig. 7) is designed for installation flexibility. Draft diverter and control-burner assemblies are field reversible, which allow for connecting gas of flue pipes on either side. These furnaces can be installed in attics, suspended from roof rafters or ceiling joists, or placed in crawl spaces.

See Fig. 8 for dimensions.

PARTS OF FURNACES

See Fig. 1, 3, 5, and 7 for the various parts of these furnaces.

Heat exchanger creates and controls the rapid swirling of gases, so

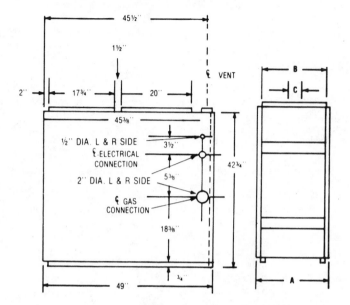

Fig. 6.

Fig. 7. Horizontal gas furnace.

that no *hot spots* occur, which can cause a failure. It also accomplishes a very high rate of heat transfer that lowers your fuel costs.

Burners are designed for both natural and propane gas.

Fully automatic controls. Air conditioning models include heavy duty transformer and blower relay.

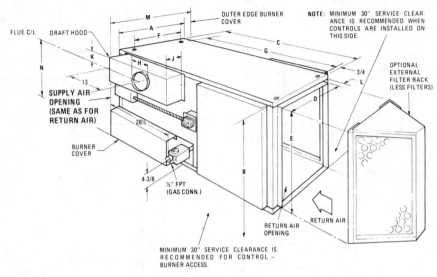

Fig. 8.

Insulation. A thick blanket of fiberglass and aluminum foil keeps the heat in the airstream where it belongs. It also helps to conserve fuel and acts as a good sound barrier.

Cabinets are welded together to keep them strong and vibration-free. The draft diverters are fully enclosed, which gives the furnace a smart, appliance look. You can install them anywhere.

Balanced air blower. Motor and blower are dynamically balanced and mounted for exceptionally quiet operation and accurate control of the air delivery.

WARRANTY

Be sure and read your warranty. The warranty for furnaces described in this chapter has a limited 10-year warranty: first year parts warranty; nine year extended warranty.

Chapter 25

Electric Furnaces (Forced Warm Air)

The *electric furnaces* shown in Figs. 1, 2, 3, and 4 deliver heat up to 45 kws and 153 Btu's/hr. When used in conjunction with air conditioning they deliver up to 60,000 Btu's/hr of cooling.

No chimney or flue is required. They are installed with zero clearance on the back and both sides and only two inches in front.

They are available in upflow, counterflow, and horizontal models, are compact in size, and are designed for installation in basement, closet, crawl space, or attic. They are also available in many heating capacities.

Features.   Figure 2 shows the various features of the electric furnace shown in Fig. 1.

1. Fully insulated steel cabinet, approved by the Underwriters Laboratories for zero clearance installation.

2. Nickel chromium elements. Resistance coils exposed to air stream for quick heat transfer, lower coil temperature.

3. Drawer-type slide-in heater strips in compact 4.8 kw elements. Elements made to give closer size kw output in accordance with heating load requirements.

4. Low-voltage (24-volt) terminal strip has slip-in screw-tight fasteners on these models. Thermostat circuit provides heat from first element $\frac{1}{20}$-second after circuit is closed.

5. Internal fusing on all models meet with UL requirements. Each furnace is properly fused at the factory. The furnace shown in Fig. 2 does not require internal fusing.

6. Relay sequencer has integral time delay between each 4.8 kw element.

7. Heavy duty 40 VA transformer on all models, such as shown in Fig. 2.

Fig. 1. Electric furnace.

8. Single-pole, double-throw fan sequencing relay on all electric furnaces.

9. Multi-speed blower assembly, direct-drive, slide-out drawer mounted for easy service. Handles up to three tons cooling on furnaces as shown in Fig. 2, and up to four tons on other models with standard equipment blower and motor.

10. Filter assembly for bottom air return is $20 \times 20 \times 1$ inches on all furnaces. No chimney or vent is required.

Figure 4 shows the various features of the electric furnace shown in Fig. 3.

1. Fully insulated steel cabinets with aluminized facing to reflect heat back into the air stream.

2. Nickel chromium elements subject to a limited five-year warranty. Resistance coils exposed to air stream for quick heat transfer, lower coil temperature.

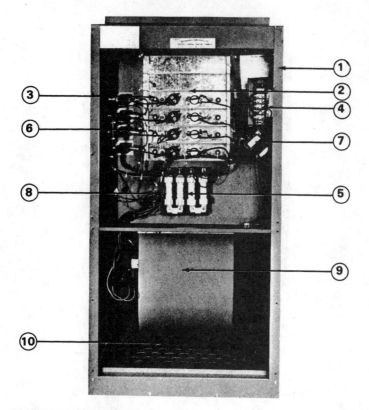

Fig. 2. Electric furnace.

3. Drawer-type slide-in heater strips in compact 5 kw elements. Elements made to give closer sized kw output in accordance with heating load requirements.

4. Internal fusing on all models meet. Underwriters Laboratories requirements. Each model is properly fused at the factory.

5. Relay sequencer has integral time delay between each 5 kw element.

6. Heavy duty 50 VA transformer on these models.

7. Single-pole, double-throw fan sequencing relay on all electric furnace models.

8. Multi-speed blower assembly, direct-drive, slide-out drawer mounted for easy service. Handles up to five tons cooling on models with standard equipment blower and motor.

Fig. 3. Electric furnace.

9. Filter assembly is disposable-hammock type with large face area for longer periods between changes.

Sequence On-Sequence Off System. The *sequence on-sequence off control system* uses a time-delay type relay to switch each heating element. Each element is turned on at a minimum of 10 seconds between stages. This process continues until all elements are energized. When the thermostat is satisfied this process is reversed and the elements sequence is reversed, the elements sequence off in the same manner they sequence on. A fan override switch is not required with this system.

Capacity Correction Factor. To obtain capacity in Btu/hr., multiply the total kw by 3.413. The capacity varies as the voltage varies. Multiply the rated capacity by the factor shown in Table 34 when voltages other than rated voltages are used.

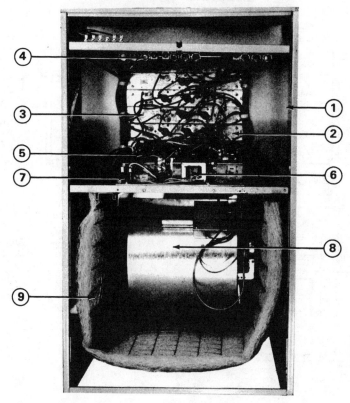

Fig. 4. Electric furnace.

TABLE 34

CAPACITY CORRECTION FACTOR

Supply Voltage	250	240	230	220	210
Multiplication Factor	1.08	1	.92	.84	.77

Furnace Dimensions. Figures 5 and 6 show dimensions for furnaces shown in Figs. 1, 2, 3, and 4.

Combustible Floor Base. *Downflow* sub-base is for use with downflow application on combustible flooring. Sub-base provides a one-inch clearance between plenum and combustible material.

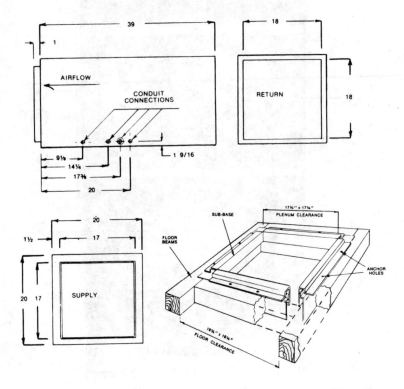

COMBUSTIBLE FLOOR BASE

Fig. 5. Furnace dimensions.

Counterflow combustible floor base is for use on combustible flooring. The sub-base provides required clearance between the plenum and combustible materials.

Cooling Coil Cabinets.   Evaporator coil cabinets (Fig. 7) for model shown in Fig. 1 are designed for installation of central air conditioning. Coils slide into position with no cabinet cutting or modification required. Cabinets are fully insulated. They are shipped assembled, ready for installation on the furnace.

Evaporator coil cabinets (Fig. 8) for model shown in Fig. 2 are shipped knocked down for field assembly. They are painted and insulated and will accept cooling coils up to 60,000 Btu's/hr

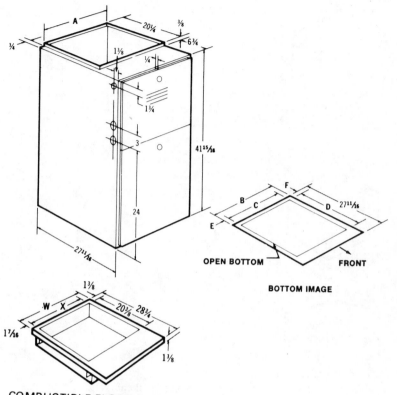

OPEN BOTTOM

FRONT

BOTTOM IMAGE

COMBUSTIBLE FLOOR BASE

Fig. 6. Furnace dimensions.

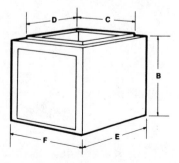

Fig. 7. Cooling coil cabinet.

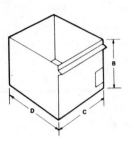

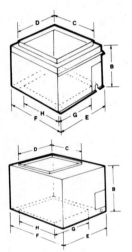

Fig. 8. Cooling coil cabinets.

capacity for central air conditioning installation. Cabinet shown in bottom illustration in Fig. 8 is assembled and galvanized.

Chapter 26

Electric Furnace Stokers

The electric furnace stoker shown in Fig. 1 is a complete automatic unit designed to feed and fire anthracite coal of economical sizes mechanically and to convey the ash into sealed containers. The unit should be installed only by the service department of the manufacturer.

Fig. 1. Electric stoker with housing.

DETERMINING FACTORS BEFORE SELECTING STOKER

Before an electric furnace stoker is selected, a preliminary survey should be made by a manufacturer's representative to determine the following factors: annual fuel consumption; living-room temperature desired; boiler water temperature or pressure maintained in severe cold weather; any deficiencies in the heating system, such as radiators that heat too slowly or not at all; sufficiency of domestic hot-water supply; and draft conditions.

An inspection of the boiler or furnace will also be necessary to determine the normal firepot diameter or width, the number of sections, and the general construction and fire travel. The clearance between the grate lugs and the base height must also be measured. The location of the coal bin and its distance from the bin feed worm should be noted, as well as any obstructions around the boiler that might interfere with stoker installation. A preliminary sketch of the proposed installation should be made. The distance from the center of the burner to the outside of the boiler or furnace fire door must be measured to determine the length of stoker required. Allow clearance for opening the fire door and clean-out doors. All deficiencies in the heating system should be corrected before the stoker is installed; otherwise, the stoker will not function properly. The function of the stoker ceases after it has delivered heat to the combustion chamber of the boiler or furnace. Absorption and distribution of heat are then dependent upon other equipment, which should be of the proper size to obtain satisfactory heating results.

OPERATING COMPONENTS

The principal operating components of most standard automatic electric stokers are the bin and burner worms, rotating burner, burner plates, coordinated coal and air supply device, speed-reduction unit, ash removal device of the scraper-chain type, fan, motor, and thermostatic controls.

The *bin* and *burner worms* (Fig. 2) conduct the coal through a fluted brass tube from the bin to the specially designed burner installed in the boiler.

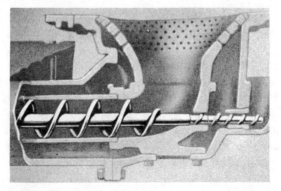

Fig. 2. Bin and burner worms.

The slowly *rotating burner* (Fig. 1, A) combined with the pinhole design of the *burner plate* is superior to the stationary burner. It creates a firebed of uniform heat density for efficient fuel consumption. The pinhole design of the burner plate provides unobstructed entrance of the forced air to the entire firebed in the burner, thus resulting in even air distribution that produces complete combustion.

The function of the *coordinated coal* and *air supply device* shown in Fig. 3 corresponds to the carburetor in an automobile. It is equipped with a single-lever control that synchronizes the supply of air and coal for perfect combustion and accurately adjusts the coal supply to varying weather conditions.

Fig. 3. Coordinated coal and air supply device.

The *speed-reduction unit* reduces the high motor speed to the required slow tempo of the coal feed and ash removal mechanisms.

The *ash removal device* (Fig. 1, B) is of the scraper-chain type that automatically removes and carries the ashes from the stoker to the covered containers that are attached to the stoker.

The *fan* operates automatically in conjunction with the coordinated coal and air supply unit to deliver the required amount of air. Fuel consumption and wear on the motor shaft and bearings can be reduced to a minimum by the use of this type of fan.

The *motor* (Fig. 3) is used to actuate the components of the electric automatic stoker. Depending on the type and size of stoker, the required horsepower rating ranges from $\frac{1}{8}$ to $\frac{1}{4}$ horsepower. All motors are equipped with thermal overload switches.

OPERATION OF STOKER

The operation of the electric stoker can be either *continuous*, with an automatically regulated coal feed, or *intermittent*, with a fixed coal feed. In small domestic installations, continuous operation maintains more efficient combustion, more uniform temperatures, and longer life of operating parts with the same economy as intermittent operation. All models of the type illustrated are designed with a regulated coal feed and coordinated air supply so that they may be operated either continuously or intermittently to suit individual requirements.

Continuous operation of the stoker is controlled by a thermostat (either plain or clock type) and a damper motor. A limit control of line voltage should always be installed and wired into the *hot* line to the stoker motor. On a warm-air system, use an Airstat; for hot-water heating boilers, use an Aquastat; and for steam boilers, install a Pressuretrol.

Intermittent operation of the stoker is normally controlled by a thermostat (either plain or clock type) and a timer relay. The timer relay operates the stoker whenever the thermostat calls for heat. It also operates the stoker at one-hour or half-hour intervals of 1 to 7 minutes to maintain a fire when no heat is desired. Various combinations of these primary controls are used in conjunction with other devices to meet the requirements of different heating systems. Wiring diagrams of the most common arrangements are shown in Figs. 4, 5, and 6. Figures 7 to 17 show the controls used in the following systems.

Low-Voltage Plain Thermostat Control of Stoker with Line Voltage Limit Control.   Figure 4 shows the common household installations used for low-pressure steam boilers, for furnaces without circulating fans, for hot-water boilers without circulating pumps, or for summer-winter, domestic, hot-water heaters. The controls in each case are the same except for the fact that the appropriate limit control for the type of heating plant used must be selected.

The system operates on a call for heat by the room thermostat, which actuates the relay to start the stoker. The stoker continues to operate until the heat required by the thermostat has been produced; then the relay is actuated to stop the stoker. In case exces-

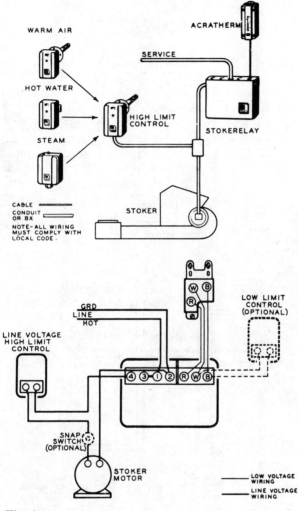

WARM AIR

ACRATHERM

SERVICE

HOT WATER

HIGH LIMIT
CONTROL

STEAM

STOKERELAY

CABLE
CONDUIT
OR BX
NOTE—ALL WIRING
MUST COMPLY WITH
LOCAL CODE.

STOKER

GRD
LINE
HOT

LOW LIMIT
CONTROL
(OPTIONAL)

LINE VOLTAGE
HIGH LIMIT
CONTROL

SNAP
SWITCH
(OPTIONAL)

STOKER
MOTOR

LOW VOLTAGE
WIRING
LINE VOLTAGE
WIRING

Fig. 4.

sively high temperatures are reached in the furnace or boiler, the high-limit control acts to stop the stoker. No operation of the stoker is possible until the furnace or boiler has cooled to the On point of the high-limit control. Between periods of thermostat operation, the relay will operate by itself at hourly or half-hour intervals, depending

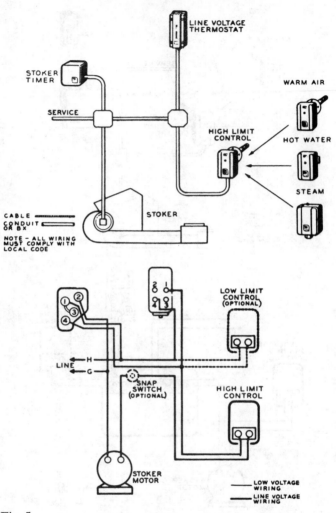

Fig. 5.

on the setting, to maintain a minimum stoker fire. Any low-pressure steam boiler can be used to supply year round hot water through the use of an indirect water heater. The only additional control needed is an immersion Aquastat installed below the water line in the boiler and wired as shown by the dotted lines in Fig. 4.

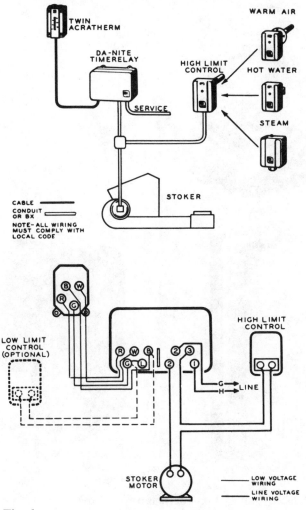

Fig. 6.

Domestic Control System for Gravity, Warm-Air, Hot-Water, or Steam Installations with the Stoker Timer. Figure 5 illustrates an inexpensive domestic installation used for warm-air furnaces without circulating fans, for hot-water boilers without circulating pumps, or for low-pressure steam boilers. It is not recommended for stokers

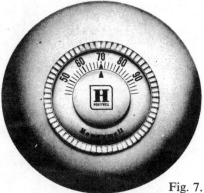

Fig. 7.

Fig. 8.   Fig. 9.

rated at more than ¼ hp. The features and the controls in each case are the same except that the limit control must be selected in accordance with the type of heating plant used.

This system operates when a call for heat by the thermostat starts the stoker directly. The stoker continues to operate until the amount of heat required by the thermostat is obtained. Should the temperature in the boiler or furnace become excessive, the high-limit control acts to stop the stoker. Between periods of thermostat operation, the

Fig. 10.

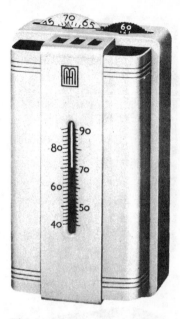

Fig. 11.

Fig. 12.

time relay will operate the stoker at intervals of every half-hour or
hour to maintain a minimum fire. In this system, the only needed

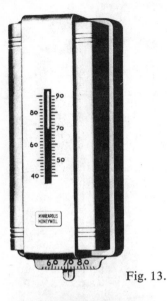

Fig. 13.

Fig. 14.

Fig. 16.

Fig. 15.

additional control for year round hot water is an immersion Aquastat installed below the water line in the boiler and wired as shown by the dotted lines in the diagram. Completely automatic day-night control can be obtained by using a Chronotherm for room temperature control and by replacing the thermostat with a relay. The terminals of the Chronotherm should be connected, color to color, to the

Fig. 17.

Fig. 18.

terminals of the relay, and the thermostat wires should be connected to terminals 3 and 4 on the relay.

Domestic System for Gravity, Warm-Air, Hot-Water, or Steam Installations with Da-Nite Time-Relay. Figure 6 shows the common installations used for warm-air furnaces without circulating fans, for hot-water boilers without circulating pumps, for summer-winter, domestic, hot-water heaters, or for low-pressure steam boilers. The controls in each case are the same except that the limit control must be selected in accordance with the type of heating plant used. This system is particularly recommended where a regular changeover from day to night temperature is desired. The changeover switch is built into the time relay so that the system can be controlled by a twin Acratherm.

This system operates on a call for heat by the Acratherm, which actuates the time relay to start the stoker. The stoker continues to run until the Acratherm requirement is satisfied, or until excessive temperature or pressure in the heating system causes the high-limit control to open the circuit. The time relay shifts control from the day setting to the night setting of the Acratherm automatically. Between periods of Acratherm operation, the time relay will operate the stoker at regular intervals to maintain a minimum fire. The *skip feature* of the relay will prevent a timer operation from immediately following an Acratherm operation. The only additional control needed to supply year round hot water is an immersion Aquastat wired into the circuit as indicated by the dotted lines on the diagram. A thermostat can be used instead of the twin Acratherm to provide temperature control during the day, with a time relay providing only intermittent timer operation at night.

LUBRICATION AND GENERAL MAINTENANCE

Lubricate components of a stoker as follows: To oil the *ash conveyor*, use any machine oil. Old oil from the crankcase of an automobile will suffice. Use as much as needed up to ¼ pint. If an oil can is used, be careful not to get the spout down into the chain. Fill the oil reservoir of the clutch bearing to the proper level. The *coal-worm bearing* and *ash-worm bearing* are equipped with fittings for high-pressure lubrication. A grease gun is usually supplied by the manufacturer. To lubricate bearings properly, turn down the handle of the gun two full turns on each fitting once a week, or follow the directions listed on the lubrication card. To fill the gun, follow the manufacturer's instructions.

After the stoker has been installed and lubricated, both *motor oil cups* should be filled until the oil runs out of the overflow hole located below the shaft bearing. This will sufficiently saturate the wool packing in the oil reservoir. Use a good grade of light machine oil. Thereafter, put 10 drops of oil in each oil cup once every month. Do not overlubricate motors, for excess oil will interfere with motor operation. Fill the *reducing unit* to the top of the filler plug twice a month with oil. Place a few drops of light machine oil on all other operating parts of the *drive mechanism* once every week.

Keep all operating parts of the stoker clean of coal, ash, and basement dust. Covers must be kept tight on the ash cans at all times to prevent ash dust from blowing throughout the basement. All bearings of the turret-type conveyor, except the ratchet drive, do not contain oil. The pawl pins should be well oiled. The drive shaft bearing should be greased in accordance with the manufacturer's instructions (Fig. 18). Put a small quantity of No. 600W nonfluid oil (supplied with the stoker) on the ratchet to silence the drive and check the pawl. The universal joint in this conveyor is filled with grease when shipped. Grease it again through the drive shaft when the grease gun is applied to the fitting.

Section 5

FOOD PREPARATION

TODAY'S MODERN GAS OR electric ranges, and electric surface ranges, offer a variety of special features in various models. They are designed to make cooking easier and more automatic than ever before.

Kerosene, coal or wood ranges are still used in some parts of the country; also gasoline ranges.

Electronic or microwave ovens cook food in one-fourth the normal time, and use less electricity than when food is cooked on a conventional range. When used with care, and according to the manufacturer's instructions, these ovens offer an easy, safe, and efficient way to cook.

Gas/electric charmettes, drop-ins, cooktops, counter built-ins, counterranges, and the like are a new concept in surface cooking containing 2 to 4 heating units.

Dishwashers are available in many models with various finishes, positions, automatic protection features, and equipped with energy saver features.

A hot-water dispenser is a compact self-contained unit for exterior mounting. It has many uses when steaming hot water is needed instantly.

Food waste disposers are available in many models for batch or continuous feed. It is easy to install your own waste disposer and save money and time.

Trash compactors are available in built-in, freestanding, and under-counter models. They use a negligible amount of energy—about 1.01 kwh per month (based on about 120 uses per month).

Chapter 27

Ranges

The secret of good cooking lies in a good range. It is the heart of the kitchen. Before you buy your first or next range learn all there is to know about them. Look for features that promise reliable performances.

When purchasing a range, keep in mind that each manufacturer offers several models—each designed to suit particular needs, adaptable to different family size, kitchen size, and cooking habits.

The kind of range you choose depends upon the kind of fuel or power you can get in your home. Your fuel may be wood, coal, kerosene, gasoline, gas, or electricity, or a combination of two of these. For best service, your range fuel should give clean, efficient heat and speedy, dependable cooking with the least amount of clean-up care.

Before you buy a range: (1) read free leaflets and literature available from range manufacturers; (2) visit demonstrations of range cooking; (3) consult users of various ranges; and (4) ask yourself this question: "Which range is best suited to my particular needs?"

SELECTING THE RANGE

For the best range to suit your needs, look for the following.

1. A reliable dealer who will give you correct information on cost of operation, local cost of fuel you select, good installation, and long-time servicing.

2. A model made by a long established manufacturer who stands behind his guarantee.

3. Safety approval seals: Underwriters Laboratories (UL) seal for electric. American Gas Association (AGA) seal for gas. CP seal is not a safety seal; it stands for cooking performance and means that the range has extra cooking conveniences.

4. One piece porcelain top and splash-back, with no hard-to-clean crevices.

5. Welded body.

Construction. A single welded frame with rounded corners, with top and back splash in one piece, with toe space at the base, and finished with stain-resistant enamel or porcelain will be easy to clean. The legs should be sturdy.

Look for snugly-fitting oven and broiler doors, rigid enough to prevent warping, and with counter-balanced springs, and for drawers that slide on rollers or bearings.

Hinges, springs, and latches should be firmly attached and non-rusting.

Oven lining should be of durable, non-rusting, enameled steel.

Special Features. An oven thermostat or a temperature indicator aids in controlling oven temperatures for baking.

A reservoir in some coal-wood combinations and kerosene ranges to heat water.

A timer clock that automatically turns oven on or off; a light on the back-splash; a deep broiler pan to reduce smoke in broiling; a deep-well cooker; glass in oven door; light in the oven; minute minders.

Extra warming ovens and drawers; griddle and toaster devices; towel racks; a storage place for utensils; and condiment sets.

A convenience outlet for plugging in other electrical appliances.

In a gas stove: A two-way burner for rapid and simmer heats; automatic lighting for top burners; oven thermostat; automatic oven lighting; smokeless broiler pan and stops on all racks and drawers; lock switches that small children cannot turn on; pilot lights that ignite gas, which may be turned on accidentally; and a built-in rectangular well master.

In an oil stove: Fuel tanks with indicator gages easily seen and reached. Built in level to help locate and keep the stove level. Adjustable legs.

COST OF RANGE

The initial cost of ranges varies considerably depending upon the kind, size, and model.

The operating cost of the range depends upon the management and skill of the user and upon the cost of the fuel. The cost of gas and electricity used in cooking depends upon the amount used in other ways in the home, and on the local rate. Coal, wood, and kerosene are less expensive than gas and electricity.

USE AND CARE

Place the range in a level position out of excessive drafts and in a light, well-ventilated place near other working areas in the kitchen.

Follow the manufacturer's directions for using and caring for the range.

Use utensils that fit the burners and that have tight-fitting lids.

Use little water in cooking.

Turn down heat after food boils, and shut off heat before cooking has been completed.

Keep your range clean. This will increase the efficiency of your range and reduce fire hazards.

When buying fuel, buy good quality for cleanliness and efficiency.

GAS RANGES

Gas ranges are available in many colors, sizes, and types, and are equipped with many features.

If your range is properly installed, adjusted, and operated under normal conditions in accordance with the manufacturer's instructions, it will satisfactorily perform the functions that are generally expected of your appliance. Most ranges have warranties for one year. Make sure your range is covered by a service contract; otherwise, you will have to pay labor charges.

INSTALLATION

The installation, adjustment, and service of a gas range must be performed by a qualified person or serviceman to insure proper operation and to avoid the possibility of injury to users or damage to the appliance.

The range must be installed in compliance with local codes. In the absence of local codes, the installation must conform with the National Fuel Code. Pipe joint compound must be resistant to the effect of liquified petroleum gases.

The maximum gas supply inlet pressure must not exceed 14 inches water column. The gas supply pressure for checking the regulator should be at least one-inch water column above the manifold pressure shown on the rating plate.

Installation in a mobile home must conform with the American National Standard for Mobile Homes.

The appliance must be electrically grounded in accordance with the National Electrical Code when installed, if an external electrical source is utilized.

If the range has electrical components, it is equipped with a three-prong grounding plug for your protection against shock hazard and should be plugged directly into a properly grounded receptacle. *Do not* cut or remove the grounding prong from this plug.

Connect range to ½-inch or ¾-inch pipe. Install manual shut-off valve in the gas lines so that it is external to the unit and in an accessible location. Because you know where the gas shut-off valve is located, you know how and where to turn off gas to the range.

Any openings in the wall behind the range and in the floor under the range must be sealed.

Minimum horizontal distance from side of range to adjacent vertical combustible wall extending above and below the cooking top must be in accordance with rating plate specifications.

TYPES OF GAS RANGES

There are many types of gas ranges available in many sizes and colors.

Built-In Double Oven. The *built-in double oven* shown in Fig. 1 has the following features: Fiberglass insulation, tempered glass control panel, indicator lights, signal timer, clock, continuous cleaning, rotisserie, removable oven door, air-cooled oven doors, shaded glass door, and others.

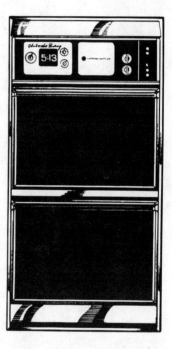

Fig. 1. Built-in double oven.

(*See* Fig. 2 for specifications and dimensions of oven shown in Fig. 1. It is recommended that this unit be vented.)

Built-In Wall Oven. The *built-in wall oven* shown in Fig. 3 is available in standard and deluxe models with many optional features. (*See* Fig. 4 for specifications and dimensions of oven shown in Fig. 3.)

Built-In Space-Saver Wall Oven. The *built-in-space-saver wall oven* shown in Fig. 5 is available with and without a continuous cleaning oven, and with other additional features.

(Figure 6 shows specifications and dimensions of oven shown in Fig. 5.)

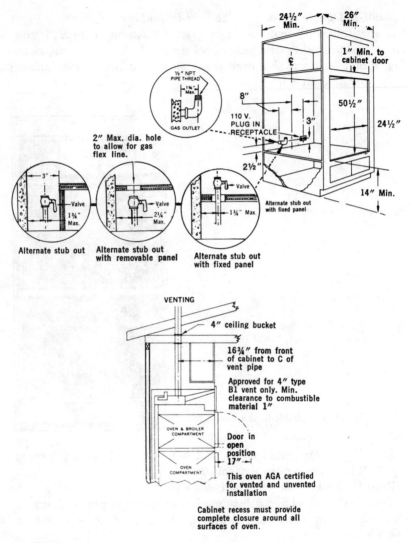

Fig. 2.

Drop-In Ranges. Figures 7 and 8 show *drop-in ranges* available in many styles, with or without a continuous cleaning feature, plus other features. (*See* Fig. 9 for specifications and dimensions of ovens shown in Figs. 7 and 8.)

Fig. 3. Gas built-in wall oven.

Freestanding Ranges. *Freestanding ranges* are shown in Figs. 10 and 11 and are available with many features; and with or without the continuous cleaning feature. (*See* Fig. 12 for dimensions and specifications.)

Eye-Level Ranges. *Freestanding* or *built-in eye-level ranges* are available with many features. Figures 13 and 14 shows freestanding ranges. Figure 15 shows a built-in range and dimensions and specifications.

Metric Pacer Gas-and-Electric Range. The *metric pacer gas-and-electric ranges* shown in Figs. 16 and 17 are available in various sizes, in many colors, and with a number of features including a metric converter, time center, and roast guide. The electric clock and four-hour interval timer (Fig. 18) with extra large numerals are very convenient. It also has an interval timer with a loud buzzer signal. The metric converter (Fig. 19) converts weights, measures, and temperatures from pounds, ounces, or Fahrenheit to the international equivalents in grains, litres or Celsius temperature at the turn of the dial. Figure 20 shows the roast guide that instantly calculates the total time required for roasting meats. To operate, just set the pointer to the weight and kind of roast to be cooked. The cooking time shows clearly in the read-out window.

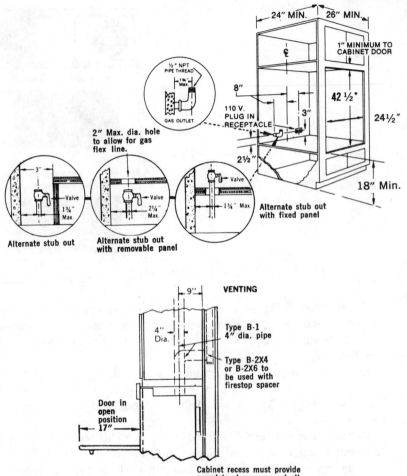

Fig. 4.

INSTALLATION

Leveling Range. All ranges must be level to obtain proper cooking results. The leveling bolts (Fig. 21) removed from the crate bottom should be screwed into the same nut in the base. Place a pan of water or spirit level on the oven rack and adjust leveling bolts until the range indicates it is level.

Fig. 5. Gas built-in space-saver wall oven.

Gas Connections on All Units. Installation must conform with local codes. In the absence of local codes, the installation must conform with the National Fuel Gas Code ANSI Z223.1, latest edition. The range should be connected to the supply line with a ½-inch black iron pipe or an approved type of flexible stove connector. To prevent gas leaks, put an approved sealing compound, which is resistant to liquified petroleum gases, on all threaded connections. It is recommended that you have the dealer where you purchased your new range install it or have him arrange with a local plumber to make the installation.

Appliances designed for installation in a mobile home must conform with American National Standard for Mobile Homes A119.1, latest edition.

Note: Check all piping connections in the unit for leaks. Never use an open flame to check for gas leaks. Use a soap solution. It is not impossible for connections made at the factory to leak, due to vibration encountered in transportation. Make certain you have checked them all, and repair any connections that leak. (*See* Fig. 22.)

Electrical Connections. All electrical wiring and attachments are 60-cycle, 125 volts, 15 amps maximum. The range should be grounded with a three-conductor (three-prong plug) supply cord that will ground the range when plugged into a *grounded* wall receptacle. If the backguard of your range has a clock or light, connect the cord from the backguard into the special terminal block

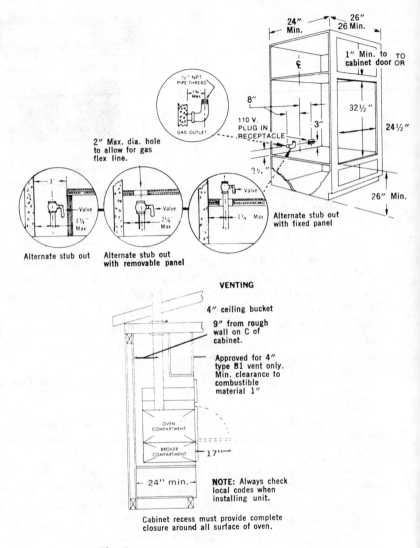

Fig. 6.

located at the top of the main back directly under the backguard supply cord. The appliance must be electrically grounded in accordance with the National Electrical Code ANSI C1–1971 when installed, if an external electrical source is utilized.

Fig. 7. Drop-in range.

Fig. 8. Drop-in range.

Wall Clearance. All units must be installed in accordance to minimum rear and side wall clearances and clearances extending vertically above cooking top, which are all stated on the rating plate. Any openings in the wall behind the unit and in the floor under the unit should be sealed.

Convertible (Universal) Range—Recessed Wall Oven—Built-In Top. The gas pressure regulator must be set for the gas with which the appliance is used.

A convertible unit can be identified by the second alpha (letter) prefix in the model number. *T* indicates convertible valves set for natural gas with convertible regulator set at four inches water column. *P* indicates convertible valves set for LP gas with convertible regulator set at 10 inches water column.

A convertible unit set for LP gas (second prefix letter P) may be converted to natural gas by opening each orifice hood approximately three-quarter turn and changing the selector key on the thermostat from LP to Natural. (To reset regulator see convertible regulator diagram.) A convertible unit set for natural gas (second prefix letter *T*) may be converted to LP gas by *screwing each orifice hood tight*, and changing selector key on thermostat from Natural to LP.

Gas Pressure Regulator. The gas pressure regulator *must* be set for the gas that the unit uses.

Convertible Regulator. The maximum pressure of the gas supply should be in accordance with the nominal inlet pressure of the regulator used on the ranges. (*See* Fig. 23.)

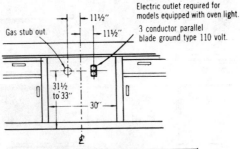

BURNER B.T.U.(HR. INPUT			
	FRONT	REAR	OVEN
Nat. Gas	12,000 ea.	9,000 ea.	18,000
L.P.G.	9,000 ea.	9,000 ea.	16,000

DIMENSIONS			
	RANGE (OVERALL)	OVEN	BROILER
HEIGHT	32⅛"	14½"	4"
WIDTH	30¾"	24"	16"
DEPTH	23-11/32"	19"	12½"

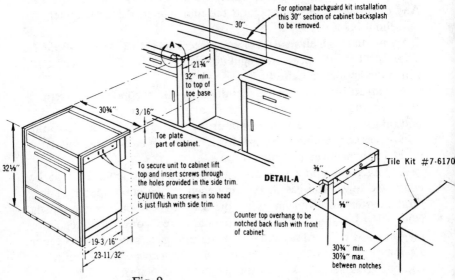

Fig. 9.

The regulator setting should be tested by pressurizing the range with manifold pressure at least one inch water column above the

Fig. 10. Freestanding gas range.

Fig. 11. Freestanding gas range.

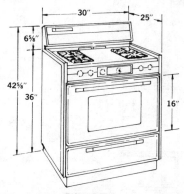

DIMENSIONS

	Overall	Oven	Broiler
Height	42⅝″	14½″	4″
Width	30″	24″	16″
Depth	25″	19″	12½″

Burners	Nat (btu)	L.P.G. (btu)
Oven	18,000	16,000
Top Front	12,000 ea.	9,000 ea.
Top Rear	9,000 ea.	9,000 ea.

Fig. 12.

Fig. 13. Gas eye-level range.

Fig. 14. Gas eye-level range.

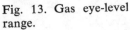

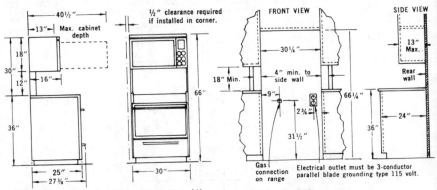

Vent Hoods available as optional accessory item. Adds 5½″ to overall height of range.

½″ clearance required if installed in corner.

B.T.U./HR. INPUT				
	Front	Rear	Upper Oven	Lower Oven
Nat. Gas	12,000	9,000	12,000	18,000
LPG	9,000	9,000	12,000	16,000

DIMENSIONS			
	Width	Height	Depth
Overall	30″	66″	25½″
Eye-level oven	21¼″	12″	13″
Lower oven	24″	14½″	19″

Fig. 15.

Fig. 16. Metric pacer gas range.

Fig. 17. Metric pacer electric range.

RANGES

Fig. 18. Electric clock and timer.

Fig. 19. Metric converter.

manufacturer's specified manifold pressure shown on the nameplate. The maximum gas supply pressure is 14 inches water column pressure.

Minimum vertical wall clearance above cooking top from cut-out to rear wall—two inches. (*See* Fig. 24.)

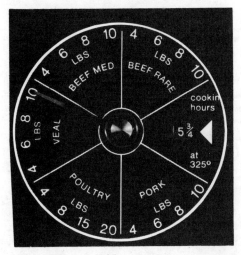

Fig. 20. Roast guide.

Fig. 21. Leveling bolts.

Minimum vertical wall clearance above cooking top from cut-out to left side—two inches. (*See* Fig. 24.)

Minimum vertical wall clearance above cooking top from cut-out to right side—one inch. (*See* Fig. 24.) *Note:* Due to potential hazards it is recommended that top cabinets not be put in above cooking surface.

Mounting the Built-In Top Unit.   *Note:* Appliance pressure regulator must be accessible through opening in cabinet (doors or removable panel).

To mount the surface unit proceed as follows:

1. Remove the top by lifting off.

2. Place burner section in cabinet opening with the valves on the right side.

3. Secure burner section to top of cabinet with four No. 8 screws.

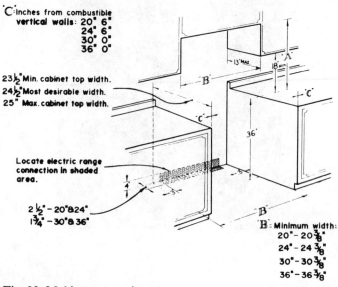

'C' Inches from combustible
vertical walls: 20" 6"
24" 6"
30" 0"
36" 0"

23½" Min. cabinet top width.
24½" Most desirable width.
25" Max. cabinet top width.

Locate electric range
connection in shaded
area.

2½" – 20"&24"
1¾" – 30"&36"

13" MAX
18" MIN

36"

'B' = Minimum width:
20" – 20⅜"
24" – 24⅜"
30" – 30⅜"
36" – 36⅜"

Fig. 22. Making connections.

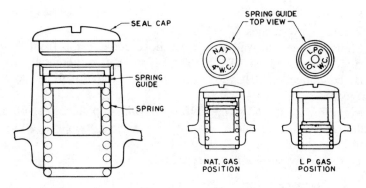

SEAL CAP

SPRING
GUIDE

SPRING

SPRING GUIDE
TOP VIEW

NAT
4" W.C.

LPG
10" W.C.

NAT. GAS
POSITION

LP GAS
POSITION

Fig. 23. Regulator.

4. The gas-pressure regulator supplied must be used with this unit. (If convertible, see section on Convertible Range previously discussed.)

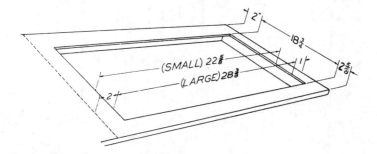

Fig. 24. Wall clearance.

Mounting the Recessed Wall Oven. Slide the oven unit into the recess as shown in Fig. 25. Secure the unit to the cabinet by placing screws through the front frame into the cabinet.

The recess in which the oven is installed should be constructed so as to provide a complete closure around the recessed portion of the unit (except for the vent thimble of a vented unit). Any openings around gas and electric service outlets should be closed at time of installation.

(A manual gas valve must be installed in an accessible location in the gas line external to the unit for the purpose of turning on or shutting off gas to the unit.)

Mounting Backguard (20- or 24-inch range). Remove the three screws in the main back located near oven outlet. Place the asbestos gasket between the vent box and vent outlet in the backguard. Secure vent box to back flange of top with two bolts found in vent box. Secure bottom of vent box to main back with the three sheet-metal screws previously removed.

Cabinet Preparation for Recessed Wall Oven. *Do not* install wall oven below work counter.

The recess should be constructed so as to provide a complete closure around the recessed portion of unit (except for vent thimble of vented unit). Any openings around gas and electrical service outlet should be closed at time of installation (Fig. 25).

Cabinet Preparation for Sit-On Unit. To properly install the sit-on range (range with upper oven), carefully follow Fig. 26. Due to potential hazards, it is recommended that top cabinets not be put in above surface.

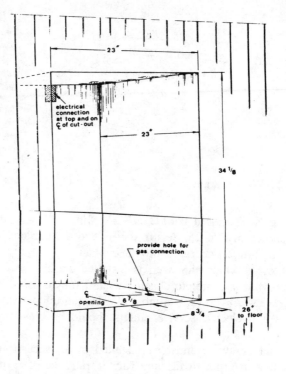

Fig. 25. Mounting recessed wall oven.

Cabinet Preparation for Double Oven.   Figure 27 shows dimensions used in preparing the cabinet for the double-oven range. Dimensions do not allow for vent-hood installation.

OPERATION

Cooking Atop Your Range.   A properly adjusted flame provides the fastest heat possible for cooking. By turning the valve knob, the amount of heat can be set to any number of different cooking speeds— from Full On to Keep Warm. Remember, when boiling food, the highest temperature that can be reached is the boiling point. When the liquid starts to boil, decrease the size of the flame until you reach the minimum flame that will hold the boil. This will save gas,

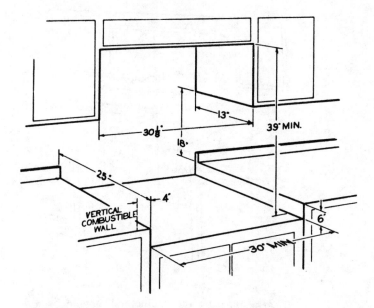

Fig. 26. Closure around recessed portion of unit.

lessen the possibility of burning or boiling food on your utensil, and keep your kitchen cooler.

Use stable utensils with flat bottoms. Unstable or rounded bottom utensils will not contact properly with the grate and will affect cooking efficiency. Always place the utensil on the burner before lighting. Select utensils large enough to avoid spillovers; however, oversized utensils (diameters exceeding 8½ inches) can cause the finish to discolor, craze, and chip.

USE OF OVEN

Preheating. Preheating is heating the oven to the temperature set on the oven knob before the intended food is placed in the oven. You should preheat for 10 to 12 minutes, although it is not necessary to preheat for broiling or roasting.

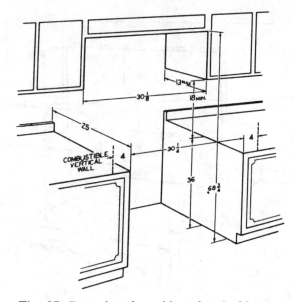

Fig. 27. Preparing the cabinet for double oven range.

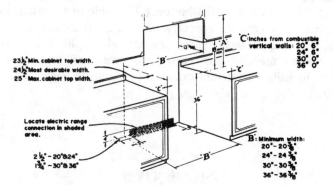

Fig. 27a. Installation of units.

Temperature Selection. It is important to select a proper temperature setting. Never set the dial to a higher degree than needed, with the intention of lowering the setting at a later time. This will not speed up the action. It can cause the oven to cycle slower and cause the temperatures to vary so that cooking results may be unsatisfactory. Imagine that the control has three sections:

1. Low temp.
2. Bake.
3. Broil.

The *low temp* has a temperature range at 140° F. to 200° F. This section is used to keep food at serving temperature. Some models have special clock equipment that performs this automatically. The *bake cycle* is from 250° F. to 550° F. This can be termed as the very slow range (250° F. to 275° F.) to extremely hot (500° F. to 525° F.). The moderate baking range is 350° F. to 425° F.

OPERATION OF ELECTRIC OVEN PILOT

The electric oven pilot operates on standard 120 volts. It does not require any special setting. Simply turn the knob counterclockwise to the temperature you prefer; ignition occurs automatically within 45 to 60 seconds.

CONTINUOUS CLEANING FEATURES

If your oven has the continuous cleaning feature, it will have a dull, brownish finish that has been blended with a special catalytic material. (If the oven has a blue-gray finish, it is standard porcelain enamelled without the continuous cleaning feature.)

Using Your Continuous Cleaning Oven.   The catalytic finish will keep your oven presentably clean with very little effort on your part. Any time the oven is in use, the catalytic action will be working to eliminate normal cooking spatters. Simply cook as you usually do. Average oven spatters must fade away. If a great deal of spattering occurs during cooking, a small amount may remain on the surface of the oven interior at the end of the cooking time. This is particularly true when you have a short cooking cycle. The longer the cooking cycle, the better the catalytic action.

USING COMMERCIAL OVEN CLEANERS

You may use commercial oven cleaner on porcelain-lined ovens; however, they are very strong, and it is essential to follow instructions carefully. Be sure to wear rubber gloves to protect your hands.

After using such cleaners, thoroughly rinse the oven with a solution of one tablespoon vinegar to one cup of water.

Oven cleaners can coat or damage the thermostat-sensing device (the long tube in the oven) so that it will not respond to temperature accurately. If you use an oven cleaner, do not let it contact the sensing bulb, or any chrome, aluminum, or plastic part of the range.

ALUMINUM FOIL IN OVEN AND BROILER

Aluminum foil, when used improperly, is a cause of many range fires. Make certain that vents or air openings are not covered by the foil. If the vents located along the sides of the oven bottom are blocked, poor cooking will result.

Never cover a rack completely. A piece of foil slightly larger than the utensil can be placed on the rack beneath the utensil.

ELECTRIC RANGES AND OVENS

Today's *electric ranges* and *ovens* are available in more makes, models, and types than ever before, all offering a combination of special features.

INSTALLATION OF UNITS

To eliminate the hazard of reaching over heated surface units, cabinet storage space located above the surface units should be avoided. If cabinet storage is to be provided, the hazard can be reduced by installing a range hood that projects horizontally a minimum of five inches beyond the bottom of the cabinets.

Be sure and keep the leg levelers. Leveling of the range is very important.

FREESTANDING AND SIT-IN UNITS

Cabinet Opening.   See Fig. 28. A—30-inch minimum clearance between the top of the cooking surface and the bottom of an unprotected wood or metal cabinet; or

A—24-inch minimum when bottom of wood or metal cabinet is protected by not less than ¼-inch asbestos millboard covered with not less than No. 28 MSG sheet steel, 0.015-inch stainless steel, 0.024-inch aluminum, or 0.020-inch copper.

B—Make opening between cabinet as shown in Fig. 27, A. Level range so the main top is level with the cabinet top.

Make electrical connection and slide range into opening.

Power Connection.   The wiring system conforms to the Underwriters Laboratories, Inc., standards and the National Electrical Code. Check your local codes regarding installation and wiring because of various code requirements.

Ranges with a *clock* or *oven light* require three wires, 120/240 volts, 60-cycle AC, single-phase current.

Ranges with only *top units*, bake and broil units, require only two wires, 240 volts, 60-cycle AC, single-phase current.

Be sure the electric power is off at the fuse box until the unit is ready to operate. See range rating plate for kw rating.

Electrical Grounding.   The range neutral is grounded to the range at the factory. Disconnect the grounding strap from the terminal block when a separate ground is required.

Check your local code for grounding requirements. Check all connections to see that they are tight and have not become loosened during transit. Each top unit is controlled by a switch and the element should heat up within a minute. The oven bake element and broil element should heat up within a minute when the temperature control is set at 400° F. in the bake area of the dial. Oven temperature should be reached within 12 to 15 minutes.

The elements are finished with a protective coating of oil. When heated up for the first time, open the oven door and allow the thermostat to operate at 400° F. for about 10 minutes. This should evaporate the oil and dissipate odors and possible smoke.

A standard electric range *pigtail* can be attached to the range by removing the lower cover and putting the supply cord through the bracket. Replace the cover after the connection is made.

Should wiring diagrams be needed, refer to the one on your particular unit. If other copies are desired, give the manufacturer the model and serial (or type) number of unit.

TOP UNITS

Cabinet Opening.   Prepare the cabinet opening accurately so your unit will fit properly. Figure 28 shows cabinet cut-out dimensions. The dimensions are for the unit to be mounted so the knobs are on the right side. If you want the knobs to be on the left, make sure the proper clearances from the cut-out to the vertical walls are maintained.

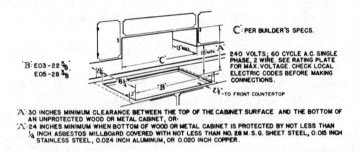

Fig. 28. Cabinet cut-out dimensions.

Mounting the Surface Unit.   For mounting the surface unit proceed as follows:

1. To raise the top of the surface unit, apply pressure by lifting up. The top is secured by spring brackets so it will be necessary to apply slight pressure to free the top.

2. Place burner section in cabinet opening. The unit can be installed with the knobs on the right or left side, but make certain the cut-out is correct for location of knobs.

3. Secure burner section to top of cabinet with four No. 8 screws.

4. Make electrical connection.

5. Electrical connection should conform to local requirements and codes.

OVEN UNITS

Prepare the cabinet opening (Fig. 29) accurately so your unit will fit properly.

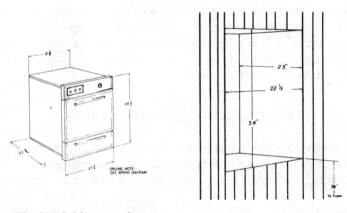

Fig. 29. Cabinet opening.

Power Connection.   *Be sure* the electric power is off from the fuse box to the junction box until the oven unit is ready to operate. The oven unit should be fused separately from other units.

The wiring system conforms to the Underwriters Laboratories, Inc., standards and the National Electrical Code. Check your local codes regarding installation and wiring because of various code requirements.

Oven units with a clock or oven light require three wires, 120/240 volts, 60-cycle AC, single-phase current. The fourth wire in the conduit is a ground wire that is grounded to the oven frame and the installer *should* connect this wire to a suitable ground.

The National Electrical Code requires use of No. 10 gage conductor when RH or RW wire insulation is used. When better insulated wire is used for the conductor, size may be smaller. *See* rating plate for kw rating.

With the oven positioned in front of the cabinet opening, connect the leads extending from the conduit to the junction box. When used, make sure the neutral (white) wire is connected to the correct terminal.

Check all connections to see that they are tight and have not become loosened during transit. When the above mentioned wire connections are made at the junction box, slide the unit in the cabinet and secure to the cabinet front with four screws. The elements are finished with a protective coating of oil. When heated up for the first time, open the oven door and allow the thermostat to operate at 400° F. for about 10 minutes. This should evaporate the oil and dissipate odors and possible smoke. No adjustment should be necessary to the oven heat control or other electrical components unless they have been damaged in transit.

SIT-ON AND DOUBLE OVENS

To install the *sit-on* range properly (range with upper oven only), *see* Fig. 30. (*See* sections on Installation of Units concerning hazard of reaching over heated surface units to reach cabinet storage space.)

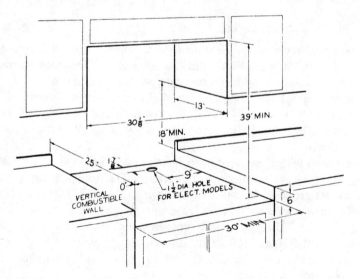

Fig. 30. Installation of sit-on range.

Power Connection. The wiring system conforms to Underwriters Laboratories, Inc., standards and the National Electrical Code. Check your local codes regarding installation and wiring because of various requirements. See rating plate for kw rating. This range requires three wires, 120/240 volts, 60-cycle AC, single-phase current.

TYPES OF ELECTRIC RANGES AND OVENS

Whatever you want in convenience and beauty you will find in the wide selection of electric ranges. They may have from 2 to 7 surface units and 1 or 2 ovens; all offer a combination of special features.

Freestanding Electric Ranges.   The complete, conventional electric range (Fig. 31) stands independently and consists of surface units, 1 or 2 ovens, and a broiler. Popular sizes are 30-inch and 40-inch widths, although economy 24-inch models are available.

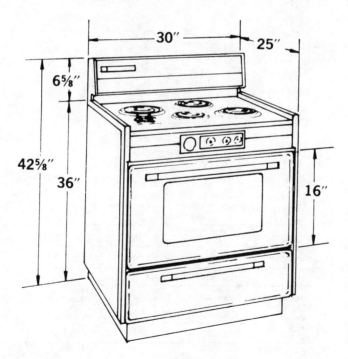

Fig. 31. Freestanding electric range.

Dimensions and specifications are shown in Fig. 32.

Self-Cleaning Freestanding Electric Ranges. The pyrolytic, self-cleaning oven (Fig. 33) cleans anything that is likely to spill. It is the most popular feature on today's electric range. Just latch the door, set the controls, and your entire oven (which includes the broiler) is cleaned automatically, electrically. Soil is decomposed at considerably above-normal baking temperatures. The oven door cannot be unlocked during the self-cleaning cycle. Extra insulation surrounds the oven walls so that exterior surfaces are no warmer than during normal baking. Soil is reduced to a tiny ash, which may be removed with a paper towel.

With the *catalytic bake clean* or *continuous clean oven*, the oven liner or panels are coated with a special porcelain containing a catalyst. This causes oven soil to oxidize from the interior surface at cooking temperatures of 425° F. to 450° F. Spots are not removed

Range is supplied with 4' flexible metal conduit

DIMENSIONS

	Range (Overall)	Oven
Height	42⅝″	14½″
Width	30″	24″
Depth	25″	19″

ELECTRICAL DATA

Models	Rated Wattage	Overall Protection	Supply Voltage
240 Volt Models	9,800	40.8 Amps.	120/240 V. 60 Cy. 3-Wire
*208 Volt Models	9,800	47.1 Amps.	120/208 V. 60 Cy. 3-Wire

Fig. 32.

Fig. 33. Self-cleaning oven.

immediately but most disappear gradually as the oven is heated and used over a period of time.

Sometimes the oven must be turned up to 500° F. or more for two hours to rid the oven of soil completely. There is no special insulation as in pyrolytic ovens. Not all of the oven interior bakes clean (racks, rack glides, oven bottom, and door liner must be hand cleaned). No warranty is given on the life of the catalytic cleaning action.

(Dimensions and specifications are shown in Fig. 34.)

Built-In Wall Ovens.   *Built-in ovens* are vented through the oven wall. The vent permits excess moisture to evaporate. They are available in standard and deluxe models, and have many features. (*See* Figs. 35 and 36.)

(Figure 37 shows specifications and dimensions.)

Built-In Self-Cleaning Wall Ovens.   The ovens shown in Fig. 38 are set to *clean* and will stay locked until cool enough to wipe clean.

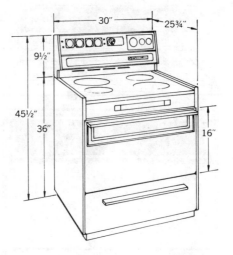

	RANGE	OVEN
WIDTH	30″	22″
HEIGHT	45½″	15″
DEPTH	25¾″	19″

Fig. 34.

Fig. 35. Built-in wall oven.

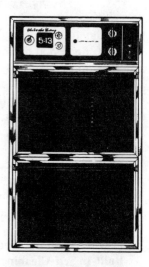

Fig. 36. Built-in wall oven.

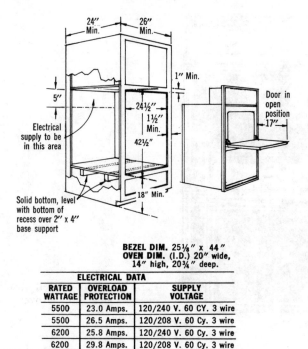

BEZEL DIM. 25⅛" x 44"
OVEN DIM. (I.D.) 20" wide,
14" high, 20¾" deep.

ELECTRICAL DATA		
RATED WATTAGE	OVERLOAD PROTECTION	SUPPLY VOLTAGE
5500	23.0 Amps.	120/240 V. 60 CY. 3 wire
5500	26.5 Amps.	120/208 V. 60 Cy. 3 wire
6200	25.8 Amps.	120/240 V. 60 Cy. 3 wire
6200	29.8 Amps.	120/208 V. 60 Cy. 3 wire

Fig. 37.

Anything you are likely to spill will clean up easily with a swish of a damp sponge. You can bake and broil in the upper oven (Fig. 38); the lower oven is used for baking only.

(Figs. 39 and 40 show specifications and dimensions.)

Built-In Space-Saver Wall Ovens. *See* Fig. 41 and Fig. 42. Figure 41 has an oven window and light. You can see what is cooking without losing oven heat and kitchen coolness. Use exterior switch to light up without opening up any doors.

(Figure 43 shows specifications and dimensions of these ovens.)

Eye-Level Ranges with Two Ovens. The eye-level range with the built-in lock may be the answer if you need facilities for multiple baking, or baking and broiling. They are available in various free-standing models including high-low ovens, or two high-ovens side-by-side. (*See* Fig. 44 showing a freestanding eye-level range.)

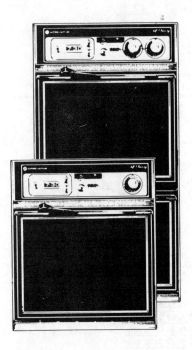

Fig. 38. Built-in self-cleaning wall ovens. Upper double oven; lower single oven.

(Figure 45 shows dimensions and specifications of this range.)

Eye-Level Range with Self-Cleaning Oven. The range shown in Fig. 46 has a self-cleaning oven with 12 other convenient ideas. It has a *hood outlet* (Fig. 46) located on the top of the range. No hook-up wiring is necessary—just plug it in as easily as a fan into a wall plug. No installation is necessary.

(*See* Fig. 47 for plugs; no hook-up wiring is necessary. Also *see* Fig. 48 for dimensions, and electrical data.)

Freestanding Smooth-Top Eye-Level Range. Figure 49 shows a *smooth-top eye-level range*. This range has fiberglass insulation, four leg levelers, tempered glass control panel, fluorescent work light, two oven broilers, new cool doors, storage drawer, oven lights, removable oven door seals, and many other features.

(*See* Fig. 50 for dimensions and specifications.)

Built-In Electric Eye-Level Ranges. Two built-in electric eye-level ranges are shown in Figs. 51 and 52. Figure 51 has blackglass oven doors, two variable temperature broilers, fluorescent panel light, and automatic cooking, along with other features. Figure 52

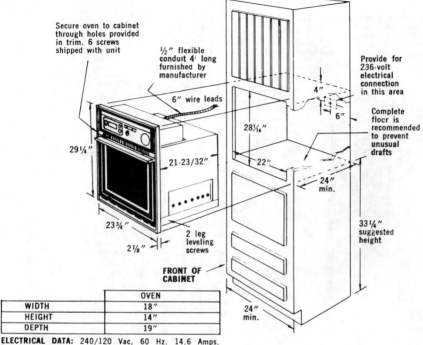

Secure oven to cabinet through holes provided in trim. 6 screws shipped with unit

½" flexible conduit 4' long furnished by manufacturer

6" wire leads

Provide for 236-volt electrical connection in this area

4"

6"

Complete floor is recommended to prevent unusual drafts

28¹⁄₁₆"

29¼"

21-23/32"

22"

24" min.

23¾"

2 leg leveling screws

2⅛"

33¼" suggested height

FRONT OF CABINET

	OVEN
WIDTH	18"
HEIGHT	14"
DEPTH	19"

24" min.

24" min.

ELECTRICAL DATA: 240/120 Vac, 60 Hz. 14.6 Amps.
Total connected load 13.5 K.W.

Fig. 39.

has blackglass oven doors, no panel light, a single broiler, and various other features.

(*See* Fig. 53 for specifications, dimensions, and electrical data.)

Drop-In Ranges.   The drop-in range (Fig. 54) is a full-feature range that slides into the counter for a compact built-in look. A variety of backguards can be added to dress up a wall installation— high or low types are available. Like other ranges, it has many important features.

(*See* Fig. 55 for specifications and dimensions.)

Smooth-Top Drop-In Ranges.   Figure 56 shows a smooth-top drop-in range. (*See* Fig. 57 for specifications, dimensions, and electrical data.)

Self-Cleaning Drop-In Range.   A self-cleaning drop-in range is

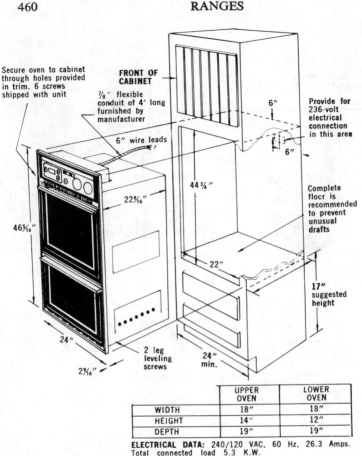

Secure oven to cabinet through holes provided in trim. 6 screws shipped with unit

FRONT OF CABINET

⅞" flexible conduit of 4' long furnished by manufacturer

6" wire leads

6"

Provide for 236-volt electrical connection in this area

6"

Complete floor is recommended to prevent unusual drafts

44¾"

22⁵⁄₁₆"

46⁵⁄₁₆"

22"

17" suggested height

24"

2 leg leveling screws

24" min.

2⁵⁄₁₆"

	UPPER OVEN	LOWER OVEN
WIDTH	18"	18"
HEIGHT	14"	12"
DEPTH	19"	19"

ELECTRICAL DATA: 240/120 VAC, 60 Hz, 26.3 Amps. Total connected load 5.3 K.W.

Fig. 40.

shown in Fig. 58. It has large elements for fast, uniform cooking; it also has smaller elements. Like other ranges it has many features, including a backguard accessory, if desired.

(*See* Fig. 59 for specifications, dimensions, and electrical data.)

BURNER OPERATION

Use of Surface Elements. The surface switches are easily operated. Simply push in and turn the switch knob. When the element

Fig. 41. Built-in space-saver wall oven.

Fig. 42. Built-in space-saver wall oven.

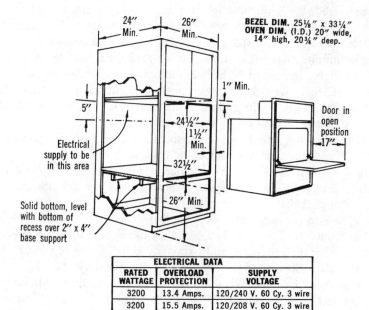

24″ Min. 26″ Min.

BEZEL DIM. 25⅛″ x 33¼″
OVEN DIM. (I.D.) 20″ wide,
14″ high, 20¾″ deep.

1″ Min.

5″

24½″
1½″ Min.

Door in open position
17″

Electrical supply to be in this area

32½″

26″ Min.

Solid bottom, level with bottom of recess over 2″ x 4″ base support

ELECTRICAL DATA		
RATED WATTAGE	OVERLOAD PROTECTION	SUPPLY VOLTAGE
3200	13.4 Amps.	120/240 V. 60 Cy. 3 wire
3200	15.5 Amps.	120/208 V. 60 Cy. 3 wire

Fig. 43.

Fig. 44. Freestanding eye-level range.

is energized, the indicator light for the surface elements will glow. For best results, use flat bottom pans of approximately the same size as the heating element. (*See* section on Safety Precautions.)

The infinite switch has a variety, or range, of heat settings from low to high. The range of heat is increased by turning the knob to High. At High, the electric power stays on continuously. At all other settings, the switch will maintain the heat selection by turning the electric power on and off to the element.

The following will help you associate the number on the knob with an approximate temperature or cooking range.

High—often used to reach boiling temperature quickly. Use this setting carefully, since the electric power stays on continuously. It has an approximate heat value of 400° F.

Fry—used for fast frying, deep fat frying, and open kettle cooking. Select from 4 to 6. Start at 5, then adjust to your personal preference. The number 6 represents approximately 350° F., 5 represents approximately 300° F., and 4 represents approximately 250° F.

Boil—used for pan frying, browning of meats, and maintaining a rolling boil in large utensils. The area is between 2 and 4. This area will give you control for most of your cooking. Two represents approximately 200° F.

Low—used for simmering vegetables, melting butter or chocolate,

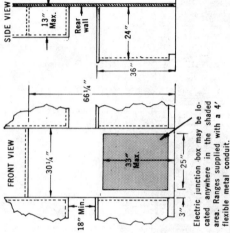

Electric junction box may be located anywhere in the shaded area. Ranges supplied with a 4' flexible metal conduit.

ELECTRICAL DATA

Rated Wattage	Overload Protection	Supply Voltage
12,400	51.7 Amps.	120/240 V. 60 Cy. 3-wire
12,400	59.6 Amps.	120/208 V. 60 Cy. 3-wire
11,800	49.2 Amps.	120/240 V. 60 Cy. 3-wire
11,800	56.7 Amps.	120/208 V. 60 Cy. 3-wire

DIMENSIONS

	Width	Height	Depth
Overall	30"	66"	25½"
Eye-level oven	21¼"	12"	13"
Lower oven	24"	14½"	19"

Fig. 45.

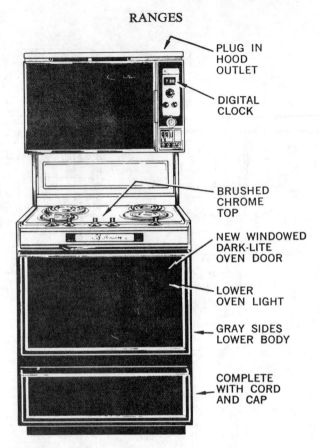

Fig. 46. Eye-level range with self-cleaning oven.

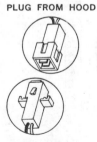

Fig. 47. Plugs.

SPECIFICATIONS & DIMENSIONS			
	RANGE	UPPER OVEN	LOWER OVEN
WIDTH	30"	21"	22"
HEIGHT	65⅝"	12"	15"
DEPTH	26⅞"	13"	19"

ELECTRICAL DATA		
RATED WATTAGE	OVERLOAD PROTECTION	SUPPLY VOLTAGE
14.7 KW	62 Amps.	120/240 VAC

Fig. 48.

Fig. 49. Freestanding smooth-top eye-level range.

and warming milk and cheese sauces. Represents a temperature of approximately 160° F.

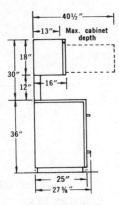
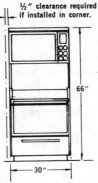
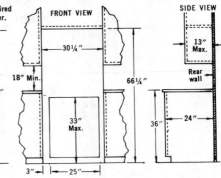

DIMENSIONS			
	Width	Height	Depth
Overall	30″	66″	25½″
Eye-Level Oven	21¼″	12″	13″
Lower Oven	24″	14½″	19″

ELECTRICAL DATA
120/240 Volt Models:
Electrical rating: 120/240 V. 60 Cycles.
Models with broiler in top oven
46.3 amps.   11.1 KW

120/208 Volt Models:
Electrical rating: 120/208 V. 60 Cycles.
Models with broiler in top oven
53.4 amps.   11.1 KW

Fig. 50.

OVEN OPERATION

Baking. By using the latest development in an electric oven heat control, a fast bake temperature is obtained; however, you should preheat. Turn the oven heat control clockwise to the temperature setting of your choice. An indicator light will glow when there is electric power to the bake element. When the oven temperature is cycled off to maintain the dial setting, the indicator light will go off; however, it relights when the power resumes.

Broiling. Broiling in these ovens may be slightly different from any previous operation you might have been acquainted with, so be sure to read the directions completely.

Fig. 51. Built-in elec-
tric eye-level range.

Fig. 52. Built-in elec-
tric eye-level range.

To broil, turn the temperature control knob clockwise to Broil. The thermostat will click when it has been set to the maximum broil setting. It is possible to broil at a low range temperature. This is accomplished with thermostatic control.

Always broil with the oven door closed. First set the thermostat to the maximum broil setting, then turn the knob back (counterclockwise) to the temperature setting of your choice. The oven thermostat will maintain the temperature while your food is broiled. Also, the temperature dial setting is now in the area that would normally be designated within the bake range temperature.

To reset the oven for baking, it is necessary to turn the oven completely off.

Oven Vent.   The oven vent tube has been eliminated. By omitting the vent tube, a greater amount of moisture is obtained, creating baked foods with greater appeal. The food itself retains more of its natural juices and has less of a tendency to dry out; as a result, the flavor is better. It also saves on fuel and is more economical. Remember, when broiling, to reset from maximum; otherwise, some excess smoking could occur. See broiling instructions for setting the thermostat.

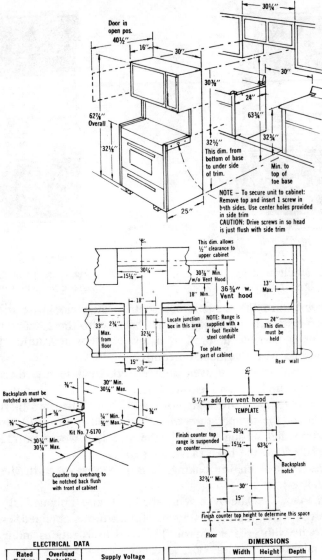

ELECTRICAL DATA

Rated Wattage	Overload Protection	Supply Voltage
12,400	51.7 Amps.	120/240 V. 60 cy. 3-wire
12,400	59.6 Amps.	120/208 V. 60 cy. 3-wire
11,800	49.2 Amps.	120/240 V. 60 cy. 3-wire
11,800	56.7 Amps.	120/208 V. 60 cy. 3-wire

DIMENSIONS

	Width	Height	Depth
Overall	30″	62⅞″	25½″
Eye-level Oven	21¼″	12″	13″
Lower Oven	24″	14½″	19″

Fig. 53.

Fig. 54. Electric drop-in range.

Oven Racks. The oven racks should be arranged before the oven knob is turned to the On range. Place the racks so the food is *centered* in the oven, not on the rack.

Where more than one utensil is used, be sure to stagger them, allowing space between each one. Do not allow the utensils to touch any part of the oven, especially the glass window. It is best to use two racks (some models are factory equipped with one rack) and place the food so one is not directly over another.

To remove the racks, lift up the back of the rack and pull forward. To replace it, place the L-shaped piece of rod (on the back of the rack) on top of the rack support and slide the rack to the rear of the oven. It will fall in place.

Never cover the oven racks with aluminum foil. Such practices will trap heat and cause intense heat, in spots, which usually give poor results. It can damage the porcelain finish as well as glass windows in the oven.

Broiler Pan and Grill. *Broiler grill.* Removing the broiler pan from the broiler compartment is a good practice. Remember never to reach into a hot oven without protecting yourself from the heat. Exercise care when removing the hot pan, especially if a considerable amount of hot fat is involved. The grease is not only flammable, but it can cause you a serious burn.

Broiler pan. Grasp the broiler pan and slide forward.

Oven Light Bulb. Only use a *range-oven* bulb. Replace, when the range is cool, by screwing out the defective bulb and screwing in a new bulb. Use a dry cloth to handle the bulb.

Element Pans. If you wrap element pans with aluminum foil,

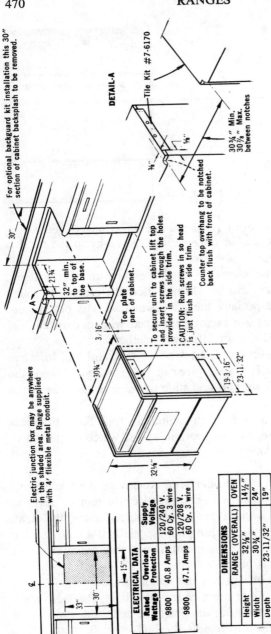

For optional backguard kit installation this 30" section of cabinet backsplash to be removed.

DETAIL-A

Tile Kit #7-6170

30¾" Min.
30⅞" Max.
between notches

⅝"

¾"

Counter top overhang to be notched back flush with front of cabinet.

30"

21¾"

A

32" min. to top of toe base.

Toe plate part of cabinet.

3 .16"

To secure unit to cabinet lift top and insert screws through the holes provided in the side trim.

CAUTION: Run screws in so head is just flush with side trim.

30¾"

19-3 .16"

23-11 .32"

32⅛"

Electric junction box may be anywhere in the shaded area. Range supplied with 4' flexible metal conduit.

33"

30"

15"

ELECTRICAL DATA			
Rated Wattage	Overload Protection	Supply Voltage	
9800	40.8 Amps	120/240 V. 60 Cy. 3 wire	
9800	47.1 Amps	120/208 V. 60 Cy. 3 wire	

DIMENSIONS		
	RANGE (OVERALL)	OVEN
Height	32⅛"	14½"
Width	30¾"	24"
Depth	23-11/32"	19"

Fig. 55.

Fig. 56. Smooth-top drop-in range.

ELECTRICAL DATA
120/240 VOLT MODELS:
Electrical rating: 120/240 V. 60 cycles.
3 wire single phase 35.4 amp. 8.5 KW

120/280 VOLT MODELS:
Electrical rating: 120/208 V. 60 cycles.
3 wire single phase 40.9 amps 8.5 KW

³⁄₈″

30″ Min.
30⅛″ Max.

³⁄₈″

¼″ Min.
⅜″ Max.

32″ min.
to top of
toe base.

A

2⅝″

30″

9½″

3/16″

32⅛″

To secure unit to cabinet lift
top and insert screws through
the holes provided in the side trim.

CAUTION: Run screws in so head
is just flush with side trim.

19-3/16″   25

33″

30″

15″

Electric junction box may be anywhere
in the shaded area. Range supplied
with 4′ flexible metal conduit.

These plates add
strength by keeping tile and
mud firm. Caution: Secure
tile plates to cabinet with
#5 flat head screws or 7D
nails.

³⁄₈″

DETAIL-A

⅝″

Counter top overhang to be
notched back flush with front
of cabinet.

30¾″ min.
30⅞″ max.
between notches

Fig. 57.

Fig. 58. Self-cleaning drop-in range.

make certain an air hole is placed in the center of the foil; otherwise, reflected heat from the foil can cause damge to the element.

Time of Day Clock.   Figure 60 shows a regular time of day clock for indicating the time of day *only*. Knob can be rotated in either direction for setting.

Clock with a Minute Minder.   These clocks are of the minute minder series (Fig. 61). Just set timer knob A for the length of time you want (Fig. 62). A signal will sound when the set time has elapsed.

This clock will also indicate the time of day. If the electric power is interrupted, you can reset the time of day by pushing the knob in and rotating the dial hands to the proper setting.

Oven with Mind Clocks.   The mind clocks (Fig. 63) can be used to automatically time the cooking of food in the oven, or as a minute minder timer.

How the Programmed Oven Works.   When the time and temperature are set, the oven burner cycles on, the oven thermostat regulates the action, and the cooking cycle begins. Shortly before the end of the time period you have selected, the clock activates a small devise that governs the thermostat so that the oven temperature is lowered and maintained at a keep-warm level. To discontinue this operation the timer knob should be placed to manual and the oven knob to Off.

Operation.   *See* Fig. 64.

1. Set knob B to the number of hours you desire the food to cook.

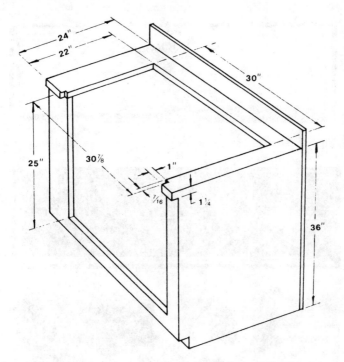

KW: 10.2
Amp: 42.5
Voltage: 120/240 Vac., 60 cycle

	OVEN
WIDTH	22"
HEIGHT	15"
DEPTH	18"
Total connected load 10.0 KW	

Fig. 59.

2. Turn oven knob to desired temperature setting.

3. To discontinue operation—turn knob B to *manual* and oven knob to off.

The minute minder operates as follows:

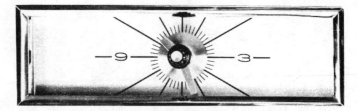

Fig. 60. Time of day clock.

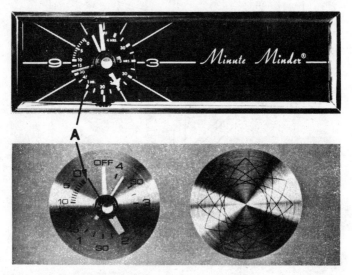

Fig. 61. Clock with minute minder.

1. Set knob A to desired minutes.

2. A signal will let you know when the set time has expired.

3. Set knob to off to set the time of day hands; push in on knob B and rotate to proper setting.

Note: The oven will not operate unless clock is turned to manual setting. If oven fails to heat, check the clock setting.

The clock control, when included on the double oven models, is for the lower oven.

Holding Times for Food. The keep-warm feature will hold foods safely for 4 to 5 hours after cooking. Some foods maintain bet-

Fig. 62. Timer knob.

Fig. 63. Mind clocks.

ter than others; however, for best results serve within 1½ to 2 hours after cooking.

Surface and Oven Lights.   The lights are push button, simple depress for on or off.

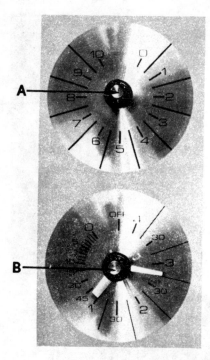

Fig. 64. Setting clock.

CARE AND CLEANING RANGE

Cleaning your range is a very easy task with the many easy-care features of today's electric ranges.

Before cleaning any part of the range, be sure all controls are off and the range is cool.

Outside Finish.   The outside of your range can be kept clean just by wiping it off regularly with warm, soapy water and a soft cloth. Wipe up spills of acidic foods, such as tomatoes, vinegar, lemon juice, and milk, immediately. Porcelain enamel is stain-resistant but not stain-proof.

The chrome trim can be kept clean by wiping with a damp cloth. Do not scour or use harsh abrasives.

For brushed aluminum or stainless steel tops, a final polish with a few drops of cooking or baby oil on a soft cloth will cut down finger marks.

The control knobs are usually removable for easy cleaning. *Surface units* are self-cleaning. Turn the unit to high until all of the food particles are burned away.

Oven.   The secret of easy oven cleaning is to wipe the oven out with warm sudsy water, rinse well, and dry after each use. This removes the grease and spillover before the oven is used again and prevents burning it into the oven liner.

When using a commercial cleaner, follow the manufacturer's directions precisely.

Do not cover the floor or the racks of the oven with foil, as this will interfere with heat distribution and browning.

Self-Cleaning Ovens.   A self-cleaning oven cleans itself electrically and eliminates the messy and difficult chore of oven cleaning.

For best results, follow the manufacturer's instructions carefully. Do not use commercial oven cleaners or oven protective coatings in or around the self-cleaning oven. Remove all utensils and excessive spillovers from the oven before cleaning. Clean the oven before it gets excessively dirty.

Remove the little ash that remains with a damp cloth.

ALIGNMENTS AND OTHER ADJUSTMENTS

Oven Hinge.   Figure 65 illustrates the hinge mechanism used on the lower oven door. The hinge spring tension can be adjusted by reaching through the broiler compartment and moving the spring to the desired notch in the lower spring anchor. The hinge pin is held in place by a wire retainer clip. To remove the hinge blade, simply unhook the spring from the rear of the hinge blade and remove the pin. If it becomes necessary to service or replace the stationary hinge bracket and roller assembly, it is recommended that the side panel be removed for better access.

Lift-Off Door.   If your range has a lift-off door it can be easily removed for oven clearing purposes. To remove, open the door to the stop position, grasp it at the top corners, and lift the door off.

Seating Top Elements.   The top elements may need initial seating after installation of the stove or after they have been unplugged and re-installed. Palm the element as shown in Fig. 66. Pick up on

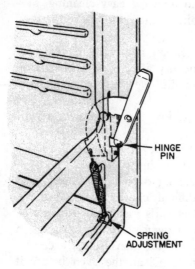

Fig. 65. Oven hinge.

Fig. 66. Seating top elements.

the rear section with your fingers while pushing down on the front of the element with the palm of your hand.

Caution: Make certain all surface elements are cool and all switches are in the Off position prior to seating the elements.

Oven Door Spring Adjustment.   The oven door springs (Fig. 67) are properly adjusted before leaving the factory. The springs

Fig. 67. Oven door springs.

should be adjusted to allow the door to remain open when pulled 90 degrees forward and yet allow you to pull the door tight against the oven front frame when closed. If adjustment should become necessary, remove the broiler and broiler cradle, grasp spring with finger, and pull down. To give more tension, push toward rear of range and attach in first slot. To make spring adjustment on ranges with a slide-out type broiler, remove end panels and follow the same procedure.

KEROSENE RANGE

Care, Cleaning, and Operation.   The kerosene range (Fig. 68) is still used in various parts of our country.

1. Be sure range is level and not located in a draft.
2. See that parts of the burner and chimney fit together properly.
3. Use a small brush or paper napkin to clean wicks (Fig. 69). Do not cut it with scissors. If the wick has a beveled edge, this should be carefully maintained. If wicks become very dirty, remove and boil in a solution of washing soda (sal soda); then rinse and dry thoroughly. In replacing a wick, adjust at level with the top of the outside of the wick tube.
4. Wipe the outside of the stove daily after it cools with a damp cloth, and dry thoroughly.
5. Keep spilled food wiped up in the oven and leave door open until it cools.
6. Clean isinglass in chimneys or oven door with vinegar.
7. Once a year, or oftener if necessary, clean range thoroughly.
   Burners and *chimneys*. Boil perforated sections in soda solu-

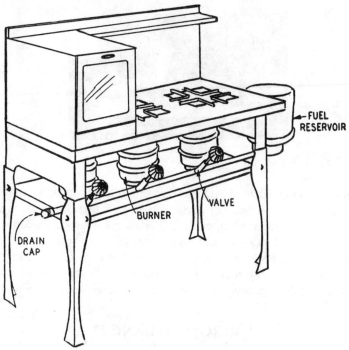

Fig. 68. Kerosene range.

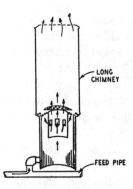

Fig. 69. Cleaning wicks.

tion, wash, and polish with a hot mixture of vinegar and salt (4 parts vinegar to 2 parts salt.) Wash and dry thoroughly. Wash chimneys with warm, soapy water; rinse and dry thoroughly. Remove rust spots with fine steel wool. (*See* Fig. 69.)

Feed pipe. Drain the feed pipe, preferably every three months, by loosening the drain cap (Fig. 68) and tilting the stove. Clean the pipe with a rag tied securely to a long wire. Flush with kerosene.

Oil tank. Drain the oil tank, then fill with washing soda solution, and let it stand 20 minutes. Wash with warm soapy water, then rinse and dry thoroughly before refilling with kerosene.

8. Adjust the flame height slowly to a blue flame that has small yellow tips.

9. To avoid odor and smoke, raise chimney on short drum burners after turning control device to Off.

10. To store kerosene range, remove wicks and clean wick tubes and feed line; drain kerosene; rub all parts likely to rust with unsalted fat and place in a clean, dry place. Wrap chimneys and grids in moisture-resistant paper.

COAL OR WOOD RANGE

Like the kerosene range, the coal or wood range is still being used in various parts of our country. (*See* Fig. 70.)

Most good stoves have several drafts and dampers, of which several are described below.

Fire control damper below the firebox admits the necessary air for combustion. Be sure to keep the ash-pit door closed.

Damper over the fuel bed admits cold air on top of the fire. Open it slightly when adding fresh fuel to aid in combustion of gases.

Oven damper reduces the draft from the chimney and draws heat around the oven.

Stove pipe drawer is used to regulate the chimney draft. When a strong wind is blowing, keep this damper partly closed, except when starting a fire. On wet days, leave this damper entirely open.

Care, Cleaning, and Operation.

1. Remove all ashes regularly from the firebox and ash pan (Fig. 70). Never allow ashes in the ash pit to remain in contact with the grates.

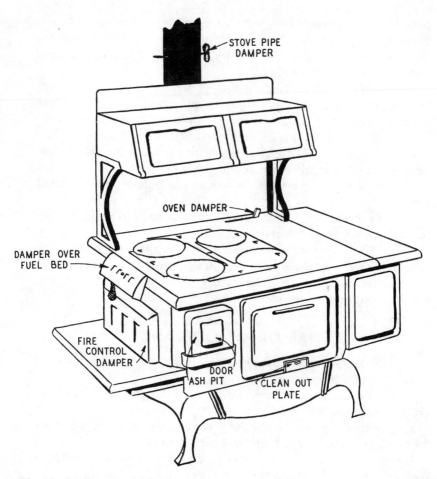

Fig. 70. Coal or wood range.

2. Clean soot from chimney, flue, and pipe once a year, and from the bottom of lids and around the oven once a week.

3. Wash the inside of the oven and racks with soap and water, rinse, and dry thoroughly. If the inside of the oven is rusted, clean with steel wool and paint with aluminum paint. Never store food in the oven. Allow oven door to remain slightly open until entirely cool.

4. Keep the top of the stove in good condition by rubbing it each day, while it is still warm, with a piece of waxed paper or unsalted fat (rather than blacking). Clean the nickel, chromium, or enamel parts with soap and whiting.

5. If stove has a water back connected with a hot water tank, be careful it does not freeze in cold weather. In severe weather, cover a bed of coals with ashes or drain the tank.

Chapter 28

Microwave Ovens

Microwaves are a form of electromagnetic energy that is intermediate in frequency and wavelength between radio waves and infrared waves.

Microwave energy is absorbed by many materials, thereby producing a temperature rise. In foods, this increase in temperature is rapid and makes it possible to cook foods quickly.

Metallic materials, such as oven walls, grids, and screens, largely reflect microwave energy. Glass and many nonmetallic wrapping materials allow microwaves to pass through them.

The *degree of heating* depends on the moisture content, shape, size, mass, and other physical features of the material.

Microwaves, a *nonionizing form of radiation*, will *not* make food and other materials radioactive.

As in any cooking process, microwave cooking has some effect on the nutritional value of the food. Most studies, however, have shown that there are no significant nutritional differences in foods heated by microwave radiation when compared to conventional cooking methods.

There have been no documented cases of *radiation injury* related to microwave ovens when these appliances were used according to the manufacturer's instructions.

Interference with certain heart pacemakers has been associated with proximity to an operating microwave oven, as it has with other kinds of electronic or electrical equipment.

The most frequent causes of *microwave leakage* have been maladjustment of oven door safety interlocks (devices to turn the oven off automatically as the door is opened), abuse of doors and door seals, buildup of dirt around door seals, improper servicing, and, with older ovens, failure to replace or repair worn-out door hinges and latches.

The Radiation Control for Health and Safety Act of 1968, enforced by the Food and Drug Administration, requires the industry to take corrective action when an electronic product fails to comply with a performance standard or has a radiation defect that relates to its safe use.

The act was passed by Congress to protect the public from exposure to radiation from electronic products, including microwave ovens. The FDA's Bureau of Radiological Health has been given responsibility for day-to-day enforcement of the act.

The bureau has issued a *radiation control standard* for microwave ovens. The standard requires that ovens manufactured after October 6, 1971, not emit radiation above specified levels, and be equipped with at least two independently operating safety interlocks to shut off radiation as oven doors are opened. Also, ovens manufactured after August 6, 1974, must become inoperable if one or both interlocks fail to function.

Every oven manufactured after October 6, 1971, must carry a label certifying compliance with the Federal standard.

The FDA tests microwave ovens in homes, commercial establishments, dealer and distributor premises, factories, and its own laboratories to assure that microwave ovens comply with Federal requirements. It also evaluates manufacturers' testing and quality control programs to assure compliance.

Microwave ovens that meet the Federal standard are *safe* for use in the home. Tests confirm that all makes and models of ovens produced since the effective date of the standard present no radiation hazard when used according to the manufacturer's instructions.

It is impossible to say that individual ovens produced *before* the effective date of the standard are not emitting radiation—unless they are tested with a properly designed instrument—as these ovens were not necessarily designed to the stringent specifications required of ovens manufactured under the standard.

In some instances, microwave oven dealers are arranging to have older ovens tested for leakage upon request. Some commercial service organizations test ovens. A number of Federal, state, and local programs also provide this service.

If you have an old oven, you should contact your state or local health department or nearest FDA district office to obtain information as to the availability of these tests in your area.

Used properly and with care, the microwave oven is a boon to homemakers. It is an unbeatable time-saver and a pleasure to use.

SELECTING A MICROWAVE OVEN

Microwave ovens have the following advantages: they cook fast (about five minutes per pound for a roast), and are especially convenient for thawing or cooking frozen foods; they save energy in cooking some food items; they keep your kitchen cool (microwaves heat the food, not the oven); clean-ups are easier (cook on disposable paper plates and just wipe the oven with a damp rag and mild detergent).

Microwave ovens have drawbacks, too: they are not all-purpose ovens (you still need a conventional oven for cooking or baking certain things); many do not brown steaks and chops; they require that you learn new cooking techniques and give special attention to certain foods (frequent turning of bulky items, for example).

When you are buying a microwave oven the following suggestions are recommended.

1. Read various manufacturers' manuals of instructions and recipes. Learn what each model offers, what wiring or special utensils it may require, and what timing to expect from it (about four minutes for one potato, for instance, but about eight minutes for two potatoes).

2. Examine various models. Will you want a tabletop (portable) oven or a freestanding range (containing both microwave and conventional ovens)? A portable plugs into any household outlet, but it does need its own 110–220-volt circuit to work efficiently? A full-size range needs a separate 220-volt line.

3. Understand what guaranties and warranties each manufacturer offers.

4. Ask about cost of replacing magnetron: that generates microwaves and other parts.

5. Ask whether technicians are available to provide servicing. What are their rates for servicing?

6. Consult your local utility company for guidance on energy

saving aspects. Will a microwave oven save energy on all cooking chores, compared with a conventional oven? Would you save more energy with a high watt or a low watt model? What might your average yearly energy savings be with a microwave oven?

7. Buy a model with additional safety interlock features.

USE AND CARE OF OVEN

The microwave oven shown in Fig. 1 is designed to give you long, safe, and peak performance. However, as with all electrical appliances, there are some things that you must follow to avoid potential personal hazards and give you the performance you expect.

Fig. 1. Microwave oven.

Visual Check After Uncrating.   After the oven is uncrated, all packing material must be removed from the oven cavity.

Inspect the oven for any damage, such as a misaligned door, damaged gasketing around the door, dents or holes in the door screen, or dents inside the oven cavity.

Any dents or breakage should be reported to your dealer and the delivering carrier immediately. The dealer will tell you if the oven will operate correctly.

Electrical Grounding.   The oven shown in Fig. 1 is equipped with a three-prong grounding plug (Fig. 2) for your protection against possible shock hazards. Where a two-prong wall receptacle is encountered, it is your personal responsibility and obligation to contact a qualified person or electrician and have it replaced with a properly grounded three-prong wall receptacle in accordance with the National Electrical Code. (*Do not* use a two-prong adaptor in Canada.) *Do not* under any circumstances cut or remove the round grounding prong from the plug shown in Fig. 2.

Fig. 2. Three-prong grounding plug.

The unit *must* be grounded at all times. If you move the oven from area to area, the receptacle you use must be fully grounded.

Electric Lock and Interlock Switch Systems.   The oven shown in Fig. 1 contains a solenoid-operated electric lock that engages when the oven is operating, and disengages when the oven is turned off. In addition, hidden back-up interlocks are activated by the motion of the door as it is opened. To check the operation of the electric lock and interlocks, proceed as follows:

1. When the oven is in operation, the electric lock is engaged.
2. Press the Stop button. The oven will shut off immediately. The cooking light on the control panel will go off; the sound of the cooking fan will cease. The electric lock is now disengaged and the door should open freely. If the oven shuts off by other means, such as the timer running out, the plug being disconnected, or if slight door motion opens a back-up interlock switch, the electric lock is also disengaged.
3. To check the operation of the back-up safety switch (interlock switch), you must have an operative oven light. If the oven light is working, press the Light button to turn the light off. Open door fully. The light should come on when the door is opened. If the oven light does not come on, the back-up safety switch is inoperative.

If under any of the preceding conditions the oven *does not* operate properly, *do not* use it. Get in touch with your dealer, or call your service man.

OPERATION

Most microwave ovens run on a frequency of 2,450 mhz, but some are available in 915 mhz. (Mhz means megahertz, such as a unit of frequency corresponding to one cycle per one-one millionth of a second.) The frequency determines the wave length; the higher the frequency, the shorter the wave length and the shallower the heat penetration. Larger meat and poultry items will cook somewhat faster in a 915-mhz unit, although the 2,450-mhz unit is adequate. Smaller meals and dishes, such as leftovers, are easier to cook and heat up in a 2,450-mhz unit.

For the first few days that you have the oven in your home, it is recommended that you keep a cup or glass of water in the oven when it is not in use. This will help protect the oven if it should accidentally be turned on by curious members of the family who might run the oven without a load in it. It is possible to damage the magnetron tube if the oven is operated without anything in it.

Be sure to fill out the registration punched card and send it to the manufacturer of the oven.

Controls. The operation of a microwave oven is very simple. All you do is select the time you desire on one of the two timers and push the start switch. Pushing the start switch with the door closed automatically engages the electric door lock.

The timer will revolve counterclockwise until the time is up and then shut off the oven. While the oven is in operation, a red light located between the two timers will be on.

Two-timer controls. The top control will allow cooking times up to five minutes (Fig. 3).

The bottom control will allow cooking times up to 30 minutes (Fig. 3).

To set either timer control, turn the control in either direction to the time you want.

Each control is numbered counterclockwise.

Note: The oven will not "see" the time on both dials. It operates only for the longest time set on *one* of the dials.

Five-minute timer control. The timer is numbered counterclockwise from 1 to 4. Each mark between the numbers represents 15 seconds. Turn the control to the time you desire. Then push the Start switch. The timer will revolve counterclockwise from the time you have set to Off. The oven will then turn off.

To set for five minutes, move the timer counterclockwise, slightly past Off.

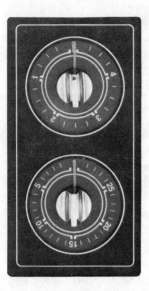

Fig. 3. Timer controls.

Thirty-minute timer control. The timer is numbered clockwise from 5 to 25. Each mark is one minute. Turn the control to the time you desire, then push the Start switch.

The timer will revolve counterclockwise from the time you have set to Off. The oven will then turn off.

To set for 30 minutes, move the timer counterclockwise, slightly past Off.

Electric lock. The electric lock is automatically engaged when the Start switch is pushed and the door closed. When the Stop switch is pushed or time runs out, the oven shuts off instantly. The electric lock disengages and the door may be opened freely.

Start switch. Push the Start switch after you have set either one of the timer controls. The Start switch will not operate the oven unless one of the timer controls has been set. (*See* Fig. 4.)

Interior light switch. The interior light switch turns the light on and off inside the oven (Fig. 5).

Stop switch. The Stop switch (Fig. 6) instantly stops the oven from operating.

Fig. 4. Start switch.

Fig. 5. Light switch.

Fig. 6. Stop switch.

Checking food while unit is operating. If at any time during the cooking cycle you wish to stir, or check food, merely push the Stop button. The electric lock will disengage and the oven will shut off.

To resume cooking, close the door and push the Start switch. You do not have to reset the timer. The oven automatically resumes time from the point it stopped when you pushed the Stop switch.

Cooking cycles. With the new Cookmatic cycle you have a choice of an additional, almost infinite, amount of cycles. For convenience and exactness in cooking, the power shift has been divided into six power settings.

The regular cook cycle, the high setting on the Cookmatic slide, means that the magnetron tube is operating 100 percent of the time. The balance of the settings are at selected levels spaced between a low level of operation and full operation.

Defrosting Food.   To defrost food proceed as follows:

Step 1. Place frozen food in the unit. Set power shift to recommended setting (Fig. 7).

Step 2. Set the timer control, either the 5-minute or 30-minute control, to the time needed for thawing or low-temperature cooking (Fig. 7).

Step 1   Step 2   Step 3

Fig. 7. Defrosting food cycle.

Step 3. Push the Start switch. The oven will then cycle on and off automatically for the full time preset on the timer control (Fig. 7).

To interrupt cycle. Push the Stop switch. This shuts off the unit immediately. The timer control will also stop at the elapsed time.

To restart cycle. Push the Start switch. The oven will continue to operate on the on-off cycle for the remaining time shown on the timer control. You do not have to reset the timer control.

CARE OF OVEN

There is little to do to keep the oven shown in Fig. 1 in tip-top condition. The inside of the oven is made of stainless steel. If it should get splattered, all you do is wipe it with a paper towel or clean with a mild detergent in warm water and a soft sponge or cloth.

To clean the glass tray, lift up and remove the tray, and wash it in warm water and detergent. Replace with the drip tray pattern up. Do not operate the oven without the tray in position.

Never pour water into the bottom of the oven.

Do not use an abrasive to clean the inside. It might damage the stainless steel.

DISHES AND COOKWARE USED

Heat-proof glass utensils such as those shown in Fig. 8 may be used.

Ceramic utensils such as Corning Ware may be used, if labeled microwave-oven safe.

Plastic containers may be used. Hot foods may distort the container of some types of plastic. Oily or greasy foods may remove glaze on some plastics.

Fig. 8. Heat-proof glass utensils.

China dishes without metal trim may be used.

Paper products, such as paper plates, toweling to cover foods that might splatter or that are used to absorb grease, may be used in the oven.

If in doubt, use this dish test: If you are questioning the type of dishes you have, this simple dish test will help you determine whether to use them in the oven.

1. Place a cup filled with water in the particular dish to be tested.

2. Place it in oven.

3. Set timer for $1\frac{1}{4}$ minutes.

Test results: If the water is very warm and the dish cool, you may use the dish. If the dish is slightly warm around the edges, use it for short term cooking. If the water is cool and the dish hot do not use the dish.

Cooking Bags, Pouch Packs, and Plastic Wraps. *Cooking bags.* Be sure to use a string tie instead of the small metal tie that is packed with cooking bags. Pierce a hole in the bag for steam to escape or it may expand and burst.

You will notice a great deal of moisture collecting in the bag. This moisture may slow the cooking somewhat. Remove excess by using a spoon or baster to remove moisture.

Pouch packs that you fill and seal at home may be used. Pierce bag before heating for steam escape, or it may expand and burst.

Plastic wraps. Use them to cover foods you are reheating. Some wraps, because of the type of plastic, will become sticky and difficult to remove after being heated. Some may shrink around the dish or food. Use plastic wrap for short-time reheating only. Be sure to pierce plastic wrap.

Cookware Not Used.
See Fig. 9.

Do not use metal pans, metal handles on ceramic dishes, or dishes having metal trim in the oven.

Do not use Corning Ware Centura.

Do not use Corelle Living Ware cups with the *closed* handles.

Do not use cooking wrap with metal foil ends.

Do not use foil pans for entrees or pot pies.

Do not use aluminum foil except in turkey roasting; small strips may be used only on wing tips and leg bones.

Do not use melamine dishes, as they usually contain some metal and may char or crack.

USE OF METAL

The use of cooking utensils or ceramic ware containing *metal*, or other *metal products* in the oven will shorten the life of the *magnetron tube* or damage the tube. Fast cooking in the microwave oven is accomplished because the microwave energy is able to penetrate the food from all sides—top, bottom, and sides. If metal is used in the oven it will reflect the microwaves and will not allow

Fig. 9. Cooking utensils not to be used.

the area that is not exposed to the microwaves to cook as well as you would like. This means that the results will not be what you anticipate. Using metal cookware or any type of glass ware, ceramic ware, or earthen ware that has metal trim or parts made of certain metal particles will shorten the life of the magnetron tube.

MAINTENANCE

How to Change the Oven Light Inside Oven. To change the oven light inside the oven shown in Fig. 1, always unplug the oven from the power source before you change the oven light.

The light bulb for the inside of the oven can be changed *only* from the back. On the upper-right-hand side of the back oven is a metal plate with two hex-head screws. The light bulb is located behind this plate. Loosen the right screw. Remove the left screw. This allows the plate to swing down. Unscrew the bulb. When replacing the lamp use a 25-watt T6-½ bulb. Reverse the procedure when putting the cover plate in position. Some ovens will use a 25-watt 25T8 DC bayonet-base bulb.

Cleaning the Discharge Air Vents.   There will be a slight build-up of cooking vapors in the discharge vent, located in the upper-right-hand corner of the oven, above the controls. These should be cleaned occasionally. Do not attempt to remove the front of the two-timer control model as it is an integral part of the oven. Clean the air vent with a damp cloth.

How to Clean the Splatter Shield Inside Oven.   The *splatter shield* keeps the top of the oven and stirrer (a fanlike blade that reflects the microwaves inside the oven) from getting dirty. Normally, a damp cloth will remove any splatter from the shield. However, if you want to clean it more thoroughly, remove the splatter shield. On the two-timer control model, remove the hex screws at the front of the oven. Pull the shield toward the front of the oven. When replacing it, be sure it fits snugly in clips at the back of the oven before replacing the screws. (Be careful not to damage stirrer blade).

Allow Air Flow Around the Oven.   Free air flow from the front and the back of oven is a must. The air flows around the electronic components. If air flow is restricted, the oven will not operate properly and the life of electrical parts is shortened.

Electrical.   The oven shown in Fig. 1 is designed to operate on 115-volt, 60 cycle current. It should be plugged into a circuit that does not have any other appliances or lights on it.

Grounding Oven.   *See* section on Electrical Grounding previously described.

SAFETY TIPS

For all owners using any brand of microwave oven—regardless of when it was made—as in the case of other major electronic appliances, you can be assured of proper oven operation by following a few simple precautions.

1. Follow the manufacturer's instruction literature for recommended operating procedures and safety precautions.

2. Examine the oven for evidence of shipping damage.

3. Never operate an oven if the door does not close firmly or is bent, warped, or otherwise damaged.

4. Never tamper with or inactivate the oven safety interlocks.

5. Frequently clean door, seals, and inside of oven with water and mild detergent. Grease around door seal can cause excess radiation emission. Do not use scouring pads, steel wool, or other abrasives.

6. Have oven regularly serviced by a qualified serviceman for signs of wear, damage, or tampering.

7. The glass oven tray must be in place when operating the oven. This allows the microwaves to be reflected up into the bottom of food that is being cooked. The tray is a special type of glass and, if it is accidently broken, it must be replaced with the same type of glass from your dealer.

8. Never insert objects through the door grill or around the door seal. Never allow even a paper towel to stick out of the door.

9. Never operate an empty oven.

Users should follow these additional precautions in the case of ovens manufactured prior to the standard (you can tell this by checking the oven for a certification label).

1. Switch the oven off before opening the door.

2. Stay at least an arm's length away from the front of an oven while it is on.

Chapter 29

Dishwashers

The purpose of a dishwasher is to save you time and relieve you of a chore. To accomplish that task, most home dishwashers are built and operate in much the same way. They wash by spraying a solution of detergent and hot water over dishes; rinse by flushing them with clean, hot water; and dry them with heated air.

SELECTING YOUR DISHWASHER

Dishwashers are classified as *portable, built-in,* or *convertible,* depending on whether they are readily movable, permanently installed, or movable but adaptable to permanent installation. The built-in type is approximately 24 inches wide, 24 inches deep, and 34 inches high. Some portables are slightly smaller than built-in models; some convertibles are larger.

In *selecting* a portable, built-in, or convertible dishwasher, consider whether you own your home or are renting. Measure the space available near a water supply and drain, and examine the arrangement of appliances in your kitchen.

PORTABLE DISHWASHERS

Portable dishwashers are usually used in apartments, mobile homes, or any kitchen where permanent installation is not practical.

Design. A portable is mounted on small wheels, or casters, so it can be rolled to a sink for washing dishes and away when not in use. On some models, the electric cord automatically retracts when it is unplugged from an outlet; on others it can be manually placed in a special storage nook. Water inlet and drain hoses are permanently attached to the machine. On most models both intake and outlet hoses are connected to a single coupling that, in turn, attaches to a sink faucet. In some models the drain hose is placed separately in the sink.

Many couplings have a device for the gradual release of water pressure that prevents water from spurting when the coupling is disconnected. It may also enable you to get water from the faucet while the dishwasher is operating, except when it is filling or draining.

Installation Requirements. Three things are needed for the operation of a portable dishwasher: space, plumbing, and electrical power.

Space. Before shopping for a portable dishwasher, measure the space in your kitchen where you plan to store the machine when it is not in use. Take the measurements with you to the store.

Consider, too, whether you will have limited or ample space for loading and unloading the dishwasher when it is in place near the kitchen sink. A front-loading portable needs space for the door to open and the racks to slide out horizontally. If the space is limited, you may want a top-loading portable. The open door takes up only air space and not floor space. However, the top cannot be used as a work surface while dishes are loaded or unloaded.

Plumbing. An adequate supply of hot water and good drainage are essential. Some faucets may require a special adaptor available at most hardware stores. The manufacturer's instructions will tell you how to use it.

Power. Power requirements for portable dishwashers differ with size and design. Some models require as little as seven amperes of electric current; others need as many as 16 amperes. A small metal plate, located either inside the door or on the back of the machine, lists the number of amperes required.

Before you buy a portable dishwasher, check to see that your kitchen wiring will carry the load. If the wiring is inadequate, buy a dishwasher that uses less current or have higher capacity wiring built into your kitchen.

Kitchen circuit capacities. Many kitchens have 15-ampere circuits; some have 20-ampere circuits. To find the *current capacity* of your kitchen wiring, check your house or apartment fuse box and read the amperes for the kitchen circuit you plan to use for your dishwasher. If you do not know how to do this, ask your local electric utility company to tell you the circuit's ampere rating or consult an electrician.

Codes.   To find out what ampere rating of dishwasher is allowable on the kitchen circuit you plan to use under local electrical codes, telephone the city or county engineer's office, a licensed electrician, or the local electric utility company.

In most areas, a dishwasher using fewer than 12 amperes can be connected to a 15-ampere circuit with more than one outlet. In other words, no special electrical installation is needed. But be careful not to use too many other appliances when the dishwasher is operating or you may blow a fuse or trip a circuit breaker.

Everywhere in the country electrical codes require that a dishwasher drawing 12 amperes must be connected either to a separate 15-ampere circuit that has no other household use or to a 20-ampere circuit. A dishwasher using 16 amperes must have a separate 20-ampere circuit. Few kitchens have separate circuits available.

The cost of installing a separate-circuit outlet may vary. If you find that you need a separate circuit, be sure to get an estimate of costs before you make your dishwasher purchase.

Grounding.   All portable dishwashers have a three-prong plug for insertion into a three-hole outlet. The third hole is for grounding; that is, it connects your dishwasher, through wiring, to the earth outside your home. Then, if an electrical fault occurs in the dishwasher, electricity flows harmlessly through this wiring to the outdoor earth rather than giving you a shock or a burn.

Grounding is particularly important for dishwashers and other appliances used in kitchens where spilled water is common. If your kitchen does not have a three-hole, grounded, electrical outlet, have an electrician install one.

Adaptors are available to connect three-prong plugs to two-hole outlets, but they are not recommended. They may or may not provide adequate grounding for your dishwasher.

Never remove the third prong from a three-prong plug to connect it to a two-hole outlet. Not only will the dishwasher be ungrounded but the plug may be damaged and, thus, dangerous.

Never use an extension cord with a dishwasher. If the connection between the dishwasher plug and the extension cord is exposed to water, a shock hazard results.

BUILT-IN DISHWASHERS

Built-in dishwashers are installed when a kitchen is being built or remodeled and operate without any further connecting or disconnecting.

Design. All built-in dishwashers load from the front and have no external hoses or cords and no casters. They may or may not have side and back panels and tops, depending upon their location in the kitchen.

Installation Requirements. A built-in dishwasher should be installed by a licensed plumber and an electrician. Power requirements are the same as for a portable dishwasher. Among other plumbing connections, you may wish to have a shut-off valve placed in the hot-water pipe leading to the dishwasher. It should be located where you can reach it quickly if the dishwasher overflows.

Installing a dishwasher in a new house or remodeled kitchen, or a replacement installation, varies in cost.

Location. Built-in dishwashers can be placed under the kitchen counter near the center or at the end; or they can be freestanding. They should be located near the kitchen sink or other plumbing so that the water inlet and drain can be easily connected. Adequate space should be allowed for loading through the front-opening door.

Kitchen location affects the cost of a built-in dishwasher. *Under-the-counter* models come with only a front panel and are the least expensive. For *end-of-counter* models, you must also pay for a side panel; for *freestanding* models, you pay for a top, one or more side panels, and a back panel.

CONVERTIBLE DISHWASHERS

Convertible dishwashers are for people who want a portable at present but expect they'll need a built-in dishwasher later. They combine the features of portable and built-in dishwashers.

Design. Convertibles are mounted on casters and are equipped with an inlet hose, a drain hose, a faucet coupling, and a power cord. Convertibles load from the front and may be identical on the inside with built-in models of the same brand.

Convertibles are sold with all sides paneled. The top panel as well as the casters, hoses, and electrical cord are removed for permanent installation; the side and rear panels may or may not be removable.

Installation Requirements.   The installation requirements for a convertible are the same as for a portable if it is being used as one. Remember, however, that convertibles may be heavier and more difficult to move than portables. If you buy a convertible, be sure you have storage space for it close to the sink.

For using a convertible as a built-in dishwasher, you need professional installation by a serviceman from an authorized service center or by a licensed plumber and an electrician.

OPERATION

Cleaning and Drying Sequence.   The specific steps to be taken after the racks are loaded with dirty dishes and pushed inside the tub, and the cleaning aids placed in the dispensers, are shown in Figs. 1 through 5.

To start the dishwasher, you first close the door and turn or push the latch that seals it. Then you activate the timer by pressing a button or turning a dial.

Hot water enters at a constant rate through the inlet valve, which compensates for fluctuations in the household water pressure. When enough water is in the tub, the valve closes. During the water fill, the dishwasher motor starts.

The motor powers the pump, which forces water through the wash arms and/or spray tower onto the dishes. At the proper time, detergent is added to the water automatically.

The pump continuously circulates water within the dishwasher, passing it through either a filter or a soft food disposer. The filter traps food particles, and the disposer pulverizes them. Both help prevent food particles from being redeposited on dishes.

When washing is completed, the pump forces the dirty water out through the drain.

Fresh, hot water then comes in through the water intake for rinsing. The motor starts, and the pump sends clear water to the wash arms and/or spray tower.

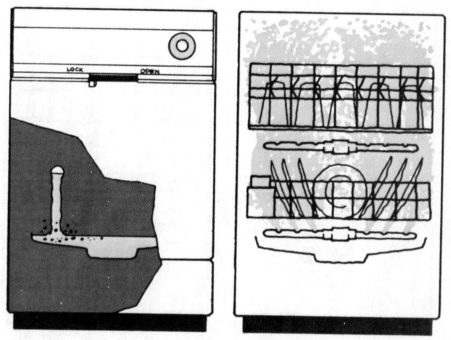

Fig. 1.   Fig. 2.

The wash and rinse steps may be repeated, depending on the model and how the controls are set. As each washing and rinsing action is completed, the water is again pumped out through the drain.

The dishes are dried by air heated by an electric heating rod or coil. The hot air either flows past the dishes because of the dishwasher's construction or is forced past by a blower.

CAPACITY

Any dishwasher provides a scrubbing that is hard to duplicate by hand washing because it uses hotter water and stronger detergents than hands can stand, and because it provides several washing and rinsing actions.

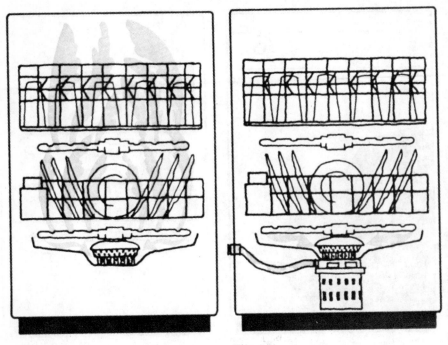

Fig. 3.   Fig. 4.

Nevertheless, dishwashers differ in their capacity, cleaning ability, and versatility.

The *capacity* of a dishwasher is the number of dishes, glasses, utensils, knives, forks, and spoons it can accommodate for a thorough washing. Sometimes capacity is listed on dishwasher hang tags in terms of *place settings*. However, because the definition of a place setting differs among dishwasher manufacturers, the capacities of different brands may be difficult to compare.

CLEANING

The satisfactory performance of a dishwasher depends on four things: forceful and thorough water action on dishes; the right amount of detergent dispensed into the water at the proper time; hot wash and rinse water; and hot air for drying.

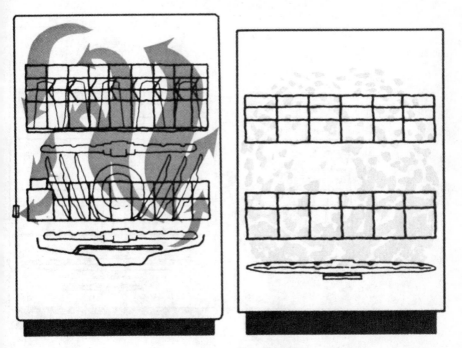

Fig. 5.   Fig. 6. Single wash arm.

Water Action. The simplest dishwashers have a single wash arm at the bottom of the tub that sprays water upward (Fig. 6).

Some dishwashers use a spray tower or tube (Fig. 7), rising upward from the bottom wash arm to the middle of the dishwasher. Water is forced to the top of the tower and sprayed sideways from holes.

More complex dishwasher models have several wash arms or a combination of two or more wash arms and a spray tower. The additional wash arms may be at the top of the tub for spraying down, between the racks for spraying up, or at one side for washing flatware (Fig. 8).

Dispensers. To insure that the water spraying over dishes during wash and rinse actions has the proper amount of cleaning and/or rinse agent in it, some dishwashers have cleaning agent and rinsing agent dispensers.

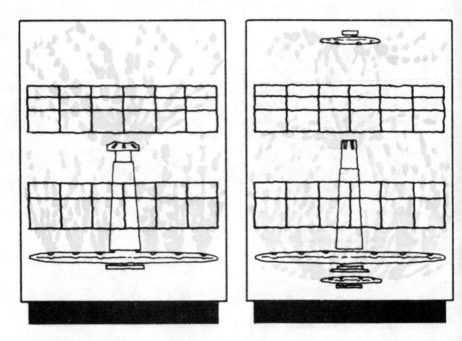

Fig. 7. Spray tower.   Fig. 8. Wash arms and spray tower.

Detergent. The detergent dispenser is usually on the inside of the dishwasher door (Fig. 9).

If the dishwasher has only one wash action, the dispenser may be a single compartment. Wash-water spraying into the compartment mixes the detergent with the water.

If the machine has repeated wash actions, the dispenser will have separate compartments for releasing detergent at each wash. One compartment empties as the first wash begins; the others empty at the start of each succeeding wash.

Rinse agent. Many dishwashers come equipped with a container on the inside of the door (Fig. 10) to hold a liquid rinse agent that helps prevent spotting by enabling water to flow off dishes in sheets instead of drops. The container automatically dispenses the proper amount of agent for the final rinse.

If the dishwasher you buy is not equipped with a rinse agent

Fig. 9. Detergent dispenser.

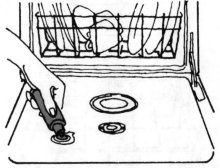

Fig. 10. Rinse agent.

dispenser, you can buy rinse agent in solid form and hang it at the top of the upper rack (Fig. 11). A small amount of the agent is dissolved each time the water circulates in the dishwasher.

Water Temperature. For effective cleaning, the water that enters the dishwasher from your home water heater should be between 140° F. and 160° F. A household water heater usually has a thermostat that indicates the temperature of the water it is providing. However, because the temperature drops a few degrees as the water passes through the pipes from the heater to the dishwasher, set the thermostat a little higher than you want the water temperature to be.

Some dishwashers have a booster heater. Controls can be set to heat water to a selected temperature before or during one or more parts of the dishwashing cycle.

Hot Air. When wash and rinse actions are completed, a heating rod or coil at the bottom of the dishwasher tub heats air to dry the dishes. Some models have a blower to circulate heated air for faster drying.

Cycles. The complete washing, rinsing, and drying actions of a dishwasher make up the dishwashing cycle. Cycles differ from brand to brand of dishwasher in sequence, number, and length of time of actions. They also differ in versatility, or the choice of actions offered.

On most dishwashers you can, by means of push buttons and dials, select, eliminate, shorten, or lengthen actions in the dishwasher

Fig. 11. Solid form rinse agent.

cycle. This results in special cycles for special purposes. The principal special cycles and their functions are as follows:

Rinse and hold. Dishes are sprayed by the rinsing action, the water is pumped out the drain, and the machine stops. The cycle is used to rinse dishes that you want to hold in the dishwasher until you accumulate a full load for a complete wash.

Pots and pans. This may also be called *powerwash, superscrub,* or a similar name. In most dishwashers it extends the time of one or more of the washes. It may also eliminate or shorten drying so that if food particles remain they will not be baked on utensils.

Short cycle. This option, also called *minicycle* or *short wash,* adjusts the machine to the final wash, one or two rinses, and drying. It is used for small loads or lightly soiled dishes.

Gentle cycle. The machine performs one or two rinses and the drying action. Some models reduce the velocity of the water spray. This cycle is for fine china, crystal, and stored items that need light cleaning before use.

Sanicycle. Sanicycle, also known as *hygienic wash,* delays the wash or the final rinse while the machine heats water to 150° F. to 180° F. The higher the water temperature, the more bacteria are removed from the dishes; but heating the water lengthens cycle time. About one minute is needed to raise dishwasher water temperature one or two degrees.

Soak cycle. One type of soak cycle extends wash action. Another stops the machine after the first wash and keeps pans and utensils in the high humidity of the tub for 10 or 12 minutes before the cycle continues. Soak cycles are for extra-dirty dishes, heavier than normal loads, and pots and pans.

Platewarmer. This is a portion of the drying stage. It is used to warm dishes or platters before serving.

CONVENIENT DISHWASHER

A *convenient dishwasher* is one that is easy to load and unload, requires little cleaning or care, and is built for trouble-free operation.

Loading and Unloading.   Whether a dishwasher is easy or hard to load and unload depends upon the accessibility of the racks and their design. Both differ among brands of dishwashers.

Top-loading portables have top racks that can either be lifted out or are attached to the lid so that they raise when the lid is opened (Fig. 12). Either arrangement gives access to the bottom racks. In some models, both top and bottom racks can be removed so you can load them at a table and unload them at a storage space.

Front-loading portables have the lower rack mounted on small wheels so that it can be rolled out onto the door for loading and unloading. Circular upper racks can be pulled part way out and rotated; rectangular upper racks can be pulled out far enough for loading. In some models, one or both of the racks can be removed. (*See* Fig. 13.)

Built-in and *convertible* dishwashers open from the front and have racks similar to those in front-loading portables.

Some dishwasher racks adjust up or down to make room for larger top or bottom loads. This flexibility is useful if you want to wash large serving plates or extra-tall glasses.

Rack design. All dishwasher racks have vinyl-covered metal pins to hold dishes in place. In some models, the pins can be turned upright, horizontal, or at an angle to accommodate dishes of unusual size or shape. (*See* Fig. 14.)

Baskets for spoons, knives, and forks are removable from most dishwashers; some baskets have covers to prevent small pieces from being forced out by spraying water. (*See* Fig. 15.)

Tubs.   The *tub* of any dishwasher that is functioning properly

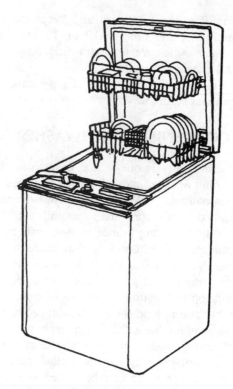

Fig. 12. Top-loading portable.

will generally be kept clean by the detergent solution and water sprayed about during washes and rinses. But the three materials commonly used in tubs—vinyl, porcelain, and stainless steel—differ somewhat in performance.

Vinyl tub coating is similar to the material used on dishwasher racks. It provides a cushion if something is dropped in the tub, but it is not as resistant to stains and scratches as porcelain or stainless steel. If the vinyl is cut, it should be repaired immediately or the tub may rust and ultimately leak. Vinyl is relatively inexpensive to repair.

Porcelain tub coating is a hard, glassy material fused onto steel. It is durable and resistant to stains and scratches. Porcelain sometimes chips. Damage that exposes the underlying steel is difficult but possible to repair. With time, porcelain may loose its glassy surface and some of its stain resistance.

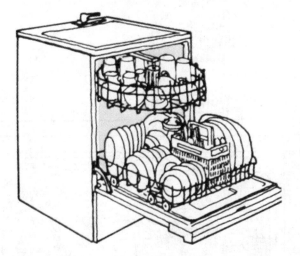

Fig. 13. Front-loading portable.

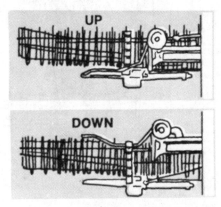

Fig. 14. Rack design.

Stainless steel tubs are stain- odor- and scratch-resistant. They are especially durable but more expensive than the other types.

Overflow Protection Device.　An important accessory found on many dishwashers prevents overflow if the timer fails while the dishwasher is filling or if the machine does not drain properly. The overflow protection may be either a float switch, located on the side of the tub, or a pressure diaphragm at the bottom of the tub. Either can cause the water inlet valve to close when the water in the tub

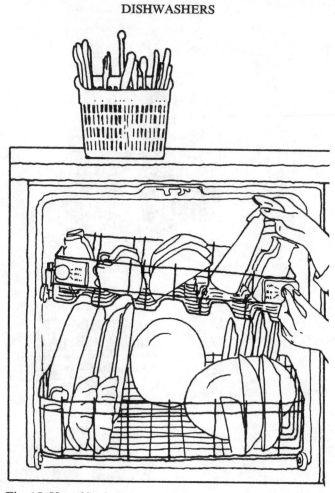

Fig. 15. Use of basket.

reaches a certain height or set the pump to work, forcing the water out through the drain.

Filter Systems.   All dishwashers have filter systems to prevent food particles from being redeposited on dishes as water is circulated during washing and rinsing, and to guard the pump and drain. There are two general types: a combination of coarse and fine filters, and soft food disposers.

Coarse and fine filter systems protect the drain and pump with a coarse filter that catches large particles while a fine filter prevents most small particles from reaching the pump and being recirculated. The fine filter is cleaned by the dishwasher's repeated washes and rinses, and the small particles go down the drain. In some models, the pump reverses at the end of a wash and forces particles off the fine filter. Filters used in this system may need occasional cleaning.

Soft food disposers pulverize food particles in the circulating water as the water enters the pump. With repeated wash and rinse actions, particles that may be temporarily redeposited on dishes are flushed down the drain. A coarse filter protects the pump and drain.

Sound and Heat Insulation. Although any dishwasher will make noise while it is operating, *good insulation* will keep the noise down. Insulation may also help washing and drying performance by reducing heat loss; and it minimizes the chance of warping or other damage to adjacent cabinets.

You can test the insulation of a portable dishwasher by opening the door, reaching in, and knocking the tub side. The less noise you hear on the outside, the better the insulation.

If you are buying a *built-in* dishwasher, you may also want to consider one that is sound insulated if a lower noise level is worth the additional cost to you.

BUYING A DISHWASHER

What you pay for a dishwasher depends on the options you choose, where you live, local competition among dealers, taxes, and maintenance service provisions and warranties.

The simplest and least expensive dishwasher you can buy, if it is made by a reputable manufacturer, will clean your dishes well. More costly machines usually have more optional features, such as special cycles, signals, or decorations. They may or may not have longer lasting materials and better workmanship.

Cycles. Think about how you will use the dishwasher, and buy only the cycles you will use regularly. If your normal load will be dishes, cups, saucers, glasses, and flatware from a day's meals, a dishwasher that has the routine wash and rinse actions may be adequate for you. Remember that some of the effects of special cycles can be obtained on simpler models by hand adjustments of the timer dial.

However, if you want the versatility of special cycles, be sure you know what each cycle will do and how much extra it costs before you buy.

Decorations and Signals.   Dishwashers are available in many colors, with the white models usually being the least expensive. Some have lights to signal the portion of the cycle the dishwasher is in while it is operating. Portables and convertibles may come with a carving board top in various types and colors of wood.

Find out how much extra these optional features cost; then decide whether you want to pay for them.

Locality and Competition.   Prices of the same model of dishwasher may differ in different parts of the country because of the cost of transportation from the factory to the dealer. Prices are likely to be somewhat higher in rural than in metropolitan areas. Within a city, prices may differ among dealers.

Go to a number of stores and compare the prices of the dishwashers with the particular features you want. Watch for newspaper advertisements, look for sales, and do not be afraid to bargain. If you find what seems to be an unusually good buy, be sure it has features equal to those you have seen in other dishwashers.

Taxes.   *Sales taxes* in some states apply only to the product sold and not to delivery or installation charges. Some dealers do not bother to separate these items when computing the sales tax. Be sure you do not pay more tax than the law requires.

Service Provisions.   Before you buy any dishwasher, check to see what service provisions are included. Examine the *warranty* carefully to be sure it will cover the cost of repairs for a reasonable time; also, make sure an authorized service center is near your home. You may want to consider buying a *service contract*.

Warranties. Most warranties guarantee that any defective dishwasher part will be replaced without charge for materials or labor for a period of one year. Some manufacturers guarantee to furnish certain free replacement parts, but not free labor, for an additional year. Others guarantee to provide selected replacement parts, but not free work, for as many as five years.

Read the warranty carefully, and ask the salesman to explain anything you do not understand. Ask if the dealer provides any services beyond those listed in the manufacturer's warranty. Ask whether the dealer or service center will charge for a service call if repairs are needed during the warranty period.

Practically all warranties specify that they do not cover damage by accident or misuse and that the product must remain in the United States.

Authorized service centers. All warranties require that repairs be done by a dealer or service center authorized by the manufacturer to service his brand. Such service centers exist in many parts of the country for all well-known brands, and some centers are authorized to perform warranty work on several brands of dishwashers.

Be sure there is a local center for the brand of dishwasher you are considering, and try to find out about its reputation and reliability before you buy your dishwasher.

Service contracts. Department stores and appliance dealers sometimes offer service contracts when they sell a dishwasher. Contracts may be for one or several years with an annual cost; costs may vary. A service contract guarantees you free repair work on the dishwasher for the contract period.

If the warranty on your dishwasher covers the cost of parts and labor for a year, be sure a service contract does not duplicate that coverage. You may wish to buy a service contract just before the expiration of the warranty.

USE AND CARE

To get the best performance from your dishwasher, learn its special capabilities and give the dishwasher the small amount of care it requires. Before you use the dishwasher for the first time, read the manufacturer's literature carefully, then follow those directions.

Use.   Here are some suggestions on how to use your dishwasher.

1. Remove all hard objects such as bone fragments, nuts, and olive pits from dishes before loading. These could damage moving parts or clog the filter or drain. You do not have to rinse dishes before loading.

2. Place glasses securely on the rack pins to keep them from toppling.

3. If your dishwasher has a rotating, circular, upper rack, place dishes on it so that their weight is distributed evenly to allow the rack to rotate freely.

4. Alternate large and small pieces to allow the water to spray freely over the entire load.

5. Use only detergents made especially for dishwashers. Try several brands to see which gives the best results with the water in your area. Never use soap or detergents that form suds. Suds can block spraying water and decrease cleaning efficiency.

6. Use only detergents that flow freely. Dishwasher detergents may become lumpy or hard if they are not used within two or three weeks after the box is opened.

7. Fill the detergent dispensers exactly as the owner's literature specifies. Too little detergent can cause spotting; too much can result in suds.

8. Find out from your local water department the hardness of the water in your area. If it is rated at more than 12 grains per gallon, you may want to obtain a water softening service for your home. Alternatively, you can occasionally add extra detergent or vinegar during the wash action to remove film and spots.

9. *Do not* put cracked glasses or dishes or slender or small items, such as cheese forks or meat pins, in the dishwasher. If the dishes break or the small items fall into the tub, the dishwasher may be damaged.

Care.   The following simple procedures will help you get better service from your dishwasher and may prevent a large repair bill.

1. Clean the inside of the door and the outside of the dishwasher occasionally with a damp cloth and mild detergent. The interior and the tub are essentially self-cleaning.

2. Check the bottom of the tub and the filter now and then to remove any insoluble food particles that may have accumulated. Be careful not to burn yourself on the heating rod or coil if the dishwasher has just stopped.

3. If you live in a hard-water area, lime deposits may form on the bottom of the tub and on the door. To remove them, start the dishwasher on the rinse action. While water is entering, open the

door and add ½ cup of white vinegar. *Do not* use detergent. Then let the dishwasher finish its cycle.

SAFETY

You want to be sure the dishwasher you buy will not give you an electric shock or cause a fire and that it will be safe for children to be around. You also want a dishwasher that is convenient to load and unload, easy to keep clean, and built so that it will not spill water on your floor.

Insist on a dishwasher with the mark of an independent testing laboratory, such as the Underwriters Laboratories, Inc. The mark indicates that the machine has been manufactured to conform to established electrical fire, and mechanical safety standards.

Such a dishwasher will also have a door seal switch. The switch turns the dishwasher off the instant the door is opened and prevents burns from sprayed hot water. It also allows you to add overlooked dishes at any time.

For *portable* or *convertible dishwashers*, the mark indicates the model has been tested for stability under normal use. Some have a front-opening door with hinges that release or legs that automatically extend if the machine is in danger of tipping from weight placed on the open door. Others are specially counterbalanced against tipping.

INSTALLATION

An installation kit for dishwashers shown in Figs. 16, 17, and 18 is available from your local dealer. This kit contains all parts and complete instructions needed for replacing almost any old dishwasher, or for a new dishwasher installation. The kit includes the following items: flexible drain hose, copper inlet tubing, double compression reduction elbow, double compression reduction union, double compression elbow, step-down adapter, test light, strain relief bushing, wire nuts, hose clamps, and barbed union connector.

Cabinetry. Opening for dishwasher should be 24 inches wide by 34½ inches high. Remove all obstructions at the upper rear of the opening. (*See* section on Preliminary Rough-In later in this chapter.)

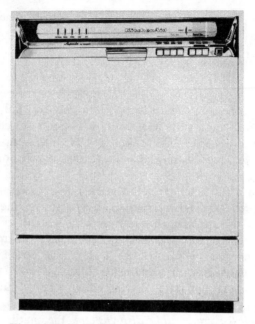

Fig. 16. Built-in dishwasher.

Electrical Specifications.   Voltage and frequency—120 volts, 60 hertz; operating load—13.5 amperes, 7.9 amperes; circuit size—20 amperes. Wiring must conform to local codes and the National Electrical Code.

Plumbing Specifications.   Plumbing must conform to local codes. Use ½-inch OD copper tube for water line. Dishwasher has ⅜-inch IPS internal thread at valve. A 90-degree compression ell (furnished) should be used to connect tubing to valve. Water flow pressure at dishwasher should be 20 psi to 120 psi. Water temperature at dishwasher should be 140° F. to 160° F. Drain size requires minimum ⅝-inch OD copper tubing without air gap. Drain line requires minimum ⅞-inch OD copper tubing with air gap, not furnished.

Caution: Avoid getting joint compound inside new joints. Hot-water fill line must be flushed of foreign matter before connection to dishwasher fill valve. A hand shut-off valve (not furnished) should be located in an easily accessible area adjacent to the dishwasher.

Fig. 17. Cabinet-sink combination.

Panel. Locate top of lower panel just below evaporation channel support (Fig. 19). Insert panel flange under evaporation channel support ends (Fig. 19, A) and push up to engage top of panel. Lift up lower bottom flange of panel, place flange (Fig. 19, B) over front face of frame and push in. Fasten panel with two screws (Fig. 19, C) furnished. If a wood or laminated front is to be used and these panels are not immediately available, use back-up panel furnished with trim kit. Stainless-steel trim should be used to assemble wood or laminate when available. Reverse procedure when removing lower panel.

PRELIMINARY ROUGH-IN

Cabinet Opening. For dishwasher to be flush with adjacent cabinets, there must be a minimum of 24 inches under counter depth available for installation (Fig. 20). When a $\frac{1}{4}$-inch wood panel (lower front panel, $8\frac{5}{16}$ inches high, $23\frac{23}{32}$ inches wide; door front panel, $16\frac{3}{32}$ inches high, $23\frac{19}{32}$ inches wide) with trim kit is used, the dishwasher must have a minimum cabinet depth of $24\frac{1}{4}$ inches.

Fig. 18. Convertible-portable dishwasher.

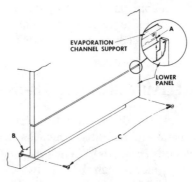

Fig. 19. Lower panel below evaporation channel.

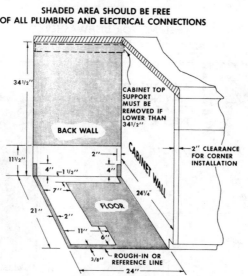

Fig. 20. Cabinet opening.

To establish a reference line for purposes of providing plumbing and electrical connections to the dishwasher, measure 21 inches from the wall. (This is the front edge of the dishwasher kick panel. There is a three-inch toe space from the front of the kick panel to the front edge of the dishwasher with a standard metal front panel.) Cabinets 23½ inches to 23⅝ inches deep from wall to front of cabinet may be accommodated by removing dry or plaster wall, with the baseboard and quarter round directly behind the dishwasher.

Note: For corner installation, allow a two-inch clearance for adjacent cabinet. *Caution:* Make sure the dishwasher is not installed under a surface burner or warming plate where the heat would damage the constant rinse (upper spray) assembly.

Hot Water Supply Line. If the fill line comes from either the right or left, it must be installed behind the vertical frame members that are 1½ inches from the wall (Fig. 21). Locate the fill line as shown in Fig. 21. For roughing-in purposes, locate a ⅝-inch hole 19¾ inches from the back wall and 6 inches from the left edge of the cabinet. For other typical fill line installations, such as water line from back, see alternate (dotted line) suggestions.

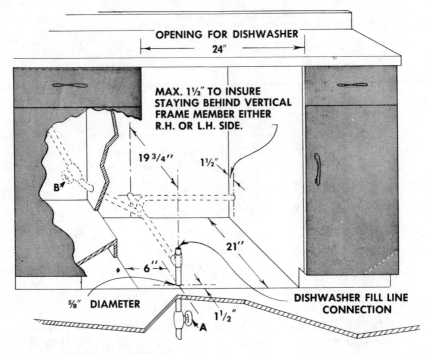

Fig. 21. Fill line connection.

All sweat fittings for ½-inch OD copper tubing must be sweated into place before attaching to the dishwasher to prevent excess heat on fill valve. Make certain that there is a hand shut-off valve (Fig. 21, A or B) in the hot water supply line.

To conveniently service the dishwasher, it is recommended a union be connected in the fill line.

Drain System. The dishwasher is equipped with a pump-type drain. During drain periods, the drain valve is closed, thus protecting the dishwasher from normal back flow from drain line. The dishwasher can be connected to a drain line through the back wall to a sink or disposer to either right or left side or to an air gap. (*See* Figs. 22 and 23 for dimensions for locations of drain line for sink connection and disposer connection.) Figure 20 shows area to be kept free of all plumbing connections. Connect a ⅟₁₆-inch ID minimum drain line (furnished by installer) to drain valve. If a flexible hose is used,

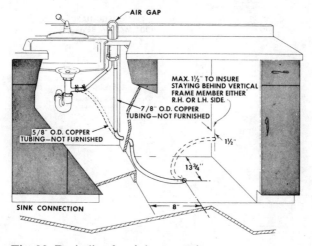

Fig. 22. Drain line for sink connection.

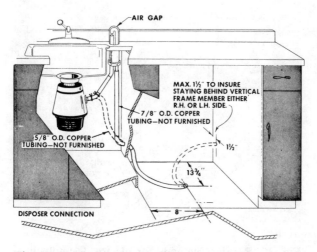

Fig. 23. Drain line for disposer connection.

it must be resistant to heat and detergent water. If copper tubing is required, make the connection to the drain valve, using a short length of flexible hose and clamps (Fig. 24). Flexible drain hose and clamps are furnished in the installation kit available from your local dealer or distributor. Drain connections must be in compliance with

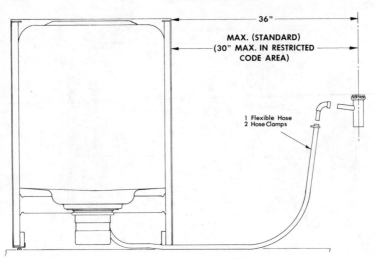

Fig. 24. Flexible hose and hose clamps.

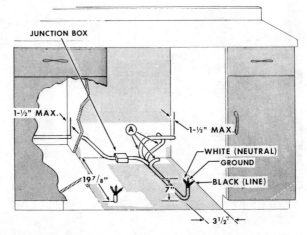

Fig. 25. Routing methods for electrical supply line hook-up to dishwasher.

local codes. *Do not install check valve in drain line.* When connecting dishwasher drain to a food waste disposer, be sure to remove the knock-out (or threaded) plug in the disposer to insure proper drainage. *Note:* Do not kink drain hose. Minimum size for all dishwasher drains is $\frac{1}{16}$-inch ID.

Note: Drain hose may be used to connect dishwasher with disposer unit, or to sink drain using tee or elbow (available as accessories).

Caution: Make sure drain hose does not touch any electrical components or terminals.

Drain hose must withstand hot water and detergent and can be obtained from a plumbing hardware or automotive supply outlet.

Other accessories available from your dealer or distributor: top kits, rinse agent kits, side panel kits, front trim kits, and front panel kits.

Electrical Supply Line. Before setting the dishwasher in place, run individual 20-amperes branch circuit of No. 12–2 wg (minimum) with ground electrical cable. Figure 25, A, shows routing methods for the electrical supply line hook-up to the dishwasher. *Caution:* No other outlets or appliances should be on this circuit.

FINAL INSTALLATION

Positioning and Anchoring Dishwasher. Remove styrofoam packing blocks and corrugated motor block packing after dishwasher is removed from skid. Remove protector panel before front panels are installed. Check the upper rear portion of the cabinet opening to make certain that area is cleared of cabinet or top support framing members. Set the dishwasher adjacent to cabinet and adjust the four leveling feet to the desired height. The four leveling feet can be used to raise the dishwasher to 35 inches or to lower it to 34 inches ($33\frac{1}{2}$ inches if leveling screws are removed). Adjust kickplate. (Kickplate can be adjusted by moving up or down.)

After the dishwasher is in position, make sure it is level from side to side and front to rear. If possible, dishwasher front should be parallel to counter top and flush with cabinets. To maintain alignment of dishwasher with adjacent cabinets, fasten dishwasher to counter top with two No. 10 flat-head wood screws (not furnished). Use these screws in the two L-shaped adjustable brackets (furnished) at the upper left and right hand corners of the dishwasher (Fig. 26). When the dishwasher is not installed beneath a continuous counter top it may be necessary to anchor the dishwasher to the floor by placing a $\frac{1}{4}$-inch lag bolt or screw in the hole provided. If door tension adjustment is required, adjust door spring (Fig. 26) so the

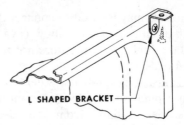

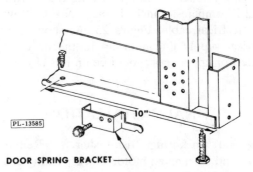

Fig. 26. L-shaped bracket and door spring
bracket.

door is counterbalanced and will remain in an open position. Adjust
tension by changing bracket to alternate holes and/or moving spring
hooks to alternate position.

Connecting Hot Water Supply Line.   Be sure that the fill line has
been flushed clear of foreign materials. Use compression ell (furnished) to connect ½-inch OD copper fill line to dishwasher fill valve.
Be sure that the fill line has no sharp bends (five inches minimum
bend radius suggested) that may produce kinks that might restrict
water flow. Connect fill line to meet local plumbing codes.

Connecting Drain Line.   Connect the dishwasher drain to meet
local plumbing code. (*See* Figs. 22 and 23.)

Connecting Electrical Power Source.

1. Remove cover from junction box on the dishwasher.
2. Install approved connector (not furnished).
3. Connect power cable (minimum No. 12–2 wg), white lead

to white lead, and black lead to black lead, and ground wire under green ground-screw or lug. (*See* Fig. 27.)

When house wiring is aluminum, use UL-approved aluminum to copper connectors.

The dishwasher must be properly grounded before operating by connecting to a suitable ground complying with the National Electrical Code and the local electrical code.

Fig. 27. Ground screw.

Testing Installation. Remove installation debris from under dishwasher, foam door pads on each side and near top of tank, and all internal packing material and labels.

Install front and lower panels according to the instructions supplied with panel kits. Turn on electrical power and water supply. Turn *action indicator* clockwise to the Off position. On some models, press *cancel-drain* button; timer will advance to Off automatically. Lift door handle. Wait for *timer* to automatically reset itself (necessary for initial installation test of some models). Then, push door handle down to lock position and press normal cycle button. Run the dishwasher through the complete cycle to make certain it is operating properly. Turn off electrical power, remove lower panel and check for leaks. Reinstall lower panel and turn on electrical power. (*See* Fig. 28 for details and connections.)

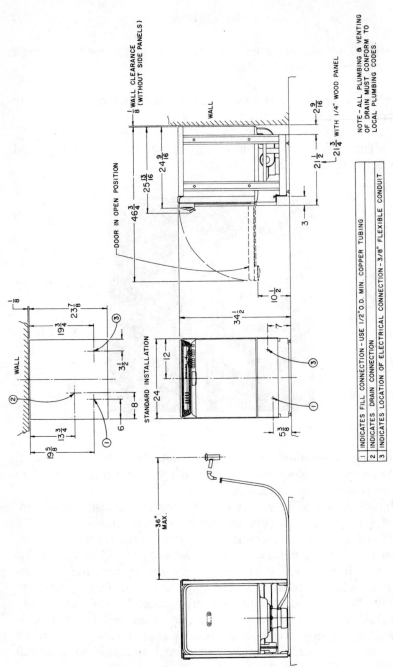

Fig. 28. Details and connections.

Caution: For installation when the dishwasher is to be left unused in freezing temperature. Turn off electrical power and shut off water supply at the hand valve. Remove lower panel. Disconnect both inlet and outlet lines at the *drain valve*. This permits water to drain from the dishwasher tank, pump, and drain line. Disconnect both the inlet and outlet lines at the *fill valve*. Make provisions to control water drained from unit. Reinstall lower panel. Turn on electrical power. Then, push door handle down to lock and push normal cycle button. Let the dishwasher run through first pre-rinse only (approximately four minutes) to drain all water trapped in the dishwasher. Turn off electricity.

To complete installation later proceed as follows:

1. Connect drain and fill valves—both inlet and outlet.
2. Reinstall lower panel.
3. Turn on water and electrical supply. Then push button for the cycle desired.

Chapter 30

Hot Water Dispenser

The *hot water dispenser* shown in Fig. 1 has an electrical heating element and electrical controls to deliver hot water immediately, for use in food and beverage preparation. Tank water is automatically maintained at selected temperatures up to 190° F. This temperature is controlled by an adjustable thermostat.

Prior to attempting installation, it will be necessary to purchase a 36-inch by ¼-inch copper tubing (.035 inch wall). A stainless-steel tip saddle valve is furnished with dispenser for easy installation.

Wiring must conform to National Electrical Code and all applicable local electrical codes.

INSTALLATION

See Fig. 2 for installation dimensions.

PLUMBING

Plumbing must conform to all applicable codes. It is recommended that installation be made to the hot-water supply line. Hot water will reduce liming in the tank because some of the lime will be deposited in the hot-water heater.

Note: Some hot-water heaters have a magnesium rod that retards corrosion of the water tank. In certain water conditions, this magnesium rod can create a rotten egg odor in the hot water. Test your hot-water supply. If this condition is noticed, connect the dispenser to the cold-water supply line. It is recommended that the copper tube be used for the water supply line. Water flow pressure at dispenser must be 20 pounds per square inch (psi) (¾-gallon per minute) to 120 psi. A hand shut-off valve (not furnished) should be

530

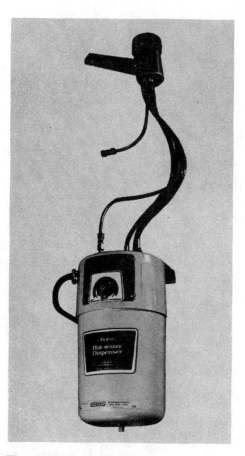

Fig. 1. Hot water dispenser.

located in the water supply line in an easily accessible area adjacent to the dispenser.

Caution: Water supply line must be flushed of foreign matter before connecting to dispenser solenoid valve.

SPOUT AND TANK ASSEMBLIES

Note: The dispenser spout assembly (Fig. 2, 1) can be mounted in either an existing hole in the sink (such as the hole formerly used

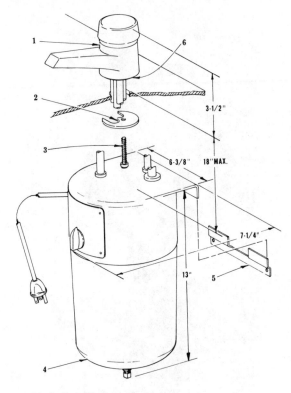

Fig. 2. Installation diagram.

for the dish sprayer) or into a 1¼-inch hole drilled through the counter on either side of the sink.

1. Unpack spout assembly with flexible tubes, hose clamps, copper tubes, and compression fittings.

2. Remove screw (Fig. 2, 3) and plate (Fig. 2, 2) from spout assembly (Fig. 2, 1).

3. Insert tubes (already attached to spout assembly) through 1¼-inch hole in sink/counter top.

4. Reinstall plate (Fig. 2, 2) and screw (Fig. 2, 3) onto spout assembly from underside of sink/counter top. It may be desirable to add a bead of sealer (such as plumber's putty) around bottom inside area of spout assembly (Fig. 2, 6) before tightening screw.

5. Attach mounting bracket (Fig. 2, 5) below spout, onto sink cabinet or wall, using necessary fasteners (Fig. 3, 2) (not furnished).

6. Hang tank and enclosure unit (Fig. 2, 4) onto bracket (Fig. 2, 5). *Note:* Tank and enclosure unit *must* be mounted in *upright* (vertical) position *only*.

7. Slide hose clamps up onto bottom end of flexible tubes, then attach flexible tubes to tank tubes (Fig. 3, 1). Fasten tubes into place with hose clamps. *Caution:* Flexible tubes supplied are of a proper length; a greater length should not be substituted. The tubes may be shortened to suit the installation. (*Do not* kink flexible tubes.)

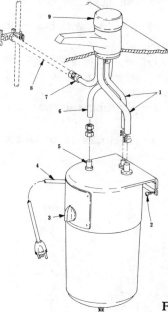

Fig. 3. Dispenser assembly.

WATER CONNECTIONS

Caution: Do not use pipe sealing compound or similar compounds because they contaminate the unit and may produce an offensive taste and odor. All water connections use compression fittings that require no sealing compounds.

1. Connect ¼-inch OD copper tubing (Fig. 3, 6) (long tubing) to water inlet tubing (Fig. 3, 5) (match green marked tubing), using ¼-inch compression union (furnished). The spout outlet tubing (Fig. 3, 6) may be cut to the length required.

2. Connect ¼-inch OD copper tubing (not furnished) (Fig. 3, 8) to the spout inlet tubing that has the factory-assembled compression union (Fig. 3, 7).

3. The compression union (Fig. 3, 7) has an internal stainless-steel filter that can be removed for cleaning if necessary. For proper performance, *always* reinstall this filter.

Installation procedure for self-drilling saddle valve.

1. Assemble valve body (Fig. 4, 1)—with pierce pin (Fig. 4, 4) retracted—to top clamp (Fig. 4, 2).

2. With rubber gasket (Fig. 4, 3) in fixed position, clamp the assembly firmly to the copper water supply line, using the screws, nuts, and base clamp provided.

3. Connect the ¼-inch copper tubing to the valve outlet (Fig. 4, 5).

4. Turn saddle valve handle clockwise to pierce the copper water supply line and close the valve.

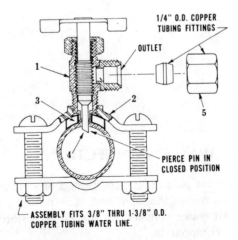

Fig. 4. Saddle valve.

5. Completely open valve by turning handle counterclockwise.

Note: No drilling or water shut-off required for copper water line. When connecting the self-piercing saddle valve to water line of other than copper tubing, it will be necessary to pre-drill a ¼-inch hole.

The water supply line must be thoroughly flushed before making the plumbing connections.

Fill tank by opening saddle valve and then turning water control knob (Fig. 3, 9) in a clockwise direction and holding it until water flows from the spout. It will take almost one minute before the two-quart tank is full and water flows from the spout. Check for leaks and make any corrections.

ELECTRICAL CONNECTIONS

Wiring must conform to the National Electrical Code and all applicable local electrical codes.

Caution: Before making electrical connections, be sure the thermostat control knob (Fig. 3, 3) is turned completely to the left (counterclockwise) to insure heating unit is turned off.

Note: If unable to use power supply cord provided, proceed as follows:

1. Remove four retaining screws (Fig. 5, 4) and lift off front cover (Fig. 5, 5).

2. Remove power supply cord (Fig. 3, 4).

3. Insert electrical power supply line (Fig. 5, 1) into cable clamp (Fig. 5, 2). Tighten cable clamp.

4. Connect the ground wire of the electrical power supply (Fig. 5, 1) to the green hex grounding screw (Fig. 5, 6) in the top enclosure (Fig. 5, 3).

5. Connect the remaining four wires in the top enclosure (Fig. 5, 3) as follows (using Underwriters Laboratory (UL) approved wire nuts or locally approved connecting methods): black to black; white to white.

6. The dispenser assembly must be properly grounded before operating by connecting the grounding conductor to a suitable ground complying with National Electrical Code and local electrical codes.

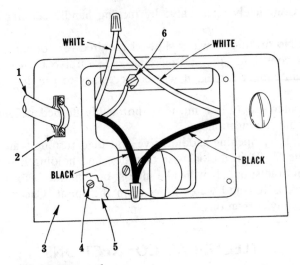

Fig. 5. Top enclosure.

7. Form and place wires in top enclosure (Fig. 5, 3) and replace front cover (Fig. 5, 5) and four retaining screws (Fig. 5, 4).

TESTING INSTALLATION

To test your installation proceed as follows:

1. Make sure the tank is filled by turning water control knob (Fig. 3, 9) in a clockwise direction and noting if water flows from the spout.

2. With tank filled, plug in the electrical supply cord or turn on the electrical power supply.

3. Turn thermostat control knob (Fig. 3, 3) fully to the right (clockwise). This starts unit heating. While unit is heating, check again to make sure that all connections have been made correctly and there are no leaks. Water may drip from the spout on initial heating. Hot water will be available in approximately 15 minutes. *Note:* Water temperature is controlled by this thermostat control knob—clockwise movement of knob increases temperature, counterclockwise movement decreases temperature. If water is too hot or boils at higher altitudes, decrease temperature setting.

4. To turn dispenser off, rotate the thermostat control knob (Fig. 3, 3) counterclockwise as far as possible.

Caution: Turn off thermostat and drain unit if left unused in freezing temperature.

COMPONENTS

Turning the water control knob (Fig. 6, 3) operates the plunger (Fig. 6, 2), opening the valve (Fig. 6, 1), allowing water from the supply line to enter the heating tank (Fig. 6, 7). The water entering the tank forces hot water up the large tube (Fig. 6, 5), and out the spout (Fig. 6, 4). The tank water is then heated by the heating element (Fig. 6, 6).

As the water enters the tank, it draws air through the air tube (Fig. 6, 9) into the air chamber (Fig. 6, 8). When the water control knob (Fig. 6, 3) returns to the Off position, the air within the air chamber (Fig. 6, 8) is forced out the air tube (Fig. 6, 9) and returns to the atmosphere, thus allowing room for water expansion within the tank. This pressure-free design permits degassing of tank water, thus eliminating most odors and taste that occur in heated tap water. This also assures safe, long-lasting operation.

OPERATION

Fill tank by turning water control knob (Fig. 7, 9) in a clockwise direction and noting that water flows from the spout.

With tank filled, plug in the electrical supply cord (Fig. 7, 6) or turn on the electrical power supply.

Turn thermostat control knob (Fig. 7, 5) fully to the right (clockwise). This starts unit heating. Water may drip from the spout on initial heating. Hot water will be available in approximately 15 minutes.

Note: Water temperature is controlled by this thermostat control knob. Clockwise movement of the knob increases temperature; counterclockwise movement decreases temperature. If water is too hot or boils at higher altitudes, decrease temperature setting.

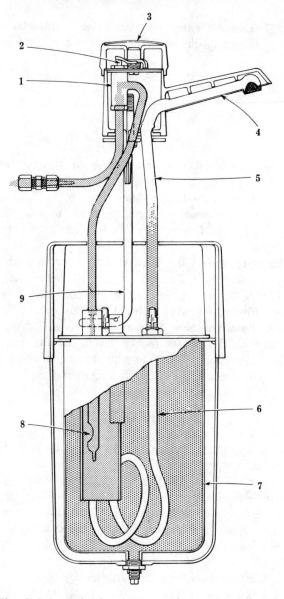

Fig. 6. Schematic showing operation.

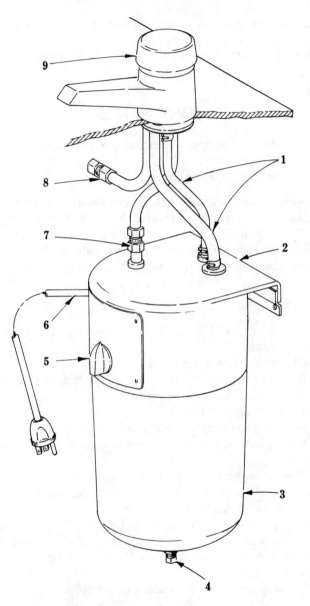

Fig. 7. Operating dispenser.

To turn the dispenser off, rotate the thermostat control knob (Fig. 7, 5) counterclockwise as far as possible.

Caution: Turn off thermostat and drain unit if not used in freezing temperature.

MAINTENANCE

Caution: Always disconnect electrical power supply before servicing hot-water dispenser.

Spout Assembly. *Flow screen* (Fig. 8, 6):

1. Remove two screws (Fig. 8, 8) and spout plate (Fig. 8, 7).
2. Remove spout flow screen (Fig. 8, 6) and O ring (Fig. 8, 5).
3. Clean spout flow screen or replace when necessary. In reassembling, carefully position O ring over outside surface of spout tube. Push screen in spout tube and assemble spout plate with two screws.

Spout tube (Fig. 8, 4).

1. Remove screw (Fig. 8, 11) and mounting plate (Fig. 8, 12) from under counter.
2. Disconnect tubing from tank.
3. Remove two screws (Fig. 8, 8) and spout plate (Fig. 8, 7).
4. Unfasten clamps and remove tubing.

Supply Line Strainer Screen.

1. Shut off water supply line at saddle valve (Fig. 9, 1).
2. Disconnect the compression union (Fig. 9, 4) from the supply line.
3. Remove supply line strainer screen (Fig. 9, 2) from the compression union body. Clean or replace the screen.

Mechanical Valve Assembly.

1. Shut off water supply line at saddle valve.
2. Disconnect the two compression nuts (Fig. 7, 7 and 8).
3. Straighten both copper tubes. Using a tubing cutter, remove nut and ferrule (Fig. 10, 1).
4. Remove water control knob cap by pulling cap straight up and off.
5. Remove the two screws (Fig. 11, 1) that retain the valve mounting plate (Fig. 11, 2).

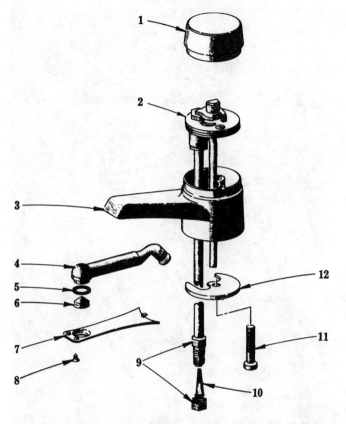

Fig. 8. Parts of a spout tube. 1. Cap assembly 2. Mechanical valve assembly 3. Spout body and insert assembly 4. Tube—spout 5. O ring 6. Screen—flow 7. Plate—spout 8. Self-tapping screw 9. Union—compression 10. Screen—supply line 11. Machine screw 12. Plate—sink mounting

6. Lift mechanical valve assembly (Fig. 12, 1) out through spout body.

7. To install a new mechanical assembly, reverse the disassembly procedure.

Tank Body Assembly.

1. Disconnect unit from electrical power supply.

2. Drain water from tank. *Note:* To drain water, place a three-

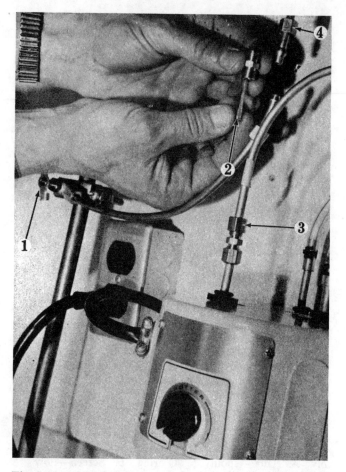

Fig. 9. Supply line strainer screen.

quart capacity container under bottom enclosure (Fig. 7, 3) and remove pipe plug (Fig. 7, 4). Allow all water to drain from tank, then replace pipe plug.

3. Disconnect flexible tubing (Fig. 7, 1) by loosening clamps and removing flexible tubing from both tubing extensions protruding from top enclosure (Fig. 7, 2). Disconnect the ¼-inch compression union at the water inlet (Fig. 7, 8).

4. Disconnect wiring as follows:

   (a) Remove the four retaining screws (Fig. 13, 4) and front

Fig. 10. Removing nut and ferrule.

cover (Fig. 13, 5), then remove knob lock screw and thermostat control knob (Fig. 13, 6) from top enclosure (Fig. 13, 3).

(b) Pull wires from the top enclosure (Fig. 13, 3) and disconnect the ground wire (Fig. 13, 7) and the connectors between black and black and white and white.

(c) Loosen the cable clamp (Fig. 13, 2), then disconnect and withdraw the electrical power supply line (Fig. 5, 1) from top enclosure (Fig. 13, 3). Remove thermostat retaining screw (Fig. 13, 25).

5. Remove tank body assembly from enclosure unit as follows:

(a) Remove tank body assembly unit from under counter location by lifting from mounting bracket (Fig. 14, 16).

(b) Remove bottom enclosure (Fig. 14, 19) from top enclosure (Fig. 14, 11) by removing special nut (Fig. 14, 18) and sliding bottom enclosure (Fig. 14, 19) and tank body insulation (Fig. 14, 20) down and off the lower part of tank body assembly (Fig. 14, 21).

(c) Remove tank body assembly from top enclosure (Fig. 14, 11) by removing three tank retaining plates and fasteners (Fig.

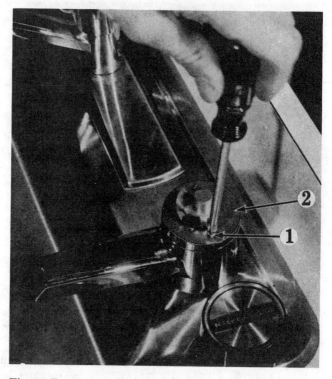

Fig. 11. Removing valve mounting plate.

14, 29 and 30), then pull tank body assembly down from top enclosure.

Note: Retain the three bushings (Fig. 14, 6, 8, and 9) to reuse during replacement of tank body assembly in top enclosure.

6. Replace tank body assembly and enclosure by reversing disassembly procedure.

Thermostat.

1. Disconnect electrical power supply.

2. Remove four retaining screws (Fig. 14, 13), front cover (Fig. 14, 14), knob lock screw, and thermostat control knob (Fig. 14, 26).

3. Remove screw (Fig. 14, 25) that holds thermostat (Fig. 14, 23) and enclosure (Fig. 14, 22) to tank mounting stud.

Fig. 12. Lifting mechanical valve assembly.

4. Pull thermostat (Fig. 14, 23) from top enclosure (Fig. 14, 11) and disconnect wires at thermostat terminals.

5. Replace thermostat by reversing disassembly procedure.

Note: At reassembly of thermostat, make certain the top insulation (Fig. 14, 28) does not project between the thermostat and mounting stud. To realign thermostat knob, rotate thermostat shaft counterclockwise to stop, then place knob on shaft with pointer at the Off position. Tighten knob lock screw.

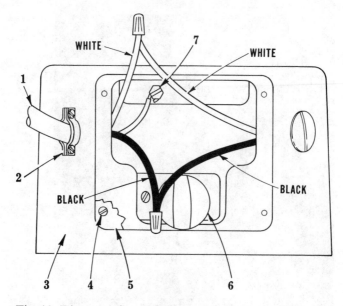

Fig. 13. Disconnecting wiring.

Tank and Enclosure Unit. *See* Fig. 14. *See* Fig. 15 for pictorial wiring diagram; *also see* Fig. 16 for schematic wiring diagram.

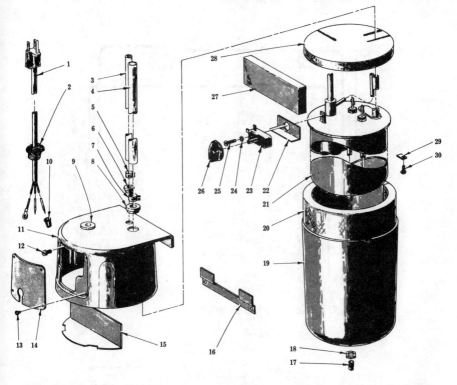

Fig. 14. Parts of a tank and enclosure unit. 1. Cord and plug 2. Strain relief 3. Tubing (¼ inch I.D.) 4. Tubing (⅜ inch I.D.) 5. Clamp—tube (⅜ inch tubing) 6. Bushing—air tube 7. Clamp—tube (½ inch tubing) 8. Bushing—water outlet tube 9. Bushing—water inlet tube 10. Wire nut 11. Enclosure—top 12. Machine screw 13. Self-tapping screw 14. Front cover and label assembly 15. Barrier—wiring compartment 16. Bracket—mounting 17. Plug—⅛ inch square head pipe 18. Special nut 19. Bottom enclosure and label assembly 20. Insulation—tank body 21. Tank assembly 22. Enclosure—thermostat 23. Thermostat 24. Lock washer 25. Machine screw 26. Knob—thermostat 27. Insulation—thermostat 28. Insulation—top 29. Strap—tank support 30. Machine screw

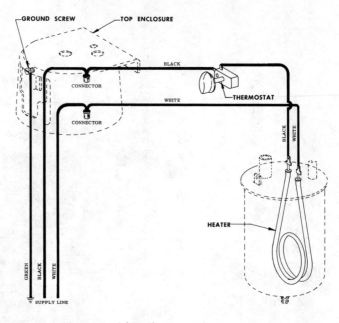

Fig. 15. Pictorial wiring diagram.

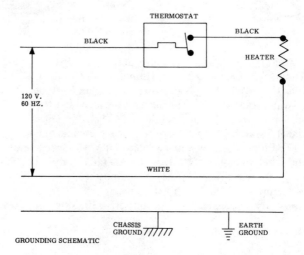

Fig. 16. Schematic wiring diagram.

Chapter 31

Food Waste Disposer

You can probably install your own food waste disposer (Fig. 1), as it is not hard work, will save time, and is inexpensive if you do it yourself.

The only tools needed are a common screwdriver, a Phillips screwdriver, a $\frac{9}{16}$-inch wrench, and a hammer (if you connect dishwasher to disposer). The only materials needed are plumber's putty and two wire nuts.

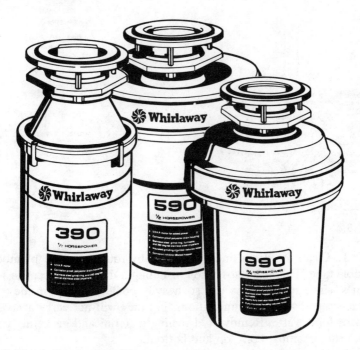

Fig. 1. Food waste disposer.

INSTALLATION

To install your food waste disposer *see* Figs. 2 and 3, and proceed as follows:

Fig. 2.

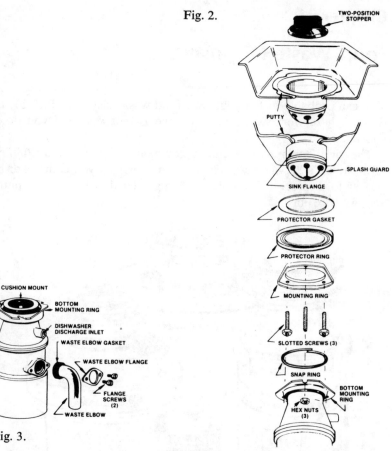

Fig. 3.

1. Clean the drain line thoroughly by routing with a plumber's flexible tape. This is a *must* when installing a disposer, except in new homes, since most drains are so heavily coated on the inside with hardened grease and accumulations that they will not carry away the flow of food waste. Remove old sealing material and gasketing from sink drain opening, both top and bottom.

2. If a dishwasher is to be used in connection with your disposer, it is suggested that the dishwasher knock-out plug be removed before installation of the disposer. The drain plug is easily knocked out by using a hammer and small chisel or screwdriver. *Be sure* to remove knock-out plug from inside disposer.

3. To install *sink flange*, form a ring of top-grade oil base putty around the underside of sink flange. Use putty that remains pliable. *Do not* use mastic. Insert sink flange once it is sealed.

4. Insert three slotted screws in the tapped holes in the mounting ring (3 or 4 turns).

5. From underneath the sink, place protector gasket over the sink flange. Follow with the protector ring (flat side up) and then the mounting ring (with screws).

6. Hold the above parts above groove in the sink flange and push snap ring over the sink flange until it seats in the groove. *Caution: Do not* spread the snap ring as it will slip easily but firmly over the sink flange without spreading.

7. Using the screwdriver, tighten the three slotted screws evenly so that gasket and protector ring are snug to the underside of the sink. *Do not* distort the protector ring.

Install two hex nuts 2 or 3 turns onto two of the slotted screws.

8. Lift the disposer and tilt and slip the slotted holes in the support ring over the slotted screws above the hex nuts. This will help support the unit.

9. Affix the other hex nut to the other slotted screw (2 or 3 turns).

10. Align disposer for proper assembly of elbow assembly.

11. Tighten the three hex nuts and slotted screws evenly to complete installation.

12. Connect flange-type elbow to disposer and connect to trap.

13. Test installation for water leaks and be sure all plumbing connections are tight.

14. Inspect inside of disposer to be certain no foreign material (screws, nails, and the like) is present. Install stopper.

15. Make all connections in accordance with local plumbing codes and ordinances where installation is made.

ELECTRICAL CONNECTION

1. Connect disposer to 115-volt, 60-cycle alternate current (AC) only.

2. A junction box should be installed either in the cabinet compartment under the sink or in a removed location.

3. Mount standard amperes toggle switch near the sink, within easy reach of the user.

4. Use BX cable. Install BX connector in hole provided in bottom of disposer. Connect white wire in BX cable to white lead and black wire in BX cable to black lead. If BX cable is not used, provide a separate ground wire to nearest cold-water pipe or other suitable ground, using screw on bottom and bell for third wire.

5. If plug-in cord is used, it should be 30 inches long with a male connection of the parallel blade two-pole, three-wire type. Ground wire should be attached to a screw on the bottom end bell (Fig. 4).

6. This appliance is equipped with copper lead wires. If connection is made to aluminum house wiring, use only special connectors that are approved for joining copper and aluminum wires in accordance with the National Electrical Code and local codes and ordinances.

7. Make all installations in accordance with local electrical codes and ordinances where installation is made.

Grounding.   It is recommended that the electrical hook-up be like the type shown in Fig. 4, with a ground wire. If the supply source does not have a ground, then a ground wire must be run from screw *inside* bottom cover of disposer to *grounded metal cold* water line. Make certain wire is securely clamped to the pipe.

(*See* specifications in Fig. 5.)

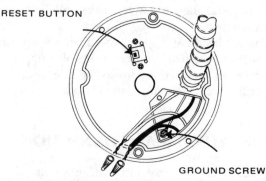

RESET BUTTON

GROUND SCREW

WIRE NUTS (OR EQUIV.)

Fig. 4.

HORSE-POWER	RPM	VOLTS 60 CYCLE	AMPS	DIMENSIONS			
				A	B	C	D
1/3	1725	115AC	6.0	$3\frac{3}{8}$	$6\frac{1}{2}$	$12\frac{3}{4}$	$6\frac{3}{4}$
1/2	1725	115AC	8.2	$3\frac{3}{8}$	$6\frac{1}{2}$	$12\frac{3}{4}$	$10\frac{1}{2}$
3/4	1725	115AC	9.2	$3\frac{3}{8}$	$7\frac{3}{4}$	$14\frac{1}{2}$	$10\frac{1}{2}$

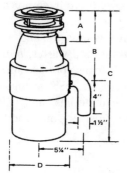

Fig. 5.

CARE AND USE OF WASTE DISPOSER

Operation.

1. *Turn the tap.* Remove drain stopper and turn on a medium flow of cold water. Keep the water running so that all ground waste particles wash through the drain.

2. *Flip the switch.* The instant you flick the electrical toggle switch, your food waste disposer is on and ready to use.

3. *Scrape in food wastes.* Down the drain go table scraps, vegetable peelings, cobs, rinds, seeds, pits, bones, and coffee grounds.

4. *Run disposer for 15 seconds after shredding stops.* Before turning the toggle switch off, let water and disposer run for about 15 seconds after shredding stops. This guarantees that all waste is thoroughly flushed through trap and drain.

Use.   Use your disposer *before* and *after meals.* While preparing food, turn on your disposer and the cold water. Let it clear your sink of vegetable peelings, meat wrappings, or salad trimmings. When the meal is over, scrape food scraps directly into the disposer.

To *speed up* food waste disposal: cut or break up large bones, melon rinds, grapefruit skins, and corn cobs; also fibrous materials such as pineapple or vegetable stalks. Items such as large bones and fibrous husks, like lima bean pods and corn husks, require considerable cutting time. For this reason, you may prefer to place them in the trash can or trash compactor along with your empty tin cans and bottles.

Your disposer is ruggedly built to give you years and years of trouble-free service. It will handle all normal food wastes, *but*, it will not grind and dispose of such items as tin cans, bottles and bottle caps, glass, china, leather, cloth, crockery, rubber, string, clams, oyster shells, or feathers. These are waste materials, and belong in the trash can, or trash compactor—not inside your food waste disposer.

CLEANING AND MAINTENANCE

1. Usually, the disposer cleans itself, but you can flush it by filling the sink with cold water, turning on the disposer and removing the stopper. While the water is draining through the disposer, allow the tap to continue running. When the sink is empty, your disposer will be clean.

2. *Removable splash guard.* Almost all disposers are equipped with the unique removable splash guard for easy cleaning or replacement. If cleaning or replacement becomes necessary, simply remove it by pulling it out from the top. To replace, snap splash guard onto beaded lip near bottom of sink flange. *Note:* Do not operate disposer without splash guard in place.

3. The refrigerator-type motor in this disposer is permanently lubricated for the life of the unit. The disposer is self-cleaning and scours itself thoroughly with each disposal.

4. *Never* put lye or other chemical drain pipe cleaners into the disposer, as they will cause serious corrosion of the alloy parts. If used, the resulting damage can be easily detected, and all guarantees are null and void.

SAFETY

1. This appliance was designed to grind food waste material. It is, therefore, equipped with sharp cutting edges and under no condition should you put your hand inside the disposer when it is running. Should any object unintentionally be dropped into the disposer, be sure to *turn off* the disposer before attempting to remove the object.

2. Make sure disposer is properly grounded.

3. Do not operate disposer unless splash guard is in place.

4. Make all installations in accordance with local electrical and plumbing codes and ordinances where installation is made.

DISPOSER WARRANTY

Most disposer manufacturers provide a one-year warranty. When purchasing a disposer, *be sure* to read the warranty carefully.

Chapter 32

Trash Compactors

The built-in freestanding compactor shown in Fig. 1 is delivered ready to plug in and use. It is approved by the Underwriters Laboratory (UL) for conversion to an undercounter unit, if you choose.

The compactor shown in Fig. 2 has safety interlocks and will not operate unless you have (1) closed the trash drawer, (2) turned key to unlocked (vertical) position, and (3) pushed the Start button. The Stop button will stop the ram movement at any point. After stopping the unit, push the start button and ram will return to its original up position. *Caution: Do not* allow children to operate compactor. It is recommended that you lock the unit, and remove the key when the unit is not in use.

Fig. 1. Trash compactor.

PREPARING FOR USE

Receptacle Outlet.   The power cord on compactor shown in Fig. 2 is equipped with a three-pronged grounding plug. The third

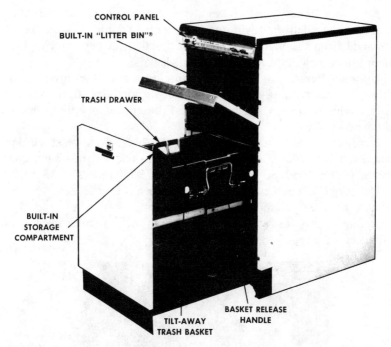

CONTROL PANEL

BUILT-IN "LITTER BIN"®

TRASH DRAWER

BUILT-IN
STORAGE
COMPARTMENT

TILT-AWAY
TRASH BASKET

BASKET RELEASE
HANDLE

Fig. 2. Features of compactor.

prong is designed to ground the cabinet electrically, thus eliminating the possibility of shocking the operator if an internal electrical malfunction should occur.

It is essential that the electrical outlet into which the three-pronged power cord is inserted by properly grounded. If in doubt, a competent electrician should be contacted to check the outlet.

Connecting Compactor to Electricity.   The compactor shown in Fig. 2 operates on regular 120-volt AC, 60-hertz house current, to be supplied by an *approved three-prong grounded receptacle.* The house current circuit should be protected by a 15-ampere fuse, or circuit breaker.

To connect the compactor to electricity (1) be sure the key is in the *locked* position, (2) and insert the three-pronged plug into a three-prong receptacle. If the wall receptacle is not a three-prong grounding type, one should be installed. *Caution:* The use of an extension cord is not recommended.

Accessory Items. Two keys, trash bags, and replacement charcoal filters are delivered with the compactor. Additional keys may be obtained from the manufacturer. Additional trash bags and replacement filters may be purchased at your dealers.

Optional Items. *Trim kit.* A trim kit is available through your dealer for use with ¼-inch wood, laminate, or other front panel of your choice to accent kitchen decor. Front panel material must be obtained locally.

Hardwood top. A finished, 1½-inch thick, hardwood cutting-board top is available through your dealer. The height of the compactor with a wood top is adjustable—from 35½ inches to 36 inches.

Leveling Compactor. The compactor has four leveling feet that will vary the height and provide level stability within a range of ½ inch. Simply raise or lower as required for your particular installation situation. (*See* Fig. 3.)

Fig. 3. Leveling compactor.

Enclosed in your owner's literature packet are four rubber caps for the leveling feet. These caps may be used on slippery surface floors to prevent compactor from moving. They will also minimize marring of the floor.

(*See* section on Installation, for assembly directions, later in this chapter.)

Converting to Undercounter. For converting the unit, the minimum size opening required is 18 inches wide, 24 inches deep, and 34¼ inches high (Fig. 4). *Note:* A minimum ¼-inch clearance should be maintained between compactor top and counter top for service accessibility, if required.

(*See* section on Installation later in this chapter.)

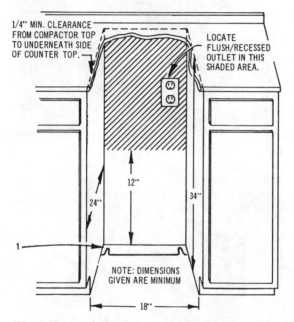

Fig. 4. Converting unit.

LOADING COMPACTOR

Built-In Litter Bin.   Small cans, paper scraps, lids, small boxes, and containers may simply be dropped into this bin (Fig. 5), rather than opening the larger trash drawer. Trash will drop automatically into the large drawer below, when the trash drawer is pulled open.

Large Capacity Trash Drawer.   Large bulky items should be placed directly into the drawer (Fig. 6). It is not necessary to run a compaction cycle every time you place trash into the drawer. However, the more often you run a cycle, the more compact the trash will be.

Fig. 5. Litter bin.

Fig. 6. Large capacity trash drawer.

Tilt-Away Trash Basket. The trash compactor (Fig. 7) is equipped with a versatile, two-piece, polypropylene basket. It is designed especially for easy use and removal of compacted trash.

The tilt-away basket may be used with or without trash bags. You will probably want to try it both ways before deciding how you wish to use your compactor.

Fig. 7. Tilt-away basket without bag.

USE OF BASKET WITHOUT BAGS

1. Be sure basket release handle is in vertical position (Fig. 8).

2. Place trash directly into the basket. It is recommended that you place several sheets of newspaper at the bottom of the basket first, when bags are not being used. This will minimize the clean-up of the basket, after emptying compacted trash. *Note:* Compacting a folded newspaper on top of loose trash in the drawer will help keep the ram clean of trash or broken glass.

3. Remove the basket when trash is compacted to about 4 or 5 inches below the top of the basket. If you find this too heavy, compact less trash the next time. *Remember*, the weight of the compacted trash will vary with the contents of the trash. Cans and bottles may weigh more than paper products. You will be able to judge the desired compacted amount after a few loads.

To *remove* the trash basket when trash is compacted to desired level, proceed as follows:

1. Place basket-release handle in Down position. Lift built-in storage compartment cover, and leave in the Up position (Fig. 9).

2. Grasp both handles of the basket and remove it from drawer (Fig. 10). Carry the basket to trash storage area.

3. Pull the handles of the two-piece basket away from each other (Fig. 11).

Fig. 8. Basket release handle.

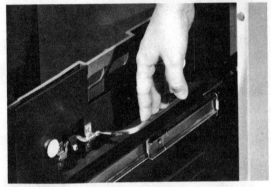

Fig. 9.

Fig. 10.

Fig. 11.

4. Dump the compacted trash from the half-basket into either the trash can or the plastic trash bag (Fig. 12). *Caution:* The compacted trash will probably contain crushed and broken glass, metal cans, and other sharp objects. Always use the half basket to handle and dump trash. *Do not* use your bare hands.

Fig. 12.

USE OF BASKET WITH BAGS

The tilt-away trash basket should *always* be in the drawer when using compactor bags.

1. Lift the built-in storage compartment cover and leave it in the Up position (Fig. 13).

2. Pull the basket-release handle down (Fig. 14).

3. Hold folded bag by the top and place it inside tilt-away trash basket (Fig. 15).

4. Open the bag and pull the top edges of bag down over the top of the drawer (Fig. 16).

5. Lock the bag in place by pulling the four outer holes of the bag down over buttons on sides of the drawer (Fig. 17). The holes will expand over buttons without damaging the bag.

6. Spread bag to fit the interior of basket (Fig. 18). Close storage compartment cover. Pull the basket-release handle up.

Fig. 13.

It is recommended, to *remove* bag when trash is compacted to about 4 or 5 inches from top of basket. If you find this too heavy, compact less the next time.

To remove the bag from the basket proceed as follows:

1. Pull basket-release handle down (Fig. 19).

2. Lift cover of the storage compartment. Release bag from buttons. Pull up top edges of the bag (Fig. 20).

3. Close the bag with twist ties provided (Fig. 21).

Fig. 14.

Fig. 15. Placing bag inside basket.

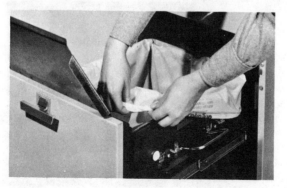

Fig. 16.

Fig. 17.

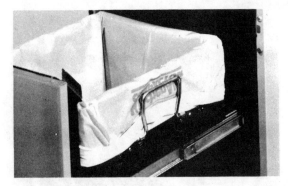

Fig. 18.

Fig. 19.

Fig. 20.

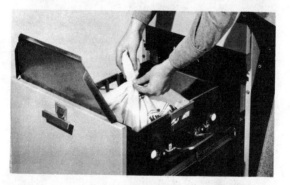

Fig. 21.

Fig. 22.

4. Grasp the handles of basket and remove from the drawer (Fig. 22). Carry the basket containing bag to trash storage area.

5. Pull the handles of two-piece basket away from each other to loosen the bag (Fig. 23).

6. Lift the bag out (Fig. 24). *Caution:* Sharp objects may protrude through the bag after removal from the trash basket; therefore, handle the bag carefully to avoid injury.

Fig. 23.

Fig. 24.

BUILT-IN CONVERSION AND INSTALLATION

Wiring must conform to the National Electrical Code, #70, 1971 Section 250–57 and/or all applicable local electrical codes. (*See* Fig. 25 for installation dimensions.)

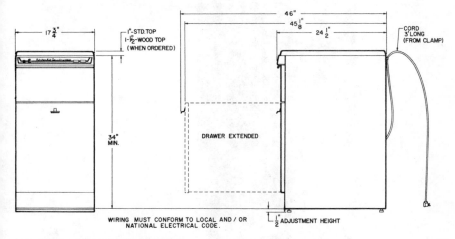

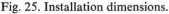

Fig. 25. Installation dimensions.

Converting Compactor. To convert compactor from freestanding to under counter built-in, proceed as follows:

1. Operate machine to place ram in the Up position.
2. Disconnect compactor from electrical power supply.
3. Compare dimensions of proposed under counter location (Fig. 4) with those of Fig. 25, and, if necessary, remove compactor top.

To remove top: Remove three top retaining screws from rear of compactor. Slide top toward rear to disengage from key slots. Lift top off.

4. Remove drawer.

(a) Pull drawer forward and remove drawer retaining screws (Fig. 26, 1) (one from each side), that hold drawer to track.

(b) Carefully remove drawer from drawer tracks. Full weight of drawer must be lifted at this time.

5. Recess kickboard to match adjoining cabinets (optional).

Fig. 26.

    (a) Tilt compactor toward rear until leveling feet (Fig. 26, 5) and foot brackets (Fig. 26, 6) are accessible.

    (b) Remove retaining screws (Fig. 26, 2 and 4) and end cap (Fig. 26, 3) (each side). Discard both end caps. Replace screws into original holes.

    (c) Remove leveling foot from foot bracket (each side) and reassemble into tapped holes of base (Fig. 27, 1).

    (d) Remove and discard retaining screws and foot brackets (Fig. 26, 6).

    (e) Remove four retaining screws (Fig. 28, 2) from kickboard (Fig. 28, 3) and kickboard support plate (Fig. 28, 1).

    (f) Replace kickboard support plate (Fig. 29, 1) in original position, then position kickboard in new reversed position (Fig. 29, 2) and reassemble the four retaining screws (Fig. 29, 3).

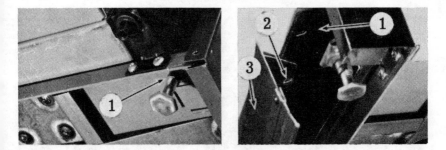

Fig. 27.   Fig. 28.

6. Using installation bracket template, locate bracket (Fig. 4, 1) in desired position.

7. Place compactor in front of proposed under counter location. Slide compactor sideways with enough room to insert three-pronged plug of the power supply cord into the three-prong wall receptacle (shown in shaded area of Fig. 4). Make certain that cord is secured in clamp at top rear of unit.

8. *See* note on caps for feet.

9. Slide compactor into under counter cavity, making sure rear leveling feet are engaged in installation bracket.

10. Level compactor by using leveling feet. A minimum $\frac{1}{4}$-inch clearance *must be maintained* between compactor top and counter top for service accessibility.

11. Check charcoal air filter (Fig. 30, 1) for proper installation.

12. Replace drawer, reassemble to track, and replace both drawer retaining screws. (*See* note on adjustable feet.)

13. If required, control panel can be moved forward for better visibility of controls. Loosen two control panel retaining screws (Fig. 31, 1) located in elongated slots of litter bin top (beneath panel). Relocate panel (Fig. 31, 2) and retighten screws (Fig. 31, 1).

Note: Four special rubber caps for the leveling feet (Fig. 29, 5) are supplied with the unit, and may be used on all four feet—or only on the front feet when moving compactor into cabinet cavity (Fig. 4). The caps will prevent the compactor from moving on slippery surfaced floors and minimize any marring of flooring.

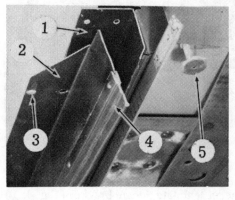

Fig. 29.

Fig. 30.

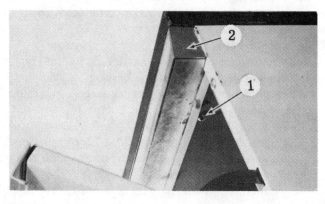

Fig. 31.

Note: For a few special installations where the adjustable feet (Fig. 29, 5) have been set to the low screwed-in position, and/or if the compactor is mounted on an extra thick shag or similar type of carpet, the rubber kickboard molding (Fig. 29, 4) might drag on the carpet when the drawer is opened. Should this happen, simply remove the kickboard (Fig. 29, 2) and cut the molding (Fig. 29, 4) with a pair of scissors to suit your installation.

OPERATING COMPACTOR

It is not necessary to run a compaction cycle every time you place trash in the drawer. However, the more often you run a cycle, the more compact the trash will be. To start the compactor, proceed as follows:

1. Close the large trash drawer (Fig. 32).
2. Turn the key to the unlocked (vertical) position (Fig. 33).
3. Push the Start button (Fig. 34).

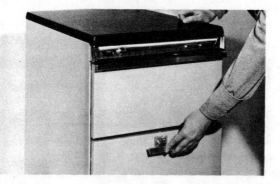

Fig. 32.

Fig. 33.

The compactor ram will move down inside the trash drawer. The complete cycle of the ram moving down, reversing, and then returning to its original position will take approximately 35 seconds. As the

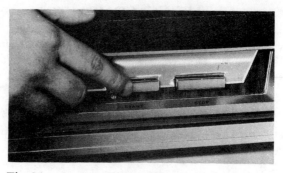

Fig. 34.

basket fills, and the ram travels a shorter distance, this time will lessen.

The ram does not go all the way to the bottom of the drawer; therefore, you can expect to cycle several loose trash loads before compaction is evident. This is normal and not a cause for concern.

As the ram compacts difficult-to-break items you may notice a downward movement of the compactor drawer. This is normal and will not cause damage. The spring-loaded drawer is specially designed to freely move down and return to its original position. As the ram compacts the contents, the entire force of the ram is absorbed by the rigid steel frame of the compactor.

Note: It is possible for a cycle to be incomplete when you have not firmly closed the drawer before pushing the Start button. If this occurs, the unit will shut off but the drawer cannot be pulled open. Close drawer firmly and push the Start button. The ram will then return to the original up position.

How to Stop Cycle and Open Drawer.   You may push the stop button at any time during operation to stop the ram (Fig. 35). Then push the Start button to return the ram to the original up position. The drawer may then be opened. To restart a compaction cycle, close the drawer and push the Start button.

Charcoal Air Filter.   The charcoal air filter (Fig. 36) absorbs and minimizes odor. It is located at the right rear section of the compactor. A fan moves air through the charcoal filter, removing odor. The degree of odor in your compactor will depend upon the type of trash you place in it. It is recommended that you use a food waste disposer for wet garbage.

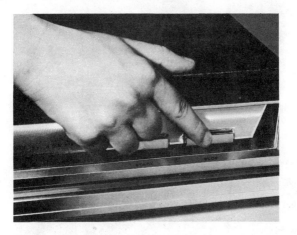

Fig. 35.

Off position (Fig. 36). Even when the fan is not running, the filter will be working to remove odor. *On position* (Fig. 36). The fan will create a fast air movement for greater efficiency.

Fig. 36. Charcoal air filter.

Odor is adsorbed into the pores of the charcoal filter. The filter need be replaced just once or twice a year. Length of time before filter replacement is necessary may vary with the types of trash compacted. (*See* Fig. 37.)

To *remove* and *replace filter*, proceed as follows:

1. After pulling trash drawer out to a fully opened position,

Fig. 37.

reach into the right rear corner where the filter is located (Fig. 38).
Note: Filter is taped into place at factory for shipping purposes.
Remove the tape from bottom of filter and filter housing.

    2. Release filter from bottom clip and pull filter down (Fig. 39).

    3. Push replacement filter up into place within top clips. Snap
securely behind bottom clip (Fig. 39).

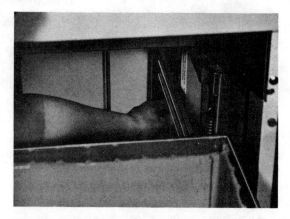

Fig. 38. Removing and replacing air filters.

Fig. 39.

CARE AND CLEANING

Inside. *Built-in litter bin.* The smooth, seamless, stainless-steel liner can be wiped clean of any spills with a cloth or sponge dipped in a mild detergent or ammonia and water (Fig. 40). Rinse with

Fig. 40. Cleaning litter bin.

clean water and then dry. Do not use abrasive cleansers that could scratch the finish.

Tilt-away trash basket. Clean as necessary, after emptying compacted trash. Using paper toweling or a damp sponge, remove any small pieces of debris from the basket, such as paper or tiny pieces of crushed glass. *Avoid contact with bare hands.* Light soil may be wiped away with a damp sponge or cloth (Fig. 41). Heavy soil may require the use of a mild detergent and warm water. Rinse with clean water, then dry.

Fig. 41. Cleaning trash basket.

Ram. Occasionally, you should check and clean the ram. Using paper toweling or a damp sponge (Fig. 42), remove any small pieces of debris from the ram, such as paper or tiny pieces of crushed glass. *Avoid contact with bare hands.* Dip sponge in mild detergent and warm water and wipe ram clean. Hard-to-remove soil may require the use of a dampened scouring pad. Rinse with clean water, then dry.

Metal drawer. Occasionally, you should use a lubricant on the drawer latch rod and slide hook located on both sides of the drawer opening, as indicated in Fig. 43, A and B. This will prevent the door latch from developing a squeak or sticking problem. It will also help insure an extended life for the latch mechanism.

We suggest the use of soap, margarine, or a solid stick lubricant that can be purchased at auto supply or some hardware stores.

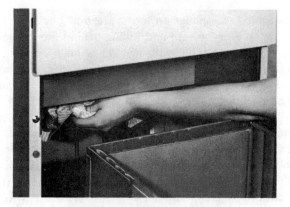

Fig. 42. Checking and cleaning ram.

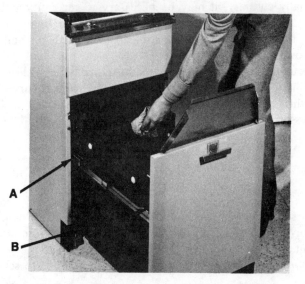

Fig. 43. Lubricating drawer latch rod and slide hook.

Metal drawer liner. This should require little cleaning. However, if spills should occur, use a cloth or sponge dipped in mild detergent and water solution. Rinse with clean water and dry. *Do not* use abrasive cleansers.

Occasionally, you should check the area behind the trash drawer and remove any small pieces of trash.

Placing a folded newspaper on top of trash will help prevent small items from sticking to the ram and falling behind the drawer.

Outside.   Wipe cabinet with a damp sponge or cloth, using a mild detergent and warm water. Rinse sponge in clean water, wipe cabinet, and dry with a soft cloth. *Do not* use abrasive cleansers that could scratch the finish.

Do not use metal top of compactor for a cutting surface as this could permanently damage the finish.

Care of Cutting Board Top.   The hardwood top is pre-finished with a protective lacquer seal. For daily care, simply wipe with a damp cloth after using. To remove stubborn stains, let dampened scouring powder remain in contact with the wood for 3 to 5 hours, then wipe away with a damp cloth. After an extended period of use (especially cutting), it may be necessary to recondition the top by sanding off all the remaining lacquer and applying mineral oil to the cutting board. Simply saturate a clean cloth with oil and wipe on. Allow overnight absorption.

Repeat this oil treatment the following day and allow to stand 4 to 6 hours before removing excess oil with a soft, dry cloth. The top is then ready for use. Repeat this treatment every 6 to 8 months, as necessary.

MAINTENANCE

This section applies to a freestanding model. If the compactor is built-in, it will be necessary to remove the unit from its installed position.

Be sure to disconnect electrical power supply before servicing the unit.

Top.
    1. Remove three top retaining screws (Fig. 44, 1) from rear of compactor.
    2. Slide top toward rear to disengage from key slots. Lift off top.
Back Panel.
    1. Remove three screws (Fig. 44, 1) at top.
    2. Remove four screws (Fig. 44, 2) from each side.
    3. Remove two screws (Fig. 44, 3 and 6) from back panel.

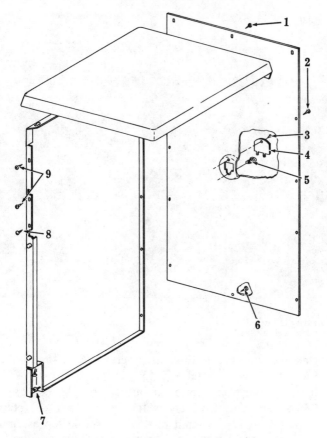

Fig. 44. Removing unit from installed position.

Remove plate (Fig. 44, 4) and slide strain relief (Fig. 44, 5) up and out of slot. Feed cord through rectangular hole in back panel.

Side Panels.

    1. Remove top and back panel.

    2. Open litter bin door and remove two retaining screws (Fig. 44, 9).

    3. Open drawer and remove remaining front retaining screws (Fig. 44, 7 and 8).

Frame Top Assembly.

    1. Remove top, back panel, and side panels.

    2. Remove three jack screw retainer nuts (Fig. 45, 4).

Fig. 45. Motor drive belt.

3. Remove two truss head retaining screws (Fig. 45, 3).

4. Lift off enclosure plate (Fig. 45, 1).

5. Remove four truss head retaining screws (Fig. 45, 2).

6. Disconnect the two ram switch leads from the start-stop program switch (Fig. 46, 3) and remove the frame top assembly.

Door Front Panel.

1. Open door and remove three retaining screws from pull handle (Fig. 47, 1).

2. Close door and open drawer to remove three screws from bottom of door panel.

3. Take out remaining two inner panel retaining screws (Fig. 47, 2) (one from each side).

4. Lift off panel.

Drawer Assembly.

1. With drawer forward, remove two drawer retaining screws (Fig. 48, 1) and nuts and lock washers from drawer tracks.

2. Remove drawer from drawer tracks.

Fig. 46. Switches-control panel.

Fig. 47. Door front panel.

Fig. 48. Drawer assembly.

Drawer Front Panel.

1. Remove drawer and take out four retaining screws (Fig. 48, 2) from each side of panel.

2. Remove two outside storage cover retaining screws (Fig. 48, 3) and loosen the two center screws (Fig. 48, 4) from inside top of panel and side storage cover.

3. Stand drawer on rear and remove the front two panel retaining screws from bottom of drawer.

4. When drawer front panel is removed, springs (Fig. 49, 3) will be disengaged from notch on each side of storage wrapper and latch rod (Fig. 49, 1) will come out of notch in storage wrapper.

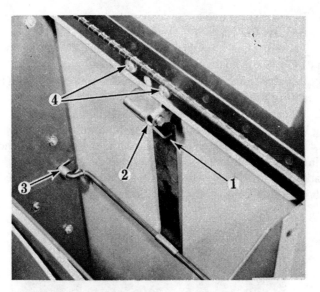

Fig. 49. Drawer handle latch mechanism.

Drawer Handle Latch Mechanism.

1. To service springs (Fig. 49, 3), and latch rod and hook sub-assembly, remove drawer front.

2. Remove springs from latch rod. When reassembling springs, be sure to install right hand and left hand springs in the correct location on rod. End of spring must be installed in notch on storage wrapper.

3. To replace latch rod and hook sub-assembly, remove springs and lift up on latch rod hook (Fig. 49, 1) to disengage it from notch in hinge and mounting bracket assembly.

4. It is not necessary to remove the drawer front to service drawer handle or hinge and mounting bracket assembly.

5. Use a short-handled Phillips screwdriver to remove retaining screws (Fig. 49, 2) so you can remove drawer handle.

6. To remove hinge and handle mounting bracket assembly, withdraw the two screws (Fig. 49, 4) from inside storage cover.

Drawer Track/Spring.

1. Remove top.

2. Remove back panel.

3. Remove side panels.

4. Remove drawer.

5. Loosen, then remove, the four track mounting nuts and washers (Fig. 50, 1) (two in front and two in back).

6. Remove bolts and washers, then disconnect springs (Fig. 50, 2) and remove drawer tracks.

7. When installing drawer tracks, first connect springs to frame (spring hooks facing out), then to track mounting brackets.

8. Force the track downward until the holes in the track mounting bracket line up with the slots in the frame, permitting installation of the bolts, washers and nuts. *Note:* At re-assembly, the bolt head should be on the inside of the frame.

Fig. 50. Drawer track spring.

Kickboard.

1. Remove drawer.

2. Stand drawer on rear and remove four retaining screws from kickboard and kickboard support plate.

3. Remove kickboard and support plate.

Control Panel.

1. Open litter bin door and remove two retaining screws (Fig. 51, 1) from inside top of litter bin.

2. Slide console forward to clear unit and disconnect wire leads from charcoal air filter switch, key interlock switch, and start-stop program switch.

3. Remove control panel (Fig. 51, 2).

Fig. 51. Control panel.

Blower Motor.

1. Connect electrical power supply and run ram to bottom position.

2. Disconnect power supply.

3. Remove back panel.

4. Disconnect three lead wires from blower motor.

5. Remove two blower motor mounting screws (Fig. 52, 1).

6. Remove blower motor and fan from housing. *Note:* The nylon blower motor fan is lightly pressed onto the motor shaft. This is removable for service replacement.

Chain Tension Regulator.

1. Remove top and top frame cover plate.

2. Remove chain tension regulator spring (Fig. 53, 2).

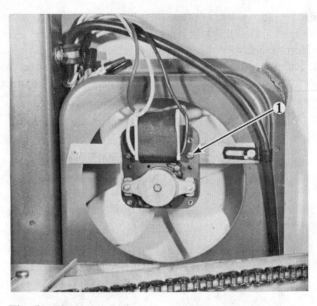

Fig. 52. Blower motor.

3. Remove retaining nut (Fig. 53, 1) and lock washer from idler sprocket arm.

4. Remove screw (Fig. 53, 5) from idler plate assembly (Fig. 53, 4). Shift idler plate to allow idler arm (Fig. 53, 3) to clear sprocket cover.

5. Lift off idler arm (Fig. 53, 3).

Drive Chain.

1. Remove top, back panel, side panels, and frame top assembly.

2. Remove chain tension regulator spring (Fig. 53, 2).

3. Pull drawer half way open. Locate ram on top of drawer. Ram can be operated manually by using the $\frac{5}{8}$-inch hexsocket on the motor sprocket (Fig. 45, 6).

4. Remove the four sprocket cover and brace screws from the ram top brace. Then loosen—(only)—the two remaining screws in the ram top brace. Remove the drive sprocket covers (Fig. 45, 1, 3, and 6).

5. Remove chain (Fig. 54, 5) from sprockets.

6. Install replacement chain, making certain chain is properly positioned onto drive and idler sprockets. Install tension regulator

Fig. 53. Chain tension regulator.

spring (Fig. 54, 4). *Note:* All three drive sprockets must be level (at the same height). Measure distance from top of each jack screw to top of drive sprocket.

7. Adjust drive chain for correct tension by loosening the four motor sprocket bracket mounting bolts (Fig. 54, 7), and moving the sprocket in the proper direction so the distance from the center of the two idler sprocket retaining screws is $6\frac{1}{4}$ inches minimum to $6\frac{1}{2}$ inches maximum, as shown in Fig. 53. It is *important* this distance be maintained.

8. The four sprocket bracket mounting bolts (Fig. 54, 7) *must* be securely tightened. Check the two side flange bearing mounting bolts (Fig. 54, 8) and, if necessary, retighten. Recheck the chain adjustment.

9. Reinstall drive sprocket covers and ram top brace.

10. Manually rotate motor sprocket clockwise to check for free operation of ram drive mechanism.

Motor Drive Belt.   To *remove* motor drive belt, proceed as follows:

Fig. 54. Drive sprocket covers and ram drive mechanism.

1. Remove top and top frame cover plate.

2. Locate ram approximately four inches from top position. Ram can be operated manually by using the $\frac{5}{8}$-inch hex socket on the motor sprocket (Fig. 45, 6).

3. Remove chain tension regulator spring (Fig. 54, 4).

4. Loosen four motor mounting bolts (Fig. 54, 2). Slide motor toward motor sprocket drive pulley and remove belt.

To *replace* the motor drive belt, proceed as follows:

1. Position belt around motor sprocket drive pulley.

2. Move belt toward motor and around motor pulley, making certain teeth in belt are meshed in both sprocket drive pulley and motor pulley.

3. Slide motor toward front and finger tighten mounting bolts (Fig. 9, 2).

4. Rotate motor sprocket manually, approximately two revolutions, to align belt.

5. Loosen motor mounting bolts (Fig. 54, 2), and slide motor toward front until belt is taut (approximately 30 to 40 pounds).

6. Replace chain tension regulator spring (Fig. 54, 4).

Ram Unit.

1. Remove top, back panel, side panels, and frame top assembly.

2. Pull drawer out half way.

3. Locate ram on top of drawer. Ram can be operated manually by using the ⅝-inch hex socket on the motor sprocket (Fig. 45, 6).

4. Remove drive chain (Fig. 45, 5).

5. Unscrew all three drive sprockets (Fig. 55, 1) from jack screws (Fig. 55, 2).

6. Remove jack screw thrust bearing assemblies (Fig. 56). *Caution: Do not interchange* jack screw sprocket and bearing assemblies. On reinstallation be sure to return each sprocket and bearing assembly to its original jack screw location.

7. Remove drawer interlock actuator bracket from rear of upper ram housing.

8. Loosen main wiring harness by removing strain relief bushing (Fig. 57, 1) from frame, and harness retainer (Fig. 60, 4) from idler plate.

9. Move wiring harness aside. Grasp side of ram and lift from jack screws. *Note:* should further disassembly be required for the ram, disconnect all ram wiring connections.

Jack Screws.

1. Remove ram. (Jack screws are now accessible for removal.)

2. Remove hex mounting bolts (Fig. 58, 2).

3. Pull jack screw (Fig. 58, 1) down through hole in frame and withdraw jack screw retainer nut (Fig. 58, 3) and screw retaining plate (Fig. 58, 4) from underside of cross member of frame. *Caution:* At reassembly of jack screw make certain square end of jack screw (Fig. 59, 1) extends through square hole and is flush with bottom of screw retainer plate (Fig. 59, 2). Screw retainer plate (Fig. 59, 2) must be drawn up tight against the mating face of the jack screw retainer nut (Fig. 59, 3).

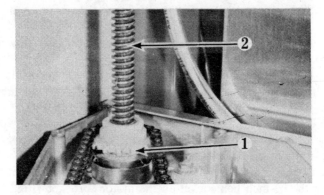

Fig. 55. Ram unit.

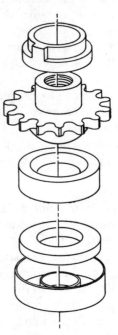

Fig. 56. Bearing assemblies.

Motor Sprocket and Drive Pulley Assembly.

1. Remove top, top frame cover plate, and one side panel.

2. Ram must be located in the top position (if necessary, use $5/8$-inch hex socket wrench to manually raise ram).

Fig. 57. Wiring harness.

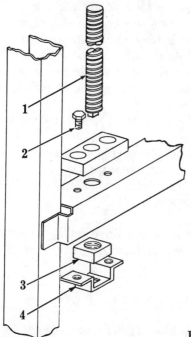

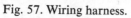

Fig. 58. Removal of jack screws.

Fig. 59. Reassembly of jack screws.

3. Remove drawer.

4. Tape the ram spacer to ram top for holding spacer in place before removing ram bottom. (Use 6 or 8 strips of masking tape.)

5. Remove four retaining screws from ram bottom. *Note:* To reassemble ram bottom, masking tape should again be used to hold ram bottom in place (6 or 8 strips are necessary). Start one of the front retaining screws to secure the ram bottom. Install remaining screws. Tighten securely and remove tape.

6. Loosen four mounting bolts (Fig. 60, 1), and slide motor sprocket bracket toward motor.

7. Remove chain tension regulator spring (Fig. 60, 2).

8. Disengage chain (Fig. 60, 5) from motor sprocket.

9. Remove four motor sprocket bracket mounting bolts (Fig. 60, 1), and lower the drive pulley assembly.

Note: Repairs to the motor sprocket and drive pulley assembly should not be attempted. If the unit is faulty, replace it with a complete new unit.

Motor and Pulley.

1. Remove top and top frame cover plate.

2. Remove drawer.

3. Locate ram in the down position. (If necessary, use ⅝-inch hex socket to manually lower ram).

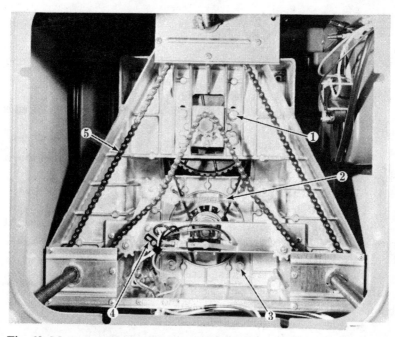

Fig. 60. Motor sprocket and drive pulley assembly.

4. Remove four retaining screws from ram bottom.

5. Remove ram bottom and the ram spacer.

6. Disconnect motor lead wires.

7. Loosen motor mounting bolts (Fig. 60, 3) and slide motor toward motor drive sprocket assembly.

8. Remove motor drive belt.

9. Insert ram bottom and spacer and place as support under motor. Remove motor mounting bolts (Fig. 60, 3). Slightly raise ram manually to clear top of motor. Lower and remove motor.

Switches-Control Panel. *See* Fig. 46—filter switch (1), key interlock switch (2), and start-stop program switch (3).

1. Remove control panel.

2. Remove lead wires from switches.

3. Remove switch retaining screws and then the switch.

Caution: Lead wire identifications *must* correspond with switch terminals.

Electrical Power Cord.

1. Remove left hand side panel.

2. Remove back panel.

3. Remove ground screw and wire connector from white neutral lead, and disconnect two switch terminal connections from drawer front interlock and bypass interlock switch.

4. Remove strain relief bushing from left front vertical frame upright.

5. Remove electrical power cord.

6. When reinstalling electrical power cord, feed cord through cord clamps.

Directional Switch.

1. Remove top and top frame cover plate.

2. Disconnect lead wires from switch (Fig. 46, 4). *Caution:* At reassembly, lead wire identification *must* correspond with switch terminals.

3. Remove switch retaining screws and the switch.

Drawer Front Interlock Switch.

1. Remove top and left side panel.

2. Remove interlock switch lead wires.

3. Remove switch mounting screws and the switch.

Interlock Bypass Switch.

1. Remove top and left side panel.

2. Disconnect two lead wires from switch (Fig. 61, 1).

3. Remove switch mounting screws and the switch.

Ram Switch.

1. Remove top and top frame cover plate.

2. Disconnect two lead wires fro switmch (Fig. 61, 1).

3. Remove switch retaining screws and the switch.

4. In reassembling switch make sure it is correctly adjusted. Rotate in slot as necessary.

WIRING DIAGRAMS

See Fig. 62 for pictorial wiring diagram of the trash compactor; *also see* Fig. 63 for schematic wiring diagram of the unit.

Fig. 61. Reassembling ram switch.

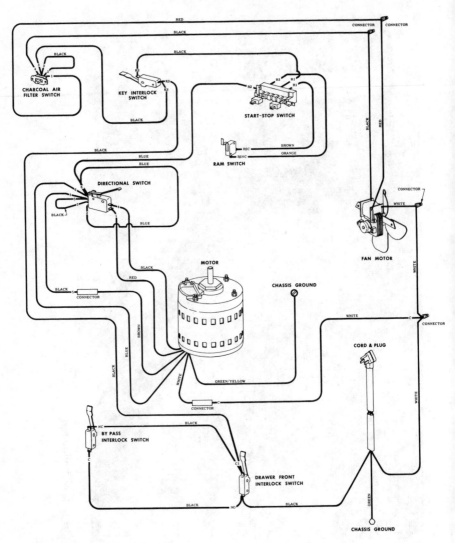

Fig. 62. Pictorial wiring diagram.

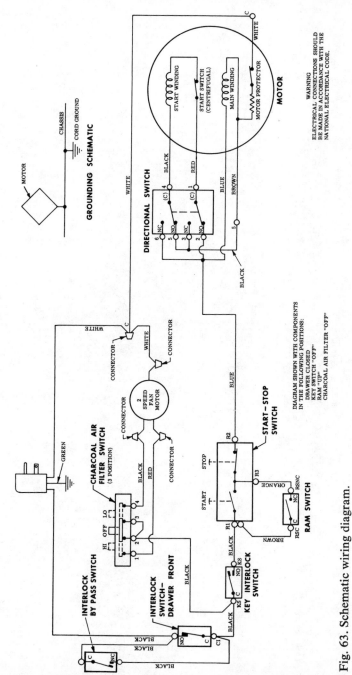

Fig. 63. Schematic wiring diagram.

Section 6

FOOD PRESERVATION

THE REFRIGERATION SYSTEMS MOST commonly used utilize R-12 as a refrigerant. Chemically, R-12 is dichlorodifluromethane ($CCl_2 F_2$). The boiling point of R-12 is so low that the substance cannot exist as a liquid unless it is confined and put under pressure. It also has the advantage of being practically nontoxic, nonflammable, nonexplosive, and noncorrosive; and it does not poison or contaminate foods.

When you buy your first or next *refrigerator*, you will want to be sure you are getting one that will hold at safe refrigerating temperatures, operate efficiently, and last for many years.

Consider the features that make a refrigerator easy to use and adaptable to the special needs of the family. Before you buy, talk with your friends and neighbors about the kind they have. Knowledge of what to look for and some shopping around are well worth your time and effort. Among the most important things to consider are type of operation, amount and kind of food storage space, overall construction, insulation, surface, surface finishes, shelf and space flexibility, and ease in cleaning.

To own a *home freezer* is a goal of many families. Possible benefits of freezer ownership are numerous; how great they will prove to be depends on the choice of freezer and the way in which it is used.

Chapter 33

Fundamentals of Refrigeration

Refrigeration is a general term used to describe the process of removing heat from spaces, objects, or materials and maintaining them at temperatures below the temperature of the surrounding atmosphere. In order to produce a refrigeration effect, it is merely necessary to expose the material to be cooled to a colder object or environment and to allow heat to flow in its *natural* direction; that is, from the warmer material to the colder material. The term is usually applied to an artificial means of lowering the temperature. *Mechanical refrigeration* may be defined as a mechanical system of apparatus so designed and constructed that, through its function, heat is transferred from one substance to another.

Refrigeration is more readily understood if you know the relationships among temperature, pressure, and volume, and how pressure affects liquids and gases.

HEAT

The purpose of refrigeration is to maintain spaces at low temperatures. Remember, however, that you cannot cool anything by adding coolness to it; you have to *remove heat* from it. *Refrigeration, therefore, is a process of cooling by removing heat.*

Heat and Temperature.   It is important to distinguish between heat and temperature. *Heat* is a form of energy. *Temperature* is the intensity of heat. The quantity or amount of heat is measured in terms of a standard unit called a *British thermal unit* (Btu). Temperature, as you know, is measured in degrees, which indicate the intensity of the heat in a given substance; it does not indicate the number of Btu's in the substance. *For example*, let us consider a spoonful of very hot water and a bucketful of warm water. Which has the higher temperature? Which has more heat? The heat in the spoonful of hot water is more intense; therefore, its temperature is higher. The bucketful of warm water has more Btu's (more heat energy), but its heat is less intense.

Sensible Heat and Latent Heat.   In the study of refrigeration, it is necessary to distinguish between sensible heat and latent heat. *Sensible heat* is the term applied to the heat that is absorbed or given off by a substance that is *not* in the process of changing its physical state. When a substance is not in the process of changing its state, the addition or removal of heat always causes a change in the temperature of the substance. Sensible heat can be sensed, or measured, with a thermometer.

Latent heat is the term used to describe the heat that is absorbed or given off by a substance while it is changing its physical state. When a substance is in the process of changing its physical state, the heat absorbed or given off does *not* cause a temperature change in the substance—the heat is latent or hidden. In other words, sensible heat is the term used to describe heat that affects the temperature of things; latent heat is the term used to describe heat that affects the physical state of things.

Specific Heat.   Substances vary with respect to their ability to absorb or lose heat. The ability of a substance to absorb heat or to lose it is known as the *specific heat* of the substance. The specific heat of water is taken to be 1.0, and the specific heat of each other substance is measured by comparison with this standard. Thus, if it takes only $\frac{1}{2}$ Btu to raise the temperature of one pound of a substance 1° F., the specific heat of that substance is 0.5, or one-half the specific heat of water. If you look up the specific heat of ice in a table, you will find it to be about 0.5.

Heat Flow.   Heat flows only from objects of higher temperature to objects of lower temperature. When two objects at different temperatures are placed near each other, heat will flow from the warmer object to the cooler one until both objects are at the same temperature. *Heat flow* takes place at a greater rate when there is a large temperature difference than when there is only a slight temperature difference. As the temperature difference approaches zero, the rate of heat flow also approaches zero. Heat flow may take place by radiation, by conduction, by convection, or by a combination of these methods.

Refrigeration Ton.   The unit that measures the amount of heat removal, and thereby indicates the capacity of a refrigeration system, is known as the *refrigeration ton*. The refrigeration ton is based on the cooling effect of one ton (2000 pounds) of ice at 32° F. melting in 24 hours. The latent heat of fusion of ice (or water) is 144 Btu's. Therefore, the number of Btu's required to melt one ton of ice is 144 × 2000, or 288,000. The standard refrigeration ton is defined as the transfer of 288,000 Btu's in 24 hours. On an hourly basis, the refrigeration ton is 12,000 Btu's per hour (288,000 divided by 24).

It should be emphasized that the refrigeration ton is the standard unit of measure used to designate the heat-removal capacity of a refrigeration unit. It is not necessarily a measure of the ice-making capacity of a machine, since the amount of ice that can be made depends upon the initial temperature of the water and other factors.

PRESSURE, TEMPERATURE, AND VOLUME

In studying refrigeration, it is important to understand some of the ways in which pressure affects liquids and gases, and some of the relationships between pressure, temperature, and volume in gases.

The boiling point of any liquid varies according to the pressure on the liquid—the higher the pressure, the higher the boiling point. It is good to remember that condensing a gas to a liquid is just the reverse process of boiling a liquid until it vaporizes, and that the same pressure and temperature relationship is required to produce either change of state.

Water boils at 80° F. under a vacuum of 29 inches of mercury; at 212° F. at atmospheric pressure; and at 489° F. at a pressure of 600 pounds per square inch gage (psig). Refrigerants used in vapor compressor cycle equipment usually have much lower boiling points than water under any given pressure, but these boiling points also vary according to pressure. R-12, for example, boils at —21° F. at atmospheric pressure; at 0° F. at 9.17 psig; at 50° F. at 46.69 psig; and at 100° F. at 116.9 psig. From these figures, you can see that R-12 cannot exist as a liquid at ordinary temperatures unless it is confined and put under pressure.

If the temperature of a liquid is raised to the boiling point corresponding to its pressure, and if the application of heat is continued, the liquid begins to boil and vaporize. The vapor that is formed remains at the same temperature as the boiling liquid, as long as it is in contact with the liquid. A vapor *cannot* be superheated as long as it is in contact with the liquid from which it is being generated.

The pressure-temperature-volume relationships of gases are expressed by Boyle's law, Charles' law, and the general gas law or equation.

Boyle's law states that the volume of any dry gas varies inversely with its absolute pressure, provided the temperature remains constant. This law may also be expressed as an equation:

$$V_1 P_1 = V_2 P_2$$

where V_1 is the original volume of the gas, P_1 its original absolute pressure, V_2 its new volume, and P_2 its new absolute pressure.

Charles' law states that the volume of a gas is directly proportional to its absolute temperature, provided the pressure is kept constant. The equation for this law is:

$$V_1 T_2 = V_2 T_1$$

The *general gas equation* combines Boyle's law and Charles' law, and expresses the relationship between the volume, the absolute pressure, and the absolute temperature of gases. The general gas law is expressed by the equation:

$$\frac{P_1 V_1}{T_1} = \frac{P_2 V_2}{T_2}$$

These equations indicate the nature of the relationship between the pressure, the volume, and the temperature of any gas. You will probably not find it necessary to use the equations themselves, but you should have a thorough understanding of the principles that they express. Let us summarize them.

1. When temperature is held constant, increasing the pressure on a gas causes a proportional decrease in volume; decreasing the pressure causes a proportional increase in volume.

2. When pressure is held constant, increasing the temperature of a gas causes a proportional increase in volume; decreasing the temperature causes a proportional decrease in volume.

3. When the volume is held constant, increasing the temperature of a gas causes a proportional increase in pressure; decreasing the temperature causes a proportional decrease in pressure.

In this discussion of the effects of pressure on a gas, we have noted that the volume and the temperature of the gas are different *after* the pressure has been changed. It is important to note, however, that a temperature change normally occurs in a gas *while* the pressure is being changed. Compressing a gas raises its temperature; allowing a gas to expand lowers its temperature.

Chapter 34

Refrigerators

Choose a refrigerator that is big enough. The size of the unit you need depends upon the following:

1. Kind of food you most often store.
2. How much frozen foods, frozen deserts, and ice cubes you use.
3. How often you buy and prepare food.
4. The size of your family.

Check your family needs in this way—a family of two needs at least a six cubic foot refrigerator. For each additional two persons, add an extra cubic foot.

Select a refrigerator that is for the specific kind of gas you are using, or type of current and voltage that you can get from your power line.

There are many types of electric refrigerators—the conventional type with increased space for frozen foods; the two-temperature refrigerator with ample space for standard refrigeration plus a large compartment for frozen foods.

Note the special features of the different models of refrigerators and consider their advantages. Remember that each adds to the cost, though it may make no difference in the actual operation. You will probably want some special features because they will help you make the best use of your refrigerator. Whether or not they are worth the extra cost to you depends on your own particular needs and what you like.

ELECTRICAL GROUNDING

The refrigerator shown in Fig. 1 is equipped with a three-prong grounding plug for your protection against possible shock hazards.

Where a two-prong wall receptacle is encountered, *be sure* to have it replaced with a properly grounded three-prong wall receptacle in accordance with the National Electrical Code. (*See* Fig. 2.)

Where a two-prong adapter is required temporarily, it is your personal responsibility and obligation to have the adapter properly grounded and polarized.

Do not cut or remove the round grounding prong from the plug. *Do not* remove the tag from the cord. *Do not* use a two-prong adapter in Canada.

The unit is designed to operate on a 115-volt, 15-ampere, 60-cycle line.

Fig. 1. Refrigerator with freezer on top.

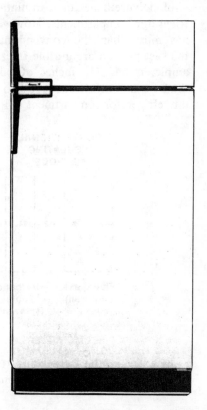

Fig. 2. Three-prong grounding plug.

INSULATION

Saving Energy.   Conventional refrigerators have the same thickness of cabinet wall insulation around the freezer compartment as around the refrigerator compartment. The freezer compartment, however, must maintain the temperature at 0° F. which is about 40 degrees colder than the 38° F. to 40° F. range of temperature maintained in the refrigerator compartment. The colder freezer temperature means there is a greater chance of heat leakage into the freezer than into the refrigerator compartment. Therefore, more insulation should be used around the freezer than around the refrigerator compartment.

The conventional refrigerator design uses either three inches of fiberglass insulation or an equivalent amount—one and three-quarters —of polyurethane foam insulation around both the freezer and refrigerator compartments. However, the refrigerator shown in Fig. 1 has more than the conventional amount of insulation—with the thickest portion around the freezer where it is needed most. For example, it has 2½ inches of polyurethane foam insulation around the freezer compartment and two inches of polyurethane foam around the refrigerator compartment (Fig. 3).

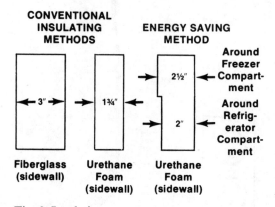

Fig. 3. Insulation.

In addition, the freezer and refrigerator doors have slab foam insulation that is superior to conventionally used fiberglass because it prevents heat leakage better. With better and more insulation, your refrigerator will maintain proper temperatures longer. This means the compressor does not have to run so often, and that means reduced energy consumption.

Other Energy Saving Features. The *radiant shell condenser* (it releases heat from food in the refrigerator to the outside air) is welded to the top and sides of the outer cabinet. This condenser saves more energy because it does not require an energy consuming condenser fan motor as is required in some *no-frost* type of refrigerators.

Magna-seal gaskets, with a magnetic strip inside the tough vinyl gasket, grip the cabinet for an airtight seal. This locks the cold in, keeps the warm air out, and reduces running time.

The *seamless, one-piece insuliner* adds extra insulating protection because it conducts less heat than either metal or porcelain-coated steel liners.

This refrigerator is a partial automatic defrost model, and has one auxiliary, moisture-preventing heater strip (center mullion). This heater is cycled with the compressor and controlled by the energy saver control so you can realize additional energy savings depending upon humidity conditions in your home. (*See* section on Energy Saver Control later in this chapter.)

How to Save Energy. *Location.* You will save energy if your refrigerator is located away from heating equipment and direct sunlight.

Keep the freezer and refrigerator sections full, The unit will operate more economically when filled to capacity, but not overfilled. When the refrigerator-freezer is full and the doors are opened, the cold food helps maintain temperature.

Control settings. You should set the freezer-refrigerator control so that it does not run colder than necessary.

Doors. Check the door gaskets to be sure they do not become blocked, dirty, or worn. Air leaks will cause the unit to operate unnecessarily.

Defrosting. You should defrost your freezer when frost has built to more than ¼-inch thick. With frost build-up, efficiency decreases and your unit must run longer to compensate for it.

HOW TO PREPARE YOUR REFRIGERATOR FOR USE WITH FREEZER ON TOP

As part of your purchase, you may have agreed to install your refrigerator yourself. If so, follow these instructions. You will also find this information useful when preparing your refrigerator for a move from one place to another.

Exterior. Remove protective packing and report any transportation damage to the selling dealer or delivery company at once.

1. If the refrigerator base skid is still attached, tip the refrigerator back, place a supporting block under the back of the unit and unbolt (Fig. 4). Bolts are ½ inch. For refrigerator shown in Fig. 1, the four leveling legs should be installed at this time by screwing them into the four outer case feet. (*See* section on How to Level later in this chapter.)

2. Save some of the heavy duty tape that you have removed and make a pad, adhesive side out, and touch it to any tape residue remaining on the unit. This should lift it off and eliminate the need for using solvents of any kind (Fig. 5).

Fig. 4.

Fig. 5.

3. Convert doors from right hand to left hand door opening if desired. This unit is delivered as a right hand opening unit. Consult instruction sheet included with the unit for reversing to a left hand opening unit.

Interior. Remove protective packing (Fig. 6). The special cardboard stripping braces that prevented damage in shipment have to be removed and discarded.

Crispers. There is packing material around the crisper pans that must be removed. Remove the tape as shown in Fig. 7, then lift up on pans and cover and carefully remove from unit. Complete the

Fig. 6.

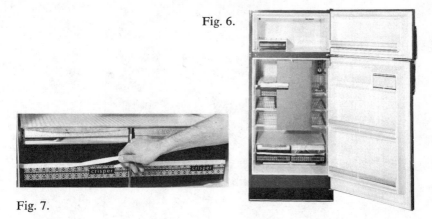

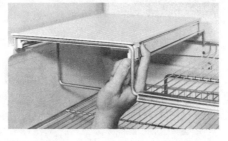

Fig. 7.

unpacking, then replace. Be sure to install shelf support between the crisper pans.

Meat pan. Remove all padding between the pan and the shelf.

To remove meat pan, slide the meat pan out till it comes into contact with the *stop* that has been built into the meat pan top. Next, reach into the pan and push up on the meat pan top while at the same time sliding the pan over the built-in stop. Then, depress plastic stopper clips (Fig. 8). Slide meat pan out of the metal holder. When reassembling, reverse the procedure.

Fig. 8.

Removable doorshelf retainer bars. Remove all tape from retainer bars on the doors. Again, use the tape to remove any residue. To remove retainer bars for cleaning, just lift and pull out from the bottom. When replacing, be sure they are snapped back in place (Fig. 9).

Fig. 9.

Cleaning. (*See* section on How to Clean Your Refrigerator.)

How to remove grill at bottom of the unit. Pull grill straight forward from the unit to release the grill clips. To replace, reverse procedure.

Condensate drain pan. The pan is located underneath the cabinet. Periodically, remove grill and clean pan. We suggest every three months. Before replacing grill, make sure the pan is in place (Fig. 10).

Fig. 10.

FINAL PLACEMENT OF REFRIGERATOR ON SOLID FLOOR

Your refrigerator must be installed on a floor strong enough to support the combined weight of the food *and* the unit in order to insure proper operation and a good door seal.

If the spot selected is next to a wall, be sure that you allow two inches of space along the side so the doors can be opened 90 degrees.

FREESTANDING INSTALLATION

The refrigerator shown in Fig. 11 must be installed as a freestanding unit. It has an efficient radiant shell condenser but there must be ample air circulation around the unit for maximum operating efficiency. Locate it away from direct sources of heat.

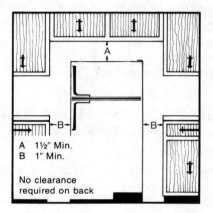

A 1½″ Min.
B 1″ Min.

No clearance required on back

Fig. 11.

Slide unit against the wall. For minimum clearances, allow 1½-inches between top of unit and overhead cabinets. Each side of the unit must have one inch between wall, counter top, or other appliance (Fig. 12). *Do not completely build in unit.*

Fig. 12.

Warm cabinet. Even when installed with proper clearance, it is normal for the sides and top of the cabinet to feel warm to the touch.

This is the heat being transferred from the food inside the unit into the air. It is warmest when the compressor motor is running.

Leveling is important for proper closing. (*See* following section on How to Level.)

How to level refrigerator. Your refrigerator should be leveled with rollers at each corner. Some models have four leveling legs. If your floor is not level from side to side, it may be necessary to shim under one of the rollers or legs at the rear.

Leveling with rollers. Each front roller (located behind the grill at the bottom of the unit) is independently adjustable. Use a screwdriver to move the front rollers up or down. Adjust until the unit tilts slightly from front to back. This allows the doors to close firmly.

Leveling unit without rollers. This model has leveling legs that must rest firmly against the floor. Adjust by turning legs until the unit tilts slightly from front to back. This allows the doors to close firmly.

HOW TO BEST STORE FOOD IN YOUR REFRIGERATOR

Freezer Storage.   *See* Fig. 13.

Ice-cube compartment and shelf. The ice compartment contains two ice-cube trays. This unit will not accept an icemaker.

Packaged frozen foods. Frozen foods from the supermarket should be placed in the freezer as soon as possible. To quickly return them to a safe 0° F. to 2° F. storage, we recommend placing them against the back wall for several hours before organizing them elsewhere in the freezer.

Fresh frozen foods. Fresh frozen foods you prepare at home should be carefully wrapped in a moisture- and vapor-proof wrap, or placed in airtight containers. Thin plastic wrap used for covering food stored in the refrigerator is *not suitable* as moisture can be drawn through it. And in some instances, the plastic wrap will produce an odor that can be absorbed by other foods.

Door storage. The door shelves are designed to hold juice cans, food packages, and the ice-cube storage bin.

How long to store frozen food. It is better to store food for shorter periods and replenish often, as needed. Use the following frozen food storage chart as a guide. The times shown in Chart 3 are approximate times for properly wrapped foods.

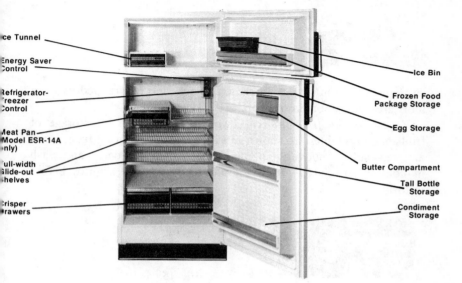

Fig. 13.

CHART 3
FROZEN FOOD STORAGE

PRODUCT	MONTHS-APPROXIMATE	PRODUCT	MONTHS-APPROXIMATE
Beef	12 months or more	Bacon, sliced	1-1½ months
Lamb		Fruits	10-12 months
Mutton	8-10 months	Vegetables	10-12 months
Pork, fresh		Eggs	6-8 months
Veal		Butter	6-8 months
Poultry		Cheese	4-5 months
Lean Fish	6-8 months		
Game		Cream	2-4 months
Ground meat		Ice Cream	1-1½ months
Sausage, unseasoned		Milk, homogenized	1 month
Shellfiish		Baked Products	6 months
Variety meats	4-6 months	Unbaked Products	2 months
Fatty fish			
Bacon, Slab		Prepared dishes	
Ham	2-4 months	(stews, casseroles, etc.)	4-6 months
Sausage, Seasoned			

Refrigerator Storage.   *See* Fig. 13.

Pre-packaged meats. The meat pan (Fig. 14) helps to keep meat fresh. Pre-packaged fresh meat may be stored in original wrapping, if used in one or two days. Otherwise, meat should be rewrapped in a moisture- and vapor-proof wrap. Meat wrapped by the butcher should

Fig. 14.

be removed from the market wrappings and rewrapped with a moisture- and vapor-proof wrap.

Vegetable and fruit storage. Two crisper drawers for storage of fruits and vegetables are shown in Fig. 15. Before storing fresh fruits and vegetables, remove wrapping, trim off damaged parts, and wash in cold water. Salad greens should be moistened slightly before restoring.

Fig. 15.

Foods stored on shelves. As you know, cold air is very dry. Foods stored on the open shelves should be covered with plastic wrap or placed in covered containers to prevent drying. This also prevents mixing of odors or flavors.

Glide-out shelves. The full-width shelves slide part way out (to a built-in stop) for easier loading (Fig. 16.) This also permits easy access to items at the back of the shelf.

Fig. 16.

Butter compartment. Foods stored in the refrigerator doors include butter in the butter compartment (Fig. 17). For your convenience, there is a sturdy melamine butter dish that can be taken to the table (Fig. 17). It is dishwasher safe.

Egg storage. An egg nest (Fig. 18) is built into the refrigerator door. Always use eggs from the front row first.

Tall bottles, milk, and condiments. Small condiment bottles, tall beverage bottles, and even half-gallon milk cartons are conveniently organized and stored in the refrigerator door (Fig. 19).

Fig. 17.

Fig. 18.

Fig. 19.

AUTOMATIC COLD CONTROL

Refrigerator-Freezer Control.   The refrigerator-freezer control (Fig. 20) senses the change in temperature of the evaporator plate, located in the refrigerator compartment. When a temperature change has been detected, the control turns the compressor on or off as required. The setting you select on the control will be maintained.

The control is numbered from 1 to 7. Number 1 is the warmest, and number 7 is the coldest setting. We recommend a setting of number 4. However, feel free to regulate the control as desired after the refrigerator and freezer compartments have cooled.

Fig. 20.

Checking the Temperature.   After several days under normal load conditions, be sure to check the temperature inside the freezer section. Use a good quality thermometer that is capable of registering below zero degrees.

Place the thermometer in the center of the freezer, surrounded by frozen packages. Leave the thermometer overnight before reading and making any control adjustments. For best storage the temperature should be in the 0° F. to 2° F. range. Adjust the refrigerator-freezer control as needed.

Three-Position Energy Saver Control for Energy Conservation.

The three-position energy saver control (Fig. 20) allows you to save electricity.

Any freezer will sweat around the doors in hot, humid weather.

This sweating is a lot like a glass of ice water in hot weather when humidity condenses on the glass.

A special *heater strip* between the doors minimizes this normal sweating during hot, humid weather.

Two Ways to Save Electricity.   *First*, the special heater strip only operates when the compressor is running.

Second, the energy saver control has three settings, so you can match the refrigerator to the humidity conditions in your house. You set the energy saver to determine the savings.

Extra High for periods of high humidity.

High reduces the electricity used by the heater strip. Should be used for modest humidity conditions.

Low shuts the special heater strip off for periods of low humidity, cold weather, or if your house is air conditioned.

The correct use of the energy saver control allows savings in the amount of electricity you will use.

The refrigerator is designed to allow a minimum amount of condensation during periods of high humidity. However, when climatic conditions exceed the design criteria, additional amounts of condensation will form on the cabinet sides, door, and other places. This is a normal condition and will disappear when climatic conditions return to normal.

HOW TO DEFROST THE FREEZER COMPARTMENT

The amount of frost in the freezer depends on the door openings, humidity, and frequency with which you freeze ice cubes. When the frost has built up to approximately ¼-inch in some parts of the freezer compartment, it should be defrosted.

For easy defrosting proceed as follows:

1. Turn unit off and unplug service cord before cleaning to avoid shock.

2. Remove food and ice cube trays from freezer.

3. Be sure to protect food during the time of defrosting. Store frozen foods so they will not thaw during the short period of time you are defrosting freezer compartment.

4. Remove drain plug from bottom of freezer liner (Fig. 21).

5. To speed up defrosting, use pans of warm water on the freezer bottom or a fan blowing air into the freezer section.

6. Remove loose frost and ice as it melts. *Do not* use sharp or pointed instruments as scrapers. You might damage the evaporator.

7. When all ice and frost has been removed, wipe shelves dry with cloth or sponge.

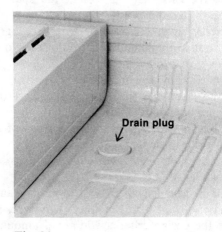

Drain plug

Fig. 21.

8. Mop up any water that may have accumulated in the bottom of the freezer. The freezer liner (Fig. 22) will allow water to drain into condensate pan located behind the grill (Fig. 22). The condensate pan will not normally hold all the water from defrosting at one time, and should be emptied several times.

9. Clean freezer drain, if necessary, using a bottle brush for cleaning. Replace drain plug.

10. Plug in service cord and turn unit on to previous setting. Close door and let freezer become chilled before replacing food packages.

DEFROSTING THE REFRIGERATOR

The refrigerator section has a *defrost cycle.* That means the refrigerator will automatically defrost itself. Whenever you defrost

Fig. 22.

the freezer, the roll-bond evaporator located at the back of the refrigerator compartment will also defrost. You will find that very little moisture collects on these coils. However, what does collect will melt and run down into the special drip tray located behind the roll-bond evaporator.

HOW TO CLEAN REFRIGERATOR-FREEZER

For your safety, unplug the service cord before cleaning to avoid any possibility of an electrical shock. (*See* Fig. 23). *Also see* section on How to Prepare your Refrigerator for Use, previously described in this chapter.

Wash the refrigerator-freezer liner, the door liners, crispers, meat tray, and *shelf*, plus *crisper pans*, with warm water and baking soda solution (about a tablespoon of soda per quart of water). This will clean and sweeten these parts. Rinse and dry thoroughly.

Do not use liquid detergent, abrasive cleaners, solvents, or polish cleaners on these parts. To do so will deteriorate them and make them susceptible to cracking, discoloring, and so on.

Do not put any of these parts in your dishwasher. To do so will cause them to warp.

Exterior. Wash with soapy water, and rinse.

Condensate pan. Remove grill and pull out condensate pan from

Fig. 23.

beneath cabinet. Empty and wash with warm sudsy water to prevent odors. Replace before replacing grill.

Door gaskets. For maximum life, the door gaskets and cabinet flanges should be washed at least twice a year with mild soap and warm water; then, rinsed and dried. A light film of petroleum jelly or vaseline must then be applied to the door gaskets.

Power cord. After cleaning, reconnect power cord to put unit back in service.

Vacation time. Empty the refrigerator compartment of all perishable items. *Do not* change the setting of the refrigerator-freezer control. (*See* the following sections on Extended Periods of Non-Use, and When You Move.)

Extended periods of non-use. If you are to be away for a long period, you will want to empty the unit. This will reduce needless energy consumption and also assure that if electrical service is interrupted or a malfunction occurs, food will not spoil. Just clean the unit as described previously in the section on How to Clean

Refrigerator-Freezer, and then place a pad or block between the doors and the frame so that air can circulate. Leave the unit unplugged.

When you move. Unplug the unit. Clean the refrigerator and freezer completely. Use strapping tape or masking tape to securely tie all the trays, shelves, and the like so they do not slide or fall. (*See* section on How To Prepare Your Refrigerator For Use, previously described in this chapter; *also see* illustrations on unpacking.)

Caution: Be sure you do not use some of the tape that has *permanent*-type adhesive.

SOUNDS YOU MAY HEAR

You may be replacing a smaller refrigerator with a larger one; therefore, it might be possible that the floor and/or wall may act as a sounding board, and you may hear the compressor during its running cycle. None of these sounds are unusual, and will soon become familiar and go unnoticed.

SERVICE PROBLEMS

Before calling your serviceman, check the following things:

1. Does the light work? (A dim light indicates low voltage or a weak bulb.)
2. Is the cord plugged in?
3. Is a fuse blown?
4. Has the freezer control been accidently turned off?

If the refrigerator section is too warm, check temperature with a good quality thermometer emersed in water.

1. Adjust the refrigerator-freezer control. (*See* section on Checking Temperature, previously described.)
2. Has the door been open a long time?
3. Have you recently added a large load of food?
4. Are any shelves covered with foil or plastic, preventing proper air flow?

If the freezer section is too warm, check temperature with a good quality thermometer.

1. Adjust control in the refrigerator section. (*See* above section on Refrigerator-Freezer Control.)
2. Has either door been open a long time?
3. Have you recently added a large load of fresh food?

If unit still will not operate, proceed as follows:

1. Unplug unit.
2. Take the steps necessary to preserve the food stored in the unit. Take frozen foods to neighbors and/or locker. Dry ice may be placed in the freezer section of the unit to preserve the food until the unit can be serviced.
3. Doors should be left closed as much as possible until unit has been placed back into service.
4. Call your dealer or service agency.

HOW TO PREPARE YOUR REFRIGERATOR FOR USE (WITH FREEZER ON THE BOTTOM)

As part of your purchase you may have agreed to install your refrigerator yourself.

EXTERIOR

Remove protective packing and report any transportation damage to the dealer or delivery company at once.

1. If the base skid is still attached, tip the refrigerator over, place a supporting block under the back of the unit, and remove the mounting bolts (Fig. 24). Bolts are $5/16$-inch. Repeat on opposite side.
2. Save some of the heavy-duty tape that you have removed and make a pad, adhesive side out, and touch it to any tape residue remaining on the unit (Fig. 25). This should lift it off, and eliminate the need for using solvent of any kind.

Fig. 24.

Fig. 25.

INTERIOR

Remove protective packing (Fig. 26). The special cardboard shipping braces that prevented damage in shipment have to be removed and discarded.

Fig. 26.

Adjustable Cantilevered Shelves. This unit features removable cantilevered shelves that are shipped in place and are held in by red plastic *hairpins*. Remove all of them by exerting finger pressure against the bowed portion while pulling toward yourself (Fig. 27).

Meat Keeper. You will need to remove all padding between the lid and the shelf (Fig. 28).

To remove meat keeper, first remove the meat pan. This is accomplished by sliding the meat pan out until it comes into contact with the stop that has been built into the meat pan top. Next, reach

Fig. 27.

Fig. 28.

into the pan and push up on the meat pan top while at the same time sliding the pan over the built-in stop. Then depress plastic stopper clips (Fig. 28) and slide the outer shell of the meat keeper out of the metal holder. The meat keeper can be disassembled further by slipping the top out of the grooves that hold it to the outer jacket. To reassemble, reverse the procedure.

Crispers.   There is packing material under and around the crisper pans that must be removed. Remove the tape as shown in Fig. 29, then lift up on pan and cover, and carefully remove from unit. Complete the unpacking, then replace. The pans have stops similar to the meat pan. Follow instructions previously given for meat pans to remove them.

Door Retainer Bars.   Remove all tape from retainer bars (Fig. 30) on the doors. Again, use the tape to remove any residue.

Cleaning.   Follow the cleaning instructions later in this chapter, or on the cleaning label attached to the unit.

Fig. 29.

Fig. 30.

FINAL PLACEMENT OF REFRIGERATOR ON SOLID FLOOR

Your refrigerator must be installed on a floor strong enough to support the combined weight of the food and the unit in order to insure proper operation and a good door seal.

If the spot selected is next to a wall, be sure that you allow a 1¾-inch space along the side so the door can be opened 90 degrees.

Leveling is important to the operation of an automatic icemaker. The correct amount of water is metered for each fill. If unit is leveled improperly, the ice cubes will not be of uniform size. In an extreme case, water could overflow.

How to remove grill at bottom of the unit. Pull straight forward from the unit to release the grill clips. *To replace,* reverse the procedure.

Level unit. The unit should be leveled. It is provided with leveling rollers (Fig. 31) located behind the grill at the bottom of the unit. If the floor is not level from side to side, it may be necessary to shim under one of the feet at the rear. Each front roller is independently adjustable. Use an adjustable wrench to move the rollers up or down. Adjust until the unit tilts slightly from front to back. This allows the doors to close firmly and helps prevent rebounding.

Fig. 31.

Brake. Your roller-equipped unit must be braked to prevent the unit from rolling forward. Adjust the wing nut, centrally located behind the front grill, until the brake is snug to the floor (Fig. 32).

Fig. 32.

Do not overtighten. *Note:* Whenever the unit is to be moved, first release the brake. It must be readjusted when the unit is back in place.

AUTOMATIC COLD CONTROLS

Set one control independent of the other. If at all possible, it is a good idea to pre-chill a new refrigeration product before loading it with a large quantity of room temperature food. This can reduce the need for excessive running time when the unit is first put into use.

Freezer Control. The *freezer control* is the master control. If it is turned off, the unit will not operate. The control has seven settings. Number 1 is the warmest; number 7 is the coldest.

It is recommended to set the control at number 4 when the unit is installed. It will take about 2 to 3 hours to cool the freezer compartment.

For the best frozen food storage, the temperature should be in the 0° F. to 2° F. range. If it is above the 0° F. to 2° F. range, turn the dial to a colder setting number (5, 6, or 7). If the thermometer reads below the 0° F. to 2° F. range, the unit is set too cold, and power is being wasted. Turn to a warmer setting number (3, 2, or 1). It is suggested that the adjustment up or down should be done one number at a time with a new temperature reading taken before further adjustment is made.

Refrigerator Control. The *refrigerator control* is designed to detect a slight rise or lowering of temperature in the refrigerator. That means that the setting you select will be maintained as the control automatically opens and closes to maintain your setting.

The control is numbered from 1 to 7. Number 1 is the warmest, and number 7 is the coldest setting. We recommend a setting of number 4.

Checking the temperature. (*See* section With Freezer On The Top.)

Thermometer. Place the thermometer in the center of the *freezer*, surrounded by frozen packages. The reason for this is that air temperature in the freezer may show a definite, brief warming during the defrost cycle. This is of very short duration, and does not harm the food, but can mislead you into believing your unit is malfunctioning when it is not. Check the reading after 15 minutes or longer. For best storage, the temperature should be in the 0° F. to 2° F. range. Adjust the control as needed.

Place the thermometer in a glass of water, and place in the *refrigerator* on the middle of the center shelf. Be sure that air can flow around it. Leave the door closed for a minimum of 15 minutes before reading. For best storage, the temperature should be in the 38° F. to 40° F. range. Adjust the control as needed.

Condensate drain pan is located underneath the cabinet (Fig. 33). Before replacing grill, make sure that it is in place. Remove grill and clean pan above every three months.

Energy saver control and *refrigerated meat keeper control.* (*See* section With Freezer On The Top.)

Fig. 33.

STORAGE OF FOOD

The following suggestions will help you fully utilize the top front preservation design and features in your unit. Features will vary by model, but for this discussion, we are illustrating a model that has all the features. (*See* Fig. 34.)

Freezer Storage. If you purchase the *add-on icemaker*, the ice tunnel holding the ice-cube trays has to be removed. (*See* section How to Operate Automatic Icemaker, described later in this chapter.)

The freezer shelf is not adjustable. *Note:* The solid bottom shelf above the glide-out basket must be in position at all times to assure proper air circulation throughout the freezer.

Fast-freeze shelf and ice tunnel. This unit is equipped with a fast-freeze shelf and ice tunnel containing two ice-cube trays. All foods you prepare for home freezing should be placed on that shelf for the quickest possible freezing. It is designed so that super cold air is blown around the packages placed on it. Inside is a *tunnel* where extremely cold air is blown across the ice-cube trays.

If you purchase the add-on icemaker, the shelf has to be removed.

Refrigerator Control

Meat Storage Control

Fresh Meat Keeper

Adjustable Cantilevered Shelves

Freezer Control

Glide-out Basket

Butter Keeper

Egg Storage

Crisper Pans

Tall Bottle Storage

Ice Storage Bin

Juice Can Storage

Stor-Mor® Door Storage

Fig. 34.

(*See* section, How To Operate Automatic Ice Maker, later in this chapter.)

Packaged frozen foods. Frozen foods from the supermarket should be placed in the freezer as soon as possible. To quickly return them to 0° F. to 2° F. storage, it is recommended that you place them on the fast freeze shelf for several hours before organizing them elsewhere in the freezer. If the wrapping material has been damaged, you should replace it with a moisture- and vapor-proof freezer wrap.

Fresh frozen foods. (*See* section, With Freezer On The Top, previously described.)

Door storage. (*See* section, With Freezer On The Top, previously described.)

How Long to Store Frozen Food. (*See* Frozen Food Storage Chart.)

Refrigerator Storage.   You will want to know about the special features that allow optimum storage of different types of foods in your refrigerator. Features will vary by size and capacity.

Adjustable cantilevered shelves. Three shelves hook into the hidden track at the back of the unit. Thus, there are no posts or mechanisms needed to support the front. This allows you to design storage to suit your needs. To remove for repositioning, use both hands to lift up on the shelf and pull toward yourself. Reverse procedure to reposition. The cantilevered shelf holding the refrigerated meat keeper cannot be repositioned without disconnecting the keeper and rendering it inoperative.

Fresh meat. The refrigerated meat keeper is designed to keep meat fresh longer. It is a refrigerator within a *refrigerator*. The meat pan fits inside its own *outer case*. On the back of the outer case is an air inlet and outlet. At the back of the refrigerator liner is a tube. This tube provides the air circulating between the meat pan and the outer case. The meat keeper must be kept in this position for proper operation. It allows you to store fresh meat in temperatures up to 8° F. colder than the refrigerator. This temperature may allow ice crystals to form. Real freezing will take place if you have set the control quite low. Meats to be stored include beef, veal, pork, lamb, hamburger, and a variety of meats such as liver, heart, and tongue. For long periods it is best to freeze the meat.

Fresh fish and seafood. Fresh fish and seafood should not be stored, but eaten the same day. Foods of this type may be stored in the freezer, if properly wrapped.

Pre-packaged meats. Pre-packaged fresh meat may be stored in original wrapping if eaten in 1 or 2 days. Otherwise, the wrapper should be loosened at both ends.

Meat wrapped by the butcher should be removed from the market wrappings and stored unwrapped or loosely wrapped in wax paper or foil.

Vegetable storage. Two crisper pans for storage of fruits and vegetables is featured on this unit. Leafy vegetables and other greens should be washed before storing. Drain excess water only. Then, if you anticipate keeping them over 6 or 7 days, wrap with plastic wrap. *Before* storing fresh fruit and vegetables, remove wrapping, trim off damaged parts, wash in cold water, and drain. Salad greens should be moistened slightly before being restored.

Foods stored on shelves. Air circulation is important in a modern refrigerator that features a true freezer. As you know, cold air is very dry. Because it is being stirred by fans, foods stored on the open shelves should be covered with plastic wrap or placed in covered containers to prevent drying. This also prevents mixing of odors or flavors.

Door. Foods stored in the doors include butter in the butter compartment. For your convenience, there is a sturdy melamine butter dish that can be taken to the table. It is dishwasher safe.

Egg storage. Take-to-counter egg tray is included in the door storage system.

Tall bottles, milk, and condiments. (*See* section, With Freezer On Top, previously described.)

HOW TO OPERATE THE AUTOMATIC ICEMAKER

The *icemaker* (Fig. 35) automatically fills and empties itself. The correct amount of water is metered by a solenoid valve. The amount of ice manufactured is sensed by a wire arm that measures the growing pile of ice. Eventually, the arm is pushed high enough to turn the icemaker off.

Fig. 35.

We suggest you discard the first several harvests of ice so any impurities flushed through the lines of the mechanism will not be consumed.

To remove the bin, you must manually lift the arm to an upright position. *Note:* As long as the arm is in this Off position, no ice will be manufactured. Always return the arm to the operating position.

Cold, dry air has to circulate in the freezer to maintain safe, zero-degree freezing temperatures. Thus, cubes stored open in the bin over several weeks will tend to evaporate.

The unit must be level to insure proper operation and manufacture of ice of even size.

Party quantities. When planning for a party, you will want to make a quantity of cubes ahead. Merely dump the full bin into a plastic bag and store in the freezer. Replace bin, lower arm, and the icemaker will resume full production. Do this several days in advance.

Ice can absorb food odors, so be sure to keep foods covered in both the refrigerator and the freezer.

SOUNDS YOU MAY HEAR

Your new refrigerator may be replacing a smaller one. Now you have two appliances in one: a true freezer, plus a refrigerator. The Free-O'-Frost feature is made possible by moving cold air fans, so you may hear those fans running. It's possible that the floor and/or wall may act as a sounding board, and you may hear the compressor during its running cycle.

You may also hear new sounds such as the icemaker filling with water or the ice cubes falling out of the automatic icemaker during a harvest cycle.

Also, there may be sounds heard during the defrost cycle.

None of these sounds are unusual, and will soon become familiar and go unnoticed.

HOW TO CLEAN THE REFRIGERATOR AND FREEZER SECTIONS

For your safety, unplug the service cord before cleaning to avoid any possibility of an electrical shock.

Remove all food and special compartments from the refrigerator and freezer sections. (*See* instructions in the section How To Prepare Your Refrigerator For Use (With Freezer On The Bottom).

CALLING SERVICEMAN

See checklist in same section With Freezer On The Top.

FROZEN FOOD STORAGE CHART

Those times shown are approximate. It is better to store foods for shorter periods and replenish more often as needed. (*See* Chart 3.)

SIDE-BY-SIDE REFRIGERATOR-FREEZER

As part of your purchase, you may have agreed to install your new refrigerator yourself.

How to Prepare Your Refrigerator for Use.   *See* Interior and Exterior sections With Freezer On The Bottom.

Wall-to-wall shelves. The freezer shelves, and the refrigerator section on some units, are wall-to-wall. They are secured with tape (Fig. 36). Remove any tape residue. Make a pad from the removed tape and touch the adhesive surface to any tape residue on cabinet or shelf.

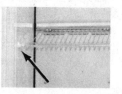

Fig. 36.

Final Placement of Refrigerator Should Be on Solid Floor.   *See* sections With Freezer On The Bottom.

Automatic Cold Controls.   *See* sections With Freezer On The Bottom.

Energy Saver.   *See* sections With Freezer On The Bottom.

Refrigerated Meet Keep Control.   *See* sections With Freezer On The Bottom.

High-Humidity Compartment Control.   *See* sections With Freezer On The Bottom.

HOW TO STORE FOOD IN
SIDE-BY-SIDE REFRIGERATOR-FREEZER

Freezer Storage.   Features will vary by model, but for this discussion, we are illustrating a model that has all the features (Fig. 37).

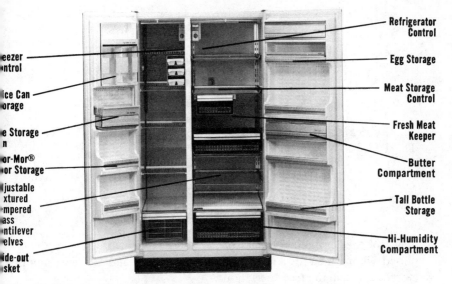

eezer
ntrol

Ice Can
orage

e Storage
n

or-Mor®
or Storage

justable
xtured
mpered
ass
ntilever
elves

de-out
sket

Refrigerator
Control

Egg Storage

Meat Storage
Control

Fresh Meat
Keeper

Butter
Compartment

Tall Bottle
Storage

Hi-Humidity
Compartment

Fig. 37. Side-by-side refrigerator-freezer.

Units have shelves that allow you to convert storage space to suit your needs of the moment. They are easily removed and replaced.

(*See* sections With Freezer On The Bottom for other suggestions.)

Refrigerator Storage. Features will vary by size and capacity of the refrigerator-freezer.

Wall-to-wall shelves. Some models are equipped with this traditional shelving style.

(*See* sections With Freezer On The Bottom for other suggestions.)

Frozen Food Storage Chart. *See* Chart 3.

HOW TO OPERATE YOUR AUTOMATIC ICEMAKER

See this section in Refrigerator-Freezer (With Freezer On The Bottom.

SOUNDS YOU MAY HEAR

See section With Freezer On The Bottom.

CLEANING

See section With Freezer On The Top.

CALLING SERVICEMAN

See checklist in section on Refrigerator-Freezers (With Freezer On The Top).

THREE-DOOR ICE-AND-WATER AUTOMATIC REFRIGERATOR

All of the icemaking and dispensing mechanisms are sensibly enclosed within their own compartment for safety and for maximum storage space in the freezer sections.

Whenever the top freezer door is opened, the electrical circuit to the icemaker and ice dispenser mechanism is interrupted. This prevents the dispensing of ice and also insures that you can service the ice bucket with complete safety. Also, the evaporator fan is turned off when the door is opened. This prevents the needless loss of cold air from the freezer when the door is opened.

The unit is completely pre-wired and plumbed at the factory. All you have to do is connect it to your household cold water supply. Water pressure rating must be 20 to 120 pounds per square inch (psi) to ensure proper operation of unit. Check all water connections to be sure there are no leaks.

Soda Fountain Convenience.   Separate dispenser bars control the release of ice cubes and cold water. They are located in a recessed alcove for safety and convenience. The dispenser bars are sculptured to fit the contours of an ordinary drinking glass. Lightly depress the appropriate dispenser bar to activate the dispensing mechanism.

The sides, top, and bottom of the recessed dispensing area are made of stainless steel. Care for it as you would any other fine stainless-steel surface. At the bottom, beneath the removable grill, is a small, heated sump to catch and evaporate small spills.

Note: There is no drain in the sump so water should not purposely be poured into it.

Control Panel Light with Switch. The dispensing areas can be illuminated at the touch of the switch. It provides *night light* convenience, if you desire. It uses a 120-volt, 6-watt bulb.

How the Dispenser Works. Behind the ice-and-water dispenser cavity is a special icemaking and storage compartment. It houses the automatic icemaker, ice storage bin, and the ice auger.

Dispensing ice. Apply pressure against the dispenser bar with a glass or other container. This activates the ice auger and ice wheel, which automatically delivers ice to the glass. *Release pressure on dispenser bar* before glass is full. *Do not* remove the glass until the last of the cubes fall.

Overload. If you hold the dispenser bar in the On position for approximately 4 to 5 minutes, the dispenser motor may trip out on overload. This could occur if you were trying to fill a large container with the ice. The overload will reset automatically in approximately three minutes, after which time ice can again be dispensed.

Care of Icemaker and Dispenser. Certain conditions will require you to service the icemaker and dispenser. These include cleaning, preparing for vacations, moving, and the like. The unit has been designed so that you can do such servicing with a minimum of effort.

First, remove all stored foods from the top and bottom shelves of the top freezer. If you have room, store them temporarily in the bottom freezer. Otherwise, place them in a cardboard container and cover with several sheets of newspaper or towels to reduce thawing to a minimum. Remove both shelves.

Icemaker Control Arm. The *wire control arm* on the automatic ice maker has three functions.

1. *Normal operation.* When the wire arm is in the down position, ice will be made. (*See* Fig. 38.)

2. *To stop ice production.* Take hold of wire arm near black housing, and lift up. There will be an audible *click* when the icemaker shuts off. The wire arm stays in the upper position (Fig. 39). As long as the arm is in this position, ice will not be made. The unit will continue to dispense cubes from the ice bin until all have been used.

3. *To remove ice bin.* The right end of the wire control arm must be inserted in the square plastic receptacle that receives water from water tube (Fig. 40). *Note:* The wire control arm *must be re-*

Fig. 38.

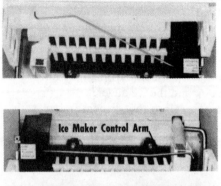

Fig. 39.

Fig. 40.

turned to its normal position after bin has been reinstalled. If not, the icemaker will continue to make cubes and possibly overfill the bin.

Pull forward on the master control lever until it slips into the *front* slot. This disengages the drive coupling to the auger. *Note:* As long as the master control is in the forward (Off) position, no ice will be manufactured or dispensed. With the master control in the Off position and the wire arm inserted in the receptacle, the entire ice storage bin can be lifted up and removed (Fig. 41).

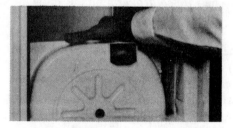

Fig. 41.

When to Remove the Bin and Empty the Contents.

1. Remove after the first few harvests of ice have been made by a newly installed unit. This will allow any impurities in the line to be thrown out, rather than being ingested.

2. If you are going to be gone for longer than a week you will want to empty the storage bin of all ice cubes and place the master control in the Off position. This will prevent the cubes from freezing into a mass around the ice auger.

3. Remove if the usage of ice becomes quite light and the ice cubes become frozen to each other and around the ice auger.

4. If you have an extended power outage (one-half hour or more), and after unit comes on and starts cooling, check to see if cubes have frozen to each other or around the auger.

Selecting Sizes of Cubes. The icemaker is equipped with a *variable size control lever* (Fig. 42).

Fig. 42. Control lever.

It lets you adjust the icemaker to provide two sizes of cubes, large or small. The unit is shipped with the control in the *larger* cube position. If you want to improve your ice-dispensing rate or desire the smaller cube size, push the control lever down to the *smaller* cube position.

Do not try to speed ice dispensing by adding cubes or ice that you may have purchased or made in some other way. The unit has been *matched* to the automatic icemaker and will not operate properly with different shaped or sized ice cubes.

Normal Operation. After installation, it will take 4 to 12 hours before the first harvest of ice will occur. Time will depend upon the amount of food that is placed in the refrigerator and freezer sections.

The ice storage bin takes about 3 or 4 days to fill, depending on how much you use it. And at first, your family will be using it quite frequently. To overcome this demand, you can speed ice production by turning the freezer control to a colder setting. For best overall operation of the unit, *be sure* to return freezer control to its normal position as soon as possible.

As previously mentioned, if you use very little ice over a period of a week or so—or if you use none at all for that period—the ice cubes may freeze into a solid mass and the unit will not dispense ice. You must then remove the ice bin (as previously described), and thaw and throw away the ice.

Under no circumstances should you use an ice pick or similar sharp instrument to break the ice. To do so could cause damage to the ice bin and/or ice auger.

Cold Water Dispenser.   To operate, press glass against cold water dispenser bar. Releasing pressure shuts off the water.

The water tank is located in the refrigerator behind the high-humidity compartment (Fig. 43). The water line to the dispenser bar is routed to prevent freeze-ups. An eight-ounce glass of cold water is dispensed in approximately six seconds.

Fig. 43. Cold water dispenser.

After the unit is connected to the household cold water pipes, it is advisable to fill and throw out the first seven glasses of water. This will cleanse the lines of impurities.

It will be approximately 24 hours after installation before the water in the tank is fully chilled. Thereafter, recovery for a completely fresh tank of water will be about 2½ to 3 hours, depending upon the temperature of the fresh water.

If you move to a new home during the winter, you should drain the dome tank before the unit is packed to prevent freezing and eventual rupturing of the tank.

To drain tank (*see* Fig. 44) proceed as follows:

1. Unplug refrigerator from household electrical supply.
2. Disconnect refrigerator from household water supply.
3. Place a large pan—with at least a 55-ounce capacity—at the rear of the unit, next to the water solenoid valve.
4. Disconnect dome water inlet line at the water solenoid valve

Fig. 44.

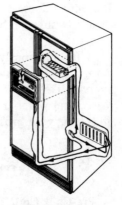

Fig. 45.

(Fig. 45). *Caution:* As you are removing the water line coupling, some water spillage is possible.

5. Place dome water inlet line in pan to catch drainage.

6. When drainage has stopped, reconnect dome water inlet line to water solenoid valve. Some water will remain in the dome, but not in sufficient amount to damage tank if freezing should occur.

Water Taste and Odor. There are many variables that can affect the taste and odor properties of the water that is being dispensed from the Ice and Water model. The following are several examples.

1. Iron and other mineral deposits normally found in water.

2. Type of tubing (copper, galvanized, plastic, and so on) used in the household water supply system as well as the type of tubing used to connect your unit to your household water supply.

3. Is the water fresh or has it been left standing unused in the dome storage tank and/or water supply line for any length of time?

To minimize taste and odor problems, it is recommended that the following steps be taken.

1. Connect your unit to the cold water line supplying water to the kitchen faucet.

2. Thoroughly rinse out the system after it has been connected to the household water supply. This can be accomplished by throwing away the first 10 to 14 eight-ounce glasses of water that are obtained from the unit.

3. If the water dispensing system is not used frequently, then

the entire dome tank and system should be flushed out. This will ensure fresh water being available in the dome tank at all times.

If the previously described suggestions do not entirely eliminate an undesirable taste or odor condition in your water, your problem is most likely a water problem. It is recommended that you contact your local water treatment company for its specialized kind of help in solving your problem.

AUTOMATIC COLD CONTROLS

Pre-Chill Unit.   If at all possible, it is a good idea to pre-chill a new refrigerator product before loading it with a large quantity of food at room temperature. Pre-chilling of the unit and pre-freezing of the food to be stored in a freezer eliminates the need for excessive running time when the unit is first put to use.

See Automatic Cold Controls in Refrigerator-Freezer (With Freezer On The Bottom) section.

Saving Energy.   *See* this section in Refrigerator-Freezer (With Freezer On The Top).

STORAGE OF FOOD

The following are suggestions to help you fully utilize top food preservation design and features for the model illustrated in Fig. 46.

Freezer Storage.   Units have a shelf system that allows you to convert storage space to suit your needs of the moment. The wire shelves are easily removed and replaced. The solid shelf above the ice storage bin, and the one above the glide-out basket, must always be in place.

See section on Refrigerator-Freezer (With Freezer On The Bottom) for the other features.

Refrigerator Storage.   *See* section on Refrigerator-Freezer (With Freezer On The Bottom) for the various features.

Frozen Food Storage Chart.   Times shown are approximate. It is better to store foods for shorter periods and replenish more often as needed. (*See* Chart 3.)

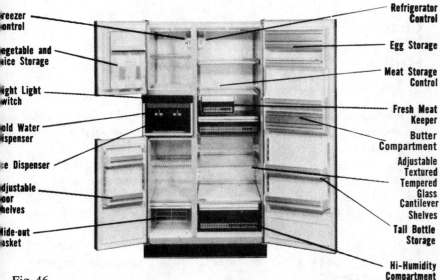

Freezer Control

Vegetable and Ice Storage

Night Light Switch

Cold Water Dispenser

Ice Dispenser

Adjustable Door Shelves

Slide-out Basket

Refrigerator Control

Egg Storage

Meat Storage Control

Fresh Meat Keeper

Butter Compartment

Adjustable Textured Tempered Glass Cantilever Shelves

Tall Bottle Storage

Hi-Humidity Compartment

Fig. 46.

Sounds You May Hear. *See* Refrigerator-Freezer (With Freezer On The Bottom) section.

Cleaning. For your safety, unplug the service cord before cleaning to avoid the possibility of an electrical shock.

See Refrigerator-Freezer (With Freezer On The Top) section to remove all food and special compartments; *also see* section for Cleaning.

Icemaker mold. If your local water supply has a high mineral content, the icemaker mold may require cleaning. Contact your local water treatment dealer.

Calling Serviceman. *See* Refrigerator-Freezer (With Freezer On The Top) section for checklist.

Chapter 35

Home Freezers

In selecting a freezer, one of the first things to think about is how the freezer will fit into the family's plan—that is, whether it will provide the amount of freezing and storage space needed.

The buyer will do well to choose a freezer made by a company likely to continue in the home freezer business. Otherwise he or she may find himself or herself with an "orphan" freezer that will be hard to keep in repair because of difficulty in getting replacement parts.

The dealer's ability to comply with any warranty or guarantee and to give prompt service is also a factor in deciding on the make of freezer to buy.

If several models are equally suited to the family's needs and if provisions for service are equally satisfactory, then design and construction features, operating characteristics, and convenience-in-use features will be the basis of choice.

CABINET DESIGN

The freezer cabinet, in which food is stored, consists of outer walls (a shell) and inner walls (liners), separated by insulation. The interior may be a single compartment or, in large freezers, the space may be divided into several compartments. Arrangements differ in different models. In some freezers a freezing compartment, separate from the storage section, is provided.

Chest and Upright Freezers. In general design, home freezers fall into two classes—chest and upright. The *chest freezer* (Fig. 1) is low, with a top opening; the *upright freezer* (Fig. 2.) is higher and opens at the front. If equally well built, the two types will operate equally well. The choice depends chiefly on the family's preference.

646

Fig. 1. Chest or deepfreeze freezer.

Fig. 2. Upright freezer.

Space requirements. An *upright freezer* occupies less floor space than a *horizontal* one of the same capacity, but additional space must be allowed for the doors to swing open. *Chest freezers,* generally counter height, provide work space—often an advantage in a kitchen or utility room.

Cost. An upright freezer usually costs a little more than a chest model. For equally effective operation, more costly construction is required in the upright type.

Efficiency. A freezer that opens at the top has a natural advantage in maintaining low temperatures. When its lid is lifted there is very little exchange of cold, dry, freezer air with warm, moist, outside air, since cold air is heavier than warm. With an upright freezer, cold air tends to spill out when the door is opened and warm air comes in to take its place. Also, in an upright freezer, the heavier hinges and supports required for the front-opening door conduct more heat to the inside of the freezer.

Convenience. Whether one type of freezer is more convenient than the other is largely a matter of personal opinion. A carryover of ideas gained from using a household refrigerator leads many persons to conclude that food stored in an upright freezer will be more easily accessible. However, problems in using refrigerators and freezers are quite different.

When a freezer is closely packed there can be no reaching over the tops of packages in front to get at those in the rear. To remove inner packages, those in front must be taken out and, if all shelves are full, placed outside the freezer where temperature is relatively high. In top-opening freezers, packages taken out in order to reach the lower layers can be placed on those in another section, even though the section is full, and will not warm up as much.

In a chest freezer, the hardest place to reach is the back part of the bottom. In an upright freezer, the back part of the top and bottom shelves are the least accessible. When a family is considering different models, it is a good idea for the persons who will use the freezer most to try reaching various locations to find out which designs are most convenient for them.

Some upright freezers have drawers instead of shelves so packages at the rear can be readily reached, and some chest freezers are equipped with baskets to make it easier to get at packages at the bottom of the freezer. Although drawers and baskets are convenient, they use space otherwise available for storage—sometimes as much as a cubic foot. Also, baskets, if fully loaded, may be difficult to lift. Irregularly shaped packages create more of a problem in an upright than in a chest freezer. They do not stack well and tend to slide out of an upright freezer when the door is opened. This is especially true if a door is frosted shut and has to be jarred or jerked loose.

Generally speaking, frost collects more rapidly in an upright than in a chest freezer. However, the upright is easier to defrost, especially when the shelves are refrigerated. The frost can be scraped to the front of the freezer where it can be taken out easily. In the chest freezer, frost falls to the bottom of the compartment as it is scraped from walls or dividers and is more difficult to remove. A few chest freezers have drains at the bottom so that water can conveniently be used in defrosting.

Separate Freezing Compartment. A freezer with a separate freezing compartment is a wise choice for the family that plans to freeze food at home.

A freezing compartment is one separated from the rest of the freezer by insulation or by a refrigerated surface. This compartment is designed to be the coldest part of the freezer, so that food will freeze more quickly in it than elsewhere.

Equally important is the fact that the separate freezing compartment protects stored frozen food from excessive temperature changes while other food is being frozen. Temperature rise in stored food is less when the freezing load is kept completely separate than when freezing is done in the compartment in which the food is stored.

CONSTRUCTION

Outer walls of home freezers are generally metal coated with porcelain or synthetic enamel, although a few manufacturers are making them of stainless steel. Enameled cabinets are usually white to match standard kitchen equipment. The base metal is often steel but sometimes aluminum or aluminum alloy. All these materials have proved satisfactory. A point for the buyer to check is whether enameled steel has been treated to resist corrosion in case the coating is scratched through or chipped.

Liners are porcelain enamel, aluminum with a nonoxidized finish, or aluminum alloy. Rounded corners make for ease in cleaning.

Toe space is a convenience in working at a chest-type freezer.

An inside light may be a desirable feature, particularly if the cabinet is in a poorly lighted place.

Insulation.   Adequate insulation is essential to efficient freezer operation. Several kinds of insulating materials are suitable for home freezers.

With any material, the thicker the insulation, the more economically a freezer will operate. However, thicker insulation means either a decrease in food-storage space or an increase in the overall size of the cabinet. In order to provide maximum storage space within the limitations of exterior dimensions that are practical and convenient in a home freezer, most manufacturers use from 3 to 6 inches of insulating material.

If the compressor unit is at the bottom of the freezer, at least as much insulation is needed between it and the food-storage compartment as in other parts of the freezer. Otherwise, heat from the compressor may make the bottom of the compartment too warm for satisfactory storage of frozen food.

In localities where electric rates are relatively high, thickness of insulation may be a major factor in the choice of a freezer. However, other factors, such as efficiency of the mechanism and design of the freezer, also affect operating costs.

Sealing of Outer Shell.   Sealing of the outer shell so that water vapor cannot pass into the insulation is important in freezer construction. The difference in temperature between the outside and inside of a freezer causes a difference in water-vapor pressure, resulting in a force that tends to drive water vapor into the freezer. Under normal conditions of operation this force is equivalent to a 70-mile-an-hour wind; in many cases it is even greater.

If water vapor gets between the freezer walls, it will eventually be deposited as ice and water and will destroy the effectiveness of the insulation. Therefore, the purchaser should ask whether precautions have been taken to vapor-seal the outer shell. The sealing can be done in several ways.

Door and Door Seals.   Home freezer cabinets, whether chest or upright, may have either *flush* or *recessed doors*. The difference in design is shown in Fig. 3. Provided the doors are well-built and tight-fitting, the two types are equally satisfactory.

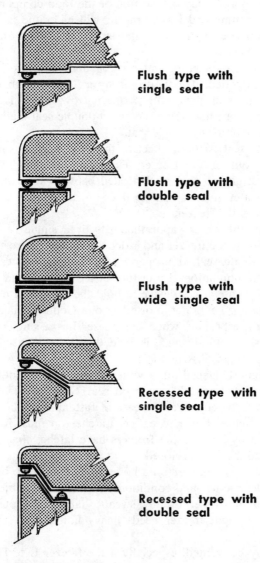

Flush type with single seal

Flush type with double seal

Flush type with wide single seal

Recessed type with single seal

Recessed type with double seal

Fig. 3. Door seals.

Large freezers are often built with multiple doors. An upright freezer sometimes has a single outer door and multiple inner doors. With multiple doors, only one section of the food compartment need be opened at a time and less warm air will enter the freezer. However, the fewer the outer doors, the less heat leakage there will be around them.

To reduce the passage of water vapor and heat into a freezer, a door seal is provided. This is ordinarily a flexible rubber or plastic gasket. A single seal consisting of one narrow gasket is most common, although some manufacturers use a double seal made up of two narrow gaskets, or a wide single seal.

The double seal is more effective than the narrow single seal in keeping heat out of the freezer. However, any water vapor that passes the first gasket may be deposited between the two gaskets in the form of water and may freeze later on; this makes it difficult to open the door of the freezer.

In contrast, the water vapor that gets by a single seal continues into the interior of the freezer and is deposited there as frost.

The wide single seal, if properly constructed, reduces both heat leakage and accumulation of moisture or ice between the surfaces.

Essential for safety is a device to hold the door of a chest freezer open while food is being put in or taken out. Counterbalancing hinges are often used, especially when the freezer has a single door. With multiple doors, the total weight is divided and the danger of a serious accident happening is lessened.

With a counterbalanced lid or with a front-opening door, a tension latch is necessary to produce a good seal. Since the latch must be tightly closed to be effective, the ease of fastening the latch is something for the freezer buyer to notice. Latches on most freezers have to be fastened by hand; some freezers have latches that catch automatically when the door is closed.

Hardware.   *Hardware* on a home freezer needs to be rugged to stand up under the use and conditions to which it is subjected. Since the outside of a freezer usually sweats, hardware should be rust-resistant. An upright freezer needs heavy hinges to keep the door from sagging.

A lock may be wanted, especially if the freezer is to be kept in a garage or on a porch.

REFRIGERATING MECHANISM

In a home freezer, as in a mechanically operated household refrigerator, refrigeration is produced by causing the refrigerant to change from a liquid to a gas and back again to a liquid. As the liquid refrigerant circulates through adjacent coils in the food compartments, under low pressure it boils and changes to a gas, absorbing heat in the process. Then, under increased pressure, the gas changes to a liquid, giving up heat.

The refrigerating mechanism includes compressor, condenser, expansion device, and evaporator. The course of the refrigerant as it circulates and changes from liquid to gas is shown in Fig. 4.

An automatic device that starts and stops the motor as the temperature changes, controls the freezer temperature. Most controls can be set by the user for the desired temperature.

Compressor. The *compressor* is the heart of the refrigerating mechanism—the part that keeps the refrigerant in circulation (Fig. 4). Two kinds of compressor units are in general use in home freezers: the hermetically sealed unit and the open type.

A *hermetically sealed unit* consists of motor and compressor sealed in a gastight compartment. A separate motor is required for operating a condenser fan. The sealed unit is more compact and quieter in operation than the open type. There is no danger of refrigerant leakage. The unit needs no oiling for the lubricant is sealed in. The unit must be returned to the factory for repairs and replaced entirely if it fails.

In the *open-unit*, motor and compressor are connected by a belt. The fan that blows air through the condenser coils is usually attached to the motor shaft. There is a possibility of refrigerant leakage at the compressor shaft seal. The unit requires oiling.

An open unit usually costs a little more than a hermetically sealed unit. In general it will operate more efficiently, although the belt may break and cause temporary failure of the mechanism. Repairs to an open unit can usually be made by a local serviceman.

In either type of unit, the motor should have an overload cut-out switch for protection against excessive current flow.

On freezers of up to 20-cubic-foot capacity, motors of $\frac{1}{8}$ to $\frac{1}{4}$ horsepower are generally used; on 15- to 30-cubic-foot freezers, the motor is usually ¼ to ½ horsepower. This overlapping of size is due to differences in manufacturers' ideas of how a freezer will be used. For maintaining storage temperature only, less power is required than for both storing and freezing food. Therefore, if the manufacturer thinks of his freezer chiefly as a storage cabinet he tends toward the lower powered compressor; if he thinks that a considerable amount of freezing will be done, he uses the higher powered unit.

A compressor unit that will run no more than 50 percent of the time in a temperature of 90° F., when no freezing is being done, will give best all-round mechanical performance. Such a unit will provide enough refrigerating power for maintaining storage temperature in the cabinet, with a sufficient reserve to take care of recommended freezing loads and any abnormal conditions requiring extra refrigeration. The buyer can find out from the manufacturer or dealer what percent of the time the compressor runs.

The buyer will also need to find out about operation of the compressor while food is being frozen. Freezing results are best when the

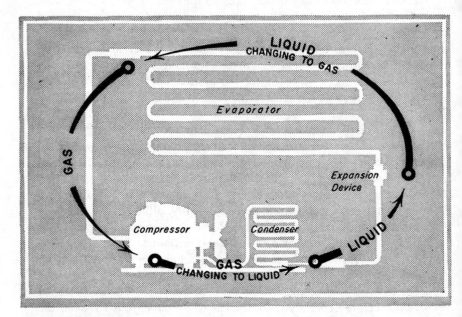

Fig. 4. Refrigeration cycle.

unit runs without stopping during the entire freezing period, so that heat is removed from the food continuously until the freezing load is reduced to storage temperature.

Condenser. The *condenser* is the mechanism in which heat, absorbed by the refrigerant, is removed. It generally consists of coils with heat-dissipating fins and may be of the fan or gravity type. In a fan-cooled condenser, a motor-driven fan forces air through the coils to cool them. A gravity-type condenser is set at an angle so that the natural flow of air can cool the coils. Compressor units with a gravity-type condenser usually cost slightly more to operate than those with a fan-cooled condenser. (*See* Figs. 5 and 6.)

Fig. 5. Open type compressor.

Evaporator. The *evaporator* is made up of coils through which the refrigerant circulates. The coils may be in the form of tubing attached to the liners or they may be stamped into plates that are used as liners, dividers, or shelves.

The area of the evaporator surface is one of the factors that determine how efficiently a freezer will operate. All other factors being equal, the freezer with the largest evaporator surface is the one to

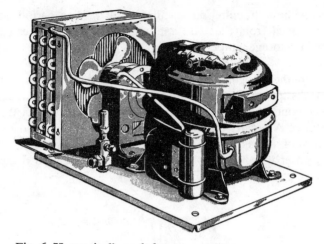

Fig. 6. Hermetically sealed type.

be preferred. A small evaporator must have a much lower temperature than a large one to produce a given freezer air temperature, and requires more extensive compressor operation. Also, the lower the evaporator temperature, the greater the tendency of the food in the freezer to dry out.

Information about relative areas of evaporator surface in different models can be obtained from the dealer or manufacturer. Length of evaporator coils or number and size of stamped plates is an indication of evaporator size.

Attached Coil. The *attached-coil evaporator* consists of metal tubing attached to freezer liners by soldering or brazing, or by clamps. Heat transmission is best when the coils are soldered or brazed to the liners along their entire length, and not so good when the coils are fastened only at intervals by clamps or soldering.

Tubing attached to liners is used most in chest freezers. Upright freezers sometimes have attached coils on three sides and sometimes on the top liner or the bottom of the food compartment.

Stamped Plates. A *stamped evaporator plate* is made of two sheets of metal, one of which is stamped to form coils that carry the refrigerant. The coils may form either a continuous serpentine path or parallel paths running between headers at opposite ends or sides of the plate. In general, the serpentine path gives a better distribution of the refrigerant. (*See* Figs. 7 and 8.)

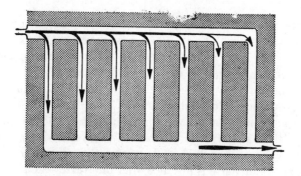

Fig. 7. Parallel refrigerant paths.

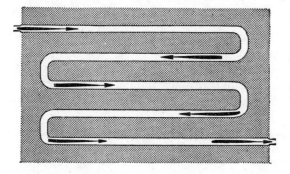

Fig. 8. Serpentine refrigerant path.

The stamped-plate evaporator is somewhat more expensive to construct than the attached-tubing type. It is usually slightly more efficient since the refrigerant path is a part of the liner or divider.

Stamped plates may be used as liners in either chest or upright freezers. In chest freezers, plates may form vertical dividers, extending either from side-to-side or from front-to-back. In upright freezers, stamped plates may be used in horizontal position as shelves; often an additional plate is placed at the top of the freezer.

Advantages of the stamped plate as divider or shelf are that both sides provide refrigerated surfaces and that the plates are readily accessible for repair. A disadvantage is that the necessary piping reduces food-storage space.

When shelves are refrigerated, food in storage is more likely to be affected by temperature changes during the operating cycle than when liners or dividers form the evaporator surfaces, since packages make firmer contact with horizontal than with vertical surfaces.

Freezer Alarms. Even though a freezer owner is careful to check on freezer operation each day, temperature rise can be so rapid in some parts of the freezer that a signal to give warning when something is wrong is a desirable feature.

The alarm should give the warning signal before the warmest package in a partly loaded freezer reaches 15° F.; otherwise, some of the food may reach such a high temperature that it would be unwise to refreeze it. If an alarm is installed after the freezer is purchased, the best place for the sensitive bulb that controls it is against a back liner level with the top layer of packages when the freezer is full.

Other desirable features in an alarm system are as follows:

1. A signal that is audible rather than visible—and loud enough to be readily heard.

2. An alarm that signals either when the circuit is broken or when the temperature rises above normal operating temperature.

3. Connections that interfere as little as possible with gasket seals.

4. Manual means for turning off the signal and for testing the alarm system.

Whether built into the freezer or installed later, the alarm system will need an occasional checking. This can be done by warming the sensitive bulb, either by taking it out or by other means, to see whether it is working.

ELECTRICAL GROUNDING

The freezers shown in Fig. 1 and 2 are equipped with a three-prong grounding plug for your protection against possible shock hazards. Where a two-prong wall receptacle is encountered, it is the personal responsibility and obligation of the customer to contact a qualified electrician and have it replaced with a properly grounded three-prong wall receptacle in accordance with the National Electrical Code (Fig. 9).

Where a two-prong adapter is required temporarily, it is the personal responsibility and obligation of the customer to contact a quali-

Fig. 9. Three-prong plug.

fied electrician and have the adapter properly grounded and polarized.

Do not under any circumstances cut or remove the round grounding prong from the plug. *Do not* remove the tag from the cord. *Do not* use a two-prong adapter in Canada.

Connect the unit to a wall outlet supply delivering a 115-volt, 15-ampere, 60-cycle current, located within five feet of the unit. For maximum security, the electric current supplying the freezer should have a 15-ampere delayed-action fuse, and should not be used for other electrical equipment.

INSTALLATION

The freezer must be installed on a floor sufficiently strong to support the combined weight of the food and the cabinet in order to insure proper operation and a good door seal. When moving the unit, do not lift or push, using the door or handle for leverage.

Leveling Upright Freezer. All upright units (Fig. 2) are equipped with leveling gliders behind the front grill at the bottom of the cabinet. Level unit by adjusting front glider bolts until sides of unit are vertical. If floor is not level from side-to-side, it may be necessary to shim under one of the feet at the rear of the unit. Two or three weeks after your freezer has been loaded with food, recheck level and correct for any setting of floor.

On all upright units, the grill can be removed by pulling straight out from the unit. To replace, reverse procedure.

Leveling Deep-Freeze Food Freezer. Each unit, except the 7 and 9 cubic foot models, is equipped with four leveling screws that must be installed on the bottom of the unit in each corner. They screw into the holes at each corner. Use the leveling feet to raise or lower the unit to help level the unit. On cement, plastic, or rubber tile, or other soft flooring, it is recommended that furniture-type coaster cups be used to protect the floor from the concentrated weight of each of the feet. Two or three weeks after it has been loaded with food, recheck level of unit to correct for any settling of floor.

Condensate drain pan. The upright freezers have a condensate pan. It must be installed before running the unit. The condensate drain pan is located behind the grill at the bottom of the unit.

Free-of Frost models. The condensate pan is used to collect moisture after each defrosting cycle. Normally it is not necessary to empty the pan. We suggest a periodic check and cleaning.

Conventional models. The condensate pan is used as an aid to defrosting the freezer. You will have to empty it frequently during manual defrosting.

Electrical Requirements. Connect the unit to a wall outlet supply delivering 115 volts, 60-cycle current, located within five feet of the unit. For maximum security, the electric circuit supplying the unit should have a 15-ampere delayed-action fuse, and should not be used for other electrical equipment.

If the cord has a plug clamp, it should be installed to prevent accidental unplugging from the electrical outlet.

Freestanding Installation. Both the upright and chest freezers must be installed as a freestanding unit. They have the efficient radiant condenser and there must be ample air circulation around the above units for maximum operating efficiency. Locate away from direct source of heat.

Upright Freezer. Allow three inches of space on both sides of the freezer and six inches above it to allow compressor and condenser cooled air to escape. Spacers on the back of the unit will provide the required 1½ inches of space from the wall.

Chest or Deep-Freeze Food Freezer. To keep your unit the correct distance from the wall two ¾-inch spacers are provided on all models except the 7 and 9 cubic foot models. They must be clipped on the back of the unit at the bottom of the hinge cover. Locate the unit where a maximum of free circulating air is available. Allow three inches between the ends of the unit and the wall, cabinets, or other appliance. Free air circulation is essential to efficient operation. *Be sure the drain plug is installed on those units with a drain.*

CLEANING

Exterior. With proper care the finish on your freezer should remain beautiful for a lifetime. Clean it regularly. Wash only with mild soap or household detergent, using a soft cloth or sponge. *Never* use abrasives, ammonia cleaners, or strong alkalis. A light coat of refrigerator wax will aid in preserving the finish. *Note:* Do not allow wax or a comparable polishing agent to come in contact with plastic parts, trim, or vinyl gaskets.

Door gaskets. The sealing gaskets around the doors or lid may be washed with mild soap or household detergent and lukewarm water. *Never use* wax, polish, or metallic cleaners on these parts.

Interior. *Deep-freeze, food-freezer, food-liner.* To clean the liner, use a solution of two tablespoons of baking soda in a quart of lukewarm water. Avoid use of soap or harsh scouring powder. *Do not* use a sharp instrument or stiff bristle brush—you might damage the finish. *Be sure* you do not damage the moisture barrier sealer around the bottom of the liner.

Upright freezer liner and *shelves* are made from stucco-embossed aluminum and may be cleaned with a cloth or sponge and a solution of lukewarm water with baking soda or mild detergent. *Never* use a cabinet cleaner to polish.

Plastic parts should be washed with mild soap or household detergent and lukewarm water only. *Do not* use hot water, wax, or polish.

WHEN SERVICING BECOMES NECESSARY

If you think an adjustment is needed, check the following list before calling your dealer service department (it may save you time and an unnecessary call).

1. Is the temperature control dial at other than the Off position?
2. Does bulb light when door is open? If not, check to see if (a) the connection between service cord and wall outlet is good, or (b) plug in a table lamp to see if fuse is blown out.
3. Has the door been open for an excessively long period of time?

If none of these conditions exist, call your dealer service department.

OPERATION AND MAINTENANCE—
UPRIGHT FREEZER

Before using unit be sure to reread installation section previously described, and check for the following.

1. Unit is level.
2. Condensate drain pan is in place.
3. Electrical requirements.
4. Storage basket (if unit has one) is in place.

Temperature Control.   The *temperature control* is located on the left side wall of the food liner. A normal setting, such as position 3, 4, or 5, is recommended, whichever gives the desired food temperature. A good quality freezer thermometer that is capable of registering below zero degrees may be used to help in selecting a control setting.

When the unit is installed, turn the control to position 7 for the first 3 or 4 hours of operation. Then, reset the control to a mid-position, such as 3, 4, or 5, for average conditions. If colder temperatures are desired, turn to a higher setting; a lower setting gives warmer temperatures.

Storing Food in the Freezer.   Be sure packages are back far enough in the freezer to allow the door to close completely. If door does not close, this will cause unit to run excessively and allow temperatures to rise in the freezer.

CONVENTIONAL FREEZERS WITH
CONTACT FREEZING

Freezing food. This freezer has fast, efficient, contact freezing. Freezing coils are attached directly to the solid aluminum shelves, plus additional coils on the top and bottom of the liner. It is not necessary to turn the temperature control to a colder setting for fast freezing. Food to be frozen should always be placed directly on the contact freezing shelves. The quantity of food packages in the door should not exceed that on the freezing shelves.

Defrosting conventional freezer. Frost build-up depends on moisture content of air, food temperature, and number of door openings. Normally, removal of frost will be required only at infrequent inter-

vals or when frost interferes with storage. See the following suggestions for defrosting conventional units.

1. Turn unit off and remove food from freezer. Take packages
from door first. Protect food during defrosting.

2. To speed defrosting, set pans of warm water on each shelf,
or direct fan into unit.

3. Remove frost and ice as it melts. *Note:* Do not use a sharp
or pointed instrument as a scraper; you might damage shelves and
freezing coils attached to them.

4. When all ice and frost have been removed, wipe shelves dry.

5. Mop up any water in bottom of freezer liner.

6. There is a drain with a cover on the bottom of the food liner.
It allows water to drain into the defrost drain pan located behind the
grill. The pan will need to be emptied frequently.

7. Clean defrost drain. Remove cover, if necessary. Use a bottle brush for cleaning. Replace cover.

8. Restart freezer on previous setting. Close door, and let
shelves chill before replacing food.

FREE-OF-FROST MODELS

Freezing Food.   Cold air at $-10°$ F. is gently, but firmly moved
into each shelf *compartment*, where it surrounds food in super
cold air. The cold air is discharged from both the top of the shelf
compartment and the bottom. The cold air flows toward the door to
give you zero degree temperatures in the door also. It flows down
the door, under the bottom shelf and back to the freezing coil between the back walls of the freezer (Fig. 10).

Defrosting.   It is never necessary to manually defrost this model.
It is done for you automatically. It keeps food packages and shelves
free from frost accumulation.

Efficient operation of the system is dependent on a free flow of air
around the fan located behind the glide-out basket. It is important
that the basket or trivet be used when foods are stored in this section
of the freezer.

Add-On Icemaker.   The icemaker may be installed at any time
—now or months from now—on certain models. Complete installation instructions are included in every kit.

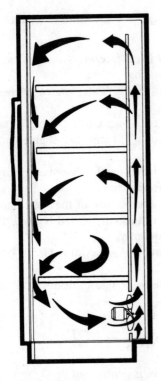

Fig. 10. Flow of cold air.

The icemaker provides crescent-shaped cubes automatically. The ice bin must be in position at all times.

When newly installed, it is suggested that you do not use the first 3 or 4 harvest cycles.

To stop the icemaker, merely lift the wire arm up until a *stop* catches it and holds it in place. This prevents any more ice cubes from being made. To restart, pull lever down.

CHEST FREEZERS

Before using unit be sure to recheck installation section previously described; and recheck installation as follows:

1. Unit is level. (All except 7 and 9 cubic foot models are equipped with levelers.)

2. Drain plug is in place. (All have defrost drains except 7 and 9 cubic foot models.)

3. Air circulation around unit.

4. Electrical requirements.

Food Storage Baskets and Storage Dividers. Food baskets and dividers may be washed with mild soap or household detergent and lukewarm water. Because of the different capacities, some models will have wire food dividers and baskets, and some models will not have dividers or a basket.

Temperature Control. The temperature control is located on the front of the unit in the lower right-hand corner.

Setting Control. The center of the control dial is recessed to allow a coin to be inserted to turn the control. This prevents unauthorized setting or resetting of the control. Set the control on a mid-position, such as 3, 4, or 5, for average conditions. For a colder temperature turn control toward setting 7; for a warmer temperature turn toward setting 1.

Freezing Food. The small compartment in the unit is the fast-freezing compartment. There are fast-freezing coils on the bottom and sides of the compartment. For maximum speed in freezing new foods, place unfrozen foods against any of the sides or on the bottom. There are also freezing coils on the entire bottom of the food liner.

Fast-Freezing Food. Set the control on setting number 7 two or three hours prior to the time food is placed in the freezer. This will insure fast freezing with a minimum of temperature rise of food already stored in the unit.

After foods are frozen, the control should be returned to the previous setting.

When freezing small quantities of unfrozen food it is not necessary to reset the dial to a colder position, just place them in the fast-freezing compartment.

Frost Removal. The frost that builds up in the freezer is the frozen accumulation of moisture removed from the air. In a chest freezer, it is entirely normal for most of the frost to form the upper portion of the food storage compartment.

A number of factors, such as the moisture content of the air, food storage temperature, and number of lid openings, govern the rapidity of the frost build-up.

Defrosting. If frost has been allowed to accumulate sufficiently to develop a glazed or icy condition, it may be necessary to remove all packages from the cabinet in order to defrost the freezer. After the freezer has been disconnected, thawing can be speeded up by means of an electric fan blowing into the cabinet. When all ice and frost are soft and loosened, remove soft frost. Excess water in the bottom of the unit will drain out through the drain hole in the lower left-hand side of the freezer compartment. Remove drain plug from outside of unit on all but 7 and 9 cubic foot models. Use shallow pan to collect water from drain. Empty pan as often as necessary. Wipe off interior with a cloth and mop up any water that remains in bottom and sides of compartments. When finished, *be sure* to replace plug on outside of unit on models equipped with a defrost drain.

Caution: When defrosting the unit, do not use a sharp or pointed instrument or scrape the liner with a stiff bristle brush. You might damage the finish of the food liner or the moisture barrier seal around the bottom of the liner.

Drain Plug. The drain plug must be in place to insure proper operation of the freezer.

Signal Light. On all except 7 and 9 cubic foot models, above the temperature control dial is a red signal light. The light will be on as long as you have power coming from the power source to the unit. When the light goes off it means you have interrupted electrical power. The light *does not* tell you when the compressor is operating.

No Sweat Cabinet. It is normal for all four sides of the cabinet to feel warm to the touch. This is the heat being transferred from the food inside the unit into the air. It is warmest when the compressor motor is running and during the summer.

Before Calling Serviceman. *If the freezer is too warm,* check the temperature with a quality thermometer.

1. Adjust freezer control.
2. Has the door been open a long time?
3. Have you recently added a large load of fresh food?
4. Does the light work? (A dim light indicates low voltage or a weak bulb.)
5. Is the cord plugged in?
6. Is a fuse blown?
7. Has the freezer control been accidentally turned off?

If the light works and the freezer control is on, but the fan and compressor in a Free-of-Frost unit are not operating, the unit is likely to be in the defrost cycle. Wait 30 minutes to see if the unit will restart. If it does not, remove the toe grill at the bottom front of the freezer. The defrost timer is located at the lower right-front corner. Turn the timer knob until your hear a click. The freezer should begin running.

If the unit still will not operate, then proceed as follows:

1. Unplug the unit.
2. Try to preserve the food stored in the unit. Take frozen foods to the neighbors and/or frozen food locker or place dry ice in the freezer until the unit can be serviced.
3. Keep the door closed as much as possible until the unit has been placed back into service.
4. Call your service dealer or service agent.

FOOD-FREEZING GUIDE

For best freezing of newly stored foods, follow the recommendations for your particular type of freezer.

Those times shown in the frozen food storage chart are approximate. It is better to store foods for shorter periods and replenish more often as needed. (*See* Chart 3.)

Freezer Wrapping or Packaging Material. Package or wrapping material must be moisture- and vapor-proof freezer wrap to protect food from absorbing flavors of other foods and to prevent the drying of food. Select only materials that are designed for freezer use and labeled as such by the manufacturer. Ordinary wax paper and butcher paper do not adequately protect food stored in your freezer. And wrapping paper not designed for freezer use may give off an offensive odor and taste. Freezer materials must be strong so there is no danger of breakage or tearing in the freezer. Wrap packages so they are easily labeled for quick identification in the freezer and seal them tightly. When lids are furnished with the packages, follow the directions for best results. Select packages or wrapping that are designed especially for the food you wish to freeze. Also keep in mind the most economical use of your freezer space and choose packages that will stack easily and fit into available space.

Freezing Meat. Meat is one of the most important foods in your freezer. It is vital in maintaining good health, the basis of all menu planning, and the largest single expenditure in the family food budget. In fact, two important reasons for buying a home freezer are the food savings made possible by purchasing meat in quantity and the convenience of a complete variety of meat at your fingertips at all times. All meats may be frozen successfully, so the following considerations will apply to any meats you buy for your freezer. Although freezing tenderizes meat to some extent, it cannot change the quality of the meat, only retain the original goodness. Choose the quality of meat you want to serve. If you are packaging your own meat for the freezer, adjust the packages to your own specifications. Use portions to fit your family's needs.

Refreezing Defrosted Meats. Examine each package carefully to determine how completely the meat is defrosted. If the package still contains some ice crystals, you can freeze it without risk. If the meat is completely thawed, the temperature of the meat is the best guide. If the temperature of the meat is under 50° F., test the meat for odor—if the meat still has a fresh odor, cook it first, then serve immediately or refreeze it. If you refreeze any meat, place the packages in direct contact with the freezing surface of your freezer so that the meat will freeze rapidly.

Freezing Poultry. The following are three ways to prepare poultry for the freezer.

1. Cut the bird in half along the backbone (if not purchased this way) and clean thoroughly. Place the halves together with a double layer of freezer paper between them. Wrap the giblets separately and place between the halves. Package the birds in moisture- and vapor-proof freezer paper or aluminum foil. Wrap well to exclude all the air possible. Package broilers in plastic freezer bags. Force out all of the air and twist the top of the bag into a *gooseneck* and fasten well. Label and date packages and freeze.

2. Cut the bird into frying pieces (if not purchased this way) and clean well. Insert each piece in a fold of freezer paper. Package in a freezer carton lined with freezer paper. Pack a complete fryer in each carton or pack thighs together, then drumsticks, and so on.

Wrap giblets separately and place in either the carton with the other pieces or in a separate carton. Fryers may also be packaged in freezer paper, foil, or freezer bags. Cartons, however, stack better in a freezer. Always label and date your packages.

3. Clean bird thoroughly. Wrap giblets separately and place in the cavity of the bird. Truss the legs and wings tightly to the body for easier wrapping and to save storage space. It is helpful to pad the protruding bony parts with small wads of freezer paper to prevent package punctures. Wrap in either freezer paper or foil, or package in plastic bags. Label and date packages and freeze.

Freezing Fish.   The secret to good frozen fish is absolute freshness. Therefore, prepare and freeze fish quickly; if possible, freeze the fish the same day you catch it. Otherwise, pack it in ice immediately until it can be frozen. Fish is extremely perishable and must never become warm.

Clean the fish and prepare for table use. Leave small fish whole for freezing. Fillet large fish or cut into steaks. Dip lean fish in a salt solution for about a minute to reduce leakage in thawing. (Use ½ cup of salt to one gallon of water for this solution.) Storage qualities of fatty fish can be improved by dipping cut pieces in an ascorbic acid solution (one tablespoon ascorbic acid to ½ gallon of water).

Freezing Small Game.   Pluck and dress game birds as soon as possible. Cut up and package small four-footed game the same as cut-up poultry; package halves and quarters the same as broilers. Prepare game birds that are quartered or cut up as suggested for cut-up poultry.

Freezing Vegetables.   To give you the best possible frozen vegetables, proceed as follows:

Select only the best vegetables for freezing. They should be slightly immature by table or canning standards, brightly colored, and of the best texture. Whenever possible, pick vegetables for freezing in the early morning before they absorb heat from the sun. If you are buying from a market, buy where fresh produce is delivered daily. Varieties of vegetables used for freezing will greatly affect the quality of the frozen product.

Blanch vegetables. To preserve freshness, blanch almost all vegetables. This slows and checks enzyme activity responsible for quality loss. It brightens color, making vegetables more attractive. It softens the products, making packaging easier. It cleans vegetables and destroys harmful bacteria. Blanching in boiling water or steam, for most vegetables, may be used.

1. *Water blanching.* Use about a gallon of boiling water for every pound of vegetables. Use a large kettle, regular blancher, or deep-well cooker for blanching. Place the vegetables in a long-handled colander, wire basket, or cheese cloth and immerse completely in rapidly boiling water for the recommended time. Start counting the blanching time as soon as the vegetables are put into the boiling water. Keep the utensil covered during blanching and keep the heat on high. Move the colander or basket several times during blanching to insure even heating. Remove vegetables promptly at the end of the blanching time. Cool quickly and thoroughly with running cold water or iced water. The cooling time should be at least 1½ to 2 times as long as the blanching period. Drain as soon as cool and start packing.

2. *Steam blanching.* A good steamer is the best equipment for this method. If you do not have one, use a large kettle, fitted with a trivet and a tight cover. Place water to a depth of one to two inches on the bottom of the steamer and bring to a full boil. Put about a pound of vegetables in a colander or wire container and place this on a rack in the steamer. Be sure the steaming compartment is filled with plenty of live steam for the entire blanching period. Cover the container tightly. After blanching for the recommended time, cool and proceed as described under water blanching.

Packing Vegetables.   After vegetables are blanched, cooled, and drained, they are ready for quick packaging and freezing.

Dry pack. Most vegetables are packed this way. After the vegetables are drained, fill the freezer cartons or containers with the vegetables, close or seal the package, and freeze. (Greens should be packed to the top of the container, leaving as little air space as possible. The greens pack solidly and therefore need no headspace.)

Loose pack. Spread vegetables (after blanching, cooling, and draining) on small trays or baking sheets and place on the shelf in your freezer. When frozen, the vegetables may be packed in freezer containers. This method takes more time but enables you to separate the vegetables easily for uniform cooking, and lets you use only part of a package rather than defrosting all of it.

Container. Vegetables may be frozen and stored in any container that is moisture- and vapor-proof. If you wish to use freezer bags for your vegetables, use a square or rectangular form for the package until the vegetables freeze. Packages will stack easily in the freezer. When deciding which freezer container to use, select a size that will adequately serve your family for a meal and leave no leftovers. An average serving of vegetables is ½ cup, so figure that a pint container will serve 3 or 4 people.

After packaging vegetables, freeze them immediately. If there is any delay before freezing, refrigerate the packaged vegetables. Label all packages before freezing. Write both the kind of vegetable and the date frozen—and use older packages first.

Freezing Fruits. Prepare and handle fruit carefully and quickly. Time is precious in retaining the freshness of fruit. The shorter the time from harvest to freezer, the better your frozen fruit will be. Always freeze the fruit the same day it is picked, or the same day that you select it at your market. If you must wait from morning until evening to freeze, refrigerate the fruit. In preparing fruit, always wash it in ice water. This firms the fruit and prevents sogginess and juice seepage. Wash about a quart of fruit at a time. Drain the fruit in a colander or on absorbent towels.

Packing Fruit. Select the method best suited to the fruit you are freezing.

Dry pack. Wash and freeze without sugar or syrup. This method is used primarily for fruits that are to be used for pies, cooked sauces, jellies, and jams.

Dry sugar pack. Use a proportion of sugar to fruit that will give the sweetness you want in your frozen fruit. (Usually a cup of sugar to 4 or 5 cups of fruit.)

Method 1 (preferred). Spread the prepared fruit in a large flat pan. Sprinkle sugar over the fruit (if desired, use a flour sifter to evenly distribute the sugar). Use a slotted spoon or spatula and turn the fruit gently until it is mixed well with the sugar. (After the fruit is packaged, invert the freezer containers several times to distribute the sugar that tends to settle.)

Method 2. Fill the freezer container about ¼ full of prepared fruit. Sprinkle in one-quarter total amount of sugar. Continue filling by sprinkling additional sugar in the fruit when the container is one-half full, three-quarters full and completely full.

Syrup pack. Method 1 (sugar syrup). Dissolve the sugar in water, using proportions given below. Make the syrup first so that it will be thoroughly cooled when you use it. The sweetness you desire in the frozen fruit will determine the syrup you use.

Thin syrup	*Medium syrup*	*Heavy syrup*
1 cup sugar to 3 cups water	1 cup sugar to 2 cups water	1 cup sugar to 1 cup water

Allow three-quarters to one cup syrup per quart container. Pour some of the syrup into the container before placing in the fruit. Add the syrup when necessary to cover the fruit completely. Add a crumpled piece of freezer paper on top to keep the fruit from bobbing out of the syrup.

Method 2 (blended syrup). Corn syrup may be substituted for one-third the sugar in syrup pack. Dissolve the sugar in the water, then add the syrup and mix.

Thin syrup	*Medium syrup*	*Heavy syrup*
3 cups sugar	4 cups sugar	3⅓ cups sugar
5 cups water	4⅓ cups water	5¼ cups water
1¼ cups corn syrup	1½ cups corn syrup	2 cups corn syrup

Section 7

LAURDRY

TODAY, AUTOMATIC WASHERS ARE available that wash, rinse, and spin loads to a damp dry; control water levels and temperatures; regulate time and power of agitation or tumbling; and add laundry aids.

As the name implies, *non-automatics* have few of the automatic's conveniences. They are motor driven machines like the automatic, but they require you to do some parts of the wash process manually, such as filling tubs and moving clothes from wash to rinse water.

To properly care for today's fabrics an *automatic dryer* is a necessity. Permanent press, wash and wear, and synthetic fabrics come out of the dryer ready to wear. Towels, shag rugs, and bedspreads are soft and fluffy when tumble dried. Much of a child's clothing, sportswear, and many work garments require no touch-up when removed from the dryer.

The *combination washer/dryer* uses the same drum for washing and drying clothes. This unit offers most of the features found in separate washers and dryers. Where space is limited or your present home is not a permanent one, the combination may be the answer. Taking up about half of the space of separate units, it is available in a freestanding or built-in under counter model.

A *portable washer* and *dryer* is smaller than the conventional washer and dryer. The portable units have some but not all of the convenience features of the full-size models. They care for about one-half the load of the regular models. In a well-ventilated room they do not have to be vented and can be plugged into a standard 120-volt line. For a small family or in crowded quarters, the

673

portables serve a real need. A growing family should consider the full-size model.

Automatic electric and *gas water heaters* are designed to provide continuous hot water for all your household needs. They fit almost anywhere in the house—e.g., in the closet or utility room. They do not require a vent or chimney, and they are automatically controlled.

Chapter 36

Washers

When you shop for a washer, the biggest decision you will have to make is the degree of automation you should buy. The more automatic features there are, the higher the price. Consider the use you will make of each control, and balance time and convenience against additional cost. To help you decide, this chapter covers the full range of controls from the simple ones to programed appliances. It also explains other aspects of washers that may be important to you—convenience features, cost, size, construction, installation, and repair.

TYPES OF AUTOMATIC WASHERS

Two basic kinds of washers are available—*automatic* and *non-automatics*. The difference between the two is in automation—how much the washer will do for you automatically. Either kind will provide satisfactory soil removal, given the proper washing conditions and a sufficient amount of detergent, water, and mechanical motion.

With the *automatic washer*, you set the controls and, without any further attention, the washer fills with water to the preselected level at a preselected temperature, washes, drains, rinses, spins the clothes to a damp dry, and stops (Fig. 1).

Automatic washers are either top loaders or front loaders.

Top Loaders.   Laundry is placed around an upright agitator in the center of the tub. Most agitators have finlike extensions to give additional movement to the water and clothes.

The *top loader* (Fig. 2) can be loaded and unloaded from a standing position, requires no extra floor space for the door to open or for work room, and usually offers a greater load capacity than the front loader. Articles may be put in or removed at any point of the cycle without spilling water.

Fig. 1. Automatic washer.

Fig. 2. Top loader.

Front Loaders. Baffle extensions in the tub help carry wash along as the tub rotates so the clothes are tumbled through the water.

Front loaders (Fig. 3) usually use less water and detergent per load than the top loaders, and their tops can be used as work surfaces.

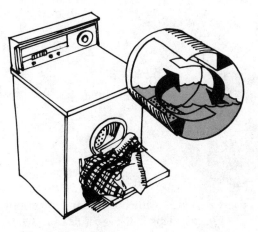

Fig. 3. Front loader.

SELECTIVE CONTROLS

Automatic washing machines have *control centers* with buttons or dials that allow you to tell the machine what you want it to do at different parts of the wash cycle. By means of these buttons and dials, you can preselect such things as water level, wash-water temperature, length of wash time, speed of agitation or tumbling, rinse-water temperature, spin speed, and special cycles.

Selecting a washer with a control center that will give you the degree of automation you want or need, within your budget limitations, is the key to buying. Here are the major points to consider when *selecting washer controls.*

Water Temperature. Most washers provide three water temperatures: hot, warm, and cold. Controls for water temperatures are set up differently on different washers. For example, some machines have controls listing combinations of wash and rinse temperatures such as *hot wash/warm rinse; warm wash/cold rinse; hot wash/cold* *rinse.* If you buy this type, be sure you buy a model with all the water temperature combinations (Fig. 4) that are important to you.

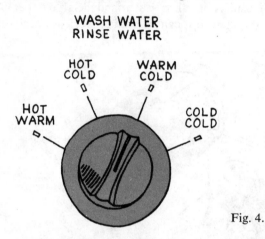

Fig. 4.

Other washers are designed with individual temperature controls for wash and rinse (Fig. 5). This is the most flexible type.

| Cold Wash | Warm Wash | Hot Wash | Cold Rinse | Warm Rinse |

Fig. 5. Individual temperature controls.

Water Fill.   An automatic washer that permits you to match the water level with the size of the wash load will save you money in the long run, even though the washer may have a slightly higher initial cost. Water just deep enough to cover the wash reduces friction and minimizes linting and wearing; it also lessens wrinkling of permanent press clothing. Too much water per load wastes both water and laundry aids.

Most machines today are *pressure (meter) filled.* No matter how low the water pressure in your home or how slow the water runs, water will enter the machine until it reaches the level of fill you have selected.

Some machines have *time fill.* Water enters only for a predetermined period regardless of the level it reaches. If the water pressure in your home happens to be low during the water fill, you will not get the preselected level of wash water unless you make a special adjustment.

If you have a water-pressure problem in your home or your area, it will be simplest to buy a washer that is pressure filled.

Wash Action. The wash action (Fig. 6) of the automatic cycle includes agitating or tumbling the wash load and extracting the soapy water.

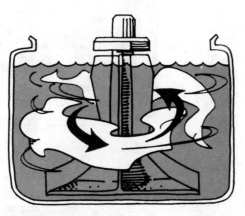

Fig. 6. Wash action.

Washing. So that you can accommodate agitation or tumbling time to the wash load, automatic washers have a time-adjustment dial. Most allow 10 to 14 minutes for the regular wash period and less time for permanent press and delicate loads. This range of time for the wash action is generally adequate.

In some washers, two speeds of washing are available: slow for delicate fabrics such as washable woolens and knits; regular for permanent press or cotton fabrics.

Water extraction. After agitation or tumbling is completed, the washer either drains wash water before spinning or as the tub spins. Spinning forces the undrained water through the holes in the outside walls of a perforated tub or up over the top of a solid tub to prepare the wash for rinsing (Fig. 7).

Rinse Action. Although most of the suds and soil empty with the wash water, plenty of clean rinse water is needed to completely rid the wash load of soap and dirt.

Rinsing. Automatics use all or some combination of three types of rinses during the rinse cycle.

1. One or more spray rinses (Fig. 8) in which water enters periodically while the tub is spinning.

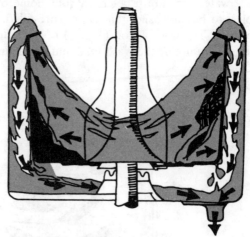

Fig. 7. Water extraction.

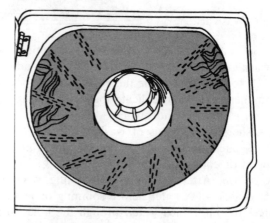

Fig. 8. Spray rinse.

2. A deep rinse that is a shortened, soapless version of washing.

3. An overflow rinse that flushes excess suds and loose lint over the top of the tub before spinning.

Some washers provide a control for an optional second deep rinse.

Water extraction. After rinsing, enough water must be forced out of the wash so that it can be dried easily. This is done by spinning. Some machines provide slow as well as regular spin speed.

Permanent Press Cycle. On some machines, a *permanent press control* programs the proper sequence for permanent press fabrics; on others, the wash temperature, the rinse temperature, and agitation and spin speeds must be set separately at the beginning of the wash. Either way, a cold rinse is always added before or at the start of a slow spin for water extraction. Permanent press fabrics tend to wrinkle if the clothes are spun without first being cooled or if they are spun too fast.

If you launder a lot of permanent press fabrics, choose a washer that has a permanent press cycle.

Delicate or Knit Cycles. *Delicate* or *knit cycles* offer protection against fabric damage by providing a warm-water wash, slow agitation, and a slow spin. In machines without these cycles, you can get good results by setting the controls with the combination previously mentioned.

Pre-Soak. A *pre-soak control* is useful if you frequently launder clothes that are exceptionally dirty or that contain food soil. Different brands of washers have different pre-soak time selections that range from five minutes to overnight. To use enzyme pre-soakers effectively, the clothes must soak at least 30 minutes and preferably longer. Some machines advance automatically from soaking to washing.

If your machine does not have a pre-soak control, you can presoak by filling the tub of soiled clothes with warm water and detergent or enzyme presoaker and then turning off the washer.

Pre-Wash. Also effective for heavily soiled clothes is a pre-wash action in which the clothes are agitated or tumbled up to five minutes in warm water and detergent. Some machines with this feature first pre-wash the clothes, then spin out the used water, and later advance automatically into the wash cycle. Such washers also automatically dispense detergent with the wash operation.

If you do not buy a washer with a pre-wash control, but occasionally have heavily soiled clothes, put the wash load in the washer with warm water and detergent and set the control for rinse. This provides a short period of agitation, or tumbling, plus water extraction. Then reset the machine for regular wash.

Programmed Cycle. Some machines are so automatic that, by selecting a single control, you can program the wash and rinse water temperatures and the agitation and spin speeds. These washers usually have the controls labeled according to types of wash loads: delicate; delicate permanent press; sturdy permanent press; regular noncolorfast; regular white; and colorfast (Fig. 9). These washers are the most expensive to buy.

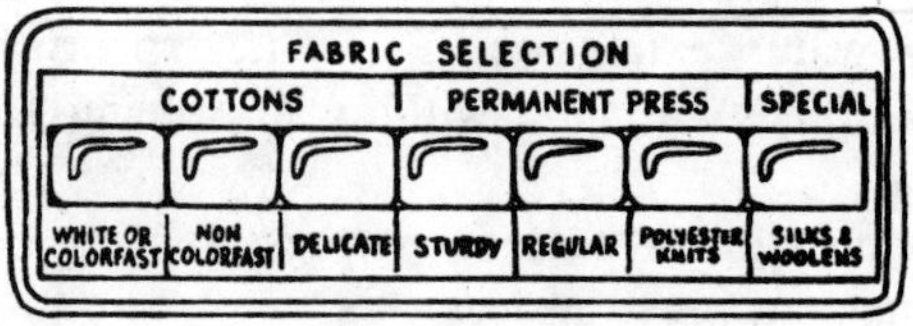

Fig. 9. Programmed cycle controls.

BUILT-IN FEATURES

Machine features that operate without dials or buttons to turn them on are as follows.

Dispensing Systems.   Three types of built-in dispensing features can save you trips to the washer by adding washing aids at the appropriate time.

1. *The automatic bleach dispenser* dilutes bleach before adding it to the wash water to avoid damage to fabrics.

2. *The automatic fabric softener dispenser* adds softener during the final deep rinse because most fabric softeners are not compatible with detergents.

3. *The automatic detergent dispenser* adds detergent after an automatic pre-soak or pre-wash when the washer cycles into the regular wash sequence. It is usually designed for liquid detergent. (*See* Fig. 10.)

Lint-Removal Systems.   Most washers have some system for lint removal, either around the top of the agitator or in the water-recirculating system. The first type requires cleaning; the second is usually self-cleaning and is effective at any water level.

Linting problems often result from improper sorting of wash loads or from machine overloading. No lint-removal system will compensate for these faults.

Off-Balance Systems.   All automatic washers have systems to protect the machine from imbalance during the spin cycle.

On the inside, the washtub is hung on some type of suspension

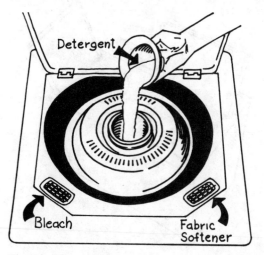

Fig. 10. Dispensing systems.

spring to allow it to adjust to various spin loads. If the load becomes seriously off balance and the tub wobbles too violently, some washers will turn off. Other washers will continue to spin but at such a reduced rate that water may remain in the clothes. You can help maintain balance by evenly distributing the wash when you load the machine.

On the outside, the machine bottom should be completely level. To accommodate the washer to slight variations in floor levels, most washers have four leveling legs. Each leg can be slightly raised or lowered. Leveling is usually done at the time of installation. However, if your washer is consistently spinning off balance, see if the machine is no longer level. See manufacturer's instructions for readjusting the legs.

Lights. An interior washbasket light that goes on whenever the lid or door is opened is a convenience on some deluxe models. Washers also may have panel and indicator lights.

NON-AUTOMATIC WASHERS

Non-automatic washers, depending on how water is extracted from wash, are either spinners (Fig. 11) or wringers (Fig. 12).

Fig. 11. Spinner.

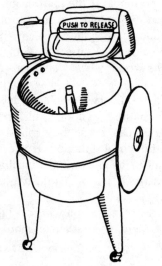

Fig. 12. Wringer.

Spinners.   Wash is put into the spinner tub and water is extracted by high-speed spinning that forces the wash to the sides of the basket and squeezes out the water. This is the same method that is used in the automatic washer.

Wringers.   Wash is fed through two rotating rollers, called wringers, attached to the top of the washtub frame. The rollers squeeze out the water, and the drainboard underneath the rollers channels the water back into the washtub. A tub of clear water is usually placed on the other side of the wringer to catch the clothes and provide a rinse.

With both spinners and wringers, handling the wash may be a problem if you have used extremely hot wash water. If you use a spinner, you can lift the wash out of the washtub and into the spinner with a wooden paddle. If you use a wringer washer and have to handle each piece of wash individually, you can use rubber gloves to help protect your hands.

CONTROLS AND ACTION

If you buy a non-automatic washer, instead of setting controls for such things as water fill, water temperature, or rinsing, you will have to handle these chores yourself.

Because non-automatics make more demands on you and your time, they are usually bought only when they fit a particular preference or need. For example, a non-automatic may be the answer when space is limited or when permanent washer installation is not practical—as in a mobile home, in a vacation home, or in a small apartment.

If you are going to buy a non-automatic, you may wish to buy one with as many automatic controls and features as you can for ease of operation. But the more controls and features, the higher the price. Non-automatics with many controls can be more expensive than automatics with few controls.

Built-in features are usually minimal. Some models have lint filters. Some have signals, such as a light showing whether the washer is plugged in or a bell alerting you that the washer has finished agitation or is off balance.

Water Fill/Water Temperature.   You control the water level and temperature on a non-automatic washer by turning faucets. Some models have waterline indicators in the tub. Always see that the water covers the wash load.

Washing.   The non-automatic resembles the automatic in its motorized agitation for washing. In addition, many non-automatics have wash controls for four-minute, six-minute, or 12-minute time settings for delicates, synthetics, and cottons (Fig. 13). More expensive models may have controls for regular and gentle wash speeds; some spinners let you run a cool-down rinse before spinning permanent press loads.

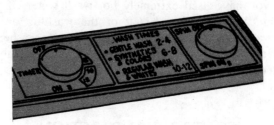

Fig. 13. Spinner wash controls.

Water Extraction.   In both spinners and wringers, a separate clothes-handling operation is needed after the wash and after each rinse process.

Spinners. You have to lift the load from the wash tub to the spinner tub. The motor spins the tub until most water is forced through the holes in the tub walls or over the tub top.

The spinner extracts water from anything that can be washed in the washer and extracts more water than the wringer.

Wringers. You feed laundry pieces through rubber rollers that squeeze out water. Once the rollers grasp fabric, they help lift it out of the water and through the wringer. The wringer can be pivoted into various positions for use over wash or rinse tubs.

The rollers are tight enough to squeeze most of the water out of the clothes but loose enough to let a variety of clothing pass through. There can be problems. Large buttons may break or pull off. Clothes may come out deeply creased. Certain fabrics and buckles, belts, and zippers may be too bulky to pass through. Some features on wringers that can minimize these difficulties are automatic or manual pressure adjustments, rollers that combine soft and hard rubber, or two large, soft rollers. Large, soft rollers most easily accommodate all thicknesses of material, but they require heavy pressure to effectively squeeze water out of clothes.

Rinsing.   After you have extracted used water and added new, you can rinse by hand, use the agitator in your wash tub, or use the spinner basket.

OTHER ASPECTS WHEN BUYING A WASHER

In addition to deciding the kind of washer you want and the controls and features, you should consider cost, size, construction quality and safety, installation, and ease of repair.

Cost.   The initial price of a washer is only part of its cost; the continuing expense is also important. Both types of cost should be examined before you purchase a washer.

Initial Cost.   Automatic washers have a wide price range, non-automatics a narrower range.

Higher prices usually indicate more choice of controls and more special features; they may also indicate quality and long life. You have to decide what kind of washer you want, which controls you want, how many features you will use, and how much you are willing to pay. Once you have decided on these things, do some comparison shopping. Prices on the same model may differ from store to store.

Prices of economy washers vary among brands because of manufacturing policy. Some manufacturers use the same internal wash systems on all models, and this increases the costs of their economy models. Others use a less expensive system on a less expensive washer.

Operating Cost.   Automatic washers will be more expensive to operate than non-automatics because they use more water. On the basis of full loads, front-loading automatics generally use less water and detergent than top-loading machines.

To determine which brand of top-loading automatic will be the most economical water user, check with the dealer or examine washer literature. The permanent press cycle is good for comparison because it requires an extra cool-down rinse. The amount of water used in this rinse varies considerably among brands without much difference in the results.

If water conservation is a special concern, you can buy a special suds-return system (Fig. 14) on some machines. It permits wash

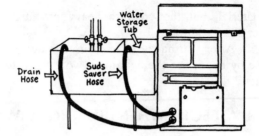

Fig. 14. Suds-return system.

water to be stored in a separate tub and then pumped back into the washbasket for reuse with additional hot water and detergent.

With the wringer, wash water may be used again if it is fairly clean. Rinse water may be used as wash water with the addition of hot water and detergent.

Size.   Two considerations are involved here—the capacity of the washer and the floor space the washer requires.

Capacity. Automatic washers are available that handle 5-pound to 20-pound loads of dry wash. Check the hang tag for the maximum load. If there is no capacity weight listed, note the water-level indicators on the controls or simply examine the washbasket to see if the washer will be large enough to handle your normal loads.

In the non-automatics, wringer washers can handle the same size loads as the average automatic. Most spinners handle loads of about five pounds.

A small family will probably require a washer with a maximum capacity of about eight pounds; for a large family, a maximum capacity of 15 to 20 pounds would be desirable.

Floor space. Be sure you coordinate the measurements of the floor space in your home with the size of the washer you buy. Floor space requirements are listed on the hang tags of models.

The depth and height of regular-sized automatic washers are usually standard—up to 28 inches deep (add a few inches for clearance) and 43 inches high. The width varies from 25 to 31 inches. Compact automatic washers as narrow as 21 inches are available.

Non-automatic two-tub spinners measure from 29 to 32 inches wide, 17 to 19 inches deep, and 30 to 33 inches high. The measurements of a spinner may be important to you not only for use but also for storage.

Most wringers have one tub. If a second tub is attached, it is used as a rinse tub to contain the load after it has been put through the wringer. A second tub is not necessary, however, if you have stationary tubs in your basement. One-tub wringers take up about 25 to 27 inches of floor width.

Construction. Quality and safety of construction are important considerations when you are selecting a washer.

Quality. Look for good workmanship in the parts you can see. Construction materials are also important, since the washer is exposed to water, high humidity, and laundry chemicals.

The exterior and interior finish on tubs, cabinet, and lid should be smooth and durable to resist chipping and rusting. Porcelain enamel is usually used. Lid hinges should be made of non-rusting materials, and controls should be easy to read and operate.

In *non-automatics*, spinners should have an aluminum spin basket. Drain-boards on wringers should be made of smooth, non-rusting material, be adjustable, and have rounded edges and corners.

An off-on switch is convenient because you will not have to leave the washer to turn off the machine at the wall switch or plug. Hooks should be provided to store the hoses and electric cord.

Casters that lock are helpful on mobile non-automatics to prevent the machine from *walking*. On wringers, washer legs that can be raised or lowered will give flexibility to machine height and also provide a way to level the washer if it has no self-leveling casters.

Safety. To be assured of the safe electrical and mechanical construction of your washer, buy one that has been listed by a testing laboratory such as the Underwriters Laboratories, Inc.

A wringer washer should provide a safety release for the rollers in case fingers get caught or fabrics get tangled. Some wringers have an emergency release bar that stops pressure and rollers instantly. Some have an instant release feature where a tug or a pull in the direction opposite to the roller feed automatically relieves pressure and stops rollers. Some have a switch that must be pressed, usually with a foot, to keep rollers operating.

Installation. Proper installation of an automatic washer is essential.

While non-automatics need no special installation, they require the same facilities as automatics—power, water, and drainage.

Power. Washers are designed to operate on ordinary household electric current. However, local electrical codes usually require that a washer be plugged into a grounded three-hole outlet on a *separate* 15- or 20-ampere circuit.

Circuits rated at 15 or 20 amperes are common in homes; but in older buildings, circuits with only one outlet are not common. If you operate a washer on a circuit with other electrical appliances, you may overload the circuit and blow the fuse or trip the circuit breaker.

A grounded outlet is particularly important for a washer, which brings together a dangerous combination—electricity and water. With a grounded outlet, you are protected against shock, even if an electrical accident occurs. If you do not have a three-hole grounded wall outlet where your washer will be placed, you should have one installed by an electrician.

In older homes, an adapter plug is sometimes used to connect a three-pronged washer plug to a two-hole wall outlet. This is not recommended, however, *unless you know that the adapter plug is attached to grounded wiring in your home or apartment.* If you are not sure, ask an electrician to check it for you.

Never use an extension cord with a washing machine. If the connection is exposed to moisture, a shock hazard will result.

Water. All washers need easily accessible sources of hot and cold water. A 40-gallon, quick-recovery, hot-water heater should be ample for a regular-size automatic and an average-size family.

Remember that the hot water in your washer will only be as hot as the water provided by your home water heater.

For a non-automatic you may want to use warm water—but do not have a mixer faucet. In that case, you can use a Y hose, where the upper ends attach to the threaded fittings on the hot and cold faucets and the stem leads to the washer (Fig. 15).

Drainage. Water pumped from an automatic washer may be released into any drain large enough to accommodate the flow, such as a laundry sink or a standpipe (Fig. 16).

Non-automatic washtubs empty from a gravity drain outlet located in the bottom of the tub or by means of a motor-driven pump (Fig. 17). If the washer has a gravity drain, you will need to use a drain

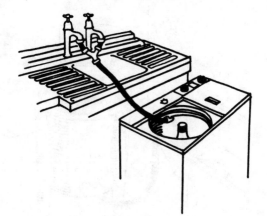

Fig. 15. Y hose attachment.

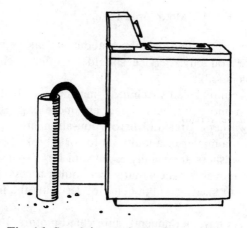

Fig. 16. Standpipe drainage.

in the floor. If the washer has a motor-driven pump, you can use a standpipe or a sink.

Any drain opening should have a screen or strainer to catch lint, buttons, and other small items.

Repair.   To minimize repair difficulties, buy a reputable brand of washer from an established local dealer and understand what the warranty guaranties before you buy. What does the warranty cover? For how long?

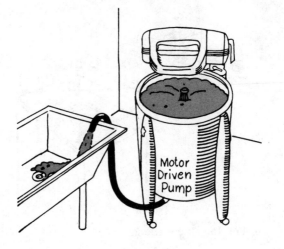

Fig. 17. Motor-driven pump.

Check with friends and neighbors about a dealer's reputation for service before you buy. Service should be quick, reliable, and as inexpensive as possible.

In general, complicated machines—machines with many controls —break down more frequently and are more expensive to repair than simple washers. Breakdowns on non-automatics are infrequent and are usually a matter of a faulty motor or a broken switch.

Automatic washers are usually easier and less expensive to service if they have removable panels that permit quick access to motors and pumps. Ask your salesman about ease of servicing the model you are considering.

Most washers have permanently lubricated motors. But, if periodic lubrication is required, find out if the lubrication points are easily accessible for home servicing. Consult the manufacturer's literature.

If your washer does break down, check some basic points yourself before you call for service. Forty percent of service calls are about simple matters.

If your washer will not run:

1. Fully depress the control button or completely turn the dial.
2. Firmly insert the electric plug into the outlet.
3. See if a fuse is blown or a circuit breaker tripped.

4. Balance the load.
5. Decrease the load in the tub.

If you are not getting enough water, or enough hot water:

1. See that hoses are attached to the right faucets.
2. Turn both faucets on fully.
3. Unkink the intake hose.
4. Look at your home water heater thermostat setting. It should be about 160° Fahrenheit.
5. See if the water pressure is low in the house.
6. See if hoses are connected tightly to faucets.
7. Clean the screens in the faucet ends of the intake hoses.

If the water does not empty properly:

1. See if the lint drain is clogged.
2. Unkink the drainage hose.
3. Check that the drain hose is correctly inserted into the drain pipe.

SERVICE PROCEDURES

Warning: Disconnect power cord and close water supply valve before servicing washer.

Timer. *See* Fig. 18, 19, or 20 for timer removal. *See* appropriate wiring diagram for rewiring timer. *Note:* When reinstalling timer knob assembly, pin-in timer shaft must be positioned in timer indicator slot.

Soak Timer. *See* Fig. 18 for soak timer removal.

Temperature or Speed/Action Switch. *See* Fig. 18, 19, or 20 for switch removal. *Note:* Refer to appropriate wiring diagram for rewiring switch.

Pressure Switch. *See* Figs. 18 and 19 for switch removal in some models. In other models remove front panel, as described in section on Front Panel later in this chapter. Disconnect pressure hose and remove two screws holding pressure switch to the left-front hold-down bracket.

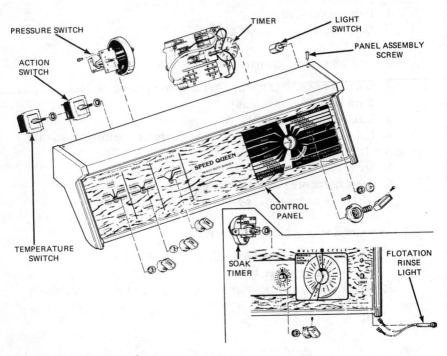

Fig. 18. Switch removal.

Light Switch.   *See* Fig. 18 for switch removal.

Flotation Rinse Light.   *See* Fig. 18 for light removal. *Note*: Be sure washer between control panel and support plate is in position when installing light.

Ballast.   *See* Fig. 21 for ballast removal.

Water Mixing Valve.   *See* Fig. 22.

1. Disconnect water hoses inlet from valve.

2. Remove panel assembly screws (Fig. 18, 19 or 20), and lift assembly off panel support.

3. Disconnect wires from valve solenoids.

4. Remove mixing valve mounting screw.

5. Disconnect filler hose from valve and lift valve out of cabinet top.

Note: See Fig. 23 for mixing valve assembly sequence.

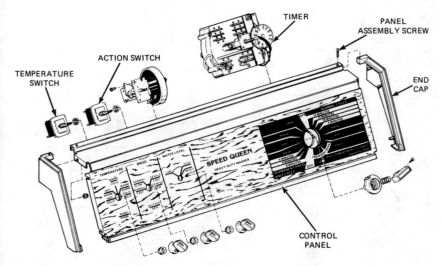

Fig. 19. Switch removal.

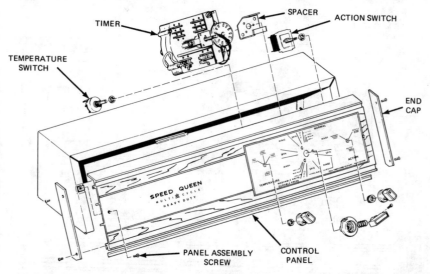

Fig. 20. Switch removal.

Control Panel.   *See* model shown in Fig. 18.

1. Remove panel assembly screws and lift assembly off panel support.

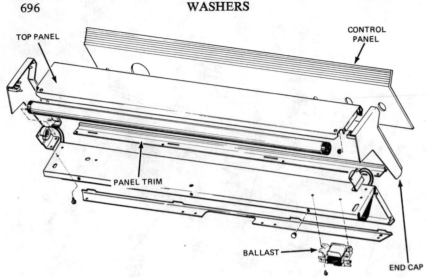

Fig. 21. Ballast removal.

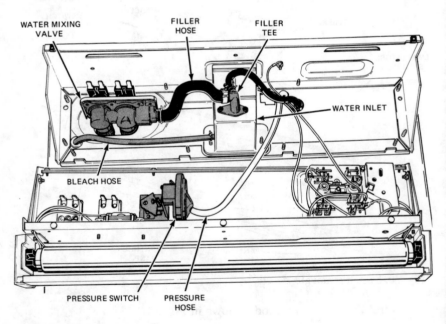

Fig. 22. Water mixing valve.

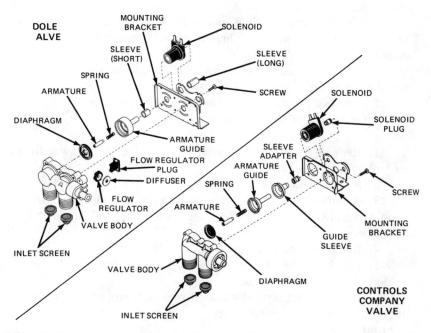

DOLE
ALVE
MOUNTING BRACKET
SOLENOID
SLEEVE (SHORT)
SLEEVE (LONG)
SPRING
ARMATURE
SCREW
SOLENOID
DIAPHRAGM
SOLENOID PLUG
ARMATURE GUIDE
FLOW REGULATOR PLUG
SLEEVE ADAPTER
ARMATURE GUIDE
DIFFUSER
SPRING
SCREW
FLOW REGULATOR
ARMATURE
VALVE BODY
MOUNTING BRACKET
INLET SCREEN
GUIDE SLEEVE
VALVE BODY
DIAPHRAGM
CONTROLS COMPANY VALVE
INLET SCREEN

Fig. 23. Dole valve and controls company valve.

2. Remove end caps (Fig. 21).

3. Lift hood top panel (Fig. 21) off panel assembly.

4. Remove timer knob assembly. *Note:* When reinstalling timer knob assembly, pin-in timer shaft must be positioned in timer indicator slot.

5. Pull knobs off switches.

6. *Models with soak timer.* Loosen soak timer knob setscrew and pull knob off shaft.

7. *Models with light switch.* Pull light switch collar off knurled nut.

8. Tilt control panel forward slightly and raise to disengage bottom edge of panel from panel trim (Fig. 21).

Control Panel.   *See* style shown in Fig. 19.

1. Remove panel assembly screws and lift assembly off panel support.

2. Remove end caps.

3. Remove timer knob assembly. *Note:* When reinstalling timer knob assembly, pin-in timer shaft must be positioned in timer indicator slot.

4. Pull knobs off temperature and speed/action switches, and remove knurled nuts holding switches to control panel.

5. Remove three screws holding timer to control panel.

Control Panel. *See* style shown in Fig. 20.

1. Remove panel assembly screws and pull assembly away from control hood.

2. Remove end caps.

3. Remove timer knob assembly. *Note:* When reinstalling timer knob assembly, pin-in timer shaft must be positioned in timer indicator slot.

4. Remove three screws holding timer to control panel.

5. Pull knob off temperature switch, and remove knurled nut holding switch to control panel.

6. Pull knob off action switch (if present), and remove knurled nut holding switch to control panel.

Front Panel.

1. Remove four screws from bottom edge of panel.

2. Pull bottom of panel slightly away from washer, and lower panel to disengage guide lugs at top of panel from cabinet top.

Bleach Pump. *See* Fig. 24.

1. Remove front panel. (*See* section on Front Panel previously described.)

2. Disconnect bleach pump wires at connectors.

3. Disconnect hoses from pump.

4. Push pump down to disengage top of pump from upper rubber isolation mount, and lift pump out of lower mount.

Note: When reinstalling, secure bleach pump in mounts with a rubber base cement.

Agitator Drive Shaft.

1. Remove front panel. (*See* section on Front Panel previously described.)

2. Open loading door and remove agitator.

3. Loosen two thrust-collar setscrews (Fig. 25).

4. Grasp agitator drive block and pull shaft out of agitator post.

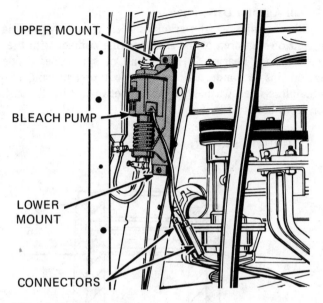

Fig. 24. Bleach pump.

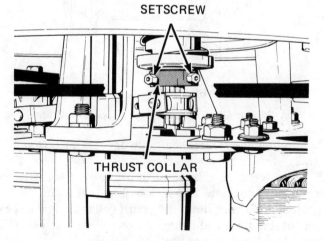

Fig. 25. Thrust collar and setscrews.

Note: Use a bearing puller to remove drive shaft from agitator post if it cannot be removed by hand.

To Install Agitator Drive Shaft.

1. Slide stainless-steel washer onto shaft, and wipe a light film of lubricant on that area of the shaft making contact with the following areas: bronze bearing in lower end of spin tube; inside sleeve bearing; on lips of water seal; and inside thrust bearing (Fig. 26). *Note:* Stainless-steel washer must be between thrust bearing and agitator drive block (Fig. 27).

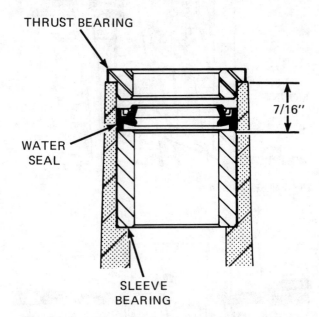

Fig. 26. Installing agitator post bearings and seal.

2. Carefully insert drive shaft into agitator post. *Do not* damage water seal.

3. Insert feeler gage between thrust bearing and stainless steel washer (Fig. 27) to allow .012 inch end-play in shaft.

4. Hold drive shaft down, lift thrust collar up against bearing in lower end of spin tube, and tighten thrust-collar set screws (Fig. 25).

Agitator Post Bearings and Seal.   *See* Fig. 26.

1. Remove front panel. (*See* section on Front Panel previously described.)

2. Remove agitator drive shaft. (*See* section on Agitator Drive

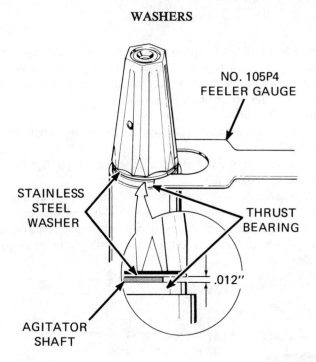

NO. 105P4
FEELER GAUGE

STAINLESS
STEEL
WASHER

THRUST
BEARING

.012"

AGITATOR
SHAFT

Fig. 27.

Shaft previously described. *Note:* Cover transmission drive clutch with piece of cloth or paper to prevent dirt from falling in.

3. Pry thrust bearing and water seal out of agitator post.

4. Use bearing puller to remove sleeve bearing from agitator post.

To Install Agitator Post Bearings and Seal. *See* Fig. 26.

Note: A new water seal must be installed in agitator post when installing new bearings.

1. Thoroughly clean opening in top of agitator post.

2. Use bearing inserter to install sleeve bearing in agitator post. *Note:* Bearing must be properly aligned when it is inserted into agitator post to avoid bearing damage. Also, after bearing is installed in agitator post, top of bearing must be no less than $\frac{7}{16}$ inch from top of agitator post.

3. Wipe a light film of lubricant on lips of water seal. Use hammer and pin punch to drive water seal down into agitator post until bottom of seal contacts top of sleeve bearing.

4. Use block of wood and hammer to drive thrust bearing down into agitator post until bearing flange contacts top of agitator post. *Note:* Use new stainless-steel washer between drive block and new thrust bearing when drive shaft is installed.

Agitator Shift Clutch.

1. Remove front panel. (*See* section on Front Panel previously described.)

2. Remove agitator drive shaft. (*See* section on Agitator Drive Shaft previously described.)

3. Remove thrust collar and pull shift clutch toward right front corner of washer to disengage clutch from shifter fork collar (Fig. 28). *Note:* If shift clutch is engaged with transmission drive clutch, grasp pump belt and rotate transmission pulley clockwise to raise shift clutch.

THRUST COLLAR

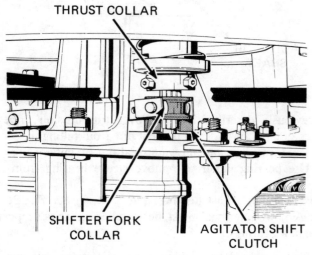

SHIFTER FORK COLLAR

AGITATOR SHIFT CLUTCH

Fig. 28.

Spin Belt.

1. Remove front panel. (*See* section on Front Panel previously described.)

2. Remove agitator drive shaft. (*See* section on Agitator Drive Shaft previously described.)

3. Run spin belt off spin pulley, and lift belt over top of fluid drive (Fig. 29).

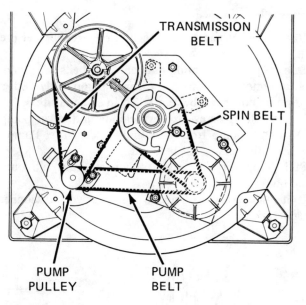

Fig. 29.

Note: After installing spin belt, adjust spin, pump, and transmission belts. (*See* section on Adjustments, on Spin Belt, and on Pump and Transmission Belts.)

Transmission Belt.   *See* Fig. 29.

1. Remove front panel. (*See* section on Front Panel previously described.)

2. Run transmission belt off pump and transmission pulleys.

Pump Belt.   *See* Fig. 29.

1. Remove front panel. (*See* section on Front Panel previously described.)

2. Run spin belt off spin pulley.

3. Loosen pump mounting nuts, and run transmission belt off pump pulley.

4. Run pump belt off pump pulley, work belt between spin belt and fluid drive, and lift belt over top of fluid drive.

Note: After installing pump belt, adjust pump and transmission belts. (*See* section on Adjustments, Pump, and Transmission Belts.)

Pump Assembly.   *See* Fig. 30.

1. Remove front panel. (*See* section on Front Panel previously described.)

2. Loosen pump mounting nuts and run belts off pump pulley. *Note:* Before removing pump cover, mark pump body and cover so clamp and pump cover can be reinstalled in same position.

3. Loosen clamp screw, remove clamp, and lower pump cover.

4. Disengage pump from mounting bolts. *Note:* Pump mounts are above mounting plate, not below it.

5. Pull pump forward, and disconnect drain tub outlet hose from pump body.

6. If it's necessary to remove pump cover, disconnect hose from cover.

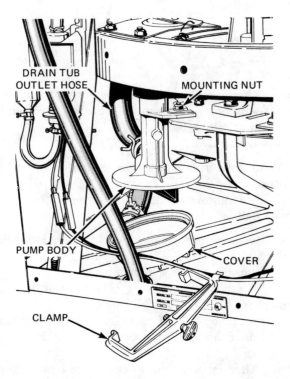

Fig. 30. Pump assembly.

Note: See Fig. 31 for pump assembly sequence.

Caution: Use new cover gasket and finger-tighten clamp screw when installing pump cover. *Do not use pliers.*

Pump Impeller and Shaft. *See* Fig. 31.

1. Remove front panel. (*See* section on Front Panel previously described.)

2. Remove pump assembly. (*See* section on Pump Assembly, steps 2 through 4, previously described.)

3. Loosen two pump pulley set screws and pull impeller and shaft out of pump body.

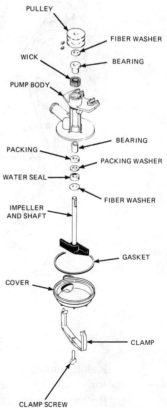

PULLEY

FIBER WASHER

WICK

BEARING

PUMP BODY

BEARING

PACKING

PACKING WASHER

WATER SEAL

FIBER WASHER

IMPELLER
AND SHAFT

GASKET

COVER

CLAMP

CLAMP SCREW

Fig. 31. Pump assembly sequence.

Note: Fiber washers must be between impeller and water seal and between upper bearing and pulley when impeller and shaft is installed. When installing pump cover, use new cover gasket and finger-tighten clamp screw. *Do not use pliers.*

Motor and Fluid Drive Assembly.

1. Remove front panel. (*See* section on Front Panel previously described.)

2. Disconnect motor wire harness plug from receptacle, bleach-pump wires at connectors, and wire-harness clip from chassis.

3. Remove motor pivot bolt, spin belt adjusting bolt, and spin belt adjusting nut (Fig. 32).

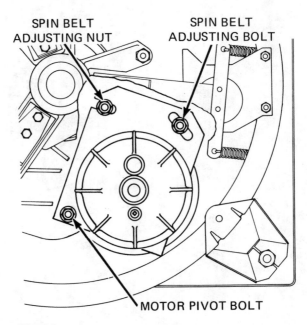

SPIN BELT ADJUSTING NUT   SPIN BELT ADJUSTING BOLT

MOTOR PIVOT BOLT

Fig. 32.

4. Run spin belt off spin pulley and pump belt off top of motor pulley.

5. Rotate motor and fluid drive assembly clockwise to disengage motor mounting plate from rear stud.

6. Rotate assembly counterclockwise and lower left front corner

of motor mounting plate, then rotate assembly clockwise until rear
of motor mounting plate clears main mounting plate.

7. Lower motor and fluid drive assembly to floor of chassis, tip
assembly toward center of washer. (Fig. 33), and lift spin belt over
top of fluid drive.

8. Lift bottom of motor out of washer first (Fig. 33), and lift
pump belt over top of fluid drive after assembly is out of washer.

Fluid Drive.   *See* Fig. 34.

1. Remove front panel. (*See* section on Front Panel previously
described.)

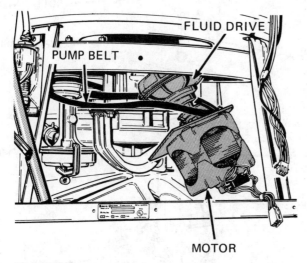

Fig. 33.

2. Remove motor and fluid drive assembly. (*See* section on
Motor and Fluid Drive Assembly previously described.)

3. While supporting fluid drive and motor shaft (to prevent
bending shaft), drive out fluid drive roll pin.

4. Pull fluid drive off motor shaft.

Drive Motor.   *See* Fig. 34.

1. Remove front panel. (*See* section on Front Panel previously
described.)

2. Remove motor and fluid drive assembly. (*See* section on
Motor and Fluid Drive Assembly previously described.)

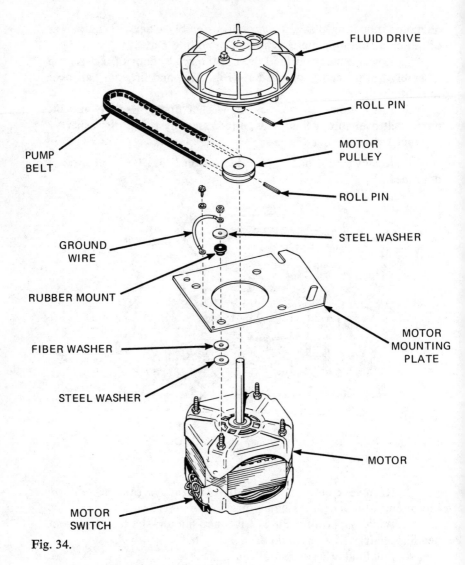

FLUID DRIVE

ROLL PIN

MOTOR PULLEY

ROLL PIN

PUMP BELT

STEEL WASHER

GROUND WIRE

RUBBER MOUNT

FIBER WASHER

MOTOR MOUNTING PLATE

STEEL WASHER

MOTOR

MOTOR SWITCH

Fig. 34.

3. Remove fluid drive. (*See* section on Fluid Drive previously described.)

4. Remove nuts, steel washers, and rubber mounts holding motor mounting plate to motor, and lift plate off motor. Remove fiber washers and steel washers from motor mounting studs.

Note: When installing motor to mounting plate, position motor with switch toward front of washer.

To remove motor pulley, support motor shaft (to prevent bending shaft) and drive out pulley roll pin.

To Remove Motor Switch. *See* Fig. 34.

1. Remove two screws holding switch to motor.
2. Disconnect motor leads from switch terminals.

Note: To rewire motor switch to motor, *see* Appendix XI for Internal Wiring of Motor Switches.

Cabinet Top Assembly.

1. Remove front panel. (*See* section on Front Panel previously described.)
2. Disconnect inlet hoses from water mixing valve.
3. Shur-Fil models: (a) Remove panel assembly screws, (Fig. 18), and lift assembly off panel support; (b) disconnect pressure hose from pressure switch (Fig. 22); (c) install panel assembly, securing it loosely to control hood.
4. Open loading door, lift lid off bleach dispenser, remove cover, compress dispenser, and push dispenser down through opening in cabinet top (Fig. 35).
5. Disconnect bleach hose from top of bleach pump (Fig. 36).

Note: Remove shipping plugs located on lower edge of cabinet top behind rear hold-down brackets, if they were not removed at time of installation.

6. Remove two cabinet top hold-down screws (Fig. 37), lift front of cabinet top slightly, and pull forward to disengage rear of top from hold-down brackets (Fig. 38).
7. Models with quick disconnect wire harness: Carefully lift rear of top assembly high enough for disconnecting the wire harness (Fig. 39), and remove clip holding the wire harness and pressure hose for cabinet top.
8. Models without quick disconnect wire harness: Carefully stand top on front edge on protective padding at right side of washer.

Note: When cabinet top assembly is removed from washer, drain tub rim gasket should be removed to prevent damage. (*See* following section on Drain Tub Rim Gasket.) When installing cabinet top

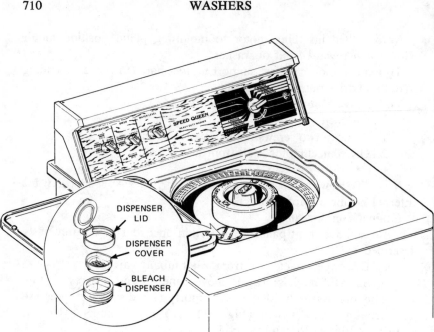

Fig. 35.

assembly, use caution to avoid moving rim gasket out of position on rim of drain tub. Gasket must provide a watertight seal when top assembly is installed

Drain Tub Rim Gasket.

1. Remove front panel. (*See* section on Front Panel previously described.)

2. Remove cabinet top assembly. (*See* section on Cabinet Top Assembly previously described.)

3. Lift gasket off drain tub rim.

Note: When installing drain tub rim gasket, tape gasket to outside of drain tub in several places to hold gasket in position.

Vinyl Clothes Guard.

1. Remove front panel. (*See* section on Front Panel previously described.)

2. Remove cabinet top assembly. (*See* section on Cabinet Top Assembly previously described.)

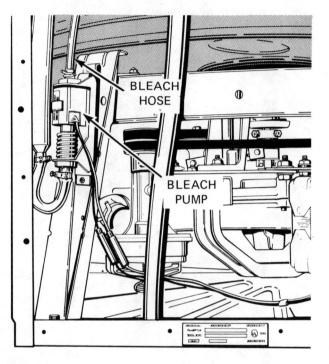

Fig. 36.

3. Disconnect spring from clothes guard retainer wire (Fig. 39), and disengage guard from cabinet top.

Bleach Dispenser.

1. Remove front panel. (*See* section on Front Panel previously described.)

2. Remove cabinet top assembly. (*See* section on Cabinet Top Assembly previously described.)

3. Disconnect bleach dispenser from bleach tube (Fig. 39), and pull dispenser out of grommet in drain tub.

Bleach Tube.

1. Remove front panel. (*See* section on Front Panel previously described.)

2. Disconnect bleach dispenser (Fig. 40), and bleach pump hose (Fig. 41) from bleach tube.

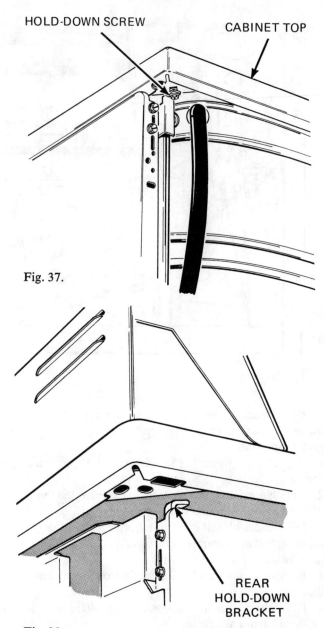

HOLD-DOWN SCREW

CABINET TOP

Fig. 37.

REAR
HOLD-DOWN
BRACKET

Fig. 38.

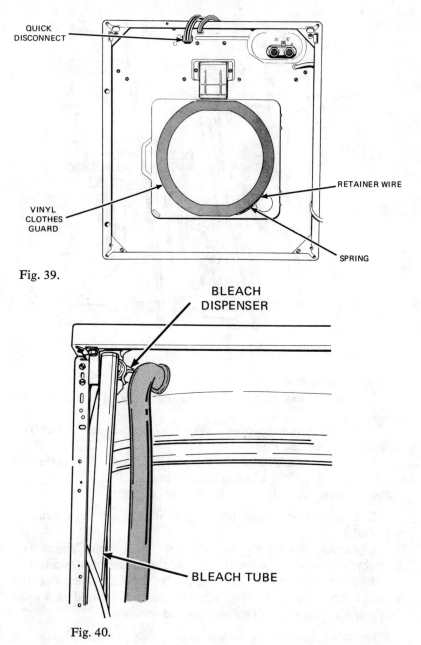

QUICK DISCONNECT

RETAINER WIRE

VINYL CLOTHES GUARD

SPRING

Fig. 39.

BLEACH DISPENSER

BLEACH TUBE

Fig. 40.

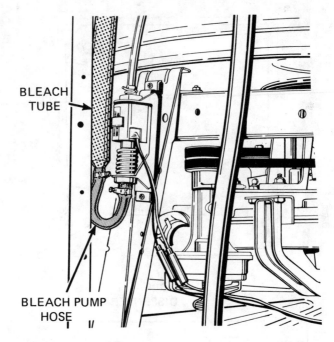

BLEACH
TUBE

BLEACH PUMP
HOSE

Fig. 41.

Door Safety Switch.

1. Remove front panel. (*See* section on Front Panel previously described.)

2. Remove cabinet top assembly. (*See* section on Cabinet Top Assembly, steps 6 and 8.)

3. Block up front of cabinet top high enough to remove two switch screws (Fig. 42), and disconnect wires.

Balance Ring Assembly.   *See* Fig. 43.

1. Remove front panel. (*See* section on Front Panel previously described.)

2. Remove cabinet top assembly (*see* section on Cabinet Top Assembly previously described), and lift rim gasket off drain tub.

3. Remove screws, washers, and nuts holding balance ring and sediment tube bracket to spin tub and carefully (avoid damaging door safety switch arm) lift balance ring off spin tub.

Note: When reinstalling, locate marked side of balance ring 180

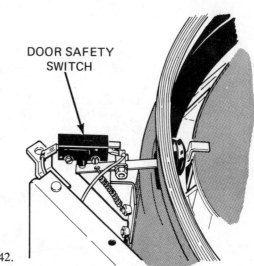

DOOR SAFETY
SWITCH

Fig. 42.

degrees from sediment tube. Also, install the steel nut on the screw holding the sediment tube bracket.

Spin Tub.

   1. Remove front panel. (*See* section on Front Panel previously described.)

   2. Remove cabinet top assembly (*see* section on Cabinet Top Assembly previously described), and lift rim gasket off drain tub.

   3. Remove screw, washer, and nut holding sediment tube bracket to spin tub (Fig. 43).

   4. Remove agitator.

   5. Remove eight spin tub screws (Fig. 44), and carefully (avoid damaging door safety switch arm and sediment tube) lift spin tub and balance ring assembly out of drain tub.

   6. Remove screws, washers, and nuts holding balance ring to spin tub.

Note: When reinstalling, locate marked side of balance ring 180 degrees from sediment tube. Also, install the steel nut on the screw holding the sediment tube bracket.

Agitator Post and Spin Tub Assembly.   *See* Fig. 44.

   1. Remove front panel. (*See* section on Front Panel previously described.)

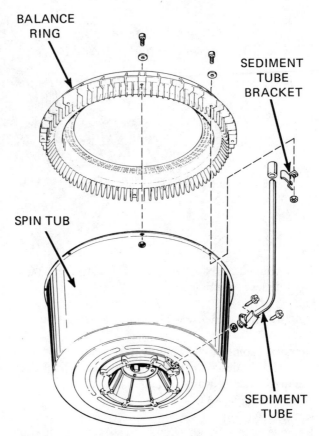

Fig. 43. Balance ring assembly.

2. Remove agitator drive shaft. (*See* section on Agitator Drive Shaft previously described.)

3. Remove cabinet top assembly. (*See* section on Cabinet Top Assembly previously described.) Then lift rim gasket off drain tub.

4. Remove four cap screws holding agitator post to spin tube flange.

5. Carefully (avoid damaging door safety switch arm) lift agitator post and spin tub assembly out of drain tub. *Note:* If agitator post sticks to spin tube flange, thread cap screws back into holes approximately halfway and rap on screw heads with hammer while

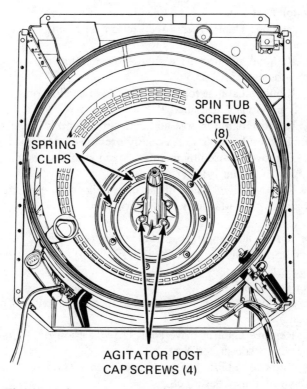

SPIN TUB
SCREWS
(8)

SPRING
CLIPS

AGITATOR POST
CAP SCREWS (4)

Fig. 44. Agitator post and spin tub assembly.

lifting edge of spin tub. This should break agitator post loose. Inspect spin tube flange gasket and replace if necessary.

Sediment Tube.   *See* Fig. 43.

1. Remove front panel. (*See* section on Front Panel previously described.)

2. Remove agitator drive shaft. (*See* section on Agitator Drive Shaft previously described.)

3. Remove cabinet top assembly. (*See* section on Cabinet Top Assembly previously described.)

4. Remove agitator post and spin tub assembly. (*See* section on Agitator Post and Spin Tub Assembly.)

5. Remove two sediment tube screws and lower tube to disengage upper end from bracket.

Agitator Post.

    1. Remove front panel. (*See* section on Front Panel previously described.)

    2. Remove agitator drive shaft. (*See* section on Agitator Drive Shaft previously described.)

    3. Remove cabinet top assembly. (*See* section on Cabinet Top Assembly previously described.)

    4. Remove agitator post and spin tub assembly. (*See* section on Agitator Post and Spin Tub Assembly previously described.)

    5. Remove two sediment tube screws and lower tube to disengage upper end from bracket (Fig. 43).

    6. Remove eight spin tub screws (Fig. 44) and lift spin tub (with balance ring attached) off agitator post.

Note: Use a new spin tub gasket when reinstalling. Install spring clips and spring over sediment zone (Fig. 44) when reinstalling spin tub.

Drain Tub Boot.

    1. Remove front panel. (*See* section on Front Panel previously described.)

    2. Remove agitator drive shaft. (*See* section on Agitator Drive Shaft previously described.)

    3. Remove cabinet top assembly. (*See* section on Cabinet Top Assembly previously described.)

    4. Remove agitator post and spin tub assembly. (*See* section on Agitator Post and Spin Tub Assembly previously described.)

    5. Remove upper and lower boot clamps (Fig. 45) and pull boot up over spin tube flange.

Note: When installing boot, do not stretch it taut. Allow boot to resume its natural shape. Replace clamps on opposite sides as shown in Fig. 45.

Drain Tub.   *See* Fig. 45.

    1. Remove front panel. (*See* section on Front Panel previously described.)

    2. Remove agitator drive shaft. (*See* section on Agitator Drive Shaft previously described.)

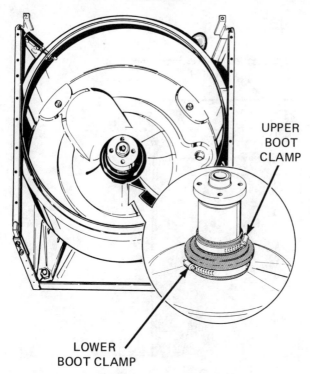

UPPER
BOOT
CLAMP

LOWER
BOOT CLAMP

Fig. 45. Drain tub.

3. Remove cabinet top assembly. (*See* section on Cabinet Top Assembly previously described.)

4. Remove agitator post and spin tub assembly. (*See* section on Agitator Post and Spin Tub Assembly previously described.)

5. Remove rear panel.

6. Remove lower boot clamp and fold bottom of boot up. *Note:* When installing boot, do not stretch it taut. Allow boot to resume its natural shape.

7. Disconnect wires from door safety switch.

8. Disconnect bleach tube from dispenser, and drain tub outlet hose from pump.

9. Shur-Fil models: Disconnect drain valve hose from drain valve (Fig. 46), and overflow hose from base of washer.

10. Remove four drain tub screws and lift drain tub off chassis.

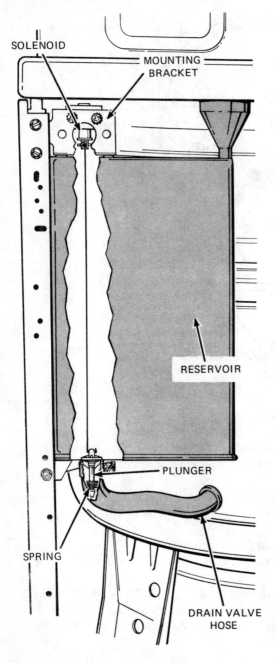

SOLENOID

MOUNTING BRACKET

RESERVOIR

PLUNGER

SPRING

DRAIN VALVE HOSE

Fig. 46. Water reservoir assembly.

Note: Rubber spacers must be between chassis legs and drain tub when tub is installed. If drain valve hose is disengaged from drain tub, use rubber base cement to form a watertight seal when hose is installed.

Water Reservoir Assembly—Shur-Fil Models. *See* Fig. 46.

1. Remove real panel.
2. Disconnect drain valve hose from drain valve and wires from solenoid.
3. Remove three screws holding reservoir assembly to side panel.
4. Remove assembly from washer far enough to disconnect pressure hose.

Reservoir Drain Valve—Shur-Fil Models. *See* Fig. 46.

1. Remove rear panel.
2. Remove water reservoir assembly. (*See* section on Water Reservoir Assembly previously described.)
3. Remove spring from drain valve plunger.
4. Remove two screws holding mounting bracket to top of reservoir, and carefully lift complete drain valve assembly out of reservoir.

Pressure Hose—Shur-Fil Models.

1. Remove rear panel.
2. Remove water reservoir. (*See* section on Water Reservoir Assembly previously described.)
3. Remove panel assembly screws (Fig. 18), and lift assembly off panel support.
4. Disconnect pressure hose from pressure switch (Fig. 22), and pull hose down through cabinet top.

Counterbalance Weight and Bracket.

1. Remove rear panel.
2. Remove two snubber springs from snubber arm closest to the rear.
3. While supporting counterbalance weight, remove two nuts and lockwashers holding weight to bracket.
4. Remove two cap screws and lockwashers holding snubber support plate, snubber arm, and counterbalance weight bracket to main bearing house.
5. Remove bolts, lockwashers, and nut holding counterbalance weight bracket to main mounting plate.

Left Side Panel.

1. Remove front panel. (*See* section on Front Panel previously described.)

2. Remove two screws holding front hold-down bracket to side panel.

3. Remove screws holding rear panel to side panel. (*Note:* Remove shipping plug located in lower edge of cabinet top behind rear hold-down bracket, if it was not removed at time of installation.)

4. Remove four screws holding side panel to base, and move panel toward rear of washer to disengage it from cabinet top.

Right Side Panel.

1. Remove front panel. (*See* section on Front Panel previously described.)

2. Remove two screws holding front hold-down bracket to side panel.

3. Shur-Fil models: Remove water reservoir assembly. (*See* section on Water Reservoir Assembly previously described.)

4. Time Fill models: Remove screws holding rear panel to side panel.

5. *Note:* Remove shipping plug located in lower edge of cabinet top behind rear hold-down bracket, if it was not removed at time of installation.

6. Remove four screws holding side panel to base, move panel toward rear of washer to disengage it from cabinet top, and remove wire harness clips from top of side panel.

Shifter Fork.

1. Remove left side panel. (*See* section on Left Side Panel previously described.)

2. Run transmission belt off transmission pulley and remove belt.

3. Remove cap screw, lockwasher, and flat washer holding stop, hub, and transmission pulley to drive pinion (Fig. 47), and lift stop-off pinion.

4. Rotate transmission pulley clockwise to lift hub and pulley off pinion (Fig. 47).

5. Remove pin holding shifter fork to pivot bracket and remove shifter fork from washer (Fig. 48).

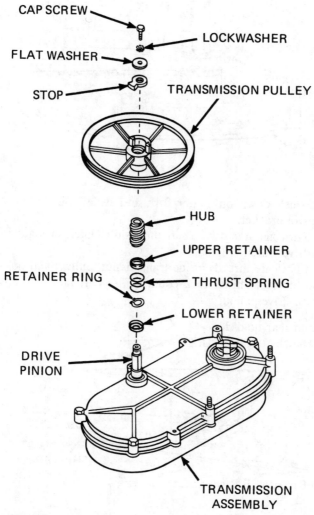

CAP SCREW

LOCKWASHER

FLAT WASHER

STOP

TRANSMISSION PULLEY

HUB

UPPER RETAINER

RETAINER RING

THRUST SPRING

LOWER RETAINER

DRIVE
PINION

TRANSMISSION
ASSEMBLY

Fig. 47.

To install shifter fork

1. With one shifter fork collar engaged in shift clutch (Fig. 48)
and the other collar positioned flat on top of the upper thrust spring

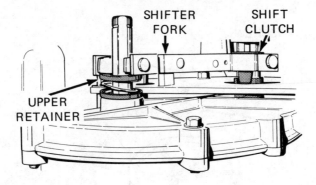

Fig. 48.

retainer, push down on shifter fork and install pin holding shifter fork to pivot bracket.

2. Turn agitator drive shaft until shift clutch engages in transmission drive clutch (Fig. 48).

3. Lubricate threads inside transmission pulley, and on top and inside surfaces of shifter fork collar (Fig. 49), and carefully place pulley over drive pinion.

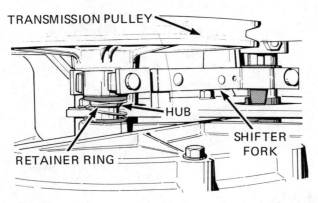

Fig. 49.

4. Lubricate threads on hub, place hub in opening in top of transmission pulley, and rotate hub until flat on inside of hub corresponds with flat on drive pinion.

5. Thread hub down inside pulley by rotating pulley counter-

clockwise. *Note:* Hold down on hub while turning pulley to prevent shift clutch from being lifted out of transmission drive clutch.

6. Turn pulley until hub just seats against retainer ring (Fig. 49).

7. Without moving pulley from position obtained in step 6, position pulley stop on drive pinion so that left side of stop is against left stop surface of pulley (Fig. 50).

8. Secure stop to drive pinion with flat washer, lockwasher, and cap screw (Fig. 50).

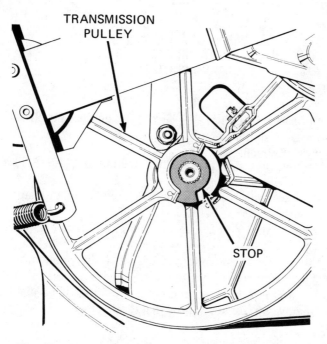

Fig. 50.

9. Check adjustment by rotating pulley in both directions. When rotating pulley in a counterclockwise (agitation) direction, the shift clutch lugs and drive clutch lugs must be firmly engaged (Fig. 49). When rotating in a clockwise (spin) direction, there must be between $\frac{1}{16}$-inch and $\frac{1}{8}$-inch clearance between lugs (Fig. 51). *Note:* If bottom of shift clutch lugs do not clear, remove pulley stop and

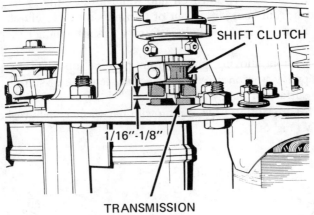

SHIFT CLUTCH

1/16"-1/8"

TRANSMISSION
DRIVE CLUTCH

Fig. 51.

reposition it one serration in a clockwise direction from its previous position.

Transmission Assembly.

1. Remove left side panel. (*See* section on Left Side Panel previously described.)

2. Remove agitator drive shaft. (*See* section on Agitator Drive Shaft previously described.)

3. Remove shifter fork. (*See* section on Shifter Fork previously described.)

4. Lift upper retainer and thrust spring off drive pinion.

5. While supporting transmission, remove two nuts, two cap screws, and washers holding transmission to mounting plate (Fig. 52), and remove transmission through left side of washer.

To remove transmission cover. (*See* Fig. 53.)

1. Remove retainer ring and lower thrust spring retainer from drive pinion (Fig. 53).

2. Remove burrs from drive pinion to prevent damage to pinion seal.

3. Remove three cap screws, and lockwashers holding transmission cover to case.

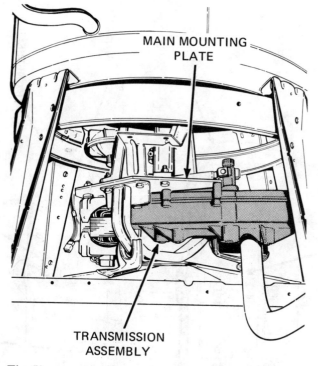

MAIN MOUNTING PLATE

TRANSMISSION ASSEMBLY

Fig. 52.

4. Hold drive pinion down to prevent its pulling out of case, and carefully lift transmission cover off case. *Do not* damage pinion seal when pulling seal over retainer ring groove in pinion.

Note: When transmission is serviced, replace cover gasket and refill transmission with new lubricant. Apply a light film of lubricant to lips of seals when installing cover.

To replace pinion and drive clutch seals. (*See* Figs. 53 and 54.)

1. Pry pinion and drive clutch seals (Fig. 53) out of top of transmission cover.

2. Thoroughly clean seal holes in cover.

3. Support transmission cover and use hammer and wood block to drive clutch seal (with lip extending upward) into top of cover

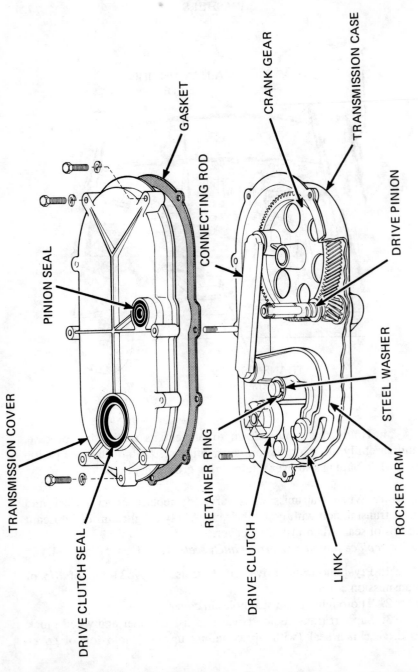

TRANSMISSION COVER

PINION SEAL

GASKET

CRANK GEAR

TRANSMISSION CASE

CONNECTING ROD

DRIVE PINION

DRIVE CLUTCH SEAL

RETAINER RING

DRIVE CLUTCH

LINK

STEEL WASHER

ROCKER ARM

Fig. 53.

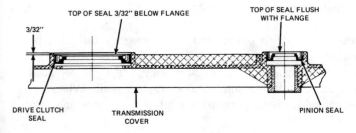

Fig. 54.

until top of outside diameter of seal is $\frac{3}{32}$ inch below top of flange of cover (Fig. 54).

4. Apply a light film of lubricant to lip of drive clutch seal (Fig. 53).

5. Install transmission cover on case, and secure with three cap screws and lockwashers (Fig. 53).

6. Apply a light film of lubricant to lip of pinion seal, and to fiber washer on top of drive pinion (Fig. 53).

7. Place pinion seal (with lip extending upward) (Fig. 54) on drive pinion, and using a hammer and wood block, drive seal down into transmission cover so that it is flush with flange.

To disassemble transmission. (See Fig. 53.)

1. Pour lubricant out of transmission case or remove with a putty knife. Clean remaining lubricant from case with solvent.

2. Remove retainer ring and steel washer holding rocker arm on shaft, and remove connecting rod and link assembly (rocker arm, drive clutch, and link). Remove fiber washers from rocker arm and drive clutch shafts, and from connecting rod on top of crank gear.

3. Remove cotter pin holding connecting rod to rocker arm, and disengage connecting rod from rocker arm. Remove fiber washer from connecting rod. (*Note:* The link assembly can be disassembled by driving or pressing link pins out top of rocker arm and drive clutch.)

4. Remove fiber washer from top of drive pinion, and lift and rotate drive pinion to remove from bearing. Remove steel washer from transmission case. (*Note:* When drive pinion is installed, bearing and hole in transmission case must be perfectly clean.)

5. Lift crank gear off crank gear shaft.

Note: Transmission drive pinion and crank gear should both be replaced if either requires replacement. Do not replace only one of the two gears. All steel and fiber washers should also be replaced if any component of transmission requires replacement. When assembling transmission, oil all parts to aid lubricant in working into moving parts.

Snubber Assembly. *See* Fig. 55.

1. Remove front panel. (*See* section on Front Panel previously described.)
2. Remove agitator drive shaft. (*See* section on Agitator Drive Shaft previously described.)
3. Remove cabinet top assembly. (*See* section on Cabinet Top Assembly previously described.)
4. Remove agitator post and spin tub assembly. (*See* section on Agitator Post and Spin Tub Assembly previously described.)
5. Remove rear panel.
6. Remove drain tub. (*See* section on Drain Tub previously described.)
7. Disconnect two snubber springs from snubber arm and frame ring.
8. Remove two cap screws and lockwashers holding snubber support plate and snubber arm to main bearing housing.
9. Remove two snubber plate cap screws, lockwashers, and nuts.

Main Bearing Assembly.

1. Remove front panel. (*See* section on Front Panel previously described.)
2. Remove agitator drive shaft. (*See* section on Agitator Drive Shaft previously described.)
3. Remove cabinet top assembly. (*See* section on Cabinet Top Assembly previously described.)
4. Remove agitator post and spin tub assembly. (*See* section on Agitator Post and Spin Tub Assembly previously described.)
5. Remove rear panel.
6. Remove drain tub. (*See* section on Drain Tub previously described.)

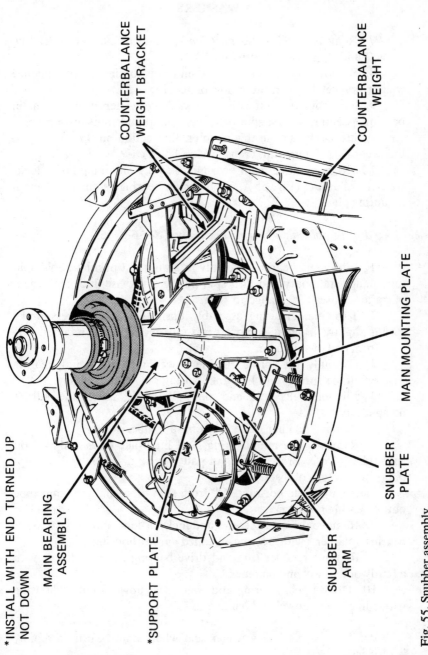

*INSTALL WITH END TURNED UP NOT DOWN

MAIN BEARING ASSEMBLY

*SUPPORT PLATE

COUNTERBALANCE WEIGHT BRACKET

COUNTERBALANCE WEIGHT

MAIN MOUNTING PLATE

SNUBBER PLATE

SNUBBER ARM

Fig. 55. Snubber assembly.

7. Remove three snubbers. (*See* section on Snubber Assembly, steps 7 and 8, previously described.)

8. Remove bolts, lockwashers, and nut holding counterbalance weight bracket to main mounting plate (Fig. 55).

9. Run spin belt off spin pulley. *Note:* After installing main bearing assembly, adjust spin belt, then pump and transmission belts. (*See* Adjustments later in this chapter, the section on Spin Belt, and the section on Pump and Transmission belts.)

10. Remove three main bearing assembly mounting bolts, lockwashers, and nuts (Fig. 55), and lift main bearing assembly off main mounting plate.

To disassemble main bearing assembly. (See Fig. 56.)

1. With main bearing assembly in an upright position, hold spin tube flange stationary and turn spin pulley clockwise until movement of pulley causes tube flange to turn.

2. Turn main bearing assembly upside-down, compress brake spring slightly using a compressor tool, and remove retainer ring "A" from end of spin tube.

3. Carefully lift spring retainer, needle bearing, and bearing race-off brake spring, and lift brake spring out of spin pulley.

4. Lift spin pulley stop and spin pulley (with hub inside pulley) off spin tube.

5. Remove retainer ring "B" from spin tube.

6. Remove wire retainer ring, and lift brake discs and pad off spin tube. (*Note:* Brake discs and pad can be disassembled by slipping clips off tabs of discs.)

7. Remove retainer ring "C" from spin tube, and pull spin tube out of bearing housing.

8. Remove three cap screws and lockwashers, and remove lower bearing retainer (with bearing installed) from housing.

9. Remove retainer ring and drive bearing out of retainer with a hardwood dowel and hammer.

10. Drive upper bearing and water seal upward out of housing with a hardwood dowel and hammer.

Note: Always install new water seal when main bearing assembly is serviced.

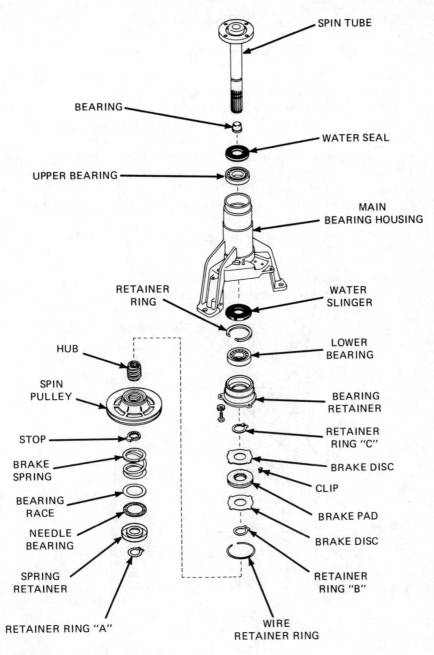

SPIN TUBE

BEARING

WATER SEAL

UPPER BEARING

MAIN BEARING HOUSING

RETAINER RING

WATER SLINGER

HUB

LOWER BEARING

SPIN PULLEY

BEARING RETAINER

STOP

RETAINER RING "C"

BRAKE SPRING

BRAKE DISC

BEARING RACE

CLIP

NEEDLE BEARING

BRAKE PAD

SPRING RETAINER

BRAKE DISC

RETAINER RING "A"

RETAINER RING "B"

WIRE RETAINER RING

Fig. 56. Main bearing assembly.

To assemble main bearing assembly. (*See* Fig. 56.)

1. Drive upper bearing down to shoulder in housing (Fig. 57) with a hardwood dowel and hammer.

2. Apply a generous amount of lubricant to groove in inside diameter of seal, and to shaded area directly above upper bearing (Fig. 57).

3. Drive water seal down into housing, using a hardwood dowel —at outside diameter of seal—and a hammer, until top of seal is set flush with top of housing (Fig. 57).

4. Carefully insert spin tube through water seal and upper bearing in bearing housing.

5. Install water slinger on spin tube using proper tool.

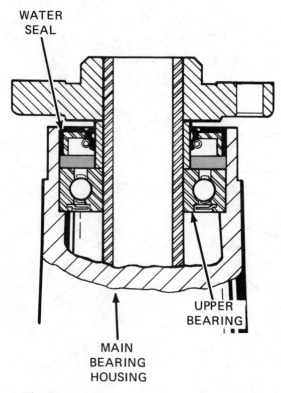

Fig. 57.

6. Press lower bearing into bearing retainer, and install retainer ring.

7. Carefully insert bearing retainer, with lower bearing, over spin tube up into bearing housing, and secure retainer to housing with three cap screws and lockwashers.

8. Install retainer ring "C" on spin tube directly below lower bearing so sharp edge of ring is away from bearing.

9. Clean foreign material off outside surfaces of brake discs and pad, then insert into bearing housing, aligning tabs on outside of discs with grooves in housing.

10. Compress wire retainer ring, and insert ring into groove in bearing housing. Position wire retainer so opening between ends of ring is not located over any brake disc tab.

11. Place retainer ring "B" on spin tube with sharp edge of ring toward brake disc.

12. Thread hub out of spin pulley, and thoroughly clean all foreign material from needle bearings, bearing race, spin pulley, pulley hub, and brake spring retainer with degreasing solvent. Remove all traces of solvent with dry compressed air or lint-free cloth.

13. Apply a light film of lubricant to splines on inside of spin pulley hub, and to threads on outside of hub and inside of spin pulley.

14. Thread hub into spin pulley until top of hub is at least ¼-inch below top surface of spin pulley.

15. Apply a small amount of lubricant to needle bearing on spin pulley.

16. Align splines on inside of spin pulley hub with splines on spin tube, and place spin pulley (with hub installed) over spin tube and into position in bearing housing.

17. Rotate spin pulley until lower flat portion in front of raised half moon on pulley is even with flat edge of hub.

18. Facing opening of raised half moon on spin pulley, position the stop so tab, if dropped into place, would be next to left side of raised half moon. Turn stop one more spline in clockwise direction and slide stop down over spin tube (Fig. 58).

19. Rotate spin pulley in clockwise direction until stop can be dropped down into position on lower flat portion of pulley. With stop against left side of raised half moon (looking at it from open end of half moon), there should be a clearance of no less than .030 inch, nor more than .050 inch between pulley and stop (Fig. 59).

SPIN PULLEY

RAISED "HALF MOON"

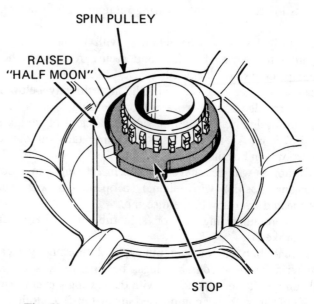

STOP

Fig. 58.

(a) If clearance is less than .030 inch, lift stop off spin tube, rotate stop one spline in clockwise direction, and replace stop over spin tube.

(b) If clearance is greater than .050 inch, lift stop off spin tube, rotate stop one spline in counterclockwise direction, and replace stop over spin tube.

20. Insert brake spring into bottom of spin pulley.

21. Apply small amount of lubricant to both sides of needle bearings, place bearing in brake spring retainer, and place bearing race on top of needle bearings. *Note:* Smoothest side of bearing race should be toward needle bearing. If area of race that contacts needle bearing is not smooth on either side, replace race.

22. Place brake spring retainer (with needle bearing in place) on spring, compress brake spring using compressor tool, and place retainer ring "A" on spin tube. *Note:* Retainer ring should be positioned on spin tube so sharp edge of ring is away from spring retainer. *Caution:* Be sure that retainer ring is firmly seated in groove in spin tube before releasing compressor tool.

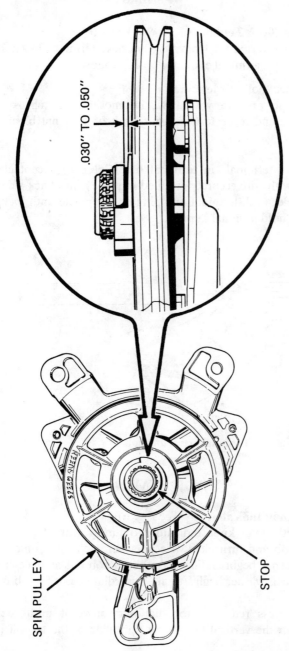

.030" TO .050"

SPIN PULLEY

STOP

Fig. 59.

Terminal Block Terminals.   *See* Fig. 60.

To *remove* terminals from wire harness terminal block plugs or receptacles, use terminal extractor tool as follows:

1. Place tool over terminal.

2. Apply pressure with a twisting motion to compress terminal locking tabs and force terminal out back of terminal block plug or receptacle.

To *install* terminals in terminal block plug or receptacle, insert terminal (with wire securely crimped in place) into back side of plug or receptacle. Push terminal into plug or receptacle until locking tabs spread and hold terminal in place.

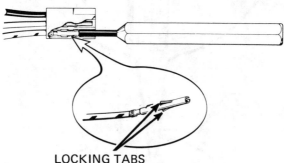

LOCKING TABS

Fig. 60. Terminal extractor tool.

ADJUSTMENTS

Timer Knob Indicator.   *See* Fig. 61.

1. With timer knob indicator pointing toward top-off position, depress knob and turn clockwise one increment at a time, checking to see if washer begins filling by pulling knob out after each click.

2. When washer begins to fill, immediately push knob in to stop washer.

3. Depress red indicator dial and move it until the slot is directly over the vertical line at the right side of the top-off position.

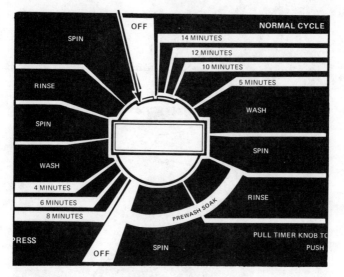

Fig. 61. Timer knob indicator.

Leveling Legs. *See* Fig. 62.

1. Loosen locknuts and thread leveling legs into washer base as far as possible.

2. Turn appropriate leveling leg(s) out of frame *only* until washer is level. Keep washer as close to floor as possible.

3. Install rubber pads over leveling legs. *Note:* All four legs must rest firmly on floor so weight of washer is evenly distributed. Washer must not rock.

4. Tighten lock-nuts securely against bottom of washer base. *Note: Do not* move washer at any time unless lock-nuts are securely tightened.

Pressure Switch. *See* Fig. 63.

The pressure switch on pressure-fill automatic washers is set at the factory for proper water fill levels. However, if there is a problem of overfilling or underfilling, the pressure switch can be adjusted in the home. The maximum water fill level can be increased by turning the adjusting screw clockwise, and decreased by turning the screw counterclockwise. One-quarter turn of the adjusting screw represents approximately a one inch increase or decrease of the water level in the tub.

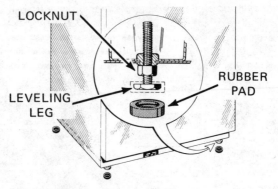

Fig. 62. Leveling legs.

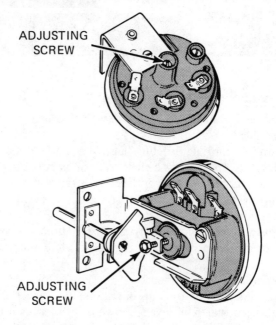

Fig. 63. Pressure switches for various models.

Note: Do not turn the adjusting screw more than three-quarters of a turn in either direction.

Spin Belt.   *See* Fig. 64.

1. Remove front panel. (*See* section on Front Panel previously described.)

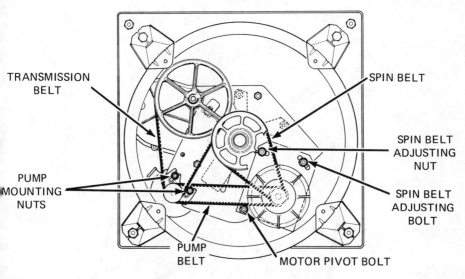

Fig. 64.

2. Loosen pump mounting nuts.

3. Loosen motor pivot bolt, spin belt adjusting bolt, and spin belt adjusting nut.

4. Shift motor to secure proper belt tension. Proper tension is attained when belt can be deflected approximately ½-inch from its normal position by applying moderate pressure (five pounds) to a point midway between pulleys (Fig. 65). *Note:* Use a belt tension meter to aid in making exact belt adjustments.

5. Tighten motor pivot bolt, spin belt adjusting bolt and spin belt adjusting nut, and adjust pump and transmission belts. (*See* following section on Pump and Transmission Belts.)

Pump and Transmission Belts. *See* Fig. 64.

1. Remove front panel. (*See* section on Front Panel previously described.)

2. Loosen pump mounting nuts.

3. Shift pump to secure proper pump and transmission belt tension. Proper tension is attained when belt can be deflected approximately ½-inch from its normal position by applying moderate pressure (five pounds) to a point midway between pulleys (Fig. 65).

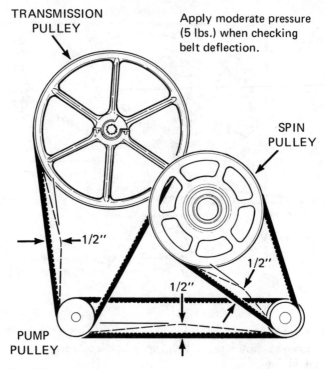

TRANSMISSION
PULLEY

Apply moderate pressure
(5 lbs.) when checking
belt deflection.

SPIN
PULLEY

←1/2″

1/2″

1/2″

PUMP
PULLEY

Fig. 65.

Note: Use a belt tension meter to aid in making exact belt adjustments.

    4. Tighten mounting nuts.

TEST PROCEDURES

Be sure to disconnect power cord and close water supply valves before testing.

Note: For electrical test procedures in this section, use a *live* test cord (Fig. 66), and an ohm meter.

Drive Motor.   *See* Fig. 67.

    1. Remove front panel. (*See* section on Front Panel previously described.)

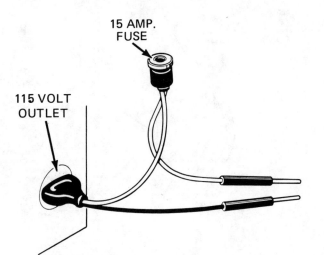

15 AMP.
FUSE

115 VOLT
OUTLET

Fig. 66.

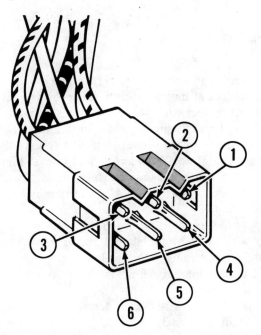

Fig. 67

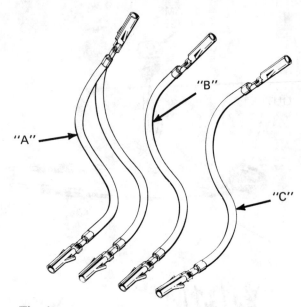

Fig. 68.

2. Disconnect motor harness plug from receptacle.

3. Assemble three motor testing wires as shown in Fig. 68.

4. Connect jumper wire "A" to terminals 3 and 4, jumper wire "B" to terminals 1 and 2, and wire "C" to terminal 6.

5. Apply *live* test cord probes to third terminal of jumper wire "A" and wire "C". Motor should run clockwise at high speed (approximately 1,725 rpm), causing fast spin.

6*. Disconnect jumper wire "A" from terminal 4, and connect that end to terminal 5.

7*. Apply *live* test cord probes to third terminal of jumper wire "A" and to wire "C". Motor should run clockwise at low speed (approximately 1,140 rpm), causing slow spin.

8*. Disconnect jumper wires "A" and "B", leaving wire "C" connected to terminal 6.

9. Connect jumper wire "A" to terminals 2 and 4, and jumper wire "B" to terminals 1 and 3.

10. Apply *live* test cord probes to third terminal of jumper wire

"A" and to wire "C". Motor should run counterclockwise at high speed causing normal agitation.

11*. Disconnect jumper wire "A" from terminal 4, and connect that end to terminal 5.

12*. Apply *live* test cord probes to third terminal of jumper wire "A" and to wire "C". Motor should run counterclockwise at low speed, causing gentle agitation.

13*. Insure that washer is not grounded through power cord or external ground wire, then apply one probe of an ohm meter to the motor case and second probe to each of the terminals in motor harness plug successively. In each instance, there should be an infinity reading on the ohm meter.

Timer. The general procedure for each testing step is as follows:

1. Remove two control panel assembly screws and lift assembly off panel support.

2. Remove timer knob from timer shaft and remove three screws holding timer to control panel. *Note:* Mark top of timer before removing it from control panel.

3. Disconnect all wires from timer except J to J jumper wire (if present). (*Note:* When rewiring timer, see appropriate wiring diagram.)

4. Reinstall timer knob on timer shaft.

5. Apply ohm meter probes to terminals as directed on Trouble and Remedy Chart 4 for specific problem.

6. Starting with timer knob pulled out and with indicator pointing toward top of timer, slowly turn timer knob indicator clockwise until indicator again points toward top of timer. Ohm meter should register a reading only when contacts in the cams in question are closed.

Example:
Problem—No Hot Water—Mallory Timer. (*See* Chart 4.)
1. Follow steps 1 through 4 above.
2. Connect jumper wire between terminals H and C.

* Not applicable to single-speed motors.

3. Connect ohm meter probes to terminals TM and W.

4. Perform step 6 above: ohm meter should indicate a closed circuit when contacts in Cam 5B (bottom) are closed. (*See* Timer Cycle Chart 4 for Mallory timer to see when contacts should be closed.)

CHART 4
TIMER CYCLE

PROBLEM	TIMER TEST	
	Kingston	Mallory
1. NO COLD WATER	TM and R	
	Cam 4B bottom	Cam 5 top
2. NO HOT WATER	Jumper H to C	
	TM and W	
	Cam 4B top	Cam 5 bottom
3. TIMER DOES NOT ADVANCE	Apply "live" test cord to terminals on timer motor wires. Timer motor should run. — AND — L1 and TM	
	Cam 2B	Cam 2
4. CONSTANT AGITATION OR NO AGITATION	Jumpers MA to K and F to G TM and L	
	Cam 3B	Cam 3 bottom
5. CONSTANT SPIN OR NO SPIN	Jumpers MS to K and F to G TM and L	
	Cam 1B	Cam 3 top
6. WATER FILL DOES NOT STOP	See numbers 1, 2 or 3	
7. INADEQUATE FILL	See numbers 1 or 2	
8. DRIVE MOTOR DOES NOT RUN	See numbers 4 or 5	

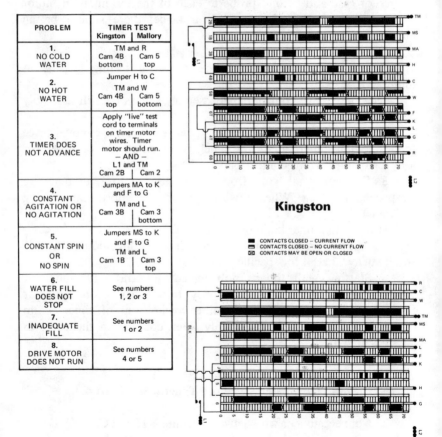

Kingston

■ CONTACTS CLOSED – CURRENT FLOW
▤ CONTACTS CLOSED – NO CURRENT FLOW
⊠ CONTACTS MAY BE OPEN OR CLOSED

Mallory

Chapter 37

Domestic Automatic Dryers

All dryers (Fig. 1) are automatic and have control centers with buttons or dials that allow you to program the dryer to handle loads of different fabrics, such as cotton, delicate, or permanent press. Different settings allow adjustment of drying temperature and time.

As with automatic washers, the more controls you buy on an automatic dryer and the more sophisticated the controls, the higher the price. So before shopping, consider both how much money you wish to pay for a dryer and the time you can afford to spend around it. Then choose the dryer that offers the best compromise between convenience and economy.

CONTROLS

Dryers have two kinds of controls: those that adjust drying temperature, and those that, after drying, time and turn the dryer off. (*See* Fig. 2 and Remedy Chart 4 for specific problem.)

Temperature. Today, dryer temperatures are low to accommodate the man made fabrics while air flow is high to hasten drying. Actually, dryer temperatures differ comparatively little, and controls are there primarily to provide the proper turn-off. Temperature control settings now available on dryers include the following. (*See* Fig. 3.)

1. Regular, or high heat, for cottons and linens.
2. Permanent press for man made fabrics. First heat relaxes wrinkles in fabrics; then, for 5 or 10 minutes clothes tumble without heat. Some dryers signal when they are near the end of the cycle. As soon as the cycle is completed, clothing should be removed to keep wrinkles from setting.

Fig. 1. Domestic automatic dryer.

Fig. 2. Dryer controls.

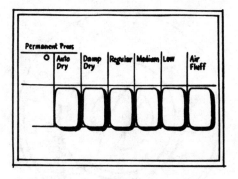

Fig. 3. Temperature selector.

3. Delicate or knit, or low heat, to prevent fabrics from over-drying, shrinking, harshness, and carrying static electricity.

4. Air fluff for freshening items like bedding, stored clothes, shag rugs, and bedspreads. This setting operates the dryer at room temperature.

5. Damp dry for clothes that will be ironed immediately. Some dryers offer as a substitute for this control a means for automatically sprinkling clothes in the dryer.

To benefit from these temperature settings, dryer loads should consist of similar fabrics. Otherwise, some clothes overdry while others remain damp.

Time.   Dryers are designed with three different kinds of timing and turn-off controls: the timer, the thermostat and timer, and the moisture-sensing system.

Timer. With this type you estimate the total drying time for a load and set the control for the number of minutes you want the dryer to operate. When the time is over, the dryer shuts off. (*See* Fig. 4.)

To help you estimate an approximate drying time for a load, the time dial is usually divided into settings for regular, delicate, and permanent press fabrics. If you still guess wrong, you may return to find the wash either overdry or still damp. Overdrying is the bigger problem because it can cause discoloring, shrinkage, and wrinkles.

Thermostat and timer. When you set these controls, you select a temperature in addition to a time (Fig. 5). When the dryer thermo-stat reaches that temperature, the heat turns off and the timer

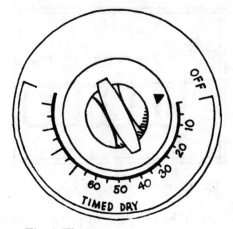

Fig. 4. Timer.

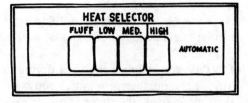

Fig. 5. Thermostat and timer.

advances. As soon as the temperature drops, the heat turns on again and the timer stops.

As the clothes dry, there is less and less heat. Dry clothes, or almost dry clothes, get hot faster and stay hot longer. When the heat is off long enough, the timer advances and completes the drying cycle.

While guesswork is not completely eliminated, the chance of an overdry or wet load is decreased to a great extent.

Moisture sensing. As moist clothes tumble in the dryer and contact built-in electronic sensors, the moisture completes an electric circuit that keeps the heat turned on (Fig. 6). As the moisture decreases during drying, the current in the circuit decreases. When the moisture in the clothes cannot complete the circuit, the heater turns off, and the tumbling continues for a short time to cool down the clothes before the tumbling stops. This kind of automatic control gives you the most accurate results.

Fig. 6. Moisture sensor.

Tumbling.   Stationary drying for woolens, canvas shoes, and other washables that should not be tumbled can be provided by a no-tumble control. Wet articles are put on a rack in the drum, which remains stationary while heated or unheated air flows past.

BUILT-IN FEATURES

Easy access to the lint filter, an inspection window in the dryer door, and lights and bells are practical convenience accessories to consider when buying a dryer.

Drum lights help you find that stray sock, and top panel lights illuminate the dryer's working surface. Many dryers also have a light on the control panel to signal when the machine is on.

A signal alerting you to the end of the drying cycle allows you to remove permanent press items before they wrinkle. Some dryers give an intermittent end-of-cycle signal and retumble the load every few minutes until it is removed.

OTHER CONSIDERATIONS

The controls and built-in features you have examined in dryers are only a few of the things you should consider before making a purchase. Some others are cost, size, construction quality and safety, installation, and repair.

Cost.   Both initial and operating costs are important considerations when buying a dryer.

Initial cost. Automatic dryer prices vary. A dryer with multiple temperature settings or a moisture-sensing time control costs more than a dryer with a manually controlled timer. The prices for gas dryers are higher than those for electric dryers. Higher initial costs, however, may be offset in some communities by lower operating costs.

Operating costs. To calculate operating costs for gas and electric dryers, here are some facts you should know.

1. Drying an average load takes about 3.4 kilowatt-hours of electricity.

2. Drying the same load takes approximately 14 cubic feet of natural gas.

3. Get information from your local utility companies about the local cost for electricity per kilowatt-hour, and the local cost of gas per cubic foot.

Fuel rates differ across the country, so your operating costs may differ from those in our samples. But the arithmetic would go like this for figuring electric dryer operating expenses per load:

3.4 kilowatt-hours to dry an average load
$\times$2.5 cents per kilowatt-hour
_____
8.5 cents total cost

And the following steps are needed to find the cost for running a gas dryer for one load:

14.0   cubic feet of gas to dry an average load
$\times$ 0.09 cents per cubic foot
_____
1.3   cents for gas
$+$ 0.4 cents for electricity per load
_____
1.7   cents total cost

When you multiply the cost per load by the number of loads you dry per year, you may find that one fuel will give a substantial saving over the other.

Size. Two things need to be considered in size—capacity and floor space.

Capacity. Dryers are available that handle maximum loads from 5 to 20 pounds dry weight. Capacities are usually listed on the dryer hang tag. Remember that wet clothes weigh at least twice as much as dry clothes.

Floor space. Check the measurements of the dryer you plan to buy to be certain it will fit your floor space. Regular dryer widths range from 26 to 31 inches, heights from 42 to 45 inches, and depths from 25 to 28 inches. Compact dryers as small as 21 inches wide and 36 inches high are available for small loads.

Construction. Both quality and safety are important construction considerations.

Quality. Both drum and cabinet should have smooth, durable finishes. Stainless steel, zinc coating, or porcelain enamel give you good corrosion protection for the drum. The finish should be listed on the dryer hang tag or in the manufacturer's brochure. Enamel is generally preferred on the dryer cabinet surface because of its resistance to common laundry chemicals and scratches.

Safety. To be assured of the electrical and mechanical safety of your dryer, buy one that carries a label of a testing laboratory, such as Underwriters Laboratories, Inc., or the American Gas Association.

Installation. Installation of an automatic dryer should be done by an experienced serviceman. Generally, your appliance dealer will make arrangements.

Electric dryers. Most regular-size electric dryers operate on 200 to 240 volts. If you do not have this service in your home, an electrician will have to wire a special outlet or your dryer will not work. Get an estimate of rewiring costs before you buy the dryer.

Although drying time is much longer, some electric dryers operate on 110 to 130 volts. This electrical service is common to most homes. However, the dryer should have a separate 15-ampere, grounded circuit, which is not common in older buildings. If you operate the dryer on the same circuit as other appliances, you may blow fuses or trip circuit breakers.

Any outlet for a dryer should be grounded; that is, it should have three holes, one of which connects to a wire leading to the earth outside the building.

Using an adapter plug will solve the problem of fitting a three-prong plug in a two-prong hole, but it may or may not provide grounding. To be sure about grounding, call an electrician.

Gas dryers. A gas dryer needs a convenient gas line. If you have a gas range or water heater in your home, gas should be accessible. You also need an ordinary household electrical outlet to operate the motor, lights, and controls.

Exhaust vents. Almost all regular-size dryers require exhaust vents to channel heat, moisture, and the lint that gets past the filter to the outdoors. To give maximum air flow, ductwork should be short; and lint buildup will be minimized by having few elbow bends. The best spot for a dryer, therefore, is next to an outside wall where a vent hole can be made (Fig. 7). Small, compact dryers may require no venting.

Repair.   Because a dryer is a relatively simple machine with few moving parts to break down or wear out, it will probably need less servicing and will last longer than your washer. But a gas model can have pilot light problems, an electric dryer may need coils repaired, and in both lint may build up in the venting.

To prevent a family crisis when the dryer breaks down, buy from a nearby dealer who has a reputation for prompt and dependable service. You can probably check by talking to your friends and neighbors who are his customers.

Read the warranty before you buy a dryer to determine how well your purchase is protected. Usually, the warranty is covered in the price of the dryer.

Fig. 7. Exhaust vent.

Ask the salesman if the model has removable panels so the motor and belt can be serviced easily. Dryers with removable panels are less expensive to repair.

You can help keep your dryer in good working order by removing lint from the lint filter and vents. If you have metal vent pipes, take them apart and clean them with a brush or a vacuum cleaner attachment. If you have inexpensive plastic vent tubing, you may wish to replace it every few years.

Most dryers have permanently lubricated motors, but if lubrication is required for the dryer you plan to buy, follow directions.

ROUGHING-IN DIMENSIONS AND SPECIFICATIONS

Electric Models.   *See* Fig. 8.

Note: Exhaust openings on sides of dryer are located in the same spot on both sides. Side, rear, and bottom exhaust openings are for four-inch ducting. (*See* installation section later in this chapter.)

Gas Models.   *See* Fig. 9.

Note: Exhaust openings on sides of dryer are located in the same spot on both sides. Side, rear, and bottom exhaust openings are for four-inch ducting. (*See* Installation section later in this chapter.)

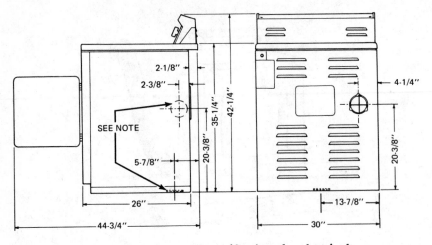

Fig. 8. Roughing-in dimensions and specifications for electric dryer.

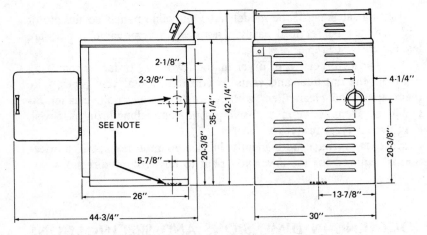

Fig. 9. Roughing-in dimensions and specifications for gas dryer.

INSTALLATION

Electric Dryers. *Electrical service.* The electrical service must be a separate branch, three-wire, 60-Hertz, single-phase circuit fused with 30-ampere fuses. Electrical service should be of the maximum rated voltage listed on the serial plate. Heating elements are available for field installation in dryers that are to be connected to electrical service of different voltages than that listed on the serial plate. (*See* Fig. 10.)

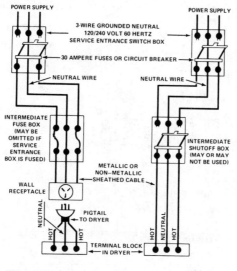

Fig. 10.

If branch circuit to dryer is 15 feet or less in length, use UL approved No. 10 wire, or as required by local codes. If over 15 feet, No. 8 UL approved wire should be used, or as required by local codes. Allow sufficient slack in wiring so the dryer can be moved from its normal location when necessary.

Remove terminal block access panel on the dryer's rear panel. Make certain inner nuts on terminal block are tight, then connect power cord or wires to terminal block posts, using nuts and washers from accessories pack. Tighten and secure outer nuts. The electrical installation should conform to the National Electric Code and such local regulations as might apply. The method of wiring is optional and subject to local code requirements.

Grounding strap. Electric dryers are grounded to neutral through a *grounding strap.* If the dryer is installed in a mobile home or if local codes do not permit grounding through the neutral, remove grounding strap from dryer. (Reinstall inner nut securely on center

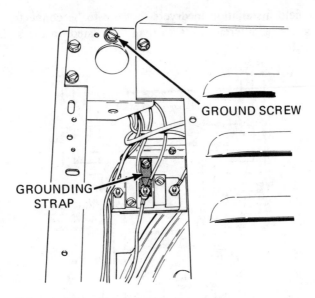

GROUND SCREW

GROUNDING STRAP

Fig. 11. Grounding strap.

post of terminal block.) Ground the dryer frame externally by connecting one end of a copper wire under the ground screw and the other end to a known ground such as a cold water pipe. (*See* Fig. 11.)

Gas Dryers.   *Note:* The gas dryer installation must conform with American National Standard Z223.1-1974 National Fuel Gas Code.

Gas service. Be sure to install dryer with sufficient clearance for servicing. (*See* Fig. 12.) *Note:* Use a pipe joint compound resistant to actions of low pressure gas.

Gas dryers installed in mobile homes *must* be exhausted to the outdoors, and *must* be permanently attached to the floor. Dryer installations kits for a mobile home installation are available from your dealer or the manufacturer.

Electrical grounding. To insure protection against shock hazards, the dryer shown in Fig. 1 *must* be grounded. The three-prong grounding plug on the power cord should be plugged directly into a grounded three-prong receptacle. *Do not*, under any circumstances, remove the round grounding prong from the plug.

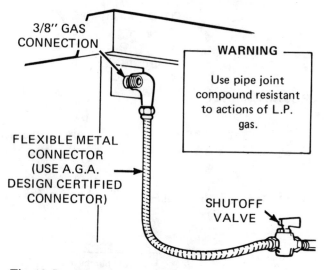

3/8" GAS CONNECTION

WARNING

Use pipe joint compound resistant to actions of L.P. gas.

FLEXIBLE METAL CONNECTOR (USE A.G.A. DESIGN CERTIFIED CONNECTOR)

SHUTOFF VALVE

Fig. 12. Installing dryer.

Any adapter or external ground wire used should be properly connected to a known ground.

Unit must be grounded in accordance with the National Electric Code and local codes and ordinances. Electrical work should be done by a qualified electrician.

The *dryer cabinet* must be grounded to eliminate any possible shock hazard. Use the enclosed ground wire and strap to ground the dryer to a known ground such as a cold water pipe (Fig. 13). *Do not ground to a gas or hot water pipe.*

Lighting pilot burner. Step 1: Open gas valve in gas supply line to dryer. (*See* steps 2, 3, and 4 in Fig. 14.) *Note:* If pilot light goes out, wait five minutes before relighting.

After dryer has run for five minutes, observe the burner flame. Adjust air shutter to obtain a soft, uniform flame (Fig. 14). (A lazy, white-tipped flame indicates lack of air; a harsh, roaring flame indicates too much air.)

All Models.   *Outdoor exhaust.* The dryer can be exhausted to the outdoors through the back, left, right, or bottom panel (Fig. 15).

Exhaust kits are available as optional equipment at extra cost. (*See* Fig. 15.) The *exhaust pipe must* be four inches in diameter. Rigid

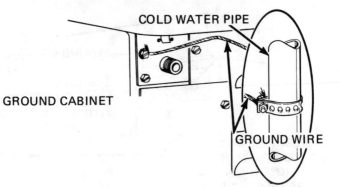

Fig. 13. Grounding dryer cabinet.

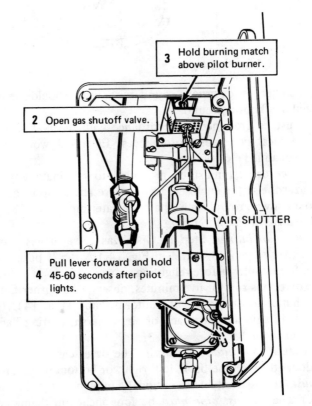

Fig. 14. Lighting pilot burner.

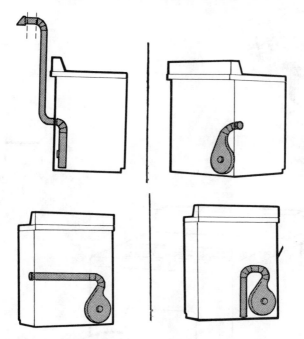

Fig. 15. Outdoor exhausts.

or flexible aluminum exhaust pipe is recommended. Maximum length of exhaust pipe is 14 feet with two elbows. Deduct two feet in length for each additional elbow. Outer end of exhaust pipe must have a weather hood with hinged damper to prevent back-draft when dryer is not in operation. The weather hood should be at least 12 inches above the ground. *Note:* Cut and remove wire guards from exhaust elbow before connecting exhaust pipe (Fig. 16).

Indoor exhaust. Use an indoor exhaust *only* if exhausting outdoors is impractical. (*See* Fig. 17.)

The room must be well ventilated. *Be sure* to use a lint bag or nylon stocking over the end of the exhaust pipe to collect lint.

Leveling dryer. To level dryer proceed as follows: Loosen locknuts; adjust legs to level dryer; tighten locknuts. Dryer must not rock. (*See* Fig. 18.)

Tape. Open loading door and remove shipping tape (Fig. 19).

Checking heat. Set temperature selector switch at Normal and set

Fig. 16. Exhaust pipe.

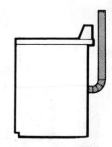

Fig. 17. Indoor exhaust.

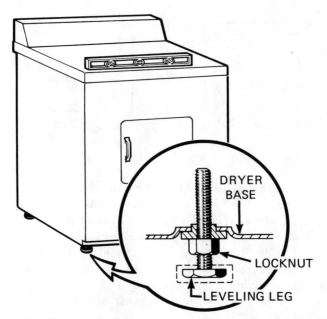

Fig. 18. Leveling dryer.

timer knob at 60. Close loading door and press start button. After dryer has operated for three minutes, exhaust air should be warm.

SERVICE PROCEDURES

Note: For safety reasons, disconnect electrical service and close valve in gas supply line to gas dryer before servicing.

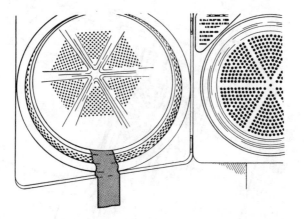

Fig. 19.

Timer. For all models except flat tops, *see* Fig. 20, 21, or 22 for timer removal.

Note: When timer knob is installed, adjust indicator. (*See* section on Adjustments, Time Knob Indicator, later in this chapter.)

Flat top models:

1. Remove front panel. (*See* section on Front Panel later in this chapter.)

2. Remove two hold-down screws (Fig. 49) and block up front of cabinet top.

3. *See* Fig. 23 for timer removal.

Temperature Selector Switch. *See* Fig. 20, 21, or 23 for switch removal.

Signal Control. *See* Fig. 20 or 21 for signal control removal.

Light Switch. *See* Fig. 20 for switch removal.

Start Switch. For all models except flat tops, *see* Fig. 20, 21, or 22 for switch removal.

Flat top models.

1. Remove front panel. (*See* section on Front Panel described later in this chapter.)

2. Remove two hold-down screws (Fig. 51) and block up front of cabinet top.

3. *See* Fig. 23 for switch removal.

Ballast. *See* Fig. 24, for ballast removal.

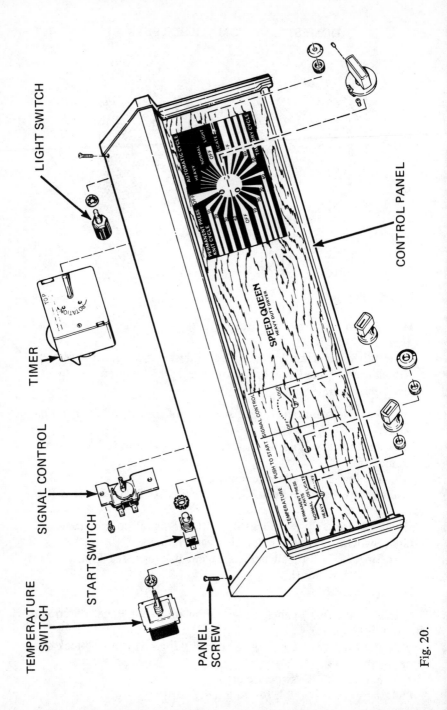

LIGHT SWITCH

CONTROL PANEL

TIMER

SIGNAL CONTROL

START SWITCH

TEMPERATURE SWITCH

PANEL SCREW

Fig. 20.

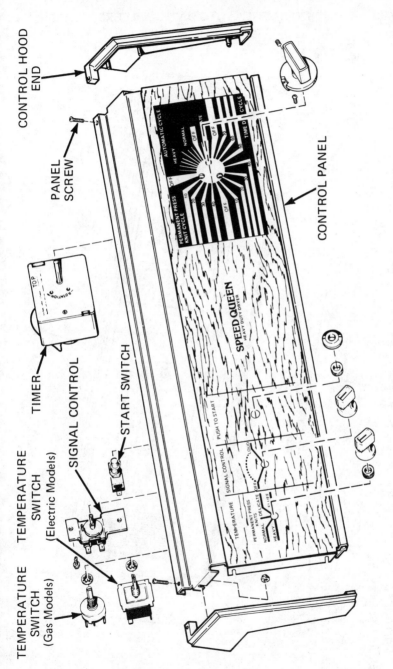

CONTROL HOOD
END

PANEL
SCREW

TIMER

TEMPERATURE
SWITCH
(Electric Models)

TEMPERATURE
SWITCH
(Gas Models)

SIGNAL CONTROL

START SWITCH

CONTROL PANEL

AUTOMATIC CYCLE

HEAVY

NORMAL

OFF

TIME D

PERMANENT PRESS
KNIT CYCLE

OFF

SPEED QUEEN
HEAVY DUTY DRYER

PUSH TO START

SIGNAL CONTROL

TEMPERATURE

PERMANENT PRESS
KNITS DELICATE

NORMAL

HEAVY

Fig. 21.

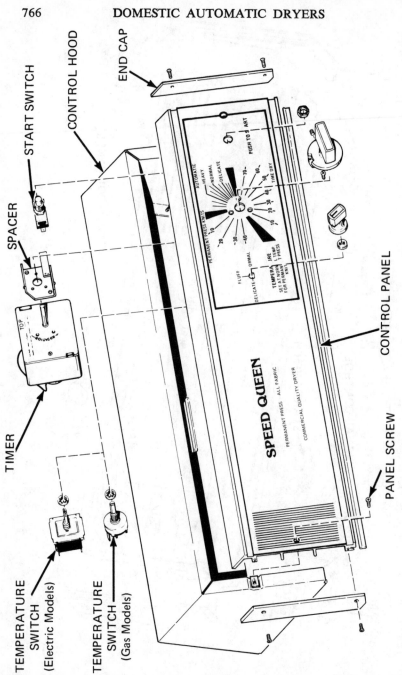

START SWITCH

CONTROL HOOD

END CAP

SPACER

TIMER

TEMPERATURE SWITCH (Electric Models)

TEMPERATURE SWITCH (Gas Models)

CONTROL PANEL

PANEL SCREW

SPEED QUEEN ALL FABRIC

PERMANENT PRESS

COMMERCIAL QUALITY DRYER

Fig. 22.

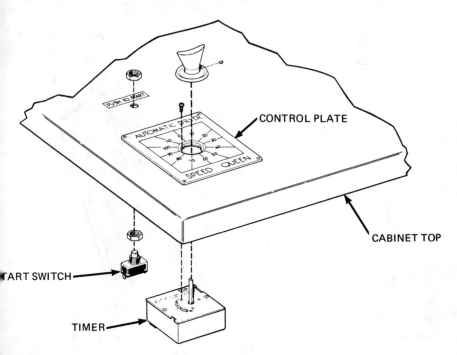

Fig. 23.

Control Panel.   *See* type shown in Fig. 21.

1. Remove panel screws and lift assembly off panel support.
2. Remove left and right control hood ends (Fig. 24).
3. Lift hood top panel (Fig. 24) off panel assembly.
4. Loosen timer knob set screw and pull knob off shaft. *Note:* When timer knob is installed, adjust indicator. (*See* section on Adjustments, Timer Knob Indicator, described later in this chapter.)
5. Models with signal buzzer: pull knob off signal buzzer and pull collar off light switch ferrule nut.
6. Pull knob off temperature selector switch and remove start switch collar.
7. Tilt control panel forward slightly and raise to disengage bottom edge of panel from panel trim (Fig. 24).

Control Panel.   *See* type shown in Fig. 21.

1. Remove panel screws and lift assembly off panel support.

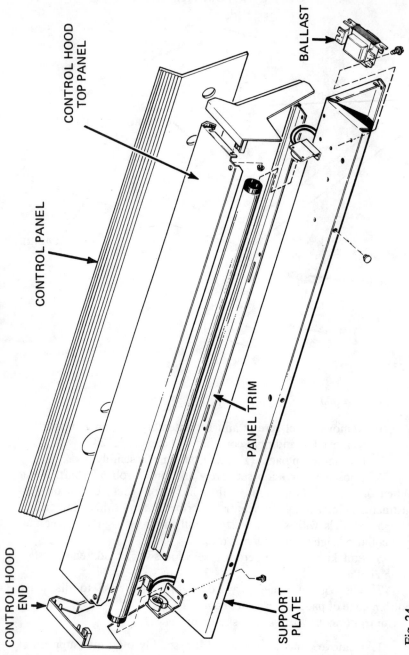

CONTROL HOOD TOP PANEL

CONTROL PANEL

BALLAST

PANEL TRIM

CONTROL HOOD END

SUPPORT PLATE

Fig. 24.

2. Remove left and right control hood ends.

3. Loosen timer knob set screw and pull knob off shaft. *Note:* When timer knob is installed, adjust indicator. (*See* section on Adjustments, Timer Knob Indicator, described later in this chapter.)

4. Pull knob off temperature selector switch and remove knurled nut holding switch in control panel.

5. Remove hex nut holding start switch in control panel.

6. Remove three screws holding timer in control panel.

Control Panel. *See* type shown in Fig. 22.

1. Remove panel screws and pull panel away from control hood as far as wires will permit.

2. Loosen timer knob set screw and pull knob off shaft. *Note:* When timer knob is installed, adjust indicator. (*See* section on Adjustments, Timer Knob Indicator, described later in this chapter.)

3. Remove three screws holding timer to control panel. *Note:* When reinstalling timer, position spacer between timer and control panel.

4. Pull knob off temperature selector switch.

5. Remove temperature selector switch knurled nut and start switch hex nut.

6. Remove left and right end caps.

Burner System Components—White-Rodgers Automatic Ignition. *See* section on Glow Bar Ignition Burner System later in this chapter.

1. Complete Burner Assembly. (*See* Fig. 25.)

   (a) Open access door and close gas shut-off valve.

   (b) Disconnect flare nut from gas shut-off valve.

   (c) Disconnect tan and white wires at connectors.

   (d) Remove screws holding gas valve bracket and igniter control bracket to burner shield.

   (e) Carefully lift burner assembly out of dryer.

2. Igniter.

   (a) Remove complete burner assembly. (*See* step 1.)

   (b) Disconnect igniter wires from igniter control. *Note:* When installing igniter, connect yellow wire to igniter control terminal IGY, and orange wire to IGO.

   (c) Remove two igniter attaching screws (Fig. 26).

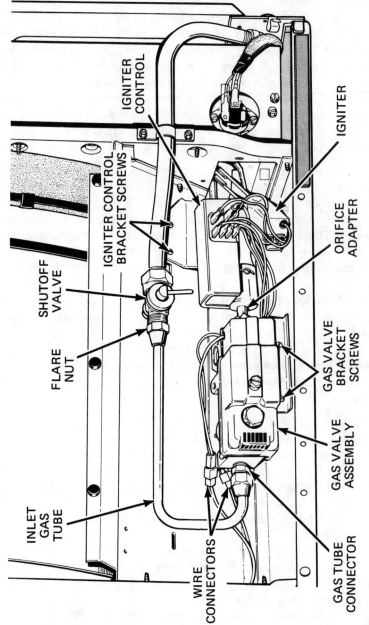

IGNITER CONTROL

IGNITER

IGNITER CONTROL BRACKET SCREWS

ORIFICE ADAPTER

SHUTOFF VALVE

FLARE NUT

GAS VALVE BRACKET SCREWS

GAS VALVE ASSEMBLY

INLET GAS TUBE

WIRE CONNECTORS

GAS TUBE CONNECTOR

Fig. 25.

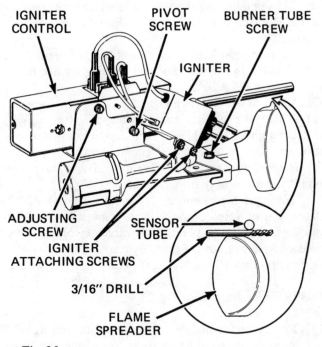

IGNITER
CONTROL

PIVOT
SCREW

BURNER TUBE
SCREW

IGNITER

ADJUSTING
SCREW

SENSOR
TUBE

IGNITER
ATTACHING SCREWS

3/16" DRILL

FLAME
SPREADER

Fig. 26.

3. Igniter Control.

(a) Remove complete burner assembly. (*See* step 1.)

(b) Disconnect all wires from igniter control.

(c) Remove igniter control pivot and adjusting screws (Fig. 26).

4. To Install Igniter Control. (*See* Fig. 26.)

(a) Insert pivot and adjusting screws through bracket and start them into igniter control to secure control to bracket. Leave adjusting screw loose, but tighten pivot screw just enough to hold control snugly against bracket.

(b) Pivot igniter control to raise sensor tube, then place $\frac{3}{16}$-inch drill (or short length of $\frac{3}{16}$-inch diameter rod) on flat surface on top of burner tube flame spreader.

(c) While holding drill in place, pivot igniter control to lower sensor tube until bottom of tube just touches drill.

(d) Tighten adjusting screw, then pivot screw without moving igniter control. Recheck clearance, and re-adjust if necessary.

5. Burner Tube

(a) Remove complete burner assembly. (*See* step 1.)

(b) Remove two screws and nut holding burner tube to igniter control bracket (Fig. 26).

6. Gas Valve Assembly. (*See* Fig. 25.)

(a) Disconnect flare nut from gas shut-off valve.

(b) Disconnect tan, black, red, and white wires from igniter control, and tan and white wires at connectors.

(c) Remove two screws holding gas valve bracket to burner shield, and lift valve assembly from dryer.

(d) Turn gas tube connector (or inlet elbow) and burner orifice adapter out of valve. *Note:* Gas valve must be installed with arrow embossed on bottom pointing in direction of gas flow. Use an approved sealer (type not dissolved by gas) on all gas connections and make certain connections are tight. Test for leaks with a soap solution.

7. Gas Valve Resistor. (*See* Fig. 27.)

(a) Open access door.

(b) Remove valve housing screw, and lift housing off valve.

(c) Remove screws holding wires to resistor and resistor to mount.

8. Gas Valve Coil. (*See* Fig. 27.)

(a) Open access door.

(b) Remove valve housing screw, and lift housing off valve.

(c) Remove screw holding red and white wires to resistor.

(d) Remove metal wire connector holding white and black wires to black coil wire, and disconnect wires.

(e) Remove two plunger guide and bracket screws, and lift bracket (with O ring, plate, and coil attached) off valve cover.

(f) Pull O ring, plate, and coil off plunger guide. *Note:* When installing coil, O ring must fit into counterbore in valve cover, and sharp edge of hole in plate must be up (away from O ring).

9. Gas Valve Spring and Plunger (*See* Fig. 27.)

(a) Open access door and close gas shut-off valve.

(b) Remove valve housing screw, and lift housing off valve.

(c) Remove valve cover screws, and lift cover and regulator spring off valve. *Note:* Regulator spring must be in place between

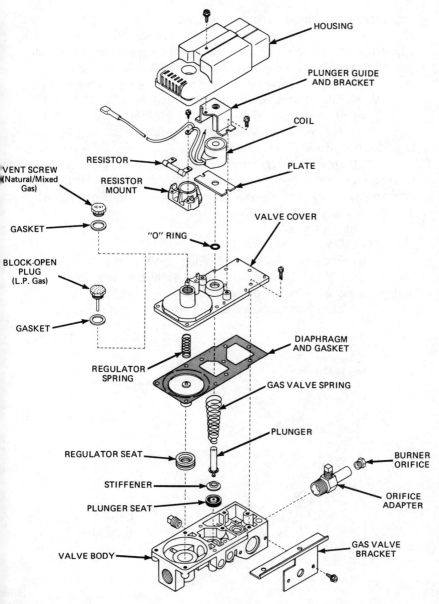

HOUSING

PLUNGER GUIDE
AND BRACKET

COIL

RESISTOR

VENT SCREW
(Natural/Mixed
Gas)

RESISTOR
MOUNT

PLATE

GASKET

VALVE COVER

"O" RING

BLOCK-OPEN
PLUG
(L.P. Gas)

GASKET

DIAPHRAGM
AND GASKET

REGULATOR
SPRING

GAS VALVE SPRING

PLUNGER

REGULATOR SEAT

BURNER
ORIFICE

STIFFENER

ORIFICE
ADAPTER

PLUNGER SEAT

VALVE BODY

GAS VALVE
BRACKET

Fig. 27.

diaphragm plate and regulator screw when valve cover is installed. *Do not* remove regulator screw from valve cover. Regulator screw is adjusted at the factory to reduce gas supply pressure to three inches water column pressure. *Do not* readjust without a *manometer*.

(d) Lift gas valve spring and plunger out of valve body.

10. Regulator Seat, Diaphragm and Gasket. (*See* Fig. 27.)

(a) Remove gas valve spring and plunger. (*See* step 8.)

(b) Pull regulator stem out of regulator seat, and lift regulator diaphragm and gasket off valve body.

(c) Disengage regulator seat from valve body. *Note:* Regulator seat must be properly inserted in valve (markings up), and stem of diaphragm must be inserted down through regulator seat when diaphragm and gasket is installed.

11. Burner Orifice.

(a) Open access door.

(b) Remove two screws holding igniter control bracket to burner shield (Fig. 25) and carefully move burner tube toward rear of dryer, away from burner orifice.

(c) Turn burner orifice out of orifice adapter (Fig. 28).

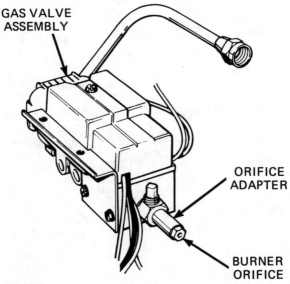

Fig. 28.

Burner System Components—White-Rodgers Standing Pilot. *See* section on Glow Bar Ignition Burner System later in this chapter.

    1. Complete Burner Assembly (*See* Fig. 29.)

        (a) Open access door and close gas shut-off valve.

        (b) Disconnect white and tan wires at connectors.

        (c) Remove two screws holding gas valve bracket to burner shield.

        (d) Remove two screws holding burner tube to burner shield.

        (e) Disconnect flare nut from gas shut-off valve and carefully lift burner assembly out of dryer. *Note:* Use caution when re-

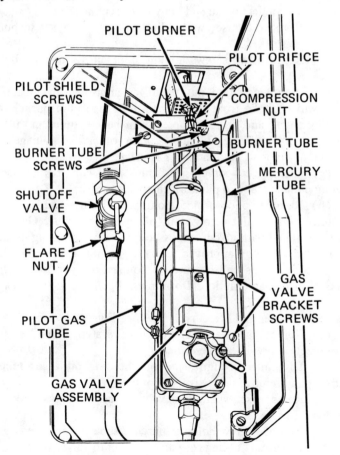

Fig. 29.

moving burner assembly to avoid damaging pilot gas tube and pilot burner mercury tube.

2. Gas Valve Assembly (*See* Fig. 29.)

(a) Open access door and close gas shut-off valve.

(b) While holding pilot orifice, carefully loosen compression nut connecting pilot gas tube to orifice, then loosen pilot orifice. *Note:* Do not damage pilot burner mercury tube when loosening compression nut and pilot orifice. When installing gas valve do not tighten compression nut and pilot orifice until pilot burner is secured to pilot burner shield.

(c) Disconnect white and tan wires at connection.

(d) Remove two screws holding gas valve bracket to burner shield.

(e) Remove two screws holding pilot burner to pilot burner shield.

(f) Disconnect flare nut from gas shut-off valve, carefully move gas valve toward front of dryer to disengage pilot burner from pilot burner shield and orifice adapter from burner tube, and lift gas valve out of dryer. *Note:* Do not kink or otherwise damage pilot burner mercury tube when removing gas valve.

(g) Disconnect compression nut and compression screw connecting pilot gas tube to pilot orifice and gas valve.

(h) Remove pilot orifice from pilot burner, and turn gas tube connector (or inlet elbow) out of gas valve. *Note:* Gas valve must be reinstalled with arrow embossed on bottom pointing in direction of gas flow. Use an approved sealer (type not dissolved by gas) on all gas connections and be sure all connections are tight. Check for leaks with a soap solution. *Do not use open flame to check for leaks.*

3. Pilot Burner and Mercury Tube. (*See* Fig. 30.)

(a) Remove gas valve assembly. (*See* step 2 in Gas Valve Assembly section previously described.)

(b) Disconnect compression nut holding pilot gas tube to pilot orifice, and remove orifice from pilot burner.

(c) Remove screw holding valve housing to gas valve and lift housing off valve.

(d) Remove screw holding mercury tube to top of gas valve and loosen two screws holding gas valve bracket to valve.

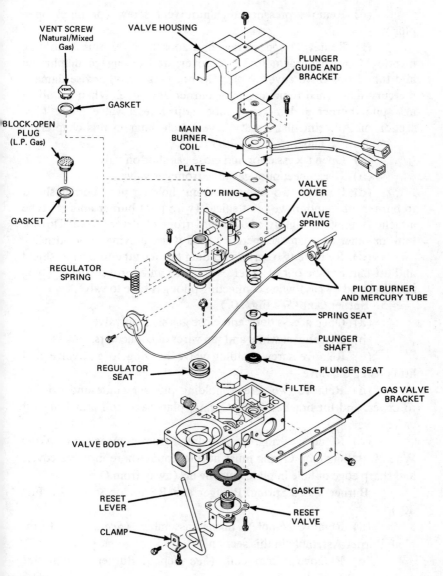

Fig. 30.

(e) Remove pressure regulator vent screw (or block-open plug).

(f) Remove upper screw and loosen lower screw holding mercury tube diaphragm to valve cover, and disengage diaphragm and tube from valve cover. *Note:* Do not kink or otherwise damage mercury tube when removing pilot burner and tube. When installing new pilot burner and mercury tube, adjust reset valve latch. (*See* section on Adjustments, Reset Valve Latch, later in this chapter.)

4. Burner Tube. (*See* Fig. 29.)

(a) Open access door and close gas shut-off valve.

(b) Disconnect pilot gas tube from gas valve.

(c) Remove two screws and nut holding pilot burner shield to burner tube, and move pilot shield (with pilot burner and gas tube attached) upward slightly and toward front of dryer. *Note:* Do not kink or otherwise damage mercury tube when moving pilot burner.

(d) Remove two screws holding burner tube to burner shield and lift burner tube out of dryer. *Note:* Use an approved sealer (type not dissolved by gas) when connecting pilot gas tube to valve.

5. Burner Coil (*See* Fig. 30.)

(a) Open access door and close gas shut-off valve.

(b) Disconnect white and tan wires at connectors.

(c) Remove screw holding valve housing to gas valve and lift housing off valve.

(d) Remove two screws holding plunger guide and bracket to cover, and lift bracket (with O ring, plate, and coil attached) off valve cover.

(e) Remove O ring, plate and coil from plunger guide. *Note:* When installing coil, O ring must fit into counterbore in valve cover, and sharp edge of hole in plate must be up (away from O ring).

6. Burner Valve Spring, Plunger and Regulator Seat. (*See* Fig. 30.)

(a) Remove complete burner assembly. (*See* step 1, Complete Burner Assembly in this section.)

(b) Remove burner coil. (*See* step 5, Burner Coil in this section.)

(c) Loosen two screws holding gas valve bracket to valve.

(d) Remove remaining screws holding valve cover to valve

body, carefully lift cover off body, and pull stem of regulator out of regulator seat. *Note:* When removing valve cover, use caution to avoid damaging diaphragm gasket. Regulator stem must be inserted down through center of regulator seat and regulator spring must be in place when valve cover is installed.

    (e) Lift spring and plunger out of valve body.

    (f) Disengage regulator seat from valve body. *Note:* When installing, insert regulator seat into valve body with markings up.

    7. Reset Valve (*See* Fig. 30.)

    (a) Remove complete burner assembly. (*See* step 1, Complete Burner Assembly, in this section.)

    (b) Remove four screws holding reset valve to gas valve and remove valve from body.

    (c) Remove two screws and clamp holding reset lever to reset valve and remove lever.

Burner System Components—Eaton Standing Pilot.   *See* section on Glow Bar Ignition Burner System later in this chapter.

    1. Complete Burner System. (*See* Fig. 31.)

    (a) Open access door and close gas shut-off valve.

    (b) Disconnect wires from gas valve burner coil.

    (c) Remove two screws holding gas valve bracket to burner shield.

    (d) Remove two screws holding burner tube to burner shield.

    (e) Disconnect flare nut from gas shut-off valve and carefully lift complete burner assembly out of dryer. *Note:* Use caution when removing burner assembly to avoid damaging pilot gas tube and pilot burner mercury tube.

    2. Gas Valve Assembly. (*See* Fig. 31.)

    (a) Open access door and close gas shut-off valve.

    (b) Disconnect wires from gas valve burner coil.

    (c) Remove two screws holding gas valve bracket to burner shield.

    (d) Remove two screws holding pilot burner to burner tube.

    (e) Disconnect flare nut from gas shut-off valve and carefully lift gas valve assembly out of dryer. *Note:* Use caution when removing gas valve assembly to avoid damaging pilot gas tube and pilot burner mercury tube.

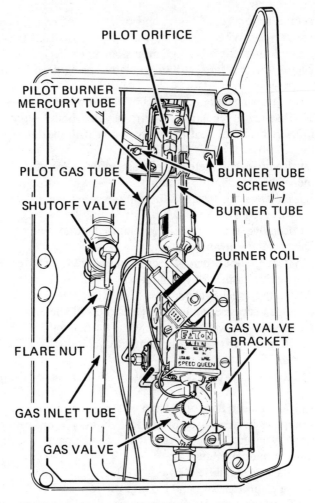

Fig. 31.

(f) While holding pilot orifice, carefully loosen compression nut holding pilot gas tube to pilot orifice.

(g) Loosen compression nut holding pilot gas tube to gas valve.

(h) Remove gas inlet tube from gas valve. *Note:* When re-installing gas valve assembly, use an approved sealer (type not dissolved by gas) on all gas connections and be sure all connections are tight. Check for gas leaks with a soap solution. *Do not use an open flame to check for leaks.*

   3. Pilot Burner and Mercury Tube. (*See* Fig. 32.)
       (a) Remove gas valve assembly. (*See* step 2, Gas Valve Assembly, in this chapter.)
       (b) Remove screw holding mercury tube clamp to gas valve.
       (c) Remove two screws holding mercury tube diaphragm to gas valve. *Note:* Be careful not to lose the actuating pin.
       (d) Remove pilot orifice from pilot burner.
   4. Burner Coil. (*See* Fig. 32.)
       (a) Open access door and close gas shut-off valve.
       (b) Disconnect wires from gas valve burner coil.
       (c) Remove two screws holding coil hold-down bracket to gas valve, and lift bracket and burner coil off plunger guide.
   5. Burner Coil Spring and Plunger. (*See* Fig. 32.)
       (a) Remove burner coil. (*See* step 4, Burner Coil, in this chapter.)
       (b) Remove remaining screws holding plunger guide to gas valve and remove plunger guide, gasket, spring, and plunger.
   6. Gas Valve Filter. (*See* Fig. 32.)
       (a) Remove complete burner system. (*See* step 1, Complete Burner System, in this chapter.)
       (b) Loosen compression not holding pilot gas tube to gas valve.
       (c) Remove three screws holding pilot gas tube outlet to gas valve, and remove outlet, gasket, filter screens, and filter from gas valve.
   7. Reset Valve. (*See* Fig. 32.)
       (a) Remove complete burner system. (*See* step 1, Complete Burner System, in this chapter.)
       (b) Remove two screws holding reset lever and bracket to reset valve.
       (c) Remove remaining screws holding reset valve to gas valve, and remove reset valve and gasket.
   8. Regulator Pin and Diaphragm. (*See* Fig. 32.)
       (a) Remove gas valve assembly. (*See* step 2, Gas Valve Assembly, in this chapter.)
       (b) Remove four screws holding regulator cover to gas valve, carefully pry off regulator cover, and remove regulator spring.

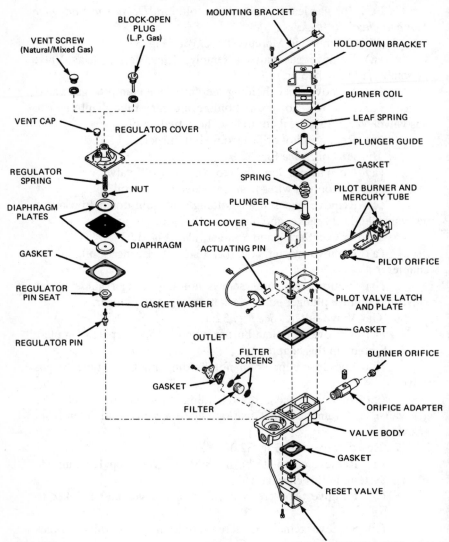

Fig. 32.

(c) Insert small punch through hole in regulator pin, and remove nut holding diaphragm plate to pin.

(d) Remove diaphragm and diaphragm plates, regulator pin seat, gasket washer, regulator pin, and gasket.

Inner or Outer Door Seal.

    1. *See* Fig. 33 for duct ring removal.

    2. Disengage outer door seal from duct ring or inner door seal from front support frame.

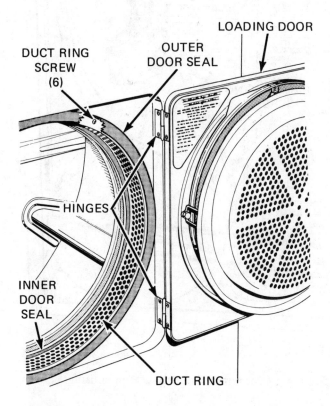

Fig. 33.

Exhaust Fan Belt.

    1. Remove rear panel.

    2. Run belt off fan pulley (Fig. 34).

Note: After installing, adjust belt. (*See* section on Adjustments, Exhaust Fan Belt, later in this chapter.)

Exhaust Fan Housing.

    1. Remove rear panel.

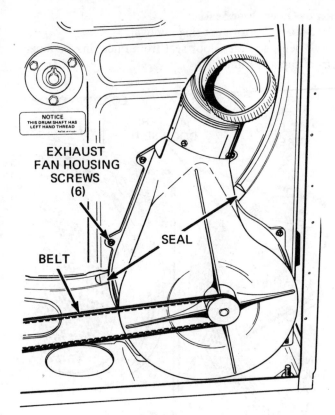

Fig. 34.

2. *See* Fig. 34 for removal of exhaust fan housing.

Note: When installing assembly, use heat-resistant cement to se-cure seal to rear support frame and gasket to frame housing.

See Fig. 35 for exhaust fan housing assembly sequence. *Do not* drive bearing out of housing—support housing and *press* bearing out; or use a bearing puller.

Drive Motor.

    1. Remove rear panel.

    2. Run belt off fan pulley (Fig. 34).

    3. Disengage idler lever spring from dryer base (Fig. 36), and slip belt off motor drum drive pulley (Fig. 37).

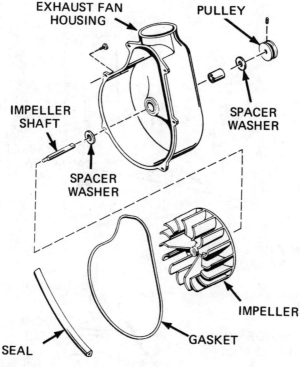

Fig. 35.

4. Disconnect wires. (*Note:* Refer to appropriate wiring diagram when rewiring motor.)

5. Remove cap screw and lockwasher holding motor bracket to base (Fig. 36), and pull motor and bracket out of rear of dryer.

6. Remove motor mounting clamps (Fig. 38), and disengage motor from bracket.

7. Loosen pulley set screws and remove pulleys.

Note: Motor drum drive pulley must be all the way on shaft and motor exhaust fan pulley must be aligned with fan pulley when motor is installed.

To remove motor switch. (*See* Fig. 38.)

1. Remove two screws holding switch to motor.
2. Disconnect motor leads from switch terminals.

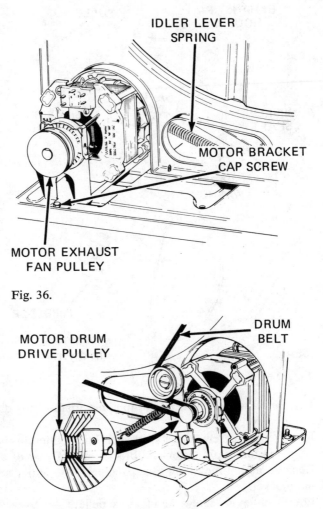

IDLER LEVER
SPRING

MOTOR BRACKET
CAP SCREW

MOTOR EXHAUST
FAN PULLEY

Fig. 36.

DRUM
BELT

MOTOR DRUM
DRIVE PULLEY

Fig. 37.

Note: See wiring schematics in Appendix **XI** to rewire motor switch to motor.

Drum Shaft Bearing.

1. Remove rear panel.
2. Disconnect idler lever spring (Fig. 36).
3. *See* Fig. 39 for bearing removal.

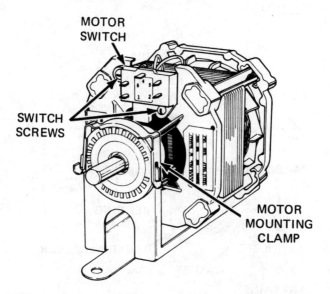

MOTOR
SWITCH

SWITCH
SCREWS

MOTOR
MOUNTING
CLAMP

Fig. 38.

Note: If bearing is the type with a hole in the housing, install bearing with the hole at the top and to the rear of the dryer.

Drum Shaft.

1. Remove rear panel.

2. Disengage idler lever spring from dryer base (Fig. 36).

3. Remove retainer ring and washer from drum shaft (Fig. 39).

4. Use a ⅝-inch open-end or adjustable wrench on flats of shaft to turn shaft clockwise out of drum (left-hand thread).

Heating Element.

1. Remove rear panel.

2. Disconnect wires from limit thermostat and heating element terminals (Fig. 40).

3. While supporting heater box, remove screws holding box to rear support frame (Fig. 40).

4. Remove two screws holding cover plate to heater box.

5. Remove nuts and washers holding element lead bolts in insulators (Fig. 41).

6. Remove four screws holding element in heater box (Fig. 40), and carefully remove element from box.

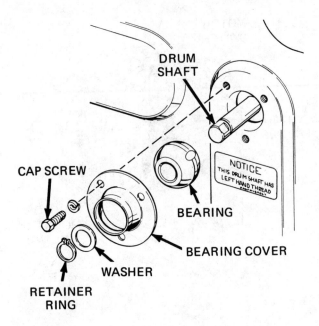

Fig. 39.

Front Panel.

1. Open loading door, remove six screws under outer door seal and remove seal and duct ring (Fig. 33).

2. Remove four screws from bottom edge of front panel.

3. Pull bottom of panel away from dryer slightly and lower panel to remove.

Loading Door.

1. Open loading door.

2. Remove four screws holding door assembly to hinges (Fig. 42).

Note: Certain dryers have a lift-off door (Fig. 42). Simply open door and lift straight up to remove door.

Door Striker.

1. Open loading door.

2. Remove six Phillips head screws from upper, lower, and outer edges of door (Fig. 43).

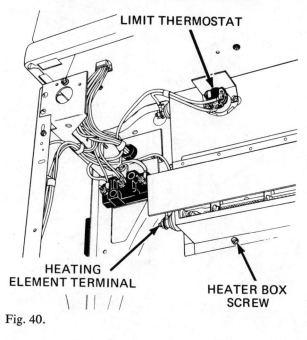

LIMIT THERMOSTAT

HEATING
ELEMENT TERMINAL

HEATER BOX
SCREW

Fig. 40.

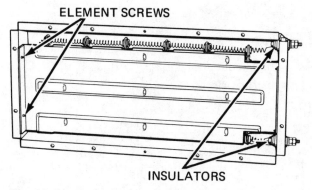

ELEMENT SCREWS

INSULATORS

Fig. 41.

3. Spread outer and inner door panels just far enough to re-move striker.

Striker Catch.

1. Remove front panel. (*See* section on Front Panel previously described.)

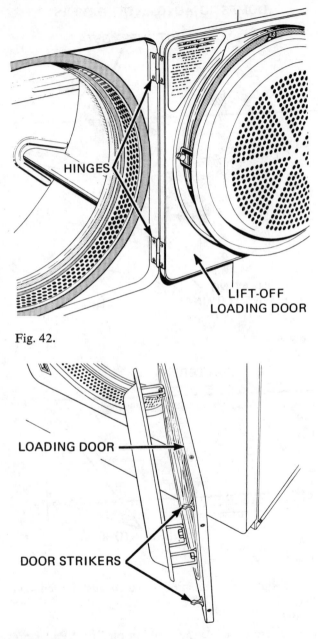

HINGES

LIFT-OFF
LOADING DOOR

Fig. 42.

LOADING DOOR

DOOR STRIKERS

Fig. 43.

2. Bend tabs of striker catch (Fig. 44) together, and disengage catch from front panel.

Door Hinge.

1. Open loading door.

2. Remove four screws holding door assembly to door hinges (Fig. 42).

3. Remove front panel. (*See* section on Front Panel previously described.)

4. Remove Phillips head screws and nuts holding hinge to front panel (Fig. 44).

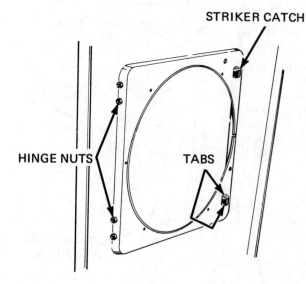

STRIKER CATCH

HINGE NUTS TABS

Fig. 44.

Door Release Assembly.

1. Remove front panel.

2. Remove adjusting nut and nylon washer from bottom end of release rod (Fig. 45).

3. Remove two door-release screws (Fig. 46), and lift assembly out of front support frame.

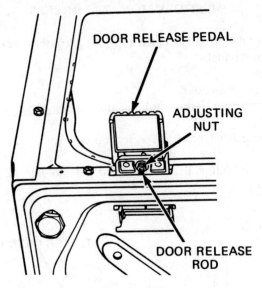

Fig. 45.

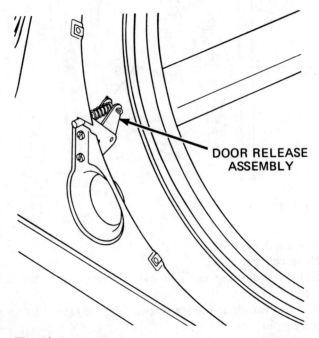

Fig. 46.

Door Switch.
1. Remove front panel.
2. *See* Fig. 47 for switch removal.

Note: Insulation must be in place between switch and front support frame (Fig. 47) when switch is installed.

Drum Light Bulb.
Open loading door and remove bulb through top opening in duct ring (Fig. 47).

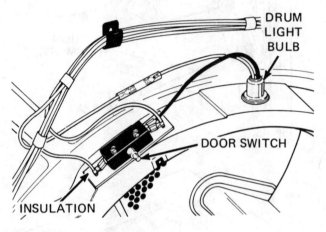

Fig. 47.

High or Low Thermostat.
1. Remove front panel.
2. *See* Fig. 48 for thermostat removal.

Exhaust Limit Thermostat.   Gas Models.

1. Remove front panel.
2. *See* Fig. 48 thermostat removal.

Cabinet Top.   All Models Except Flat Tops.

1. Remove panel screws (Fig. 20, 21, or 22) and lift assembly off panel support.
2. Disconnect wires from timer and switches, and remove panel assembly from top.
3. Remove front panel.
4. Remove two cabinet top hold-down screws (Fig. 49).

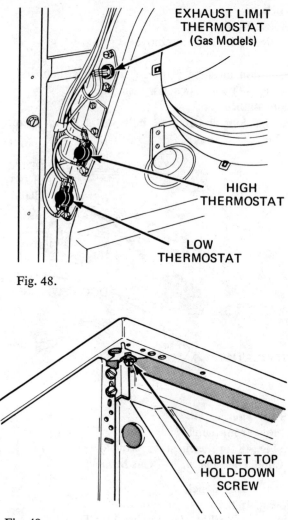

EXHAUST LIMIT
THERMOSTAT
(Gas Models)

HIGH
THERMOSTAT

LOW
THERMOSTAT

Fig. 48.

CABINET TOP
HOLD-DOWN
SCREW

Fig. 49.

5. Lift front of cabinet top slightly and pull forward to disengage rear of top from rear hold-down brackets (Fig. 50).

6. Models with quick disconnect wire harness: Disconnect wire harness at terminal block and remove top. Models without quick disconnect wire harness: Position top toward rear of top of dryer.

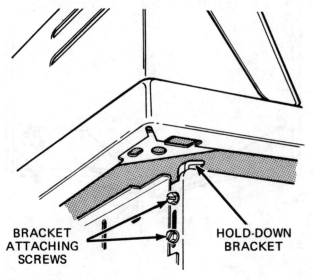

BRACKET ATTACHING SCREWS

HOLD-DOWN BRACKET

Fig. 50.

7. *Electric Models:* Remove seven screws holding control hood to cabinet top (Fig. 51).

8. *Gas Models:* Remove two screws holding top baffle to cabinet top (Fig. 52) and remove baffle.

9. *Gas Models:* Remove seven screws holding control hood to cabinet top (Fig. 52).

10. Remove screw, nut, and lockwasher holding ground wire(s) to control hood and lift hood and spacers off cabinet top.

11. Remove screw holding ground wire(s) to cabinet top and disengage wire harness strain relief (or terminal block) from top.

12. Lift cabinet top off dryer.

Flat Top Models.

1. Remove two screws holding control panel to cabinet top.

2. Remove timer.

3. Remove start switch (Fig. 23).

4. Remove four screws holding control plate to cabinet top (Fig. 23).

5. Pull forward on top to disengage rear of top from hold-down brackets, and position top toward left front of top of dryer.

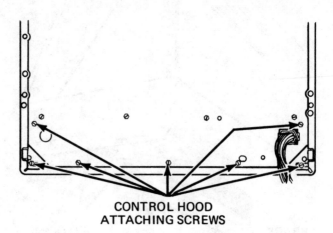

**CONTROL HOOD
ATTACHING SCREWS**

Fig. 51.

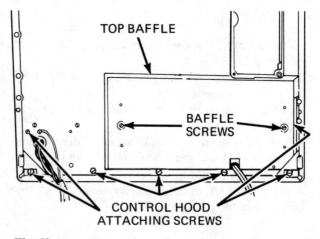

TOP BAFFLE

**BAFFLE
SCREWS**

**CONTROL HOOD
ATTACHING SCREWS**

Fig. 52.

6. Remove two screws and nuts holding wire harness clamp and ground wire(s) to cabinet top flange.

7. *Electric Models:* Lift cabinet top off dryer.

8. *Gas Models:* Disconnect power cord wires at connectors and disengage wire harness and clips from flange on left side of cabinet top.

9. *Gas Models:* Lift cabinet top off dryer, turn upside down on protective padding, disengage power cord strain relief from cabinet top flange, and remove cord.

10. *Gas Models:* Remove two nuts holding baffle to underside of cabinet top.

Limit Thermostat.   *Electric Models.*

1. Remove rear panel.

2. *See* Fig. 53 for thermostat removal.

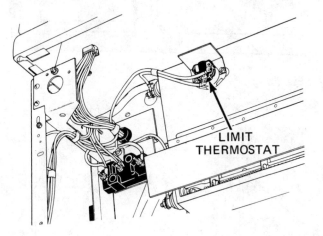

LIMIT
THERMOSTAT

Fig. 53.

Gas Models. (*See* section for models with Glow Bar Ignition later in this chapter.)

1. Remove cabinet top. (*See* section on Cabinet Top, steps 3, 4, 5.) Position top toward left front of top of dryer.

2. *See* Fig. 54 for thermostat removal.

Side Panel (Left or Right).

1. Remove front panel.

2. Remove two cabinet top hold-down screws (Fig. 49).

3. Lift front of cabinet top slightly, pull forward to disengage rear of top from rear hold-down brackets (Fig. 50), and position top toward side of dryer opposite side panel being removed.

4. Remove screws holding side panel to front support frame, and remove front cabinet top hold-down bracket (Fig. 55 or 56).

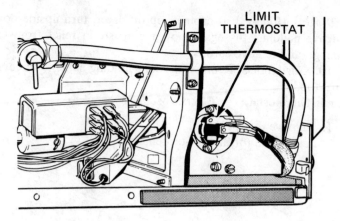

Fig. 54.

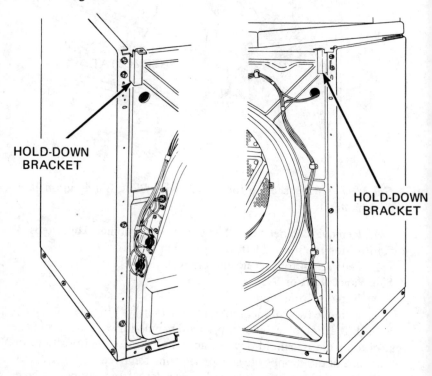

Fig. 55.

Fig. 56.

5. Remove screw holding side panel to top of rear support frame (Fig. 57).

6. If present, disengage wire harness clips from top flange of side panel (Fig. 57).

7. Remove screws holding rear cabinet top hold-down bracket to side panel (Fig. 50).

8. Remove screws holding rear panel to side panel, and side panel to dryer base (Fig. 55 or 56).

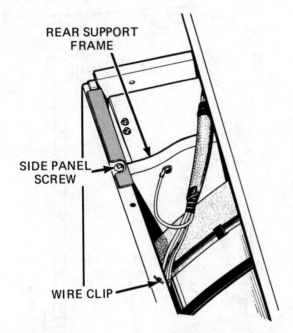

REAR SUPPORT
FRAME

SIDE PANEL
SCREW

WIRE CLIP

Fig. 57.

Drum.   *Note*: Do not damage drum seals or wires when removing or installing drum. When installing, rotate drum to check and position front and rear drum seals.

Electric Models.

1. Remove rear panel.

2. Remove front panel. (*See* section on Front Panel previously described.)

3. Remove two cabinet top hold-down screws, lift front of

cabinet top slightly, and pull forward to disengage rear hold-down brackets (Fig. 50).

4. Models with quick disconnect wire harness: Disconnect wire harness at terminal block and remove top. Models without quick disconnect wire harness: Stand top on edge on protective padding at rear of dryer (Fig. 58). *Note:* Padding must be high enough to prevent strain on wire harness.

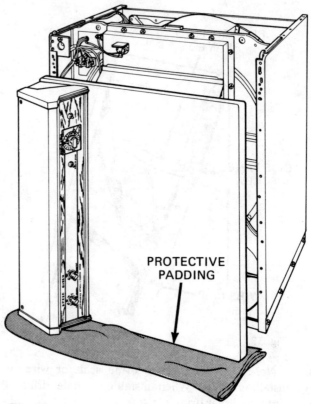

PROTECTIVE PADDING

Fig. 58.

5. Disengage idler lever spring from dryer base (Fig. 36) and slip belt off motor drum drive pulley (Fig. 37).

6. Use ⅝-inch open-end or adjustable wrench on flats of drum shaft to turn shaft clockwise out of drum (left-hand thread).

7. Disengage wire harness from clips at top flange of right side panel.

8. Tilt forward slightly, and carefully lift it out of dryer.

Gas Models.

1. Remove rear panel.

2. Remove front panel. (*See* section on Front Panel previously described.)

3. Remove left side panel. (*See* section on Side Panel (left or right) previously described.)

4. Remove screws holding left support channel to front and rear support frames (Fig. 59).

5. Models *with* quick disconnect wire harness: Remove screw holding ground wire to rear support frame. Disconnect wire harness at terminal block and remove top. Models *without* quick disconnect wire harness: Remove screw holding ground wire to rear support frame, lift cabinet top assembly off dryer, and stand it on right edge on protective padding at front of dryer (Fig. 59).

6. Disengage idler lever spring from dryer base (Fig. 36) and slip belt off motor drum drive pulley (Fig. 37).

7. Use ⅝ inch open-end or adjustable wrench on flats of drum shaft to turn shaft clockwise out of drum (left-hand thread).

8. Tilt drum forward slightly, and carefully lift it out left side of dryer.

Drum Belt.

1. Remove rear panel and run exhaust fan belt off motor pulley.

2. Remove broken drum belt, or cut and remove worn or frayed belt.

3. Remove three cap screws and lockwashers holding bearing retainer to rear frame, and remove retainer ring, washer, and bearing from drum shaft (Fig. 39).

4. Straighten out new belt so there are no twists in it, and work belt through drum shaft opening in rear frame until only a small loop of belt remains (Fig. 60).

5. Lift up on drum shaft and push remaining loop of belt through rear frame under shaft.

6. Reach through lower opening in rear frame and up past drum seal to pull belt down through rear frame opening (Fig. 61).

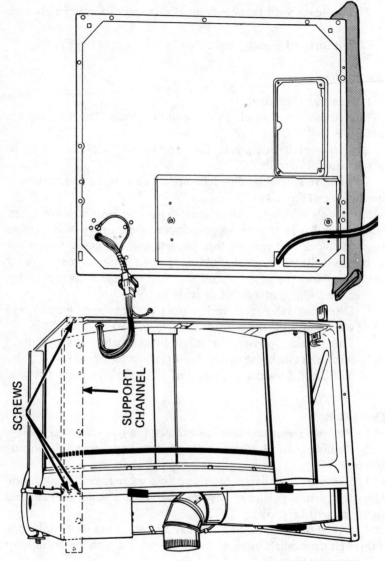

SCREWS

SUPPORT
CHANNEL

Fig. 59.

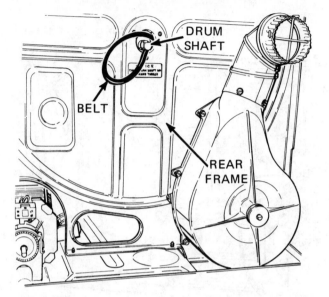

Fig. 60.

Note: Straighten belt and pull down on one side; belt should slide around top of drum shaft in the same direction. Slide complete length of belt over drum shaft to eliminate any possible twists.

7. Reinstall bearing and bearing retainer.

8. Grasp right side of belt (Fig. 61), reach in through lower opening in rear frame and hold belt (with grooves up) against bottom of drum approximately two inches past drum seal.

9. Use ⅝-inch open-end or adjustable wrench on flats of drum shaft and turn shaft in counterclockwise direction while holding belt firmly against drum. *Note:* It will be necessary to stop turning drum 2 or 3 times during first revolution and pull down on left side of belt to get entire length of belt past drum seal.

10. When belt is completely around drum, hold it against dryer base and give drum a turn in counterclockwise direction. Belt should slide freely around drum.

11. Install belt around motor and idler pulleys (Fig. 37).

12. Turn down slowly in counterclockwise direction to give belt a chance to position itself properly around drum.

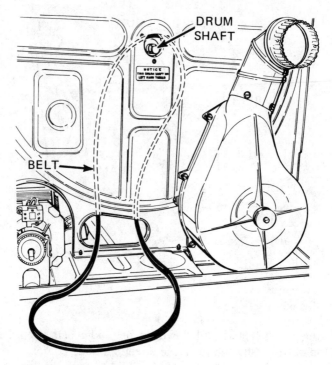

Fig. 61.

13. Reinstall exhaust fan belt and rear panel.

Drum Support Roller and Shaft.
1. Remove drum. (*See* section on Drum previously described.)
2. Remove roller and shaft from frost support frame.

Front or Rear Drum Seal.
1. Remove drum. (*See* section on Drum previously described.)
2: Front drum seal: Disconnect spring (Fig. 62).

3. Rear drum seal: Cut retainer strap (Fig. 62) and remove seal from drum.

Note: When rear drum seal is installed, forward edge must be properly positioned under clips (Fig. 62). Secure seal with retainer strap and spring supplied with replacement seal.

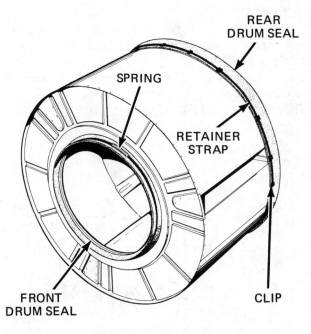

Fig. 62.

ADJUSTMENTS

Timer Knob Indicator. For all models except flat tops.

1. With timer knob indicator pointing toward top Off position, push and hold the start-switch button in, slowly turn timer knob clockwise only until dryer starts, then immediately open loading door to stop dryer.

2. Carefully—do not turn knob—loosen timer knob set screw, then retighten it just enough to hold knob snugly on timer shaft.

3. Carefully—do not turn knob—move indicator until it is directly over the vertical line at the right side of the top Off position. *Note:* If indicator cannot be moved, loosen timer knob set screw slightly.

4. Tighten timer knob set screw securely.

Leveling Legs.

1. Thread lock-nuts (Fig. 63) down to heads of leveling legs, then thread legs into dryer base until heads extend out of base approximately ¾ inch.

2. Turn legs in or out of base as necessary to level dryer. All four legs must rest firmly on the floor.

3. Tighten lock-nuts (Fig. 63) securely against dryer base.

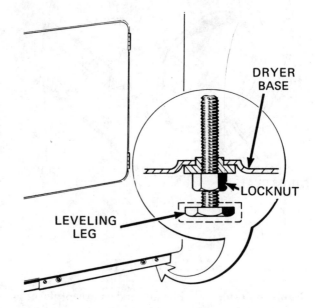

Fig. 63.

Burner Flame—Gas Models.

1. Close loading door, set temperature selector switch at *normal*, set timer at 70, and push start switch button to start dryer.

2. Allow dryer to operate for approximately five minutes, then open access door and loosen air shutter lock screw (Fig. 64).

3. Turn air shutter to the right to open or to the left to close as necessary. (A lazy, orange-tipped flame indicates lack of air. A harsh, roaring flame indicates too much air.)

4. Tighten air shutter lock screw (Fig. 64) securely.

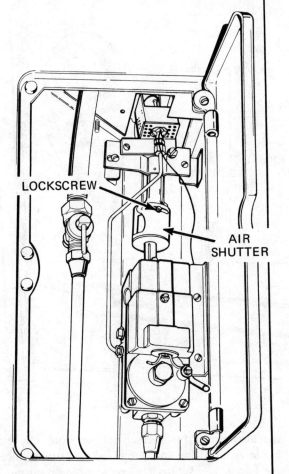

LOCKSCREW

AIR
SHUTTER

Fig. 64.

Exhaust Fan Belt.

1. Remove rear panel.

2. Loosen exhaust fan housing screws (Fig. 65) and shift housing to tighten or loosen belt.

Note: If exhaust fan belt is adjusted too tight, drive motor and exhaust fan bearings may be damaged. The drive motor overload

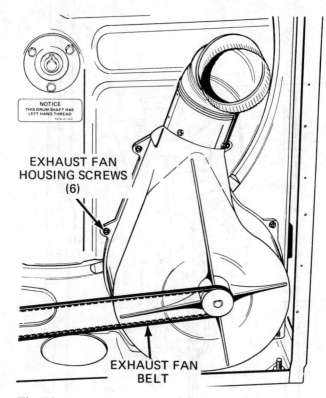

NOTICE
THIS DRUM SHAFT HAS
LEFT HAND THREAD

EXHAUST FAN
HOUSING SCREWS
(6)

EXHAUST FAN
BELT

Fig. 65.

protector may also cycle. Insufficient belt tension may allow slippage, resulting in reduced fan speed and reduced dryer efficiency.

Reset Valve Latch.   White-Rodgers standing pilot models (Fig. 66).

1. Open access door and close gas shut-off valve.

2. Remove screw holding valve housing to gas control valve, and lift housing off valve. *Note:* Do not attempt to adjust reset valve latch until at least 15 minutes has elapsed since pilot flame went out.

3. Insert .025-inch feeler gage between latching cap and end of pin in lower end of latching lever, and turn adjusting screw to adjust gap to thickness of feeler gage. (Turn screw clockwise to decrease gap, or counterclockwise to increase gap.)

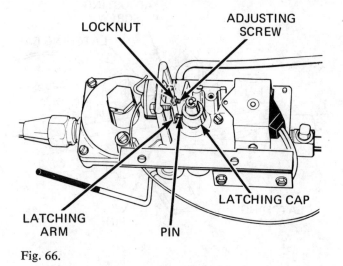

LOCKNUT   ADJUSTING SCREW

LATCHING CAP

LATCHING ARM   PIN

Fig. 66.

4. If adjusting screw lock-nut is loose, hold screw and tighten lock-nut.

McQuay-Norris (Eaton) standing pilot models (Fig. 67).

1. Open access door and close gas shut-off valve.
2. Remove latch cover from gas valve (Fig. 32). *Note:* Do not attempt to adjust reset valve latch until at least 15 minutes has elapsed since pilot flame went out.
3. Insert .010-inch feeler gage between latching cap and end of latching lever, and turn adjusting screw to adjust gap to thickness of feeler gage.

TEST PROCEDURES

For safety reasons, close valve in gas supply line to gas dryer and disconnect electrical power before performing test procedures.

Electrical test procedures in this chapter are performed using a live test cord, a test lamp, a live test lamp, or combinations of these (Fig. 68).

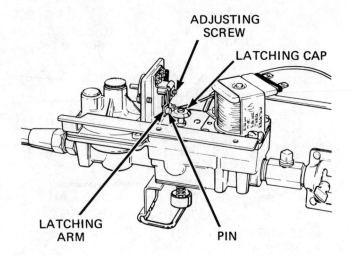

ADJUSTING
SCREW

LATCHING CAP

LATCHING
ARM

PIN

Fig. 67.

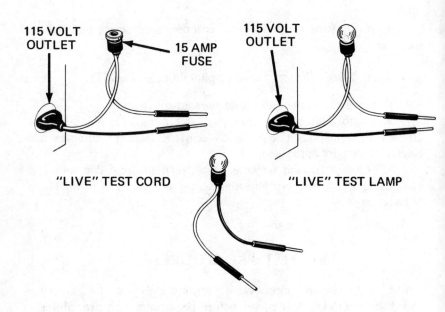

115 VOLT
OUTLET

15 AMP
FUSE

115 VOLT
OUTLET

"LIVE" TEST CORD

"LIVE" TEST LAMP

TEST LAMP

Fig. 68.

Drive Motor. *See* Fig. 69.

1. Remove rear panel.
2. Run exhaust fan belt off exhaust fan pulley and remove belt.
3. Disconnect base harness wires from motor switch.
4. Connect a *live* test cord to terminals 4 and 5.
5. While motor is running, apply test lamp probes to terminals 4 and 6. Lamp should light.
6. While motor is running, apply *live* test lamp probes to terminals 1 and 2. *Live* test lamp should light.

DRIVE MOTOR

Fig. 69.

Timer Contact Points. *See* Fig. 70.

1. All models except flat top models: Remove panel screws (Fig. 20, 21, or 22) and lift assembly off panel support.

Flat top models: Remove front panel (*see* section on Front Panel), remove two cabinet top hold-down screws (Fig. 71), and block up front of top.

2. Disconnect wires from timer.

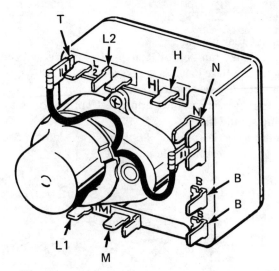

Fig. 70.

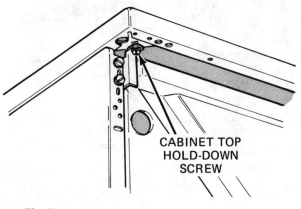

Fig. 71.

3. Apply *live* test lamp probes to terminals:
   (a) L1 and M to test drive motor circuit.
   (b) L2 and H to test heat circuit.
   (c) L2 and T to test timer motor circuit.
   (d) D and B to test buzzer circuit.

4. Starting with timer knob indicator pointing toward Off position at top of timer, slowly turn timer knob clockwise until indicator is again pointing toward Off position at top of timer. *Live* test lamp should light when circuit being tested is completed by timer. (*See* appropriate Wiring Diagram for Timer Cycle Chart supplied by manufacturer.)

Burner System Components—White-Rodgers Automatic Ignition. *See* Fig. 72. (*See* section for models with Glow Bar Ignition described later in this chapter.)

Note: Before testing individual components of burner system, perform the following checks: Carefully open access door and, without jarring igniter control, apply *live* test lamp probes to igniter control terminals B and IGY. If live test lamp does not light, replace igniter control. Next, very carefully, remove the wire from igniter control terminal IGY. Apply *live* test lamp probes to igniter control terminal IGO and to terminal on igniter wire removed from igniter control. If live test lamp does not light, replace igniter.

1. Igniter.

(a) Open access door and disconnect igniter wires from igniter control (Fig. 25).

(b) Apply *live* test cord probes to terminals on pink and yellow wires. Movable igniter arm should open and remain open until electrical power is removed.

(c) Apply *live* test cord probes to terminals on yellow and orange wires. Movable igniter arm should vibrate, producing an arc as the contact points open and close.

2. Igniter Control.

(a) Open access door and disconnect all wires from igniter control (Fig. 25).

(b) Apply *live* test lamp probes to terminals W and R. *Live* test lamp should not light.

(c) Apply *live* test lamp probes to terminals PK and W. Live test lamp should light.

(d) Apply *live* test lamp probes to terminals B and IGY. Live test lamp should light.

(e) With *live* test lamp probes applied to terminals B and IGY, heat outer end of sensor tube with a small flame. Live test lamp

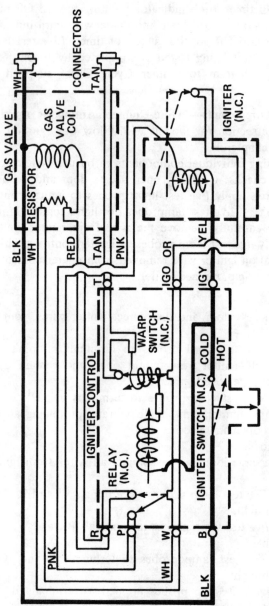

Fig. 72.

should go out a few seconds after heat is applied and light again a few seconds after heat is removed.

(f) Connect a *live* test cord to terminals T and IGY. Relay should close with an audible click. Immediately apply test lamp probes to terminals R and IGY. Test lamp should light.

(g) Disconnect *live* test cord and allow an approximate five-minute cooling-off period.

(h) Connect *live* test cord to terminals T and IGY and immediately apply test lamp probes to terminals IGO and B. Test lamp should light and remain lit for approximately 35 seconds until the warp switch cycles. (Time required will vary with voltage.)

3. Gas Valve Coil.

(a) Open access door and close gas shut-off valve.

(b) Disconnect red, white, and black wires from igniter control and white wire at connector.

(c) Apply *live* test cord probes to terminals on red and black wires. Coil should open valve with an audible click and valve should remain open until live test cord probes are removed.

4. Gas Valve Resistor.

(a) Test gas valve coil, step 3, in section on Gas Valve Coil.

(b) Connect a *live* test cord to terminals on white and black wires. Valve should not open.

(c) Momentarily touch terminal on red wire to test cord probe connected to white wire. Valve should open with an audible click and remain open until test cord is removed.

GLOW BAR IGNITION BURNER SYSTEM

Note: For safety reasons, disconnect electrical service and close valve in gas supply line before servicing.

REMOVAL PROCEDURES

Gas Valve Assembly. *See* Fig. 73.

1. Open access door and close gas shut-off valve.
2. Disconnect flare nut from shut-off valve.

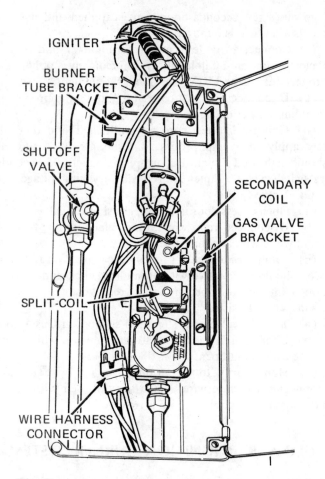

IGNITER

BURNER
TUBE BRACKET

SHUTOFF
VALVE

SECONDARY
COIL

GAS VALVE
BRACKET

SPLIT-COIL

WIRE HARNESS
CONNECTOR

Fig. 73.

3. Disconnect wires from igniter and gas valve wire harness at connector.

4. Remove two screws holding gas valve bracket to burner shield and carefully lift assembly out of dryer.

Note: The split-coil, secondary coil, and wire are replaced as a kit.

Burner Tube and Igniter.   *See* Fig. 73.

Caution: Use extreme care when handling the igniter as it is very fragile.

    1. Open access door and disconnect wires from igniter.

    2. Remove two screws holding burner tube bracket to burner shield.

    3. Move burner tube assembly toward rear of dryer to disengage the tube from orifice adapter, and carefully remove assembly from dryer.

    4. Remove igniter by carefully spreading mounting clip with pliers. *Note:* Always handle igniter by ceramic end, keeping fingers off of the silicon carbide portion.

Flame Sensor.   *See* Fig. 74.

    1. Remove cabinet top. (*See* section on Cabinet Top, steps 1 through 4, previously described.)

    2. Disconnect wires from sensor, and remove screw holding sensor to heater box.

Limit Thermostat.   *See* Fig. 74.

    1. Remove cabinet top. (*See* section on Cabinet Top, steps 1 through 4, previously described.)

    2. Disconnect wires from thermostat and remove two screws holding thermostat to heater box.

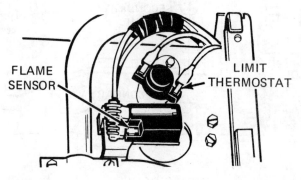

Fig. 74.

Burner System Operation.   *See* Fig. 75 or 76.

Components. This burner has four basic components: a silicon carbide (glow bar) igniter, burner tube, flame sensor, and a two-stage gas valve consisting of a split-coil valve and a secondary coil valve. The split-coil valve is opened when the dryer thermostat calls for heat, while the secondary valve does not open until the igniter has attained ignition temperature.

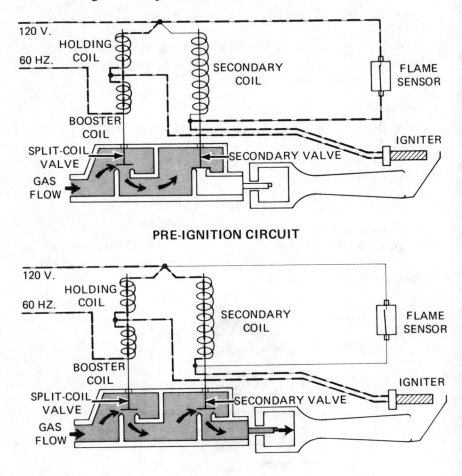

Fig. 75.

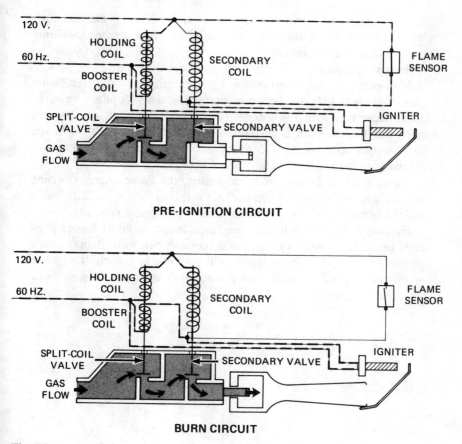

Fig. 76.

Pre-Ignition Circuits. When the dryer thermostat calls for heat, circuits are completed through the holding coil, flame sensor, booster coil, and igniter. Both coils must be energized to open split-coil valve. Once opened, the holding coil can hold the valve open without assistance from the booster coil. The current, shunted around the secondary coil by the flame sensor, passes through the igniter, causing it to get hot.

Burn Circuit. In approximately 30 seconds, the igniter attains ignition temperature and the flame sensor (located directly above igniter) contacts open. A circuit is then completed through the secondary valve coil, opening the valve and allowing gas to flow. Ignition is made and the heat from the burner flame causes the flame sensor contacts to remain open.

System Features. *See* Fig. 75 or 76.

Momentary Power Interruption. Upon resumption of power, flame sensor contacts will still be open, permitting the secondary valve to open. However, with the secondary coil in the circuit, the booster coil cannot draw enough current to open the split-coil valve. When flame sensor contacts do reclose, the secondary valve will close, and the burner system will be in the normal pre-ignition circuit.

Flame Failure. In case of flame failure, the flame sensor contacts will reclose in about 45 seconds. This will close the secondary valve and the burner system will be in the normal pre-ignition circuit.

Ignition Failure. If a flame is not established as flame sensor contacts open, the secondary valve will remain open until flame sensor contacts reclose. The flame sensor will continue to recycle the igniter and secondary valve about once per minute until ignition is made or the dryer is turned off.

Chapter 38

Automatic Water Heaters

All water heaters must be installed in accordance with local codes and utility company requirements, or in accordance with the National Code.

ELECTRIC WATER HEATERS

Location.   Select a location accessible to water lines and power supply where the floor is level. Do not locate the heater where water lines could be subjected to freezing temperatures. It is recommended that the heater be located near the center of greatest hot water usage to prevent heat loss through the pipes. Locate the heater so that access panels and drain valves are accessible.

Note: Do not use or store gasoline or other flammable liquids in the vicinity of this heater.

The heater should be located in an area where leakage of the tank or connections will not result in damage to the area adjacent to the heater or to lower floors of the structure. When such locations cannot be avoided, a suitable drain pan should be installed under the heater. Such pans should be at least two inches deep, have a minimum length and width at least two inches greater than the diameter of the heater, and should be piped to an adequate drain.

Note: Before proceeding with the installation, close the main water supply valve, open a water faucet to relieve the house pressure, and then close the faucet.

Note: Do not turn on electrical current to the water heater until the tank has been completely filled with water. Open several hot water faucets to allow air to escape from the system while the heater is filling. The heating elements will burn out if not immersed in water.

Types of Models.   *Upright or lowboy*. The hot and cold water connections are identified on the top of the upright or lowboy heater. Connect the hot and cold water lines to the installed nipples using unions. Install a listed temperature-pressure relief valve in the opening on the side of the heater. (*See* Fig. 1.)

Fig. 1. Upright and lowboy electric water heaters.

Utility. The hot and cold water connections are identified on the side of the utility heater. Connect the hot and cold water lines to the installed nipples using unions. Install a listed temperature-pressure relief valve in the opening on the side of the heater. (*See* Fig. 2.)

Tabletop. The hot water outlet and cold water inlet are identified on the back panel of the tabletop heater (Fig. 3). Remove the porcelain top by sliding it forward and lifting it off the cabinet. Care should be taken in handling the porcelain top to prevent chipping of the porcelain. Remove the four front-panel screws; two at the top flange. Check drain valve to make sure that it is closed. Remove the top fiberglass insulation to allow access to the plumbing and electrical

Fig. 2. Utility water heater.

Fig. 3. Tabletop water heater.

connections. Connect the cold water supply line and hot water outlet lines using elbows, nipples, and unions as shown in Fig. 4. Install a temperature-pressure valve in the remaining fitting. Replace the top fiberglass insulation in its original location.

Note: Be sure to install an approved AGA or ASME ¾-inch by ¾-inch temperature-pressure relief valve.

Do not install a check valve or any other device that would prevent a reverse flow of water unless required by local codes. A closed system will result and frequent operation of the relief valve will occur.

The end of the relief pipe opening should terminate near the floor drain or other suitable location not subject to blocking or freezing. *Do not* thread, plug, or cap the relief pipe opening. Leave an air gap of approximately six inches between the end of the relief pipe and the floor drain.

After the installation of all water lines, open the main water supply valve and fill the heater. Open several hot water faucets to allow air to escape from the system while the heater is filling. When water passes through the faucets, close them and check for possible leaks in the system.

If sweat fittings are used in models shown in Figs. 4, 5, and 6, do not apply heat to the nipples on top of the heater. Sweat tubing to adapter before fitting adapter to water connection. It is imperative that no heat be applied to the water connection as nipples contain a plastic liner.

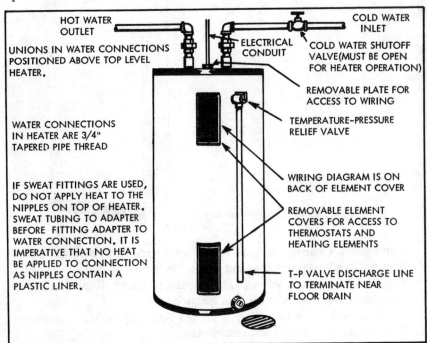

Fig. 4.

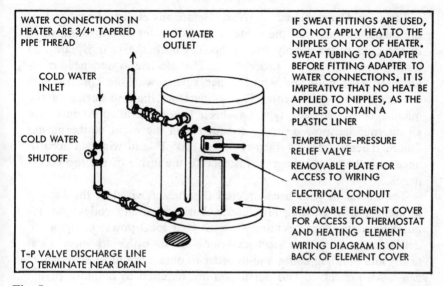

WATER CONNECTIONS IN HEATER ARE 3/4" TAPERED PIPE THREAD

HOT WATER OUTLET

COLD WATER INLET

COLD WATER SHUTOFF

IF SWEAT FITTINGS ARE USED, DO NOT APPLY HEAT TO THE NIPPLES ON TOP OF HEATER. SWEAT TUBING TO ADAPTER BEFORE FITTING ADAPTER TO WATER CONNECTIONS. IT IS IMPERATIVE THAT NO HEAT BE APPLIED TO NIPPLES, AS THE NIPPLES CONTAIN A PLASTIC LINER

TEMPERATURE-PRESSURE RELIEF VALVE

REMOVABLE PLATE FOR ACCESS TO WIRING

ELECTRICAL CONDUIT

REMOVABLE ELEMENT COVER FOR ACCESS TO THERMOSTAT AND HEATING ELEMENT

WIRING DIAGRAM IS ON BACK OF ELEMENT COVER

T-P VALVE DISCHARGE LINE TO TERMINATE NEAR DRAIN

Fig. 5.

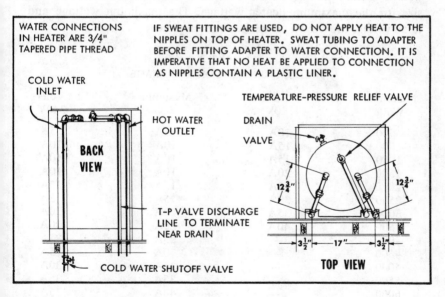

WATER CONNECTIONS IN HEATER ARE 3/4" TAPERED PIPE THREAD

IF SWEAT FITTINGS ARE USED, DO NOT APPLY HEAT TO THE NIPPLES ON TOP OF HEATER. SWEAT TUBING TO ADAPTER BEFORE FITTING ADAPTER TO WATER CONNECTION. IT IS IMPERATIVE THAT NO HEAT BE APPLIED TO CONNECTION AS NIPPLES CONTAIN A PLASTIC LINER.

COLD WATER INLET

BACK VIEW

HOT WATER OUTLET

TEMPERATURE-PRESSURE RELIEF VALVE

DRAIN VALVE

T-P VALVE DISCHARGE LINE TO TERMINATE NEAR DRAIN

$12\frac{3}{4}"$ $12\frac{3}{4}"$

$3\frac{1}{2}"$ 17" $3\frac{1}{2}"$

COLD WATER SHUTOFF VALVE

TOP VIEW

Fig. 6.

Electrical Connections. *Note:* Before any electrical connections are made, be sure that the heater is full of water and that the valve in the cold water supply line is open. Check the rating plate and wiring diagram before proceeding. The electric water heaters illustrated were built and wired in accordance with the Underwriters Laboratories' requirements. The temperature limiting device of the manual reset, trip-free type has been factory-installed to interrupt all ungrounded power supply conductors in the event of thermostat failure. Thermostats are factory set at 150° F. and wired in accordance with the wiring diagram fastened to the inside of the top access panel.

The dealer in your area ordered this heater wired at the factory to comply with existing area codes, but local utility codes may require or allow other circuitry. Consult your local power company to determine the correct electrical hook-up in order to meet local utility and building codes and in order to obtain the most economical rates. Also check to find out if you are required to obtain a permit before starting the installation. Chart 5 shows the recommended fuse size for the maximum heater wattage. The maximum wattage and rated voltage are shown on the heater data plate.

CHART 5
RECOMMENDED FOR AMPERAGE

Maximum Watts	120V	Maximum 208V	Volts 240V
500	10A	5A	5A
1000	15A	10A	10A
1250	15A	10A	10A
1500	20A	10A	10A
2000	25A	15A	15A
2500	30A	15A	15A
3000	35A	20A	20A
3500	40A	20A	20A
4000	—	25A	25A
4500	—	30A	25A
5000	—	35A	30A
5500	—	35A	35A
6000	—	40A	35A

Grounded. The heater must be well grounded. A green ground screw is provided at the electrical connection point for connecting a ground wire to the upright and tabletop units. A green ground wire is provided at the electrical connection point on utility models for connections to a ground.

Operation. *Note:* Before closing the switch to allow electric current to flow to the heater, make certain that the heater is full of water and that the cold water inlet valve is open. Complete failure of the heating elements will result if they are not completely immersed in water at all times. When the switch is closed, the operation of this electric water heater is automatic.

The temperature of the water can be changed by adjusting the thermostats. Before any work is done on the heater, disconnect all power to the heater by opening the switch at the main electrical panel. Remove the access panels (or front panel on *tabletops*), and fold the insulation outward and away from the controls. Set the thermostats to the desired water temperature, using a screwdriver, to move the thermostat pointer, and replace the insulation, making sure the controls are well covered and that the plastic terminal shield has not been displaced; then replace the access panel, or front panel. The heater is now ready for operation and the main switch can be closed.

When it's necessary to completely drain the heater, shut off the electric power supply to heater, close the cold water inlet valve, open a hot water faucet to allow air to enter the system, and open the drain valve, which is threaded to receive a standard hose coupling. On tabletop models, the front panel must be removed to gain access to the drain valve.

Maintenance. Shut off the electric power whenever the water supply is turned off.

Whenever the building is left unoccupied during the cold weather months, shut off the electric power and water supply, and drain the heater completely to prevent freezing.

In order to insure efficient operation and long tank life, drain the heater through the drain valve until water runs clear. Drain it at least once a month. Failure to do this may result in noisy operation and lime and sediment build-up in the bottom of the tank. At the same time, check the temperature-pressure relief valve by raising the test lever at the top of this valve to make certain that waterways are clear.

Service. The manual reset, trip-free, temperature-limiting devices on heaters illustrated will cut off all power to the heater if temperature of water exceeds 190° F. If there is no hot water after a reasonable period of time, check the main fuse box. In the event that the fuses have not blown, call a serviceman and have him check the entire circuit, including the elements and thermostats, before resetting the temperature limiting device. The heater must be disconnected from its power supply before servicing the switch. Consult your plumber or electric service company in your area for all service, replacement parts, or any questions you might have regarding your heater. Insist on factory inspected and approved replacement parts.

Warranty. Read the warranty attached to the water heater for a full explanation of the time period that parts and heater are guaranteed. Removal of the magnesium anode will terminate the warranty.

GAS WATER HEATER

The *installation* of a gas water heater should conform with the National Fuel Gas Code, ANSI Z223.1-1974, and with the requirements of the authority having jurisdiction. Figure 7 shows a standard, tabletop, and lowboy gas water heater.

Location. Select a location accessible to water and gas supply lines near the chimney where the floor is level. Do not locate the heater where water lines could be subjected to freezing temperatures. If the water heater is installed in an enclosed area, two ventilation openings must be provided. The total area of each opening must be equal to at least one square inch per 1,000 Btu's/hr of the rated input of all gas appliances installed in the same room. Locate one opening near the floor and the other opening above the level of the heater top.

The heaters shown in Fig. 7 are certified for installation on combustible flooring. See the clearance label attached to the unit for proper clearances to combustible construction and type of installation.

The installation should allow access to the front of the heater and adequate clearance should be provided for servicing and operating the heater.

The heater should be located in an area where leakage of the tank or connections will not result in damage to the area adjacent to the

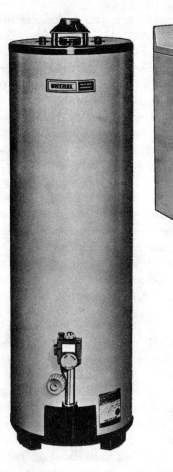

Fig. 7. Types of gas heaters.

heater or to lower floors of the structure. When such locations cannot be avoided, a suitable drain pan must be installed under the heater. Such pans should be at least two inches deep, have a minimum length and width at least two inches greater than the heater, and should be piped to an adequate drain.

Note: Do not use or store gasoline or other flammable liquids in the vicinity of the heater.

Warranty. The warranty is void if the heater is exposed to a corrosive atmosphere containing chlorinated hydrocarbons. Removal of the magnesium anode will terminate the warranty.

Venting. Position the draft diverter over the flue opening at the top of the heater by inserting the tips of the legs on the diverter into the four holes in the jacket top. All four feet of the diverter should rest squarely on the jacket top. Connect the draft diverter to the chimney flue using pipe of the same diameter as the outlet of the diverter and using the least number of vent pipe elbows possible. All horizontal runs should have a minimum rise of $\frac{1}{4}$-inch per foot. The vent pipe should not exceed 15 feet in length and should not project into the chimney beyond the inner wall.

Water Connections. *Note:* Before proceeding with the installation, close the main water supply valve and gas supply cock. Open a water faucet, relieve the house pressure, and then close the faucet. The cold water inlet and hot water outlet are identified on the top of the heater. Connect the cold and hot water supply lines, using a union. Install a temperature pressure relief valve in the opening at side of heater near the top.

Failure to install ASME or AGA certified $\frac{3}{4}$-inch by $\frac{3}{4}$-inch temperature-pressure relief valve will release the manufacturer from any claims that might result from excessive temperatures and pressures.

Do not install a check valve or any other device that would prevent reverse flow of water unless required by local codes. A closed system will result and frequent operation of the relief valve will occur.

The end of the relief pipe opening should terminate near the floor drain or other suitable location not subject to blocking or freezing the relief opening. *Do not* thread, plug, or cap the relief pipe opening. Leave an air gap of approximately six inches between the end of the relief pipe and the floor drain.

After the installation of all water lines, open the main water supply valve and fill the heater. Open several hot water faucets to allow air to escape from the system. When water passes through the faucets, close them and check for possible leaks in the system. Check for water leaks at the gas thermostat, heater drain valve, and the pipe connections at the top of the heater.

Figure 8 shows installation arrangement of a gas heater.

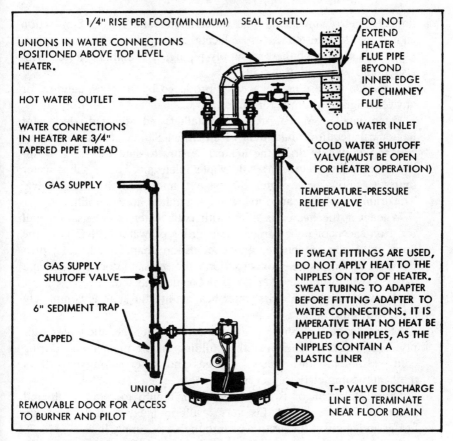

1/4" RISE PER FOOT(MINIMUM) SEAL TIGHTLY

DO NOT EXTEND HEATER FLUE PIPE BEYOND INNER EDGE OF CHIMNEY FLUE

UNIONS IN WATER CONNECTIONS POSITIONED ABOVE TOP LEVEL HEATER.

HOT WATER OUTLET →

WATER CONNECTIONS IN HEATER ARE 3/4" TAPERED PIPE THREAD

COLD WATER INLET

COLD WATER SHUTOFF VALVE(MUST BE OPEN FOR HEATER OPERATION)

TEMPERATURE-PRESSURE RELIEF VALVE

GAS SUPPLY

GAS SUPPLY SHUTOFF VALVE

6" SEDIMENT TRAP

CAPPED

IF SWEAT FITTINGS ARE USED, DO NOT APPLY HEAT TO THE NIPPLES ON TOP OF HEATER. SWEAT TUBING TO ADAPTER BEFORE FITTING ADAPTER TO WATER CONNECTIONS. IT IS IMPERATIVE THAT NO HEAT BE APPLIED TO NIPPLES, AS THE NIPPLES CONTAIN A PLASTIC LINER

UNION

REMOVABLE DOOR FOR ACCESS TO BURNER AND PILOT

T-P VALVE DISCHARGE LINE TO TERMINATE NEAR FLOOR DRAIN

Fig. 8. Installation arrangement.

Gas Connections. The gas supply lines must meet all requirements of the National Fuel Gas Code.

Connect the water heater only to the type of gas (natural or propane) shown on rating plate. Use clean ½-inch black iron pipe. (Dirt and scale from the pipe can enter the thermostat and cause a malfunction, resulting in overheating.) The inlet gas line should have a sediment trap (drip leg)—ahead of a union connection of the metal-to-metal type—in the supply line feeding the thermostat to permit servicing of the appliance. The compound used on the threaded joints of gas piping should be resistant to the action of liquefied petroleum gases. The water heater and its gas connection should be leak-tested before placing the appliance in operation. Upon completion of the gas supply piping, it should be tested with a soap-and-water solution only.

Note: Do not use an open flame produced by matches, candles, or any other ignition source for this purpose.

Operation.   When properly installed and adjusted, the water heater will require a minimum of attention. Should it become necessary to completely drain the heater, be sure to shut off the gas supply to the heater, close the cold water inlet valve, open a hot water faucet to allow air to enter the system, and open the drain valve. The drain valve is threaded to receive a standard hose coupling.

Whenever the heater is filled with cold water, condensation will form on the cool tank surfaces and drops of water will fall on the floor or on the hot burner and combustion chamber surfaces, producing a sizzling noise. Condensation is normal and does not indicate a leak. It will disappear when the tank becomes heated.

Note: Do not operate the water heater until the tank is completely filled with water.

Maintenance.   Shut off the gas supply whenever the water supply is turned off. Whenever the building is left unoccupied during cold weather months, shut off the gas and water supply and drain the heater completely to prevent freezing.

Drain off a pail or two of water each month to remove silt and sediment. Failure to do this may result in noisy operation of the heater and allow sediment to pass into the water supply lines.

Check the temperature-pressure relief valve (Fig. 8) each month to insure that the valve has not become encrusted with lime. Lift the lever at the top of the valve several times until the valve seats properly without leaking and operates freely.

Normal maintenance of this water heater should include shutting off gas, removing the main burner, and cleaning the inside of the combustion chamber with a wire brush.

Periodic examination of the flue pipe and chimney should be made to make sure that the flue passages are clear of foreign matter. (*See* Fig. 8.)

Care should be taken to see that the area around the heater is kept free of combustible material and that the flow of combustion and ventilating air is not obstructed.

Warranty. Read the warranty for a full explanation of the length of time that parts and heater are guaranteed.

Lighting and Relighting, and Flame Patterns. *See* thermostat in Fig. 9. The procedure for lighting or relighting is as follows:

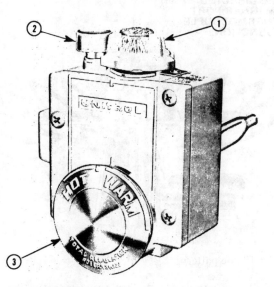

Fig. 9. Thermostat.

1. Turn gas cock dial (1) to Off position.

2. Wait a sufficient length of time (at least five minutes) to allow gas that may have accumulated in burner compartment to escape.

3. Turn gas cock dial (1) to Start position. Depress and hold set button (2) while lighting burner. Place match next to ports underneath the flame spreader on the burner. (*See* Fig. 11.)

4. Allow standby flame to burn approximately one-half a minute before releasing reset button. If burner does not remain lighted, repeat operation, allowing a longer period of time before releasing reset button.

5. Turn gas cock dial (1) to On position and turn temperature dial (3) to desired position.

A periodic visual check of the main burner and stand-by flame should be made to determine if they are burning properly. The flame should be blue with yellow tips and should not be blowing off of the burner. The main burner flame should light smoothly from the stand-by flame. (*See* Fig. 10.)

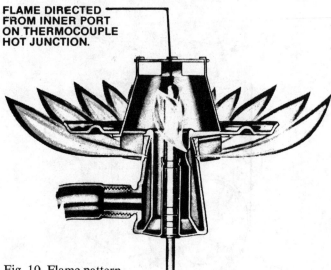

FLAME DIRECTED FROM INNER PORT ON THERMOCOUPLE HOT JUNCTION.

Fig. 10. Flame pattern.

The water heater shown in Fig. 12 is equipped with a thermostat having a built-in regulator. Replacing this thermostat with an un-regulated one or one with the pressure setting other than that indicated on the thermostat could result in a hazard to life, property, and health.

Contact your dealer or plumber for replacement parts or contact the manufacturer.

SAFETY

If you smell gas:

1. Open windows.
2. Do not touch electrical switches.
3. Extinguish any open flame.
4. Immediately call your gas supplier.

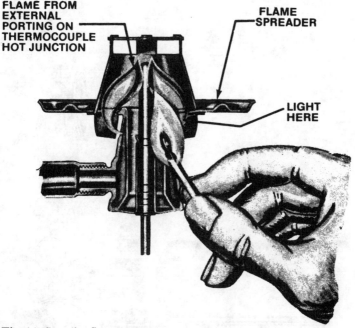

FLAME FROM
EXTERNAL
PORTING ON
THERMOCOUPLE
HOT JUNCTION

FLAME
SPREADER

LIGHT
HERE

Fig. 11. Standby flame pattern.

OIL FIRING WATER HEATERS

The oil firing water heater (Fig. 13) must be installed in accordance with the National Fire Protection Association rules or local codes and utility requirements.

The heater shown in Fig. 13 is available in three sizes. It has sufficient capacity to provide an ample supply of hot water for any single residence or small apartment house. Its rugged design provides the maximum practical contact between hot gases and heating surface, so as to put the most heat into the water and the least up the flue.

See Fig. 14 and chart for horizontal types with storage capacities for 45 gallons, 75 gallons, and 100 gallons of water.

Flammable items, pressurized containers, or any other potential fire hazardous articles must never be placed on or adjacent to the water

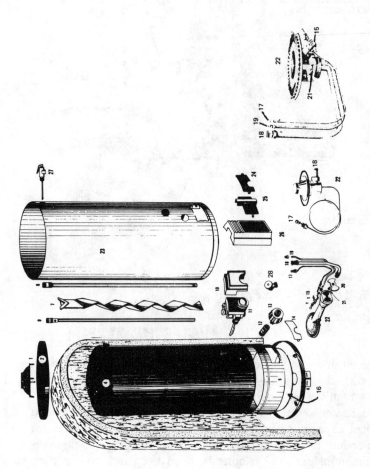

Fig. 12. Gas water heater showing different parts.

1. Draft hood 2. Jacket top assembly 3. Fiberglass insulation 4. Glass lined tank 5. Tank skirt assembly 6. Jacket base assembly 7. Flue baffle 8. Cold water intake tube with nipple 9. Magnesium anode with hot water outlet 10. Thermostat cover 11. Thermostat W/E.C.O. and full regulation or thermostat-unifire R120 rtp for B100 burner 12. Drain valve nipple assembly 13. Drain valve head assembly 14. Inner door 15. Pilot assembly 16. Radiation shield 17. Thermocouple lead 18. Gas feed line (burner) 19. Gas feed line (pilot) 20. Air shutter 21. Main burner orifice 22. Burner 23. Jacket assembly 24. Outer door with knob 25. Outer door with channel 26. Pouch door 27. T & P relief valve 28. Brass drain valve

Fig. 13. Oil firing water heater.

heater. Open containers of flammable material should not be stored or used in the same room with the water heater.

Some models must be installed on noncombustible floors.

SIZE OF HEATER	A	B	C	D	E	F	G	H	J	K	L	M
45 GAL.	60¼	29¼	24	48¾	12¼	12¼	18¼	27¾	18	5	8⅜	7
75 GAL.	72½	32¾	28	60¼	12¼	12⅜	18⅜	40	20	6	9⅜	8
100 GAL.	81½	36	30	69⅜	12⅛	13¾	19¾	40	22	8	8	8

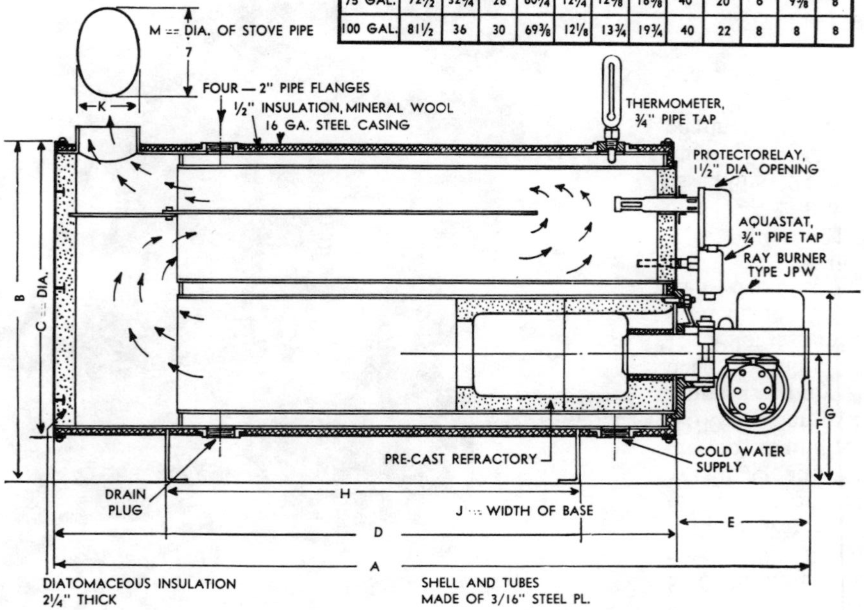
M = DIA. OF STOVE PIPE
7
K
FOUR — 2" PIPE FLANGES
½" INSULATION, MINERAL WOOL
16 GA. STEEL CASING
THERMOMETER, ¾" PIPE TAP
PROTECTORELAY, 1½" DIA. OPENING
AQUASTAT, ¾" PIPE TAP
RAY BURNER TYPE JPW
B
C = DIA.
G
F
COLD WATER SUPPLY
PRE-CAST REFRACTORY
DRAIN PLUG
H
J = WIDTH OF BASE
E
D
A
DIATOMACEOUS INSULATION 2¼" THICK
SHELL AND TUBES MADE OF 3/16" STEEL PL.

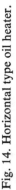

Fig. 14. Horizontal type oil heater.

Chapter 39

Solar Hot Water Systems and Your Home

The conversion of solar radiation to thermal energy and the use of this energy to meet all or part of a dwelling's heating and domestic hot water requirements has been the primary application of solar energy in buildings.

This chapter will help you to understand the basic facts about solar hot water heating. It points out some of the technical details you should know, and discusses design and choice of different solar hot water systems.

FUNCTION

The basic function of a domestic solar hot water system is the collection and conversion of solar radiation into usable energy. This is accomplished—in general terms—in the following manner: Solar radiation is absorbed by a *collector*, placed in storage as required, with or without the use of a *transport* medium, and *distributed* to points of use. The performance of each operation is maintained by automatic or manual controls. An *auxiliary energy system* is usually available both to supplement the output provided by the solar system and to provide for the total energy demand should the solar system become inoperable.

The parts of a solar system—collector, storage, distribution, transport, controls and auxiliary energy—may vary widely in design, operation, and performance. They may be arranged in numerous combinations depending on function, component compatibility, climatic conditions, required performance, site characteristics, and architectural requirements.

Of the numerous concepts presently being developed for the collection of solar radiation, the relatively simple flat-plate collector has the widest application. It consists of an absorber plate, usually made of metal and coated black to increase absorption of the sun's energy. The plate is insulated on its underside and covered with one or more transparent cover plates to trap heat within the collector and reduce convective losses from the absorber plate. The captured heat is removed from the absorber plate by means of a heat transfer fluid, generally air or water. The fluid is heated as it passes through or near the absorber plate and then transported to points of use, or to storage, depending on energy demand. (Most solar hot water systems use liquid heat transfer fluids.)

The storage of thermal energy is the second item of importance since there will be an energy demand during the evening, or on sunless days when solar collection cannot take place. Heat is stored when the energy delivered by the sun and captured by the collector exceeds demand. In some cases, it is necessary to transfer heat from the collector to storage by means of a heat exchanger. In other cases, transfer is made by direct contact of the heat transfer fluid with the storage medium.

The *distribution* component receives heat energy from the collector or storage, and dispenses it at points of use as hot water.

The *controls* of a solar system perform the sensing, evaluation, and response functions required to operate the system in the desired mode. For example, when the collector temperature is sufficiently higher than the storage temperature, the controls will cause the heat transfer fluid in storage to circulate through the collector and accumulate solar heat.

An *auxiliary energy* system provides the supply of energy when stored energy is depleted due to severe weather or clouds. The auxiliary system, using conventional fuels such as oil, gas, electricity, or wood, provides the required heat until solar energy is available again.

Most solar systems can be characterized as either active or passive.

An *active solar system* is generally classified as one in which an energy resource—in addition to solar—is used for the transfer of thermal energy. This additional energy, generated on or off the site, is required for pumps or other heat transfer medium moving devices for system operation. Generally, the collection, storage, and distribution of thermal energy is achieved by moving a transfer medium throughout the system with the assistance of pumping power.

A *passive solar system*, on the other hand, is generally classified as one where solar energy alone is used for the transfer of thermal energy. Energy other than solar is not required for pumps or other heat transfer medium moving devices for system operation. Collection, storage, and distribution is achieved by natural heat transfer phenomena employing convection, radiation, and conduction.

OPERATION

The solar hot water system is usually designed to preheat water from the incoming water supply prior to its passage through a conventional water heater. The domestic hot water preheating system can be combined with a solar heating system or designed as a separate system. Both situations are illustrated in Figs. 1 and 2.

Domestic Hot Water Preheating—Separate System. Domestic hot water preheating may be the only solar system included in many designs. An active solar system is shown in the upper illustration, and a passive thermosyphoning arrangement in the lower illustration in Fig. 1.

Domestic Hot Water Preheating—Combined System. Domestic hot water is preheated as it passes through heat storage en route to the conventional water heater. An active solar system using air for heat transport is shown in the upper illustration, and a passive solar system in the lower illustration in Fig. 2.

BASICS OF SOLAR ENERGY UTILIZATION

Solar collectors must be oriented and tilted within prescribed limits to receive the optimum level of solar radiation for successful system operation and performance.

Collector Orientation and Tilt. *Collector tilt for domestic hot water.* The optimum collector tilt for domestic water heating alone is usually equal to the site latitude (Fig. 3). Variations up to 10° F. on either side of the optimum is acceptable.

Collector orientation. A collector orientation of 20° F. to either side of true South is acceptable (Fig. 4). However, the local climate and the type of collector may influence the choice between East or West deviations.

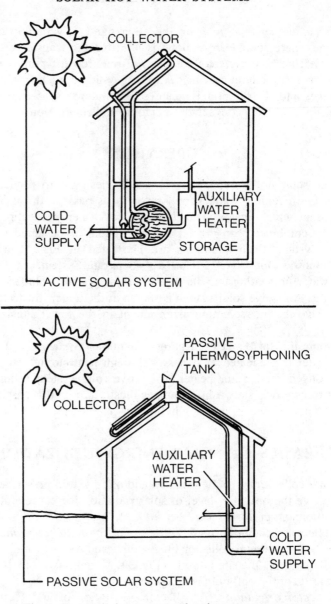

Fig. 1. Domestic hot water preheating—separate system.

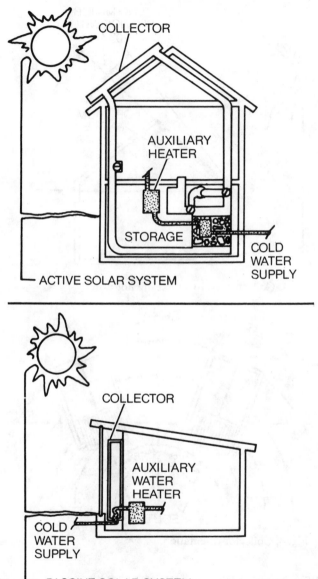

Fig. 2. Domestic hot water preheating—combined system.

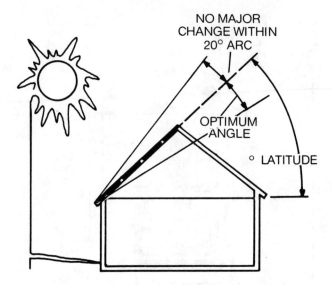

Fig. 3. Collector tilt for domestic hot water.

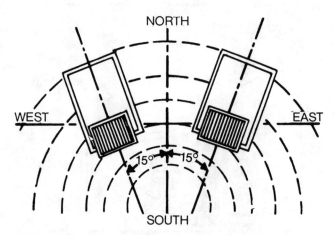

Fig. 4. Collector orientation.

Modification of optimum collector tilt. A greater gain in solar radiation collection may sometimes be achieved by tilting the collector away from the optimum in order to capture radiation reflected from adjacent ground or building surfaces (Fig. 5). The corresponding

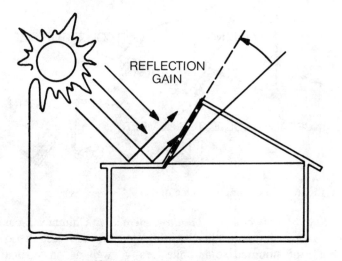

REFLECTION GAIN

Fig. 5. Modification of optimum collector tilt.

reduction of radiation directly striking the collector, due to non-optimum tilt, should be recognized when considering this option.

Snowfall consideration. The snowfall characteristics of an area may influence the appropriateness of these optimum collector tilts. Snow build-up on the collector, or drifting in front of the collector, should be avoided.

Shading of Collector. Another issue related to both collector orientation and tilt is shading. Solar collectors should be located on the building or site so that unwanted shading of the collectors by adjacent structures, landscaping, or building elements does not occur. In addition, considerations for avoiding shading of the collector by other collectors should also be made. Collector shading by elements surrounding the site must also be addressed.

Self-shading of collector. Avoiding all self-shading for a bank of parallel collectors during useful collection hours (between 9 AM and 3 PM) results in designing for the lowest angle of incidence with large spaces between collectors. It may be desirable therefore to allow some self-shading at the end of solar collection hours in order to increase collector size or to design a closer spacing of collectors, thus increasing the solar collection area. (*See* Fig. 6.)

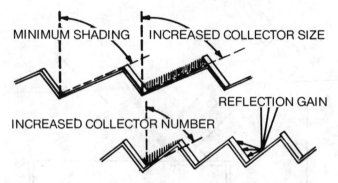

MINIMUM SHADING   INCREASED COLLECTOR SIZE

INCREASED COLLECTOR NUMBER

REFLECTION GAIN

Fig. 6. Self-shading of collector.

Shading of collector by building elements. Chimneys, parapets, fire walls, dormers, and other building elements can cast shadows on adjacent roof-mounted solar collectors, as well as on vertical wall collectors. Figure 7 shows a house with a 45 degree south-facing collector at latitude 40° North. By mid-afternoon, portions of the collector are shaded by the chimney, dormer, and the off-set between the collector on the garage. Careful attention to the placement of building elements and to floor plan arrangement is required to assure that unwanted collector shading will not occur.

COLLECTORS

Fig. 7.

ACTIVE SOLAR SYSTEMS

Active solar systems are characterized by collectors, thermal storage units, and transfer media in an assembly that requires additional mechanical energy to convert and transfer the solar energy into thermal energy. The following discussion of active solar systems serves as an introduction to a range of active concepts that have been constructed.

Domestic hot water can be preheated either by circulating the potable water supply itself through the collector, or by passing the supply line through storage en route to a conventional water heater. Storage-related preheating systems are shown in Figs. 8, 9, and 10.

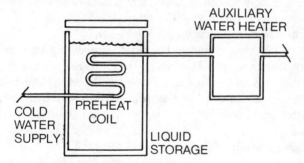

Fig. 8. Preheat coil in storage.

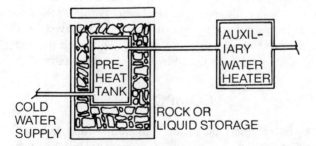

Fig. 9. Preheat tank in storage.

Preheating Coil in Storage.   *See* Fig. 8.

Water is passed through a suitably sized coil placed in storage en route to the conventional water heater. Unless the preheat coil has a

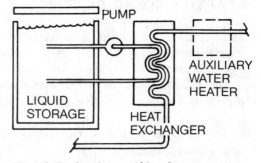

Fig. 10. Preheating outside of storage.

protective double-wall construction, this method can only be used for solar systems employing non-toxic storage media.

Preheating Tank in Storage.   *See* Fig. 9.

In this system, the domestic hot water preheating tank is located within the heat storage. The water supply passes through storage to the preheating tank where it is heated and stored, and later piped to a conventional water heater as needed. A protective double-wall construction again will be necessary unless a non-toxic storage medium is used.

Preheating Outside of Storage.   *See* Fig. 10.

In this preheating method, the heat transfer liquid in storage is pumped through a separate heat exchanger to be used for domestic hot water preheating. This separate heat exchanger could be the conventional water heater itself. However, if the liquid from storage is toxic, the required separation of liquids is achieved by the use of a double-wall exchanger, as shown in Fig. 18, which the water supply passes through en route to the conventional water heater.

COMPONENTS

As previously described in the Function section, a solar domestic hot water system is composed of numerous individual parts and pieces: collectors; storage; a distribution network with pipes, pumps and valves; insulation; a system of manual or automatic controls; and possibly heat exchangers, expansion tanks, and filters. These parts are assembled in a variety of combinations, depending on function, component compatibility, climatic conditions, required performance, site characteristics, and architectural requirements to form a solar domestic hot water system. Some components that are unique to the collector system or that are used in an unconventional manner are briefly illustrated and described in this section.

Flat-Plate Collectors. The flat-plate collector (Fig. 11) is a common solar collection device used for domestic water heating. Most collectors are designed to use liquid (usually treated water) as the heat transfer medium. However, air systems are available for domestic water heating. Most flat-plate collectors consist of the same general components.

Batten. Battens (Fig. 11) serve to hold down the cover plate(s) and provide a weathertight seal between the enclosure and the cover.

Cover plate. The cover plate (**Fig. 11**) usually consists of one or more layers of glass or plastic film or combinations thereof. The cover plate is separated from the absorber plate to reduce reradiation and to create an air space, which traps heat by reducing convective losses. This space between the cover and absorber can be evacuated to further reduce convective losses.

Heat transfer fluid passage. Tubes are attached above, below, or integral with an absorber plate for the purpose of transferring thermal energy from the absorber plate to a heat transfer medium (Fig. 11).

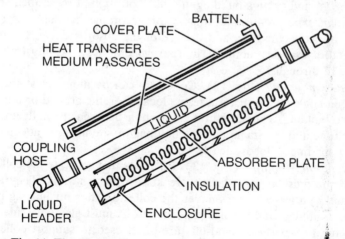

Fig. 11. Flat-plate collectors.

The largest variation in flat-plate collector design occurs with this component and its combination with the absorber plate. Tube on plate, integral tube and sheet, open channel flow, corrugated sheets, deformed sheets, extruded sheets, and finned tubes are some of the techniques used.

Absorber plate. Since the absorber plate must have a good thermal bond with the fluid passages, an absorber plate integral with the heat transfer media passages is common. The absorber plate is usually metallic, and normally treated with a surface coating that improves absorptivity. Black or dark paints or selective coatings are used for this purpose. The design of this passage and plate combination helps determine a solar system's effectiveness (Fig. 11).

Insulation. Insulation is employed to reduce heat loss through the back of the collector (Fig. 11). The insulation must be suitable for the high temperature that may occur under no-flow or dry-plate conditions, or even normal collection operation. Thermal decomposition and outgassing of the insulation must be prevented.

Enclosure. The enclosure (Fig. 11) is a container for all the above components. The assembly is usually weatherproof. Preventing dust, wind, and water from coming in contact with the cover plate and insulation is essential to maintaining collector performance.

Collector Mounting.   Flat-plate collectors are generally mounted on the ground or on a building in a fixed position at prescribed angles of solar exposure—angles that vary according to the geographic location, collector type, and the use of the absorbed heat. Flat-plate collectors may be mounted in four general ways as illustrated in Figs. 12 through 15.

Rack mounting (Fig. 12). Collectors can be mounted at the prescribed angle on a structural frame located on the ground or attached to the building. The structural connection between the collector and the frame and the frame and the building or site must be adequate to resist any impact loads such as wind.

Stand-off Mounting (Fig. 13). Elements that separate the collector from the finished roof surface are known as stand-offs. They allow air and rain water to pass under the collector, thus minimizing problems of mildew and leakage. The stand-offs must also have adequate structural properties. Stand-offs are often used to support collectors at an angle other than that of the roof to optimize collector tilt.

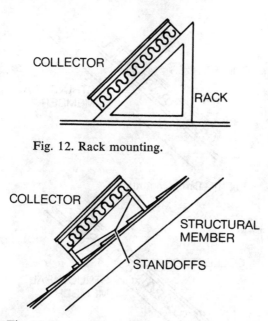

Fig. 12. Rack mounting.

Fig. 13. Stand-off mounting.

Direct mounting (Fig. 14). Collectors can be mounted directly on the roof surface. Generally, the collectors are placed on a waterproof membrane on top of the roof sheathing. The finished roof surface, together with the necessary collector structural attachments and flashing, are then built up around the collector. A weatherproof seal between the collector and the roof must be maintained, or leakage, mildew, and rotting may occur.

Integral mounting (Fig. 15). Unlike the previous three component collectors that can be applied or mounted separately, integral mounting places the collector within the roof construction itself. Thus the collector is attached to and supported by the structural framing members. In addition, the top of the collector serves as the finished roof surface. Weather tightness is again crucial to avoid problems of water damage and mildew. This method of mounting is frequently used for site built collectors.

Heat Exchangers. A *heat exchanger* is a device for transferring thermal energy from one fluid to another. In some solar systems, a

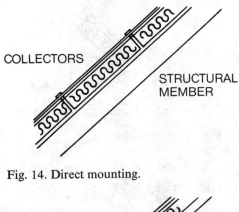

Fig. 14. Direct mounting.

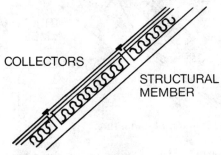

Fig. 15. Integral mounting.

heat exchanger may be required between the transfer medium—circulated through the collector—and the storage medium, or between the storage and the distribution medium. There are three types of heat exchangers that are the most commonly used for these purposes: the shell and tube, the shell and double tube, and the double wall, as shown in Figs. 16, 17, and 18.

Shell and tube (Fig. 16). The shell and tube heat exchanger is used to transfer heat from a circulating transfer medium to another medium used in storage or in distribution. Shell and tube heat exchangers consist of an outer casing or shell surrounding a bundle of tubes. The water to be heated is normally circulated in the tubes and the hot liquid is circulated in the shell. Tubes are usually metal, such as steel, copper, or stainless steel. A single shell and tube heat exchanger *cannot be used* for transfering heat from a toxic liquid to potable water because double separation is not provided and the

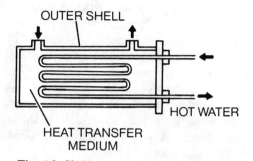

Fig. 16. Shell and tube heat exchanger.

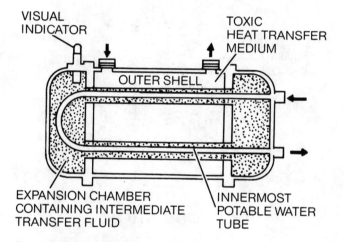

Fig. 17. Shell and double tube heat exchanger.

toxic liquid may enter the potable water supply in the event of tube failure.

Shell and Double Tube (Fig. 17). The shell and double tube heat exchanger is similar to the previous one, shell and tube, except that a secondary chamber is located within the shell to surround the potable water tube. The heated toxic liquid then circulates inside the shell but around this second tube. An intermediary non-toxic heat transfer liquid is then located between the two tube circuits. As the toxic heat transfer medium circulates through the shell, the intermediary liquid is heated, which in turn heats the potable water supply circulating through the innermost tube. This heat exchanger can be equipped with a sight glass to detect leaks by a change in color—toxic liquid often contains a dye—or by a change in the liquid level in the intermediary chamber, which would indicate a failure in either the outer shell or intermediary tube lining.

Double wall (Fig. 18). Another method of providing a double separation between the transfer medium and the potable water supply consists of tubing or a plate coil wrapped around and bonded to a tank. The potable water is heated as it circulates through the coil or through the tank. When this method is used, the tubing coil must be adequately insulated to reduce heat loss.

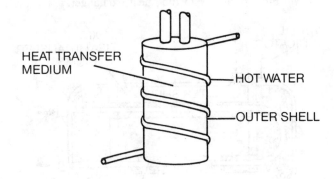

Fig. 18. Double wall.

CONSIDERATIONS

Cost. The cost of a typical, uninstalled, solar domestic hot water system for an average family depends on geographic location, collector efficiency, and other factors. Installation costs vary greatly on a case-by-case basis, depending on the design of the home and on any structural modifications required.

Evaluating Solar Hot Water Systems. Two important factors are *first cost* and *collector efficiency*. Both factors must be considered when comparing collectors. Thus, a relatively inexpensive collector with low efficiency may be a poor choice when compared to a more expensive one that captures and delivers the sun's energy more efficiently. All other things being equal, the collector that delivers more *heat per dollar* should be selected.

However, it must be stressed that there are other considerations besides first cost and efficiency. The question of *warranties* is an important one. Is the collector covered by a warranty, what is specifically covered, and for what period of time? Warranties on equipment now available are generally limited. That is, they cover only certain features. The two following warranties are both limited, but provide very different coverage. Knowing the differences can make a big difference in your pocketbook.

1. This product is guaranteed against all defects in construction and against corrosion for a period of five years. Manufacturer will pay for all labor and parts costs to correct problems.
2. This product is guaranteed to be one of the finest solar systems ever manufactured. Manufacturer will pay for costs of parts to correct any problem.

Choosing a Solar Hot Water System. The following should be considered in choosing a solar hot water system:

Durability. How long is it expected to last? Is it weatherproof; does it shed water?

Ease of repair. If something goes wrong, who will fix it, and are repair parts easy to obtain? What will various repairs cost?

Susceptibility to either freezing or overheating. There are a number of adequate solutions to both problems, and the collector must have protection for both extremes built in. In addition, if antifreeze fluid is used in the collector, it must not mix with water for domestic use.

Protection against corrosion. Metal corrosion can cause irreparable damage to a solar heating system and shorten its life span. More importantly, corrosion can cause serious health problems if the water is used directly by the user. The three metals commonly used in collectors are copper, steel, and aluminum. Inhibitors are usually added to prevent corrosion in most systems. Copper will function over a long period without inhibitors, while steel and aluminum may fail quickly without special protection. With inhibited water, all three will last indefinitely as long as inhibition is maintained.

Protection against leaks. The greater the number of joints, the greater the possibility of leakage. Some liquid collectors using channel systems have reduced the need for soldered joints considerably without affecting efficiency. Know what happens if a leak occurs, how it will be fixed, who will fix it, and how much it will cost.

Consumer protection. Try to obtain the names of other buyers, and learn whether the buyer is satisfied with its performance and whether the collector has lived up to the claims of the seller.

Insulation. The pipes, ducts, back parts of collectors, and storage tank should be insulated to prevent heat loss. This is true of inside and outside pipes and ducts. Avoid use of heating tapes to prevent freezing. They may use more energy than the solar system saves.

Pitch of pipes. The flow of water in pipes has to be positive if the collector is the drain-down type. There cannot be any traps in the external pipes where water can collect and possibly freeze. Pipes and collectors need to be pitched to achieve drain-down.

Bleeding mechanism. Air has a habit of getting into systems even though they are watertight. A facility should be provided for bleeding the system. An expansion tank, or room in storage for expansion, should also be included.

Fans and pumps. Fans and pumps use electricity, and hence should not be any bigger than necessary to perform. If they are too big then they will reduce the total energy savings. A time elapsed meter can be installed to see if the fans or pumps are running for too long a period. Sometimes they can be on when not needed but, since they are quiet, the homeowner is not aware that they are on. Pumps should be located below tank water level.

Tests. The system should be taken through a complete operating test before acceptance by the owner. All controls should be confirmed as working and all leaks should be fixed. There should be confirmation that the collector does increase the temperature in storage. If the system is a drain-down type, there should be evidence that the system will drain down properly.

Controls and valves. These items should be corrosive-resistant and as silent as possible. In a system that connects directly to the potable water supply, inhibitors or anti-freeze cannot be used. In this case, the controls and valves should be brass.

All installations should be done in a thoroughly workmanlike manner. Holes made in the roof or foundation should be well calked to prevent leaks, the collectors should be properly anchored to prevent being blown away, and all plumbing joints should be well soldered. These are things to look for in any water or air system, not just solar systems. Remember, the system has to last for many years and unless the workmanship is of high quality, unnecessary leaks and malfunctions can develop. These items do not usually show up in the first year.

Standards. Ask whether the collector will meet the intermediate Minimum Property Standards for Solar Heating and Domestic Hot Water Systems. If the manufacturer claims such standards are met, get that in writing. These standards provide a degree of assurance for the consumer, and if a seller claims that such standards are met, he is legally accountable for that claim.

In summary, the most important points in buying a solar hot water system are:

1. The total costs, including installation.
2. The expected performance of the system all year round.
3. The expected lifetime of the system.

HOW TO BUY SOLAR

To get your money's worth, three main obstacles must be overcome:

1. The consumer's own lack of knowledge and inexperience in the field.
2. Manufacturers who unintentionally build shoddy products.
3. Deliberate fraud and misrepresentation.

By relying on competent engineering advice, many potential problems can be avoided. Additional steps to take include the following:

1. *Ask for proof that the product will perform as advertised.* The proof could come from an independent laboratory or a university. You should have the report itself, not what the manufacturer states the report claims.

2. *Examine the warranty carefully.* Remember that, according to the law, the manufacturer must state that the warranty is *full or limited.* If it is limited, know what the limitations are. How long does the warranty last? Are parts, service, and labor covered? Who will

provide the service? Does the equipment have to be sent back to the manufacturer for repairs? Make sure you understand the terms of the warranty before you buy. Ask the seller what financial arrangements, such as an escrow account, have been made to honor the warranties.

3. *Solar components are like stereo components—some work well together, others do not.* If the system you are purchasing is not sold as a single package by one manufacturer, be certain that the seller has strong experience in choosing compatible components.

4. *Be sure you will know specifically who will service the solar system if something goes wrong.* Do not settle for a response that any plumber or handyman will do.

5. *Do not try a do-it-yourself kit, unless you really have a very solid background as a handyman.* One or two mistakes could make a system inoperable and you will have no one to blame but yourself.

6. *Do not forget your local consumer protection office or your Better Business Bureau.* Both may be able to help you determine whether a seller is reputable or not. Check, too, to see whether there is a local volunteer citizens solar organization around. If so, it can probably give you plenty of good advice.

7. *If the seller makes verbal claims that are not reflected in the literature handed out, ask him to write those claims down, and to sign his name to it.* Compare what he said with what he wrote and save that statement.

8. If you have what appears to be a *legitimate complaint*, immediately notify the local district attorney's office, the Better Business Bureau, and the local consumer protection agency. Be as specific in your complaint as possible, and give as much documentation as you can.

Section 8

HOUSEWARES

HOUSEHOLD VACUUM CLEANERS CAN be divided into three basic categories: canister tank (suction-type cleaner), upright (agitation-type cleaner), and a combination cleaner (suction plus agitation cleaner).

Today there are many choices of *sewing machines* in a wide range of prices. No one machine is likely to have all the features you might desire. Buying a sewing machine for home use is a long-time investment. Reputable manufacturers build machines to last for many years with only minor replacements of parts. Usually you can clean, oil, and adjust the machine yourself.

With the increasing rate of residential burglary, homeowners are becoming more and more concerned for the security of their homes and personal belongings. Therefore, many homeowners are considering the installation of *home security alarm systems.*

The statistics on the loss of life and property due to fire are grim. However, there is an inexpensive and dependable way to protect your home, yourself, and your family with *smoke detectors.*

There are three classes of home-type fires. Your ability to identify the type of fire *quickly* may save your home—or your life. The reason is that most extinguishers are designed to fight particular classes of fires. Some fight only one class; some fight two classes; *only one home-type extinguisher* fights all three classes of fires.

Chapter 40

Vacuum Cleaners

When you go out to buy a vacuum cleaner, do not forget the following *basic questions* to ask.

How well does the cleaner pick up granular material like sand or salt? How large is the dust bag? Is the bag easy to empty or replace? What is the cost of disposable bag replacements? Does the cleaner roll easily? Does it have a hand grip so that it can be carried? Is the on-off switch conveniently located? How much noise does the cleaner make when operated in a small room? Is the cleaner comfortable to operate? What are the guarantees? Will servicing be convenient? Is the cleaner labeled as electrically safe?

Canister/tank. How well does the model clean the rug, the floor, above the floor? How many attachments are supplied? Are the tools made of durable material? Do the cleaning tools lock securely on the wands? Are tools for bare floor and rugs designed to swivel? What provision is made for tool carrying and storage? Is the hose flexible but durable? Are the wands made of strong material? Do they have a positive means of locking? Are all the connections tight? Is the housing stable, smooth, and surrounded by resilient bumpers? Does the cleaner exhaust air in a way that will not scatter dust? Is the shape of the canister/tank suited to your particular needs? Does the cleaner have a motor inlet filter?

Upright. Does the upright clean beneath the surface of the rug pile? Is the nozzle about 11 inches wide? If not, cleaning may be slow. Are the brushes thick? Do they extend to both ends of the agitator? Can the brushes be adjusted or replaced? Is the nozzle edged with resilient bumpers? Is there a tight connection between the dust bag and the nozzle? Is the cleaner stable, regardless of the handle position?

Combination cleaner. Since the combination cleaner has the features of both the canister/tank and the upright, use the same questions if you plan to buy this type.

TYPES OF VACUUM CLEANERS

Canister/Tank.   The cleaning ability of the canister/tank model comes from the suction produced by the motor driven fan. This suction pulls at the surface, and the air flow carries the litter and dust into the dust bag.

Upright.   The cleaning ability of the upright comes from both agitation and suction. The suction lifts the rug against the nozzle; the brushes and/or beater bars vibrate the dirt and litter loose from the rug; the air flow carries the dirt into the dust bag.

Combination Cleaner.   Some manufacturers take the strong suction of the canister/tank and the powered agitator head of the upright and combine them. They do this by adding a powered rug nozzle to the canister/tank models.

FACTS YOU SHOULD KNOW ABOUT CLEANERS

Cleaning Ability.   Buying a new cleaner would be simple if manufacturers rated the cleaning ability of their models in some meaningful way. But since horsepower, revolutions per minute, sealed suction, working suction, and water lift ratings of themselves tell the non-technical person very little about how well a particular model cleans, you will have to measure its cleaning ability in a very practical way—by observing its performance. Operate the cleaner yourself to be sure it meets your needs.

If possible, get a home demonstration. See how well the cleaner works on your rugs and floors, and areas above the floor.

If you cannot get a home demonstration, get a demonstration in the store, but try to use the cleaner on rugs similar to the kind you have in your home.

The best material to use for testing a cleaner's efficiency is granular material like sand or salt. After the cleaner is run over this kind of material, check below the rug pile to see that the material has been picked up, not just pushed down.

Beware of the following popular demonstration gimmicks:

1. *Picking up some heavy object with the cleaner.* This is not a meaningful test. Working suction against a rug or carpet is what you need to measure cleaning efficiency.

2. *Picking up fine powder or filmy cotton fiber.* This is no test for cleaning efficiency, either. Very little suction is required to pick up this kind of material.

3. *Using the new cleaner after your old cleaner has worked over an area of the rug.* The salesman will empty the dust bag of the new cleaner to show you how much additional dirt it has picked up. You could get the same result if you had used the new cleaner first, and then the old one. No cleaner will pick up all the dirt in just a few strokes.

Dust Bag.   The dust bag capacity should be large. The larger the capacity, the less frequently will you have to empty or change the bag. Dust bags should be large also to maintain an adequate filter area for air as the bag fills with dirt. When you consider a cleaner, compare dust bag sizes among various models. The salesman or the owner's manual should give you the capacities of the bags.

Ease of emptying or changing the dust bag should be a point of comparison when you buy. Also, in the case of disposable bags, the cost of the bags should be a consideration.

There are some advantages to using disposable bags. They are less messy to handle, naturally, since the bags are throwaways. In addition, the disposable bag inside the cloth bag provides the motor in a canister/tank model with a second layer of protection against dust. Some canister/tank models also have a motor inlet filter to further protect the motor.

Noise.   If you get a home demonstration, you will be able to judge the level of noise in which you will be working. In a store demonstration, the noise of the cleaner may be minimized because of background sounds and the store size. If you are limited to a store demonstration, ask the salesman to operate the cleaner in a stock room or a small closed off area before you buy the cleaner. In this way you can get an approximation of the noise level you will be working with in your home.

Ease of Operation.   Before you buy any cleaner, use it yourself to see if you feel comfortable with the machine. In the upright types, consider the weight and length of the handle. In the canister/tank types, consider the ease of movement. In both types, consider the convenience of operating latches and switches.

Features. Features such as a full bag indicator, automatic cord reel, and a regulation for high and low suction are available on some models. Selection here is a matter of personal preference. Is the added feature worth the extra cost? Convenience features do not necessarily add to the quality of the cleaner.

Small Commercial Cleaner. If color and styling are not essential to you, you may wish to consider a relatively small commercial cleaner and compare it to the household type for cleaning efficiency, durability, service, and attachment features.

Guarantees and Service. Buying a product from a reputable manufacturer is itself some guarantee, but to know exactly what you can depend on, read the guarantee.

Most cleaners have a guarantee of one year on parts and labor. Check to see if some parts are guaranteed for less time. Remember that unauthorized servicing or unauthorized replacement of parts may void your guarantee.

To measure the convenience of future servicing, look into the location of service centers for the model you are considering. You can find these listed either in the owner's manual or in the Yellow Pages of your telephone directory.

Safety. Electrical safety is an important consideration when selecting a cleaner.

Independent testing laboratories have established standards for testing many products with regard to electrical safety. If a particular brand and model of a vacuum cleaner has been tested by one of these laboratories and is acceptable, it will carry the laboratory's seal or marker. In the absence of any safety seal of approval, check with the dealer to see if the cleaner has been tested by a nationally recognized laboratory.

Disconnect electrical appliances before cleaning them with vacuum cleaner tools.

Unless the cleaner is advertised for wet pick-up, it should never be used to pick up water, nor should it be used outside on a patio carpet even if the carpet looks dry. *Moisture can cause a dangerous short circuit.*

Frayed or cracked cords should be replaced immediately.

SELECTING A VACUUM CLEANER

Canister/Tank. Versatility and maneuverability make the canister/tank the most desirable if you are a one-vacuum family and if you need a cleaner predominantly for general floor care and above-the-floor cleaning. This kind of cleaner is very good for surface litter and light, clinging dust.

Versatility. High suction and the tool attachments give the canister/tank its versatility. The attachments connect to the housing of the cleaner by means of a hose.

Hose. The hose should be flexible, but made from, or reinforced by, a strong, durable material.

In some models, you can get either suction or blowing action by attaching the hose to the inlet or exhaust connections.

Tools. The tools should be made of a synthetic material or of a non-corroding metal. Some tools come as a two-in-one combination; some have brushes that are removable or replaceable. Check to see which tools are included in the purchase price, and how they are made.

The *rug cleaning tool* should swivel to permit rug cleaning under furniture. Most have a trailing brush or comb to help dislodge clinging litter and to give the cleaned rug pile a finished look.

The *bare floor tool* should swivel. In some models it is edged with fixed brushes that help gather surface litter into the path of suction.

The *upholstery tool* is designed to clean fabric and drapes. It may include a device that prevents the fabric or trim from being drawn into the nozzle.

The *dusting brush* is intended for use on surfaces such as wooden furniture, pictures, books, blinds, and screens that would ordinarily be cleaned with a dust cloth.

The *crevice tool* is shaped to clean hard-to-reach spots—between radiator coils, edges of wall-to-wall carpeting, cushion crevices, and refrigerator or freezer grilles.

Wands. The wands connect the hose of the canister/tank to the attachments, providing a handle. The wands should be made of finished or plated metal or a strong synthetic material, and should have a positive means of locking.

Maneuverability and *portability*. To provide cleaning maneuverability, the canister/tank should have wheels sufficiently large to roll easily. The housing of the cleaner should be smooth and stable, and surrounded with resilient bumpers to protect furniture.

The cleaner should have a good-sized handle so that it can be carried. If you intend to use it on stairs, consider the shape of the model when you shop.

Air flow. All connections should be air-tight. This is especially important for maximum effectiveness in a canister/tank because of all the attachable parts. It is also important with an upright if you are using the attachments.

Be aware that the exhaust air of the canister/tank may scatter dust. Possible problems will be minimized if the exhaust is deflected upward.

On-off switch. A foot operated on-off switch, conveniently located, is probably the most satisfactory.

Upright.   The upright cleaner with its agitator action is generally recognized for its ease of operation on carpeting and its rug cleaning efficiency. If you have many square feet of carpets and rugs, a good upright may be the cleaner you need to remove embedded gritty dirt—which is the most destructive kind.

Rug cleaning ability. The rug cleaning ability of the upright lies in the nozzle. The nozzle is a part of the frame that encloses the motor, the fan, and the agitator. The agitator, which is turned by a belt from the motor, is lined with brushes and/or beater bars.

Nozzle head. The nozzle width should be about 11 inches. This width is important to minimize the time and energy spent in cleaning. The head should adjust, manually or automatically, to various rug piles. A correct adjustment is essential for deep rug cleaning. The nozzle should be edged with resilient bumpers for furniture protection.

Brushes. Brushes should be thick, extending to both ends of the agitator. Cleaners that have brushes that are self-adjusting, or that can be adjusted or replaced when they become worn, offer a practical advantage. Otherwise, when the brush wears down, the whole agitator has to be replaced.

The *beater bars* come in addition to the brushes on some models. They supply beating action to the rug.

Air flow and *suction*. All connections should be air-tight.

Generally, suction is best if the internal design channels the dust to the top or middle of the bag, especially if granular material like sand or salt is to be picked up. Heavy dirt will fall to the bottom of the bag, leaving the rest of the dust bag free to act as a filter.

The attachments for above-the-floor cleaning are not as effective in the upright as in the canister/tank, even in uprights with a two-speed motor. This is because most of the power of the upright is directed toward running the agitator.

If you buy an upright cleaner with optional attachments, those which permit connection of attachments closest to the fan generally give the best suction. But even if a particular upright has good suction, the use of attachments with an upright is more cumbersome than with a canister/tank model.

Handle. The cleaner should be stable regardless of the position of the handle. For storage, the handle should lock in an upright position.

The hand grip is considered by many to be the most convenient place for the on-off switch.

Maneuverability and portability. In the heavy upright, wide wheels offer the best maneuverability. It is convenient if the upright has a grip, probably where the handle attaches to the cleaner body, to make it easier to carry.

Combination Cleaner. Double duty is the feature of this combination unit. The canister, with attachments, offers the powerful suction that is important for general floor care and above-the-floor cleaning, and the versatility that is unique to the canister. The powered nozzle attachment with its separate motor-driven brush agitates the rug and provides rug cleaning efficiency. In this way, the combination unit is similar to the upright but differs in its ease of operation.

To be sure that you will get effective double service from the combination unit, check through the basic questions at the beginning of this chapter. If the combination cleaner meets these points, it should be a good buy, unless you object to working with the attachments.

If you want a dual approach to cleaning, you will need both a canister/tank and an upright, or a combination. Check for a comparative convenience, quality, and cost.

USE AND CARE

Vacuum cleaners consist of three working parts: a motor that drives the fan, the fan that produces the necessary suction to draw the dirt into the bag or tank, and a separator to retain the dirt while permitting the air to escape.

Many of the operations employed in checking and repairing upright or conventional-type cleaners apply to the tank type as well.

UPRIGHT CLEANER

Cautions: When using electrical appliances, basic safety cautions should always be followed.

Most domestic vacuum cleaners and dirt collection bags are not designed to handle liquid or for use *outside* the home. The intake of liquid in this cleaner or use outside may create an electrical shock hazard and can cause damage to the cleaner.

For your own safety, always disconnect the cleaner cord from the electrical outlet before removing any parts to check the cleaner or to perform minor maintenance operations.

Do not operate any appliance with a damaged cordset or after it has been dropped or damaged in any manner. Return it to the nearest authorized service facility for examination and repair.

How to Assemble Cleaner.

1. Remove all parts carefully from carton. Remove cardboard inserts from lower and upper handle sections and discard packing materials.

2. To assemble handle (Figs. 1 and 2): Remove nut and bolt from lower handle section (handle bracket); insert straight handle section into handle bracket, with cord hook to the side and pointing down; align handle holes.

Fig. 1. Assembly of upright cleaner handle.

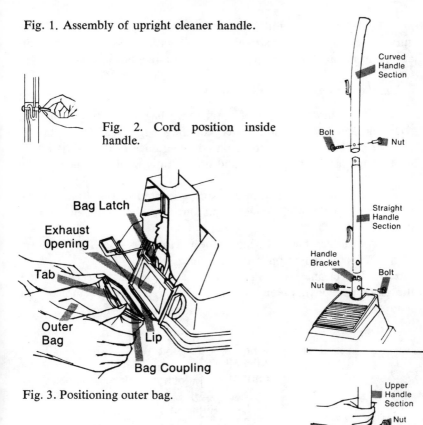

Fig. 2. Cord position inside handle.

Bag Latch

Exhaust Opening

Tab

Outer Bag

Lip

Bag Coupling

Curved Handle Section

Bolt

Nut

Straight Handle Section

Handle Bracket

Nut

Bolt

Upper Handle Section

Nut

Bolt

Lower Handle Section

Fig. 3. Positioning outer bag.

3. Form the excess length of cord in a loop. Position upper handle section above lower handle, push cord loop into lower handle and join handle sections. Align the large and small handle holes. Figure 2 shows the cross-section that shows the cord position inside the handle for easy insertion of the nut and bolt.

4. Insert bolt in small hole and nut in large hole. Tighten nut with coin or screwdriver.

5. Remove nut and bolt from straight handle section. Join curved handle section to straight section, with cord hook to the side and pointing up. Align handle hole. Repeat directions in step 4.

Vinyl outer bag. (See Figs. 3 and 4.)

1. Grip the open end of vinyl outer bag with the tab on bag coupling upward. Position lower coupling edge over lower lip of exhaust opening. Place thumbs on coupling edge next to center tab, push coupling toward cleaner, and press firmly until tab snaps under bag latch.

2. Grip the upper end of coil spring located at top of vinyl outer bag. Gently pull spring upward and slip ring over hook on rear of upper handle.

3. Refer to the following section, How To Use The Cleaner, Carpet Selector, before operating cleaner.

4. The cleaner is equipped with a disposable filter bag inside the zippered, vinyl, outer bag. The cleaner is now assembled and ready for use.

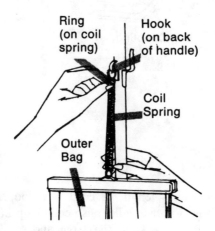

Fig. 4. Positioning outer bag.

How to Use the Cleaner.   *Automatic cord reel.*

1. To unwind cord from automatic cord reel, pull cord upward from the cord guide located near handle grip (Fig. 5). Remove only

the amount of cord needed for the cleaning job. (When 18 feet of cord has been extended, a yellow band will appear on the cord—a warning that six inches of cord are left. Do not pull cord beyond the yellow band as this may result in damage to the cleaner.)

2. To automatically rewind the cord, remove plug from electrical outlet and drape cord across the palm of your hand. It is important to position this hand near the cleaner handle in order to maintain proper cord control during rewind. Press the lever on the cord guide (Fig. 5). If cord retracts too fast, either close your hand around the cord or release the lever; if cord retracts too slowly, straighten the cord above the cord guide.

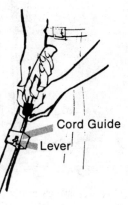

Cord Guide

Lever

Fig. 5. Automatic cord reel.

Handle position adjustments.

The cleaner is equipped with three handle positions, as shown in Fig. 6. To adjust handle, depress handle release pedal on left rear of cleaner housing with your toe, then lower handle.

Upright position. Handle locks in this position for cleaner storage and for easily maneuvering cleaner on its rear wheels. When using the optional kit of attachments, it is desirable to leave the handle in the upright position for easy maneuverability around furniture.

Middle position. The middle position is the operating position for rug and carpet cleaning. A handle stop at the lower end of this position enables raising the front of the motor housing to easily pass over door sills or across rug edges and for quick pick-up of large litter.

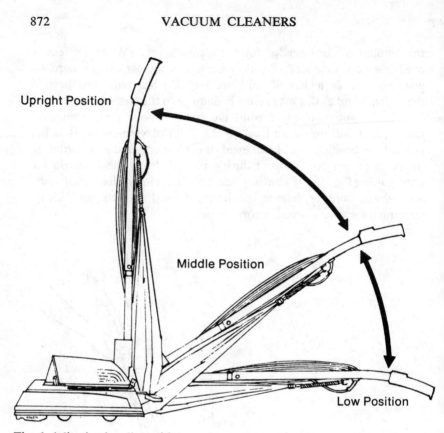

Upright Position

Middle Position

Low Position

Fig. 6. Adjusting handle position.

Low position. This position is used for vacuuming under some furniture. The handle release pedal must be depressed and the handle further lowered to attain this position.

Carpet selectors and levers.

Rug and hose lever. The rug and hose lever located to the left side of the motor housing should be adjusted for the type of cleaning to be done. When cleaning rugs and carpeting the word Rugs should be exposed. When using the optional kits of cleaning attachments the word Hose should be exposed. To adjust this lever, slide it forward or backward with your hand or foot.

Suction control lever. The suction control lever located to the right of motor housing provides a high and low suction setting. This lever may be adjusted by moving it with your foot (Fig. 7). Use the high setting for low pile and multi-level carpeting for most effective cleaning. Use the low setting for deep pile carpeting and light throw rugs to make cleaning strokes easier.

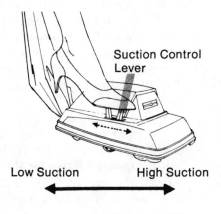

Fig. 7. Adjusting suction control lever.

Carpet selector. The carpet selector located at the far left side of motor housing provides four selective positions to adjust the cleaner for effective cleaning on different types of rugs and carpeting. Positions are designated Indoor-Outdoor Pile, Average Pile, High Pile and Shag Pile.

To adjust cleaner, make sure rug-hose lever has Rug exposed, then grip handle, tilt cleaner forward, and move lever with your finger until it clicks into the desired carpet position (Fig. 8).

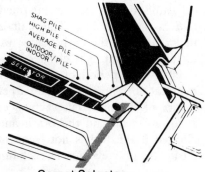

Fig. 8. Adjusting carpet selector.

Carpet Selector

Guide for using carpet selector.

Indoor-outdoor pile. Select this position to vacuum low, tight, or flat surface carpet of the indoor-outdoor type.

Average pile. Use this position to vacuum carpet of average pile height. If cleaner does not push easily, reduce suction control to Low or adjust carpet selector to High Pile.

High pile. Use this position to vacuum deep, luxurious carpet pile. Reduce suction control to Low if necessary for easier cleaning strokes.

Shag pile. Choose this position to vacuum shag or other long pile carpets and rugs.

Edger. The edger, located on each side of the cleaner soleplate, provides improved cleaning of carpeting next to walls and baseboards. Simply move the cleaner slowly along the edge of the carpet.

How to Operate Cleaner for Rug Cleaning.

1. Slide switch on front of handle to Off and place handle in upright position. Plug cord into a 120-volt, 50-60 cps (cycles per second), AC outlet.

2. Grip handle and depress handle release pedal. As handle is lowered, slide switch to On position.

3. To vacuum rugs, maneuver the cleaner back and forth using short, relaxed, overlapping strokes. Use repetitive strokes for cleaning traffic lanes where tracked-in dirt is heaviest.

4. When cleaning is finished, slide switch to Off and return handle to upright position. Remove plug from electrical outlet and store cleaner cord. On non-cord reel model, wrap cord around handle hooks, then attach end of cord by using the clip-on plug.

New Carpeting.   After using your upright vacuum cleaner on new carpeting, do not become alarmed over the large quantity of carpet *fluff* in the filter bag. This fluff is simply loose fiber ends and lint that remain in the carpet after weaving and shearing by the manufacturer. The upright cleaner will eventually remove this loose material over a period of many months of cleaning. Removal of this material does not injure the carpet in any way. Because of the fluffy nature of the material, vacuum cleaner bags will fill more rapidly. Also, areas around the brush and belt of the cleaner may become clogged if the bag is not frequently replaced. Examine these areas during the first few months each time the bag is changed.

When vacuuming new, sheared carpeting, you can minimize clogging in the interior dirt channel by following this procedure: After vacuuming about six square feet of carpeting, lower cleaner handle to the middle handle stop, which will raise the front of the cleaner. Keep cleaner in this position a few seconds. This allows a rush of air through the cleaner that will draw carpet fluff into the filter bag.

How to Use Cleaner with Attachments. If your upright cleaner has a two-speed motor, one speed is employed for cleaning carpets and rugs and a second, higher speed is utilized when the cleaner is adjusted to attachment use. If your cleaner has a single-speed motor, the same speed is used for both types of cleaning.

Custom accessory kit (Fig. 9). The kit includes a flexible hose, molded wands, dusting brush, upholstery nozzle, and crevice tool.

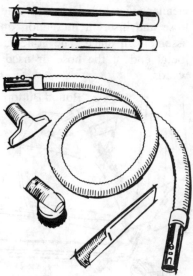

Fig. 9. Accessories.

To operate cleaner with attachments:

1. Position cleaner handle upright and plug cord into a 120-volt, 50–60 cps, AC outlet.

2. Adjust cleaner to the attachment setting by sliding the rug-hose lever to expose the word *hose* (Fig. 10). When the rug-hose lever is adjusted the carpet selector will shift automatically to the shag pile position, which provides easy maneuvering of cleaner.

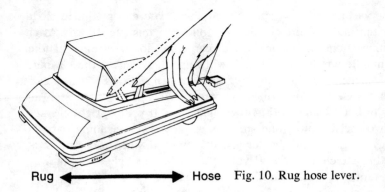

Rug ◄─────────────► Hose   Fig. 10. Rug hose lever.

3. Pull plug from suction opening located on right rear of cleaner (Fig. 11). Depress round button on long metal end of flexible hose and insert it in suction opening. Release button to lock hose assembly in place. The attachments may be connected to the short metal end of the hose or used in combination with the extension wands.

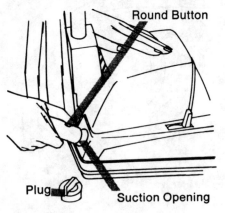

Round Button

Plug   Suction Opening   Fig. 11. Suction opening.

4. Slide switch to On position and commence using attachments. For convenience during room cleaning, the upright cleaner may be quickly adjusted for rug and carpet cleaning without removing the attachment hose from the cleaner. Simply loop the hose around the handle and drape hose over the front of vinyl outer bag. Tilt motor housing forward and first adjust the rug-hose lever to

expose the word Rugs, then readjust carpet selector to desired setting and begin rug cleaning. You may find it convenient to store the cleaner with the hose attached, so it is ready for rug and carpet cleaning or for quick adjustment for attachment use when you need it.

5. When cleaning is finished, slide switch to Off position, remove cord from electrical outlet, and store cord on cleaner. It is important to readjust rug-hose lever to expose the word rugs as carpet selector cannot be adjusted with the lever in the Hose position.

Disposable Filter Bag. Always operate the cleaner with a disposable filter bag installed. Periodically the bag should be checked for dirt accumulation. Position handle upright and unzip outer bag. When dirt level has reached the *fill line* indicated on the disposable bag, the bag should be replaced. It is important to remember that some types of fine dirt particles quickly cover the inner pores of the filter bag, thus reducing air flow. This may be the problem if the cleaner is not cleaning efficiently and dirt is below the bag fill line. When this occurs, the disposable bag should be removed and discarded, and a new disposable filter bag installed.

How to Remove Disposable Filter Bag. *See* Fig. 12.

1. Position handle upright and unzip the vinyl outer bag. Separate the outer bag opening and carefully lift out the bottom, then the top of the disposable bag.

2. Gently pull bag connector between zipper opening and roll down the coiled spring.

3. Gently remove the disposable bag fill tube from the bag connector and discard the dirt filled bag.

How to Install Disposable Filter Bag. *See* Fig. 12.

1. With disposable bag fill tube toward cleaner handle and the word Top printed on the bag clearly evident, as shown in Fig. 12, slip fill tube completely over bag connector. Carefully fold excess paper to one side for a snug fit, then roll coil spring upward until it is positioned in groove.

2. Arrange disposable filter bag inside vinyl outer bag and with word Top printed on bag, at top of outer bag. Disposable bag should be between zipper of outer bag and bag connector. Zip outer bag closed.

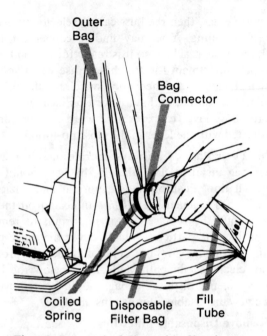

Outer Bag

Bag Connector

Coiled Spring

Disposable Filter Bag

Fill Tube

Fig. 12. Removal of disposable filter bag.

Operating Efficiency.   When the cleaner fails to pick up surface dirt and litter efficiently, check the following areas and refer to the section discussing each area.

Disposable filter bag.
Drive belt.
Vibrator bar brush assembly.

It is important to occasionally check the area of the cleaner fan, especially if metal objects have been picked up accidentally. Large or sharp metal objects should be avoided as they can damage the cleaner fan.

Periodically the cleaner exhaust opening should be checked—particularly during the first few months when using the cleaner to vacuum new, cut-pile carpeting. To release bag coupling from exhaust opening see Fig. 3 and press bag latch toward cleaner handle. To attach bag coupling see step 1 under Vinyl Outer Bag.

How to Remove and Replace Soleplate. *See* Fig. 13.

1. Lower cleaner handle to floor and turn cleaner upside down. Rotate the three metal tabs and lift off soleplate.

2. Check gasket on inner edge of soleplate and wipe off any dirt accumulation.

3. To replace soleplate, fit front edge under the two clips on edge of motor housing. Lower soleplate, then rotate the metal tabs to lock soleplate securely.

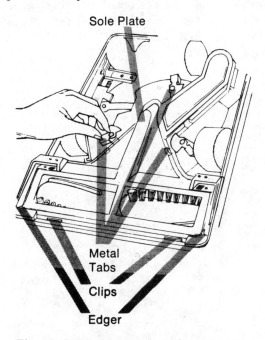

Fig. 13. Removing and replacing soleplate.

Drive Belt.   The drive belt controls the proper rotation of the bar brush assembly. If the belt is stretched or has obvious surface abrasion, the bar brush assembly will not clean efficiently. The worn belt should be replaced with a drive belt that is specifically designed for use with a cleaner.

How to Replace Drive Belt.

1. Remove soleplate (Fig. 13). Slip drive belt off pulley (Fig. 14).

2. Lift out vibrator bar brush assembly and remove worn belt. Slip new belt over assembly.

3. Replace the bar brush assembly by lowering the black rubber mounts in the channels on each side of cleaner housing. Be sure each mount has the same adjustment setting exposed, that is, number 1, 2, or 3 (Fig. 14). Also check to make sure that the letters R and L indicated on the black rubber mounts coincide with the words Right and Left marked inside the cleaner housing.

4. Center drive belt (on bar brush assembly) and replace belt on pulley. See Fig. 14 and the guide printed near the pulley on the cleaner base for correct belt installation.

5. Replace soleplate.

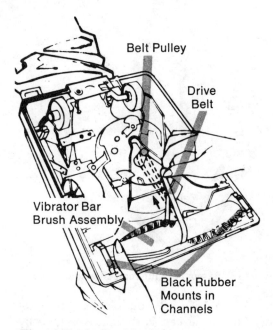

Fig. 14. Replacing drive belt.

Vibrator Bar Brush Assembly. Check vibrator bar brush assembly periodically for the accumulation of threads. If threads cannot be pulled off, snip them carefully with scissors.

After continued cleaner use, the brush bristles will become worn and such may be evident when the cleaner fails to pick up obvious dirt and litter. The bar brush assembly of the upright cleaner provides three adjustments to compensate for bristle wear. Adjust as follows:

1. Remove soleplate (Fig. 13). Slip drive belt off pulley (Fig. 14).

2. Lift out bar brush assembly. On each end of the assembly the black rubber mounts will have number 1 exposed. Rotate the mounts to expose the number 2. The next time a brush adjustment is required the number 3 should be exposed. Make sure the letters R and L on the mounts coincide with the words right and left marked inside the cleaner. Slide the bar brush assembly mounts into the cleaner channels (Fig. 14).

3. Replace drive belt on pulley, then replace soleplate.

4. After the vibrator bar brush assembly has been used at the number 3 setting and the bristles become worn, a new bar brush assembly is required.

How to Replace Headlight Bulb. Remove soleplate, then loosen and remove the two screws shown in Fig. 15. Turn cleaner over and

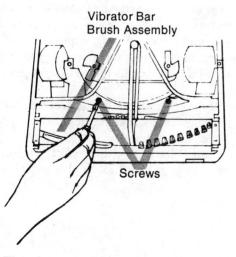

Fig. 15. Replacing headlight bulb.

gently pull out translucent light diffuser (Fig. 16). To remove old bulb, hold socket with fingers, push bulb toward socket, then turn bulb counterclockwise. Insert new bulb in the reverse order of removal procedures. The replacement bulb must not exceed 25 watts. Turn cleaner over, replace and tighten screws, then replace soleplate.

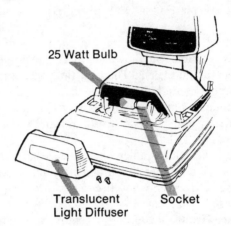

25 Watt Bulb

Translucent   Socket
Light Diffuser

Fig. 16. Removing old bulb.

Care and Storage of Cleaner and Attachments.   *Cleaner.*
The motor bearings are factory sealed and require no lubrication. To clean handle and motor housing, wipe with a soft moist cloth.

To store cleaner, hang from the opening provided on rear of handle grip or leave on floor with handle in upright position.

Attachments.
To clean hose and wands, wipe with a soft, moist cloth.

Remove lint accumulation from brush bristles by vacuuming the bristles with the open end of the hose.

Cleaning tools may be wiped with a moist cloth or washed periodically in warm, sudsy water. Rinse and allow to dry thoroughly before using.

Chapter 41

Selecting a Sewing Machine

Buying a sewing machine for home use is a long-time investment. Reputable manufacturers build machines to last for many years with only minor replacement parts. Usually you can clean, oil, and adjust the machine yourself.

Today there are many choices of machines in a wide range of prices. No one machine is likely to have all the features you might desire. This chapter and Chapter 42 can help you select the machine best suited to your present and future sewing needs.

Figure 1 shows the essential parts of a sewing machine.

Choosing a Machine. There are four main categories of sewing machines from which to choose:

1. Straight stitch.
2. Basic zig zag.
3. More versatile zig zag.
4. Most versatile zig zag.

Straight stitch machine. Most home sewing needs can be filled by the most simple and least expensive machine—one that does only straight stitching, forward and reverse. This is called a straight stitch machine (Fig. 2). With this machine, attachments are provided or can be bought to make a zig zag stitch, buttonholes, ruffles, overcasting, or blind hemming. However, if you have to buy too many extra attachments for your simple sewing machine, the cost may be more than a machine with a few more built-in stitches.

Basic zig zag stitch machine. A more versatile and somewhat more expensive machine is a basic zig zag stitch type (Fig. 3). This sews a straight stitch, but can also be set to sew a zig zag stitch with the needle swinging from side to side. The basic zig zag stitch is used for overcasting, blind stitching, darning, satin stitching, buttonholing, and sewing on buttons.

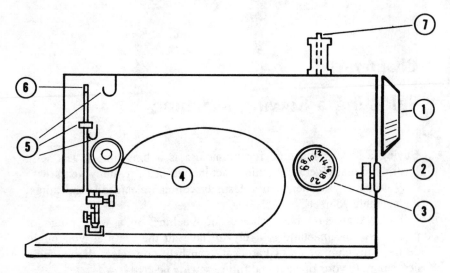

Fig. 1. Essential parts of a sewing machine.
1. Hand wheel   2. Bobbin winder   3. Stitch length dial   4. Tension regulator
5. Thread guides   6. Takeup lever   7. Spool pin

Fig. 2. Straight stitch.

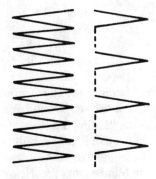

Fig. 3. Basic zig zag stitch.

A greater variety of decorative stitches is possible with a zig zag machine. It takes some skill to develop a uniform pattern or design.

Some more *versatile zig zag machines* offer special stitch possibilities (Fig. 4). In addition to the operations of the simple zig zag machine, this kind of machine has from 1 to 25 or more stitch possibilities. The needle movements are guided by cams, which may be built in or added separately (Fig. 5). Extra cams may be available to make more stitch types possible. Some of the special stitches you can make on this machine are blind hem, buttonhole, multiple zig zag, and a variety of decorative stitches. Although considered automatic, you need a complete knowledge of this machine to make the best use of its varied operations. Be sure to get personal instruction from the seller.

Fig. 4. More versatile zig zag stitches.

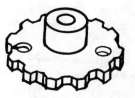

Fig. 5. Cam.

When buying a zig zag machine, test it for good straight stitch and for ease in switching from straight to zig zag stitching.

There is a fourth type of zig zag machine, which might be called a *most versatile zig zag* (Fig. 6). In most zig zag machines, the needle motion is side-to-side while the fabric moves under the presser foot, but this machine has a mechanism for moving the fabric automatically back and forth while the needle swings from side to side. This makes possible a new range of practical stitches, including some of the special stitches recommended for sewing stretch fabric. Some of these machines can be updated with cams as new features are developed.

Weigh carefully your decision as to whether you use special stitches often enough to warrant the added initial cost and the increased amount of service that will probably be necessary. It is logical that a more complicated machine will take more skill to adjust. You may not have this skill. Straight stitch machines are simpler to use than zig zag machines, easier to take care of, and less likely to need adjustment. Why buy a machine with capabilities you will never want to use?

Attachments. Some attachments come with the machine. Most straight stitch sewing machines can be fitted with additional attachments, such as one for buttonholes and one for zig zag stitch. These attachments shift the cloth when making the buttonhole or a stitch. Only a limited number of buttonhole sizes can be made. These are the most commonly used, however, and with a little practice you can make a good buttonhole on them (Fig. 7). This buttonhole attachment can also be used on many zig zag machines (Fig. 8). Some prefer the buttonhole made with this attachment, since it makes a buttonhole with rounded ends, similar to one made by hand.

An open arm machine. Some makes of machines come in an *open arm model* (Fig. 9). This style allows you to slip tubular parts of a garment, such as a sleeve, pant leg, cuff, and so on, over the arm in order to sew them more easily. A *sewing bed extension*, which can be attached, is usually provided to enlarge the sewing surface (Fig. 10).

Sewing machine for disabled persons. Machines have been developed for use by handicapped persons who have impaired vision and for those with limited use of hands, arms, or legs.

For a person with restricted use of the hands, the speed control is designed to be operated by the foot, the arm, or the knee (Fig. 11). Knobs are fitted with projecting spokes (Fig. 12). Levers have knobs at the end; clamp screws hold the needle in place.

A slow-speed control makes operation by a disabled person easier. A special tong makes removal and fitting of bobbin and bobbin case easier. A guide bar for guiding fabric under the needle is attached to the bed of the machine.

Cabinet or portable machine. A further choice is between a cabinet or a portable model. A cabinet should have well-supported leaves and sturdy legs. This gives good sewing support with a flat surface at the same height as the surface of the sewing machine. It has the added advantage of always being ready to use. A machine is a permanent cabinet or table is more convenient and time-saving for anyone who sews frequently. Choose the cabinet for sturdiness, and convenience, since its main purpose is to house the machine.

Fig. 7. Buttonhole stitch.

Fig. 6. Most versatile zig zag stitches.

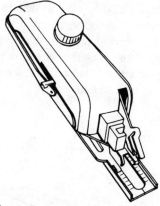

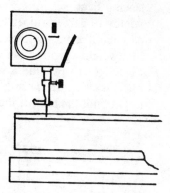

Fig. 8. Buttonhole attachment.

Fig. 9. Open arm sewing machine.

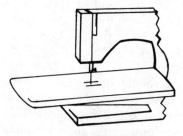

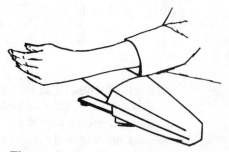

Fig. 10. Sewing bed extension.

Fig. 11. Speed control operated by arm.

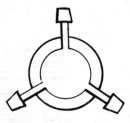

Fig. 12. Knobs with projecting spokes for disabled person.

The extra cost of a fancy cabinet may better be invested in useful furniture. You will have several choices of style and price of cabinet to house the machine you select (Fig. 13).

The portable is the usual choice where space is limited, as in small homes and apartments, or where a machine must often be moved from place to place (Fig. 14). Some portables are merely the regular sewing head set into a carrying case. Though this is heavy and unwieldy to carry, it does have the advantage of being able to fit into a cabinet if you want one at a future time. Some portables are of lightweight construction with an attached carrying case, which opens on hinges to provide a working surface. If the machine is too compact in size, the space between the bed and the arm of the machine might limit the bulk of the material that can be handled.

Fig. 13. Cabinet.

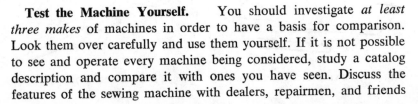

Fig. 14. Portable.

Test the Machine Yourself.   You should investigate *at least three makes* of machines in order to have a basis for comparison. Look them over carefully and use them yourself. If it is not possible to see and operate every machine being considered, study a catalog description and compare it with ones you have seen. Discuss the features of the sewing machine with dealers, repairmen, and friends whose opinion you value. This will give you some basis for deciding on the machine that will best fill your particular needs.

You will want to choose a machine at which you can sit comfortably when operating the controls—one which is easy to handle and operate, and is not too noisy. Select one that is readily adjusted to your varying sewing needs and is easy to care for and keep in perfect running condition.

The person who will *use* the machine should be the one to *select* it, even if it is intended as a gift.

A well-written instruction book with many illustrations should accompany every sewing machine. It should clearly explain how to operate, adjust, and care for the machine. You are entitled to free personal instruction on operating your new machine. The more versatile your machine, the more important it is to have this instruction.

How Does Machine Operate?

1. Is the machine quiet, free from objectionable sounds and vibration at all speeds?

2. Does it change readily from one speed to another? Does it start easily? Will it operate slowly?

3. Try the machine on some of your fabrics, stitching both straight and curved seams.

    (a) Do the individual stitches form a straight line?

    (b) Does the fabric have a tendency to drift to the right or left?

    (c) Is the fabric easy to guide when stitching curved seams?

    (d) Do unlike fabrics feed under the needle at the same rate? (Sew together two pieces of fabric of different weights, such as lining and a heavy outer fabric.)

    (e) Stitch together two pieces of like fabric of the same length. Do they feed under the needle at the same rate?

    (f) Try sewing with a variety of the fabrics you will be apt to work with—thick and thin, loosely woven and tightly woven, leather or leather-like fabric, knits, a combination of fabrics.

4. Can the presser foot be easily adjusted to adapt to various weights of fabrics?

5. Is the knee or foot control comfortable to use?

6. When the bobbin is being wound, does it fill evenly (Fig. 15)?

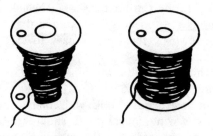

Fig. 15. Bobbin wound unevenly and evenly.

Lighting.

1. Does the lamp throw light on the stitching where it is needed (Fig. 16)?

2. Is the lamp in a position where it will not burn you when you raise the presser foot or when threading?

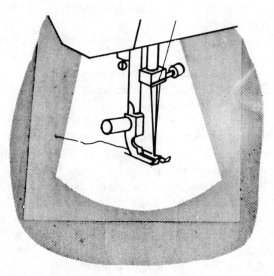

Fig. 16. Proper lighting.

The sewing machine light helps when threading and using the machine. It does not provide enough illumination for regular sewing and should be supplemented by a good local light, such as a floor lamp. The sewing machine lamp, its position, and the type of paint finish on the machine sometimes combine to reflect sufficient light to produce an objectionable glare. A frosted lamp bulb, a diffusing cover for the lamp, or a choice of paint finish can reduce this glare.

Is the finish glossy or flat? Machines finished with a smooth, glossy surface are easiest to keep clean, but light reflections may prove annoying. Some manufacturers recognize the effect of color in causing eyestrain, and finish their machines in green, brown, or tan. Others use a crackle surface to prevent glare, but this may reflect many points of light just as disturbing as the glare from a glossy finish.

Threading.

1. Is the machine easy to thread?
2. Is the bobbin easy to take out and put back?
3. Is the bobbin easy to thread?

Stitching.

1. Is the stitch length control scale easy to read (Fig. 17)?

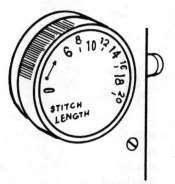

Fig. 17. Control scale.

2. Is the upper tension adjustment shown by numbers that are easy to read?

3. Will the machine stitch backwards?

4. Are there adjustable lock positions for the forward and reverse stitching control?

5. Are the tension adjustments clearly explained in the instruction book? Are the upper and lower tensions easy to adjust (Fig. 18)?

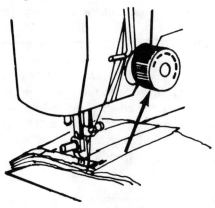

Fig. 18. Adjustment of tension gage.

6. Is there a quick feed dog and presser bar release mechanism for darning and embroidery? If there is no feed dog release, is there a plate to cover the feed dog?

7. Can pressure of presser foot be easily adjusted?

Controlling Speed.

The speed of the sewing machine motor is controlled by a foot pedal (Fig. 19) or a knee lever. This control mechanism may be either a *step control* or a *carbon control.*

The *step control* changes the speed in a series of steps or intervals, usually from 5 to 8, from slow speed or top speed. With some step controls, the first step does not provide the slow speed you sometimes want in sewing. The *carbon control,* however, adjusts the speed from slow to fast smoothly and uniformly, especially when starting, and at very slow speed. On either type of control the power is reduced at low speeds.

Sometimes you need to sew slowly so that you can place stitches carefully. This is a great advantage for one who is learning to sew. On machines that have this governing feature you will find a button, dial, or knob on the head or foot control of the machine (Figs. 20 and 21). This is in addition to the speed control you operate with your foot or knee.

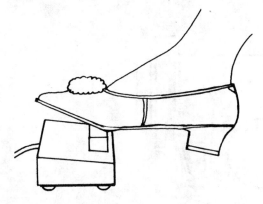

Fig. 19. Foot pedal control.

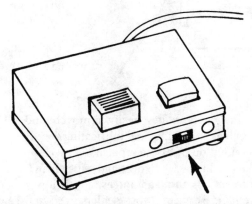

Fig. 20. Speed governor on foot control.

There are three ways of doing this available on machines today.

1. Controlling speed by withholding electrical current. This will reduce the power of the machine as well as the speed.

2. Control of speed by a transmission with a gear reduction system, which provides slower speed with increased power. This is similar to the gear system in an automobile. Full or greater power and slow speed are sometimes needed at the same time.

3. Solid state electronic control system that maintains full power at various speeds.

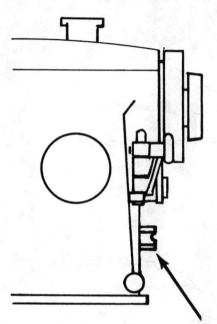

Fig. 21. Speed governor on machine head.

Care.

1. Are the cover plates easily removed and all parts readily accessible for cleaning, oiling, and lubricating?

2. Is the light bulb easy to replace?

3. Is the machine easy to dust and wipe clean?

Service Agreements and Guarantees. Know your dealer. Can he give good reliable service? Most dealers who sell sewing machines offer some form of guarantee and free-service agreement. The best guarantee is one from the manufacturer. Dealers move. You may move. Buy a machine from a company with service centers in many places. Would you have to pay the cost of shipping the machine to the factory for service? How far away is the factory?

The guarantee protects the buyer for varying periods of time after purchase against the possibility of inferior or defective parts or concealed damage. Make sure that this guarantee protects you for a reasonable length of time. The free-service period places the responsibility on the seller to correct any defect in adjustment or parts, other than normal wear, at no charge to the buyer. These agreements *should be in writing.* Verbal agreements are unsatisfactory because they may be impossible to prove or because the exact sense of such agreements depends upon memory.

Tips on Buying.

1. Understand the total cost. Understand all costs in addition to the retail price.

2. Nothing is free. Do not be misled by proposals that you are paying only for a cabinet or service charge. The machine is included in the price.

3. A machine should last for a number of years. Buying from a well-established manufacturer will more likely provide a continuing source of parts.

4. Test the machine yourself before you buy it.

5. After you have made your purchase, take the time to study your instruction book and learn its proper use, otherwise you might damage the machine.

Chapter 42

Basic Functions and Adjustment of a Sewing Machine

For sewing a normal seam, the material must be fed regularly for the formation of each stitch. The feed dog does the conveying, together with the presser bar, on which a presser foot has been fastened.

FEED DOG

The task of the *feed dog* is to move the cloth on for a certain distance after each stitch. This distance, called *stitch length*, can be accurately adjusted by means of a lever or a knob, which acts on the feed mechanism. The feed dog is equipped with small, sharp teeth. Figure 1 shows the most common types of feed dogs.

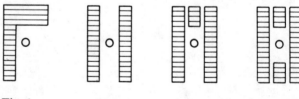

Fig. 1.

The *L-shaped* feed dog is one of the oldest types and common to sewing machines with vibrating shuttles. It has the disadvantage that it does not feed all kinds of work, such as collar points, evenly.

The *H-shaped* feed dog, with a row of teeth on either side of the needle plate hole, is an improvement on the L-shaped feed dog, but does not feed narrow strips or hems well.

The *M-* and *O-shaped* feed dogs guarantee the uniform feed of any kind of work or material.

TWIST OF THE THREAD

Depending on the kind of shuttle used, the twist of the thread is important.

If thread with a right-hand twist is used, it will unravel slightly when the stitch is formed, due to the direction of rotation of the shuttle. This naturally reduces the tensile strength of the thread. For sewing, the question whether a left- or right-hand twist is used, is of lesser importance. It is recommended, however, to use a left-twist thread for darning with fine thread.

The difference between the two kinds of twist is best determined in the following manner.

The thread is left-twist if, when held horizontally, the individual strands slant to the left from bottom to top (Fig. 2, A).

A thread is right-twist if, when held horizontally, the individual strands slant to the right from bottom to top (Fig. 2, B).

Fig. 2.

PARTS USED FOR STITCH FORMATION

The Needle.   To become acquainted with the structure of the sewing machine needle in detail, and to be able to understand better how the stitch is formed, different systems and sizes are described.

Needles have existed since ancient times. They were made of thorns, horn, fish-bones, gold, and ivory. The first steel needles were made in Germany.

The needle with the eye near the point became more widely used with the introduction of the lock-stitch sewing machine. At first, each manufacturer used a needle that could only be used on his own models. The different kinds of needles have since been standardized by an international agreement.

Needle Systems.   There exist approximately 2,000 different types of needles, amongst which system 705 (U.S.A., style 15 × 1) is the most frequently used for household sewing machines. This needle is described in detail in Fig. 3.

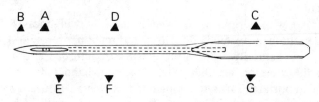

Fig. 3. Parts of needle. (A) Eye, (B) point, (C) body, (D) shaft, (E) short groove, (F) long groove, and (G) flat.

What happens if the upper tension is too weak?
At the moment the lower thread should be drawn from the bobbin to finish the stitch, its resistance *becomes too strong* in relation to the upper tension. Thus the upper thread is unwound before the lower thread is drawn into the material. The thread take-up lever no longer meets with enough resistance from the upper tension to enable the thread to cross in the material, and the lower thread remains stretched (Fig. 4, C).

What happens if the upper tension is too tight?
At the moment the lower thread should be drawn from the bobbin to finish the stitch, its resistance is *too weak* in relation to the upper tension. The lower thread thus unwinds too freely and does not offer enough resistance to the pull of the upper thread. The upper thread withdraws entirely from the material and remains stretched on top of it while the lower thread crosses right through (Fig. 4, B).

Figure 5 shows a perfect seam, then a skipped stitch (A), and then a broken thread (B). Skipped stitches are caused when, for one reason or another, the point of the hook does not catch the loop of the upper thread.

On all lock-stitch machines, regardless of what shuttle systems they may have, the upper thread has to form the loop.

When a threaded needle pierces the material, the thread will slip into the two grooves on the needle, in order to offer the least resistance when passing through the material. However, this resistance increases on the side of the short groove, as the latter disappears in the material, because the thread is now no longer in the groove but is

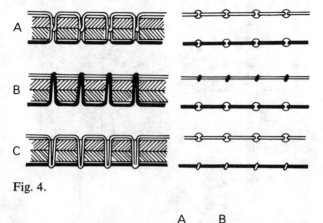

Fig. 4.

Fig. 5.

jammed between the body of the needle and the material. Thus the thread remains stretched, until the needle reaches its lowest point (Fig. 6).

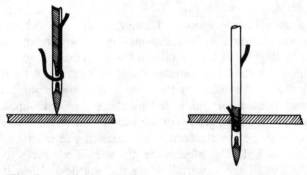

Fig. 6.

When the needle starts moving upward again, the thread in the long groove (Fig. 7, F) can slide without difficulty between the needle and the material (Fig. 7). As on the short-grooved side (E),

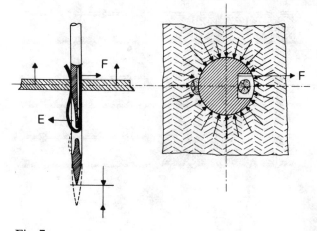

Fig. 7.

the thread is jammed, it can not slide along with the needle, and, therefore, forms a small loop on the same side.

Now the different shuttle systems come into play. They all have the same task, which is to pass the bobbin with the lower thread through the loop. This is what is called *stitch formation*.

To make it easier for you to understand how the stitches are formed an explanation follows of how this was done with Howe's invention, the *long (boat-shaped) shuttle*.

This shuttle has an elongated shape, with one end pointed. In effecting its already described up-and-down movement, the needle is grazed by the point of the shuttle at the moment the loop is formed, upon which the shuttle penetrates the loop (Fig. 8, A). In moving forward, the shuttle enlarges the loop and passes right through it. The thread needed for this is fed by the thread take-up lever and slides easily in the long groove of the needle, due to the pull exercised by the body of the shuttle (which increases in size from the point to the end) (Fig. 8, B, C). Meanwhile, the needle continues its upward movement out of the material, while the shuttle finishes its course and then starts back again. The thread take-up lever, after first having released enough upper thread for the formation of the stitch, now tightens this thread and, at the same time, pulls the lower thread up into the material with it (Fig. 8, D).

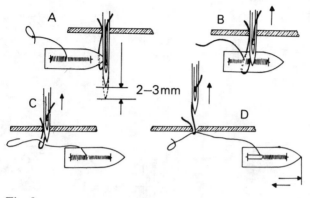

Fig. 8.

The *present modern shuttle* forms the stitch in much the same manner. However, it is not the whole shuttle with the bobbin that goes through the loop. The mobile part, such as the point of the shuttle hook, picks up the loop at the right moment, enlarges it, and conducts it around the fixed part of the shuttle, such as the assembled guard rings or the bobbin case—which hold the bobbin with the lower thread. The performance of the thread take-up lever does not change.

Without going into the operation of the feed dog and the tensions, study the various phases of the stitch formation illustrated in Figs. 9 and 10.

Phase 1:
Needle: Needle is at its lowest position.
Shuttle hook: The point of the shuttle hook approaches the needle.
Thread take-up: It moves downward, thus releasing the upper thread.
Phase 2:
Needle: Needle has risen slightly in the meantime and the loop has been formed (timing).
Shuttle hook: The point of the shuttle hook is now facing the needle and starts to penetrate the loop.
Thread take-up: It keeps moving down in order to supply enough upper thread to enlarge the loop.

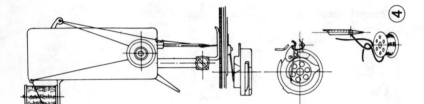

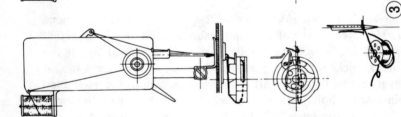

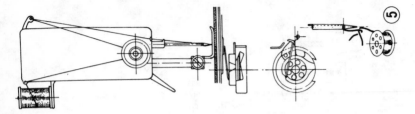

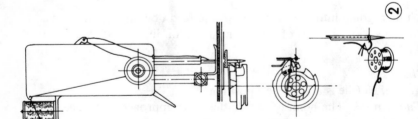

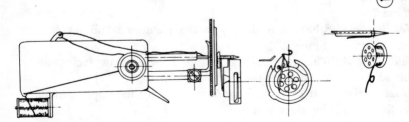

Fig. 9.

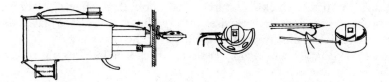

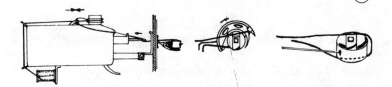

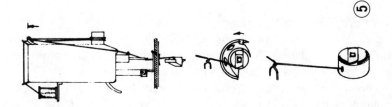

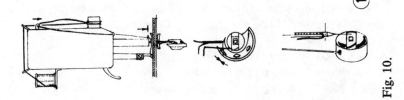

Fig. 10.

Phase 3:

Needle: The needle continues its upward movement.

Shuttle hook: In continuing its revolving movement the hooks conical point enlarges the loop and guides it around the satisfactory part, which contains the bobbin with the lower thread.

Thread take-up: It gets to its lowest point and starts to rise again, as soon as the loop can slide off the stationary part of the shuttle and is ready to be drawn up.

Phase 4:

Needle: Still moving upward, the needle comes out of the material and reaches its highest point.

Thread take-up: It rises more quickly and pulls the upper thread taut, thus closing the loop and drawing the lower thread into the material.

Shuttle hook: In the meantime the upper thread has been drawn off from the point of the shuttle by the thread take-up lever, and it now runs without thread.

Phase 5:

Thread take-up: It now pulls the lower thread completely into the material.

Needle: The needle starts moving downward again to begin the next stitch.

Shuttle hook: During the first four phases, the hook made approximately one revolution in case of rotary shuttle or, in case of oscillating shuttle, a clockwise turn. The hook then effects a second revolution or counterclockwise turn without thread, to give the needle sufficient time to prepare the loop for the next stitch.

Cloth feed: The feed dog (will be discussed later) now pushes the material on.

For easier memorizing, these five phases can also be grouped according to the work to be performed by the various parts:

1. Phase 1 and 2: Work of the needle.
2. Phase 3: Work of the shuttle.
3. Phase 4: Work of the take-up lever.
4. Phase 5: Work of the cloth feed.

It is evident from the foregoing that the rotary shuttle hook revolves twice or oscillates one time during the formation of each stitch. These two revolutions or one oscillation are necessary to ensure a uniform speed and to avoid vibration. There are also machines whose shuttle hooks only perform one revolution for each stitch, but then the speed is not uniform.

PRESSER BAR HEIGHT

Proper *presser bar height* is about ¼ inch between needle plate and bottom portion of presser foot when presser bar is in the Up position.

Adjustment.   *Step 1*. Open face plate, release pressure regulator, and lift up presser bar to the Up position.

Step 2. Loosen set screw (Fig. 11, 2) and lower or lift presser bar to proper height. Adjust alignment (simply to eliminate loosening set screw again) before tightening screw. Tighten screw (Fig. 11, 2).

PRESSER FOOT ALIGNMENT

Presser foot should be aligned parallel with feed dog slots, allowing for clearance of needle plate hole.

Adjustment.   *Step 1*. Open face plate, release pressure regulator.

Step 2. Carefully loosen set screw (Fig. 11, 2) a little as not to vary the set position of the screw, and align presser foot correctly. Tighten screw (Fig. 11, 2).

BASIC NEEDLE POSITION FOR ZIG ZAG SEWING

The basic Straight Stitch position is in the left position on side-load type machines, and in the center position on front-load type machines. Erratic sewing in zig zag and straight stitch may occur if needle is incorrectly set.

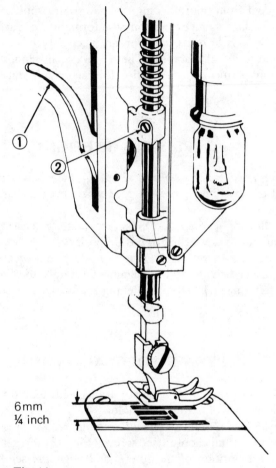

6mm
¼ inch

Fig. 11.

Adjustment for Side-Load Type Machines.   *Step 1.* Set stitch width to Maximum and turn hand wheel until the needle bar is at the bottom of its down stroke in its left swing. Leave in this position.

Step 2. Reset stitch width to 0. Grasp zig zag lever or knob and move from 0 to 5. If the needle moves from its original set (step 1), needle position is incorrect.

Step 3. Remove top cover, loosen set screw (Fig. 12, 1), and rotate collar (Fig. 12, 2) slightly. Move knob or lever several times

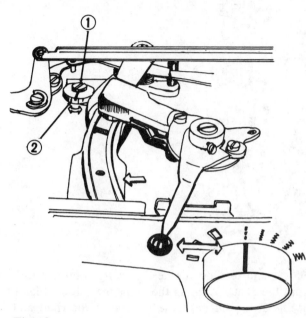

Fig. 12.

during adjustment until needle remains stationary. Tighten screw (Fig. 12, 1) firmly.

Step 4. Needle clearance to hook may be affected by this adjustment and it may be necessary to reset hook (check adjustment of needle and shuttle hook clearance).

Adjustment for Front-Load Type Machines.   *Step 1.* Set needle position change control at C. Set stitch width to 0. Turn hand wheel to lower the needle down.

Step 2. If the needle is not exactly at the center of needle hole of needle plate, open face cover, remove light bulb, then loosen set screw (Fig. 13, 1), and turn eccentric connecting stud (Fig. 13, 2) so that the needle positions exactly at the center of needle hole of needle plate. Firmly tighten set screw (Fig. 13, 1).

Step 3. Machines with a needle-position-change device do not require additional adjustment since the correction of the center needle position will straighten up both left and right needle positions. However, for the machine without a needle-position-change device, re-

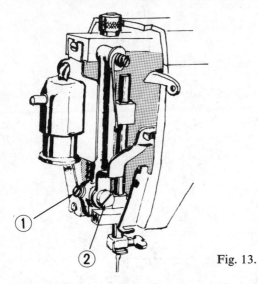

Fig. 13.

move top cover and readjust the needle swing allotment toward right and left from the center, turning the adjusting screw (Fig. 14, 1) so that the needle swings in the same volume to the right and the left from the center in zig zag sewing. After adjustment, firmly tighten the lock-nut (Fig. 14, 2).

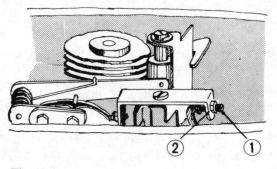

Fig. 14.

NEEDLE POSITION IN STRAIGHT SEWING

The correct needle position in straight sewing is .032 inch to .04 inch clearance between needle and needle plate in case of *side-load* type zig zag machines.

That of *front-load* type machines is at the center of needle hole of needle plate, exactly the same as its basic needle position.

Caution: Basic needle position for zig zag sewing should be checked prior to setting needle position in straight sewing.

Adjustment for Side-Load Type Machines.   *Step 1.* If needle is out of position, remove top cover and loosen set screw (Fig. 16, 1) of needle bar connecting rod.

Step 2. With stitch width control at Straight Stitch position, adjust needle bar connecting rod so that the needle falls in the correct position (Fig. 15), then fasten set screw.

Step 3. Readjust the needle and shuttle clearance as explained in that section.

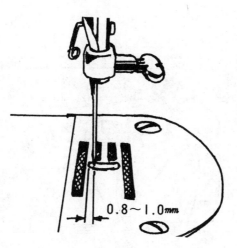

Fig. 15.

UNEVEN (WAVERING) STRAIGHT STITCH

Needle bar must not waver in straight sewing. If needle wavers sideward in straight sewing the following adjustments must be made.

Adjustment for Side-Load Type Machines.   *Step 1.* Check the basic needle position for zig zag sewing as previously explained.

Step 2. Remove top cover and observe the position of zig zag origin slide block. This slide block should be directly over fulcrum screw

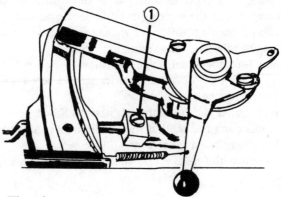

Fig. 16.

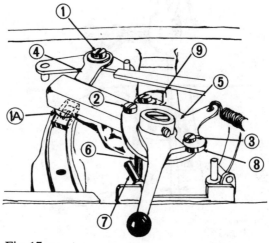

Fig. 17.

on zig zag channel casting (Fig. 17, 1A). This slide block should not move when hand wheel is turned.

Step 3. If movement occurs loosen screw (Fig. 17, 1) and readjust stopper (Fig. 17, 4) checking the motion. Then tighten the screw.

Step 4. Direct contact between zig zag origin and zig zag control lever or knob must be maintained (Fig. 17, 6 and 7). Any gap must be removed by adjusting screw (Fig. 17, 2).

Step 5. Eccentric collar stop (Fig. 17, 9) should be aligned after settings.

Adjustment for Front-Load Type Machines.

Example A.

Step 1. Remove top cover and observe the position of the roller (Fig. 18, 1). This roller should accurately align to the fulcrum stud (Fig. 18, 2) of zig zag oscillator and should not move when hand wheel is turned.

Step 2. If movement occurs, loosen stitch-width control-knob set-screw, readjust the position of the roller in zig zag oscillator, then, contacting the pin (Fig. 18, 4) directly to 0-width position stopper (Fig. 18, 3) without any gap, firmly tighten stitch-width control-knob set screw.

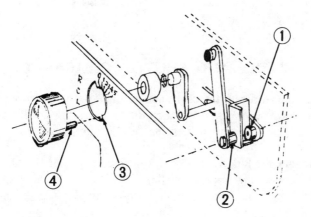

Fig. 18.

Example B.

Step 1. Same as Example A, but refer to Fig. 19.

Step 2. If movement occurs, remove stitch-width control and loosen set screw (Fig. 19, 5). Readjust the position of the roller (Fig. 19, 1), checking the motion; then, readjust the stopper (Fig. 19, 3) to directly contact to the pin (Fig. 19, 4) without any gap, maintaining the roller at the corrected position. Firmly tighten the screw (Fig. 19, 5) and reset stitch-width control-knob.

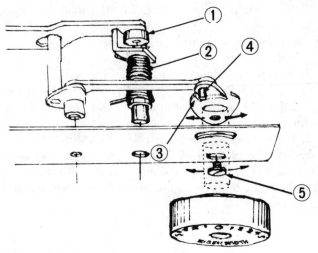

Fig. 19.

NEEDLE AND SHUTTLE CLEARANCE

The needle and shuttle clearance is one of the most important factors to good sewing performance. In all cases the needle must be new and perfect, clearance between needle and hook .001 inch or the thickness of a hair.

Adjustment for Side-Load Type Machines.   *Step 1.* Always replace needle with new unused needle.

Step 2. Check the correct needle position for Zig Zag sewing (Fig. 12).

Step 3. Check the correct needle position for Straight Sewing. (Fig. 15).

Step 4. Check the correct needle bar height.

Step 5. Set stitch width at Maximum, check race body (Fig. 20, 1) for looseness. Tighten body (Fig. 20, 3) with screw (Fig. 20, 2) or vertical shaft set screw (Fig. 21, 4).

Step 6. Adjust for needle and shuttle cap clearance as noted in Fig. 25.

Step 7. Confirm the correct clearance between the needle and the shuttle hook point.

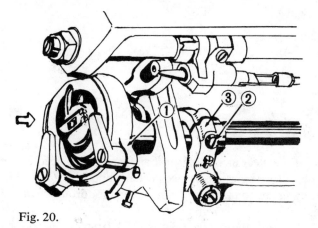

Fig. 20.

Step 8. If incorrect, loosen clamping screw (Fig. 21, 4) and move shuttle body (Fig. 20, 1) either in or out as needed. Hold race firmly and tighten clamping screw (Fig. 21, 4).

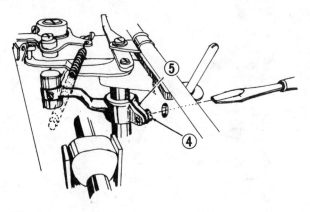

Fig. 21.

Adjustment for Front-Load Type Machines.   *Step 1*. Set stitch width at Maximum and stitch pattern at Regular Zig Zag sewing. Turn hand wheel by hand to raise the needle up in its left-side upward stroke until shuttle hook point reaches just behind the needle. Check the needle and shuttle clearance at this time (Fig. 22).

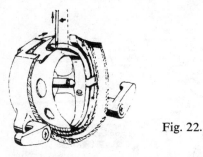

Fig. 22.

Step 2. If the clearance is bigger than standard or needle rubs hook point, open face cover. Press needle bar supporter (Fig. 23, 1) to the right by finger to check and remember the torque of its sideward movement.

Step 3. Unhook the spring (Fig. 23, 2) from the needle bar supporter and very slightly loosen the set screw (Fig. 23, 3).

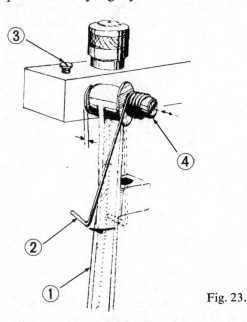

Fig. 23.

Step 4. Carefully shift, in or out, the needle bar supporter shaft (Fig. 23, 4) together with the needle bar supporter, by very lightly knocking on the end of the supporter shaft or slightly enlarging the distance of the supporter shaft from machine casting by inserting a screwdriver to correct the needle and shuttle clearance. Do not turn the angle of slot on the shaft end for insertion of the spring in this step.

Step 5. Check the torque of sideward movement of the needle bar supporter, tighten the set screw (Fig. 23, 3), hook the spring (Fig. 23, 2), and check the pressure of the spring to spring the supporter back to the left.

If the clearance is off to either extreme, this method may not correct the situation, as the needle may in fact strike the needle plate. In this event it becomes necessary to move not the *needle* in relation to the hook, but the entire shuttle body (with the needle remaining stationary) in relation to the hook.

Also, moving the shaft (Fig. 23, 4) to an extreme may cause the entire needle bar to bind (will not return freely). The bar becomes *cocked* (Fig. 24).

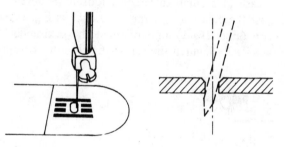

Fig. 24.

NEEDLE AND SHUTTLE CAP SPRING CLEARANCE

This clearance between the needle and the cap spring on the shuttle race cover is a factor to prevent skip stitches.

Adjustment for Side-Load Type Machines.   *Step 1.* Set machine on Wide Zig Zag and slightly loosen set screw (Fig. 20, 2) of face guide.

Step 2. Without change of needle and shuttle hook clearance, turn shuttle body so that needle is centered in slot opening (Fig. 25) when rotated in left and right side of cap spring.

Step 3. Tighten clamp set screw (Fig. 20, 2).

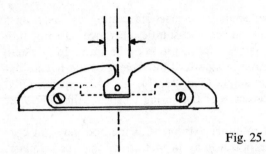

Fig. 25.

Adjustment for Front-Load Type Machines.   *Step 1*. Remove bobbin case and shuttle hook from shuttle race and set the race cover only to race. Lower the needle-turning-hand wheel by hand.

Step 2. Press the needle bar to the right and check if the distance between needle and right edge of shuttle cap spring is .02 inch (Fig. 26).

Step 3. In case of a small difference, loosen set screws (Fig. 26, 1) and readjust the clearance. If the difference is big, loosen shuttle race set screws (Fig. 26, 2) and readjust the clearance by turning the shuttle race itself. Tighten the screws firmly after readjustment.

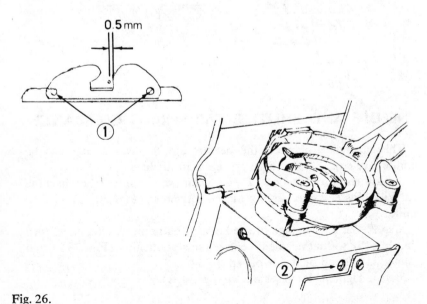

Fig. 26.

NEEDLE BAR HEIGHT AND
NEEDLE TIMING TO SHUTTLE

The timing of the shuttle hook to catch the upper thread is one of the most important keys for perfect stitch performance. Many machines have a preset system where the driver is locked into position by drive pins. This is fixed so that the shuttle hook at the end of its leftward position is as shown in Fig. 27, A, making it necessary to change the needle bar height or clearance in case of timing problems. The setting for the needle bar height is generally checked on the distance of the top of needle eye from the shuttle hook point when the shuttle point comes to the center of the needle line in the upward stroke of the needle—in case of a side loader, in any needle position or needle fall, and, in case of a front loader, in the left-side needle-stroke of a maximum zig zag sewing condition, as shown in Fig. 27, B.

Adjustment.   *Step 1.* Set machine in the widest zig zag setting in case of a front loader. Turn hand wheel slowly to turn shuttle hook to its leftward oscillating end with needle bar in its lowest position. In case of front loader in the left-side needle-stroke of maximum zig zag sewing, check if the distance between shuttle hook point and needle line is about .104 inch. Clearance between shuttle driver spring and shuttle hook is about .016 inch as shown in Fig. 19, A.

Step 2. Turn hand wheel until the shuttle point comes to the center of needle line, and check the vertical distance between shuttle hook point and the top end of thread hole of needle to make sure it is in the range between .04 inch and .08 inch or, more accurately, about .064 inch as shown in Fig. 19, B.

Step 3. If height is incorrect, turn hand wheel to the lowest end of its stroke, loosen set screw (Fig. 27, 1, C), side loader, or front loader (Fig. 27, D), and adjust needle bar height.

Step 4. After adjustment, tightly fasten set screw (Fig. 19, 1, C or D).

Step 5. Clearance between shuttle driver spring and shuttle hook can be adjusted as follows: Rotate wheel until shuttle driver is at low end of raceway, place screwdriver blade between shuttle driver and race, and bend driver slightly upward for less clearance; then use a pair of snub-nosed pliers and grasp shuttle driver and raceway and apply pressure to increase clearance. Care should be taken not to scar raceway surface.

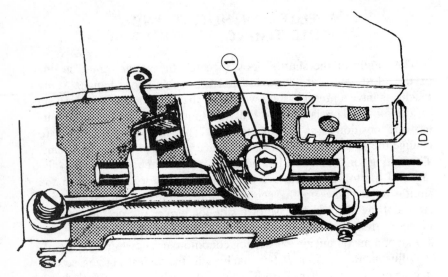

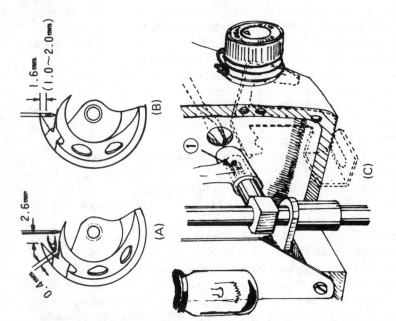

Fig. 27. Upper thread tension control.

NEEDLE BAR SWING TIMING

The coordination of the vertical needle bar movement and its sideward movement is one of the most important elements for good zig zag sewing performance.

The ideal movement of the needle bar is that the needle point falls straight down vertically from the level of 0.04 inch above the needle plate face and rises up from the needle plate face up to .04 inch high with no needle point side movement or less than 0.014 inch as shown in Fig. 28, under a maximum zig zag sewing condition.

If the needle point moves aside in the above range exceeding the above limit, readjust as described in the following adjustments.

Adjustment for Side-Load Type Machines.   *Step 1.* Set stitch width at Maximum, take off arm cover, and turn hand wheel to bring the gear set-screws (Fig. 28, 1) to the top in right-side down stroke of needle.

Step 2. Loosen set screws (Fig. 28, 1) and holding the gear stationary by screwdriver, turn hand wheel back in case of excessive side movement of needle in its down stroke, or forward in case of excessive side movement of needle in its upward stroke. Repeat the adjustment until the down and up movement of the needle point in the check range becomes equal. Firmly tighten up set screws (Fig. 28, 1).

Adjustment for Front-Load Type Machines.   *Step 1.* Set the stitch pattern at Regular Zig Zag stitch, take off arm cover, and check if the cam follower (Fig. 29, 1) faces to the center of the recess portion of the cam with the needle at the bottom of its stroke, or to the center of projecting portion of cam when the needle is at the top of its stroke.

Step 2. If it does not, loosen gear set-screws (Fig. 29, 2), inserting the screwdriver from back of the arm, and readjust by turning hand wheel so that when needle is at the bottom of its stroke, the cam follower faces to the center of the recessed portion of the cam, and when needle is at the top of its stroke, the follower faces to the center of the projecting portion of the cam. Firmly tighten set screws (Fig. 29, 2) after adjustment.

(The proper adjustment of this timing on front-load type machines will normally control malfunction of any special pattern stitches made by the cam.)

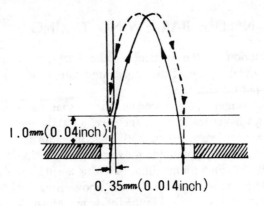

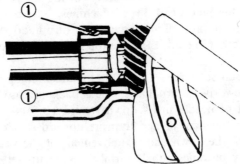

Fig. 28.

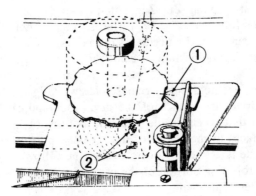

Fig. 29.

FEED DOG HEIGHT

Feed dog height is one of the key elements for proper feeding. The correct height of the feed dog from the needle plate surface is .032 inch to .04 inch with the feed in the high position and it should be below the needle plate surface when in the Darn or Off position. Before any adjustments are made on the feed height, it is important to clean out all lint accumulation between feed dog teeth.

Adjustment for Side-Load Type Machines. *Step 1.* Turn hand wheel counterclockwise to raise feed dog to its highest position.

Step 2. Loosen set screw (Fig. 30, 1) of drop feed unit, and turn the unit clockwise in case of insufficient height and counterclockwise in case of excessive height, until the correct height is obtained.

Step 3. Tighten set screw (Fig. 30, 1) after adjustment.

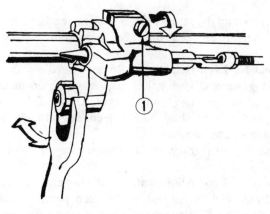

Fig. 30.

Adjustment for Front-Load Type Machines. *Caution:* Incorrect up-and-down motion timing may look like incorrect feed dog height on front-load type machines. Check it before adjusting feed dog height and, if wrong, correct it first of all. (*See* section on Feed Motion Timing—Up-Down Motion Timing for Front-Load Type Machines).

Step 1. Turn hand wheel to raise the feed dog to its highest position.

Step 2. Loosen set screw (Fig. 31, 1) of drop feed unit and rotate the eccentric holder (Fig. 31, 2) as needed for correct height.

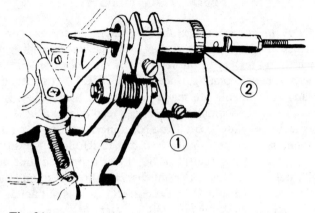

Fig. 31.

Step 3. Tighten up the screw (Fig. 31, 1) after adjustment.

(Uneven height of feed may be another cause of improper feeding.)

Adjustment for Even Height.   Remove needle plate and loosen both feed dog screws. Use either paper, fiber, or metal as shim material on corner needing more height. Use a flat piece of steel about four inches long, laid across feed dog, to check for even height. Tighten screws securely.

(Feed misalignment may be another cause of uneven feeding, especially on buttonholes.)

Adjustment for Feed Alignment.   Remove needle plate, loosen feed dog screws slightly, and align the feed parallel with feed dog slots on needle plate. Tighten screws when correct.

(Sharp feed may be a cause of snags and tears on sheer material.)

Adjustment for Feed Sharpness.   Use a fine honing stone and rub across the feed in both directions. Check often for sharpness as continuous rubbing may ruin feed dogs.

FEED MOTION TIMING

The horizontal backward movement of the feed dog starts roughly simultaneously with or a little bit earlier than the start of the needle bar's downward movement.

Many machines will have a timing mark on the feed cam and a corresponding mark on the shaft. A rough position can be made by turning the upper shaft to bring the crank portion to a 3:00 o'clock position; the feed-cam set-screw should be at the 12:00 o'clock position.

If the feed dog starts its horizontal backward movement too early, or its forward movement too late, check and readjust as follows.

Adjustment for Horizontal Motion Timing.   *Step 1.* Take off the top cover plate, and check if the gage line (Fig. 32, 1) on the right side of the feed cam is aligned with the gage line (Fig. 32, 2) on the arm shaft within the tolerance of about .04 inch.

Step 2. Loosen feed-cam set screw (Fig. 32, 3) and readjust the alignment of two gage lines, then tighten the set screw (Fig. 32, 3).

Note: Do not touch feed motion timing unless feeding starts while needle is still into fabric, or needle pierces fabric before feeding finishes, or irregular reverse stitch feed motion in stretch stitching is observed.

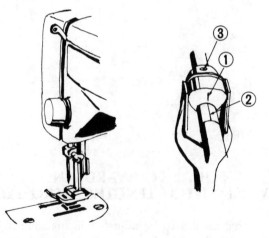

Fig. 32.

PROCEDURE USED WHEN
NO TIMING LINE IS PRESENT

1. Turn hand wheel counterclockwise until needle point is exactly even with top of needle plate.

2. Feed dog should be slightly below the surface of needle plate.

3. If feed dog is not, adjust as follows: Turn hand wheel until heaviest portion of take-up counterbalance is at the 12:00 o'clock position, screw (Fig. 32, 3) should be at the 1:00 o'clock position.

4. A very slight adjustment may be needed either way for the exact position as described in steps 1 and 2.

Adjustment for Up-Down Motion Timing in Front-Load Type Machines. On side-load type machines, feed-dog up-down motion timing cannot be adjusted, but on front-load type machines, it can be adjusted by the following steps. (The correct up-down motion timing may be often misjudged as the incorrect feed-dog height.)

Step 1. With the needle bar at its highest position, check if the cam on the feed lift shaft touches the bar of the feed lifting device, and the gage line (Fig. 33, 2) makes a right angle against the bar (Fig. 33, 1).

Step 2. If not, loosen set screw (Fig. 33, 3) and correct the cam angle against the bar. Firmly tighten screw after adjustment.

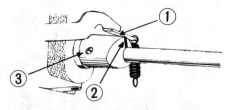

Fig. 33.

EQUAL FORWARD AND
REVERSE STITCH LENGTHS (ZERO FEED)

There are three factors to be adjusted in machine in relation to stitch length: no feeding in either forward or reverse (zero feeding), maximum stitch length, and equality of forward and reverse stitch length. However, it seems the most important practice is to provide correct zero feeding.

On most machines, with the correct zero feeding, the stitch lengths of both forward and reverse stitches become the same within a tolerance of .003 inch for the difference between maximum forward and reverse stitch lengths, and the maximum stitch length becomes about six stitches per inch on paper.

There are several different styles of reverse mechanisms but you must remember they will all originate from a pivot point on the crank.

If forward and reverse stitch lengths are much different, and fabric moves with the stitch length control knob at 0, readjust as follows.

Adjustment.   *Example A*. Take off the top cover, set the stitch length control at 0, place a piece of paper under the presser foot, and run the machine. If the paper moves back, turn the feed regulating screw (Fig. 34, 1) clockwise; if the paper moves forward, turn the screw counterclockwise until the paper stops moving.

Example B.

Take off the top cover, test for movement as described in Example A, (Fig. 34a). This type of reverse mechanism is at 0 feeding when rod C is centered exactly in the bottom of the *V portion* of B.

To achieve this position the body (A) of the assembly has to be rotated for rod C to fall exactly into the V-slot and then locked into position with the set screw.

Example C.

Take off the top cover and test for movement as described in Example A. This type of reverse mechanism is activated by a push rod with an activating finger held on to the rod with two set screws. This finger pushes the linkage reverse mechanism. If machine is feeding at zero setting, loosen screws and move finger (Fig. 35, 1) either forward or back, as needed. Tighten screws securely.

STRETCH STITCH DEVICE

There are three important elements for perfect stretch stitch performance:

1. Perfect needle bar swing timing.
2. Perfect synchronization of stretch stitch cam rotation timing for its reverse feed with basic horizontal feed motion timing.
3. Equal stretch stitch forward and reverse length.

For malfunctions of stretch stitch performance other than unequal forward and reverse stretch stitch lengths, first check needle bar swing

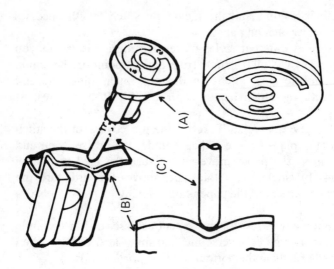

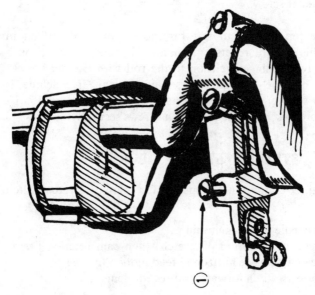

Fig. 34.

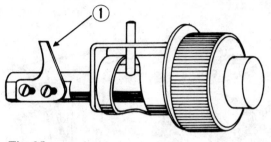

Fig. 35.

timing and feed motion timing and correct them. If a malfunction other than unequal stretch stitch length is still observed on side-load type machines with correct needle bar timing and feed motion timing, the cause in most cases is incorrect synchronization of *stretch stitch* cam rotation, which must be corrected by changing the position of the worm gear on the upper shaft.

If stretch stitch forward and reverse lengths are not equal, readjust as follows.

Adjustment for Side-Load Type Machines.

Example A.

Step 1. Take off arm cover and set stitch length control knob to Longest Stitch, stitch width control at Straight Stitch position, and stitch pattern control to Stretch Stitch.

Step 2. Place a paper under presser foot and check the difference between forward and reverse stretch stitch lengths.

Step 3. Turn the adjusting screw rod (Fig. 36, 1) clockwise in case of a longer forward stitch, or counterclockwise in case of a shorter forward stitch. Repeat the adjustment until both stitch lengths become equal.

Note: If the coil spring (Fig. 36, 2) is broken or worn out, replace it, or the corrected condition may vary later while the machine is running.

Example B. Other Models.

Step 1. Take off arm cover and motor cover, and set stitch length control knob to Longest Stitch, stitch width control at Straight Stitch position, and stretch stitch lever at S position.

Step 2. Same as step 2 in Example A.

Step 3. Loosen set screws (Fig. 37, 1) and turn the shaft (Fig. 37, 2) clockwise in case of longer forward stitch, or counterclockwise

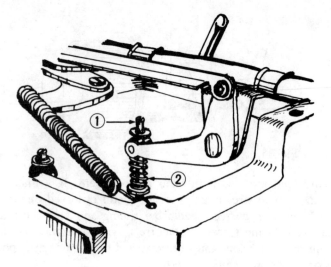

Fig. 36.

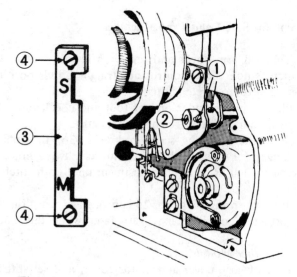

Fig. 37.

in case of shorter forward stitch. Repeat the adjustment until both
stitch lengths become equal. Firmly tighten set screws (Fig. 37, 1).

If adjustment needed is slight, it can be adjusted by relocating plate (Fig. 37, 3). Screws (Fig. 37, 4) are set in elongated slots, for this purpose, instead of above procedure.

Adjustment for Front-Load Type Machines (Various Models).
Steps 1 and 2. Same as Example A.

Step 3. Loosen lock-nut (Fig. 38, 1) and turn the eccentric adjusting pin (Fig. 38, 2) as needed for equal forward and reverse stretch stitch length. Firmly tighten up lock nut (Fig. 38, 1) after adjustment.

(On some models the elongator should be in the center.)

Fig. 38.

BLIND STITCH MECHANISM

It is rarely required to adjust the *blind stitch mechanism.* The basic adjustments of needle position for zig zag sewing, needle position in straight sewing, the test for uneven straight stitch on side loader, and the basic adjustment of needle bar swing timing on front loader will normally control any malfunction. It is possible that wavering or uneven stitching will occur if linkage is worn or loose.

Adjustment for Side-Load Type Machines.   *Step 1.* Remove top cover, set stitch pattern to Regular Stitch and stitch control at 0,

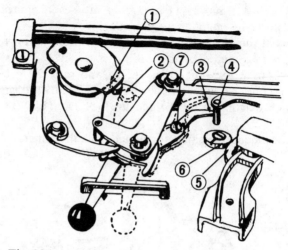

Fig. 39.

turn hand wheel toward you until the blind-stitch cam-recessed portion meets the follower pin or finger and the needle bar is at the low
end of its stroke.

Step 2. Shift lever on knob to Blind-Stitch position. There should
be direct contact between pin and cam (Fig. 39, 1 and 2) plus lever
and pin (Fig. 39, 3 and 4). Linkage should be adjusted to compensate for any clearances.

BUTTONHOLER

The basic adjustments of the basic needle position, needle position
in straight sewing, and equal forward and reverse stitch lengths (zero
feed) will normally correct any malfunction of the buttonholer. If
the center open space of the buttonhole is still too narrow or none
at all, or the reverse stitch length is too loose or too short, readjust
as follows.

Adjustment for Narrow Center Open Space.
Example A.
Step 1. Take off arm cover and check if there is no play between
the pins (Fig. 40, 1 and 2); also, no shift of the link of the pin
(Fig. 40, 1) by the pin (Fig. 40, 2) with the stitch-width control-
knob at the Straight-Stitch position.

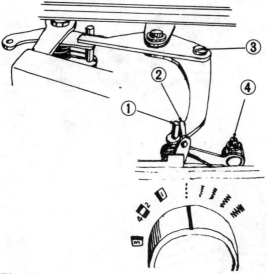

Fig. 40.

Step 2. If there is movement, loosen set screw (Fig. 40, 3) and adjust the connection between the two pins to eliminate any play of the prior shift of the link. Tighten set screw (Fig. 40, 3).

Example B. Other Models.

Take off arm cover and loosen set screw (Fig. 41, 1). Shift the stopper (Fig. 41, 2) to the left to increase center open space and to the right to decrease it.

If the pre-set reverse buttonhole stitch length is too long or too short despite of correct zero feeding adjustment, adjust as follows.

Adjustment for Buttonhole Reverse Stitch Length.

Example A.

Step 1. Take off arm cover and set the control at buttonhole mark 3.

Step 2. Turn the screw (Fig. 40, 4) to the right to increase stitch length and to the left to decrease it. (Standard length is 50 to 60 stitches per inch.)

Example B. Various Models.

Step 1. Take off arm cover and set the stitch control knob at buttonhole mark 3 position. For the machine with an elongator, set the elongator lever at the center.

Step 2. Turn tuner (Fig. 42, 1) or adjusting screw (Fig. 43, 1)

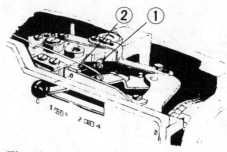

Fig. 41.

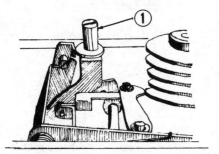

Fig. 42.

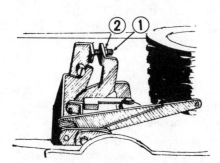

Fig. 43.

upon loosening lock-nut (**Fig. 43, 2**) as needed for proper button-hole reverse stitch length, then tighten lock-nut (**Fig. 43, 2**).

UPPER THREAD TENSION CONTROL

To *disassemble* the upper thread tension control (**Fig. 44**) proceed as follows:

1. Pull out cap (17) and remove screw (16).

2. Remove dial (14), washer (13), stopper (12), nut (11), spring (10), tray (9), pin (8), disc (6), washer (7), and disc (6) in this order.

3. Loosen screw (3), remove stud (5), and check spring (4).

For *assembly* and *adjustment* (Figs. 44, 45, and 46), proceed as follows:

1. Insert check spring (4) onto stud (5), then insert the stud into barrel (2). Tighten screw (3). At this time stud (5) should be located as shown in Fig. 45. Adjust the position of check spring (4) against stud (5) so that the tension of check spring is between .175 ounce and .35 ounce at the beginning tension.

2. Insert disc (6), washer (7), disc (6), pin (8), tray (9), and spring (10) onto stud (5).

3. Tighten nut (11) being sure that any pressure does not work to the beehive tension spring. (*See* Fig. 46.)

4. Insert stopper (12) with the raised part to the upper side and the washer (13).

5. Insert the lower raised part of dial (14) into the slot of nut (11) with the number 0 to the upper side.

6. Insert washer (15) and tighten screw (16).

7. Check the tension of upper thread. The tension of the upper thread should be between 0 and .35 ounce when dial is set at 0, and more than 7.7 ounces when set at 9.

If it is not, adjust the tension by turning nut (11). Maximum tension is too loose . . . turn nut clockwise. Maximum tension is too tight . . . turn nut counterclockwise.

8. Put on cap (17) and base (1).

HOW TO REGULATE BELT TENSION ON MOTOR

To adjust the belt tension, take off the belt cover and loosen the fixing screw about one turn with a screwdriver. This will allow the motor to move downward or upward. Then firmly tighten the screw, and belt should have the correct tension. (*See* Figs. 47 and 48.) When replacing motor belt leave $\frac{3}{16}$ inch slack.

Caution: Do not tighten the belt too tightly.

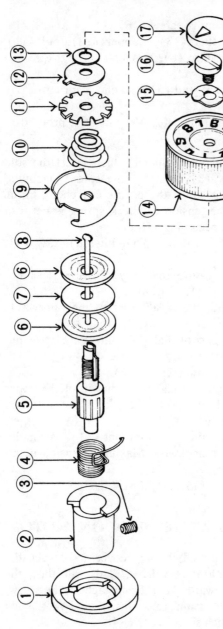

Fig. 44. Upper thread tension controls:
1. Base   2. Tension barrel   3. Set screw   4. Check spring   5. Tension stud   6. Tension disc   7. Tension washer   8. Tension release pin   9. Tension presser tray   10. Beehive tension spring   11. Nut   12. Tension dial stopper   13. Adjusting washer   14. Tension dial   15. Spring washer   16. Set screw   17. Cap

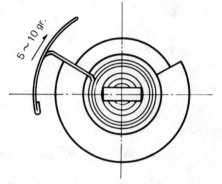

Fig. 45.

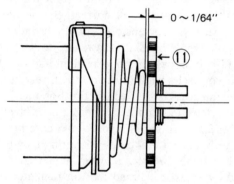

Fig. 46.

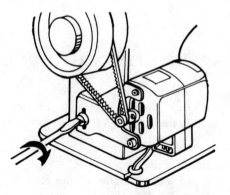

Fig. 47.

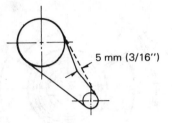

Fig. 48.

HOW TO REGULATE THREAD TENSIONS

Correct tensions (Fig. 49) are important for good appearances of stitches. If the tensions are not correct, the results will be imperfect stitching. Generally, the tensions should be adjusted by the upper thread tension regulator dial. However, to test the bobbin thread tension, hold bobbin case in your left hand and pull out a few inches of thread. If you feel a slight pull and the thread is supplied smoothly, it is usually unnecessary to adjust the bobbin thread tension (Fig. 49). If lower tension cannot be maintained, check for bent spring, thread lodged between spring and bobbin case body, or groove worn into spring or bobbin. In all cases the spring may have to be replaced.

To regulate bobbin thread tension. When correct tensions cannot be obtained by adjusting thread tension regulator or when the fabric will need a special bobbin thread tension, adjust the bobbin thread tension as shown in Fig. 49.

HOW TO CLEAN FEED DOG

Lint and loose thread are liable to collect on the feed dog from time to time. Therefore, it is necessary that the feed dog be cleaned from time to time. (*See* Fig. 50 and 51.)

1. Loosen thumb screw and remove the presser foot.
2. Remove needle plate.
3. Clean lint and loose threads in the feed dog with a brush. Special attention should be given to feed channels.
4. After cleaning, reset the needle plate and presser foot.

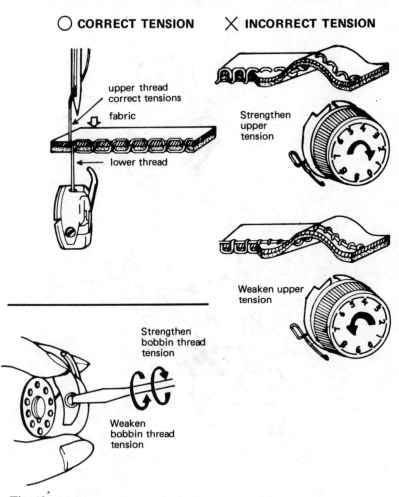

○ **CORRECT TENSION**   ✕ **INCORRECT TENSION**

upper thread
correct tensions

fabric

lower thread

Strengthen
upper
tension

Weaken upper
tension

Strengthen
bobbin thread
tension

Weaken
bobbin thread
tension

Fig. 49.

HOW TO OPEN AND CLEAN SHUTTLE RACE

Because your machine is specially equipped with the shuttle thread ejector that prevents jamming of the shuttle, it will rarely be necessary to open and clean the shuttle race. (*See* Fig. 52.)

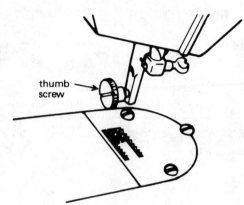

Fig. 50.

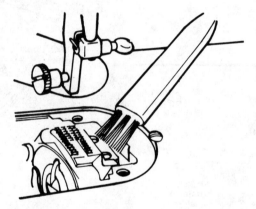

Fig. 51.

However, if for some reason it should be required to open and clean the shuttle race, proceed as follows:

1. First raise the needle bar to its highest point and remove the bobbin case.

2. Next, twist the shuttle race ring clasps outward and take out the shuttle race ring.

3. Carefully remove shuttle hook and clean out shuttle race.

4. Replace shuttle hook and shuttle race ring and lock with clasps. Be careful not to drop the shuttle to avoid possible damage.

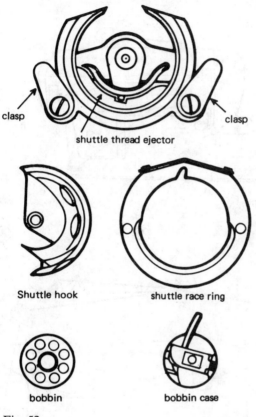

clasp   clasp

shuttle thread ejector

Shuttle hook   shuttle race ring

bobbin   bobbin case

Fig. 52.

WINDING THE BOBBIN THREAD

There are two basic bobbin winders on most machines: a type below the wheel on the arm, another mounted on the top. In both cases, there is an adjustment for even winding.

Bobbin Winder Mounted on Arm.   Adjustment for even and tight winding of bobbin is located at (Fig. 53, 2) on bed plate. Loosen screw and adjust to left or right as needed.

Bobbin Winder on Top Cover.   Adjustment for even and tight winding of bobbin is located at (Fig. 54, 2) on arm. Loosen screw and adjust the guide up or down as needed.

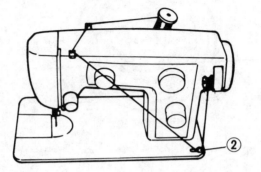

Fig. 53.

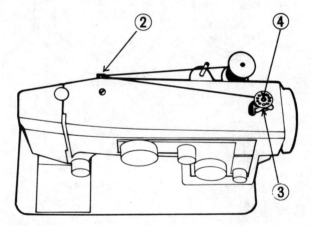

Fig. 54.

SETTING PROPER RELEASE OF CLUTCH NUT

At times it is necessary to remove the wheel for cleaning out thread, lint, or any other foreign object. Proper placement of lock-nut washer-and-screw is needed for free release.

1. Clutch sleeve should be free from thread and rust or burrs, and should be oiled.

2. Wheel should be mounted on sleeve (Fig. 55, 1) and free running.

3. Lock-nut washer should be placed on the bushing with two inner lugs, bent portion faced out (Fig. 55, 2).

4. Clutch nut should be secured into sleeve (Fig. 55, 1) and small set screw tightened.

5. Correct spacing (Fig. 55, 3) is needed between clutch-nut set-screw (Fig. 55, 4) and lock-nut washer-lug for proper wheel release in order to wind bobbin.

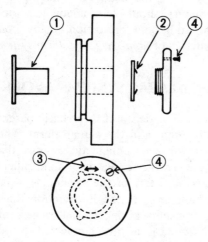

Fig. 55.

Chapter 43

Home Security Alarms

With the increasing rate of residential burglary, homeowners are becoming more and more concerned for the security of their homes and personal belongings. A solidly constructed door, hung on a well-fitted frame and secured with a good deadbolt lock, along with windows that will resist forced entry, should offer adequate protection for your home. However, for additional protection, many homeowners are considering the installation of *home security alarm systems.*

HOW ALARM SYSTEMS WORK

All security alarms are made up of three basic parts: the detectors or sensors, the control unit, and the actual alarm. The detectors or sensors are electronic or electromagnetic devices that act as observers by detecting the presence or action of an intruder.

The control unit is the heart of the system, to which all sensors are connected. The unit receives the information that a sensor has been disturbed and transmits a signal that triggers the alarm. Devices called *panic buttons* can also be connected to the control unit. These devices allow you to activate the alarm manually and are usually placed at the front door or in the bedroom.

The alarm reports that a sensor has been disturbed. It can sound at your home, or the signal can be transmitted to a remote location.

HOW DETECTORS OR SENSORS WORK

The following are some of the more commonly available sensors or detectors.

Switch Sensors.   *Switch sensors* are electromagnetic devices that are installed at all entry points considered to the accessible from the ground. When a door or window is opened the alarm is triggered. It is advisable to install sensors on windows or balcony doors adjacent to trees. Switch sensors are the most frequently used alarm sensors in residences (**Fig. 1**).

Fig. 1.

Pressure Mats. *Pressure mats* (Fig. 2) are used to protect specific areas of the home. The mats can be hidden under a carpet or rug in a frequently traveled corridor or can be used near items of value such as your TV set or stereo system. When pressure is exerted on the mat, the alarm is triggered.

Fig. 2.

Ultrasonic Motion Detectors. *Ultrasonic motion detectors* (Fig. 3) fill the room with sound waves too high for most humans to hear. Any movement in the room disturbs the wave pattern and triggers the

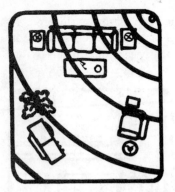

Fig. 3.

alarm. As some people and most animals are bothered by the high-pitched sounds, an in-home demonstration before purchasing is advisable.

Infrared Photoelectric Sensors.   *Infrared photoelectric sensors* (Fig. 4) project an infrared light beam between two points. Anything interrupting the beam will trigger an alarm. They are effective when installed at entry points as well as specific areas inside your home.

Fig. 4.

Connecting Sensors and Panic Buttons to Control Unit.   The *sensors* and *panic buttons* can be connected to the control unit either by direct wiring or lay a wireless system.

The *wireless system* operates on batteries that must be charged periodically. Transmitters are installed at each sensor or panic button and a receiver is installed in the control unit. The *wireless panic button* can be carried from room to room. Wired and wireless systems are equally effective.

TYPES OF ALARMS

There are two types of reporting alarms available—local and remote.

Local Alarm.   The *local* alarm is the simplest to install and the least expensive. When the system detects an intruder the alarm signal is heard at or near your home. Its effectiveness depends on the intruder being frightened away, or neighbors calling the police. The alarm device is generally located in the attic or under the eaves of the roof.

Remote Alarm.   The *remote* alarm transmits the alarm signal to a location away from your home, but can be combined with a local alarm. Several types of remote alarms are available.

The *automatic dialer* sends a prerecorded message or signal over telephone lines to a person you choose—an answering service, a neighbor, or a relative. The effectiveness of this system depends on someone being present to answer the telephone and call the police. The telephone company requires that the installation of a dialer system meet its specifications.

Note: Do not direct your alarm to the local police department without its prior approval. Several of the first dialer alarms were so unreliable that many jurisdictions continue to prohibit directing an alarm from a dialer to a police department.

The *direct-connect system* transmits the alarm signal to the police department. This type of service provides very good protection, but often is not available to the private homeowner. Most jurisdictions limit the direct-connect service to financial institutions and commercial establishments. The signals are transmitted over leased lines and there is a monthly charge to the subscriber.

The *central station system* is a commercial service. The alarm signal is transmitted to a private security company that monitors the system. In addition to notifying the police that your system has sent an alarm, the central station will dispatch guards to your home. Central stations will normally include the maintenance and repair of your alarm system as a part of your contract and will charge a monthly service fee.

COST OF ALARM SYSTEM

The cost of purchasing and installing a system can range from several hundred dollars to more than a thousand dollars. In addition, a monthly service fee of from 10 to more than 50 dollars may be charged for some remote alarm systems.

Your security alarm should be approved by a major testing laboratory, such as Underwriters Laboratories, Inc. (UL).

OPERATION OF ALARM SYSTEM

To get the best service from your alarm system, establish and follow a routine. When activating the system, make sure that doors and windows are closed and that pets are removed from protected areas. Nine out of ten alarms transmitted are false, half of which are caused by improper operation.

Do not treat the system like a new toy or demonstrate it to your friends. If your system sends alarms unnecessarily, it will lose credibility.

Improperly selected or installed sensors can also cause false alarms. For example, some sensors may react to changes in temperature or humidity, or to a draft from heating and air conditioning vents. Similarly, the motion of a billowing curtain or a ringing telephone bell may cause an ultrasonic motion detector to signal an alarm. In addition, your system should not be operated on the same electrical circuit as kitchen appliances or your heating and cooling system. The cyclic operation of these appliances may trigger an alarm. Your installer can advise you on the *selection* and *placement of sensors* that will best suit your needs.

Some detectors have sensitivity adjustments. Do not set them too high; they could become an almost constant source of false alarms. Also, do not try to increase the area of protection of a detector by increasing its sensitivity. Either use two detectors, or buy one that will meet your needs.

PURCHASING AN ALARM SYSTEM

Consider the following factors when purchasing an alarm system.

Local Laws. The system you purchase should conform to local ordinances. Make sure and check the local laws regarding noise (some jurisdictions limit the time that an alarm can sound) and licensing of installers. Get price quotations from several companies before your install your system; costs for equipment and installation will vary.

Installation. Discuss installation and maintenance with the installer before you sign a contract. Know how the system will be installed. Will the wiring be concealed or exposed? Will touchup painting be needed when the installation is complete? Ask to see how the sensors will look—you may find their appearance unacceptable. The more you know before you sign a contract, the better.

Optional Features. There are a few optional features that you may want to consider adding to your system: (1) A key-activated switch that allows you to turn the system on and off from the outside (Fig. 5); (2) a test switch that allows you to check all sensors without sending an alarm; and (3) a battery-powered back-up that allows the system to continue to operate during a power failure.

Fig. 5.

Maintenance. Once the system is installed, follow the manufacturer's instructions carefully, and be sure that all the members of your family know how to operate the system.

WHAT TO DO WHEN ALARM GOES OFF

When an intruder hears the alarm, his primary interest is getting out of the house as quickly as possible. If you are in the house, *stay out of the way*. If you can, lock yourself in your bedroom. The intruder is more likely to hurt you if confronted. Telephone the police as soon as possible.

Chapter 44

Smoke Detectors and Fire Extinguishers

SMOKE DETECTORS

The statistics on the loss of life and property due to fire are grim. However, there is an inexpensive and dependable way to protect your home, yourself, and your family—smoke detectors. They provide a reliable early warning system in the event of fire.

HOW SMOKE DETECTORS WORK

Smoke detectors work by sensing the rising smoke from a fire and sounding an alarm. They can detect smoke far from the origin of the fire. Smoke detectors are most valuable at night—alerting family members to the presence of fire when they are asleep.

There are presently two types of smoke detectors on the market— the photoelectric smoke detector, and the ionization chamber smoke detector.

The *photoelectric smoke detector* uses a photoelectric bulb that sends forth a beam of light. When smoke enters the detector, light from the beam is reflected from smoke particles into a photocell, and the alarm is triggered.

The *ionization chamber smoke detector* contains a small radiation source that produces electrically charged air molecules called ions. The presence of these ions allows a small electric current to flow in the chamber. When smoke particles enter the chamber they attach themselves to these ions, reducing the flow of electric current. The change in the current sets off the alarm.

SAFETY ANALYSIS

Before smoke detectors containing radioactive materials are placed on the market, the United States Nuclear Regulatory Commission (NRC) performs a radiation safety analysis to make sure that the detectors meet safety requirements.

EFFECTIVENESS OF DETECTORS

Both types of detectors are equally effective in the home. If properly installed, they can provide adequate warning for the family. Some differences exist between the two when they operate close to the origin of the fire. Ionization detectors will respond more quickly to flaming fires. Photoelectric detectors will generally respond faster to smoldering fires. These differences, however, are not critical. The detector you buy should be approved by a major testing laboratory such as Underwriters Laboratories, Inc. (UL).

INSTALLATION

Because smoke rises, the best place to install a detector is on the ceiling or high on an inside wall just below the ceiling. However, if the ceiling is below an uninsulated attic or in a mobile home, the detector should be placed on the wall 6 to 12 inches below the ceiling. In a multi-level air conditioned home, a detector is needed on each level. On the first floor, the detector should be placed on the ceiling at the base of the stairwell.

Sleeping Areas.   Detectors should be installed close enough to the bedrooms so that the alarm can be heard if the doors are closed. Do not install a smoke detector within three feet of an air supply register that might blow the smoke away from the detector. A detector should be installed between the air return to the furnace and the sleeping area as the smoke will be recirculated and diluted, resulting in a delayed alarm (Fig. 2). If you usually sleep with your doors closed, you might consider installing an additional detector inside the bedroom. If a fire starts in the bedroom, the detector inside that room will respond faster than the one in the hallway.

In a one-bedroom area on one level, locate a smoke detector between the sleeping area and living area (Fig. 1).

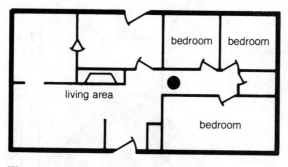

Fig. 1.

Basement.   For the best protection, the detector should be located on the basement ceiling at the bottom of the stairway.

If you are sleeping, it may be difficult to hear a detector located away from the bedroom area. If you are installing more than one detector, consider purchasing units that can be interconnected. That way, when one unit detects smoke, all the detectors will sound an alarm.

Connecting Detectors.   Smoke detectors can be connected in two ways: (1) By pulling wires through the walls, or (2) by a wireless system. Pulling the wires through the walls is a more permanent method and may require the services of an electrician. The wireless system operates on the same principle as home wireless intercoms. Either procedure is effective.

OPERATION

Detectors can be powered in two ways: By batteries or by household electric current. *Battery-operated detectors* are the easiest to install. They require no outlets or connections to household wiring. However, the batteries must be replaced approximately once a year to keep the detector operating properly. The cost of replacing batteries varies.

All Underwriters Laboratories approved battery-operated smoke

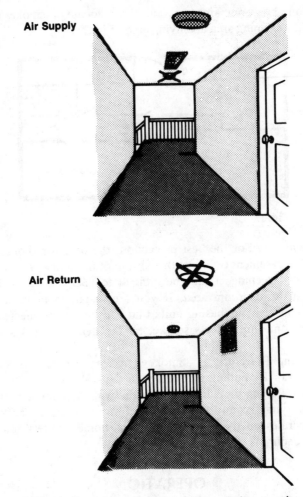

Air Supply

Air Return

Fig. 2. Location of detectors in relation to air supply and air return registers.

detectors are required to sound a trouble signal when the battery needs to be replaced. This *chirp* signal usually lasts seven days. If you are away from home for an extended period of time, it is advisable when you return to check your detector, according to the manufacturer's instructions, and to make sure the battery has not lost power.

Smoke detectors that operate on *household current* can be powered in two ways. The detector, equipped with an 8 to 9 foot electrical cord, can be plugged into an existing wall outlet. A detector powered in this way should not be operated with an on-off switch, as it may be accidentally turned off. It can also be wired permanently into your home's electrical system. This procedure requires an electrician, and the cost may vary.

A fire in the home electrical circuit that would interrupt power to a smoke detector is a remote possibility. If an appliance, such as a TV set in the living room, starts the fire, a smoke detector located outside the bedroom area should sound an alarm before the fire reaches the electrical wiring. This is particularly true if the TV set and smoke detector are on different circuits.

Dirt, extreme changes in temperature, and cooking exhaust smoke can cause a false alarm or a malfunction of a smoke detector. To prevent false alarms, locate the detector away from air vents, air conditioners, and fans. Keep the grillwork of the detector free of dirt by dusting or vacuuming regularly. Check and replace batteries periodically. Test your detectors every 30 days by using the test button, if provided, or by blowing smoke into the unit.

The best fire detection equipment can only tell you that there is a fire. All fire alarms should be used with a family escape plan. A smoke detector in working condition will usually give you at least three minutes to evacuate the house. Fire drills should be held so that all family members know what to do. Each person should be aware of all escape routes in the home, including bedroom windows. Do not try to fight the fire yourself. Choose a meeting place outside so you will know everyone in the house has escaped. *Do not* stop to call the fire department from your home—use a neighbor's telephone.

FIRE EXTINGUISHERS

If there is a fire in your house, you should get all the people out of the house fast, and immediately call the fire department.

Then—and only then—if the fire is small, and if your own escape route is clear, should you fight the fire yourself with a special tool designed for the job—a fire extinguisher. You may be able to put out the fire, or at least hold damage to a minimum, *but do not take chances.*

If you can attack a fire fast enough, your success with a fire extinguisher may depend upon one or more of the following:

1. Your ability to quickly identify the type of fire.
2. The availability of the right kind of extinguisher for that particular kind of fire.
3. Your knowledge of how to use the extinguisher; and how well the extinguisher has been maintained.

CLASSES OF FIRES

There are three classes of home-type fires. Your ability to *quickly* identify the type of fire may save your home—or your life. The reason is that most extinguishers are designed to fight particular classes of fires. Some fight only one class; some fight two classes; only one home-type extinguisher fights all three classes of fires.

Class A fires. Fire in ordinary combustible materials—paper, wood, cloth, and many plastics.

Class B fires. Fire in flammable liquids, gases, and greases—a flash fire in your frying pan or oven, or in paint or solvents.

Class C fires. Fire in electrical appliances and equipment—fire caused by faulty wiring, as in a TV.

FIRE EXTINGUISHERS FOR DIFFERENT CLASSES OF FIRES

Fire extinguishers are labeled to indicate the class or classes of fires they are designed to fight. While there are other kinds of extinguishers on the market, the following types are the kind recommended for home use.

SELECTING A FIRE EXTINGUISHER

Read the Labels.   Fire extinguisher labels indicate by their letters, A, B, or C, the *classes* of fires they fight. They also indicate by

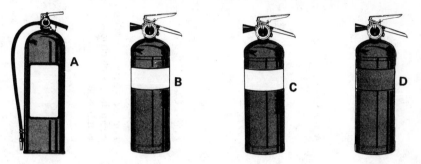

Fig. 3.

the numbers in front of the letters, 2-A: 10-B:C, the approximate *size* of the fire they can extinguish. The numerical ratings are established by Underwriters Laboratories, Inc. The actual size of fires indicated by each numerical rating is not listed here because too many variables are involved. Rather, we suggest particular fire extinguisher sizes for particular fire hazard areas.

The numerical ratings. The numerical code starts with 1 and increases by whole numbers. The higher the number, the greater the ability of the extinguisher to put out a fire. For example, an extinguisher with a 10-B:C on its label will extinguish approximately twice the size fire as will an extinguisher marked 5-B:C.

Combinations. Certain extinguishers for home use not only have multiple alphabetical ratings, A:B:C or B:C, but multiple numerical ratings as well, 2-A 10-B:C. This means that the extinguisher can be used against any Class A fire, Class B fire, or Class C fire of a size that you would attempt to combat in your home.

Match the Extinguisher to Your Need.   Before you invest in fire extinguishers for your home, think carefully about where you intend to use them. What are the hazard areas where fires are likely to start? What class of fire most likely to occur in each area?

General recommendations. You can approach the problem of selection in three ways. You can buy all-purpose extinguishers that are effective against all types of fires; you can buy extinguishers designed especially for specific types of fires likely to occur in particular areas; or you can buy a combination of the two.

For Class A:B:C all-purpose fire protection. In areas where you

Type of Extinguisher	Classes of Fires		
	A	*B*	*C*
Water	*Fights Class A fires only*	*Not effective*	*Not effective*
Freezes in low temperature unless treated with anti-freeze solution. Usually weighs over 20 pounds and is heavier than any other extinguisher mentioned.	For use in bedrooms, living rooms, recreation room, dining room; wherever paper, wood, cloth, and plastic materials predominate.		
Standard dry chemical; also called ordinary or regular dry chemical. (Sodium bicarbonate.)	*Not effective.*	*Fights Class B fires.*	*Fights Class C fires.*
Clean residue immediately after using the extinguisher so that sprayed material will not be affected.		For use in kitchen, workshop, garage, furnace or laundry areas; wherever there are flammable liquids, gases, or grease.	For use wherever fire may occur in live electrical equipment.

Purple K dry chemical (Potassium bicarbonate)

Not effective.

Fights Class B fires.

For use in kitchen, workshop, garage, furnace or laundry area; wherever there are flammable liquids, gases, or grease.

Fights Class C fires.

For use wherever fire may occur in live electrical equipment.

Has greatest initial fire-stopping power of the extinguishers mentioned for class B fires.

Clean residue immediately after using the extinguisher so sprayed material will not be affected.

Multipurpose dry chemical (Ammonium phosphates)

Fights Class A fires.

For use in any room in house to fight fire in paper, wood, cloth, rubbish, and many plastics.

Fights Class B fires.

For use in any room in house to fight fire in flammable liquids, gases, or grease.

Fights Class C fires.

For use in any room in house to fight fire in live electrical equipment.

Only extinguisher that fights all three classes of fires.

Clean residue immediately after using the extinguisher so sprayed material will not be affected.

are likely to have combustible materials such as wood, paper, cloth, or plastics; or where flammable liquids, gases, grease, or electrical apparatus are stored or used, select the *multipurpose dry chemical extinguisher* with a minimum 2-A: 10-B:C rating.

For Class A fire protection. In areas where you are likely to have only ordinary combustible materials such as wood, paper, cloth, or plastics, select a *water-type extinguisher* with a minimum 2-A rating.

For Class B and Class C fire protection. In areas where flammable liquids, gases, grease, or electrical apparatus is stored or used, select an extinguisher with a minimum 5-B:C rating.

A FIRE EXTINGUISHER PLAN FOR YOUR ENTIRE HOME

If you decide to buy fire extinguishers to match your home hazard areas, the house plan would look as illustrated.

In the *utility room or workshop* (Fig. 4), where old paint cans and solvents are stored, and in the laundry and furnace area where fire might start in electrical equipment, a B:C hazard area extinguisher is recommended, with at least a 5-B:C rating.

Fig. 4.

In the *kitchen* (Fig. 5), because of the possibility of grease fires or possible fires in the electrical appliances, a B:C hazard area extinguisher is recommended, having at least a 5-B:C rating.

In the *living room*, where fire might break out in ordinary combustible materials such as an upholstered chair or a rug, or in live electrical equipment such as the TV, an all-purpose extinguisher is recommended (Fig. 6). It should have a rating of at least 2-A: 10-B:C.

Fig. 5.

Fig. 6.

In the *bedroom area*, where fire might break out in ordinary combustible material such as bedding and clothing, or in electrical equipment (Fig. 7), an all-purpose extinguisher is recommended. It should
have at least a 2-A: 10-B:C rating.

Because *attics* usually have only one entrance/exit door, you
should not attempt to fight an attic fire.

In the *garage* (Fig. 8), a B:C hazard area extinguisher with at
least a 5-B:C rating is recommended to fight a fire in flammable liquids
and gases and fire in electrical equipment.

Place the extinguisher away from the hazard area but convenient
to reach and nearby an escape route.

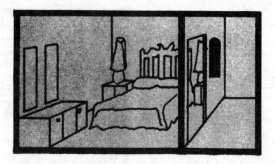

Fig. 7.

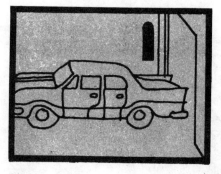

Fig. 8.

SELECTING A FIRE EXTINGUISHER

After you decide which kind and how many extinguishers you need, take a close look at the labels before you make your purchase. (*See* Fig. 9.)

USE OF FIRE EXTINGUISHER

After you buy a fire extinguisher and install it in a good location, learn how to use it. Because extinguishers vary in their operations, we will not attempt to cover the operating instructions for each type, but general remarks on use are described. Read the owner's manual

Are the operating instructions clearly marked on the extinguisher? *If not, don't buy it.*

Does the extinguisher clearly state what to do after it has been used? *If not, don't buy it.*

Does the extinguisher clearly state how it should be maintained? *If not, don't buy it.*

Is the extinguisher approved or listed by Underwriters' Laboratories? A marking on the extinguisher should clearly indicate this. *If not, don't buy it.*

Is the numerical and alphabetical rating clearly marked on the extinguisher name plate? *If not, don't buy it.*

Fig. 9.

that comes with your extinguisher, and the operating instructions that appear on the extinguisher label. Explain how to use the extinguisher to everyone in the family who is mature enough to cope with a fire.

Just as there are different fire extinguishers for different classes of fires, so there are different ways of fighting fire with different types of extinguishers.

On Class A Fires.   *Use of water-type extinguisher.* Direct the stream of water at the *base* of the fire (Fig. 3, A), using a side-to-side motion to wet the burning surface. Separate and soak the burning material. The water will cool and saturate the burning material to quench the fire.

Caution: Do not use water on flammable liquids, gases, or grease (Class B fires), or on fires in live electrical equipment (Class C fires).

Use of multipurpose dry-chemical-type extinguisher. From a distance of about six feet, aim the nozzle directly at the *base* of the burning material, coating it with the chemical (Fig. 3, D). The chemical will smother the fire.

On Class B Fires.   *Use of dry chemical extinguishers.* Direct the discharge at the *base* of the flames, moving the dry chemical extinguisher or its nozzle from side-to-side so that the discharge *sweeps* in front of the fire area. Stand back at least six feet; otherwise, the force of the discharge will *splash* the fire into other areas.

On Class C Fires.   *Use of dry chemical extinguishers.* Shut off electrical power. If possible, pull the plug. Direct the discharge at the *base* of the flames.

Caution: In fighting a home fire that is spreading:

1. Keep near a door to use as an escape route.
2. Stay low. Avoid breathing the heated smoke, vapors, or fumes as much as possible.
3. If the fire gets too big, get out, closing the door behind you.

LOCATION

A fire extinguisher should be in plain view, in an accessible spot, near a room exit that provides an escape route. Locate your extinguisher away from fire hazard spots (the stove, the paint shelf) because if a fire should start there your extinguisher would be useless to you. If you do not intend to mount the unit, remove the mounting brackets. Brackets on an unmounted extinguisher may complicate its use. Keep the extinguisher out of reach of small children.

MAINTENANCE

Follow the directions in the owner's manual and on the label of the fire extinguisher regarding its maintenance. They vary from unit to unit. The gage on a pressurized unit should be checked regularly to see that its pressure is maintained.

Have the extinguisher recharged promptly *after each use*, according to the directions on the label. You can do this by calling an authorized fire extinguisher service center listed in the telephone directory, or by calling or writing the manufacturer for information about your closest servicing center. A dry chemical extinguisher should be recharged with the same kind of chemical agent as shown on the nameplate.

Some extinguishers come with disposable cylinders so no recharging is necessary. For this type, you need buy only a replacement unit.

Never attempt to use a physically damaged extinguisher until it has been tested by an approved fire extinguisher service center.

There are many additional kinds of extinguishers made for specific purposes: for your car, for your boat, for particular home applications.

Section 9

HOW TO SAVE ENERGY IN AND AROUND YOUR HOME

ENERGY CONSERVATION WILL HELP us extend our supplies and reduce our import burdens until we develop new energy technologies and resources. Without personal hardship, we could easily cut our energy use by an estimated 30 percent or more—saving energy for our country and money for ourselves. The energy we use for our homes and automobiles—gas, oil, electricity—draws on all of our energy resources. Cutting back on these uses is the simplest, most effective way to make our resources last longer. And each individual conservation effort, multiplied by millions, can serve as an *energy bank*—a supply that can be used to help balance our energy accounts.

We can conserve if we make energy thrift a part of our way of life—adopting common sense energy habits.

The use of *thermal insulation*, properly specified and installed, has long been recognized as the most rewarding of all means of saving energy and money, and enhancing comfort, in homes of all types and during all seasons of the year. Now, persistent escalation in the cost of energy, regardless of its form, has intensified the appreciation of insulation's benefits. Federal and state governments, public service commissions, utility companies, and consumer-interest groups are recommending the installation of insulation in greater amounts than ever before.

By fixing up your home, you win in a lot of ways: You use less energy and save money year after year; since your energy is the country's energy, you help your country; and you add resale value to your home—it will cost the next owner less to heat and cool, so he or she will probably be willing to pay you more.

Chapter 45

Energy Savers

Most of our residential energy, 70 percent in fact, is used to heat and cool our homes. An additional 20 percent goes for heating water, the second-largest home energy user and expense. The remaining 10 percent goes into lighting and running small appliances.

We can cut our energy use and family costs by making our homes energy efficient, even if we have to spend some money to do it. The money we spend now will be returned in a few years through lower utility bills month after month. And then the savings are all ours.

PROTECTING YOUR HOME FROM OUTSIDE HEAT AND COLD

About 40 million single-family homes in the United States are not adequately protected from outside weather, according to Federal Department of Energy estimates.

Insulation. *R-Values.* You can reduce the load on your heating and cooling equipment by as much as 20 to 30 percent by investing a few hundred dollars in insulation. That is about as much as it would cost to buy a television set. But the benefits of insulation—lower utility costs—continue for years. Research the following areas.

1. *Insulating your home.* Your needs will depend on the climate in which you live and the amount of insulation, if any, you already have. For guidance, consult a reputable insulation dealer in your community or your local building inspector or county agent.

2. *R-values.* Find out about R-values before you buy your insulation materials. Then buy the thickness of insulation that will give you the R-value you should have. (*See* Fig. 1, Heating Zone map and data.) *R-values or numbers* are insulation efficiency ratings. The R stands for resistance to winter heat loss or summer heat gain. The

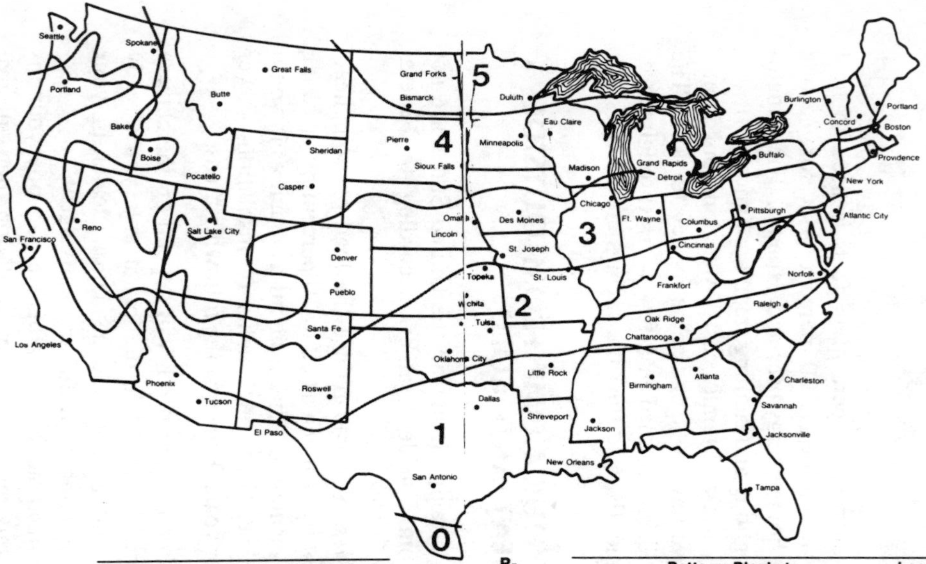

Heating Zone	Recommended for	
	Ceiling	Floor
0,1	R-26	R-11
2	R-26	R-13
3	R-30	R-19
4	R-33	R-22
5	R-38	R-22

R-Values	Batts or Blankets		Loose Fill (Poured In)		
	glass fiber	rock wool	glass fiber	rock wool	cellulosic fiber
R-11	3½"-4"	3"	5"	4"	3"
R-13	4"	4½"	6"	4½"	3½"
R-19	6"-6½"	5¼"	8"-9"	6"-7"	5"
R-22	6½"	6"	10"	7"-8"	6"
R-26	8"	8½"	12"	9"	7"-7½"
R-30	9½"-10½"	9"	13"-14"	10"-11"	8"
R-33	11"	10"	15"	11"-12"	9"
R-38	12"-13"	10½"	17"-18"	13"-14"	10"-11"

Fig. 1. Heating zone map and data.

higher the R-number, the more effective the insulating capability. The numbers should appear on packages of all insulation materials: mineral, glass fiber, or rock wool batts or blankets; foam or loose-fill materials that are poured or blown into insulation spaces; or rigid board insulation. If the insulation you buy does not have the R-value written on the package, ask the salesperson to write the R-value on your receipt for future references.

3. *Insulating attic floors or top floor ceilings.* Current Federal Housing Administration standards for new houses call for a minimum of R-19 for these spaces, and this can serve as a good guide for existing houses as well.

If you have old insulation in your attic, you probably will not be able to judge its R-value. But, if you have less than six inches of old insulation, chances are you need more. If you have no insulation, or less than three inches, add a minimum of R-19. For 3 to 6 inches, add at least R-11.

Amounts of more than R-19 are often justifiable if your climate is colder or warmer than average.

Investment costs vary. Heating and cooling savings should range from somewhere around five percent, if you are adding to present insulation, to as much as 30 percent if you have no insulation.

4. *Insulating exterior walls* if you live in a climate that requires a good deal of heating or air-conditioning and if there is space in the walls for blown-in insulation. You will need to employ a contractor to do this job. R-values recommended for most wall insulation range from R-11 to R-13.

5. *Insulating floors over unheated spaces,* such as crawl spaces and garages.

Draft-Proof Windows and Doors. Savings in reduced space heating costs for any of the following types of protection can amount to as much as 15 percent a year.

1. *Test your windows and doors for air-tightness.* Move a lighted candle around the frames and sashes of your windows. If the flame dances around, you need calking and/or weatherstripping. Try slipping a quarter under the door. If it goes through easily, you need weatherstripping.

2. *Calk and weatherstrip doors and windows.* It is easy to do this yourself. Savings in annual energy costs could amount to 10 per-

cent or more than the calking and weatherstripping materials cost for the average house (12 windows, 2 doors).

3. *Install storm windows.* Combination screen-and-storm windows (triple-track glass combination) are the most convenient and energy efficient because they can be opened easily when there is no need to run heating or cooling equipment.

Alternatives range from single-pane storm windows that have to be removed to admit outside air, to clear plastic film that can be taped tightly to the inside of the window frames.

Note: If every gas heated home were properly calked and weatherstripped, we would save enough natural gas each year to heat about four million homes.

Heating and Cooling Your Home. Heating and cooling our homes account for most of our energy costs. Do not waste any of that precious conditioned air, whether you pay for it yourself or pay your landlord for it.

During both heating and cooling seasons:

1. *Close off unoccupied rooms* and shut their heat or air conditioning vents; or turn off room air-conditioners.

2. *Use kitchen, bath, and other ventilating fans sparingly.* In just one hour these fans can blow away a houseful of warmed or cooled air. Turn them off just as soon as they have done their job.

3. *Keep your fireplace damper closed unless you have a fire going.* An open damper in a 48-inch square fireplace can let up to eight percent of your heat out the chimney.

HEATING ENERGY SAVERS

1. *If you use electric heating, consider a heat-pump system.* The heat pump uses outside air for both heating and cooling. Costs for these pumps vary for a whole-house unit or for room size. These pumps can cut your use of electricity for heating by 30 to 40 percent and can also provide some savings in cooling costs.

2. *Consider the advantages of a clock thermostat for your heating system.* The clock thermostat will turn the heat down for you automatically at a regular hour before you retire and turn it up

again before you wake. While you can easily turn your thermostat back at night and up again in the morning yourself, the convenience of a clock thermostat may be worth the cost to you.

3. *Consider buying a furnace that incorporates an automatic flue gas damper.* This device reduces the loss of heat when the furnace is off.

4. *Do not use your fireplace for supplemental heating when your furnace is on,* unless you take one of the measures suggested below to lessen the loss of heated air from the house.

The warmth from a fire on the hearth generally does not radiate through the house; the heat gain is confined to the room with the fireplace. Also, when your furnace is on, a considerable amount of heated air from the rest of the house flows into the fireplace and goes wastefully up the chimney. Then the temperature in other rooms of the house goes down, and the furnace uses more fuel to raise it to the level controlled by the thermostat. So you use more fuel, rather than less, when the furnace and fireplace are both going.

5. *Lessen heat loss when you use your fireplace when the furnace is on.*

Lower the thermostat setting to 50° F. to 55° F. Some warmed air will still be lost, but the furnace will not have to use as much fuel to heat the rest of the house to these temperatures as it would to raise the heat to 65° F. or 68° F.

Close all doors and warm air ducts entering the room with the fireplace and open a window near the fireplace about ½ to 1 inch. Air needed by fire will be provided through the open window and the amount of heated air drawn from the rest of the house will be reduced.

If you have a simple open masonry fireplace, consider installing a glass front or a glass screen. This will cut down on the loss of warmed air through the flue.

When the heat is on.

1. *Lower your thermostat to 65° F. during the day and 55° F. at night.* You can save about three percent on your fuel costs for every degree you reduce the *average temperature* in your home. You can save about one percent on your heating bills for every degree you dial down *only at night.*

2. *Keep windows near your thermostat tightly closed*; otherwise, it will keep your furnace working after the rest of the room has reached a comfortable temperature.

3. *Have your oil furnace serviced at least once a year*, preferably each summer to take advantage of off-season rates. This simple precaution could save you 10 percent in fuel consumption.

4. *Clean or replace the filter in your forced-air heating system each month.*

5. *Check the duct work for air leaks about once a year if you have a forced-air heating system.* To do this, feel around the duct joints for escaping air when the fan is on. You could save almost nine percent in heating fuel costs this way.

6. *If you have oil heat, check to see if the firing rate is correct.* Chances are it is not. A recent survey found that 97 percent of the furnaces checked were overfired.

If your oil furnace does not run almost constantly on a very cold day, call a service man.

7. *Do not let cold air seep into your home through the attic access door.* Check the door to make sure it is well insulated and weatherstripped; otherwise, you will be wasting fuel to heat that cool air.

8. *Dust or vacuum radiator surfaces frequently.* Dust and grime impede the flow of heat. If the radiators need painting, use flat paint; it radiates heat better than glossy paint does.

9. *Keep draperies and shades open in sunny windows; close them at night.*

10. *For comfort in cooler indoor temperatures, use the best insulation of all—warm clothing.* The human body gives off heat, about 390 Btu's for a man, 330 Btu's for a woman. Dressing wisely can help you retain natural heat. Wear closely woven fabrics; they add at least half a degree in warmth.

For women. Slacks are at least a degree warmer than skirts.

For men and women. A light long-sleeved sweater equals almost two degrees in added warmth; a heavy long-sleeved sweater adds about 3.7 degrees; and two lightweight sweaters add about five degrees in warmth because the air between them serves as insulation to keep in more body heat.

Note: If every household in the United States lowered its average heating temperatures six degrees over a 24-hour period, we would save more than 570,000 barrels of oil per day, or more than 3.5 percent of our current oil imports.

COOLING ENERGY SAVERS

Air-conditioning equipment.

1. *If you need central air-conditioning, select the smallest and least powerful system that will cool your home adequately.* A larger unit than you need not only costs more to run but probably will not remove enough moisture from the air.

Ask your dealer to help you determine how much cooling power you need for the space you have to cool and for the climate in which you live. (*See* section on Energy-Efficiency Ratios for Air Conditioners later in this chapter.)

2. *Make sure the ducts in your air conditioning system are properly insulated,* especially those that pass through the attic or other uncooled spaces. This could save you almost nine percent in cooling costs.

3. *If you do not need central air-conditioning, consider using individual window or through-the-wall units* in rooms that need cooling from time to time. Select the smallest and least powerful units for the rooms you need to cool. As a rule, these will cost less to buy and less to operate.

4. *Install a whole-house ventilating fan* in your attic or in an upstairs window to cool the house when it is cool outside, even if you have central air-conditioning. It will pay to use the fan rather than air conditioning when the outside temperature is below 82° F. When windows in the house are open, the fan pulls cool air through the house and exhausts warm air through the attic.

When you use air conditioning.

1. *Set your thermostat at 78° F.,* a reasonably comfortable and energy-efficient indoor temperature. The higher the setting and the less difference between indoor and outdoor temperature, the less out-

door hot air will flow into the building. If the 78° F. setting raises your home temperature six degrees (from 72° F. to 78° F., for example), you should save between 12 and 47 percent in cooling costs, depending on where you live.

2. *Do not set your thermostat at a colder setting than normal when you turn your air conditioner on.* It will *not* cool faster. It *will* cool to a lower temperature than you need and use more energy.

3. *Set the fan speed on High except in very humid weather.* When it is humid, set the fan speed at low; you will get less cooling but more moisture will be removed from the air.

4. *Clean or replace air-conditioning filters at least once a month.* When the filter is dirty, the fan has to run longer to move the same amount of air, and this takes more electricity.

5. *Turn off your window air-conditioners when you leave a room for several hours.* You will use less energy cooling the room down later than if you had left the unit running.

6. *Consider using a fan with your window air-conditioner* to spread the cooled air farther without greatly increasing your power use. But be sure the air conditioner is strong enough to help cool the additional space.

7. *Do not place lamps or TV sets near your air-conditioning thermostat.* Heat from these appliances is sensed by the thermostat and could cause the air conditioner to run longer than necessary.

With or without air conditioning.

1. *Keep out daytime sun* with vertical louvers or awnings on the outside of your windows, or draw draperies, blinds, and shades indoors. You can reduce heat gain from the sun by as much as 80 percent this way.

2. *Keep lights low or off.* Electric lights generate heat and add to the load on your air conditioner.

3. *Do your cooking and use other heat-generating appliances* in the early morning and late evening hours whenever possible.

4. *Open the windows instead of using your air conditioner or electric fan* on cooler days and during cooler hours.

5. *Turn off the furnace pilot light* in summer, but be sure it is reignited before you turn the furnace on again.

6. *Dress for the warmer indoor temperatures.* Neat but casual clothes of lightweight open-weave fabrics are the most comfortable.

Without air conditioning.

1. *Be sure to keep windows and outside doors closed during the hottest hours of the day.*

2. *Use window or whole-house ventilating fans* to cool the house when it is cool outside. (*See* section on Whole-house Fans previously discussed.)

3. *Use vents and exhaust fans* to pull heat and moisture from the attic, kitchen, and laundry directly to the outside.

Note: If everyone raised their home's air conditioning temperature six degrees, we would save the equivalent of 36 million kilowatt-hours of electricity used in the nation in one year.

Hot Water Energy Savers.   Heating water accounts for about 20 percent of all the energy we use in our homes. Do not waste it.

1. *Repair leaky faucets promptly.* One drop a second can waste as much as 60 gallons of hot or cold water in a week.

2. Do as much household cleaning as possible with *cold water.*

3. *Insulate* your hot water storage tank and piping.

Water heaters. Energy-efficient water heaters may cost a little more initially, but reduced operating costs over a period of time can more than make up for the higher outlay.

1. *Buy a water heater with thick insulation on the shell.* While the initial cost may be more than one without this conservation feature, the savings in energy costs over the years will more than repay you.

2. *Add insulation around the water heater you now have if it is inadequately insulated,* but be sure not to block off needed air vents. That would create a safety hazard, especially with oil and gas heaters. When in doubt, get professional help. When properly done, you should save in energy costs.

3. *Check the temperature on your water heater.* Most water heaters are set for 140° F. or higher, but you may not need water

that hot unless you have a dishwasher. A setting of 120° F. can provide adequate hot water for most families.

If you reduce the temperature from 140° F. (medium) to 120° F. (low), you could have over 18 percent of the energy you use at the higher setting. Even reducing the setting 10° F. will save more than six percent in water heating energy.

If you are uncertain about the tank water temperature, draw some water from the heater through the faucet near the bottom and test it with a thermometer.

4. *Do not let sediment build up in the bottom of your hot water heater*, as it lowers the heater's efficiency and wastes energy. About once a month, flush the sediment out by drawing several buckets of water from the tank through the faucet.

KITCHEN ENERGY SAVERS

1. *Use cold water rather than hot to operate your food disposer.* This saves the energy needed to heat the water, recommended for the appliance, and aids in getting rid of grease. Grease solidifies in cold water and can be ground up and washed away.

2. *Install an aerator in your kitchen sink faucet.* By reducing the amount of water in the flow, you use less hot water and save the energy that would have been required to heat it. The lower flow pressure is hardly noticeable.

3. If you need to purchase a *gas oven* or *range*, look for one with an *automatic* (electronic) *ignition system* instead of a pilot light. You will save up to 30 percent on gas.

4. If you have a *gas stove*, make sure the *pilot light* is burning efficiently—with a *blue flame*. A yellowish flame indicates that an adjustment is needed.

5. *Never boil water in an open pan.* Water will come to a boil faster and use less energy in a kettle or covered pan.

6. *Keep range-top burners and reflectors clean.* They will reflect the heat better, and you will save energy.

7. *Match the size of pan to the heating element.* More heat will get to the pan; less will be lost to surrounding air.

8. *If you cook with electricity, get in the habit of turning off the burners several minutes before the allotted cooking time.* The heating

element will stay hot long enough to finish the cooking for you without using more electricity.

9. *When using the oven, make the most of the heat from that single source.* Cook as many foods as you can at one time. Prepare dishes that can be stored or frozen for later use or make all oven-cooked meals.

10. *Watch the clock or use a timer.* Do not continually open the oven door to check food. Every time you open the door heat escapes and your cooking uses extra energy to compensate.

11. *Use small electric pans or ovens for small meals* rather than the kitchen range or oven. They use less energy.

12. *Use pressure cookers and microwave ovens if you have them.* They can save energy by reducing cooking time.

Dishwashing energy savers.

The average dishwasher uses 14 gallons of hot water per load. Use its energy efficiently.

1. When you turn it on, *be sure your dishwasher is full,* but not overloaded.

2. *When buying a dishwasher, look for a model with air-power and/or overnight dry settings.* These features automatically turn off the dishwasher after the rinse cycle. This can save you up to one-third your total dishwashing energy costs.

3. *Let your dishes air dry.* If you do not have an automatic air-dry switch, turn off the control knob after the final rinse. Prop the door open a little and the dishes will dry faster.

4. *Do not use the rinse-hold cycle on your machine.* It uses 3 to 7 gallons of hot water each time you use it.

5. *Scrape dishes before loading them into the dishwasher* so you will not have to rinse them. If they need rinsing, use cold water.

Note: If every dishwasher user in the country cut out just one load a week, we would save almost 15 million kilowatt-hours of electricity every day or the equivalent of about 9,000 barrels of oil a day.

Refrigerator/freezer energy savers.

1. *Do not keep your refrigerator or freezer too cold.* Recommended temperatures: 38° F. to 40° F. for the fresh food compartment of the refrigerator; 5° F. for the freezer.

2. *If you are buying a refrigerator, it is energy wise economically to buy one with a power-saver switch.* Most refrigerators have heating elements in their walls or doors to prevent sweating on the outside. In most climates, the heating element does not need to be working all the time. The power-saver switch turns off the heating element. By using it, you could save about 16 percent in refrigerator energy costs.

3. *Consider buying refrigerators and freezers that have to be defrosted manually.* Although they take more effort to defrost, these appliances use less energy than those that defrost automatically.

4. *Regularly defrost manual-defrost refrigerators and freezers.* Frost buildup increases the amount of energy needed to keep the engine running. Never allow frost to build up more than ¼-inch.

5. *Make sure your refrigerator door seals are air-tight.* Test them by closing the door over a piece of paper or a dollar bill so it is half in and half out of the refrigerator. If you can pull the paper or bill out easily, the latch may need adjustment or the seal may need replacing.

Laundry energy savers.

You can save considerable amounts of energy in the laundry through conservation of hot water and by using your automatic washers and dryers less often and more efficiently.

Wash clothes in warm or cold water, rinse in cold. You will save energy and money. Use hot water only if absolutely necessary.

Washing machines.

1. *Fill washers* (unless they have small-load attachments or variable water levels), but do not overload them.

2. *Use the suds saver if you have one.* It will allow you to use one tubful of hot water for several loads.

3. *Do not use too much detergent.* Follow the instructions on the box. Oversudsing makes your machine work harder and use more energy.

4. *Pre-soak or use a soak cycle when washing heavily soiled garments.* You will avoid two washings and save energy.

Clothes dryers.

1. *Fill clothes dryers but do not overload them.*
2. *Keep the lint screen in the dryer clean.* Remove lint after each load. Lint impedes the flow of air in the dryer and requires the machine to use more energy.
3. *Keep the outside exhaust of your clothes dryer clean.* Check it regularly. A clogged exhaust lengthens the drying time and increases the amount of energy used.
4. *If your dryer has an automatic dry cycle,* use it. Overdrying merely wastes energy.
5. *Dry your clothes in consecutive loads.* Stop-and-start drying uses more energy because a lot goes into bringing the dryer up to the desired temperature each time you begin.
6. *Separate drying loads into heavy and lightweight items.* Since the lighter ones take less drying time, the dryer does not have to be on as long for these loads.
7. *If drying the family wash takes more than one load, leave small, lightweight items until last.* You may be able to dry them, after you turn off the power, with heat retained by the machine from earlier loads.
8. *Save energy by using the old-fashioned clothesline.* As a bonus, clothes dried outdoors often seem fresher and cleaner than those taken from a mechanical dryer.

Ironing.

1. *Remove clothes that will need ironing from the dryer while they still are damp.* There is no point in wasting energy to dry them thoroughly if they only have to be dampened again.
2. *You can save ironing time and energy by pressing sheets and pillow cases on the warm top of your dryer.* Fold them carefully, then smooth them out on the flat surface.
3. *Save energy needed for ironing by hanging clothes in the bathroom while you are bathing or showering.* The steam often removes the wrinkles for you.

Bathroom Energy Savers.

1. *Take showers rather than tub baths,* but limit your showering

time and check the water flow if you want to save energy. It takes about 30 gallons of water to fill the average tub. A shower with a flow of four gallons of water a minute uses only 20 gallons in five minutes. Assuming you use half hot and half cold water for bathing, you would save about five gallons of hot water every time you substitute a shower for a bath. Thus, if you substituted just one shower for one bath per day, you would save almost 2,000 gallons of hot water in a year.

2. *Consider installing a flow restrictor in the pipe at the shower-head.* These inexpensive, easy-to-install devices restrict the flow of water to an adequate 3 to 4 gallons per minute. This can save considerable amounts of hot water and the energy used to produce them over a year's time.

LIGHTING ENERGY SAVERS

It is easy to use more light than you need. More than 16 percent of the electricity we use in our homes goes into lighting. Most people overlight their homes, so lowering lighting levels is an easy conservation measure.

Indoor Lighting.

1. *Light-zone your home and save electricity.* Concentrate lighting in reading and working areas and where it is needed for safety reasons (stairwells for example). Reduce lighting in other areas, but avoid very sharp contrasts.

2. *To reduce overall lighting in non-working spaces,* remove one bulb out of three in multiple light fixtures and replace it with a burned-out bulb for safety. Replace other bulbs throughout the house with bulbs of the next lower wattage.

3. *Consider installing solid-state dimmers or high-low switches* when replacing light switches. They make it easy to reduce lighting intensity in a room and thus save energy.

4. *Use one large bulb instead of several small ones in areas where bright light is needed.*

5. *Use long-life incandescent lamps only in hard-to-reach places.* They are less energy efficient than ordinary bulbs.

6. *New lamps.* Consider the advantages of those with three-way switches. They make it easy to keep lighting levels low when intense

light is not necessary, and that saves electricity. Use the High switch only for reading or other activities that require brighter light.

7. *Always turn three-way bulbs down to the lowest lighting level when watching television.* You will reduce the glare and use less energy.

8. *Use low-wattage night-light bulbs.* These now come in four-watt as well as seven-watt sizes. The four-watt bulb with a clear finish is almost as bright as the seven-watt bulb but uses about half as much energy.

9. *Try 50-watt reflector floodlights in directional lamps* (such as pole or spot lamps). These flood lights provide about the same amount of light as the standard 100-watt bulbs but at half the wattage.

10. *Try 25-watt reflector flood bulbs in high-intensity portable lamps.* They provide about the same amount of light but use less energy than the 40-watt bulbs that normally come with these lamps.

11. *Use fluorescent lights whenever you can; they give out more lumens per watt.* For example, a 40-watt fluorescent lamp gives off 80 lumens per watt and a 60-watt incandescent gives off only 14.7 lumens per watt. The 40-watt fluorescent lamp would save about 140 watts of electricity over a seven-hour period. These savings, over a period of time, could more than pay for the fixtures you would need to use fluorescent lighting.

12. *Consider fluorescent lighting for the kitchen sink and countertop areas.* These lights set under kitchen cabinets or over counter tops are pleasant and energy efficient.

13. *Fluorescent lighting is also effective for makeup and grooming areas.* Use 20-watt deluxe warm-white lamps for these areas.

14. *Keep all lamps and lighting fixtures clean.* Dirt absorbs light.

15. *You can save on lighting energy through decorating.* Remember, light colors for walls, rugs, draperies, and upholstery reflect light and therefore reduce the amount of artificial light required.

Outdoor Lighting.

1. *Have decorative outdoor gas lamps turned off unless they are essential for safety or convert them to electricity.* Keeping just 6 or 7 gas lamps burning uses as much natural gas as it takes to heat an average-size home.

2. *Use outdoor lights only when they are needed.* One way to make sure they are off during the daylight hours is to put them on a photocell unit or timer that will turn them off automatically.

APPLIANCE ENERGY SAVERS

About eight percent of all the energy used in the United States goes into running electrical home appliances, so appliance use and selection can make a considerable difference in home utility costs. Buying energy-efficient appliances may cost a bit more initially but that expense is more than made up by reduced operating costs over the lifetime of the appliance.

Energy efficiency may vary considerably though models seem similar. In the next few years it will be easier to judge the energy efficiency of appliances with the government's appliance labeling program. (*See* section on Appliance Labeling Program later in this chapter.) In the meantime, wise selection requires a degree of time and effort.

You will find a number of tips on how to save energy when buying or using appliances in other sections of this chapter, but here are a few general ideas to consider.

1. *Do not leave your appliances running when they are not in use.* It is a total waste of energy. Remember to turn off your radio, TV, or record player when you leave the room.

2. *Keep appliances in good working order* so they will last longer, work more efficiently, and use less energy.

3. *When buying appliances, comparison shop.* Compare energy-use information and operating costs of similar models by the same and different manufacturers. The retailer should be able to help you find the wattage of the appliance. With that information, and the following chart, you should be able to figure out how much it will cost you to run the appliance you choose.

Chart 6 shows the estimated annual energy use of some household appliances. With this information, you should be able to figure your approximate energy use and cost for each item listed. You should also get a good idea which appliances in your home use the most energy and where energy conservation practices will be the most effective in cutting utility costs.

CHART 6

ANNUAL ENERGY REQUIREMENTS OF ELECTRIC HOUSEHOLD
APPLIANCES

	Est. kWh used annually		Est. kWh used annually
Major Appliances		Washing Machine—non-automatic	2,497
Air-Conditioner (room) (Based on 1000 hours of operation per year. This figure will vary widely depending on geographic area and specific size of unit)	860	(including energy to heat water) washing machine only	76
		Water Heater	4,811
		Kitchen Appliances	
Clothes Dryer	993	Blender	15
Dishwasher including energy used to heat water	2,100	Broiler	100
		Carving Knife	8
Dishwasher only	363	Coffee Maker	140
Freezer (16 cu. ft.)	1,190	Deep Fryer	83
Freezer—frostless (16.5 cu. ft.)	1,820	Egg Cooker	14
		Frying Pan	186
Range with oven with self-cleaning oven	700 730	Hot Plate	90
		Mixer	13
Refrigerator (12 cu. ft.)	728	Oven, Microwave (only)	190
Refrigerator—frostless (12 cu. ft.)	1,217	Roaster	205
Refrigerator/Freezer (12.5 cu. ft.)	1,500	Sandwich Grill	33
		Toaster	39
Refrigerator/Freezer—frostless (17.5 cu. ft.)	2,250	Trash Compactor	50
		Waffle Iron	22
Washing Machine—automatic (including energy used to heat water) washing machine only	2,500 103	Waste Disposer	30

Chart 6 (continued)

	Est. kWh used annually		Est. kWh used annually
Heating and Cooling		Toothbrush	.5
Air Cleaner	216	Vibrator	2
Electric Blanket	147	**Home Entertainment**	
Dehumidifier	377	Radio	86
Fan (attic)	291	Radio/Record Player	109
Fan (circulating)	43	Television	
Fan (rollaway)	138	Black & white	
Fan (window)	170	Tube type	350
		Solid state	120
Heater (portable)	176	Color	
Heating Pad	10	Tube type	660
Humidifier	163	Solid state	440
Laundry		**Housewares**	
Iron (hand)	144	Clock	17
		Floor Polisher	15
Health & Beauty		Sewing Machine	11
Germicidal Lamp	141	Vacuum Cleaner	46
Hair Dryer	14		
Heat Lamp (infrared)	13		
Shaver	1.8		
Sun Lamp	16		

Note:
When using these figures for projections, such factors as the size of the specific appliance, the geographic area of use, and individual use should be taken into consideration.

4. *Before buying new appliances with special features, find out how much energy they use compared with other, perhaps less convenient, models.* A frost-free refrigerator, for example, uses more energy than one you have to defrost manually. It also costs more to purchase. The energy and dollars you can save with a manual-defrost model may be worth giving up the convenience.

5. *Use appliances wisely;* use the one that takes the least amount of energy for the job. For example, toasting bread in the oven uses three times more energy than toasting it in a toaster.

6. *Do not use energy-consuming special features on your appliances if you have an alternative.* For example, do not use the *instant-on* feature of your TV set. *Instant-on* sets, especially the tube types, use energy even when the screen is dark. *Use the vacation switch,* if you have one, to eliminate this waste; plug the set into an outlet that is controlled by a wall switch; or have your TV service man install an additional on-off switch on the set itself or in the cord to the wall outlet.

BUILDING OR BUYING A HOME

Energy-wasting mistakes can be avoided if you consider climate, local building codes, and energy-efficient construction when you build or buy a home. In either case, the following energy conservation ideas should help you keep down home utility bills.

Considerations when building a home.

1. *Consider a square floor plan.* It is usually more energy efficient than a rectangular plan.

2. *Insulate walls and roof to the highest specifications* recommended for your area. (*See* Fig. 1, Heating Zone Map.)

3. *Insulate floors,* too, especially those over crawl spaces, cold basements, and garages.

4. *If the base of a house is exposed,* as in the case of a mobile home, build a *skirt* around it.

5. *Install louvered panels or wind-powered roof ventilators* rather than motor-driven fans to ventilate the attic. Only use a motor-driven fan if it can be used for whole-house ventilating during cool periods.

6. *Consider solar heat gain when you plan your window locations.*

In *cool climates,* install few windows in the north wall, because there is little solar heat gain there in winter.

In *warm climates,* put the largest number of windows in the north and east walls to reduce heating from the sun.

7. *Install windows you can open* so you can use natural or fan-forced ventilation in moderate weather.

8. *Use double-pane glass throughout the house.* Windows with

double-pane heat-reflecting or heat-absorbing glass provide additional energy savings, especially in south and west exposures.

9. *Place your refrigerator in the coolest part of the kitchen*, well away from the range and oven.

10. *Install the water heater as close as possible to areas of major use* to minimize heat loss through the pipes and insulate the pipes.

11. *If you live in a warm climate, remember that* light-colored roofing can help keep houses cooler.

When buying a home. Consider all the ideas mentioned for building a home.

1. *Ask for a description of the insulation and data on the efficiency of space heating, air conditioning, and water heating plants*, or have an independent engineer advise you about the efficiency of the equipment. Ask to see the utility bills from the previous year but remember to adjust them for current utility rates. Even some new houses do not have insulation in the exterior walls. Be sure to check.

2. *Consider the need for additional insulation or replacement of equipment*. If improvements are necessary, you may want to seek an adjustment in the purchase price to cover all, or a reasonable share, of the costs.

APPLIANCE LABELING PROGRAM

This labeling program is designed to help consumers shop for energy-saving household appliances and equipment. It is being developed by the Federal Department of Energy and the Federal Trade Commission as a result of the Energy Policy and Conservation Act, signed into law on December 22, 1975.

Under that law, manufacturers must place labels showing estimated annual operating costs on all models of the following:

Central air-conditioners
Clothes dryers
Clothes washers
Dishwashers
Freezers

Furnaces

Home heating equipment, not including furnaces

Humidifiers and dehumidifiers

Kitchen ranges and ovens

Refrigerators and refrigerator-freezers

Room air-conditioners

Television sets

Water heaters

Energy-Efficiency Ratios for Air-Conditioners. If you are in the market for a room air-conditioner before the new labels are in place, you should be aware of the *energy efficiency ratio numbers* that were developed for these appliances during an earlier voluntary appliance labeling program. They may still be in use in your community.

The Energy Efficiency Ratio (EER) is a number that rates the energy efficiency of similar appliances. The higher the EER number, the more efficient the appliance. The EER numbers are approved by the U.S. Department of Commerce's National Bureau of Standards before they are used.

Example: EER's for room air-conditioners can be as low as 5.4 and as high as 11.5. The 11.5-rated room air-conditioner is more than twice as efficient as the 5.4 unit and uses less than half the electrical energy.

Manufacturer and dealers display the EER numbers in different ways. If you cannot find the EER number of the models you are considering, you should be able to get the information from the dealer.

Chapter 46

How to Insulate Your Home for Electric Heating and Air Conditioning

The use of thermal insulation, properly specified and installed, has long been recognized as the most rewarding of all means of saving energy and money, and enhancing comfort, in homes of all types and during all seasons of the year. Now, persistent escalation in the cost of energy, regardless of its form, has intensified the appreciation of insulation's benefits. Federal and state governments, public service commissions, utility companies, and consumer-interest groups are recommending the installation of insulation in greater amounts than ever before.

TYPES OF MINERAL WOOL

Mineral wool is inorganic. According to federal specifications, it "shall be made from mineral substances such as rock, slag, or glass processed from a molten state into an incombustible form." Batts and blankets are available with attached vapor barriers or unfaced. Loose fill mineral wool is meant to be blown or poured into the space to be insulated.

Thermal resistance values for insulation in both new and existing construction are shown in Table 35.

Slab-on-Grade Insulation. The edges of concrete slabs on grade should be insulated to these R-values: more than 8,000 heating degree days per year, R-8; 4,500 to 8,000 degree days, R-6; fewer than 4,500 degree days, R-4.

Determining Thermal Performance. How well insulation will resist the flow of heat is determined accurately only by resistance (R) values, which are printed prominently on all mineral wool insulation

TABLE 35
THERMAL RESISTANCE OF INSULATION

	Ceilings[1]	Walls[2]		Floors Over Vented Crawl Spaces	Floors Over Unheated Basements	Floors and Walls Between Separately Heated Units[3]
		New Const.	Existing Const.			
ELECTRIC HEATING						
Degree Days/Year						
Over 5500	30	18	11	19	19	11
3500 – 5500	30	18	11	19	11	11
Under 3500	19	11	11	19	11	11
ELECTRIC COOLING						
All climates	30	18	11	19	11	11

[1]Under some conditions, according to EEI, R-38 ceiling insulation, rather than the R-value listed, may be advantageous.

[2]Insulation with a thermal resistance of R-18 is not a standard product. Ways of achieving that resistance value are explained on Page 10. In homes with heated basements, basement walls should be insulated to a minimum value of R-11.

[3]Including walls between heated and unheated portions of a basement.

packages and vapor barriers. The greater the R value, the greater the insulating value.

WHERE TO INSULATE A HOME

(Numbers refer to Fig. 1 and 2.)

1. Exterior walls. Sections sometimes overlooked are the wall between living space and an unheated garage or storage room, dormer walls, and the portion of wall above the ceiling of an adjacent lower section of a split-level home.

2. Ceilings with cold spaces above, including dormer ceilings.

3. Knee walls when attic space is finished as living quarters.

4. Between collar beams and rafters, leaving open space above for ventilation.

5. The perimeter of a slab on grade.

6. Floors above vented crawl spaces. When a crawl space is used as a plenum, insulation is applied to crawl space walls instead of the above floor.

7. Floors over an unheated or open space such as over a garage or a porch. Floors over unheated basements. The cantilevered portion of a floor.

8. Basement walls when below-grade space is finished for living purposes.

9. Band or header joists and the wall sections at floor levels.

Although they are not shown, common walls and floors between separately heated apartment or townhouse units should be insulated. In addition to its thermal effect, the insulation aids in sound attenuation and fire resistance.

GUIDELINES FOR INSTALLING MINERAL WOOL BLANKETS

1. Install insulation so the vapor barrier side faces the living space of the home.

2. Insulate all large and small spaces of the building section.

3. Place insulation on the outside of pipes and ducts.

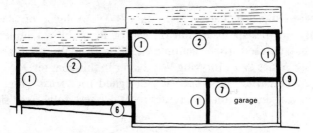

Fig. 1. Where to insulate.

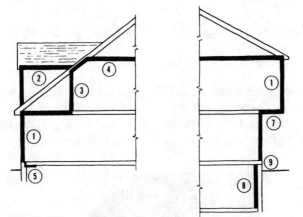

Fig. 2. Where to insulate.

4. Staple flanges snugly against the sides of framing members.

5. Repair rips or tears in the vapor barrier by stapling vapor barrier material over the tear or taping the torn barrier back into place.

6. When two layers of batts or blankets are being installed in a ceiling, unfaced (no vapor barrier) insulation should be used as the top layer. If faced insulation is used, the vapor barrier should be slashed freely with a knife.

7. In habitable spaces, vapor barriers should always be covered with standard finish material.

Insulating Ceilings. Two layers of mineral wool batts or blankets, or R-22 or R-30 batts, may be used to achieve recommended thermal resistance values greater than R-19. A layer of blanket insulation with blown insulation on top of it, or blown mineral wool alone, may be used. (*See* section on Ceiling Insulation and section on Insulating Attics With Blowing Wool later in this chapter.)

In new construction, a specially designed roof truss (Fig. 3) permits applying insulation of any desired thickness fully over sidewalls.

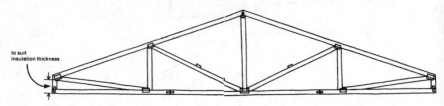

to suit
insulation thickness

Fig. 3. Roof truss.

Mineral wool batts and blankets are installed in ceilings by stapling vapor barrier flanges from below (Fig. 4), installing unfaced blankets between joists or bottom chords of trusses (Fig. 5), or laying the insulation in from above after the ceiling is in place (Fig. 6).

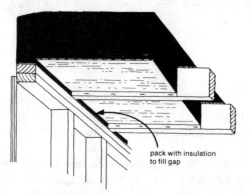

pack with insulation
to fill gap

Fig. 4. Installing mineral wool batts and blankets in ceilings.

With two layers of insulation (Fig. 4), the top layer may be installed crosswise to the bottom layer.

When thick blankets (R-19, R-22, or R-30) are installed in roof truss construction (Fig. 5), the blankets will normally expand above

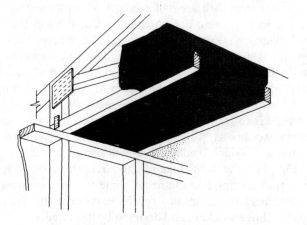

Fig. 5. Installing unfaced blankets.

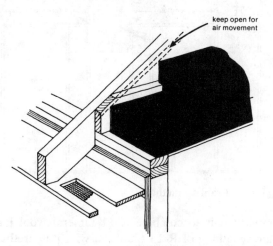

keep open for
air movement

Fig. 6. Use of batt insulation in joist and
rafter construction.

the bottom chord sufficiently to meet and close the gap, except where
truss webs meet the chord. Filling any voids with loose mineral wool
is recommended.

Figure 6 shows two layers of batt insulation in joist-and-rafter
constructions. If there are eaves vents, the insulation should not ob-

struct the ventilation path. A baffle board of scrap lumber may be used as a retainer. If there are no eaves vents, the top layer should be pushed tightly against the sheathing. The wedge-shaped space above the end of the bottom layer may be filled with loose wool.

Insulating Frame Walls.   Many recommended thermal resistance values for sidewalls cannot be achieved with conventional construction. Either of two advanced building methods can be used.

One method is to frame the wall with six-inch lumber, then install R-19 mineral wool batts, which have a resistance of R-18 when compressed into a 5½-inch (nominal 6-inch) stud space. A framing method (Fig. 7) takes advantage of the strength of six-inch lumber to increase stud spacing and eliminate some framing members. Note that plywood headers are applied on the exterior of the framing, allowing spaces above windows and doors to be insulated.

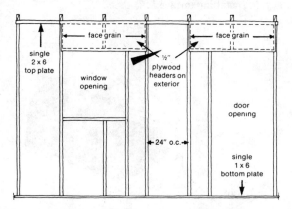

Fig. 7. Framing method.

Another method is to combine R-11 mineral wool blankets with polyurethane sheathing of R-13 blankets, with polyurethane or polystyrene sheathing of appropriate thermal resistance value (Fig. 8).

To install batts or blankets in a stud cavity, push them against the exterior sheathing. Insulation with a vapor barrier may be stapled to the sides of the studs (Fig. 9) or to the faces of the studs (Fig. 10). Use enough staples to hold the vapor barrier flanges snugly against the wood. Blanket ends should be cut to fit tightly against the plates without stapling or the vapor barrier may be pulled to the plates and stapled.

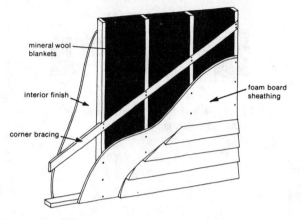

Fig. 8. Combining mineral wool blankets with poly-urethane sheathing.

Fig. 9. Insulating stud cavity.

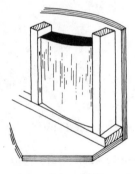

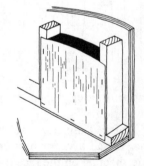

Fig. 10.

When pieces of blanket meet within a stud space, they may be butted together and the joint taped (recommended for blankets with vapor barriers) or the top section may be applied to overlap the bottom one or two inches or more (recommended only for unfaced R-11 blankets).

Insulation should be installed behind pipes and ducts. The space behind an electrical box should be packed with loose mineral wool. Then the blanket should be cut to fit neatly against the box at top, the bottom, and the exposed side (Fig. 11).

Small spaces between rough framing and windows and doors should be packed with loose mineral wool (Fig. 12). Insulation

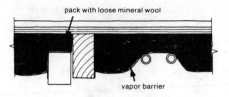

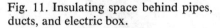

Fig. 11. Insulating space behind pipes,
ducts, and electric box.

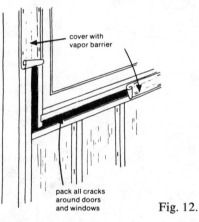

Fig. 12.

vapor barrier paper or polyethylene should be stapled over the
insulation.

Unfaced mineral wool blankets should fit tightly against all framing. Install a vapor barrier by stapling .08 inch-or-thicker polyethylene sheeting on the face of the studs (Fig. 13). A foil-backed gypsum
board may be used instead.

Insulating Masonry Walls.   The preferred method of insulating
a masonry wall of any type, above or below grade, is to build a frame
wall of 2 × 3 studs, 24 inches oc with 1 × 3 top and bottom plates,
set one inch in from the masonry (Fig. 14). Plates are nailed, top
and bottom, to joists (or blocking between joists) and the floor. R-11
or R-13 insulation is installed as in any other wall.

Insulating Floors and Crawl Space Walls.   To insulate floors
above vented crawl spaces or other cold spaces, push R-19 batts or
blankets, with vapor barriers up, tightly against the subflooring above
(Fig. 15). Hold the insulation in place with stiff, pointed, wire fast-

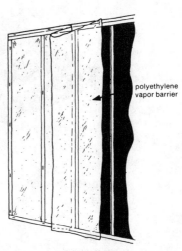

polyethylene
vapor barrier

Fig. 13. Use of polyethylene sheeting.

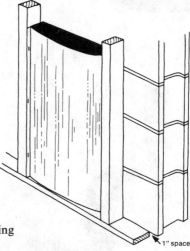

1" space

Fig. 14. Method used for insulating
masonry wall.

eners cut slightly longer than joist spacing. The wires are installed
by jamming one end into each joist, letting the wire bow upward.
An alternative method is to lace flexible wire underneath the joists.

Install R-11 blankets as in Fig. 16. An end of the blanket is
turned up to insulate the header joist; a piece of blanket cut to fit may
be used instead.

To insulate crawl space walls (Fig. 17), first lay a ground cover

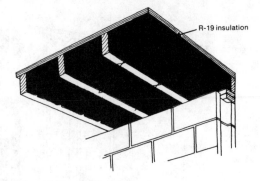

R-19 insulation

Fig. 15. Insulating floors.

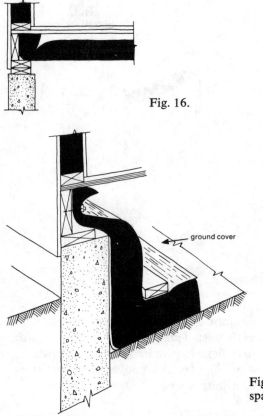

Fig. 16.

ground cover

Fig. 17. Insulating crawl space walls.

of polyethylene, lapping adjoining strips at least two inches and taping the edges to foundation walls. Then, using wood nailing strips, nail one end of blanket insulation to the header joist, making sure that the insulation touches the subflooring above. Drape the blanket down the wall and extend it two feet along the crawl space floor. Hold the blanket in place at the wall-floor joint with scrap lumber, bricks, or rocks.

INSTALLING MINERAL WOOL BLANKETS AND PERIMETER INSULATION

Insulating Slab Perimeters and Overhangs.   In slab-on-grade construction, perimeter insulation is installed as in Fig. 18, with the horizontal insulation extending two feet back from the slab edge. An alternative method is to apply the insulation vertically on the outside of the foundation wall, with appropriate protective exterior facing; the insulation should extend to the frostline, but at least two feet down from the top of the slab.

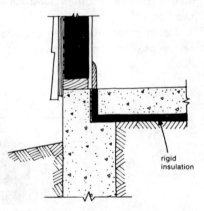

rigid insulation

Fig. 18. Insulating slab perimeters.

Cantilevered overhangs (Fig. 19) are insulated either with R-19 batts (righthand portion of drawing) or with R-11 blankets. With R-11 insulation, the band joist should be insulated to its full depth with a piece of blanket cut to size before the horizontal blanket is laid in place. An alternative is to turn the end of the blanket up as in Fig. 16.

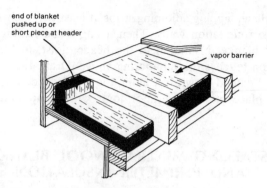

Fig. 19. Insulating cantilevered overhangs.

Insulating Ceilings with Blowing Wool.   Blowing wool should be installed by an experienced contractor to ensure proper density, coverage, and thickness and to be certain all hollow spaces are filled. Pouring wool may be applied in unfinished attic areas by emptying the bags between ceiling joists, paying attention to the manufacturer's instructions and recommendations as to proper thickness, and coverage per bag.

Be sure that eaves vents are not blocked. A way to shield these openings is shown in Fig. 20.

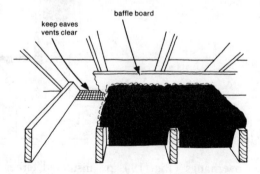

Fig. 20. Shielding eaves vents.

Small openings, such as those around a chimney, should be hand packed with mineral wool.

Cavities, drops, and scuttles should be covered with insulation, or sides and bottoms should be insulated.

Recessed lighting fixtures and fan motors protruding into the ceiling should not be covered with insulation, and insulation should be held three inches away from their sides. The purpose is to prevent overheating of the fixture.

In floored attics, floor boards may be removed as required for access to the space to be insulated. Check for obstructions, such as bridging and conduit.

Insulating Attics with Blowing Wool. When blowing wool is used to insulate attic rooms (Fig. 21), the collar beam area and the floor areas at the sides are blown in the normal manner. If the space is insufficient for the needed depth of blowing wool, batts may be used instead. Knee walls and rafters are insulated with blankets. Space for ventilation should be maintained between rafter insulation and roof sheathing.

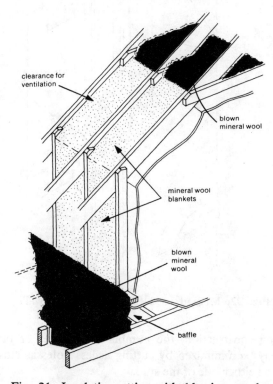

clearance for
ventilation

blown
mineral wool

mineral wool
blankets

blown
mineral
wool

baffle

Fig. 21. Insulating attics with blowing wool.

Insulating Sidewalls with Blowing Wool.   All exterior wall areas should be insulated.

Whenever the vertical space to be insulated is more than four feet high, the *double blow* method, with at least two access holes to each stud space, should be used. Check each space with a plumb bob for possible obstructions within the wall. Details of the insulating method are shown in Fig. 22.

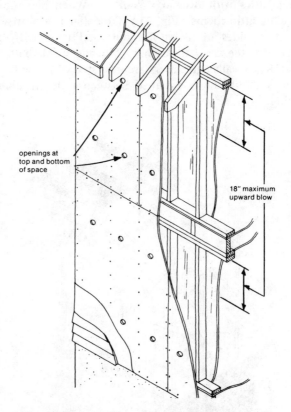

openings at
top and bottom
of space

18" maximum
upward blow

Fig. 22. Method used for insulating sidewalls.

In existing construction, the number of shingles or bricks to be removed may be minimized by cutting access holes as close together as possible on either side of the stud.

VAPOR PROTECTION

Vapor Barriers.   Vapor barriers should be placed on the warm side of walls, ceilings, and floors (those heated in winter). The materials used as membrane coverings on mineral wool blankets do not completely bar moisture vapor transmission. A vapor barrier is considered to have a vapor permeance of not more than one perm. Consequently, the materials commonly called vapor barriers are really vapor-resistant membranes. *Vapor-barrier* is used here because it is a conventional term in construction. It is recommended that vapor barriers having a flame spread greater than 200 be marked with the following statement: "This vapor barrier is flammable and should not be left exposed. Special care should be taken when working close to the facing with an open flame."

Where no vapor barrier is attached to the insulation, separate vapor barriers are necessary. These materials are satisfactory:

1. Polyethylene sheeting, .08 inch or thicker in walls and ceiling, and thicker as ground covers under slabs or over crawl space earth.
2. Foil-backed gypsum board.
3. Waterproof, laminated asphalt-coated paper.

Any vapor barrier damaged during installation should be repaired by replacing the damaged section or mending it with tape.

When blown insulation is to be used in new work, continuous vapor barriers should be applied to the underside of ceiling joists where specified and to the inside of wall studs. The barrier should be brought tightly against electrical outlets, registers, door and window frames, and other openings.

In existing houses, vapor protection may be obtained by painting interior walls and ceilings with two coats of vapor-resistant paint. If blankets with vapor barriers are to be installed on top of existing insulation in an attic floor, the vapor barriers should be removed or slashed freely with a knife, and the blankets should be laid in place with the vapor barriers facing down.

VENTING ATTICS AND CRAWL SPACES

Ventilation.   Attic vents should meet the following minimum requirements.

Gable vents only. (*See* Fig. 23.)

With vapor barrier—one square foot inlet and one square foot outlet for each 600 square feet of ceiling area.

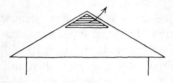

Fig. 23. Use of gable vents.

Without vapor barrier—one square foot inlet and one square foot outlet for each 300 square feet of ceiling area.

Combination of eaves and gable vents (no vapor barrier). (*See* Fig. 24.)

One square foot inlet and one square outlet for each 600 square feet of ceiling area, with at least half of the vent area at the top of the gables and the balance at the eaves. Continuous ridge vent may be used instead of gable louvers.

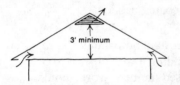

Fig. 24. Use of combination of eaves and gable vents.

Minimum requirements for crawl space vents are as follows: (*See* Fig. 25.)

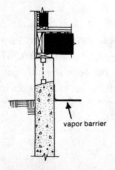

Fig. 25. Use of crawl space vents.

With ground cover—at least two vents are required, one near each of two diagonally opposite corners, with one square foot of vent area for each 1,500 square feet of crawl space.

Without ground cover—at least four vents are required, one near each corner of the space, with one square foot of vent area for each 150 square feet of crawl space.

SAFETY PRECAUTIONS

If you are installing insulation yourself, by all means follow the instructions which most insulation manufacturers provide for their products.

Here are a few safety precautions for do-it-yourselfers.

1. Provide good lighting while you work.

2. If the attic is not floored, lay boards or plywood sheets down over the tops of joists or trusses to make a walkway (the ceiling cannot be trusted to support the weight of even a slightly-built person).

3. Be careful of roofing nails protruding through the roof sheathing.

4. Wear gloves, eye protection (such as goggles or glasses), a breathing mask, loose-fitting old clothes, with a long-sleeved shirt, buttoned at the wrists. Hard hats should be worn and a respirator used.

5. Keep the insulation material wrapped until you are ready to use it.

6. *Be fire-conscious.* If you are installing insulation around electrical wires, do not pull or twist these wires. Carefully handpack insulation around electrical cables. Allow at least three inches between insulation and any recessed lighting fixture or any kind of heat-producing equipment, and a space of at least two feet above an electrical unit.

7. Use *only* materials certified as resistant to all types of corrosion and infestation.

Appendix I

Common Abbreviations

AC	Alternating current
BTU	British thermal unit
BTU'S $\times$ 10^6	Millions of Btu's
BTU'S $\times$ 10^3	Thousands of Btu's
CFM	Cubic feet per minute
COP	Coefficient of performance
CU	Coefficient of utilization
DB	Dry bulb temperature
DC	Direct current
DX	Direct expansion
EMF	Electromotive force
ESI	Equivalent sphere illumination
HID	High intensity discharge (lamps)
HVAC	Heating, ventilating, and air conditioning
HZ	Hertz
KVA	Kilovoltampere
KW	Kilowatt
KWH	Kilowatt hour
OA	Outside air
PF	Power factor
PSI	Pounds per square inch
PSIG	Pounds per square inch gage
SQ. FT.	Square foot
TD	Temperature difference
TE	Total energy (system)
WB	Wet bulb temperature

Appendix II

Energy Conservation

Leave your *dial down* set for night-time operation only or, to save even more energy and heating costs, readjust the dial so the system works while no one is at home. Depending on your geographical location, the following chart shows the approximate savings that you can realize by using the dial down. Each setback period is of eight hours duration.

The dial down also works with air conditioning systems. Just set your home thermostat to 80° F. (or higher). Set the timer to turn the dial down on when cooling is desired (one hour before getting home). The higher the dial down is set the more the thermostat is fooled and the cooler the room gets (up to approximately 11° F. below the thermostat setting). When the timer shuts the dial down off, the room temperature will return to the thermostat setting. *Example:* Set your home thermostat at 80° F. and set the dial down to turn on one hour before you return home. This way your air conditioner will not turn on unless the temperature inside your home gets to 80° F. One hour before you get home, the dial down will activate, making the thermostat think it is warmer in the house than it really is. Your air conditioner will then turn on, cooling your house down to 69° F. (when dial down is set on High). You will return to a cool home and, because your air conditioner did not run during the day, you will have saved energy and money.

There is a myth that says you will not save energy by turning down your thermostat at night because it takes so much energy to warm the building in the morning: This is untrue. Setting the thermostat back for several hours at a stretch each day during the heating season and up during the cooling season will, in a centrally heated and cooled building, save energy. Depending on your geographical location, the amount of energy you can save will range from 9 to 15 percent of what you used before adopting this energy-conserving habit.

ENERGY CONSERVATION

City	Nighttime Setback from 65°F. * Percentage Saved with Setback of —		Daytime AND Nighttime Setback Daytime Setback from 72°F. to 68°F. Nighttime Setback from 68°F. to 60°F. ** Percentage Savings
	5°F.	10°F.	
Atlanta, GA	11	15	20
Boston, MA	7	11	12
Buffalo, NY	6	10	10
Chicago, IL	7	11	11
Cincinnati, OH	8	12	14
Cleveland, OH	8	12	12
Columbus, OH	7	11	12
Dallas, TX	11	15	23
Denver, CO	7	11	12
Des Moines, IA	7	11	10
Detroit, MI	7	11	11
Kansas City, MO	8	12	14
Louisville, KY	9	13	15
Madison, WI	5	9	9
Milwaukee, WI	6	10	9
Minneapolis, MN	5	9	8
New York, NY	8	12	14
Omaha, NE	7	11	12
Philadelphia, PA	8	12	14
Pittsburgh, PA	7	11	13
Portland, OR	9	13	15
Salt Lake City, UT	7	11	12
San Francisco, CA	10	14	22
Seattle, WA	8	12	15
St. Louis, MO	8	12	14
Syracuse, NY	7	11	11
Washington, DC	9	13	15

* "Energy Savings Through Automatic Thermostat Controls" Energy Research and Development Administration, Washington D.C. 20545.

** "The Energy Conservation Potential of Winter Thermostat Reductions and Night Setback" Oak Ridge National Laboratory, Oak Ridge, Tenn. 37830.

There are two ways you can accomplish temperature setback and setup: (1) by adjusting the thermostat manually at the proper times, or (2) by installing a device that makes the adjustments automatically. The manual technique requires no special equipment, but it does demand a greater degree of daily time and attention than many people are willing to put forth. An automatic control device, on the other hand, involves some initial investment, but this outlay is more than repaid in dependability and energy savings over a period of time.

Setback Device. The exact energy and cost savings from a setback device (Figs. 1 and 2) are dependent on building design,

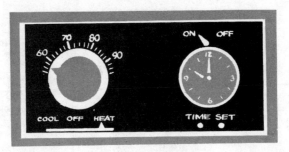

Fig. 1. Replacement setback device.

amount of insulation, climate, temperature setting, and utility rate structures. Several studies have been conducted to estimate the fuel and cost savings that can be realized by using a setback device during both the heating and cooling seasons. The chart shown represents the approximate percentage of your heating costs that can be saved in various cities throughout the country for an eight-hour night-time thermostat setback of 5° F. and 10° F.

How to Estimate Cost Savings. From the chart you can estimate what you are likely to save by automatically setting back your thermostat during the heating season from 65° F. to 55° F. (you could save as much as 11 percent of $300, or $33 a heating season). These estimated figures are based on an assumed day-time setting of 65° F.

Types of Automatic Controls. Two types of automatic controls are now available on the commercial market. One is a device that works with a conventional thermostat. The other type requires replacing the existing thermostat.

Converter setback device. This type of control converts any existing thermostat to a timed device. Several variations are available. One is a two-component system in which a temperature control is mounted below the existing thermostat and is connected by wires to a separate timer unit that is plugged into a wall outlet. If the wires carry low voltage current, they can be concealed in the wall, if desired, but 110-volt power cords cannot be so concealed. Another is a single-unit device that is attached to the wall below the thermostat and is either plugged into a nearby wall outlet or operated by self-contained batteries. (*See* Fig. 2.)

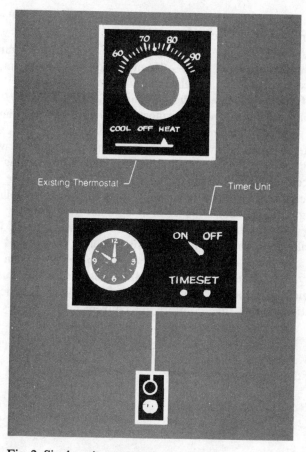

Fig. 2. Single unit converter setback device.

Replacement setback device. This type of control replaces the conventional thermostat entirely and is generally wired to the building's electrical system and heating/cooling system. Several types are available, but this type of device is usually more expensive to buy and costly to install, since it usually requires additional wiring in existing walls. Its main advantage is that, having all its wires hidden, it gives a neater appearance. (*See* Fig. 1.)

Automatic setback devices are sold in many hardware and department stores as well as building material outlets. In general, converter types sell for less than replacement types and can be installed by a do-it-yourselfer. Most converters retail for less than $40 whereas the initial cost plus the cost of installing a replacement unit may range from $75 to over $100—depending on the model and type, and the extent of installation labor required.

A No-Cost Alternative to the Automatic Setback Device.   You can continue to adjust your thermostat by hand, morning and evening, or whenever leaving your home or business for an extended period of time, and still achieve the same energy savings as with an automatic setback device. Manual setting costs you nothing. However, since the automatic setback device pays for itself rather quickly and will continue to return savings for years to come, you might prefer the regularity and convenience of an automatic control.

Saving Energy with an Automatic Setback Device.   If you are responsible for the operation of a heating/cooling system and occupy a home, apartment, office, store, or factory where the system is controlled by a wall thermostat, you should consider an automatic setback device as a tool for saving fuel and money. The benefits are conservation, cost savings, comfort, and convenience.

Appendix III

Heating With Oil—Servicing Cuts Cost and Pollution

In several studies of residential heating equipment (warm air furnaces and boilers) sponsored by government and industry, it has been found that homeowners can save money and reduce pollution by having their oil burners serviced annually.

Oil Burning Equipment Serviced Annually. The amount of money a homeowner could save will vary depending on the geographical location, present condition of the heating equipment, the price of fuel, and other factors. For example, a homeowner burning 1,300 gallons of oil per year in a very inefficient heating system could save $260 in fuel costs at a price of 80 cents per gallon with proper servicing. This is a 25 percent saving in the total fuel bill as the efficiency of the oil burner is increased from 60 to 80 percent.

Pollution Reduction. In a recent study it was found that by identifying and replacing non-tuneable units, carbon monoxide (CO) was reduced by more than 65 percent, gaseous hydrocarbons (HC) were reduced by 87 percent, and filterable particulate was reduced by 17 percent. By tuning the remaining burners in addition to replacing non-tuneable units, the total reductions were as follows: smoke—59 percent, CO—81 percent, HC—90 percent, and filterable particulate —24 percent.

Service. Many people do not call for service until the heating equipment fails. Unless this occurs during normal working hours, the homeowner will usually have to pay for the service at higher hourly rates. By having annual maintenance during the summer months, unexpected equipment failures are less likely to occur. Also, burner performance can deteriorate over a period of time. Nozzles and oil filters should be replaced annually to ensure proper burner performance.

It is recommended that a qualified oil burner service technician service the oil burner equipment. When nozzles are changed the excess air level normally needs to be adjusted. To do this properly, special instruments are used to measure the following:

1. Carbon dioxide (CO_2).
2. Flue gas temperature in the stack.
3. Smoke number.
4. Stack draft.

Most homeowners do not have access to the equipment needed to make these measurements and may not know how to use the equipment properly. Also, the service technician has a better understanding of how to diagnose problems that may be encountered, and should be familiar with any safety codes or standards that apply to the heating equipment.

The furnace owner should inspect air filters monthly during the heating season and change them as necessary. This should be done at least twice during the heating season, and more often in some cases. Dirty filters reduce furnace efficiency.

Furnace Inspection to Determine Vacuuming. Furnace vacuuming should be done periodically. Soot serves as an insulator and significantly reduces the amount of heat transferred to the house. Therefore, when needed, vacuuming can save the homeowner in fuel costs. Depending on the smoke level, a furnace may need vacuuming yearly or as infrequently as once every five years. Ask the service technician for a furnace inspection to determine whether vacuuming is needed. If the burner is properly maintained by keeping the smoke number below No. 2, the furnace should not require vacuuming very often.

Values of CO_2. A new oil burner with a properly matched furnace or boiler should operate with a minimum of 10 percent CO_2 at a maximum smoke number of 1. The following table provides a general range for a typical (gun-type) oil burner.

Combustion-Efficiency. An efficiency of 80 percent or above is excellent. This means 80 percent of the heat received from the oil goes into the house, while only 20 percent is lost to the atmosphere. Seventy-five to 79 percent is good, 70 to 74 percent is fair, and below 70 percent is poor. If the efficiency is below 70 percent, the burner should be readjusted. If an efficiency of 70 percent or better cannot be achieved or if adjustment increases the smoke number significantly, the burner should be replaced. The savings in fuel cost will offset the cost of the burner over a period of time.

If your service technician does not measure the CO_2, smoke number, stack temperature, and draft, request the company to send another technician who can and will make the measurements. If the company cannot provide proper service, it is recommended that you find a company that can. These measurements are essential for proper burner servicing.

TABLE

CO_2 (percent)	11	Excellent
	9	Average
	6	Poor
Smoke spot	0	Excellent
number	1	Excellent
	2	Good
	3	Average for untuned burners
	4	Poor
	5 or higher	Unacceptable
Net stack*	400 to 600	Average for original equipment**
Temperature	600 to 700	Average for replacement burner**
(° F.)		
Stack draft	0.04 to 0.06	Average for non-forced draft units.
(A measure of		For forced units and other types,
inches of water		follow recommendation of manu-
on gage)		facturer.

* Net stack temperature is actual stack temperature minus furnace room temperature.
** Higher temperatures require adjustment.

Keep the following chart near your furnace or boiler so that measurements can be entered during each service visit.

Burner Service Record

Date	CO$_2$ %	Smoke No.	Stack Temp.	Stack Draft	Efficiency %

Appendix IV

Electricity and Natural Gas Public Utilities

State agencies regulate both electricity and natural gas public utilities. If you have a complaint or question about the legal rates a utility company charges for electricity or natural gas, contact the utility commission in your state capital. Since these agencies have public hearings before permitting a utility to increase its rates, you and other consumers have a chance to make your views known. Also, you may want to get more information about surcharges or fuel adjustment charges added to utility bills.

The Environmental Action Foundation has names, addresses, and telephone numbers of state utility regulatory commissions. It also has information about private organizations that represent consumers or help consumers in dealing with these commissions. For the list of commissions and utility organizations in your state, write to Environmental Action Foundation, 724 Dupont Circle Building, Washington, D.C. 20046, or call 202-659-9682.

For information about taxes on utility bills, first contact your local government's tax office. That office can explain the local utility tax, if any, and direct you to other government offices that tax bills.

READING ELECTRIC AND GAS METERS

With utilities taking a larger chunk of everyone's monthly budget, it makes sense to understand how to read your gas and electric meters. You can keep tabs on your own conservation of energy and also double-check the utility companies' bills. (*See* Figs. 1, 2, 3, and 4.)

Checking Electric Meter. The electricity you use is measured in kilowatt-hours (kwh). (A watt is a measure of electricity and a kilowatt is 1,000 watts.) You will use one kwh of electricity if you leave a 100-watt light bulb burning for 10 hours.

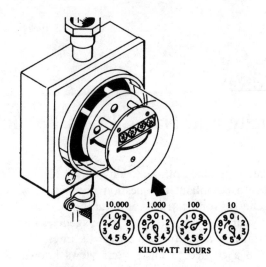

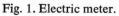

Fig. 1. Electric meter.

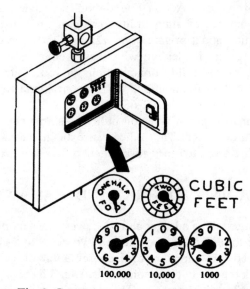

Fig. 2. Gas meter.

Each dial on your meter shows that you have used a certain number of kwh of electricity. (*See* Fig. 1.)

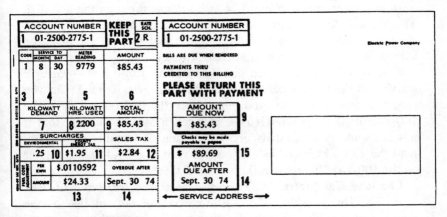

Fig. 3. Sample electric bill.

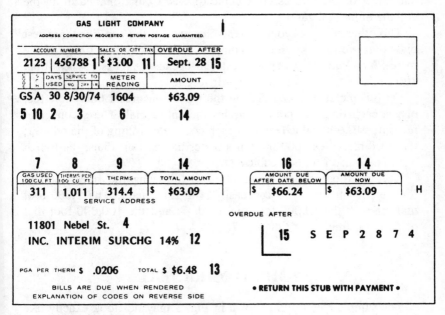

Fig. 4. Sample gas bill.

Always start to read your meter with the first dial on the right (Fig. 1); it measures a total of 10 kwh. Each time the pointer moves from one number to another on this first dial, you have used one kwh.

In the meter shown in Fig. 1, 4 kwh are measured on the first dial. The second dial on this meter—measuring a total of 100 kwh—shows that 80 kwh have been used. (Note that some of the dials run clockwise, while others run counterclockwise.)

When you check the third dial—measuring 1,000 kwh—you will see that the pointer is barely a hair's-breadth away from 5. Do you read this as 5 or 4? First you must check the dial on the right, the 100-kwh dial. Its pointer is now between 8 and 9, showing that it has not quite completed its present circling of the dial. Thus, you read the 1,000-kwh dial as 4. You will read it as 5 after the pointer on the 100-kwh dial reaches 0.

Checking Gas Meter.   Your gas meter has two types of dials (Fig. 2). The recording dials—shown on the bottom line of the meter shown in Fig. 2—are the ones that measure the amount of cubic feet of gas you use. (A cubic foot is a unit for measuring the volume of natural gas.)

The other dials on your meter—the two on the top line—are test dials that are used by the gas company to check the accuracy of the meter. You can always spot a test dial because it measures less than 100 cubic feet, and you can always ignore it.

On this meter, the first dial on the right measures 1,000 cubic feet of gas each time the pointer circles the entire dial. The second dial measures 10,000 cubic feet with each complete circling of the pointer; the third measures 100,000. On a meter having four dials, the fourth would measure 1 million cubic feet.

Keeping those figures in mind—and following the rules outlined for electric meters—you can easily read this meter. The 1,000-foot dial reads 7; the 10,000-foot dial reads 7; and the 100,000-foot dial reads 1. The meter reading is 177.

YOUR ELECTRIC BILL

The sample electric bill shown in Fig. 3 may not look exactly like the one you receive in the mail, but it probably includes many of the same items that appear on your own bill. Although utility rates, taxes, and other charges vary in different communities, this sample should help to explain your bill. If you still have questions, call your local electric company. Their consumer service department can answer•your questions and may also be able to send you a sample bill that will explain the exact items for which you are charged. (Numbers listed below describe numbered items on sample bill Fig. 3.)

1. This is the number of the consumer's account with the electric company. Use it for identification when making an inquiry or paying a bill.

2. This code indicates the rate schedule that is used in billing the consumer. This rate is usually not shown on the bill; but you do need to know what it is if you want to compute your own bill. You can find the rate at which you are charged by calling your electric company. Usually, electric rates are set on a sliding scale, with the rate per kilowatt-hour (kwh) decreasing as you use more kwh of electricity.

3. This code indicates the kind of bill this is—a regular monthly bill or an adjustment bill. The code is explained on the reverse side of the bill.

4. Cut-off date for billing.

5. Meter reading on which a bill is based. You can double-check this figure by reading your meter the same day the electric company reads it. This should be the cut-off date (*see* item 4); call the company to learn your cut-off date each month.

6. Consumer's monthly charge for electricity.

7. This applies only to commercial installations using more than 6,000 kwh per month.

8. To verify the kwh for which you are charged, subtract last month's reading (item 5 on last month's bill) from item 5 on this month's bill.

9. This is the total of the following items on the bill: item 8 multiplied by the rates charged per kwh; item 10; item 11; item 12; and item 13. (*See* section on Adding It All Up.)

10. This state's residents pay an environmental surcharge—collected for the state by the electric company—that helps defray costs of deciding where to locate electric plants.

11. This county levies an energy tax that is collected for the county by the electric company.

12. State sales tax of four percent.

13. The fuel cost adjustment is a *pass-through charge* that represents the electric company's increased costs for the coal and oil

used to generate electricity. This state's utility commission allows the electric company to pass along its increased costs to the consumer. The fuel cost increase is figured as a certain amount per kwh (on this bill, it is $.0110592, slightly over 1¢ per kwh). Multiply that figure by kwh used to get fuel cost adjustment ($24.33 on this bill).

    14. Date after which bill is overdue.

    15. After overdue date, an additional five percent is added to the bill.

For a detailed explanation of the steps to take in computing your own electric bill, *see* section Adding It All Up.

YOUR GAS BILL

When you receive your next gas bill take a few minutes to find out exactly what it is telling you. You might even take time to compare it with last month's bill—and with last year's bills if you still have them (you should). How much energy are you using these days? Have you cut down during the past year? If so, are you saving money, as well as energy?

The sample bill shown in Fig. 4 should guide you through your own bill. If you have further questions, call your local gas company. (Numbers listed below describe numbered items on sample bill.)

    1. Consumer's account number.

    2. Shows how many days' service are covered by bill.

    3. Cut-off date for billing.

    4. Gas service for consumer's home is connected to plant at this address.

    5. Code indicating charges covered by bill—gas usage, fee for repairs or merchandise. Code is explained on reverse side of bill.

    6. Meter reading on which bill is based.

    7. This is the quantity of gas—expressed in hundreds of cubic feet—that went through the meter during the billing period. This number should equal the difference between this month's meter reading (item 6) and last month's meter reading.

    8. This tells how many therms (therm is a measure of heat

energy) were supplied in the average 100 cubic feet of gas during the billing period. A therm is a significant measure for you because consumers of gas are charged by the therm, not by the cubic foot of gas.

9. This shows how many therms the consumer is being charged for. This figure is arrived at by multiplying item 7 by item 8.

10. Code for rate schedule that applies to this consumer's type of gas service; rate schedules are built on sliding scales. To learn how much you are being charged per therm of gas, telephone your gas company.

11. Sales tax of five percent.

12. This item represents an increase in the consumer's bill—a 14 percent interim surcharge granted to the company by the utility commission, until the commission has time to rule on the company's request for an increased rate schedule.

13. This is a *pass-through charge* reflecting increases in the wholesale costs paid for gas by the gas company. (*See* item 13, Your electric bill.) These increases in wholesale costs are passed on to the consumer in the form of an additional charge—a *purchase gas adjustment charge* (PGA)—for each therm of gas used. Here, the charge per therm is $.026 (slightly over two cents)—a total of $6.48 for 314.4 therms.

14. The amount of the bill is the total of the following items: item 9 multiplied by the rates charged per therm; item 11; item 12; item 13.

15. Date after which bill is overdue.

16. After overdue date, an additional five percent is added to the bill.

ADDING IT ALL UP

Do you know how to figure your monthly electric costs? First, of course, you should learn how to read your electric meter. (*See* Fig. 1.) Also see Fig. 1 on how to understand all the items on your electric bill. You will also need the rate schedule used by your local electric company. (*See* Fig. 1.) Then you can figure your electric costs by following the step-by-step procedure outlined here. (Numbers in parentheses refer to items on sample electric bill.)

First, take your meter reading, doing it the same day the electric company reads it.

Today's meter reading: 9,779.

Second, figure out how many kilowatts you have used since the previous month's reading. Remember, your electric meter gives a cumulative reading. To find kwh used for the current month (item 8), subtract last month's meter reading from today's reading (item 5).

Today's meter reading:	9,779
Last month's reading:	−7,579
Kwh used this month	2,200

Third, figure your costs for kwh used, on the basis of the rate schedule now in use by your electric company.

(The following figures are based on a sample rate schedule.)

20 kwh	@	$2.25 (flat rate)	=	$ 2.25
80 kwh	×	3.55	=	2.84
100 kwh	×	3.21	=	3.21
200 kwh	×	2.96	=	5.92
400 kwh	×	2.65	=	10.60
1,400 kwh	×	2.20	=	+30.80
+2,200 kwh				$55.62

Thus, $55.62 is your basic electricity cost.

Fourth, figure out the fuel cost adjustment charge (item 13) by multiplying the utility company's fuel adjustment rate by the kwh used.

$$\$.0110592 \times 2,200 = \$24.33$$

Fifth, figure out the county energy tax (item 11) by multiplying the tax rate (ask electric company) by kwh used.

$$\$.0008855 \times 2,200 = \$1.95$$

Sixth, add basic electricity cost, fuel cost adjustment, and county energy tax.

$55.62 basic electricity
24.33 fuel cost adjustment
+ 1.95 county energy tax
$81.90

Seventh, figure out the state sales tax (item 12) and add it to the previous total.

$81.90 $ 3.28
×   .04   + 81.90
$ 3.28 $85.18

Eighth, figure environmental surcharge (item 10) by multiplying tax rate (ask electric company) by kwh.

$.00011234 × 2,200 = $.25

Ninth, add environmental surcharge to previous total to get the total amount due on your bill (item 9).

$85.18
+   .25
$85.43 total amount due on bill.

Tenth, to find out the amount charged if the bill is paid after the overdue date, subtract the environmental surcharge from the total amount and figure five percent of that. Then add the five percent to the total amount of the bill.

$85.43
−   .25
$85.18 $ 4.26
×   .05   + 85.43
$ 4.26 $89.69 total late payment.

CHART

SAMPLE SUMMARY* RATE SCHEDULE FOR ELECTRIC SERVICE

Minimum charge (including the first 20 kwh, or fraction thereof)
$2.25 per month

Next 80 kwh	$3.55 per kwh
Next 100 kwh	3.21 per kwh
Next 200 kwh	2.96 per kwh
Next 400 kwh	2.65 per kwh
Consumption in excess of 800 kwh	2.20 per kwh

* Electric companies often charge somewhat higher rates in summer when demand for electricity is higher. Reason: To meet increased demand, company must use additional generators—older ones that are less efficient and produce electricity at a higher cost than newer generators do.

Appendix V

Air Pollutant Effects of Different Burner Adjustment Procedures

Information on the air-pollutant effects of different burner adjustment procedures has been developed in recent field and laboratory investigations, including those conducted cooperatively by the United States Environmental Protection Agency and the American Petroleum Institute. The findings of these investigations, combined with good field practice, are described in this appendix.

POLLUTANTS OF MAIN CONCERN

Pollutants and Their Measurement.   The air pollutants of main concern for the purposes of these guidelines can be divided into three broad classes, depending upon how much the serviceman can control them by his adjustments.

Class 1. Pollutants that may result from incomplete combustion and are generally *strongly affected* by burner adjustment procedures.

1. Smoke and particulate. (Particulate that is formed from the ash content of the fuel oil is not affected by burner adjustment. However, the carbon or soot portion of particulate, usually the larger portion, can be strongly affected by burner adjustments.)
2. Carbon monoxide, CO.
3. Hydrocarbons, HC.

Class 2. Pollutants only *partially affected* by burner adjustment procedures but depending only on sulfur content of the fuel.

1. Sulfur oxides (SO_2 and SO_3).

See the following descriptions of the Class 1 pollutants from the viewpoints of definition, hazards associated with the pollutant, how it is detected or measured, and how emissions of the pollutant are affected by service adjustments. (The Class 2 and 3 pollutants are not discussed further here, because the serviceman has little or no control over them through adjustment.)

Smoke and Particulate. *Smoke* consists mainly of tiny unburned particles of carbon. Smoke has long been an important factor in the adjustment of oil-burning equipment to avoid fouling of heat-transfer passages with soot, to achieve efficient fuel utilization, and to avoid general complaints resulting from visible smoke and fallout of large particles.

Over the past 25 years, the development and use of the filter-paper method of smoke measurement (as used, for example, in the Bacharach Smoke Tester) has allowed a much more sensitive measurement than by visual means such as the Ringlemann Scale. The method is now an accepted ASTM standard and is widely used in the oil-burning industry to assist in field adjustments.

Particulate is the common scientific term applied to air-pollution measurements in terms of weight of solid and liquid materials being emitted to the atmosphere. *Particulate* is defined by the U.S. Environmental Protection Agency as any finely divided solid or liquid material, other than uncombined water, as measured by EPA method 5.

Particulate is composed of unburnt fuel, carbon or soot, ash constituents in the fuel, (ash is extremely low for No. 2 heating oil, usually below 0.005 percent) and noncombustible-air-borne dust that enters with the combustion air.

Coarse particles do not carry far in the atmosphere and usually fall out near the stack. Fine particles, the predominant portion of particulate from oil burning, can remain in the atmosphere for long periods and can obscure long-range visibility. In addition, particulate can deposit on lung tissues and, therefore, result in respiratory impairment if present in high concentrations. These are the reasons particulate is of concern to air-pollution control.

Smoke and CO_2 measurements provide a simple and relatively reliable means to avoid high emissions of pollutants (including particulates associated with incomplete combustion). The service technician can exert considerable control over particulates by ensuring that the fuel pump and safety shut-off valve have good cut-off characteristics and by the burner adjustments he chooses.

For steady operation, smoke measurements by the filter-paper method are the most practical method to warn of high particulate levels, as discussed later in the section on Typical Emission Characteristics of Residential Oil Burners. Particulate measurements by standard EPA measuring techniques require special equipment and techniques, plus long sampling periods—which are not practical for most residential burner adjustments.

Carbon Monoxide (CO).   CO is a toxic gas formed by incomplete combustion. When oil-burning equipment is in good adjustment, the CO level is very low. But with improper combustion, CO can reach levels that can be dangerous if gases should leak into living spaces. When the low levels of CO that are emitted by properly operating residential oil heating equipment are diluted in the atmosphere, CO is not considered dangerous and is depleted with time in the atmosphere.

For field adjustment of most conventional oil-fired residential equipment by methods suggested in this appendix, it is seldom necessary to measure CO. Smoke measurement can be used as a detector of poor combustion that could lead to the onset of CO at low excess air levels (high CO_2 levels). However, if the serviceman increases the air setting too far, CO levels will occasionally increase rapidly without smoke; therefore, the air setting should not be increased beyond that necessary to obtain a satisfactory smoke reading below the *knee*. (*See* Chap. 21, Fig. 3.)

Hydrocarbons (HC).   Emissions of hydrocarbons from oil-burning equipment occur when combustion is incomplete; they can be accompanied by unpleasant odors and can contribute to photochemical smog in the atmosphere. Essentially, no hydrocarbons are emitted when equipment is properly adjusted.

If large amounts of unburned oil vapor should be emitted from an improperly operating installation, this can be detected as oily or yellow deposits on the filter paper during smoke measurements. At lower levels of hydrocarbon emissions, the emissions generally follow trends of smoke or CO emissions, and, hence, these measurements are usually a good indicator of whether hydrocarbon emissions are high or low (except at extremely high air settings where smoke readings may fail to indicate a rise in hydrocarbons).

For routine adjustment of residential oil burners, it is not necessary to measure hydrocarbons by chemical or analytical means. If the service technician detects hydrocarbon odors (unburned oil vapor) near the burner or near the barometric draft control, he should check for flame impingement, improper nozzle size, improper adjustment of the combustion head, or improper pump cut-off.

FIELD-TYPE INSTRUMENTS AND SIGNIFICANCE OF MEASUREMENTS

For the adjustment procedures outlined in this appendix, it is assumed that the oil-burner service technician is accustomed to using field-type instruments. A typical kit includes the following.

1. CO_2 tester for stack-gas analysis.

A simple wet-chemical absorbent-type analyser (for example, Pyrite or Orsat apparatus). CO_2 readings are used to provide an indication of the combustion air setting.

2. Smoke tester and shade scale.

Hand-pump version of the ASTM filter-paper method for smoke determination. Includes a shade scale for evaluating smoke spots from 0 to 9 (Bacharach or ASTM scale). (This is not a Ringlemann scale. Smoke levels below 5 on the Bacharach scale are generally not visible from a residential-size stack against the sky.)

3. Thermometer for measuring stack temperature.

Usually a dial type, but liquid thermometers are more accurate.

4. Draft gage.

For draft measurements in the stack or overfire.

5. CO detector for dual-fuel commercial boilers.

Usually color-sensitive chemical in tubes.

Instruments that combine several of these readings in one device are being introduced on the market and offer convenience in use.

The Significance of CO_2 Measurements. CO_2 readings are used to identify how much combustion air is being supplied to the burner, compared to the theoretical amount required for combustion. It is seldom possible to burn a fuel completely and cleanly unless air in excess of the theoretical amount is provided. The values in Table 24 will illustrate the relationship between excess air supplied for combustion and the CO_2 concentration in the flue gas for residential oil burners firing No. 2 heating oil.

The overall efficiency of fuel utilization is lowest at the low levels of CO_2 (high excess air), because the products of combustion are diluted by the excess combustion air and carry more heat up the stack.

The Significance of Smoke Measurements. The filter-paper method of smoke measurement is useful in assessing the sooting characteristics of a combustion process. In this method, a measured sample is drawn through a filter paper and smoke spots are compared to a standard shade scale (commonly known in the oil-heating trade as the Bacharach shade scale). The method offers a practical and sensitive means of judging the combustion of fuel oils and can be used as a rough indicator of particulate emissions during steady-state operation. (*See* Table 25 on Smoke scale.)

For reliable smoke readings, it is important that the manufacturer's instructions with the smoke tester be followed carefully. For example, the sample should be pumped slowly from the stack with full strokes, with several seconds pause at the end of the pullstroke to allow a full sample.

The Significance of Stack Temperature: Its Effect on Efficiency. Stack temperature is significant in determining the effectiveness of fuel utilization because it is an indicator of the amount of heat lost up the stack.

Stack temperature can be considered abnormally high if the net stack temperature (stack temperature minus room air temperature) should exceed 400°–600° F. for matched package units, or 600°–700° F. for conversion units.

A high stack temperature may indicate one of the following conditions:

1. Excessive firing rate for furnace or boiler size.
2. Dirty or soot-covered heating surfaces.
3. Need for effective baffling of flue passes.
4. Improper adjustment of the draft regulator; usually excessive draft through the unit.

These points should be checked and remedied if stack temperature is abnormally high.

TABLE 24
EXCESS AIR SUPPLY AND COMBUSTION

Air/Fuel Mixture Settings	Excess-Air Supply (percent above theoretical)	CO_2 in flue gas,	Comments on Combustion Performance (assuming satisfactory smoke levels)
Theoretical or "Chemically Correct"	0	15 %	"Stoichiometric mixture" (cannot be achieved for reliable operation in practice)
Typical for Residential Equipment	35 %	11 %	Excellent performance
	70 %	9 %	Average performance
	150 %	6 %	Poor performance

TABLE 25

SMOKE SCALE

Bacharach Smoke	Comments on Combustion Performance (assuming satisfactory CO_2 level)	Comments on Sooting of Heating Surfaces Anticipated[2]
No. 0	Excellent	None
No. 1	Excellent	Extremely light if at all
No. 2	Good	Slight sooting which will not increase stack temperature appreciably
No. 3	Average for untuned burners	May be some sooting but will rarely require cleaning more than once a year
No. 4	Poor	Borderline condition. Some units will require cleaning more than once a year
No. 5 or higher	Very Poor	Potential for rapid and heavy soot buildup

Overall thermal efficiency is defined as the proportion of the heat energy to fuel that is actually available for heating the dwelling during continuous burner operation. Two factors can be used to determine the heat lost up the stack and, therefore, the overall thermal efficiency. (*See* Fig. 1.) These factors are as follows:

1. Net stack temperature (actual stack temperature reading minus the room temperature).
2. Percent CO_2 in the flue gases.

Figure 1 shows the combined effects of these two factors on overall thermal efficiency. This figure is based on continuous operation and use of No. 2 heating oil. It also assumes that heat from the unit jacket is available for heating some portion of the dwelling; otherwise, the overall thermal efficiency will be reduced by this jacket loss (usually only a few percent).

The overall thermal efficiency is sometimes referred to as *combustion efficiency*; however, it is also dependent on the effectiveness of the heat transfer surfaces in the boiler or furnace.

Seasonal thermal efficiency is less than the continuous thermal efficiency shown in Fig. 1 because of lower efficiency during cyclic operation (such as, additional losses up the stack from the unit during off-periods). Seasonal efficiency will be highest for units that:

1. Have high overall thermal efficiency during continuous operation.
2. Have good starting and shut-down characteristics.
3. Have firing rates matched to the design load. (Overfiring results in excessively long shut-down periods.)

Figure 1 shows the stack temperature and CO_2 on overall thermal efficiency. Basis (1) continuous operation; (2) No. 2 heating oil; (3) heat from unit jacket contributes to heating dwelling, so the only loss is of stack heat.

TYPICAL EMISSION CHARACTERISTICS OF RESIDENTIAL OIL BURNERS

Figure 2 illustrates the performance characteristics of three different but typical gun-type oil burners. This illustration shows the

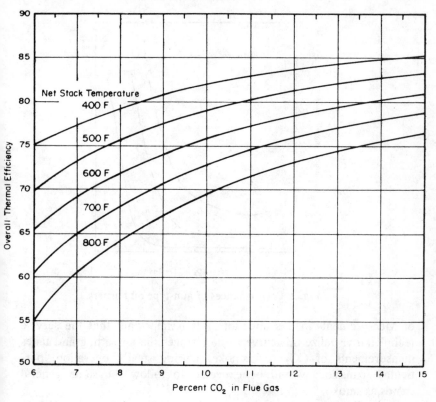

Fig. 1. Effect of stack temperature and CO_2 on overall thermal efficiency.

relationship between smoke and carbon dioxide, as measured with field-type measurements.

The three burners represent different and unique characteristics. Burner C in Fig. 2 has superior operating characteristics in that the combustion air can be set to a higher CO_2 level and still maintain a low smoke level. Other burners could have still other characteristics, but these are typical. It is possible to shift from one characteristic curve to another in *tuning*, such as by a nozzle change by burner cleaning.

Low CO_2 levels indicate an excess in combustion air; high CO_2 levels indicate an approach to the theoretical air requirement for combustion. (*See* section on Field-Type Instruments and Significance

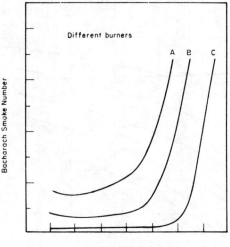

Fig. 2. Performances of gun-type oil burners.

of Measurements in this appendix.) It is important that the service technician visualize this curve as he changes the air setting and takes measurements of CO_2 and smoke. During steady operation, particulate emissions would be expected to follow the same general trends as smoke.

Particulate matter is also formed during burner starting and shutdown. Poor starting performance by ignition delay or resulting from shifts in nozzle delivery rates can result in high levels of smoke and particulate over a period of cyclic operation. Poor pump cut-off can also result in increased smoke and particulate generation at the end of a cycle.

Figure 3 illustrates typical trends of CO and HC in relation to smoke as the CO_2 setting is varied. *Note* the following trends.

    1. As CO_2 is *increased* (by closing the combustion air setting):

        (a) Smoke rises sharply beyond the normal operating CO_2 range.

        (b) CO and HC begin to rise. Here smoke has served as an indicator to forewarn of this increase.

    2. As CO_2 is *decreased* (by opening the combustion air setting):

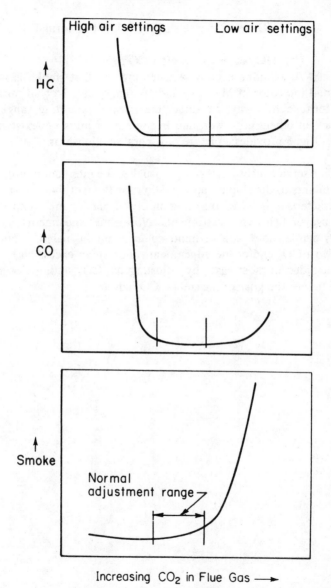

Fig. 3. Trends of CO and HC in relation to smoke as CO_2 setting is varied.

(a) CO starts to rise sharply below the normal operating CO range.

(b) HC begins to rise after CO rises.

(c) Smoke usually remains low, so that smoke is no longer a good indicator of high CO and HC emissions. Not all burners will perform in this way. In some, the *normal operating* range will be wider, in others narrower, and in some poor units nonexistant. However, Fig. 3 provides a picture of general relationships.

The service technician should visualize the interaction of the various pollutants to develop an appreciation for the fact that the smoke-CO_2 characteristic is basic to setting an oil burner for minimum emissions by use of field-type instruments. *Note* that adjustments made with only smoke limitation in mind *could* result in high CO and HC at the low CO_2 end of the adjustment range (high excess air). This can be avoided in most cases by adjusting the CO_2 setting closer to, but still below, the *knee* of the smoke-CO_2 curve.

Appendix VI

How Many Kilowatt Hours Are You Using?

The wattage rating of an appliance determines how much energy in watts per hour it uses. The table provided, based on data supplied by the Electric Energy Association, shows you the average usage of the most common electrical home appliances. The cost per year is based on an electrical rate (five cents per kilowatt hour) recommended for estimating the consumption of power.

If you wish to estimate the average hours of usage of an appliance and calculate the cost yourself, see the following directions:

Find the wattage of your appliance (from the serial plate). Estimate the number of hours you use your appliance during the week. Multiply this figure by 52 to find the total number of watts per hour (the rate at which you will use the electrical energy). Next divide the total number of watts per hour by 1,000 to find the number of kilowatt hours of energy that your appliance will use per year.

Using five cents per kilowatt hour as an approximation of your power company's rate, simply multiply the number of kilowatt hours your appliance will use over the next year to find out how much your appliance will cost you to operate for one year.

Most observers view energy conservation as a helpmate to environmental quality. Usually the two go hand-in-hand. It has been the extravagant use of energy that has pushed man toward heavy exploitation of his natural resources. Domestic oil shortages are forcing us to turn more to coal as an energy source. Eventually, research will almost certainly lead to development of cleaner ways to mine and burn coal. Research will also lead to greater utilization of energy sources such as geothermal power, solar energy, and others not yet in widespread use, and will be both economically and environmentally acceptable. Development of more efficient gasoline engines, improved insulation of buildings, and new industrial processes will enable us to maintain our standard of living with lower energy expenditure. Less

FOOD PREPARATION

Item	Average Wattage	Average Hours Per Year	Estimate Kw Hr Used Per Year	Cost Per Year (at 5 cents)
Blender	386	39	15	.75
Broiler	1,436	70	100	5.00
Carving knife	92	87	8	.40
Coffee maker	894	119	106	5.30
Deep fryer	1,448	57	83	4.15
Dishwasher	1,201	302	363	18.15
Egg cooker	516	27	14	.70
Frypan	1,196	155	186	9.30
Hot plate	1,257	72	90	4.50
Mixer	127	102	13	.65
Oven, microwave	1,450	131	190	9.50
Range with oven*	12,200	96	1,175	58.75
Range with self-cleaning oven*	12,200	99	1,205	60.25
Roaster	1,333	154	205	10.25
Sandwich grill	1,161	28	33	1.65
Toaster	1,146	34	39	1.95
Trash compactor	1,380	24	36	1.80
Waffle iron	1,116	20	22	1.10
Waste disposer	445	67	30	1.50

*Thermostatically controlled units cycle on and off. Estimates of "hours of use" are based on the time the heat element is "on" and will be less than actual switch-on time.

Item	Average Wattage	Average Hours Per Year	Estimate Kw Hr Used Per Year	Cost Per Year (at 5 cents)
FOOD PRESERVATION				
Freezer (15 cu. ft.)*	341	3,504	1,195	59.75
Freezer (frostless, 15 cu. ft.)*	440	4,002	1,761	88.05
Refrigerator (12 cu. ft.)*	241	3,021	728	36.40
Refrigerator (frostless, 12 cu. ft.)*	321	3,791	1,217	60.85
Refrigerator/freezer (14 cu. ft.)*	326	3,488	1,137	56.85
Refrigerator/freezer (frostless, 14 cu. ft.)*	615	2,974	1,829	91.95
LAUNDRY				
Clothes dryer	4,856	205	993	49.65
Iron (hand)	1,008	143	144	7.20
Washing machine (automatic)	512	201	103	5.15
Washing machine (non-automatic)	286	266	76	3.80
Water heater**	2,475	1,705	4,219	137.12
Water heater (quick recovery)**	4,474	1,075	4,811	156.35

TABLE (continued)

COMFORT CONDITIONING

Air cleaner	50	4,320	216	10.80
Air conditioner (room)	860	1,000	860	43.00
Blanket	177	831	147	7.35
Dehumidifier	257	1,467	377	18.85
Fan (attic)	370	786	291	14.55
Fan (circulating)	88	489	43	2.15
Fan (roliaway)	171	807	138	6.90
Fan (window)	200	850	170	8.50
Heater (portable)	1,322	133	176	8.80
Heating pad	65	154	10	.50
Humidifier	177	921	163	8.15

**The electric rate for heating hot water, as recommended by Public Service Co. of N. H. averages .0325 including the fuel adjustment charge.

TABLE (continued)

Item	Average Wattage	Average Hours Per Year	Estimate Kw Hr Used Per Year	Cost Per Year (at 5 cents)
HEALTH & BEAUTY				
Hair dryer	750	51	38	1.90
Heat lamp (infared)	250	52	13	.65
Shaver	14	129	1.8	.09
Sun lamp	279	57	16	.80
Toothbrush	7	71	0.5	.03
Vibrator	40	50	2	.10
HOME ENTERTAINMENT				
Radio	71	1,211	86	4.30
Radio/record player	109	1,000	109	5.45
B/W TV (tube)	160	2,188	350	17.50
B/W TV(solid state)	55	2,182	120	6.00
Color TV (tube)	300	2,200	650	33.30
Color TV (solid state)	200	2,200	440	22.00
HOUSEWARES				
Clock	2	8,760	17	.85
Floor polisher	305	49	15	.75
Sewing machine	75	147	11	.55
Vacuum cleaner	630	73	46	2.30

energy growth means important environmental savings. Truly, a barrel saved is worth *more* than a barrel found.

A nation that runs on energy cannot afford to throw it away!

Appendix VII

Glossary

Absolute humidity. The amount of humidity in a given volume of air.

Absolute pressure. The amount of gage pressure plus 14.7 pounds per square inch.

Absolute zero temperature. The temperature at which all molecular action ceases ($-460°$ F.).

Absorption. When light strikes an object, some of the light is reflected and some is absorbed. The darker the object, the more light it absorbs. Dark colors absorb large amounts of light, much as a blotter soaks up ink.

Absorption chiller. A refrigeration machine using heat as the power input to generate chilled water.

Absorption coefficient. The fraction of the total radiant energy incident on a surface that is absorbed by the surface.

Absorptivity. The physical characteristic of a substance describing its ability to absorb radiation.

Accessible (wiring methods). Not permanently closed in by the structure or finish of the building. Capable of being removed without disturbing the building structure or finish.

Accumulator. A tank that receives excess liquid refrigerant from the evaporator and prevents it from entering the compressor.

Activated carbon. A form of carbon capable of absorbing odors and vapors.

Active materials (storage battery). Materials of plates reacting chemically to produce electrical energy during the discharge.

Agitator. A device used to move confined fluid in a system.

Air changes. Expression of ventilation rate in terms of room or building volume. Usually air changes/hour.

Air coil. A coil that is sometimes used in heat pumps such as an evaporator or condenser.

Air-conditioner. A device that cleans and circulates air within a certain area and controls temperature and humidity.

Algebraic. Pertaining to that branch of mathematics which uses letters and symbols.

Algebraic sum. The addition of letters or numbers where some of them may represent negative quantities.

Alternating current (AC). A current of electrons that move in one direction and then another, alternating 60 times a second.

Alternation. One-half cycle of alternating current.

Alternator. An alternating current generator.

Ambient. Surrounding (i.e., ambient temperature is the temperature in the surrounding space).

Ammeter. Current meter with a scale calibrated in amperes.

Ampacity. Current-carrying capacity expressed in amperes.

Ampere. Unit of electric current equal to a coulomb per second.

Ampere hour. Unit of electrical energy used in rating storage batteries; the product of amperes and hours.

Ampere-hour capacity. The number of watt-hours which can be delivered by a cell or battery under specified conditions as to temperature, rate of discharge, and final voltage.

Ampere-hour-efficiency (electrochemical efficiency). The ratio of the ampere-hours output to the ampere-hours of the recharge.

Ampere turn. Unit of magnetizing force; the product of amperes and turns.

Amplidyne. A rotary magnetic or dynamo-electric amplifier used in servomechanism and control applications.

Amplification. The process of increasing the strength (current, power, or voltage) of a signal.

Amplifier. A device used to increase the signal voltage, current, or power, generally composed of a vacuum tube and associated circuit called a stage. It may contain several stages in order to obtain a desired gain.

Amplitude. In connection with alternating current or any other periodic phenomena, the maximum value of the displacement from the zero position.

Anode. The electrode in a cell (voltaic or electrolytic) that attracts the negative ions and repels the positive; the positive pole.

Antenna. A device used for sending or receiving radio waves.

Apparent power. Product of volts and amperes in AC circuits where the circuit and voltage are out of phase.

Appliance. Current-consuming equipment, fixed or portable.

Appliance, fixed. An appliance which (because of its size, its function and its location) is fixed in position in the home.

Appliance, portable. An appliance capable of being readily moved where established practice or the conditions of use make it necessary or convenient for it to be detached from its source of current by means of flexible cord and attachment plug.

Appliance, stationary. An appliance which is not easily moved but can be moved if necessary.

Approved. Acceptable to the authority enforcing the National Electrical Code.

Arc. A flash caused by an electric current ionizing a gas or vapor.

Armature. The rotating part of an electric motor or generator; also the iron part which completes the magnetic circuit in certain apparatus.

Atom. One of the minute particles of which the universe is composed; a natural group of electrons and protons.

Attenuator. A network of resistors used to reduce voltage, current, or power delivered to a load.

Auto-transformer. A transformer in which the primary and secondary are connected together in one winding.

Average voltage. The average value of the voltage during the period of charge or discharge. It is conveniently obtained from the time integral of the voltage curve.

Ballast. A device used in starting circuit for fluorescent and other types of lamps.

Bare lamp. Incandescent-filament or fluorescent lamp with no shielding.

Barrels (bbls) (energy measurement). 1 barrel equals 42 gallons.

Battery. A device for converting chemical energy into electrical; two or more cells.

Battle. A plate, wall, screen, or vane used to deflect or direct the flow of air or fluid.

Beam spread. In any plane, the angle between the two directions in which the candlepower is equal to a stated percentage (usually 10 percent) of the maximum candlepower in the beam.

Bearing. A machine part that supports or aligns a pen or other moving part.

Belt. V-type for efficient power transmission.

Bi-metal strip. A temperature-indicating apparatus that operates on the theory that when two pieces of dissimilar metal are welded together, they will bend when the temperature changes.

Blow down. The discharge of water from a boiler or cooling tower sump that contains a high proportion of total dissolved solids.

Bobbin case. Holds bobbin.

Bobbin case tension adjusting screw. For tightening or loosening tension on bobbin thread.

Bobbin winder. For winding bobbin.

Bobêche. A saucer-shaped element at the base of or below the candle socket in a candle-type fixture. In some modern fixtures of traditional styling the bobêche is often used to conceal light sources.

Boiling temperature. The temperature at which a given liquid is changed into a gas.

Bonnet. The part of a furnace casing that forms a plenum chamber from which supply ducts receive warm air.

Boost charge (storage battery). A partial charge, usually at a high rate for a short period.

Bowl. Diffusing glass or plastic used to shield light sources from view.

Boyle's law. With the temperature constant, the volume of a gas will vary in direct proportion to the pressure.

Branch circuit. The portion of the wiring system extending beyond the final overcurrent device protecting the circuit.

Branch circuit light panel. Takes the power from the main switch and feeds it to the light and receptacle circuits through separate circuit breakers or fuses.

Breaker points. Metal contacts that open and close a circuit at timed intervals.

Bridge circuit. The electrical bridge circuit is a term referring to any one of a variety of electric circuit networks, one branch of which, the "bridge" proper, connects two points of equal potential and hence carries no current when the circuit is properly adjusted or balanced.

Brightness. The degree of apparent lightness of any surface emitting or reflecting light. Everything that is visible has some brightness.

British thermal unit (Btu). A standard measurement of energy content no matter what its source. The energy required to increase the temperature of one pound of water by 1° Fahrenheit.

Brush. The conducting material, usually a block of carbon, bearing against the commutator or sliprings through which the current flows in or out.

Building envelope. All external surfaces which are subject to climatic impact; for example, walls, windows, roof, floor, and the like.

Building load. *See* Cooling load and Heating load.

Bulb. Glass enclosure of incandescent-filament lamp.

Bus bar. A primary power distribution point connected to the main power source.

BX cable. Trade name for armored cable.

Cable. A standard conductor (single-conductor cable); or a combination of conductors insulated from one another (multiple-conductor cable).

Calorie. The amount of heat required at a pressure of one atmosphere to raise the temperature of one gram of water one degree centigrade.

Candela. A unit of luminous intensity, equal to $\frac{1}{60}$ of the luminous intensity of a square centimeter of a black body heated to the temperature of the solidification of platinum (1773.5° C).

Candlelight. Fluorescent lamp color similar to deluxe warm white.

Candlepower. Luminous intensity.

Candlepower distribution curve. A curve showing the variation of luminous intensity of a lamp or luminaire.

Canopy. Shield (usually metal) covering joint of lighting fixture to ceiling.

Capacitance. Property of a circuit that opposes any change of voltage.

Capacitive reactance. The effect of capacitance in opposing the flow of alternating or pulsating current.

Capacitor. A device that stores electrical energy and is used for starting or running circuits on electrical motors.

Capacitor-start motor. An electric motor that uses a capacitor in the starting circuit.

Capacity. Output capability over a period of time, expressed in ampere-hours.

Capillary tube. A device used to restrict the flow of refrigerant so that the high side and low side pressure are properly maintained while the compressor is running.

Cathode. A fluorescent lamp part which serves to conduct the electricity from the wires into the gas.

Cavity ratio. Number indicating room cavity proportions, which is calculated using length, width, and height.

Cell. A combination of electrodes and electrolyte which converts chemical energy into electrical energy.

Centimeter. Metric measuring unit that equals .3937 inches.

Centrifugal chiller. A refrigeration machine using mechanical energy input to drive a centrifugal compressor to generate chilled water.

Centrifugal fan. Device for propelling air by centrifugal action. Forward curved fans have blades which are sloped forward relative to direction of rotation. Backward curved fans have blades which are sloped backward relative to direction of rotation. Backward curved fans are generally more efficient at high pressures than forward curved fans.

Certified. Term applied to portable lamps and fixtures made to meet certain specifications for quantity of light, quality of lighting, sturdy construction, and safety. Fluorescent ballasts and starters meeting certain performance requirements are also *certified*. Such products usually carry a certification tag or label.

Channel. A common term for the metal enclosure containing the ballast, starter, lampholders, and wiring for a fluorescent lamp.

Charge. The process of sending an electric current through a storage battery to renew its action.

Charge, state of. Condition of a cell in terms of the capacity remaining in the cell.

Charging. Process of supplying electrical energy for conversion to stored chemical energy.

Charging rate. The current expressed in amperes at which a battery is charged.

Charles' law. The volume of a gas at a constant pressure will vary according to temperature.

Chemical energy. Energy stored in molecules, such as in fossil fuels. (*See* Fossil fuels.)

Choke coil. A coil of low ohmic resistance and high impedance to alternating current.

Chroma. The attribute of perceived color used to describe its departure from gray of the same lightness.

Circuit. A closed path or mesh of closed paths usually including a source of electromotive force (emf).

Circuit, branch. That portion of a wiring system extending beyond the final overcurrent device protecting the circuit.

Circuit breaker. A safety device that will open an electrical circuit when it becomes overloaded.

Circular mil. An area equal to that of a circle with a diameter of 0.001 inch. It is used for measuring the cross section of wires.

Closed circuit. A circuit in which electrons are traveling.

Closed-circuit voltage. The voltage at the terminals of a cell or battery when current is flowing.

Coaxial cable. A transmission line consisting of two conductors concentric with and insulated from each other.

Coefficient of utilization. Ratio of lumens on a work plane to lumens emitted by the lamps.

Coffer. Recessed panel in ceiling or dome.

Cold deck. A cold-air chamber forming part of a ventilating unit.

Collector rings. Means of conveying current to or from rotating parts of alternate current machinery.

Color rendering. General expression for the effect of a light source on the color appearace of objects in conscious or subconscious comparison with their color appearance under a reference light source.

Commutation. The process of converting alternating current which flows in the armature of direct current generators to direct current.

Commutator. The part of direct current rotating machinery which makes electrical contact with the brushes and connects the armature conductors to the external circuit.

Commutator ripple. The small pulsations which take place in the voltage and current of direct current generators.

Compartment cover. For insertion or removal of automatic stitch discs.

Compression. A process of increasing pressure by using mechanical energy.

Compressor. A pump in an air-conditioning system that draws a vacuum of low pressure on the cooling side of the refrigerant cycle and squeezes the gas into the high pressure side of the cycle.

Compressor, hermetic. A compressor that has the drive motor sealed in the same housing that contains the compressor.

Compressor, open-type. A compressor that has a crankshaft extending through the crankcase that an outside motor drives.

Compressor, reciprocating. A compressor that uses a piston and cylinder to provide pumping action.

Compressor, rotary. A compressor that utilizes electric machinery, vanes, or other revolving mechanisms to create pumping action.

Concealed circuit. A circuit that is hidden by the structure or finish of the building.

Concentric-lay cable. A single-conductor cable composed of a central core surrounded by one or more layers of helically laid groups of wires.

Concentric strand. A strand composed of a control core surrounded by one or more layers of helically laid wires or groups of wires.

Condensate. Water obtained by changing the state of water vapor (i.e., steam or moisture in air) from a gas to a liquid, usually by cooling.

Condensation. Liquid that is formed when a gas is cooled below its dew point.

Condenser. The refrigeration device that gets high pressure, hot refrigerant gas from a compressor and cools the gas until it turns to a liquid.

Condenser fan. A mechanism used to force air through an air-cooled condenser.

Condensing unit. The refrigeration part that pumps the vaporlike refrigerant from the evaporator, compresses it, turns it into a liquid in the condenser, and returns the liquid to the refrigerant control.

Conductance. The ability of a material to conduct or carry an electric current. It is the reciprocal of the resistance of the material, and is expressed in units of conductance ohms.

Conductance, thermal. A measure of the thermal conducting properties of a single material expressed in units of Btu inch thickness per (square foot) (hour) (degree F temperature difference).

Conduction. The transfer of heat from a warmer to a cooler particle by direct contact.

Conductivity. The ease with which a substance transmits electricity.

Conductivity, thermal. A measure of the thermal conducting properties of a single material expressed in units of Btu per inch thickness (sq.ft.), (hour), (degree F. temperature difference).

Conductor. A wire or combination of wires not insulated from one another, suitable for carrying a single electric current.

Conductor—bare. A conductor with no covering or insulation whatsoever.

Conductor—covered. A conductor with one or more layers of nonconducting material which is not recognized as insulation.

Conductor—insulated. A conductor covered with a recognized insulation.

Conduit. A metal pipe used to enclose electrical conductors.

Constant-current charge. A charge in which the current is maintained at constant value.

Constant-voltage charge. A charge in which the voltage at the terminals of the battery is held at a constant value.

Contactor. A device for closing and opening electrical circuits remotely; a magnetically operated switch.

Contaminant. A substance such as dirt or moisture, which may accumulate in the refrigerant or refrigerant oil in an air conditioning system.

Continuous load. A load where the maximum current is expected to continue for three or more hours.

Control. The manual or automatic device used to start, regulate, and stop the flow of gas, electricity, or liquid.

Control-center, branch. The term applied to an assembly of circuit breakers for the protection of branch circuits feeding from the control-center.

Control-center, main. The term applied to an assembly of circuit breakers for the protection of feeders and branch circuits feeding from the main control-center.

Control panel. An upright panel, open or closed, where switches, rheostats, and meters are installed for controlling and protecting electrical devices.

Convector. A surface that is designed to release heat by the process of convection.

Convenience outlet. Electric receptacle (often along baseboard) used for connecting portable lamps and appliances.

Converter, rotary. An electrical machine having a commutator at one end and sliprings at the other end of the armature, used for the conversion of alternating to direct current.

Cool white. Fluorescent lamp *whiter* than filament lamp. Blends well with daylight; red colors may not appear as red under it.

Cooling load. The rate of heat gain to the building at a steady state condition when indoor and outdoor temperatures are at their selected design levels, solar gain is at its maximum for the building configuration and orientation, and heat gains due to infiltration, ventilation, lights, and people are present.

Cooling tower. Device that cools water directly by evaporation.

Cord. A small cable, flexible and substantially insulated to withstand wear.

Core. A magnetic material that affords an easy path for magnetic flux lines in a coil.

Cornice. The crown molding used both to cover and to embellish the intersection between side walls and ceiling. In modern lighting practice, it is a horizontal member of wood or plaster attached to the ceiling approximately 6 to 8 inches from the wall, with lighting incorporated between it and the wall.

Cornice lighting. Comprises light sources shielded by a panel parallel to the wall and attached to the ceiling, distributing light downward over the vertical surface.

Coulomb. The unit of static electricity; the quantity of electricity transferred by one ampere in one second.

Counter electromotive force. An emf induced in a coil or armature that opposes the applied voltage.

Couple (storage battery). The element of a cell containing two plates, one positive and one negative. This term is also applied to a positive and a negative plate connected together as one unit for installation in adjacent cells.

Coupling. Term used to represent the means by which energy is transferred from one circuit to another.

Cove. In modern lighting practice, an element of design mounted on an upper wall to conceal light sources and provide indirect lighting.

Cove lighting. Comprises light sources shielded by a ledge and distributing light upward over the ceiling.

Crude oil or **"crude."** Petroleum in its natural state.

Cubic foot (cf). 1 cubic foot = the volume of a cube whose length, width, and breadth each measure 1 foot.

Current. Gradual drift of free electrons along a conductor; electrical volume.

Current limiter. A protective device similar to a fuse, usually used in high amperage circuits.

Cut-off voltage. Voltage at the end of useful discharge. (*See* End-point voltage.)

Cycle. In periodic phenomena, one complete set of recurring events: one complete positive and one complete negative alternation of a current or voltage.

Damper. A device used to vary the volume of air passing through an air outlet, inlet, or duct.

D'Arsonal galvanometer. A galvanometer in which a moving coil swings between the poles of a permanent horseshoe magnet.

Deep discharge. Withdrawal of all electrical energy to the end-point voltage before the cell or battery is recharged.

Degree day. The difference between the median temperature of any day and 65° F. when the median temperature is less than 65° F.

Degree hour. The difference between the median temperature for any hour and selected datum.

Dehumidifier. A device that removes moisture from the air in an enclosed space such as a room.

Deluxe. Trade term applied to fluorescent lamps with good color rendition of all colors. There are cool white and warm white deluxe lamps.

Demand factor. The ratio of the maximum demand of a system, or part of a system, to the total connected load of a system or part of the system under consideration.

Density. Concentration of anything; quality per unit volume or area.

Desiccant. A substance possessing the ability to absorb moisture.

Dew point. The temperature at which vapor turns into liquid (at 100 percent humidity).

Dial selector for patterns. Provides various automatic stitching patterns.

Dielectric. An insulator; a term that refers to the insulating material between the plates of a capacitor; material which will not conduct an electric current.

Dielectric constant. Ratio of the capacitance of a condenser with a dielectric between the plates to the capacitance of the same condenser with a vacuum between the plates.

Diffuse reflection (diffusion). That process by which incident flux is redirected over a range of angles.

Diffuser. A device to scatter the light from a source primarily by the process of diffuse transmission.

Dimmer. A device for providing variable light output from lamps.

Diode. Vacuum tube—a two-element tube that contains a cathode and plate; semi-conductor—a material of either germanium or silicon that is manufactured to allow current to flow in only one direction. Diodes are used as rectifiers and detectors.

Direct current (DC). Current which is constant in magnitude and direction.

Direct expansion. Generic term used to describe refrigeration systems where the cooling effect is obtained directly from the refrigerant (e.g., refrigerant is evaporated directly in a cooling coil in the air stream).

Direct glare. Glare resulting from areas of excessive luminance and insufficiently shielded light sources in the field of view.

Direct lighting. A lighting system in which all or nearly all of the light is distributed downward by the luminaire. Fixtures that send somewhat more light upward but are still predominantly of the direct type are called semi-direct.

Disability glare. Spurious light from any source, which impairs a viewer's ability to discern a given object.

Discharge. Withdrawal of electrical energy from a cell or battery, usually to operate connected equipment.

Diversity factor. The ratio of the sum of the individual maximum demands of the various subdivisions of a system, or a part of a system, to the maximum demand of the whole system, or part under consideration.

Double bundle condenser. Condenser (usually in refrigeration machine) that contains two separate tube bundles allowing the option of either rejecting heat to the cooling tower or to another building system requiring heat input.

Double heat transfer. The transfer of heat from the plant to the heated medium and from the medium to the air in the conditioned space.

Double pole (D.P.). Having two contacts; e.g., a double pole switch.

Downlight. Luminaire which directs all the luminous flux down. Usually recessed, though it may be surface mounted.

Drain. Withdrawal of current from a cell.

Drop feed key. For lowering feed dog.

Dry battery. A battery in which the electrolyte in a cell is immobilized, being either in the form of a paste or gel or absorbed in the separator material.

Dry bulb temperature. The measure of the sensible temperature of air.

Duplex cable. Two insulated single-conductor cables twisted together.

Duplex receptacle. A double outlet receptacle used in house wiring.

Dynamo. A machine for converting mechanical energy into electrical energy or vice versa.

Economizer cycle. A method of operating a ventilation system to reduce refrigeration load. Whenever the outdoor air conditions are more favorable (lower heat content) than return air conditions, outdoor air quantity is increased.

Eddy current. Induced circulating currents in a conducting material that are caused by a varying magnetic field.

Edison socket. A socket that accepts a light bulb with a screw-in base.

Efficacy of fixtures. Ratio of usable light to energy input for a lighting fixture or system (lumens/watt).

Efficiency. The ratio of the output of a cell or battery to the input required to restore the initial state of charge under specified conditions of temperature, current rate, and final voltage.

Electric circuit. A completed conducting pathway, consisting not only of the conductor, but including the path through the voltage source.

Electric power. Rate of doing electrical work.

Electricity. One of the fundamental quantities in nature consisting of elementary particles, electrons, and protons, which is manifested as a force of attraction or repulsion, and also in work that can be performed when electrons are caused to move; a material agency which exhibits magnetic, chemical, and thermal effects when in motion, and when at rest is accompanied by an interplay of forces between associated localities in which it is present.

Electrodes. The solid conductors of a cell or battery which are placed in contact with the liquid conductor that makes electrical contact with a liquid or gas.

Electrolyte. A solution of a substance which is capable of conducting electricity. An electrolyte may be in the form of either liquid or paste.

Electromagnet. Temporary magnet which is constructed by winding a number of turns of insulated wire about an iron core.

Electromotive force (emf). Difference of electrical potential or pressure measured in volts.

Electron. One of the ultimate subdivisions of matter having about $\frac{1}{1845}$ of the mass of a hydrogen atom (carrying a negative charge of electricity); one of the negative particles of an atom.

Electronics. That brand of science and technology which relates to the conduction of electricity through gases or in vacuum.

Electro-strip wall receptacle. An insulated strip where several receptacles are installed on the wall for convenience.

Element (storage battery). The positive and negative groups with separators assembled for a cell.

End cells. The cells of a battery which may be cut in or out of the circuit for the purpose of adjusting the battery voltage.

End-point voltage. Cell voltage below which operation is not recommended.

Energy. The capacity to perform work.

Energy density. Ratio of cell energy to weight or volume (watt-hours per pound or watt-hours per cubic inch).

Energy requirement. The total yearly energy used by a building to maintain the selected inside design conditions under the dynamic impact of a typical year's climate. It includes raw fossil fuel consumed in the building and all electricity used for lighting and power. Efficiencies of utilization are supplied, and all energy is expressed in the common unit of Btu's.

Energy units translated into Btu's:
1 bbl crude oil—5,800,000 Btu's.
1 cubic foot of natural gas—1,024 Btu's.
1 gallon of gasoline—125,000 Btu's.
1 gallon of No. 2 fuel oil—139,000 Btu's.
1 kilowatt-hour—3,413 Btu's.
1 Mcf natural gas—1,024,000 Btu's.
1 therm of gas (or other fuel)—100,000 Btu's.
1 ton of bituminous coal—23,730,000 Btu's.

Enthalpy. For the purpose of air conditioning enthalpy is the total heat content of air above a datum usually in units of Btu/lb. It is the sum of sensible and latent heat and ignores internal energy changes due to pressure change.

Equalizing charge. An extended charge given to a battery to ensure the complete restoration of the active materials in all the plates of all the cells.

Equipment, electrical. The term (as used in this handbook) applies to electrical appliances and lighting fixtures—fixed and portable.

Equivalent sphere illumination. That illumination which would fall upon a task covered by an imaginary transparent hemisphere which passes light of the same intensity through each unit area.

Evaporative condenser. Apparatus that uses open spray or spill water to cool the condenser.

Evaporator. A heat exchanger which adds latent heat to a liquid, changing it to a gaseous state. (In a refrigeration system it is the component which absorbs heat.)

Evaporator coil. A part of the evaporator that evaporates refrigerant. It is made of coils of tubing.

Excitor. Small generator for supplying direct current to the alternator's field windings.

Face plate and sew light. Snap opens for changing bulb. Provides easy access to needle and presser bar assembly for oiling or adjustment.

Fahrenheit scale. A scale for temperature measurement that places the freezing point of water at +32 degrees and the boiling point of water at +212 degrees at standard atmospheric pressure.

Farad. Unit of capacitance equal to the amount of capacitance present when one volt can store one coulomb of electricity.

Feed dog. For feeding material through sewing machine.

Feedback. A transfer of energy from the output circuit of a device back to its input.

Feeders. Any conductors of a wiring system between the service equipment and the branch circuit overcurrent device.

Field. The space containing electric or magnetic lines of force.

Field of force. Region in space filled with force which spreads out in all directions and will act through a vacuum.

Field magnet. The magnet used to produce a magnetic field (usually in motors or generators).

Field winding. The coil used to provide for magnetizing force in motors and generators.

Filter. A device which changes, by transmission, the magnitude and/or the spectral composition of the flux incident upon it.

Final voltage. The prescribed voltage upon reaching which the discharge is considered complete. The final voltage is usually chosen so that the useful capacity of the cell is realized. Final voltages vary with the type of battery, the rate of the discharge, temperature, and the service in which the battery is used.

Finishing rate. The rate of charge expressed in amperes to which the charging current for some types of lead batteries is reduced near the end of charge to prevent excessive gassing and temperature rise.

Fixture. *See* Luminaire.

Flame test for leaks. A method of testing for refrigerant leaks by using a torch.

Flare. Flares are made by a special tool that, when properly used, forms a 45 degree angle on the end of tubing.

Flare nut. A fitting used with a flare that makes a connection with another flare fitting.

Float charging. Method of recharging in which a secondary cell is continuously connected to a constant-voltage supply that maintains the cell in fully charged condition.

Floating. A method of operation in which a constant voltage is applied to the battery terminals sufficient to maintain an approximately constant state of charge.

Flood lamp (Resistance or Parabolic). Incandescent filament lamp providing a relatively wide beam pattern.

Floor duct. Large square conduit buried under a concrete floor. It has receptacle outlets flush with the floor.

Flue. An enclosed passage in a chimney that carries exhaust smoke and fumes to the outer air.

Fluorescence. A property of phosphorus which, under controlled conditions, radiates light when absorbing electrons.

Fluorescent lamp (tube). A low-pressure mercury electric-discharge lamp in which a fluorescing coating (phosphor) transforms ultraviolet energy into visible light.

Flux. Magnetic field which is established in a magnetic circuit.

Flux brazing, soldering. A substance applied to metal in order to facilitate a good brazing joint.

Foot-candle. Energy of light at a distance of one foot from a standard (sperm oil) candle.

Footlambert (fL). A quantitative unit for measuring luminance. The foot-candles striking a diffuse reflecting surface, times the reflectance of that surface, equals the luminance in footlamberts.

Force. That which tends to change the state of rest or motion of matter.

Fossil fuels. Fuels derived from the remains of carbonaceous fossils, including petroleum, natural gas, coal, oil shale (a fine-grained laminated sedimentary rock that contains an oil-yielding material called kerogen), and tar sands.

Free electrons. Electrons which are loosely held and consequently tend to move at random among the atoms of the material.

Frequency. In periodic phenomena the number of complete reoccurences in unit time; in alternating current the number of cycles per second.

Full-wave rectifier circuit. A circuit which utilizes both the positive and the negative alternations of an alternating current to produce a direct current.

Furnace. That part of a warm air heating system in which combustion takes place.

Fuse. A safety apparatus in an electrical circuit that breaks when overloaded.

Gage manifold. A device that is designed to hold compound and high pressure gages and is equipped with valves for control purposes.

Gain. The ratio of the output power, voltage, or current to the input power, voltage, or current, respectively.

Galvanometer. An instrument used to measure small DC currents.

Gassing (storage battery). The evolution of oxygen or hydrogen, or both.

General lighting. The lighting designed to provide a substantially uniform level of illumination throughout an area, exclusive of any provision for special local requirements.

Generator. A device for converting mechanical energy into electrical energy.

Geothermal energy. Energy extracted from the heat of the earth's interior.

Glare. Any brightness or brightness relationship that annoys, distracts, or reduces visibility.

Glitter. Small areas of high brightness, sometimes desirable to provide sensory stimulation.

Grid. A metal wire mesh placed between the cathode and plate.

Grid battery. The battery used to supply the desired potential to the grid.

Grid leak. A very high resistance placed in parallel with the grid condenser.

Ground wire. The connection of an electrical current with the earth through a conductor.

Group (storage battery). Assembly of a set of plates of the same polarity for one cell.

Halide torch. A torch-like device used to detect halogen refrigerant leaks.

Hand wheel. For turning mechanism by hand to bring needle and take-up to High positions, and for testing. This wheel turns toward operator.

Hand-wheel clutch nut. For disengaging the hand wheel from mechanism when winding bobbin without sewing.

Harp. A rigid wire device which fits around the socket and bulb and supports the shade on some styles of floor and table lamps.

Heat gain. As applied to heating, ventilating, and air conditioning (HVAC) calculations, it is that amount of heat gained by a space from all sources, including people, lights, machines, sunshine, and so on. The total heat gain represents the amount of heat that can be removed from a space to maintain indoor comfort conditions.

Heat, latent. Heat that changes the form of a substance without changing its temperature.

Heat loss. The sum cooling effect of the building structure when the outdoor temperature is lower than the desired indoor temperature. It represents the amount of heat that must be provided to a space to maintain indoor comfort conditions.

Heat pump. A compression cycle system that distributes heat to a space. It can also remove heat from the same space.

Heat, sensible. Heat that changes the temperature of a substance without changing its form.

Heat, specific. Ratio of the amount of heat required to raise a unit mass of material one degree to that required to raise a unit mass of water one degree.

Heat transmission coefficient. Any one of a number of coefficients used in the calculation of heat transmission by conduction, convection, and radiation, through various materials and structures.

Heating load. The rate of heat loss from the building at steady state conditions when the indoor and outdoor temperatures are at their selected design levels (design criteria). The heating load always includes infiltration and may include ventilation loss and heat gain credits for lights and people.

Hg (mercury). A metallic element that is a heavy silver white liquid at room temperature.

Henry. Unit of inductance; the inductance present which will cause one volt to be induced if the current changes at the rate of one ampere per second.

Hertz. A unit of frequency equal to one cycle per second.

Hickey. A tool used to bend metal pipe or conduit (commonly called a pipe bender).

High-rate discharge. Withdrawal of large currents for short intervals of time, usually at a rate that would completely discharge a cell or battery in less than one hour.

High side. The parts of an air-conditioning system that are under high pressure.

Horsepower. The English unit of power, equal to work done at the rate of 550 foot-pounds per second. Equal to 746 watts of electrical power.

Horsepower-hour. Energy expended if work is done for one hour at the rate of one horsepower (hp).

Hot deck. A hot-air chamber forming part of a ventilating unit.

Hue. The attribute of perceived color which determines whether it is red, yellow, green, blue, or the like.

Humidifier. A device designed to increase the humidity within a room or a house by means of the discharge of water vapor. It may consist of individual room-size units or larger units attached to the heating plant to condition the entire house.

Humidity, relative. A measurement indicating moisture content of air.

Hydrometer. Device for measuring the specific gravity of liquids.

Hydropower energy. Energy possessed by matter in motion.

Hysteresis. A lagging or retardation of effect when the forces acting upon a body are changed; encountered both in magnetic and dielectric phenomena.

Induction motor. The most common type of single phase motor. It operates on the principle of a rotating magnetic field.

Illumination. The density of luminous flux on a surface.

Impedance. The total opposition that a battery offers to the flow of alternating current or any other varying current at a particular frequency. Impedance is a combination of resistance and reactance.

Incandescent filament lamp (bulb). A lamp in which light is produced by a filament heated to incandescence by an electric current.

Indirect lighting. Lighting provided by luminaires which distribute all light upward. Luminaires sending some luminous flux downward but still predominantly of the indirect type are called semi-direct.

Inductance. The property of a circuit which tends to oppose a change in the existing current.

Induction. The act or process of producing voltage by the relative motion of a magnetic field across a conductor.

Induction coil. Two coils so arranged that an interrupted current in the first produces a voltage in the second.

Inductive reactance. The opposition to the flow of alternating or pulsating current caused by the inductance of a circuit. It is measured in ohms.

Infiltration. The process by which outdoor air leaks into a building by natural forces through cracks around doors and windows, and the like.

Initial drain. Current that a cell or battery supplies at nominal voltage.

Initial voltage. The voltage of a cell or battery at the beginning of a charge or discharge. It is usually taken after the current has been flowing for a sufficient period of time for the rate of change of voltage to become practically constant.

Inphase. Applied to the condition that exists when two waves of the same frequency pass through their maximum and minimum values of like polarity at the same instant.

Insolation. The amount of solar radiation on a given plane. Expressed in Langleys or Btu/ft.^{2}.

Instantaneous value. The value at any particular instant of a quantity that is continually varying.

Insulation board, rigid. A structural building board made of coarse wood or cane fiber in ½- and $^{25}/_{32}$-inch thicknesses.

Insulation, reflective. Sheet material with one or both surfaces of comparatively low heat emissivity, such as aluminum foil.

Insulation, thermal. Any material high in resistance to heat transmission that, when placed in the walls, ceiling, or floors of a structure, will not conduct electricity.

Insulator. A substance containing very few free electrons (a nonconductor); e.g., plastic, rubber.

Intercom. An audio communication system.

Internal resistance. Opposition to current flow within a cell (ohms).

Interreflectance. The portion of the lumens reaching the work plane that has been reflected one or more times in the space.

Interrupter. A device for the automatic making and breaking of an electrical circuit.

Inversely. Inverted or reversed in position or relationship.

Ion. An electrically charged atom.

Isogonic line. An imaginary line drawn through points on the earth's surface where the magnetic variation is equal.

Jar (storage battery). The container for the element and electrolyte of a cell. Specifically a jar for lead-acid cells is usually of hard-rubber composition or glass; but for nickel-iron-alkaline cells it is a nickel-plated steel container frequently referred to as a "can."

Joule. A unit of energy or work. A joule of energy is liberated by one ampere flowing for one second through a resistance of one ohm.

Junction box. A box in which connections of several wires are made.

Kilo. A prefix meaning 1,000.

Kilowatt (kw). A common unit of measurement of electrical energy, equal to 1,000 watts. One kilowatt is the equivalent of about 1½ horsepower.

Kilowatt-hour (kwh). 1,000 watt-hours. A unit of electrical energy equal to the energy delivered by the flow of 1 kilowatt of electrical power for 1 hour. (A 100-watt bulb burning for 10 hours will consume 1 kilowatt-hour of energy.) One barrel of oil equals 500 kwh. (Rounded from 492.7 kwh.)

Kinetic energy. Energy possessed by matter in motion.

Lag. The amount one wave is behind another in time; expressed in electrical degrees.

Laminated core. A core built up from thin sheets of metal and used in transformers and relays.

Laminations. The thin sheets or discs making up an iron core.

Lamps. A generic term for a man-made source of light. By extension, the term is also used to denote sources that radiate in regions of the spectrum adjacent to the visible. (A lighting unit consisting of a lamp with shade, reflector, enclosing globe housing, or other accessories is also called a *lamp*. To distinguish between the assembled unit and the light source within it, the latter is often called a *bulb* or a *tube*, if it is electrically powered).

Langley. Measurement of radiation intensity. One Langley = 3.68 Btu/ft.^{2}.

Lead. The opposite of Lag. Also, a wire or connection.

Leakage. Term used to express current loss through imperfect insulators.

Lens. Device for optical control of luminous flux by the process of refraction.

Life cycle cost. The cost of the equipment over its entire life including operating and maintenance costs.

Lighting outlet. Means by which branch circuits are made available for connection to lampholders, to surface-mounted fixtures, to flush or recessed fixtures, or for extension to mounting devices for light sources in valances, cornices, or coves.

Line of force. A path through space along which a field of force acts, as shown by a line on a sketch.

Load. The power that is being delivered by any power-producing device. The equipment that uses the power from the power-producing device.

Load leveling. Deferment of certain loads to limit electrical power demand to a predetermined level.

Load profile. Time distribution of building heating, cooling, and electrical load.

Local action or **self-discharge.** The internal loss of charge which goes on continuously within a cell regardless of connections to an external circuit.

Local lighting. The lighting that illuminates a relatively small area or confined space.

Louver. A series of baffles used to shield a source from view at certain angles or to absorb unwanted light.

Low-rate discharge. Withdrawal of small currents for long periods of time, usually longer than one hour.

Low side. The parts of an air-conditioning system that are under low pressure.

Lumen. The unit of luminous flux.

Lumiline. A tubular incandescent lamp with a filament extending the length of the tube and connected at each end to a disc base.

Luminaire. A complete light unit consisting of a lamp, or lamps, together with parts designed to distribute the light, to position and protect the lamps and to connect the lamps to the power supply.

Luminaire efficiency. The ratio of the luminous flux leaving a luminaire to that emitted by the lamp, or lamps, used therein.

Luminance (photometric brightness). The luminous intensity of any surface in a given direction per unit area of that surface as viewed from that direction.

Luminous ceiling. A ceiling area lighting system comprising a continuous surface of transmitting material of a diffusing or light-controlling character with light sources mounted above it.

Luminous flux. The descriptive term for the time rate of flow of light.

Lux (lx). A quantitative unit for measuring illumination; the illumination on a surface of one meter square on which there is a uniformly distributed flux of one lumen.

Magnetic amplifier. A saturable reactor-type device that is used in a circuit to amplify or control.

Magnetic circuit. The complete path of magnetic lines of force.

Magnetic field. The space in which a magnetic force exists.

Magnetic flux. The total number of lines of force issuing from a pole of a magnet.

Magnetic pole. Region where the majority of magnetic lines of force leave or enter the magnet.

Magnetism. The property of the molecules of certain substances, such as iron, by virtue of which they may store energy in the form of a field of force; it is caused by the motion of the electrons in the atoms of the substance, a manifestation of energy due to the motion of a dielectric field of force.

Magnetize. To convert a material into a magnet by causing the molecules to rearrange.

Magneto. A generator which produces alternating current and has a permanent magnet as its field.

Magnetomotive force. The force necessary to establish flux in a magnetic circuit or to magnetize an unmagnetized object.

Main. A main is a supply circuit to which other energy-consuming circuits are connected through automatic cutouts, such as fuses or breakers.

Main disconnect switch. Cuts off the power to the entire building. Its fuses will blow if a major short occurs, thus protecting the wiring.

Make-up. Water supplied to a system to replace that lost by blow down, leakage, evaporation, and the like.

Matter. Anything which has weight and occupies space.

Maximum value. The greatest instantaneous value of an alternating voltage or current.

Mcf. 1,000 cubic feet (of natural gas).

Measuring energy. Specific forms of energy are measured in different ways —barrels of oil, therms of cubic feet of gas, kilowatts or kilowatt-hours of electricity, and tons of coal, for example.

Megawatt (mw). 1 million watts, or 1,000 kilowatts.

Megger. A test instrument used to measure insulation resistance and other high resistances. It is a portable hand-operated DC generator used as an ohmmeter.

Megohm. A large unit of resistance; equal to one million ohms.

Micro. A prefix meaning one-millionth.

Microfarad. Practical unit of capacitance; one-millionth of a farad.

Mil. A prefix meaning one-thousandth.

Milliammeter. An ammeter that measures current in thousandths of an ampere.

Milliampere. Small unit of electric current; equal to one one-thousandth of an ampere.

Millivoltmeter. A voltmeter reading thousandths of a volt.

Modular. A system arrangement whereby the demand for energy (heating, cooling) is met by a series of units sized to meet a portion of the load.

Molecule. A small natural particle of matter, usually composed of two or more atoms.

Motor. A device for converting electrical energy into mechanical energy.

Motor, capacity. A single-phase induction motor that has a starting winding connected to a capacitor for better starting.

Motor control. An apparatus used to stop, start, or reverse a motor. It operates at certain predetermined temperatures or pressures.

Motor-generator. A motor and a generator with a common shaft used to convert line voltages to other voltages or frequencies.

Motor starter. Device for protecting electric motors from excessive current while they are reaching full speed.

Multimeter. A combination volt, ampere, and ohm meter.

Multiple or **parallel circuits.** Those circuits in which the components are so arranged that the current divides between them.

Munsell color system. A system of object color specification based on perceptually uniform color scaled for the three variables—hue, value, and chroma.

Mutual inductance. Inductance associated with more than one circuit.

Mutual induction. The inducting of an electromotive force (emf) in a circuit by the field of a nearby circuit.

Needle clamp. For attaching needle to lower end of needle bar.

Needle clamp thumb screw. For fastening needle in needle clamp.

Needle plate. For supporting material when sewing.

Needle positioning lever. Moves needle to three positions—left, right, and center.

Negative charge. The electrical charge carried by a body which has an excess of electrons.

Negative plate (storage battery). The grid and active material from which the current flows to the external circuit when the battery is discharging.

Neon-glow lamp testers. Device for determining if a circuit is live, for determining polarity of DC circuits, and for determining if a circuit is alternating or direct current.

Neutron. A particle having the weight of a proton but carrying no electric charge. It is located in the nucleus of an atom.

Nominal voltage. Voltage of a fully charged cell when delivering rated capacity.

Non-ferrous. Any metal or metal alloy that does not contain iron.

Nuclear energy. Energy, largely in the form of heat, produced during nuclear chain reaction. This thermal energy can be transformed into electrical energy. (*See* Power.)

Nucleus. The central part of an atom that is mainly comprised of protons and neutrons. It is the part of the atom that has the most mass.

Null. Zero.

Office lights. Usually fluorescent fixtures hung end to end so that the power feeds into the end fixtures and the wires are run from fixture to fixture in troughs or housings. This is also called trough wiring.

Ohm. Fundamental unit of resistance.

Ohm meter. Device for measuring resistance by merely placing test prods across the resistor to be measured and reading the indication on a calibrated scale.

Ohm's law. The relationship which exists among current, pressure, and resistance.

Open-circuit voltage. The voltage of a cell or battery at its terminals when no current is flowing.

Orifice plate. Device inserted in a pipe or duct which causes a pressure drop across it. Depending on orifice size it can be used to restrict flow or form part of a measuring device.

Orsat apparatus. A device for measuring the combustion components of boiler or furnace flue gases.

Outlet. Point on wiring system at which current is taken to supply fixtures, heaters, motors, and current-consuming equipment generally.

Outline lighting. An arrangement of incandescent lamps or gaseous tubes used to outline or call attention to certain features such as the shape of a building or the decoration of a window.

Overload. A greater load applied to a circuit than it was designed to carry.

Parabolic lamp (PAR). Parabolic aluminized reflector lamp, spot or flood distribution, made of hard glass for indoor or outdoor use.

Parallel circuit. Two or more paths for electrons to follow.

Peak value. (*See* Maximum value.)

Perceived object color. The color perceived to belong to an object, resulting from characteristics of the object, of the incident light, and of the surroundings, the viewing direction, and observer adaptation.

Period. The time required for the completion of one cycle.

Permalloy. An alloy of nickel and iron having an abnormally high magnetic permeability.

Permanent magnet. Piece of steel or alloy which has its molecules lined up in such a way that a magnetic field exists without the application of a magnetizing force.

Permeability. Reciprocal of reluctance; a measure of the ease with which flux can be established in the magnetic circuit; a ratio of the flux produced by a current-carrying coil with a core to one without a core.

Phase. The portion of a whole period which has elapsed since the thing in question passed through its zero position in a positive direction.

Phase difference. The time in electrical degree by which one wave leads or lags another.

Physical. Of or pertaining to matter and material things involving no chemical changes.

Piggyback operation. Arrangement of chilled-water generation equipment whereby exhaust steam from a steam turbine-driven centrifugal chiller is used as the heat source for an absorption chiller.

Pigtail. A flexible wire extending from a component for ease of connection.

Pilot cell. A selected cell whose temperature, voltage, and specific gravity of electrolyte are assumed to indicate the condition of the entire battery.

Pinch-off tool. A tool used to pinch tubing walls together to stop all fluid flow.

Polarity. An electrical condition determining the direction in which current tends to flow.

Pole. The section of a magnet where the flux lines are concentrated; also, where they enter and leave the magnet. An electrode of a battery.

Polyphase. A circuit that utilizes more than one phase of alternating current.

Portable batteries. Batteries designed to be transported during service.

Portable lighting. Table or floor lamp, or unit, which is not permanently affixed to the electrical power supply.

Positive charge. The electrical charge carried by a body which has become deficient in electrons.

Positive plate (storage battery). The grid and active material to which the current flows from the external circuit when the battery is discharging.

Potential. A characteristic of a point in an electric field or circuit indicated by the work necessary to bring a unit positive charge to it from infinity; the degree of electrification as referred to some standard as that of the earth.

Potential difference. The arithmetical difference between two electrical potentials; same as electromotive force, electrical pressure, or voltage.

Potential energy. Energy that is stored in matter because of its position or because of the arrangements of its parts.

Potentiometer. A variable voltage divider; a resistor which has a variable contact arm so that any portion of the potential applied between its ends may be selected.

Power. The rate at which work is done. Power commonly is measured in units such as horsepower or kilowatts. Most bulk electric power is generated in this country by converting chemical energy to thermal, then mechanical, then electrical energy in steam, gas turbine, or large diesel powerplants, all requiring coal or petroleum resources. A lesser amount of the nation's electricity is generated by nuclear power.

Power distribution panel. A panel that takes the power from the main switch and feeds it to the utilization equipment through separate circuit breakers or fuses.

Power factor. Ratio of true power to apparent power; equal to the cosine of the phase angle between the voltage and current.

Presser bar. For controlling the pressure exerted on various materials being sewn. Pressure adjustable through spring tension controlled by presser bar cap.

Presser bar cap. To adjust pressure on presser foot, by turning down for more pressure or up for less pressure.

Presser foot. When lowered onto material, it holds material against feed dog.

Presser foot and attachment thumb screw. For fastening presser foot and attachments to presser bar.

Presser foot lifter. For raising and lowering presser bar and presser foot. When raised, tension is released. When lowered, tension is engaged.

Pressure. That which causes the current to flow.

Primary. Cell or battery which cannot be recharged efficiently or safely after any amount of discharge.

Primary line of sight. The line connecting the point of observation and the fixation point.

Prime mover. The source of mechanical power used to drive the rotor of a generator.

Protective disconnect (modern). *See* Circuit breaker.

Proton. The positive particles of an atom.

Pulsating direct current. Current which varies in magnitude but not in direction.

Purging. Releasing a compressed gas through a system for the purpose of removing contaminates.

Quad. One quadrillion Btu's.

Quality of lighting. The distribution of brightness and color rendition in a visual environment. The term is used in a positive sense and implies that these attributes contribute favorably to visual performance, visual comfort, ease of seeing, safety, and aesthetics for the specific visual tasks involved.

R.11: Trichloromonofluoromethane. A low pressure refrigerant.

R.12: Dichlorodifluoromethane. A refrigerant known as Freon 12.

Race. Groove in which shuttle turns.

Race cover. For holding shuttle in race.

Raceway. Any channel for holding wires, cables, or bus bars, designed expressly for, and used solely for, this purpose.

Radiant heating. A method of heating, usually consisting of a forced hot-water system with pipes placed in the floor, wall, or ceiling, or with electrically heated panels.

Radiation. Use of heat rays to transfer heat.

Range outlet. An electrical cook stove connection.

Ratio. The value obtained by dividing one number by another, indicating their relative proportions.

Raw source energy. The quantity of energy input at a generating station required to produce electrical energy, including all thermal and power conversion losses.

Reactance. The opposition offered to the flow of an alternating current by the inductance, capacitance, or both, in any circuit.

Readily accessible. Capable of being reached quickly for operation, renewal, or inspection, without requiring those to whom access is requisite to climb over or remove obstacles or to resort to portable ladders, chairs, and the like.

Receptacle. A contact device installed at an outlet for the connection of plug and flexible cord.

Recessed or flush unit. A luminaire mounted above the ceiling (or behind a wall or other surface) with the opening of the luminaire level with the surface.

Rechargeable. Capable of being recharged; refers to secondary cells or batteries.

Rectifier. Device for changing alternating current to pulsating direct current.

Reflectance. The ratio of the flux reflected by a surface or medium to the incident flux. This general term may be restricted by the use of one or more of the following adjectives: specular (regular), diffuse, and spectral.

Reflected glare. A glare resulting from specular reflections of high luminance in polished or glossy surfaces in the field of view.

Reflection. The process by which flux leaves a surface or medium from the incident side.

Reflector. A device used to redirect the luminous flux from a source by the process of reflection.

Reflector lamp (R). Incandescent filament lamp with reflector of silver or aluminum on inner surface.

Refraction. The process by which the direction of a ray of light changes as it passes obliquely from one medium to another.

Refrigerant. A substance used in air-conditioning systems to absorb heat in the evaporator by changing from a liquid to a gas, and for releasing heat in the condenser by changing from a gas to a liquid.

Refrigeration oil. A specially refined oil that is free from moisture and other contaminants and is used in air-conditioning systems.

Regressed unit. A luminaire designed with the control medium above the ceiling line.

Relay. Device for controlling electrical circuits from remote position; a magnetic switch.

Reluctance. The opposition to magnetic flux.

Resistance. The opposition to the flow of current caused by the nature and physical dimensions of a conductor.

Resistor. A circuit element whose chief characteristic is resistance; used to oppose the flow of current.

Retentivity. The measure of the ability of a material to hold its magnetism.

Reversal. Change in normal polarity of a storage cell.

Rheostat. A variable resistance for limiting the current in a circuit.

Roof spray. A system that reduces heat gain through a roof by cooling the outside surface with a water spray.

Rope-lay cable. A single-conductor cable composed of a central core surrounded by one or more layers of helically laid groups of wires.

Rotor. The rotating part of an AC induction motor.

Run windings. Those windings of large wire in an electric motor which are energized throughout the motor.

R-value. The resistance to heat flow expressed in units of square foot hour degree F/Btu.

Saturable reactor. A control device that uses a small DC current to control a large AC current by controlling core flux density.

Saturation. The condition existing in any circuit when an increase in the driving signal produces no further change in the resultant effect.

Schematic. A diagram of electronic circuits showing connections.

Seasonal efficiency. Ratio of useful output to energy input for a piece of equipment over an entire heating and cooling season. It can be derived by integrating part load efficiencies against time.

Secondary. Cell or battery which can be recharged; refers to secondary cells or batteries.

Self-inductance. Inductance associated with only one circuit.

Self-induction. The process by which a circuit induces an emf into itself by its own magnetic field.

Sensitivity. The degree of responsiveness measured inversely; in connection with current meters it is the current required for full-scale deflection; in connection with voltmeters it is the ohms per volt of scale on the meter.

Separator (storage battery). A device for preventing metallic contact between the plates of opposite polarity within the cell.

Series circuit. A circuit that contains only one possible path for electrons to follow.

Series connection. An arrangement of cells, generators, condensers, or conductors so that each carries the entire current of a circuit.

Series-wound. A motor or generator in which the armature is wired in series with the field winding.

Service. The conductors and equipment necessary for delivering electrical energy from the electrical source to the wiring system of the premises served.

Service cable. Service conductors (wires) made into cables.

Service conductors. That portion of the supply conductors which extends from the street main or duct or from transformers to the service equipment of the premises supplied. For overhead conductors this includes the conductors from the last line pole to the service equipment.

Service drop. That portion of overhead service conductors between the pole and the first point of attachment to the building.

Service drop line. The line that carries power from the transformer to the building.

Service entrance. The equipment needed to bring power into the building.

Service entrance conductors. That portion of service conductors between the terminals of service equipment and a point outside the building, clear of building walls, where joined by tap or splice to the service drop or to street mains or other source of supply.

Service equipment. The necessary equipment, usually consisting of circuit breaker or switch and fuses, and their accessories, located near point of entrance of supply conductors to a building and intended to constitute the main control and means of cutoff for the supply to that building.

Service feeders. Lines that carry power from the service drop to the meters.

Service manifold. An apparatus equipped with valves and gages, used for servicing air-conditioning systems.

Servo. A device used to convert a small movement into a greater movement or force.

Servomechanism. A closed-loop system that produces a force to position an object in accordance with the information that originates at the input.

Shelf life. For a dry cell, the period of time (measured from date of manufacture), at a storage temperature of 70°F., after which the cell retains a specified percentage (usually 90 percent) of its original energy content.

Shielding angle (of a luminaire). The angle between a horizontal line through the light center and the line of sight at which the bare source first becomes visible.

Short circuit. A direct connection across the source of current.

Short cycling. An air-conditioning system that starts and stops more than it should.

Shuttle. Used for forming lock stitch.

Shuttle driver. Used for turning shuttle in race.

Sight glass. A glass window that shows the amount of refrigerant, oil, or bubbles in the system.

Silica gel. A chemical compound that is used to absorb moisture from a refrigerant.

Silver bowl lamp. Incandescent filament lamp with silver reflector on the lower half of bowl. Provides indirect distribution.

Silver brazing. A brazing process that uses a filler rod that contains about 45 percent silver.

Single phase. Standard alternating current which phases from positive to negative in a sine curve at the rate of 60 times per second.

Single-pole switch. A switch which has open and closed positions only.

Sol-air temperature. The theoretical air temperature that would give a heat flow rate through a building surface equal in magnitude to that obtained by the addition of conduction and radiation effects.

Solar energy. Energy radiated directly from the sun.

Soldering. Using a relatively low temperature (less than 800 degrees Fahrenheit) to melt an adhesive (the solder) and join together two pieces of metal.

Solenoid. A tubular coil for the production of a magnetic field; electromagnet with a core which is free to move in and out.

Space charge. The cloud of electrons existing in the space between the cathode and plate in a vacuum tube, formed by the electrons emitted from the cathode in excess of those immediately attracted to the plate.

Special-purpose outlet. A point of connection to the wiring system for particular equipment.

Specific gravity. The ratio of the mass of a body to the mass of an equal volume of water at four degrees centigrade.

Specular angle. That angle between the perpendicular to a surface and the reflected ray. It is numerically equal to the angle of incidence.

Specular reflection. That process by which incident flux is redirected at the specular angle.

Specular surface. Shiny or glossy surfaces (including mirror and polished metals) that reflect incident flux of a specular angle.

Speed. Time rate of motion measured by the distance moved in unit time; in rotating equipment it is the revolution per minute, or rpm.

Spool pin bracket. Removable for access to needle positioning screw, if available.

Spool pins. One for sewing, one for winding bobbin, or both for sewing with two threads and two needles.

Spot lamp (R or Par). Incandescent filament lamp providing a relatively narrow beam pattern.

Start windings. Those windings of smaller wire in an electric motor which are energized only to start the motor and which are turned off after the motor has achieved a set number of revolutions per minute.

Starter. A device used in conjunction with a ballast for the purpose of starting an electric discharge (fluorescent) lamp.

Stationary batteries. Batteries designed for service in a permanent location.

Stator. The part of an AC generator or motor that has the stationary winding on it.

Step-down transformer. A transformer with fewer turns in the secondary than in the primary.

Step-up transformer. A transformer with more turns in the secondary than in the primary.

Stitch length adjusting lever or knob. For changing length of stitch in either forward and reverse direction.

Stitch length numbered plate. Moving lever up, turning knob, or pressing button or key increases reverse stitch length. Moving lever or turning knob from 0 down to 5 increases forward stitch length.

Stitch width lever or knob. For setting width of zig zag stitching.

Stitch width limit control. Used for pre-setting zig zag stitch to specific width limits.

Storage battery. A device which may be used repeatedly for storing energy at one time in the form of chemical energy, for use at another time in the form of electrical energy.

Storage cell. Fundamental unit of any storage battery.

Stranded conductor. A conductor composed of a group of wires or any combination of groups of wires. (These wires are usually twisted or braided together.)

Stranded wire. A group of small wires, used as a single wire.

Subjective brightness. The subjective attribute of any light sensation giving rise to the percept of luminous intensity including the whole scale of of qualities of being bright, light, brilliant, dim, or dark. (The term brightness occasionally is used when referring to measurable *photometric brightness.*)

Suction line. The tubing in an air-conditioning system that carries the refrigerant from the evaporator to the compressor.

Superheat. To raise the temperature of a liquid above the boiling point.

Surface-mounted unit. A luminaire mounted directly on the ceiling.

Suspended unit. A luminaire hung from the ceiling by supports.

Switch. A device for opening or closing an electric circuit.

Synchronous. Having the same period and phase; happening at the same time.

Synchroscope. An instrument used to indicate a difference in frequency between two AC sources.

Synchro system. An electrical system that gives remote indications or control by means of self-synchronizing motors.

System ground wire. A wire that grounds the entire conduit system so that a shorted or grounded hot wire will blow a fuse or breaker rather than electrifying the entire conduit system.

Tachometer. An instrument for indicating revolutions per minute.

Task plane. *See* Work plane.

Take-up lever. For drawing up top thread to form tight stitch.

Temperature. The condition of a body which determines the transfer of heat to or from other bodies; condition as to heat or cold; degree of heat or cold.

Tension assembly. Use separately for single or two-thread sewing. Auxiliary spring is included in this assembly.

Terminal posts. The points of the cell or battery to which the external circuit is connected.

Test light. A light with two leads used to test a circuit and determine if it is in line.

Tertiary winding. A third winding on a transformer or magnetic amplifier that is used as a second control winding.

Test lamp. A weatherproof rubber-insulated socket into which is screwed an incandescent lamp of the highest voltage rating of the circuits involved. Used for rough tests on interior-lighting and motor-wiring systems.

Therm. A unit of heat equal to 100,000 Btu's.

Thermal energy. A form of energy whose effect (heat) is produced by accelerated vibration of molecules.

Thermal insulation. A material used to resist the flow of heat from one space to another. Usually used between walls or partitions.

Thermistor. A resistor that is used to compensate for temperature variations in a circuit.

Thermocouple. A device for directly converting heat energy into electrical energy.

Thermostatic expansion valve. A valve located in the evaporator coil that operates by temperature and pressure to control the flow of refrigerant.

Thread tension guide for winding bobbin. Holds thread taut for even winding.

Three-phase. Alternating current with staggered phases of 120 degrees in a sine curve. Each operates similarly to a single phase.

Three-way switch. A three-screw switch in which the current may take either of two paths.

Thumb locks. For fastening race cover onto race.

Time rate. The rate in amperes at which a battery will be fully discharged in a specified time, under specified conditions of temperature and final voltage.

Tons of refrigeration. A means of expressing cooling capacity—1 ton = 12,000 Btu/hour cooling.

Torchere. An indirect floor lamp which directs all, or nearly all, of the luminous flux upward.

Torque. The effectiveness of a force to produce rotation about a center.

Transformer. An apparatus for converting electrical power in an AC system at one voltage or current into electrical power at some other voltage or current without the use of rotating parts; a device for raising or lowering AC voltage.

Transmission. The characteristic of many materials such as glass, plastics, and textiles. The process by which incident flux leaves a surface or medium on a side other than the incident side.

Transmission lines. Any conductor or system of conductors used to carry electrical energy from its source to a load.

Transmittance. The ratio of the flux transmitted by a medium to the incident flux.

Tray (storage battery). A support or container for one or more cells.

Trickle charging. Method of recharging in which a secondary cell is either continuously or intermittently connected to a constant-current supply that maintains the cell in fully charged condition.

Triplex cable. Three insulated single-conductor cables twisted together.

Troffer. A long recessed lighting unit, usually installed with the opening flush with the ceiling.

True power. The actual power consumed by an AC circuit, equal I^2R; expression used to distinguish from apparent power.

Tube. *See* Fluorescent lamp.

Tungsten halogen lamp. Compact incandescent filament lamp with initial efficacy essentially maintained over life of the lamp.

Twin cable. Two insulated single-conductor cables laid parallel, having a common covering.

Twin wire. Two small insulated conductors laid parallel, with a common covering.

Two-phase current. Two different alternating currents out of phase 90 degrees with each other.

Unidirectional. As applied to a current of electricity, a current that flows in one direction only.

Usable wall space. Where this term is used as the basis of requirements for spacing of outlets, it is defined as all portions of the wall except that which is not usable when a door is in its normal open position.

"U" valve. A coefficient expressing the thermal conductance of a composite structure in Btu per square foot hour degree F temperature difference.

Vacuum. A state in which pressure is below atmospheric pressure.

Vacuum pump. A special compressor used to create vacuums.

Vacuum tube. A tube from which the air has been pumped out. The tube contains an element that emits electrons when properly excited and an electrode to attract the electrons and set up a current in an external circuit.

Valance. A longitudinal shielding member mounted across the top of a window. Usually parallel to the window, it conceals the light sources and usually gives both upward and downward distributions. The same device applied to a wall is a wall bracket.

Value. The attribute of perceived color by which it seems to transmit, or reflect, a greater, or lesser, fraction of the incident light.

Vapor. A substance in a gaseous state that, under ordinary circumstances, is a liquid or a solid. In this context, it usually refers to a vaporized refrigerant.

Vapor barrier. A moisture-impervious layer designed to prevent moisture migration.

Vars. Abbreviation for volt-ampere, reactive.

Vector. A line used to represent both direction and magnitude.

Veiling reflection. Reflection of light from a task, or work surface, into the viewer's eyes.

Visual acuity. The ability to distinguish fine details.

Visual angle. The angle which an object or detail subtends at the point of observation.

Visual field. The focus of objects or points in space which can be perceived when the head and eyes are kept fixed.

Visual surround. All portions of the visual field except the visual task.

Visual task. Those details and objects which must be seen for the performance of a given activity.

Volt. Unit of potential, potential difference, electromotive force, or electrical pressure.

Volt efficiency (storage battery). The ratio of the average voltage during the discharge to the average voltage during the recharge.

Voltage. Electromotive forcing electrical pressure.

Voltage regulator. Device used in connection with generators to keep voltage constant as load or speed is changed.

Voltages. When described as 115 or 230 volts, voltages should be understood to be nominal voltages and to include, respectively, voltage of 110 to 125 and 220 to 250. In any location in which the electrical service is furnished at 120/208 volts from a three-phase, four-wire system, the local utility should be consulted regarding necessary changes in the requirements.

Voltmeter. An instrument for measuring potential difference or electrical pressure.

Wall switch. A switch on the wall, not a part of any fixture for the control of one or more outlets.

Watt. A unit of measure of electrical power; equal to a joule per second.

Watt-hour capacity. The number of watt-hours which can be delivered by a cell or battery under specified conditions as to temperature, rate of discharge, and final voltage.

Watt-hour efficiency (energy efficiency). The ratio of the watt-hours output to the watt-hours of the recharge.

Wattmeter. An instrument for measuring electrical power in watts.

Weight. The force with which a body is attracted toward the center of the earth by the gravitational field of force.

Wet. Indication that the liquid electrolyte in a cell is free-flowing.

Wet bulb temperature. The lowest temperature attainable by evaporating water in the air without the addition or subtraction of energy.

Wind energy. Energy derived from the wind.

Wire. A slender rod or filament of drawn metal.

Wire sizes. The size of wire is usually expressed according to some wire gage.

Work. The result of a force acting against opposition to produce motion; it is measured in terms of the product of the force and the distance it acts.

Work centers, kitchen. Refrigerator and preparation center; sink and dishwashing center; range and serving center.

Work plane. The plane at which work is done and at which illumination is specified; this is assumed to be a horizontal plane at the level of the task.

Appendix VIII

Trigonometric Functions

NATURAL SINES, COSINES, AND TANGENTS   0°–14.9°

Degs.	Function	0.0°	0.1°	0.2°	0.3°	0.4°	0.5°	0.6°	0.7°	0.8°	0.9°
0	sin	0.0000	0.0017	0.0035	0.0052	0.0070	0.0087	0.0105	0.0122	0.0140	0.0157
	cos	1.0000	1.0000	1.0000	1.0000	1.0000	1.0000	0.9999	0.9999	0.9999	0.9999
	tan	0.0000	0.0017	0.0035	0.0052	0.0070	0.0087	0.0105	0.0122	0.0140	0.0157
1	sin	0.0175	0.0192	0.0209	0.0227	0.0244	0.0262	0.0279	0.0297	0.0314	0.0332
	cos	0.9998	0.9998	0.9998	0.9997	0.9997	0.9997	0.9996	0.9996	0.9995	0.9995
	tan	0.0175	0.0192	0.0209	0.0227	0.0244	0.0262	0.0279	0.0297	0.0314	0.0332
2	sin	0.0349	0.0366	0.0384	0.0401	0.0419	0.0436	0.0454	0.0471	0.0488	0.0506
	cos	0.9994	0.9993	0.9993	0.9992	0.9990	0.9990	0.9990	0.9989	0.9988	0.9987
	tan	0.0349	0.0367	0.0384	0.0402	0.0419	0.0437	0.0454	0.0472	0.0489	0.0507
3	sin	0.0523	0.0541	0.0558	0.0576	0.0593	0.0610	0.0628	0.0645	0.0663	0.0680
	cos	0.9986	0.9985	0.9984	0.9983	0.9982	0.9981	0.9980	0.9979	0.9978	0.9977
	tan	0.0524	0.0542	0.0559	0.0577	0.0594	0.0612	0.0629	0.0647	0.0664	0.0682
4	sin	0.0698	0.0715	0.0732	0.0750	0.0767	0.0785	0.0802	0.0819	0.0837	0.0854
	cos	0.9976	0.9974	0.9973	0.9972	0.9971	0.9969	0.9968	0.9966	0.9965	0.9963
	tan	0.0699	0.0717	0.0734	0.0752	0.0769	0.0787	0.0805	0.0822	0.0840	0.0857
5	sin	0.0872	0.0889	0.0906	0.0924	0.0941	0.0958	0.0976	0.0993	0.1011	0.1028
	cos	0.9962	0.9960	0.9959	0.9957	0.9956	0.9954	0.9952	0.9951	0.9949	0.9947
	tan	0.0875	0.0892	0.0910	0.0928	0.0945	0.0963	0.0981	0.0998	0.1016	0.1033
6	sin	0.1045	0.1063	0.1080	0.1097	0.1115	0.1132	0.1149	0.1167	0.1184	0.1201
	cos	0.9945	0.9943	0.9942	0.9940	0.9938	0.9936	0.9934	0.9932	0.9930	0.9928
	tan	0.1051	0.1069	0.1086	0.1104	0.1122	0.1139	0.1157	0.1175	0.1192	0.1210
7	sin	0.1219	0.1236	0.1253	0.1271	0.1288	0.1305	0.1323	0.1340	0.1357	0.1374
	cos	0.9925	0.9923	0.9921	0.9919	0.9917	0.9914	0.9912	0.9910	0.9907	0.9905
	tan	0.1228	0.1246	0.1263	0.1281	0.1299	0.1317	0.1334	0.1352	0.1370	0.1388
8	sin	0.1392	0.1409	0.1426	0.1444	0.1461	0.1478	0.1495	0.1513	0.1530	0.1547
	cos	0.9903	0.9900	0.9898	0.9895	0.9893	0.9890	0.9888	0.9885	0.9882	0.9880
	tan	0.1405	0.1423	0.1441	0.1459	0.1477	0.1495	0.1512	0.1530	0.1548	0.1566
9	sin	0.1564	0.1582	0.1599	0.1616	0.1633	0.1650	0.1668	0.1685	0.1702	0.1719
	cos	0.9877	0.9874	0.9871	0.9869	0.9866	0.9863	0.9860	0.9857	0.9854	0.9851
	tan	0.1584	0.1602	0.1620	0.1638	0.1655	0.1673	0.1691	0.1709	0.1727	0.1745
10	sin	0.1736	0.1754	0.1771	0.1788	0.1805	0.1822	0.1840	0.1857	0.1874	0.1891
	cos	0.9848	0.9845	0.9842	0.9839	0.9836	0.9833	0.9829	0.9826	0.9823	0.9820
	tan	0.1763	0.1781	0.1799	0.1817	0.1835	0.1853	0.1871	0.1890	0.1908	0.1926
11	sin	0.1908	0.1925	0.1942	0.1959	0.1977	0.1994	0.2011	0.2028	0.2045	0.2062
	cos	0.9816	0.9813	0.9810	0.9806	0.9803	0.9799	0.9796	0.9792	0.9789	0.9785
	tan	0.1944	0.1962	0.1980	0.1998	0.2016	0.2035	0.2053	0.2071	0.2089	0.2107
12	sin	0.2079	0.2096	0.2113	0.2130	0.2147	0.2164	0.2181	0.2198	0.2215	0.2232
	cos	0.9781	0.9778	0.9774	0.9770	0.9767	0.9763	0.9759	0.9755	0.9751	0.9748
	tan	0.2126	0.2144	0.2162	0.2180	0.2199	0.2217	0.2235	0.2254	0.2272	0.2290
13	sin	0.2250	0.2267	0.2284	0.2300	0.2318	0.2334	0.2351	0.2368	0.2385	0.2402
	cos	0.9744	0.9740	0.9736	0.9732	0.9728	0.9724	0.9720	0.9715	0.9711	0.9707
	tan	0.2309	0.2327	0.2345	0.2364	0.2382	0.2401	0.2419	0.2438	0.2456	0.2475
14	sin	0.2419	0.2436	0.2453	0.2470	0.2487	0.2504	0.2521	0.2538	0.2554	0.2571
	cos	0.9703	0.9699	0.9694	0.9690	0.9686	0.9681	0.9677	0.9673	0.9668	0.9664
	tan	0.2493	0.2512	0.2530	0.2549	0.2568	0.2586	0.2605	0.2623	0.2642	0.2661
Degs.	Function	0′	6′	12′	18′	24′	30′	36′	42′	48′	54′

NATURAL SINES, COSINES, AND TANGENTS

15°–29.9°

Degs.	Function	0.0°	0.1°	0.2°	0.3°	0.4°	0.5°	0.6°	0.7°	0.8°	0.9°
15	sin	0.2588	0.2605	0.2622	0.2639	0.2656	0.2672	0.2689	0.2706	0.2723	0.2740
	cos	0.9659	0.9655	0.9650	0.9646	0.9641	0.9636	0.9632	0.9627	0.9622	0.9617
	tan	0.2679	0.2698	0.2717	0.2736	0.2754	0.2773	0.2792	0.2811	0.2830	0.2849
16	sin	0.2756	0.2773	0.2790	0.2807	0.2823	0.2840	0.2857	0.2874	0.2890	0.2907
	cos	0.9613	0.9608	0.9603	0.9598	0.9593	0.9588	0.9583	0.9578	0.9573	0.9568
	tan	0.2867	0.2886	0.2905	0.2924	0.2943	0.2962	0.2981	0.3000	0.3019	0.3038
17	sin	0.2924	0.2940	0.2957	0.2974	0.2990	0.3007	0.3024	0.3040	0.3057	0.3074
	cos	0.9563	0.9558	0.9553	0.9548	0.9542	0.9537	0.9532	0.9527	0.9521	0.9516
	tan	0.3057	0.3076	0.3096	0.3115	0.3134	0.3153	0.3172	0.3191	0.3211	0.3230
18	sin	0.3090	0.3107	0.3123	0.3140	0.3156	0.3173	0.3190	0.3206	0.3223	0.3239
	cos	0.9511	0.9505	0.9500	0.9494	0.9489	0.9483	0.9478	0.9472	0.9466	0.9461
	tan	0.3249	0.3269	0.3288	0.3307	0.3327	0.3346	0.3365	0.3385	0.3404	0.3424
19	sin	0.3256	0.3272	0.3289	0.3305	0.3322	0.3338	0.3355	0.3371	0.3387	0.3404
	cos	0.9455	0.9449	0.9444	0.9438	0.9432	0.9426	0.9421	0.9415	0.9409	0.9403
	tan	0.3443	0.3463	0.3482	0.3502	0.3522	0.3541	0.3561	0.3581	0.3600	0.3620
20	sin	0.3420	0.3437	0.3453	0.3469	0.3486	0.3502	0.3518	0.3535	0.3551	0.3567
	cos	0.9397	0.9391	0.9385	0.9379	0.9373	0.9367	0.9361	0.9354	0.9348	0.9342
	tan	0.3640	0.3659	0.3679	0.3699	0.3719	0.3739	0.3759	0.3779	0.3799	0.3819
21	sin	0.3584	0.3600	0.3616	0.3633	0.3649	0.3665	0.3681	0.3697	0.3714	0.3730
	cos	0.9336	0.9330	0.9323	0.9317	0.9311	0.9304	0.9298	0.9291	0.9285	0.9278
	tan	0.3839	0.3859	0.3879	0.3899	0.3919	0.3939	0.3959	0.3979	0.4000	0.4020
22	sin	0.3746	0.3762	0.3778	0.3795	0.3811	0.3827	0.3843	0.3859	0.3875	0.3891
	cos	0.9272	0.9265	0.9259	0.9252	0.9245	0.9239	0.9232	0.9225	0.9219	0.9212
	tan	0.4040	0.4061	0.4081	0.4101	0.4122	0.4142	0.4163	0.4183	0.4204	0.4224
23	sin	0.3907	0.3923	0.3939	0.3955	0.3971	0.3987	0.4003	0.4019	0.4035	0.4051
	cos	0.9205	0.9198	0.9191	0.9184	0.9178	0.9171	0.9164	0.9157	0.9150	0.9143
	tan	0.4245	0.4265	0.4286	0.4307	0.4327	0.4348	0.4369	0.4390	0.4411	0.4431
24	sin	0.4067	0.4083	0.4099	0.4115	0.4131	0.4147	0.4163	0.4179	0.4195	0.4210
	cos	0.9135	0.9128	0.9121	0.9114	0.9107	0.9100	0.9092	0.9085	0.9078	0.9070
	tan	0.4452	0.4473	0.4494	0.4515	0.4536	0.4557	0.4578	0.4599	0.4621	0.4642
25	sin	0.4226	0.4242	0.4258	0.4274	0.4289	0.4305	0.4321	0.4337	0.4352	0.4368
	cos	0.9063	0.9056	0.9048	0.9041	0.9033	0.9026	0.9018	0.9011	0.9003	0.8996
	tan	0.4663	0.4684	0.4706	0.4727	0.4748	0.4770	0.4791	0.4813	0.4834	0.4856
26	sin	0.4384	0.4399	0.4415	0.4431	0.4446	0.4462	0.4478	0.4493	0.4509	0.4524
	cos	0.8988	0.8980	0.8973	0.8965	0.8957	0.8949	0.8942	0.8934	0.8926	0.8918
	tan	0.4877	0.4899	0.4921	0.4942	0.4964	0.4986	0.5008	0.5029	0.5051	0.5073
27	sin	0.4540	0.4555	0.4571	0.4586	0.4602	0.4617	0.4633	0.4648	0.4664	0.4679
	cos	0.8910	0.8902	0.8894	0.8886	0.8878	0.8870	0.8862	0.8854	0.8846	0.8838
	tan	0.5095	0.5117	0.5139	0.5161	0.5184	0.5206	0.5228	0.5250	0.5272	0.5295
28	sin	0.4695	0.4710	0.4726	0.4741	0.4756	0.4772	0.4787	0.4802	0.4818	0.4833
	cos	0.8829	0.8821	0.8813	0.8805	0.8796	0.8788	0.8780	0.8771	0.8763	0.8755
	tan	0.5317	0.5340	0.5362	0.5384	0.5407	0.5430	0.5452	0.5475	0.5498	0.5520
29	sin	0.4848	0.4863	0.4879	0.4894	0.4909	0.4924	0.4939	0.4955	0.4970	0.4985
	cos	0.8746	0.8738	0.8729	0.8721	0.8712	0.8704	0.8695	0.8686	0.8678	0.8669
	tan	0.5543	0.5566	0.5589	0.5612	0.5635	0.5658	0.5681	0.5704	0.5727	0.5750
Degs.	Function	0'	6'	12'	18'	24'	30'	36'	42'	48'	54'

APPENDIX VIII

NATURAL SINES, COSINES, AND TANGENTS

30°–44.9°

Degs.	Function	0.0°	0.1°	0.2°	0.3°	0.4°	0.5°	0.6°	0.7°	0.8°	0.9°
30	sin	0.5000	0.5015	0.5030	0.5045	0.5060	0.5075	0.5090	0.5105	0.5120	0.5135
	cos	0.8660	0.8652	0.8643	0.8634	0.8625	0.8616	0.8607	0.8599	0.8590	0.8581
	tan	0.5774	0.5797	0.5820	0.5844	0.5867	0.5890	0.5914	0.5938	0.5961	0.5985
31	sin	0.5150	0.5165	0.5180	0.5195	0.5210	0.5225	0.5240	0.5255	0.5270	0.5284
	cos	0.8572	0.8563	0.8554	0.8545	0.8536	0.8526	0.8517	0.8506	0.8499	0.8490
	tan	0.6009	0.6032	0.6056	0.6080	0.6104	0.6128	0.6152	0.6176	0.6200	0.6224
32	sin	0.5299	0.5314	0.5329	0.5344	0.5358	0.5373	0.5388	0.5402	0.5417	0.5432
	cos	0.8480	0.8471	0.8462	0.8453	0.8443	0.8434	0.8425	0.8415	0.8406	0.8396
	tan	0.6249	0.6273	0.6297	0.6322	0.6346	0.6371	0.6395	0.6420	0.6445	0.6469
33	sin	0.5446	0.5461	0.5476	0.5490	0.5505	0.5519	0.5534	0.5548	0.5563	0.5577
	cos	0.8387	0.8377	0.8368	0.8358	0.8348	0.8339	0.8329	0.8320	0.8310	0.8300
	tan	0.6494	0.6519	0.6544	0.6569	0.6594	0.6619	0.6644	0.6669	0.6694	0.6720
34	sin	0.5592	0.5606	0.5621	0.5635	0.5650	0.5664	0.5678	0.5693	0.5707	0.5721
	cos	0.8290	0.8281	0.8271	0.8261	0.8251	0.8241	0.8231	0.8221	0.8211	0.8202
	tan	0.6745	0.6771	0.6796	0.6822	0.6847	0.6873	0.6899	0.6924	0.6950	0.6976
35	sin	0.5736	0.5750	0.5764	0.5779	0.5793	0.5807	0.5821	0.5835	0.5850	0.5864
	cos	0.8192	0.8181	0.8171	0.8161	0.8151	0.8141	0.8131	0.8121	0.8111	0.8100
	tan	0.7002	0.7028	0.7054	0.7080	0.7107	0.7133	0.7159	0.7186	0.7212	0.7239
36	sin	0.5878	0.5892	0.5906	0.5920	0.5934	0.5948	0.5962	0.5976	0.5990	0.6004
	cos	0.8090	0.8080	0.8070	0.8059	0.8049	0.8039	0.8028	0.8018	0.8007	0.7997
	tan	0.7265	0.7292	0.7319	0.7346	0.7373	0.7400	0.7427	0.7454	0.7481	0.7508
37	sin	0.6018	0.6032	0.6046	0.6060	0.6074	0.6088	0.6101	0.6115	0.6129	0.6143
	cos	0.7986	0.7976	0.7965	0.7955	0.7944	0.7934	0.7923	0.7912	0.7902	0.7891
	tan	0.7536	0.7563	0.7590	0.7618	0.7646	0.7673	0.7701	0.7729	0.7757	0.7785
38	sin	0.6157	0.6170	0.6184	0.6198	0.6211	0.6225	0.6239	0.6252	0.6266	0.6280
	cos	0.7880	0.7869	0.7859	0.7848	0.7837	0.7826	0.7815	0.7804	0.7793	0.7782
	tan	0.7813	0.7841	0.7869	0.7898	0.7926	0.7954	0.7983	0.8012	0.8040	0.8069
39	sin	0.6293	0.6307	0.6320	0.6334	0.6347	0.6361	0.6374	0.6388	0.6401	0.6414
	cos	0.7771	0.7760	0.7749	0.7738	0.7727	0.7716	0.7705	0.7694	0.7683	0.7672
	tan	0.8098	0.8127	0.8156	0.8185	0.8214	0.8243	0.8273	0.8302	0.8332	0.8361
40	sin	0.6428	0.6441	0.6455	0.6468	0.6481	0.6494	0.6508	0.6521	0.6534	0.6547
	cos	0.7660	0.7649	0.7638	0.7627	0.7615	0.7604	0.7593	0.7581	0.7570	0.7559
	tan	0.8391	0.8421	0.8451	0.8481	0.8511	0.8541	0.8571	0.8601	0.8632	0.8662
41	sin	0.6561	0.6574	0.6587	0.6600	0.6613	0.6626	0.6639	0.6652	0.6665	0.6678
	cos	0.7547	0.7536	0.7524	0.7513	0.7501	0.7490	0.7478	0.7466	0.7455	0.7443
	tan	0.8693	0.8724	0.8754	0.8785	0.8816	0.8847	0.8878	0.8910	0.8941	0.8972
42	sin	0.6691	0.6704	0.6717	0.6730	0.6743	0.6756	0.6769	0.6782	0.6794	0.6807
	cos	0.7431	0.7420	0.7408	0.7396	0.7385	0.7373	0.7361	0.7349	0.7337	0.7325
	tan	0.9004	0.9036	0.9067	0.9099	0.9131	0.9163	0.9195	0.9228	0.9260	0.9293
43	sin	0.6820	0.6833	0.6845	0.6858	0.6871	0.6884	0.6896	0.6909	0.6921	0.6934
	cos	0.7314	0.7302	0.7290	0.7278	0.7266	0.7254	0.7242	0.7230	0.7218	0.7206
	tan	0.9325	0.9358	0.9391	0.9424	0.9457	0.9490	0.9523	0.9556	0.9590	0.9623
44	sin	0.6947	0.6959	0.6972	0.6984	0.6997	0.7009	0.7022	0.7034	0.7046	0.7059
	cos	0.7193	0.7181	0.7169	0.7157	0.7145	0.7133	0.7120	0.7108	0.7096	0.7083
	tan	0.9657	0.9691	0.9725	0.9759	0.9793	0.9827	0.9861	0.9896	0.9930	0.9965
Degs.	Function	0'	6'	12'	18'	24'	30'	36'	42'	48'	54'

NATURAL SINES, COSINES, AND TANGENTS

45°–59.9°

Degs.	Function	0.0°	0.1°	0.2°	0.3°	0.4°	0.5°	0.6°	0.7°	0.8°	0.9°
45	sin	0.7071	0.7083	0.7096	0.7108	0.7120	0.7133	0.7145	0.7157	0.7169	0.7181
	cos	0.7071	0.7059	0.7046	0.7034	0.7022	0.7009	0.6997	0.6984	0.6972	0.6959
	tan	1.0000	1.0035	1.0070	1.0105	1.0141	1.0176	1.0212	1.0247	1.0283	1.0319
46	sin	0.7193	0.7206	0.7218	0.7230	0.7242	0.7254	0.7266	0.7278	0.7290	0.7302
	cos	0.6947	0.6934	0.6921	0.6909	0.6896	0.6884	0.6871	0.6858	0.6845	0.6833
	tan	1.0355	1.0392	1.0428	1.0464	1.0501	1.0538	1.0575	1.0612	1.0649	1.0686
47	sin	0.7314	0.7325	0.7337	0.7349	0.7361	0.7373	0.7385	0.7396	0.7408	0.7420
	cos	0.6820	0.6807	0.6794	0.6782	0.6769	0.6756	0.6743	0.6730	0.6717	0.6704
	tan	1.0724	1.0761	1.0799	1.0837	1.0875	1.0913	1.0951	1.0990	1.1028	1.1067
48	sin	0.7431	0.7443	0.7455	0.7466	0.7478	0.7490	0.7501	0.7513	0.7524	0.7536
	cos	0.6691	0.6678	0.6665	0.6652	0.6639	0.6626	0.6613	0.6600	0.6587	0.6574
	tan	1.1106	1.1145	1.1184	1.1224	1.1263	1.1303	1.1343	1.1383	1.1423	1.1463
49	sin	0.7547	0.7559	0.7570	0.7581	0.7593	0.7604	0.7615	0.7627	0.7638	0.7649
	cos	0.6561	0.6547	0.6534	0.6521	0.6508	0.6494	0.6481	0.6468	0.6455	0.6441
	tan	1.1504	1.1544	1.1585	1.1626	1.1667	1.1708	1.1750	1.1792	1.1833	1.1875
50	sin	0.7660	0.7672	0.7683	0.7694	0.7705	0.7716	0.7727	0.7738	0.7749	0.7760
	cos	0.6428	0.6414	0.6401	0.6388	0.6374	0.6361	0.6347	0.6334	0.6320	0.6307
	tan	1.1918	1.1960	1.2002	1.2045	1.2088	1.2131	1.2174	1.2218	1.2261	1.2305
51	sin	0.7771	0.7782	0.7793	0.7804	0.7815	0.7826	0.7837	0.7848	0.7859	0.7869
	cos	0.6293	0.6280	0.6266	0.6252	0.6239	0.6225	0.6211	0.6198	0.6184	0.6170
	tan	1.2349	1.2393	1.2437	1.2482	1.2527	1.2572	1.2617	1.2662	1.2708	1.2753
52	sin	0.7880	0.7891	0.7902	0.7912	0.7923	0.7934	0.7944	0.7955	0.7965	0.7976
	cos	0.6157	0.6143	0.6129	0.6115	0.6101	0.6088	0.6074	0.6060	0.6046	0.6032
	tan	1.2799	1.2846	1.2892	1.2938	1.2985	1.3032	1.3079	1.3127	1.3175	1.3222
53	sin	0.7986	0.7997	0.8007	0.8018	0.8028	0.8039	0.8049	0.8059	0.8070	0.8080
	cos	0.6018	0.6004	0.5990	0.5976	0.5962	0.5948	0.5934	0.5920	0.5906	0.5892
	tan	1.3270	1.3319	1.3367	1.3416	1.3465	1.3514	1.3564	1.3613	1.3663	1.3713
54	sin	0.8090	0.8100	0.8111	0.8121	0.8131	0.8141	0.8151	0.8161	0.8171	0.8181
	cos	0.5878	0.5864	0.5850	0.5835	0.5821	0.5807	0.5793	0.5779	0.5764	0.5750
	tan	1.3764	1.3814	1.3865	1.3916	1.3968	1.4019	1.4071	1.4124	1.4176	1.4229
55	sin	0.8192	0.8202	0.8211	0.8221	0.8231	0.8241	0.8251	0.8261	0.8271	0.8281
	cos	0.5736	0.5721	0.5707	0.5693	0.5678	0.5664	0.5650	0.5635	0.5621	0.5606
	tan	1.4281	1.4335	1.4388	1.4442	1.4496	1.4550	1.4605	1.4659	1.4715	1.4770
56	sin	0.8290	0.8300	0.8310	0.8320	0.8329	0.8339	0.8348	0.8358	0.8368	0.8377
	cos	0.5592	0.5577	0.5563	0.5548	0.5534	0.5519	0.5505	0.5490	0.5476	0.5461
	tan	1.4826	1.4882	1.4938	1.4994	1.5051	1.5108	1.5166	1.5224	1.5282	1.5340
57	sin	0.8387	0.8396	0.8406	0.8415	0.8425	0.8434	0.8443	0.8453	0.8462	0.8471
	cos	0.5446	0.5432	0.5417	0.5402	0.5388	0.5373	0.5358	0.5344	0.5329	0.5314
	tan	1.5399	1.5458	1.5517	1.5577	1.5637	1.5697	1.5757	1.5818	1.5880	1.5941
58	sin	0.8480	0.8490	0.8499	0.8508	0.8517	0.8526	0.8536	0.8545	0.8554	0.8563
	cos	0.5299	0.5284	0.5270	0.5255	0.5240	0.5225	0.5210	0.5195	0.5180	0.5165
	tan	1.6003	1.6066	1.6128	1.6191	1.6255	1.6319	1.6383	1.6447	1.6512	1.6577
59	sin	0.8572	0.8581	0.8590	0.8599	0.8607	0.8616	0.8625	0.8634	0.8643	0.8652
	cos	0.5150	0.5135	0.5120	0.5105	0.5090	0.5075	0.5060	0.5045	0.5030	0.5015
	tan	1.6643	1.6709	1.6775	1.6842	1.6909	1.6977	1.7045	1.7113	1.7182	1.7251
Degs.	Function	0'	6'	12'	18'	24'	30'	36'	42'	48'	54'

APPENDIX VIII

NATURAL SINES, COSINES, AND TANGENTS

60°–74.9°

Degs.	Function	0.0°	0.1°	0.2°	0.3°	0.4°	0.5°	0.6°	0.7°	0.8°	0.9°
60	sin	0.8660	0.8669	0.8678	0.8686	0.8695	0.8704	0.8712	0.8721	0.8729	0.8738
	cos	0.5000	0.4985	0.4970	0.4955	0.4939	0.4924	0.4909	0.4894	0.4879	0.4863
	tan	1.7321	1.7391	1.7461	1.7532	1.7603	1.7675	1.7747	1.7820	1.7893	1.7966
61	sin	0.8746	0.8755	0.8763	0.8771	0.8780	0.8788	0.8796	0.8805	0.8813	0.8821
	cos	0.4848	0.4833	0.4818	0.4802	0.4787	0.4772	0.4756	0.4741	0.4726	0.4710
	tan	1.8040	1.8115	1.8190	1.8265	1.8341	1.8418	1.8495	1.8572	1.8650	1.8728
62	sin	0.8829	0.8838	0.8846	0.8854	0.8862	0.8870	0.8878	0.8886	0.8894	0.8902
	cos	0.4695	0.4679	0.4664	0.4648	0.4633	0.4617	0.4602	0.4586	0.4571	0.4555
	tan	1.8807	1.8887	1.8967	1.9047	1.9128	1.9210	1.9292	1.9375	1.9458	1.9542
63	sin	0.8910	0.8918	0.8926	0.8934	0.8942	0.8949	0.8957	0.8965	0.8973	0.8980
	cos	0.4540	0.4524	0.4509	0.4493	0.4478	0.4462	0.4446	0.4431	0.4415	0.4399
	tan	1.9626	1.9711	1.9797	1.9883	1.9970	2.0057	2.0145	2.0233	2.0323	2.0413
64	sin	0.8988	0.8996	0.9003	0.9011	0.9018	0.9026	0.9033	0.9041	0.9048	0.9056
	cos	0.4384	0.4368	0.4352	0.4337	0.4321	0.4305	0.4289	0.4274	0.4258	0.4242
	tan	2.0503	2.0594	2.0686	2.0778	2.0872	2.0965	2.1060	2.1155	2.1251	2.1348
65	sin	0.9063	0.9070	0.9078	0.9085	0.9092	0.9100	0.9107	0.9114	0.9121	0.9128
	cos	0.4226	0.4210	0.4195	0.4179	0.4163	0.4147	0.4131	0.4115	0.4099	0.4083
	tan	2.1445	2.1543	2.1642	2.1742	2.1842	2.1943	2.2045	2.2148	2.2251	2.2355
66	sin	0.9135	0.9143	0.9150	0.9157	0.9164	0.9171	0.9178	0.9184	0.9191	0.9198
	cos	0.4067	0.4051	0.4035	0.4019	0.4003	0.3987	0.3971	0.3955	0.3939	0.3923
	tan	2.2460	2.2566	2.2673	2.2781	2.2889	2.2998	2.3109	2.3220	2.3332	2.3445
67	sin	0.9205	0.9212	0.9219	0.9225	0.9232	0.9239	0.9245	0.9252	0.9259	0.9265
	cos	0.3907	0.3891	0.3875	0.3859	0.3843	0.3827	0.3811	0.3795	0.3778	0.3762
	tan	2.3559	2.3673	2.3789	2.3906	2.4023	2.4142	2.4262	2.4383	2.4504	2.4627
68	sin	0.9272	0.9278	0.9285	0.9291	0.9298	0.9304	0.9311	0.9317	0.9323	0.9330
	cos	0.3746	0.3730	0.3714	0.3697	0.3681	0.3665	0.3649	0.3633	0.3616	0.3600
	tan	2.4751	2.4876	2.5002	2.5129	2.5257	2.5386	2.5517	2.5649	2.5782	2.5916
69	sin	0.9336	0.9342	0.9348	0.9354	0.9361	0.9367	0.9373	0.9379	0.9385	0.9391
	cos	0.3584	0.3567	0.3551	0.3535	0.3518	0.3502	0.3486	0.3469	0.3453	0.3437
	tan	2.6051	2.6187	2.6325	2.6464	2.6605	2.6746	2.6889	2.7034	2.7179	2.7326
70	sin	0.9397	0.9403	0.9409	0.9415	0.9421	0.9426	0.9432	0.9438	0.9444	0.9449
	cos	0.3420	0.3404	0.3387	0.3371	0.3355	0.3338	0.3322	0.3305	0.3289	0.3272
	tan	2.7475	2.7625	2.7776	2.7929	2.8083	2.8239	2.8397	2.8556	2.8716	2.8878
71	sin	0.9455	0.9461	0.9466	0.9472	0.9478	0.9483	0.9489	0.9494	0.9500	0.9505
	cos	0.3256	0.3239	0.3223	0.3206	0.3190	0.3173	0.3156	0.3140	0.3123	0.3107
	tan	2.9042	2.9208	2.9375	2.9544	2.9714	2.9887	3.0061	3.0237	3.0415	3.0595
72	sin	0.9511	0.9516	0.9521	0.9527	0.9532	0.9537	0.9542	0.9548	0.9553	0.9558
	cos	0.3090	0.3074	0.3057	0.3040	0.3024	0.3007	0.2990	0.2974	0.2957	0.2940
	tan	3.0777	3.0961	3.1146	3.1334	3.1524	3.1716	3.1910	3.2106	3.2305	3.2506
73	sin	0.9563	0.9568	0.9573	0.9578	0.9583	0.9588	0.9593	0.9598	0.9603	0.9608
	cos	0.2924	0.2907	0.2890	0.2874	0.2857	0.2840	0.2823	0.2807	0.2790	0.2773
	tan	3.2709	3.2914	3.3122	3.3332	3.3544	3.3759	3.3977	3.4197	3.4420	3.4646
74	sin	0.9613	0.9617	0.9622	0.9627	0.9632	0.9636	0.9641	0.9646	0.9650	0.9655
	cos	0.2756	0.2740	0.2723	0.2706	0.2689	0.2672	0.2656	0.2639	0.2622	0.2605
	tan	3.4874	3.5105	3.5339	3.5576	3.5816	3.6059	3.6305	3.6554	3.6806	3.7062
Degs.	Function	0′	6′	12′	18′	24′	30′	36′	42′	48′	54′

NATURAL SINES, COSINES, AND TANGENTS.

75°–89.9°

Degs.	Function	0.0°	0.1°	0.2°	0.3°	0.4°	0.5°	0.6°	0.7°	0.8°	0.9°
75	sin	0.9659	0.9664	0.9668	0.9673	0.9677	0.9681	0.9686	0.9690	0.9694	0.9699
	cos	0.2588	0.2571	0.2554	0.2538	0.2521	0.2504	0.2487	0.2470	0.2453	0.2436
	tan	3.7321	3.7583	3.7848	3.8118	3.8391	3.8667	3.8947	3.9232	3.9520	3.9812
76	sin	0.9703	0.9707	0.9711	0.9715	0.9720	0.9724	0.9728	0.9732	0.9736	0.9740
	cos	0.2419	0.2402	0.2385	0.2368	0.2351	0.2334	0.2317	0.2300	0.2284	0.2267
	tan	4.0108	4.0408	4.0713	4.1022	4.1335	4.1653	4.1976	4.2303	4.2635	4.2972
77	sin	0.9744	0.9748	0.9751	0.9755	0.9759	0.9763	0.9767	0.9770	0.9774	0.9778
	cos	0.2250	0.2232	0.2215	0.2198	0.2181	0.2164	0.2147	0.2130	0.2113	0.2096
	tan	4.3315	4.3662	4.4015	4.4374	4.4737	4.5107	4.5483	4.5864	4.6252	4.6646
78	sin	0.9781	0.9785	0.9789	0.9792	0.9796	0.9799	0.9803	0.9806	0.9810	0.9813
	cos	0.2079	0.2062	0.2045	0.2028	0.2011	0.1994	0.1977	0.1959	0.1942	0.1925
	tan	4.7046	4.7453	4.7867	4.8288	4.8716	4.9152	4.9594	5.0045	5.0504	5.0970
79	sin	0.9816	0.9820	0.9823	0.9826	0.9829	0.9833	0.9836	0.9839	0.9842	0.9845
	cos	0.1908	0.1891	0.1874	0.1857	0.1840	0.1822	0.1805	0.1788	0.1771	0.1754
	tan	5.1446	5.1929	5.2422	5.2924	5.3435	5.3955	5.4486	5.5026	5.5578	5.6140
80	sin	0.9848	0.9851	0.9854	0.9857	0.9860	0.9863	0.9866	0.9869	0.9871	0.9874
	cos	0.1736	0.1719	0.1702	0.1685	0.1668	0.1650	0.1633	0.1616	0.1599	0.1582
	tan	5.6713	5.7297	5.7894	5.8502	5.9124	5.9758	6.0405	6.1066	6.1742	6.2432
81	sin	0.9877	0.9880	0.9882	0.9885	0.9888	0.9890	0.9893	0.9895	0.9898	0.9900
	cos	0.1564	0.1547	0.1530	0.1513	0.1495	0.1478	0.1461	0.1444	0.1426	0.1409
	tan	6.3138	6.3859	6.4596	6.5350	6.6122	6.6912	6.7720	6.8548	6.9395	7.0264
82	sin	0.9903	0.9905	0.9907	0.9910	0.9912	0.9914	0.9917	0.9919	0.9921	0.9923
	cos	0.1392	0.1374	0.1357	0.1340	0.1323	0.1305	0.1288	0.1271	0.1253	0.1236
	tan	7.1154	7.2066	7.3002	7.3962	7.4947	7.5958	7.6996	7.8062	7.9158	8.0285
83	sin	0.9925	0.9928	0.9930	0.9932	0.9934	0.9936	0.9938	0.9940	0.9942	0.9943
	cos	0.1219	0.1201	0.1184	0.1167	0.1149	0.1132	0.1115	0.1097	0.1080	0.1063
	tan	8.1443	8.2636	8.3863	8.5126	8.6427	8.7769	8.9152	9.0579	9.2052	9.3572
84	sin	0.9945	0.9947	0.9949	0.9951	0.9952	0.9954	0.9956	0.9957	0.9959	0.9960
	cos	0.1045	0.1028	0.1011	0.0993	0.0976	0.0958	0.0941	0.0924	0.0906	0.0889
	tan	9.5144	9.6768	9.8448	10.02	10.20	10.39	10.58	10.78	10.99	11.20
85	sin	0.9962	0.9963	0.9965	0.9966	0.9968	0.9969	0.9971	0.9972	0.9973	0.9974
	cos	0.0872	0.0854	0.0837	0.0819	0.0802	0.0785	0.0767	0.0750	0.0732	0.0715
	tan	11.43	11.66	11.91	12.16	12.43	12.71	13.00	13.30	13.62	13.95
86	sin	0.9976	0.9977	0.9978	0.9979	0.9980	0.9981	0.9982	0.9983	0.9984	0.9985
	cos	0.0698	0.0680	0.0663	0.0645	0.0628	0.0610	0.0593	0.0576	0.0558	0.0541
	tan	14.30	14.67	15.06	15.46	15.89	16.35	16.83	17.34	17.89	18.46
87	sin	0.9986	0.9987	0.9988	0.9989	0.9990	0.9990	0.9991	0.9992	0.9993	0.9993
	cos	0.0523	0.0506	0.0488	0.0471	0.0454	0.0436	0.0419	0.0401	0.0384	0.0366
	tan	19.08	19.74	20.45	21.20	22.02	22.90	23.86	24.90	26.03	27.27
88	sin	0.9994	0.9995	0.9995	0.9996	0.9996	0.9997	0.9997	0.9997	0.9998	0.9998
	cos	0.0349	0.0332	0.0314	0.0297	0.0279	0.0262	0.0244	0.0227	0.0209	0.0192
	tan	28.64	30.14	31.82	33.69	35.80	38.19	40.92	44.07	47.74	52.08
89	sin	0.9998	0.9999	0.9999	0.9999	0.9999	1.000	1.000	1.000	1.000	1.000
	cos	0.0175	0.0157	0.0140	0.0122	0.0105	0.0087	0.0070	0.0052	0.0035	0.0017
	tan	57.29	63.66	71.62	81.85	95.49	114.6	143.2	191.0	286.5	573.0
Degs.	Function	0'	6'	12'	18'	24'	30'	36'	42'	48'	54'

Appendix IX

Symbols

VARIABLE FREQUENCY GENERATOR		BATTERY	
AIR INDUCTANCE		FIXED CAPACITOR	
PIE-TYPE CHOKE COIL (SECTIONAL)		VARIABLE RESISTOR	
VARIABLE CAPACITOR		FIXED RESISTOR	
MULTIPLE SECTION FIXED CAPACITOR		VARIO-COUPLER	
VARIABLE SPLIT-STATOR		IRON CORE INDUCTANCE	
HORSESHOE MAGNET		AIR CORE TRANSFORMER	
BAR MAGNET		IRON CORE TRANSFORMER	
SOURCE OF ALTERNATING VOLTAGE		SINGLE POLE SINGLE THROW SWITCH	
METERS ✳ MILLIAMETER-M VOLTMETER-V AMMETER-A		DOUBLE POLE SINGLE THROW SWITCH	
MOTORS OR GENERATORS ✳ D-C GENERATOR-D-C GEN D-C MOTOR - D-C MOT A-C MOTOR - A-C MOT A-C ALTERNATOR-A-C ALT		SINGLE POLE DOUBLE THROW SWITCH	

ANTENNA ⋔

GROUND ⏚

DIPOLE ⊤⊤

MULTIPLE-WINDING TRANSFORMER

Appendix X

The SI System of Metric Conversions

ENGLISH TO METRIC				METRIC TO ENGLISH			
inches (ins.)	X	25.4	= millimetres (mm)	mm	X	0.04	= ins.
feet (ft.)	X	0.3	= metres (m)	m	X	3.3	= ft.
yards (yds.)	X	0.9	= metres (m)	m	X	1.1	= yds.
miles (mi.)	X	1.6	= kilometres (km)	km	X	0.6	= mi.
sq. inch (in²)	X	6.5	= sq. centimetres (cm²)	cm²	X	0.16	= in²
sq. feet (ft²)	X	0.09	= sq. metres (m²)	m²	X	11.00	= ft²
sq. yard (yd²)	X	0.8	= sq. metres (m²)	m²	X	1.2	= yd²
acre (a)	X	0.4	= hectares (ha)	ha	X	2.5	= a
cu. in. (in³)	X	16.0	= cu. centimetres (cm³)	cm³	X	0.06	= in³
cu. ft. (ft³)	X	0.03	= cu. metres (m³)	m³	X	35.0	= ft³
cu. yd. (yd³)	X	0.8	= cu. metres (m³)	m³	X	1.3	= yd³
(liq) quart (qt)	X	0.9	= litre (l)	l	X	1.05	= qt
gallon (gal)	X	0.004	= cu. metre (m³)	m³	X	264.2	= gal
(avdp) ounce (oz)	X	28.3	= grams (g)	g	X	0.035	= oz
(avdp) pound (lb)	X	0.45	= kilogram (kg)	kg	X	2.20	= lb
horsepower (h.p.)	X	0.75	= kilowatt (kW)	kW	X	1.34	= h.p.
ft. per sec. (ft/s)	X	0.304	= met. per sec. (m/s)	m/s	X	3.280	= ft/s
ounce-force (ozf)	X	0.278	= newtons (N)	N	X	3.597	= ozf
pounds-force (lbf)	X	4.448	= newtons (N)	N	X	0.224	= lbf
foot-pounds (ft. lb)	X	1.355	= newton-metres (N.m)	N.m	X	0.737	= ft. lb.
foot-pounds (ft. lb)	X	1.355	= joules (J)	J	X	0.737	= ft. lb.
in.-pounds (in. lb.)	X	0.112	= newton-metres (N.m)	N.m	X	8.850	= in. lb
lb. per foot (lb/ft)	X	14.593	= new. per metre (N/m)	N.m	X	0.068	= lb/ft
cycles per sec. (cps)	X	1.0	= hertz (Hz)	Hz	X	1.0	= cps
Brit. Therm Unit (Btu)	X	1 055.06	= joules (J)	J	X	0.000 94	= Btu
Degrees Fah. (°F)	X	5/9 after sub. 32	= deg. Celsius (°C)	°C	X	9/5 then add 32	= °F

Note: Conversion from inches to millimetres (ins. X 25.4) is exact. Conversion from millimetres to inches (mm X 0.04) is approximate; (mm X 0.039 370 1) is accurate to six significant figures for mm/in.

Converted units should be rounded off to values consistent with the original accuracy.

COMMON METRIC EXPRESSIONS

MULTIPLES		DIVISIONS	
Prefix	means	Prefix	means
tera (10^{12})	One trillion times	deci (10^{-1})	One tenth of
giga (10^{9})	One billion times	centi (10^{-2})	One hundredth of
mega (10^{6})	One million times	milli (10^{-3})	One thousandth of
kilo (10^{3})	One thousand times	micro (10^{-6})	One millionth of
hecto (10^{2})	One hundred times	nano (10^{-9})	One billionth of
deka (10)	Ten times	pico (10^{-12})	One trillionth of

COMMON LENGTH MEASURES AND ABBREVIATIONS

1 micrometre	= 1/1,000,000 of 1 metre $(10^{-6}$ metre)	... μm
1 millimetre	= 1/1000 of 1 metre $(10^{-3}$ metre)	... mm
10 millimetres	= 1 centimetre $(10^{-2}$ metre)	... cm
10 centimetres	= 1 decimetre $(10^{-1}$ metre)	... dm
10 decimetres	= 1 metre $(10^{0}$ metre)	... m
10 metres	= 1 dekametre $(10^{1}$ metres)	... da
10 dekametres	= 1 hektometre $(10^{2}$ metres)	... hm
10 hektometres	= 1 kilometre $(10^{3}$ metres)	... km

NOTE: 1 metre = 1,650,763.73 Wavelengths of Krypton-86 Orange-Red Radiation.

Measures of Surface are expressed as square millimetres (mm^2); square centimetres (cm^2); square metres (m^2), etc.

Measures of Volume are expressed as the cube of the unit; e.g. 1 cubic centimetre (cm^3); 1 cubic metre (m^3), etc.

Measures of Capacity are expressed in multiples or divisions of one litre by addition of a prefix as above; e.g., **deci**litre for 1/10 of a litre; **kilo**litre for 1000 litres, etc.

NOTE: 1 litre = volume occupied by 1 cubic decimetre.

Measures of Weight are expressed in multiples or divisions of one gram by addition of a prefix as above; e.g., **milli**gram for 1/1000 of a gram; **kilo**gram for 1000 grams, etc.

NOTE: 1 gram = weight of 1 cubic centimetre of pure distilled water at a temperature of 4° C.

Appendix XI

Internal Wiring of Motor Switches

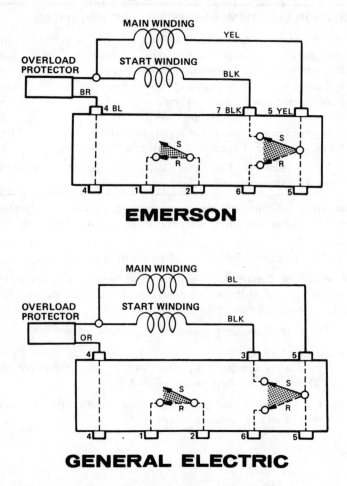

EMERSON

GENERAL ELECTRIC

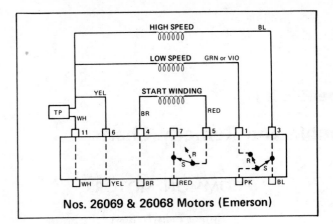

Nos. 26069 & 26068 Motors (Emerson)

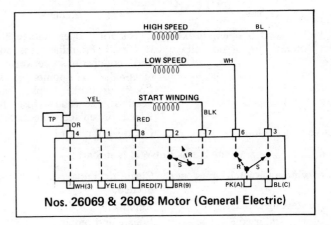

Nos. 26069 & 26068 Motor (General Electric)

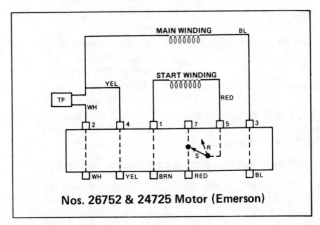

Nos. 26752 & 24725 Motor (Emerson)

Appendix XII

Trouble and Remedy Charts

COMMON MOTORS

Motor Fails To Start

Cause	Remedy
Fuses blown, switch open, broken or poor connections, or no voltage on line.	Check for proper voltage at motor terminals. Examine fuses, switches, and connections between motor terminals and points of service. Look for broken wires, bad connections, corroded fuse holders. Repair or replace as necessary.
Defective motor windings	Locate and repair.[1]

Motor Hums But Will Not Start

Starting winding switch does not close.	Clean or replace and lubricate if needed.
Defective starting capacitor.	Replace.[1]
Open rotor or stator coil.	Locate and repair.[1]
Motor overloaded.	Lighten load. Check for low voltage.
Overloaded line or low voltage.	Reduce electrical load. Check wiring. Increase wire size. Notify power company.
Bearings worn so that rotor rubs on starter.	Replace bearings. Center rotor in stator bore.[1]
Bearings too tight or lack of proper lubrication.	Clean and lubricate bearings. Check end bells for alignment.
Burned or broken connections.	Locate and repair.

Motor Will Not Start With Rotor In Certain Position

Burned or broken connections; open rotor or stator coil.	Inspect, test, and repair.[1]

Motor Runs But Then Stops

Motor overloaded.	Lighten motor load. Check for low voltage.
Defective overload protection.	Locate and replace.[1]

Slow Acceleration

Overloaded motor.	Lighten motor load.
Poor connections.	Test and repair.
Low voltage or overloaded line.	Lighten line load. Increase size of line wire.[1]
Defective capacitor.	Replace.[1]

Excessive Heating

Overloaded motor.	Reduce motor load.
Poor or damaged insulation; broken connections; or grounds or short circuits.	Locate and repair.[1]
Wrong connections.	Check wiring diagram of motor.
Worn bearings or rotor rubs on stator.	Renew or repair bearings. Check end bell alignment.[1]
Bearings too tight or lack of proper lubrication.	Clean and lubricate bearings. Check end bell alignment.
Belt too tight.	Slacken belt.
Motor dirty or improperly ventilated.	Clean motor air passages.
Defective capacitor.	Replace.

Excessive Vibration

Unbalanced rotor or load.	Rebalance rotor or load.
Worn bearings.	Replace.[1]
Motor misaligned with load.	Align motor shaft with load shaft.
Loose mounting bolts.	Tighten.
Unbalanced pulley.	Have pulley balanced or replaced.
Uneven weight of belt.	Get new belt.

Low Speed

Overloaded.	Reduce load.
Wrong or bad connections.	Check for proper voltage connections and repair.

[1] These repairs should be made by an experienced electrician.

| Low voltage, overloaded line, or wiring too small. | Reduce load. Increase size of wire.[1] |

WOUND-ROTOR MOTORS

Motor Fails To Start

Cause	Remedy
Worn brushes.	Renew brushes.
Brushes stuck in holder.	Adjust brushes.[1]
Brushes not properly set.	Check with marks on frame.

Slow Acceleration

Dirty or rough commutator.	Clean and sandpaper.
Worn or stuck brushes.	Renew or adjust.[1]
Brushes not set properly.	Adjust brushes.[1]

Low Speed

Dirty or rough commutator.	Clean and sandpaper.[1]
Badly worn brushes.	Replace with new brushes.[1]
Brushes not properly set.	Adjust brushes.[1]
Brushes stuck.	Clean and adjust.

Excessive Sparking When Starting

Dirty or rough commutator.	Clean and sandpaper.[1]
Worn or stuck brushes.	Renew or adjust brushes.[1]
High or low commutator bars.	Turn off in lathe.[1]
Excessive sparking at one place on commutator.	Check for shorted rotor winding or loose winding to bar connection.[1]
High mica.	Undercut mica.[1]
Overloaded.	Lighten load.
Open rotor or stator coil, grounds, or poor connections.	Inspect, test, and repair.[1]
High or low voltage.	Check size of wiring. Notify power company.

[1] These repairs should be made by an experienced electrician.

Excessive Sparking At Normal Speed

Cause	Remedy
Dirty short-circuiting device.	Clean with acceptable solvent; do not use carbon tetrachloride.
Governing mechanism sticks or is badly adjusted.	Readjust mechanism.[1]
Worn brushes.	Replace.

Excessive Speed

Dirty short-circuiting device.	Clean with acceptable solvent; do not use carbon tetrachloride.
Governing mechanism sticks or is badly adjusted.	Readjust mechanism.[1]

Rapid Brush Wear

Rough commutator.	Smooth with fine (00) sandpaper. Do not use emery cloth.
High or low bars.	Turn off in lathe.[1]
High mica.	Undercut mica.[1]
Overload.	Lighten motor load.
Poor connections.	Test and repair.
Low voltage.	Increase size of wire.[1]
Commutator not round.	Test and repair.[1]

CASEMENT AIR CONDITIONERS

Compressor Does Not Run

Cause	Remedy
Low voltage.	Check for voltage at compressor. 115 volt and 230 volt units will operate at 10% voltage variance.
Thermostat not set cold enough or inoperative.	Set thermostat to coldest position. Test thermostat and replace if inoperative.
Compressor hums but cuts off on overload.	Hard start compressor. Direct test compressor. If compressor starts, add starting components.
Open or shorted compressor windings.	Check for continuity and resistance.

Open overload.	Test overload protector and replace if inoperative.
Open capacitor.	Test capacitor and replace if inoperative.
Inoperative system switch.	Test for continuity in all positions. Replace if inoperative.
Broken, loose, or incorrect wiring.	Refer to appropriate wiring diagram to check wiring.

Fan Motor Does Not Run

Inoperative system switch.	Test switch and replace if inoperative.
Broken, loose, or incorrect wiring.	Refer to applicable wiring diagram.
Open capacitor.	Test capacitor and replace if inoperative.
Fan speed switch open.	Test switch and replace if inoperative.
Inoperative fan motor.	Test fan motor and replace if inoperative (be sure internal overload has had time to reset).

Does Not Cool, Or Cools Only Slightly

Undersized unit.	Replace with proper size unit.
Thermostat open or inoperative.	Set to coldest position. Test thermostat and replace if necessary.
Dirty filter.	Clean as recommended in Owner's Manual.
Dirty or plugged condenser or evaporator coil.	Use steam or detergent to clean.
Poor air circulation in area being cooled.	Adjust discharge air louvers. Use high fan speed.
Fresh air or exhaust air door open on applicable models.	Close doors.
Low capacity—undercharge.	Check for leak and make repair.
Compressor not pumping properly.	Check amperage draw against nameplate. If not conclusive, make pressure test.

Unit Does Not Run

Fuse blown or circuit tripped.	Replace fuse, reset breaker. If repeats, check fuse or breaker size.

Check for shorts in unit wiring and components.

Power cord not plugged in.	Plug in power cord.
System switch in Off position.	Set switch correctly.
Inoperative system switch.	Test for continuity in each switch position.
Loose or disconnected wiring at switch or other components.	Check wiring and connections. Reconnect per wiring diagram.

Evaporator Coil Freezes Up

Dirty filter.	Clean as recommended in Owner's Manual.
Restricted air flow.	Check for dirty or obstructed coil —clean as required.
Inoperative thermostat.	Test for shorted thermostat or stuck contacts.
Short of refrigerant.	De-ice coil and check for leak.
Inoperative fan motor.	Test fan motor and replace if inoperative.
Partially restricted capillary.	De-ice coil. Check temperature differential across coil. Touch test coil return bands for same temperature. Test for low running current.

Compressor Runs Continually—Does Not Cycle Off

Excessive heat load.	Unit undersized. Test cooling performance of unit. Replace with larger unit.
Restriction in line.	Check for partially iced coil. Check temperature split across coil.
Refrigerant leak.	Check for oil at silver soldered connections. Check for partially iced coil. Check split across coil. Check for low running amperage.
Thermostat contacts stuck.	Check operation of thermostat. Replace if contacts remain closed.
Thermostat incorrectly wired.	Refer to appropriate wiring diagram.

Thermostat Does Not Turn Unit On

Loss of charge in thermostat bulb.	Place jumper across thermostat terminals to check if unit operates.

	If unit operates, replace thermostat.
Loose or broken parts in thermostat.	Check as above.
Incorrect wiring.	Refer to appropriate wiring diagram.

Excessive Moisture

Insufficient air circulation through area to be air conditioned.	Adjust louvers for best possible air circulation.
Oversized unit.	Install correctly sized unit.
Inadequate vapor barrier in building structure, particularly floors.	Install vapor barrier.

Compressor Attempts To Start, Or Runs For Short Periods Only. Cycles On Overload

Overload inoperative. Opens too soon.	Check operation of unit. Replace overload if system operation is satisfactory.
Compressor attempts to start before system pressures are equalized.	Allow a minimum of 2 minutes to allow pressures to equalize before attempting to restart. Always remember waiting period.
Low or fluctuating voltage.	Check voltage with unit operating. Check for other appliances on circuit. Air conditioner should be on separate circuit for proper voltage and fused separately.
Incorrect wiring.	Refer to appropriate wiring diagram.
Shorted or incorrect capacitor.	Check by substituting a known good capacitor of correct rating.
Restricted or low air flow through condenser coil.	Check for proper fan speed or blocked condenser.
Compressor running abnormally hot.	Check for kinked discharge line or restricted condenser. Check amperage.

Noisy Operation

Poorly installed unit.	Refer to installation instructions for proper installation.

Fan blade striking chassis.	Reposition—adjust motor mount.
Compressor vibrating.	Check that compressor grommets have not deteriorated. Check that compressor mounting parts are not missing.
Improperly mounted or loose cabinet parts.	Check assembly and parts for looseness, rubbing, and rattling.

Water Leaks Into Room

Evaporator drain pan overflowing.	Clean obstructed drain trough.
Condensation forming on base pan.	Evaporator drain pan broken or cracked. Reseal or replace.
Poor installation resulting in rain entering room.	Check installation instructions. Reseal as required.
Condensation on discharge grilles.	Dirty evaporator coil—clean. Very high humidity level.

Thermostat Does Not Turn Unit Off

Thermostat contacts stuck.	Disconnect power to unit. Remove cover of thermostat and check if contacts are stuck. If so, replace thermostat.
Thermostat set at coldest point.	Turn to higher temperature setting to see if unit cycles off.
Incorrect wiring.	Refer to appropriate wiring diagram.
Unit undersized for area to be cooled.	Install properly sized unit.

Thermostat Short Cycles

Thermostat differential too narrow.	Replace thermostat.
Plenum gasket not sealing, allowing discharge air to short cycle thermostat.	Check gasket. Reposition or replace.
Restricted coil or dirty filter.	Clean and remember periodic cleaning necessity.

Prolonged Off Cycles (Automatic Operation)

Anticipator (resistor) wire disconnected at thermostat or system switch.	Refer to appropriate wiring diagram.

Anticipator (resistor) shorted or open.

Disconnect plug from outlet. Remove resistor from bracket. Insert plug. Place thermostat to warmest setting. Feel resistor for temperature. If no heat, replace resistor.

Partial loss of charge in thermostat bulb causing a wide differential.

Replace thermostat.

Outside Water Leaks

Evaporator drain pan cracked or obstructed.

Repair, clean, or replace as required.

Water in compressor area.

Detach shroud from pan and coil. Clean and remove old sealer. Reseal, reinstall, and check.

Obstructed condenser coil.

Steam clean.

Fan blade and slinger ring improperly positioned.

Adjust fan blade to ½″ of condenser coil.

COMMON AIR CONDITIONERS

Compressor And Condenser Motor Will Not Operate

Cause	Remedy
Thermostat temperature setting.	Check temperature setting. Set temperature below room ambient.
Thermostat system switch.	Check system switch setting. Set system to Cool.
Fuses blown.	Check fuses. Replace fuses.
High pressure switch open.	Check high pressure switch. Reset high pressure switch.
Thermostat not level.	Check thermostat. Is it level? Level thermostat.
Loose low voltage connections.	Check low voltage wiring. Tighten loose connections.
Defective low voltage transformer.	Check low voltage transformer. Replace transformer.
Contactor defective.	Check contactor. Replace defective contactor.
Low voltage.	Check voltage. Replace with adequate size wire. Notify power company.

Float switch open.

Check voltage at float switch terminals. Clean condensate drain line and trap. Replace defective float switch. Level unit & drain connections.

Anti-frost control open.

Check voltage at anti-frost switch terminals. Replace defective switch. Check return air filter. Clean filter. Check system for proper air flow. Take necessary steps to assure proper air flow.
Check for proper refrigerant charge. Evacuate and weigh in proper refrigerant charge.
Check for a restriction in refrigerant line. Remove restriction.

Defective condenser fan motor. Compressor cycling on motor overload.

Check resistance of condenser fan motor. Replace defective motor.

Condenser Fan Motor Operates But Compressor Will Not Run

Compressor run capacitor bad.

Check the capacitor for open, short, or low value. Replace defective capacitor.

Compressor internal overload tripped.

With an ohm meter check the continuity of the compressor motor. If an open winding is indicated, allow approximately 30 min. for compressor overload to re-set.

Loose wiring.

Check high and low voltage wiring. Tighten loose connections.

Compressor motor stuck.

Make a mechanical check on compressor. Replace stuck compressor.

Compressor motor failure.

With an ohm meter check resistance of compressor motor. If sufficient amount of time was allowed for the internal overload to reset— replace compressor.

Low voltage.

Check line voltage. Replace with adequate size wiring. Add start components to PSC compressors.

Defective start relay.

Make continuity check on start relay. Replace defective relay.

Compressor Operates But A Condenser Motor Will Not Operate

Fan motor run capacitor defective.	Check the capacitor for open, short, or low value. Replace defective capacitor.
Defective fan switch.	Check fan switch. Replace defective fan switch.
Condenser fan motor tripped on overload.	Check condenser motor capacitor. Could be weak, open, or shorted. Replace capacitor. Check motor bearings. If bearings are bad, replace motor. Excessive load on condenser motor. VCR access door must be in place. Re-install door.
Condenser motor failure.	Check resistance of condenser motor. Replace defective motor.
Defective contactor.	Check contactor. Replace defective contactor.

Compressor Goes Off On High Pressure Switch Or Internal Relief

Overcharge of refrigerant in the system.	Check head pressure, suction pressure, subcooling, and superheat. Evacuate and weigh in proper refrigerant charge.
Non-condensable gasses in system.	Check system for non-condensables. Discharge refrigerant, install drier, evacuate and charge.
Fins on condenser clogged or bent.	Visual check. Clean and/or straighten condenser fins.
Drier restricted.	Check temperature or pressure difference across drier. Replace drier.
Liquid line restricted.	Check liquid line for kinks, etc. Straighten and/or remove restriction.
Liquid line base valve partially closed.	Check base valve. Open base valve. Must be fully back seated (fully counterclockwise).
Liquid line quick connect fitting did not pierce.	Remove liquid line, check quick fittings. Remove obstruction, replace line, and evacuate evaporator and lines before opening service valves.

Capillary tube strainer plugged.

Visually check strainer, capillary may have ice formed on them or be excessively cold. Clean and/or replace capillary tube strainer. Install drier, evacuate lines and evaporator.

Capillary tube plugged.

Check each circuit of the evaporator for a temperature difference between circuits. Clean and/or replace capillary tube. Install drier, evacuate lines and evaporator.

Expansion valve stuck in closed position or loss of charge in feeler bulb.

Check superheat on evaporator. Refer to system curves, replace defective expansion valve.

Condenser fan switch did not switch to High.

Check fan switch. Replace defective fan switch.

Fan motor failure.

Check condenser motor capacitor. Could be weak, open or shorted. Replace capacitor.
Check motor bearings. If bearings are bad, replace motor.
Excessive load on condenser motor. VCR access door must be in place. Re-install door.
Check resistance of condenser motor. Replace defective motor.

VCR 60 belt broken or loose.

Check belt. Tighten or replace.

Re-circulation of air.

Check for obstruction such as shrubbery, etc. Remove obstructions.

VCR access doors not in place.

Check doors. Re-install doors.

Excessive air leak in VCR cabinets.

Check for leaks. Seal leaks.

Shipping support not removed from VCR fan assembly.

Check for shipping support. Remove.

Compressor Hums But Will Not Start

Low voltage.

Replace with adequate size wiring. Check line voltage. Install start kit on PSC compressors.

Start or run capacitor defective.

Check the capacitor for an open, short, or low value condition. If bad, replace capacitor.

Compressor motor internally shorted.	With an ohm meter check resistance of compressor. Replace defective compressor.
Start relay bad.	Make a continuity check on start relay. Replace defective relay.
Stuck compressor.	Make a mechanical check on compressor. Replace stuck compressor.

Compressor Starts But Immediately Cuts Off On Overload

Low voltage.	Check line voltage. Replace with adequate size wiring.
Compressor start or run capacitor bad.	Check the capacitors for open, short, or low value condition. Replace defective capacitor.
Defective start relay.	Make a continuity check on start relay. Replace defective relay.
System low on refrigerant.	Check suction pressure, head pressure, sub-cooling, and superheat. Refer to system curves. Evacuate and weigh in proper refrigerant charge.

Condenser Motor Does Not Switch To High Speed

Ambient not high enough for fan switch to high.	Check ambient temperature. Should be above 90° F.
Refrigerant sensing fan switch not connected to condenser coil.	Visual check of fan switch. Reinstall fan switch.
System low on refrigerant.	Check suction pressure, heat pressure, sub-cooling, and superheat. Evacuate and weigh in proper refrigerant charge.
Defective fan switch.	Check fan switch. Replace fan switch.

Condenser Motor Will Not Run After Switching To High Speed

Fan motor failure.	Make an electrical check on motor. Replace motor.

Condenser Motor Trips On Internal Overload

Loose wiring connections.	Check wiring. Tighten loose connections.
Condenser motor pulling excessive current.	Check for air leaks (in VCR cabinet). Seal air leaks.

Check bearings on motor. If bad, replace motor.

Defective capacitor.

Check capacitor for an open, short, or low value condition. Replace capacitor.

VCR access door not in place.

Check access door. Re-install access door.

Contactor Will Not Energize

Thermostat temperature setting.

Check temperature setting. Set temperature below room ambient.

Fuses blown.

Check fuses. Replace fuses.

Low voltage.

Check line voltage. Replace with adequate size wiring.

Low voltage wiring.

Check connections. Tighten connections.

High pressure switch open.

Check high pressure switch. Re-set high pressure switch and correct condition.

Compressor external overload opened (VCR 48 & 60 only).

With an ohm meter check for resistance across external overload. Wait sufficient amount of time for overload to reset.

Contact points on contactor burned.

Check contacts. Replace defective contactor.

Contactor coil bad.

Check for resistance across contactor coil. Replace defective contactor.

Low voltage transformer.

With a volt meter check low voltage transformer. Replace defective transformer.

Float switch open.

Check voltage at float switch terminals. Clean condensate drain line and trap. Replace defective float switch. Level unit and drain connections.

Anti-frost control open.

Check voltage at anti-frost switch. Replace defective anti-frost switch terminals.
Check filter. Clean filter.
Check for proper air flow. Take necessary steps to assure proper air flow.

Check for proper refrigerant charge. Evacuate and weigh in proper charge.

Check for restriction in refrigerant system. Remove restriction, add drier, evacuate, and charge system.

Thermostat system switch. Check system switch setting. Set system switch to cool.

Thermostat not level. Check thermostat. Is it level? Level thermostat.

Low Suction Pressure

Service valves not completely open. Check service valves. Open service valves. Valve stem must be completely back seated (fully counterclockwise).

Leak in system. Repair leak, add drier, evacuate, charge. Check leak system.

Quick connect did not pierce. Remove suction line, check quick connect fittings. Remove obstruction, add liquid line drier, replace line, and evacuate evaporator and line before opening service valves.

Suction line restricted. Check suction line for kinks, etc. Remove restrictions.

System low on refrigerant. Check head pressure, suction pressure, sub-cooling, and superheat. Refer to system curves. Evacuate and weigh in proper refrigerant charge.

Non-condensable gases or moisture in system. Check system for non-condensables. Discharge refrigerant, install drier, evacuate, and charge.

Condenser fan switch did not switch to low speed. Check condenser fan switch. Replace defective switch.

Evaporator motor failure. Check evaporator motor. Replace defective motor.

Low air flow across evaporator. Check static pressure on system, refer to cfm vs. static curves for air handler. Take necessary steps to assure proper air flow across evaporator.

Mismatched system.

Check evaporator and condensing unit. Are they compatible? Install correct units.

Expansion valve stuck in closed position or loss of charge in feeler bulb.

Check superheat on evaporator and expansion valve. Replace expansion valve.

Capillary tube strainer plugged.

Visually check strainer. Capillary tubes may have ice formed on them or be excessively cold. Replace strainer.

Capillary tubes plugged.

Check each circuit of the evaporator for a temperature difference between circuits. Clean and/or replace capillary tube.

Suction Pressure Too High

Overcharge of refrigerant.

Check suction pressure, head pressure, sub-cooling, and superheat. Refer to system curves. Evacuate and weigh in proper refrigerant charge.

Condenser fan switch did not switch to high speed.

Check condenser fan switch. Replace defective switch.

Expansion feeler valve bulb not securely fastened to suction line or improperly positioned.

Check expansion feeler valve bulb for loose mounting clamps. Position bulb and tighten clamp on expansion feeler valve bulb.

Expansion valve stuck in Open position.

Check superheat on evaporator. Refer to system curves. Replace defective expansion valve.

Fins or condenser clogged or bent.

Visual check. Clean and/or straighten condenser fins.

Compressor suction valves leaking.

Make mechanical check on compressor. Replace defective compressor.

Head Pressure Too High

Overcharge of refrigerant in system.

Check head pressure, suction pressure, sub-cooling, and superheat. Refer to system curves. Evacuate and weigh in proper refrigerant charge.

Non-condensable gases or moisture in system.	Check system for non-condensables. Discharge refrigerant, install drier, evacuate, and charge.
Condenser fins clogged or bent.	Visual check. Clean and/or straighten condenser fins.
Drier restricted.	Check temperature or pressure difference across drier. Replace drier, evacuate, and charge.
Base valves partially closed.	Check base valves. Open base valves. Valve stem must be back seated (fully counterclockwise).
Quick connect fittings did not pierce.	Check quick connect fittings. Remove obstruction, add drier, replace line, and evacuate evaporator and lines before opening service valves.
Liquid line restricted.	Check liquid line for kinks. Straighten and/or remove restriction. If system is opened, add drier, evacuate, and charge.
Expansion valve stuck partially closed.	Check superheat on evaporator and valve operation. Replace defective expansion valve.
Condenser blower switch did not switch to high.	Check blower switch. Replace defective switch.
Condenser motor does not come up to speed.	Check condenser motor capacitor. Could be weak, open, or shorted. Replace capacitor. Check motor bearings. If bearings are bad, replace motor. Excessive load on condenser motor. On VCR, access door must be in place. Re-install door.
Capillary tube restricted.	Check each circuit of the evaporator for a temperature difference between circuits. Clean and/or replace capillary tube. Add drier, evacuate and charge.
Capillary tube strainer partially restricted.	Visually check strainer. Capillary tubes may have ice formed on them or be excessively cold. Clean and/or replace capillary tube strainer. Add drier, evacuate and charge.

Re-circulation of air.

Check for obstruction such as shrubbery, etc. Remove obstruction.

Excessive air leaks in VCR cabinet.

Check for leaks. Seal leaks.

VCR 60 belt not properly adjusted.

Check belt. Tighten loose belt.

Head Pressure Too Low

Leak in system.

Repair leak, add drier, evacuate, and charge. Check system for leaks.

System low on refrigerant.

Check suction pressure, head pressure, sub-cooling, and superheat. Refer to system curves. Evacuate and weigh in proper refrigerant charge.

Suction and/or discharge valves in compressor leaking.

Make a mechanical check on compressor. Replace defective compressor.

Condenser fan switch did not switch to low.

Check condenser fan switch. Replace defective switch.

Suction service valve closed.

Check service valve. Open service valve. Valve stem must be back seated (fully counterclockwise).

Suction line quick connects did not pierce.

Remove suction line check quick connect fittings. Remove obstruction, add drier, replace line, and evacuate evaporator and line before opening service valve.

Suction line restricted.

Check suction line for kinks, etc. Remove restrictions. If system is opened install drier, evacuate and charge.

Expansion valve stuck in open position.

Check superheat on evaporator, and operation of expansion valve. Replace expansion valve.

Thermostat Never Satisfied

System improperly sized.

Re-check heat gain. Take necessary action.

| System not producing rated capacity. | Make performance check on system. Take appropriate action based upon problem analysis. |

Condensing Unit Continues To Operate After Thermostat Is Satisfied

Contact points on condensing unit contactor welded together.	Check contactor. Replace defective contactor.
Defective low voltage wiring.	Check continuity of low voltage wiring for short circuits. If short is indicated, replace low voltage wires.
Defective thermostat.	Check resistance of thermostat contacts. Replace thermostat.

Condensing Unit Noisy

Fan blade out of balance.	Check for excessive vibration. Replace defective fan.
Fan motor bearings bad.	Check motor bearings. Replace defective motor.
Compressor vibration isolators bad.	Check vibration isolators. Replace vibration isolators.
Loose parts on condensing units.	Check for loose parts. Secure loose parts.
Refrigerant piping chafing.	Check refrigerant piping. Isolate refrigerant piping.

Evaporator Coil Icing

Evaporator blower belt loose or broken.	Check evaporator blower belt. Tighten or replace belt.
Evaporator motor failure.	Check evaporator motor. Replace defective motor.
Leak in system.	Leak-check system. Repair leak, install drier, evacuate, and charge.
System low on refrigerant.	Check suction pressure, head pressure, sub-cooling, and superheat. Refer to system curves. Evacuate

and weigh in proper refrigerant charge.

Non-condensable gasses or moisture in system.

Check system for non-condensables. Discharge refrigerant, install drier, evacuate, and charge.

Service valves not completely open.

Check service valves. Open service valves. Valve stems must be back seated (fully counterclockwise).

Quick connects did not pierce.

Remove suction line, check quick connect fitting. Remove obstruction, odd drier, replace line, evacuate evaporator and lines before opening service valves.

Suction line restricted.

Check suction line for kinks, etc. Remove restriction. If system is opened, install drier, evacuate, and charge.

Low air flow across evaporator.

Check static pressure on system, refer to cfm vs. static curves for air handler. Take necessary steps to assure proper air flow across evaporator.

Dirty filter.

Check filters to see if clean. Replace dirty filters.

Expansion valve stuck in closed position or loss of charge in feeler bulb.

Check superheat on evaporator, and expansion valve operation. Replace defective expansion valves.

Capillary tube strainer restricted.

Visually check strainer. Capillary tubes may have ice formed on them or be excessively cold. Replace defective strainer, add drier, evacuate, and charge.

Capillary tubes restricted.

Check each circuit of the evaporator for a temperature difference between circuits. Clean or replace capillary tube, add drier, evacuate, and charge.

System improperly sized.

Re-check heat gain. Take necessary action.

Mis-matched system.

Check evaporator and condenser. Are they compatible? Install correct units.

Condensate Blowing Off Coil

Excessive air flow across evaporator.	Check static pressure on system. Refer to cfm vs. static curves for air handler. Take necessary steps to assure proper air flow across evaporator.
Evaporator fins bent, unevenly spaced, or dirty.	Visually check evaporator. Clean and/or straighten fins using a fin comb.

Condensing Unit Runs Continuously But Does Not Adequately Cool

System low on refrigerant.	Check suction pressure, head pressure, sub-cooling, and superheat. Evacuate and weigh in proper refrigerant charge.
Leak in system.	Leak-check system. Repair leak, install drier, evacuate and charge.
System improperly sized.	Re-check heat gain. Take necessary action.
Mis-matched system.	Check evaporator and condensing unit. Are they compatible? Install correct units.
Suction and/or discharge valves in compressor leaking.	Make mechanical check on compressor. Replace defective compressor.

Condensing Unit Short Cycles

System low on refrigerant.	Check suction pressure, head pressure, sub-cooling, and superheat. Refer to system curves. Evacuate and weigh in proper refrigerant charge.
Thermostat differential too close due to defective cooling anticipator.	Check cooling cycle with a reliable thermometer. Replace defective thermostat.

Compressor Short Cycles, Condenser Fan Motor Runs

System low on refrigerant.	Check suction pressure, head pressure, sub-cooling and superheat. Refer to system curves. Evacuate and weigh in proper refrigerant charge.
Compressor overload bad.	Check amp draw on compressor.

Compressor motor bad.

If internal overload is bad, it will require replacing the compressor.
Check amp draw on compressor. Replace defective compressor.

Evaporator Blower Runs, Condensing Unit Off

Power not restored after winter shutdown.

Check power. Restore power.

Fuses blown.

Check fuses. Replace fuses.

Thermostat system switch on heating, blower on manual.

Check system switch. Set system switch to Cool Automatic.

Defective contactor.

Check contactor. Replace defective contactor.

Loose low voltage connections.

Check low voltage wiring. Tighten loose connections.

High pressure switch open.

Check high pressure switch. Re-set high pressure switch and correct condition.
Check return air filter. Clean filter. Check system for proper air flow. Take necessary steps to assure proper air flow.
Check for proper refrigerant charge. Evacuate and weigh in proper refrigerant charge.
Check for restriction in refrigerant system. Remove restriction.

Condensing Unit Runs, Evaporator Motor Off

Fuses blown.

Check fuses. Replace fuses.

Defective motor.

Check resistance of motor windings. If an open winding is indicated replace motor.

Defective fan motor, run capacitor.

Check the capacitor for open, short or weak condition. Replace defective capacitor.

Cooling fan relay defective.

Check resistance across coil and contacts. Replace defective fan relay.

Supply Duct And Plenum Sweating

Ducts and plenums not insulated.

Inspect. Insulate ducts and plenums.

HUMIDIFIERS

Neither Air Cleaner Nor Humidifier Will Operate

Cause	Remedy
Selector switch in Off position.	Turn selector switch to desired mode of operation.
Power cord not plugged in.	Plug in power cord.
Blown fuse or tripped circuit breaker.	Replace fuse or reset breaker.
Electrical disconnect on tilt-out back panel not engaged.	Close tilt-out panel securely to engage electrical disconnect.

Small Volume Of Air Discharge From Unit

Dirty prefilter of air inlet holes in back panel.	Clean per instructions.
Unit placed with back too close to wall or draperies.	Position unit minimum of 3" from wall.

Fan Motor Slows Down Or Stops

Motor bearings oil supply exhausted.	Oil motor bearing.

Humidifier Does Not Maintain Adequate Humidity Level

Humidistat set too low.	Set at higher number.
Drum-filter clogged with minerals and other deposits.	Replace with new filter.

Condensation Forms On Inside Of Windows And Walls

Humidity level too high for structure.	Set humidistat at a lower number.

Water Level Indicator Does Not Move

Float lever hooked in upper position.	Free float lever per instructions.

Humidifier Does Not Turn Off When Water Level Is Low

Float lever hooked in upper position.	Free float lever per instructions.

Humidifier Drum Will Not Turn

Humidistat has turned unit off.	Set humidistat at higher number

Drum is not properly positioned in the two pulleys.

if additional humidification is needed.

Position drum per instructions.

Mineral build-up.

Clean pulleys and inside rim of drum.

Stale Water Odor Emitted From Unit

Characteristic of local water conditions.

Use water odor control tablets.

Reservoir requires cleaning.

Clean per instructions.

Unit Does Not Effectively Clean The Air

Dirty prefilter or air inlet holes in back panel.

Clean per instructions.

Cell ON Signal Light Flickers Continuously Or Goes Out

Dirty electronic cell.

Wash per instructions.

Continuous Or Very Frequent "Arcing" Or Snapping Sound

Excessive accumulation of dirt on prefilter and/or electronic cell.

Clean per instructions.

Electronic cell not completely dry after washing.

Operate unit on dry cycle.

OIL FURNACES

Burner Motor Does Not Start

Cause	Remedy
Incomplete electrical circuit.	Check main disconnect switch, fuse and/or circuit breaker, thermostat, and limit control position.
Primary control off on 'safety' reset.	Wait five minutes and actuate external reset button. If primary control goes off on safety reset again, check line voltage under a load. 115 volts is minimum. Check running amps of burner motor according to motor data plate.
Primary control relay contacts badly pitted.	Replace primary control.

Burner motor bearing frozen.	Free shaft, check bearing lubricant, or replace motor.
Burner motor off on thermo-overload protector.	Allow motor to cool and push motor reset button. Check line voltage and motor running amps. Lubricate motor bearings as per instructions.
Burner intermittently locks out on 'safety' reset, motor off on thermo-overload protector.	Check cad cell connections and operation. Check for flat spot on motor armature or replace motor.

Burner Motor Operates But No Oil Is Delivered To Nozzle

Fuel oil storage tank low or empty.	Fill tank with oil and bleed air from the system at fuel pump bleed spot.
Clogged fuel line strainer.	Clean or replace strainer.
Clogged nozzle.	Remove and clean or replace nozzle.
Kinked oil lines.	Replace any kinked tubing.
Air leak in the inlet line.	Tighten all fittings, including the unused inlet port on fuel pump.
Slipping or broken coupling on motor and pump assembly.	Tighten or replace coupling assembly.
Frozen pump shaft.	Replace pump assembly.
Fuel pump indicates excessive vacuum reading at inlet side.	Improperly sized fuel lines.
Suction line oil filter cartridge dirty.	Replace cartridge.

Burner Motor Operates And Delivers Oil But There Is No Flame

No spark.	Check ignition transformer or substitute with good one.
Poor oil atomization.	Adjust fuel pump pressure. Check for oil line restrictions and defective nozzle.
Improper electrode setting.	Remove drawer assembly and adjust.

Burner Starts But Flame Blows Away From Nozzle

| Excessive combustion air. | Adjust air shutter. Check draft overfire. |
| Excessive draft overfire. | Adjust barometric damper −.03 to −.04 inch water column, maximum. |

Barometric damper will not maintain −.03 to −.04 inch water column.

Draft still too high.

Poor Light Off And Shut Down

Air pocket between shutoff valve and nozzle.

Cycle burner on/off occasionally until pulsation eliminates. Bleed air from fuel pump at bleed port.

Water in fuel tank.

Drain storage tank. Replace fuel filter cartridge. Add moisture inhibitor, refill fuel tank.

Defective nozzle assembly.

Clean nozzle and strainer or replace.

Oil Odors In House

Oil leaks at piping connections.

Check fittings, valve packing, pump seals.

Poor burner shutoff.

Check fuel pump. Check valve cutoff pressure. Check nozzle and strainer assembly. Replace or clean.

Smoky fire.

Check combustion efficiency, draft, CO_2, and smoke.

Down draft causing smoke to enter the furnace area through barometric damper.

Regulate to proper draft.

ELECTRIC FURNACE STOKERS

Lag In Motor Speed

Cause   Remedy

Obstruction in bin or burner worms.

*Disassemble and remove obstruction.

Motor overload caused by excessive tension on V-belt.

*Check motor and make necessary adjustments.

Noisy Reduction Unit

Insufficient lubrication.

Proper lubrication with lubricant specified by manufacturer.

Oil leakage.

*Check and repair or replace as directed by manufacturer.

Excessive Dust

A *plus* pressure in furnace or boiler.

Adjust flue damper so that there will always be a slight *minus* pressure as directed by manufacturer.

Gas In Cellar

Improper setting of damper in flue.

Check and reset as directed by manufacturer.

Dirty or plugged-up holes in burner plates.

Stop stoker; check and clean.

Wet or damp coal.

Use only dry coal.

Worn bin and burner worms.

*Check and replace.

Excessive Vibration Or Noise

Improper setting of the motor and reduction unit.

*Check and reset.

Motor and reduction unit are not in perfect alignment.

*Check and align as directed by manufacturer.

Loose bolts, nuts, and support legs.

Tighten.

Improper adjustment of tension on elevator of ash removing device.

*Adjust tension.

Worn V-belt.

*Check and replace.

Lack of periodic lubrication.

Lubricate at intervals specified by manufacturer.

Noisy Ash Removal

Hard ash or clinker formation caused by excess air supply to burner.

*Check and make necessary adjustment to reduce air supply.

Use of poor grade anthracite.

Use type specified by manufacturer.

Stoker Does Not Operate

Fuse blown.

Check and replace.

Loose connection.

Check and tighten.

Motor failure.

*Check and make necessary repairs or replacements.

Operating on wrong control.

*Check wiring diagram furnished with stoker and correct.

Power supply failure.

Call power supplier.

No Heat

Switch is off.	Set switch.
Thermostat set too low.	Reset.
Inoperative or defective thermostat.	*Check all connections. Make necessary tests; replace if necessary.
Empty hopper.	Fill.
Thermal cut-out released because of obstruction in bin worm.	Clean out obstruction.

Too much Heat

Thermostat set too high.	Reset.
Reversed clock cycle.	*Check and correct.
Shorted control circuit.	*Check and test thermostat and hold fire-control lines. Make necessary adjustments.
Control failure.	*Check connections and test controls. Make adjustments. If necessary, replace defective controls.
Improper location of thermostat.	*Install thermostat as shown in wiring diagram furnished with equipment.

Not Enough Heat

Air-bound and noisy radiators.	Install valves on radiators.
Thermostat set too low.	Reset thermostat.
Dirty flues and boiler.	Clean out.
Slow coal feed.	*Check and make adjustments.
V-belt slipping.	Tighten.
Hole worn in coal tube.	*Replace.
Insufficient air.	*Adjust.
Motor and fan rotating in wrong direction.	Readjust motor and fan to run in opposite direction.
Inadequate heating plant.	Check with heating contractor.
Poor coal.	Use type specified by manufacturer.

* Consult service department of manufacturer.

DISHWASHERS

Upper Rack Binds

Cause	Remedy
Binding due to user's pushing from side, not center.	Push from center. (Rack flexible for user's convenience in use/loading.)
Binding due to distortion. (Has been forced out of shape.)	Align rack wheels into same plane on each side (by eye). Use hands (rack is flexible).
Binding due to distortion. (Distance between upper rack rollers changed.)	Stretch or squeeze rack to make dimension 20⅝" (over outside edge of rollers).
Binding due to improper distance between upper rack track roller screws.	Add or remove spacers to align tracks and remove distortions: a. There should always be one LESS spacer on the rear track roller screws than on the front. Actual numbers differ depending on production location.

Visible Water Vapor Exhausting From Under Door ("Steam")

Cause	Remedy
High relative humidity and/or cool room temperature (air conditioning, etc.).	Some visible water vapor is normal for brief time—no correction required or possible.
	Change room conditions as necessary (decrease humidity and/or increase room temperature).
	Make certain room air conditioner outlet does not blow directly onto face of dishwater.
Excessive water supply temperature.	Lower water temperature as necessary but not below 140° F. at dishwasher.
Dishwasher installed against outside cold wall.	Insulate dishwasher from cold, as required.

4-Way Hydro Sweep Does Not Turn At Proper Speed
(30-43 RPM Speed For Wash Arm Operating In Clean/Clear Water)

Cause	Remedy
Not enough water.	See "Insufficient fill" and "Water does not remain in tank".
Worn wash arm.	Replace Hydro Sweep wash arm and/or support.

Strainer clogged.

Clean strainer and strainer cleaning nozzle.

4-Way Hydro Sweep nozzles clogged.

Clean nozzles.

Too much suds.

Correct the amount and type of detergent or try different brand using varying amounts.

Water Does Not Remain In Tank

Foreign matter on seat of drain valve.

Remove foreign matter.

Faulty drain valve spring.

Replace drain valve.

Drain valve inoperative.

Replace drain valve.

Timer malfunctioning.

Replace timer.

Water On Floor After Fill Cycle

Water inlet tube damaged during installation.

Replace water inlet tube and/or air gap as necessary.

Fill tube of air gap clogged with foreign matter.

Clean fill tube.

Water "splashing-out" of air gap (rare).

Replace air gap.

Leaks Water At The Motor

Shaft seal leaking.

Replace motor shaft seal.

Excessive Noise or Vibration During Drying Cycle

Fan loose on shaft.

Remove and re-tighten fan.

Heater fan out of balance.

Replace fan.

Shaft bent on fan motor.

Replace fan motor.

Dishes Do Not Dry

Water not hot enough.

Set water heater so that water temperature is 140–160° F. at the dishwasher.

Dryer heater element burned out.

Replace heater element.

Fan motor inoperative.

Replace fan motor.

Dryer thermal protector inoperative.

Replace protector.

Erratic timer operation.	Replace timer.
Energy saver mechanism malfunctioning.	Check switch and cancel mechanism. Replace any broken parts or switch.
Air inlet check valve assembly stuck. (If dishwasher equipped with check valve.)	Check to see if valve operates freely.
Blower fan improperly positioned on shaft.	Locate fan as close to motor as possible without touching motor.

Dishwasher Fails To Pause in Sani Cycle

Water too hot.	Set water heater so that water temperature is 140–160° F. at the dishwasher.
Thermostat inoperative.	Replace thermostat.
Program switch malfunctioning.	Replace switch.
Erratic timer operation.	Replace timer.

Dishware Not Clean After Completed Cycle

Not enough water.	See "Insufficient fill" and "Water does not remain in tank.".
4-Way Hydro Sweep turning too slowly.	See "4-Way Hydro Sweep does not turn at proper speed".
Incorrect quantity of detergent.	See "Use and Care Guide".
Low water temperature.	Set water heater so that water temperature is 140–160° F. at the dishwasher.
Improper detergent.	Try various brands of detergents. (See "Use and Care Guide").
Incorrect loading.	See operating instructions. ("Use and Care Guide").
Clogged strainer.	Remove and clean strainer assembly.
Middle wash arm not rotating, therefore not enough water.	Check fill system.

Soak Cycle Does Not Clean Pots And Pans

Insufficient detergent.	Add more detergent. See "Use and Care Guide".

Charred food soils.   Pre-condition charred areas.

Tableware Spotting

Overloading or improper loading.   See "Use and Care Guide".

Low water temperature.   See "Does not wash clean".

Incomplete fill.   See "Insufficient fill" and "Water does not remain in tank".

Excessive water hardness.   Install water softener or check existing softener for proper regeneration.

Incorrect quantity or improper detergent.   See "Does not wash clean" and "Use and Care Guide".

Mineral solids (dissolved minerals may exist in both hard and soft water).   Water may require installation of external special filter.

Rinse agent depleted in dispenser.   Refill dispenser.

Action Indicator Light(s), Power-On Light, Etc. Inoperative

Lamps burned out.   Replace lamp and/or socket assembly. (Does not affect machine operation).

Dishwasher Does Not Operate

No electrical power at dishwasher.   Make sure Portable "plugged in". Check fuse or circuit breaker and correct.

Door not latched or cycle selector button not pushed.   Latch door and push button.

Timer has not reset.   Unlatch door, wait approximately 1 minute, re-latch door, and push button.

Spring that activates door interlock switch bent or broken.   Replace door interlock switch.

Door interlock switch inoperative.   Replace door interlock switch.

Program switch has not reset because switch cancelling lever is misaligned, preventing program switch from cancelling (button remains depressed).   Check program switch cancelling lever and correct or replace lever.

Program switch malfunctioning.

Check program switch cancelling lever and correct or replace lever.

Timer inoperative.

Replace timer.

Timer has not reset.

Check program switch cancelling lever and correct or replace lever.

Make sure torsion bar reset has reset the timer.

Motor Does Not Operate

Improper electrical connection(s).

Check and correct.

Timer malfunctioning.

Replace timer.

Motor inoperative.

Replace motor and shaft seal.

Obstruction in drain pump.

Remove obstruction.

Cycle Does Not Stop When Door Is Open

Door interlock switch and/or program switch inoperative.

Replace door interlock switch and/or program switch.

Loud Humming During Drain Cycle

Drain valve solenoid vibrating.

Replace drain valve assembly.

Obstruction between armature and frame.

Remove obstruction.

Cycle Starts But Timer Will Not Advance
(Resulting In Continuous Fill)

Timer malfunctioning.

Replace timer.

Insufficient Fill (Low Fill Line Should Be At Top Of Vertical Wall On Strainer; Normal Fill Line Should Be 2″ Up On Incline Plane Of Strainer)

Low water flow pressure.

Have water pressure tested by plumber. If below 20 lbs. per sq. in. flow pressure take corrective measures.

Fill valve strainer dirty.

Remove strainer and clean.

Fill tube of air gap clogged.

Clean fill tube.

Fill valve or overfill control switch inoperative.

Replace inoperative parts. Also check timer.

Timer inoperative on fill cycle.

Replace timer unit.

Kinked hose (portable).

Remove kinks.

Faucet adapter clogged (portable).   Clean adapter screens.

Detergent Dispenser Does Not Operate

Dispenser shaft "frozen" in housing.	Disassemble and clean shaft.
Torsion spring disassembled or broken.	Replace dispenser assembly.
Timer malfunctioning.	Replace timer.
Inoperative bimetal unit.	Replace bimetal unit.
Bimetal unit not properly adjusted.	Adjust bimetal unit.

Water In Tank During Drying Cycle And At End Of Complete Operation

Clogged drain.	Remove obstruction.
Drain pump malfunctioning.	Replace damaged impeller.
Drain valve inoperative or clogged.	Remove obstruction or replace drain valve.
Program switch malfunctioning.	Replace program switch.
Timer inoperative or malfunctioning.	Replace timer.

Inadequate Drain

Installation deficiency (drain tubing too small or too long).	Check drain size $\%_{16}''$ I.D. min.
Drain tubing kinked.	Remove kinks.
Disposer "knockout plug" not removed.	Check for removal of plug (if disposer installed).
Drain air gap, external to dishwasher, clogged or improper size ($\%''$ I.D. min. required).	Have air gap cleaned or corrected by plumber (required on some installations; not responsibility of dishwasher service technician).
Program switch has been bumped after program selected or switch malfunctioning.	Check program switch cancelling lever and correct or replace lever. Replace program switch.
Timer malfunctioning.	Check timer for continuity; replace if necessary.
Damaged drain impeller.	Replace drain impeller.

HOT WATER DISPENSERS

No Water From Spout When Water Control Knob Is Turned On

Cause	Remedy
Water supply turned off.	Turn water on.
Water supply inlet screen clogged.	Replace water inlet flow screen.
Mechanical valve inoperative.	Replace mechanical valve assembly.

Water Drips From Spout

Insufficient air in air chamber.	Normal during initial heating.
	Normal if repeated small water quantities are drawn.
Water pressure (supply line) less than 20 psi.	Restore adequate pressure.
Water spout restricted.	Clean spout flow screen.
Tube(s) to tank kinked.	Remove kink(s).
Vent hole (spout body) clogged.	Clean vent hole.

Water Seeps From Vent Hole (Spout Body)

Water spout or large flexible tube restricted.	Remove and clean spout flow screen.
	Check tube for kinks or clogs.

Water Does Not Heat

Thermostat control knob loose or out of alignment on thermostat shaft.	Realign and tighten knob screw.
Thermostat turned off.	Rotate thermostat control knob fully clockwise to turn on.
Thermostat inoperative.	Replace thermostat.
Heater element inoperative.	Replace tank body assembly.

Water Overflows Or Steam Spits From Spout

Thermostat control knob set too high for altitude.	Rotate thermostat control knob slightly counterclockwise (to lower temperature setting).
Thermostat malfunction.	Replace thermostat.

Water Overheats With Thermostat Control Knob Set To Minimum

Thermostat malfunction.	Replace thermostat.

Water Contains "Black Specks," "Bad" Taste, Or Odor

Sediments introduced during plumbing/installation.	Turn off thermostat control knob and water supply.
	Remove plug from tank and drain water.
	Refill tank, heat water, and re-drain tank as necessary.
Dirty water spout screen.	Remove and clean spout flow screen.

FREESTANDING TRASH COMPACTORS

Motor Runs But Ram Inoperative

Cause	Remedy
Motor pulley, motor sprocket, drive sprocket, or drive pulley is inoperative.	Replace pin(s).
	Replace drive belt.
	Replace drive chain.
	Replace pulleys or sprockets.

Ram Stuck In Down Position

Malfunction of directional switch.	Replace directional switch.

Ram Operates Continuously

Malfunction of ram switch.	Adjust or replace ram switch.
Misalignment of start switch button.	Realign start switch button.

Drawer Will Not Close

Drawer latch mechanism misaligned.	Adjust latch rod for proper alignment with drawer track hooks.
Drawer track malfunction.	Clean and loosen or replace drawer track.
	Replace drawer spring.
Drawer latch rod will not slide over cam on drawer slide hooks.	Apply a small amount of lubricant (grease) on the drawer slide hook cam surface to allow drawer latch rod to slide on cam surfaces.

Drawer Will Not Open

Drawer kickboard drags on floor.	Adjust leveling legs.

Malfunction of directional switch.

Drawer latch mechanism malfunctions.

Trash jamming drawer.

Malfunctioning tracks.

Track spring inoperative.

Replace drawer springs, if required.

See "Ram stuck in Down position."

Adjust or replace malfunctioning parts.

Remove trash.

Clean, lubricate, or replace, as required.

Correct or replace.

Compactor Will Not Operate

No electric power to compactor.

Drawer not completely closed.

Key in Lock position.

Make sure compactor "plugged in." Check fuse or circuit breaker.

Close drawer.

Turn key to unlock.

Motor Will Not Operate

Improper electrical connections.

Motor inoperative.

Check and correct.

Replace motor.

Odor

Fully adsorbed charcoal air filter.

Inoperative blower motor.

See "Use and Care Guide."

Check electrical connection.

Replace motor.

REFRIGERATORS

Motor Will Not Run

Cause	Remedy
Fuse blown; loose connection at wall outlet or motor; cord or plug needs repair.	Repair connection. Replace cord or plug.

Motor Runs Too Much

Condenser dirty.

Clean condenser once or twice a year with a long handled brush or vacuum cleaner attachment.

Caution: Always disconnect refrigerator from power supply before cleaning condensers.

Refrigerator overcrowded.

Remove foods that do not need refrigeration, such as jams and jellies. See that dishes are not crowded against each other or against the sides of the refrigerator. Do not place hot foods in the refrigerator.

Door leaking air. Test by closing the door on a dollar bill or a piece of paper of the same thickness. If you can pull the paper out easily, there is a poor fit at this point. Test at several points around the door.

Adjust the door latch. On some models this may require a serviceman. Door may need a new rubber gasket. The old gasket can usually be taken off by removing the screws around the door edges.

Door opened too frequently or allowed to stand open.

Have all foods ready to place in the refrigerator before opening the door. Locate the refrigerator so that door opens conveniently to a nearby work surface. Close the door immediately after the foods are placed inside.

Refrigerator improperly located.

See that refrigerator is not too close to a coal or wood stove, or too close to the wall or cabinets. Allow a 12-inch space above the refrigerator and a 4-inch space at the back and sides.

Noisy Refrigerator

Refrigerator not level.

Adjust leveling screws or place thin piece of wood under the legs. Metal discs may be obtained from dealer.

Food containers may shake or rattle.

Move containers so they do not touch each other or the cooling unit.

Loose parts.

Tighten any loose bolts or screws.

Loose or worn belt.

Tighten or replace. If squeaking noise develops rub soap or belt dressing on the belt.

Motor Runs But Will Not Freeze Ice

Float valve stuck.

Fill ice trays with hot water and place in the freezing compartment. Repeat if necessary.

Freezing Unit Collects Too Much Frost Or Moisture Condensers In Cabinet

Door leaking air.	Adjust door latch or replace rubber gasket, if worn.
Uncovered foods in refrigerator.	Cover all foods.
Incomplete defrosting.	Defrost completely; see directions given under care and cleaning.
Temperature too low in refrigerator.	Set temperature control to obtain 35° F. to 45° F.

Foods Will Not Keep

Improper storage or too high temperature.	Remove vegetables from packages, discard wilted leaves and spoiled parts, wash thoroughly, drain, and store in covered pan or hydrator in bottom of refrigerator. Unwrap meat, cover with waxed paper or butter paper, and place in the coldest part directly under freezing unit. Keep temperature between 35° F. to 45° F. Defrost when frost becomes ¼-inch on freezing unit.

Odor In Cabinet

Uncovered foods.	See that all foods with a strong odor are covered.
Cabinet needs cleaning.	Clean thoroughly according to directions found under care and cleaning.
Mechanical trouble.	Call serviceman.

AUTOMATIC WASHERS

No Hot Water

Cause	Remedy
Hot water supply valve is closed.	Open valve.
Water supply is cold.	Check water heater.
Kinked hot water inlet hose.	Straighten or replace hose.

Clogged mixing valve screen.	Disconnect hot water inlet hose, and clean or replace screen.
Inoperative hot water mixing valve solenoid.	Test solenoid and replace if inoperative.
Inoperative timer.	Test timer and replace if inoperative.
Inoperative temperature switch.	Test switch and replace if inoperative.
Water remaining in reservoir due to inoperative drain valve solenoid, or clogged hoses or drain valve.	Test solenoid, or remove and disassemble valve to clean valve and hoses.
Inoperative pressure switch.	Test switch and replace if inoperative.
Clogged pressure hose.	Remove and clean hose.
Broken, loose, or incorrect wiring.	Refer to appropriate wiring diagram.

No Cold Water

Cold water supply valve is closed.	Open valve.
Kinked cold water inlet hose.	Straighten or replace hose.
Clogged mixing valve screen.	Disconnect cold water inlet hose, and clean or replace screen.
Inoperative cold water mixing valve solenoid.	Test solenoid and replace if inoperative.
Inoperative timer.	Test timer and replace if inoperative.
Inoperative temperature switch.	Test switch and replace if inoperative.
Inoperative pressure switch.	Test switch and replace if inoperative.
Water remaining in reservoir due to inoperative drain valve solenoid, or clogged hoses or drain valve.	Test solenoid or remove and disassemble valve to clean valve and hoses.
Clogged pressure hose.	Remove and clean hose.
Broken, loose, or incorrect wiring.	Refer to appropriate wiring diagram.

No Warm Water

No hot water.	Refer to "No hot water."
No cold water.	Refer to "No cold water."

Water Fill Does Not Stop At Proper Time

(Wash and rinse fill level should range from minimum of a half a tub at LO [or SMALL] setting, to maximum of forty seconds fill over water line on agitator at HI [or LARGE] setting—with no clothes in tub)

Inoperative timer.	Test timer and replace if inoperative.
Inoperative pressure switch.	Test switch and replace if inoperative.
Reservoir filler hose kinked, clogged, or leaking water.	Replace hose.
Water reservoir is leaking.	Replace reservoir.
Reservoir drain valve or reservoir drain hose is leaking.	Remove drain valve and replace valve or hose.
Air leak in pressure hose.	Replace hose.
Clogged or partially clogged water inlet tee.	Replace tee.
Sediment on or under mixing valve diaphragm, defective diaphragm, or armature binding in armature guide.	Disassemble and clean mixing valve. Replace deteriorated or not easily cleaned components.
Broken, weak, or missing mixing valve armature spring.	Disassemble valve and replace spring.
Timer does not advance.	Refer to "Timer does not advance."
Broken, loose, shorted or incorrect wiring.	Refer to appropriate wiring diagram.

Timer Does Not Advance

Inoperative timer.	Test timer and replace if inoperative.
Broken, loose, or incorrect wiring.	Refer to appropriate wiring diagram.

No Agitation

Inoperative timer.	Test timer and replace if inoperative.
Inoperative action switch.	Test switch and replace if inoperative.
Inoperative motor.	Test motor and replace if inoperative.

Inoperative pressure switch.	Test switch and replace if inoperative.
Broken, loose, or incorrect wiring.	Refer to appropriate wiring diagram.
Loose or broken pump or transmission belt.	Adjust or replace belt.
Transmission pulley binding on hub.	Remove transmission pulley, and inspect threads on inside of pulley and outside of hub for burrs or excessive wear. Remove burrs and clean threads, or replace pulley and hub.
Inoperative transmission assembly.	Repair or replace transmission assembly.
Agitator shift clutch binding on agitator shaft.	Remove agitator shift clutch and inspect splines on inside of shift clutch and on drive shaft for burrs. Remove burrs and clean splines or replace shift clutch or shaft. Apply a light film of lubricant to splines before installing shift clutch.
Sheared motor pulley roll pin.	Remove drive motor, and replace roll pin and any other damaged parts.
Drive motor overload protector has cycled.	Refer to "Drive motor overload protector cycles repeatedly."
Transmission pulley stop incorrectly positioned.	Reposition stop.

Constant Agitation

Inoperative timer.	Test timer and replace if inoperative.
Inoperative drive motor.	Test motor and replace if inoperative.
Shorted or incorrect wiring.	Refer to appropriate wiring diagram.
Broken agitation shifter fork pivot pin.	Replace pin.
Bent agitation shifter fork, or worn collar on shifter fork.	Replace shifter fork.

Transmission pulley binding on hub.	Remove transmission pulley and inspect threads on inside of pulley and on outside of hub for burrs or excessive wear. Remove burrs and clean threads, or replace pulley and hub.
Agitator shift clutch binding on drive shaft.	Remove agitator shift clutch, and inspect splines on inside of clutch and on drive shaft for burrs. Remove burrs and clean splines, or obtain new clutch or shaft. Apply a light film of lubricant to splines before installing shift clutch.

Slow Spin Or No Spin

Inoperative timer.	Test timer and replace if inoperative.
Inoperative action switch.	Test switch and replace if inoperative.
Loading door is open or door safety switch is inoperative.	Close loading door, or test switch and replace if inoperative.
Bind in pump.	Disassemble and clean pump.
Inoperative drive motor.	Test motor and replace if inoperative.
Broken, loose, or incorrect wiring.	Refer to appropriate wiring diagram.
Loose or broken spin belt.	Adjust or replace spin belt.
Spin brake does not release due to bind between spin pulley and hub, or incorrectly positioned spin pulley stop.	Disassemble main bearing assembly. Inspect threads on inside spin pulley and on outside of hub for burrs or excessive wear. Remove burrs and clean threads, or replace pulley and hub.
Fluid level in fluid drive is low.	Remove motor and fluid drive assembly, and check fluid level using dip stick. Add fluid drive fluid if necessary.
Broken fluid drive roll pin.	Remove motor and fluid drive assembly, and replace roll pin and any other damaged parts.
Inoperative fluid drive.	Replace fluid drive.

Constant Spin

Inoperative timer.	Test timer and replace if inoperative.
Inoperative drive motor.	Test motor and replace if inoperative.
Shorted or incorrect wiring.	Refer to appropriate wiring diagram.
Spin brake does not hold due to broken brake spring, worn brake pad or discs, bind between spin pulley and hub, or incorrectly positioned spin pulley stop.	Disassemble main bearing assembly. Inspect threads inside pulley and on outside of hub for burrs or wear, and spring, brake pad and discs for breakage or wear. Remove burrs and clean threads, or replace pulley and hub as well as other worn or broken parts.
Inoperative fluid drive. (Fluid drive should operate only when motor runs clockwise and should freewheel when motor runs counterclockwise.)	Replace fluid drive.

Drive Motor Overload Protector Cycles Repeatedly

Low voltage.	Install Low Voltage Kit.
Excessive belt tension.	Adjust belts.
Inoperative overload protector.	Replace motor.
Bind in pump.	Disassemble and clean pump.
Bind in transmission.	Disassemble transmission and locate cause of bind.
Spin brake dragging due to bind between spin pulley and hub, or incorrectly positioned spin pulley stop.	Disassemble main bearing assembly, inspect threads inside of pulley and on outside of hub for burrs or excessive wear. Remove burrs and clean threads, or replace pulley and hub.
Inoperative fluid drive. (Fluid drive should operate only when motor runs clockwise, and should freewheel when motor runs counterclockwise.)	Replace fluid drive.

Drain Tub Does Not Empty

Kinked drain hose.	Straighten hose.
Inoperative water pump.	Remove pump impeller and shaft, and clean pump or replace impeller and shaft.
Obstruction in drain tube outlet hose.	Remove obstruction.
Loose pump belt.	Adjust belt.

Sediment Remains In Bottom Of Spin Tub

Plugged sediment tube.	Remove sediment tube to clean.

Excessive Vibration

Unbalanced load in tub.	Stop washer, redistribute load, then restart washer.
Sticky snubber assembly.	Replace snubber assembly.
Broken or disconnected snubber spring.	Connect or replace snubber spring.
Broken snubber arm.	Replace snubber assembly.
Washer is not properly leveled.	Adjust leveling legs.
Washer is installed on weak, "spongy," or built-up floor.	Relocate washer or support floor to eliminate weak or "spongy" condition.
Balance ring is installed incorrectly. (Marked side of balance ring should be located 180 degrees from sediment tube.)	Remove balance ring, and reinstall correctly.

Does Not Dispense Bleach

Inoperative timer.	Test timer and replace if inoperative.
Obstruction in bleach hose(s), dispenser, or tube.	Remove bleach dispenser or bleach tube, and remove obstruction.
Inoperative bleach pump.	Test pump and replace if inoperative.
Broken, loose, or incorrect wiring.	Refer to appropriate wiring diagram.

DRYERS

Motor Does Not Run

Cause	Remedy
Electrical power off, fuse blown, or power cord not plugged in.	Plug in, replace fuse, or restore power as necessary.
Loading door not closed, or inoperative door switch.	Close door, or test switch and replace if inoperative.
Motor overload protector has cycled.	Wait two or three minutes for overload protector to reset. See "Motor overload protector cycles repeatedly."
Timer improperly set.	Reset timer.
Inoperative motor switch.	Test switch and replace if inoperative.
Start circuit not completed.	Press start switch button, or test switch and replace if inoperative.
Exhaust fan housing bearing binding.	Replace bearing.
Drum shaft bearing binding.	Replace bearing.
Inoperative motor.	Test motor and replace if inoperative.
Inoperative timer.	Test timer and replace if inoperative.
Broken, loose, or incorrect wiring.	Refer to appropriate wiring diagram.

Motor Overload Protector Cycles Repeatedly

Cause	Remedy
Shipping tape has not been removed.	Open loading door and remove tape holding drum to front panel.
Low voltage.	Refer to electrical requirements.
Clothes load too large.	Remove part of load. A normal washer load is a normal dryer load.
Exhaust fan belt is too tight.	Adjust belt.
Exhaust fan housing bearing binding.	Replace bearing.
Clothes drum is binding.	Check for rear drum shaft bearing binding. Also inspect drum support rollers for binding, and inspect

Inoperative motor overload protector.

area between rear of drum and rear support frame for binding.
Replace drive motor.

Motor Runs But Drum Does Not Turn

Shipping tape has not been removed.

Open loading door and remove tape holding drum to front panel.

Loose motor drum drive pulley.

Tighten setscrew.

Broken drum belt.

Replace belt.

Clothes drum is binding.

Check for rear drum shaft bearing binding. Also inspect area between rear of drum and rear support frame for binding.

Broken or disconnected idler lever tension spring.

Replace or reconnect spring.

Motor Does Not Stop

Incorrect wiring.

Refer to appropriate wiring diagram.

Motor centrifugal switch sticky or plugged with lint.

Remove dust or lint and clean and lubricate.

Inoperative door switch.

Test switch and replace if inoperative.

Inoperative timer.

Test timer and replace if inoperative.

Heating Element Does Not Heat Or Burner Does Not Ignite

Improper or inadequate exhaust system.

See "Installation."

Blown house fuse or tripped circuit breaker.

Check fuses or circuit breakers.

Temperature selector switch set at Air Fluff, or inoperative.

Reset switch, or test switch and replace if inoperative.

Timer improperly set.

Reset timer.

Electric models: Inoperative heating element.

Replace element.

Gas models (Standing Pilot): Pilot is not ignited.

Refer to light pilot.

Gas models (Standing Pilot): Inoperative reset valve.	Replace reset valve.
Gas models (Standing Pilot): Inoperative burner coil.	Test burner coil and replace inoperative components.
Inoperative drive motor switch.	Test switch and replace if inoperative.
Gas models: Insufficient gas supply.	Open partially closed gas shutoff valve, or correct low gas pressure.
Inoperative limit thermostat.	Test thermostat and replace if inoperative.
Gas models (White-Rodgers Automatic Ignition): Inoperative gas valve coil.	Test coil and replace if inoperative.
Gas models (White-Rodgers Automatic Ignition): Inoperative igniter.	Test igniter and replace if inoperative.
Gas models (White-Rodgers Automatic Ignition): Inoperative igniter control.	Test control and replace if inoperative.
Inoperative high or low thermostat.	Test thermostat and replace if inoperative.
Gas models: Inoperative exhaust limit thermostat.	Test thermostat and replace if inoperative.
Inoperative timer.	Test timer and replace if inoperative.
Broken, loose, or incorrect wiring.	Refer to appropriate wiring diagram.

Pilot Does Not Ignite Gas Models (Standing Pilot)

Gas shutoff valve is closed.	Open valve.
Air is present in gas lines.	Purge air from gas lines until odor of gas is detected.
Incorrect pilot orifice.	Refer to "Conversion Kits" for correct orifices.
Clogged pilot gas filter.	Follow procedure for burner valve spring and plunger and replace filter pad.
Clogged pilot gas tube or pilot orifice.	Clean or replace tube or orifice.
Inoperative pressure regulator.	Remove cover and replace defective parts.

Pilot Goes Out Gas Models (Standing Pilot)

Improper or inadequate exhaust system.	See "Installation."
Clogged lint screen.	Remove and clean lint screen.
Improperly adjusted air shutter.	Close air shutters slightly—a harsh-roaring flame will draw pilot flame out.
Improperly installed or defective exhaust system.	Outer end of exhaust system must have a weather hood with hinged damper to prevent back-draft when dryer is not in operation. Install or replace weather hood if missing or inoperative.
Exhaust fan belt loose or broken.	Adjust or replace belt.
Motor pulley or exhaust fan pulley loose or off shaft.	Tighten or replace pulley.
Soot or carbon accumulation on heated end of pilot burner mercury tube.	Wipe soot or carbon off end of tube.
Incorrect pilot orifice.	Refer to "Conversion Kits" for correct orifices.
Incorrect vent screw on gas valve pressure regulator.	Replace with correct vent screw.
Incorrectly adjusted reset valve latch.	Adjust reset valve latch.
Inoperative reset valve.	Replace reset valve.

Heating Element Or Burner Shuts Off Prematurely

Improper or inadequate exhaust system.	See "Installation."
Gas models: Insufficient gas supply.	Open partially closed gas shutoff valve, or correct low gas pressure.
Gas models: Dryer not properly equipped for type of gas used.	Convert burner.
Gas models: Improperly adjusted burner flame.	Adjust flame.
Cycling off on limit thermostat.	Momentarily connect a jumper wire across thermostat terminals. If heating element heats or burner ignites when jumper wire is con-

nected, refer to section "Heating element or burner repeatedly cycles off-on limit thermostat."

Gas models (White-Rodgers Automatic Ignition): Igniter control incorrectly installed.	Check installation.
Gas models (White-Rodgers Automatic Ignition): Inoperative gas valve resistor.	Test resistor and replace if inoperative.
Gas models (White-Rodgers Automatic Ignition): Inoperative igniter control.	Test control and replace if inoperative.
Inoperative high or low thermostat.	Test thermostat and replace if inoperative.
Gas models: Exhaust limit thermostat cycling at too low a temperature.	Replace thermostat.
Broken, loose, or incorrect wiring.	Refer to appropriate wiring diagram.
Inoperative timer.	Test timer and replace if inoperative.

Igniter Does Not Shut Off After Gas Ignition
(Automatic Ignition)

Dryer not properly equipped for type of gas being used.	Refer to "Conversion Kits" to convert burner.
Insufficient gas supply.	Open partially closed gas shut off valve, or correct low gas pressure.
Improperly adjusted burner flame.	Adjust flame.
Igniter control incorrectly installed.	Check installation.
Inoperative igniter control.	Test control and replace if inoperative.
Incorrect wiring.	Refer to appropriate wiring diagram.

Heating Element Or Burner Repeatedly Cycles Off On
Limit Thermostat

External exhaust system longer or providing greater restriction than recommended.	See "Installation."

Clogged lint screen.

Remove and clean lint screen.

Lint in internal dryer ductwork.

Disassemble dryer and clean ductwork.

Lint in external exhaust system.

Disassemble and clean exhaust system.

Hinged damper on exhaust system weather hood not free to open.

Free hinged damper or replace weather hood.

Loose exhaust fan pulley or motor exhaust fan pulley.

Tighten setscrew.

Loose or broken exhaust fan belt.

Adjust or replace belt.

Limit thermostat cycling at too low a temperature.

Replace thermostat.

Air leak around loading door. (Door not sealing properly against outer door seal due to damaged seal or inoperative catches.)

Replace seal or catch(es).

Air leak at front or rear drum seal.

Check and replace seal if necessary.

Heating Element Or Burner Does Not Shut Off

Inoperative motor switch.

Test switch and replace if inoperative.

Motor does not stop.

Refer to section "Motor does not stop."

Incorrect wiring.

Refer to appropriate wiring diagram.

Gas models (White-Rodgers Automatic Ignition): Impurities on burner valve seat, preventing valve from closing.

Disassemble and clean valve.

Gas models (Standing Pilot): Inoperative burner valve, impurities on valve seat, or deteriorated valve plunger seat.

Test burner coil and replace if inoperative. Clean impurities from valve seat with a clean cloth.

Clothes Do Not Dry

Heating element does not heat or burner does not ignite.

Refer to section "Heating element does not heat or burner does not ignite."

Too much water in articles being dried.	Remove excess water.
Clothes load too large.	Remove part of load. A normal washer load is a normal dryer load.
Clothes load too small.	Enlarge load. A normal washer load is a normal dryer load.
Improper or inadequate exhaust system.	See "Installation."
Heating element or burner shuts off prematurely.	Refer to section "Motor does not run."

Timer Does Not Advance Automatic Cycle

Broken, loose, or incorrect wiring.	Refer to appropriate wiring diagram.
Inoperative high or low thermostat.	Test thermostat and replace if inoperative.
Heating element does not heat or burner does not ignite.	Refer to "Heating element does not heat."
Heating element or burner cycles off repeatedly.	Refer to "Heating element does not heat."

AUTOMATIC WATER HEATERS

No Hot Water

Cause	Remedy
No power.	Check fuses, or circuit breakers. Replace or reset. Check with utility if necessary.
Loose wiring connection.	Locate loose connections. Clean carefully (remove all oxidation). Reconnect properly.
Lighting.	Inspect: (1) fuse (or circuit breaker); (2) heater elements; and (3) thermostat. Replace if necessary.
High voltage.	Check utility for correction.
Short.	Locate short circuit and correct.
Element failure.	Replace element. Check "Complaint–Element Failure."

Wrong piping connections.	Reconnect pipes to proper fittings according to manufacturer's instructions.
Improper calibration of thermostat.	Replace thermostat.
Faulty thermostat.	Replace thermostat.
Undersized service wiring.	Check with utility.
Faulty hi-limit switch.	Replace high limit switch.
Open hi-limit switch.	Reset. Check. "Complaint–Overheated Water."

Insufficient Hot Water

Undersized heater.	Replace with one of adequate capacity—for future as well as present needs.
Element too small.	Replace with elements of higher watt rating—check with utility for proper service wiring.
Wrong wiring connections at heater terminal.	Correct according to manufacturer's instructions.
Insulation improperly replaced.	Adjust insulation to original factory condition—add new insulation if necessary.
Wasted water.	Call serviceman.
Sediment or lime in tank.	Shut off power, drain tank, check to see if water treatment is necessary.
Lime formation on elements.	Clean elements, replace if burned out. Check to see if water treatment is necessary.
Thermostat not flush to and in contact with tank.	Position properly. Be sure insulation covers thermostat before replacing access panel.
Loose wiring connection.	Locate loose connections. Clean carefully (remove all oxidation). Reconnect properly.
Poor ground.	Install proper ground.
Thermostat set too high.	Turn temperature knob to desired temperature—warm–120° F; normal–140° F; hot–160° F.

Top inlet heater: Dip tube in "Hot" fitting.

Remove and replace in cold water inlet.

Side inlet heater: Cold water pipe connected to fitting at top of heater without dip tube.

Connect cold water line to side inlet.

Wrong piping connections.

Reconnect pipes to proper fittings according to manufacturer's instructions.

Long run of exposed piping.

Insulate piping.

Hot water piping in outside walls.

Insulate piping.

Faulty thermostat.

Replace thermostat.

Leaking faucets, leaking heater nipples, and/or leaking tank drain.

Locate and correct.

Slow Hot Water Recovery

Element too small.

Replace with elements of higher watt rating—check with utility for proper service wiring.

Insulation improperly replaced.

Adjust insulation to original factory condition—add new insulation if necessary.

Wasted water.

To be serviced.

Lime formation on elements.

Clean elements, replace if burned out. Check to see if water treatment is necessary.

Thermostat not flush to and in contact with tank.

Position properly. Be sure insulation covers thermostat before replacing access panel.

Loose wiring connection.

Locate loose connections. Clean carefully (remove all oxidation). Reconnect properly.

Poor ground.

Install proper ground.

Thermostat set too high.

Turn temperature knob to desired temperature—warm–120° F; normal–140° F; hot–160° F.

Wrong piping connections.

Reconnect pipes to proper fittings according to manufacturer's instructions.

Excessive mineral deposits.

(1) Flush tank thoroughly; (2) install water filter if necessary. Tank should be flushed periodically.

Improper calibration of thermostat.	Replace thermostat.
Long run of exposed piping.	Insulate piping.
Hot water piping in outside walls.	Insulate piping.
Faulty thermostat.	Replace thermostat.

Overheated Water—Steam

Wrong wiring connections at heater terminal.	Correct according to manufacturer's instructions.
No temperature and pressure relief valve.	Install proper relief valve according to manufacturer's instructions and local codes.
Thermostat not flush to and contact with tank.	Position properly. Be sure insulation covers thermostat before replacing access panel.
Thermostat not properly insulated.	Adjust insulation to cover thermostat and element terminals—add insulation if necessary.
Short.	Locate short circuit and correct.
Thermostat set too high.	Turn temperature knob to desired temperature—warm–120° F; normal–140° F; hot–160° F.
Wrong piping connections.	Reconnect pipes to proper fittings according to manufacturer's instructions.
Improper calibration of thermostat.	Replace thermostat.
Faulty thermostat.	Replace thermostat.
Faulty hi-limit switch.	Replace high limit switch.
No hi-limit switch.	Install high limit switch in accordance with manufacturer's instructions.

High Operation Costs

Undersized heater.	Replace heater with one of adequate capacity—for future as well as present needs.
Insulation improperly replaced.	Adjust insulation to original fac-

	tory condition—add new insulation if necessary.
Wasted water.	To be serviced.
Thermostat not flush to and in contact with tank.	Position properly. Be sure insulation covers thermostat before replacing access panel.
Thermostat not properly insulated.	Adjust insulation to cover thermostat and element terminals—add insulation if necessary.
Short.	Locate short circuit and correct.
Poor ground.	Install proper ground.
Thermostat set too high.	Turn temperature knob to desired temperature—warm–120° F; normal–140° F; hot–160° F.
Improper calibration of thermostat.	Replace thermostat.
Long run of exposed piping.	Insulate piping.
Hot water piping in outside walls.	Insulate piping.
Faulty thermostat.	Replace thermostat.
Leaks around heating elements.	(1) Tighten bolts; (2) if necessary clean and smooth face of tank flange and gasket.
Leaking faucets, leaking heater nipples, and/or leaking tank drain.	Locate and correct.

Drip From Relief Valve Operation

Sediment or lime in tank.	Shut off power, drain tank, check to see if water treatment is necessary.
Excessive water pressure.	Install proper pressure reducing valve and proper pressure relief valve.
Surge from automatic washer solenoid valve.	Install blind pipe air cushion.
Check valve in water line.	Install proper pressure relief valve.
Improper calibration of thermostat.	Replace thermostat.
Faulty thermostat.	Replace thermostat.

Excessive Relief Valve Operation

Excessive water pressure.	Install proper pressure reducing valve and proper pressure relief valve.
Surge from automatic washer solenoid valve.	Install blind pipe air cushion.
Check valve in water line.	Install proper pressure relief valve.
Improper calibration of thermostat.	Replace thermostat.
Faulty thermostat.	Replace thermostat.

Condensation

Insulation improperly replaced.	Adjust insulation to original factory condition—add new insulation if necessary.
Hot water piping in outside walls.	Insulate piping.
Leaks around heating elements.	(1) Tighten bolts; (2) if necessary, clean and smooth face of tank flange and gasket.

Tank Bulged—Bottom Reversed

Excessive water pressure.	Install proper pressure reducing valve and proper pressure relief valve.
Surge from automatic washer solenoid valve.	Install blind pipe air cushion.
Check valve in water line.	Install proper pressure relief valve.
Pressure reducing valve installed in water line.	Install temperature and pressure relief valve according to manufacturer's instructions and local codes.
Faulty thermostat.	Replace thermostat.

Element Failure

Cause	Remedy
Wrong wiring connections at heater terminal.	Correct according to manufacturer's instructions.
Sediment or lime in tank.	Shut off power, drain tank, check to see if water treatment is necessary.
Lime formation on elements.	Clean elements, replace if burned out. Check to see if water treatment is necessary.

Loose wiring connection.	Locate loose connections. Clean carefully (remove all oxidation) Reconnect properly.
Lighting.	Inspect: (1) Fuse or circuit breaker; (2) heater elements; and (3) thermostat. Replace if necessary.
Power surge.	See "Lighting" above.
Low voltage.	Check utility for correction.
High voltage.	Check utility for correction.
Short.	Locate short circuit and correct.

Singing Elements

Lime formation on elements.	Clean elements, replace if burned out. Check to see if water treatment is necessary.
Damage from electrolysis.	Install dielectric unions or bushings.

Blown Fuse Or Circuit Breaker Cutout

No Power.	Check fuses or circuit breakers. Replace or reset—check with utility if necessary.
Loose wiring connection.	Locate loose connections. Clean carefully—remove all oxidation. Reconnect properly.
Lighting.	Inspect: (1) fuse or circuit breaker; (2) heater elements; and (3) thermostat. Replace if necessary.
Power surge.	See "Lighting" above.
Low voltage.	Check utility for correction.
High voltage.	Check utility for correction.
Short.	Locate short circuit and correct.
Undersized service wiring.	Check with utility.
Faulty thermostat.	Replace thermostat.

Service Wires—Charred Or Hot

Wrong wiring connections at heater terminal.	Correct according to manufacturer's instructions.
Loose wiring connection.	Locate loose connections. Clean carefully—remove all oxidation. Reconnect properly.

Poor ground.

Install proper ground.

Lighting.

Inspect: (1) fuse or circuit breaker; (2) heater elements, and (3) thermostat. Replace if necessary.

Power surge.

See "Lighting" above.

Low voltage.

Check utility for correction.

High voltage.

Check utility for correction.

Short.

Locate short circuit and correct.

Undersized service wiring.

Check with utility.

Smoking Wiring

Wrong wiring connections at heater terminal.

Correct according to manufacturer's instructions.

Loose wiring connection.

Locate loose connections. Clean carefully—remove all oxidation. Reconnect properly.

Poor ground.

Install proper ground.

Lighting.

Inspect: (1) fuse or circuit breaker, (2) heater elements; and (3) thermostat. Replace if necessary.

Power surge.

See "Lighting" above.

Low voltage.

Check utility for correction.

High voltage.

Check utility for correction.

Variable voltage.

Check utility for correction.

Undersized service wiring.

Check with utility.

Faulty thermostat.

Replace thermostat.

Continuous Operation

Undersized heater.

Replace heater with one of adequate capacity—for future as well as present needs.

Element too small.

Replace with elements of higher watt rating—check with utility for proper service wiring.

Thermostat not flush to and in contact with tank.

Position properly. Be sure insulation covers thermostat before replacing access panel.

Thermostat not properly insulated.

Adjust insulation to cover thermostat and element terminals—add insulation if necessary.

Element failure.	Replace element. Check "Complaint—Element Failure."
Thermostat set too low.	Turn temperature knob to desired temperature—warm–120° F.; normal–140° F.; hot–160° F.
Improper calibration of thermostat.	Replace thermostat.
Faulty thermostat.	Replace thermostat.
Faulty Hi-Limit switch.	Replace High Limit switch.

Wet Insulation

Undersized heater.	Replace heater with one of adequate capacity—for future as well as present needs.
Leaks around heating element.	(1) Tighten bolts; (2) if necessary clean and smooth face of tank flange gasket.
Leaking faucets, leaking heater nipples, and/or leaking tank drain.	Locate and correct.

Thermostat Failure

No power.	Check fuses or circuit breakers. Replace or reset. Check with utility if necessary.
Loose wiring connection.	Locate loose connections. Clean carefully—remove all oxidation. Reconnect properly.
Lighting.	Inspect (1) fuse or circuit breaker; (2) heater elements; and (3) thermostat. Replace if necessary.
Power surge.	See "Lighting" above.
Low voltage.	Check utility for correction.
High voltage.	Check utility for correction.
Short.	Locate short circuit and correct.
Faulty thermostat.	Replace thermostat.

Singing Thermostats

Thermostat not flush to and in contact with tank.	Position properly. Be sure insulation covers thermostat before replacing access panel.
Loose wiring connection.	Locate loose connections. Clean carefully—remove all oxidation. Reconnect properly.

Rusty Or Discolored Water

Sediment or lime in tank.	Shut off power, drain tank, check to see if water treatment is necessary.
Lime formation on elements.	Clean elements, replace if burned out. Check to see if water treatment is necessary.
Damage from electrolysis.	Install dielectric unions or bushings.
Rusted supply lines.	(1) Thoroughly clean and flush entire system; (2) replace rusted lines if necessary.
Water too soft.	Install, or replace, anode rod to protect tank.
Excessive mineral deposits.	(1) Flush tank thoroughly; (2) install water filter if necessary. Tank should be flushed periodically.
Air trapped in water system.	Locate and eliminate.
Defective tank.	Replace.
Dissipated anode rod.	Replace.

Gas, Odor Or Taste In Water

Gas from magnesium anode rod combining with sulphur in water.	Replace with zinc anode rod.

Rumbling Or Pounding Water Heater

Sediment or lime in tank.	Shut off power, drain tank, check to see if water treatment is necessary.
Lime formation on elements.	Clean elements, replace if burned out. Check to see if water treatment is necessary.
Excessive water pressure.	Install proper pressure reducing valve and proper pressure relief valve.
Gas from magnesium anode rod combining with sulphur in water.	Replace with zinc anode rod.
Surge from automatic water solenoid valve.	Install a blind air cushion.

Check valve in water line.

Install a proper pressure relief valve.

Pressure reducing valve installed in water line.

Install temperature and pressure relief valve according to manufacturer's instructions and local codes.

Wrong piping connections.

Reconnect pipes to proper fittings according to manufacturer's instructions.

Air trapped in water system.

Locate and eliminate.

Dissipated anode rod.

Replace.

Fluctuating Temperature

Undersized heater.

Replace heater with one of adequate capacity—for future as well as present needs.

Insulated improperly replaced.

Adjust insulation to original factory condition—add new insulation if necessary.

Thermostat not flush to and in contact with tank.

Position properly. Be sure insulation covers thermostat before replacing access panel.

Thermostat not properly insulated.

Adjust insulation to cover thermostat and element terminals—add insulation if necessary.

Loose wiring connection.

Locate loose connections. Clean carefully—remove all oxidation. Reconnect properly.

Top inlet heater: Dip tube in "Hot" fitting.

Remove and replace in cold water inlet.

Side inlet heater: Cold water pipe connected to fitting at top of heater without dip tube.

Connect cold water line to side inlet.

Wrong piping connections.

Reconnect pipes to proper fittings according to manufacturer's instructions.

Long run of exposed piping.

Insulate piping.

Hot water piping in outside walls.

Insulate piping.

Faulty thermostat.

Replace thermostat.

VACUUM CLEANERS

Cleaner Refuses To Pick Up Dirt

Cause	Remedy
Cleaner bag may need emptying.	Empty bag, turn wrong side out, and brush or clean.
Improper adjustment of cleaner nozzle.	Find the nozzle adjustment on your cleaner (some cleaners do not have an adjustment). Adjust so that a quarter slides easily between cleaner nozzle and rug. On cleaners with a rotating brush or roll, the clearance should be the thickness of a half dollar.
Improper adjustment of cleaner brush.	Hold machine with nozzle up, lay a ruler or piece of stiff cardboard over the nozzle. The bristles should not quite touch the ruler; a space of $\frac{1}{32}$-inch is desirable. The adjustment is usually made by moving a pin, screw, or lever at each end of the brush.
Broken belt or belt not revolving.	Examine the belt. Make sure it is around both the brush and motor shaft and is not tangled with hair and strings. It after cleaning the brush it still will not turn with the motor, the belt is probably stretched and should be replaced with a new belt. To replace belt: (a) Slip belt off motor shaft; (b) remove brush and belt from cleaner; (c) slip new belt over brush; (d) place brush back in cleaner.

Index